male fantasies

Theory and History of Literature
Edited by Wlad Godzich and Jochen Schulte-Sasse

volume 2
male bodies:
psychoanalyzing
the
white
terror

klaus theweleit

translated by erica carter
and chris turner
in collaboration with stephen conway

foreword by anson rabinbach
and jessica benjamin

university of minnesota press
minneapolis

Originally published as *Männerphantasien*, Volume 2. *Männerkörper: Zur Psychoanalyse des weissen Terrors* by Klaus Theweleit, copyright © 1978 by Verlag Roter Stern.

Published by the University of Minnesota Press,
2037 University Avenue Southeast, Minneapolis, MN 55414.

Printed in the United States of America.

Library of Congress Cataloging-in-Publication Data
Theweleit, Klaus.
  Male fantasies.
  (Theory and history of literature; v. 22-23)
  Translation of: Männerphantasien.
  Vol. 2: foreword by Jessica Benjamin and Anson
Rabinbach.
  Bibliography: v. 1, p. [489]-501; v. 2, p.
  Includes indexes.
  Contents: v. 1. Women, floods, bodies, history—
v. 2. Male bodies, psychoanalyzing the white terror.
  1. Germany. Heer. Freikorps. 2. Soldiers—
Germany—Sexual behavior. 3. Fascism and sex.
4. Fascism and women. 5. Psychoanalysis and culture—
Germany. 6. Fantasy. 7. Sex in literature. I. Title.
II. Series.
UA717.T47 1987   355.1'2'0943   86-25052
ISBN 0-8166-1448-2 (v. 1)
ISBN 0-8166-1449-0 (pbk.: v. 1)
ISBN 0-8166-1450-4 (v. 2)
ISBN 0-8166-1451-2 (pbk.: v. 2)

Text designed by Gale Houdek.
Cover designed by Craig Carnahan.
Cover illustration: "Santo Domingo" by Mary Griep, courtesy of MC Gallery, Minneapolis, Minnesota

Contents

Foreword
Jessica Benjamin and Anson Rabinbach

Some intangible impulse within the masses has long wished to rid itself of the wretched belief that life is intended for pleasure—a contagious belief which is truly Jewish in nature. Today, the idyll of "heaven on earth" has lost much of its attraction.

(Alfred Rosenberg)

Ernst Jünger, the most imaginative and philosophically interesting writer of the interwar German right, called his reflections on World War I "Battle as Inner Experience" (*Der Kampf als inneres Erlebnis*). Klaus Theweleit's *Male Fantasies* might be subtitled "fascism as inner experience." It explores an uncharted territory: the turbulent emotional world of the fascist man. More than any other writer, Theweleit penetrates beneath the skin of the "fascist warrior" to find the desires and anxieties that are at the core of his mystique of war and violence. And he does this (in contrast to Hans Jürgen Syberberg's film *Our Hitler*) without ever finding his fascists seductive and without succumbing to their charms. Even more remarkably, Theweleit's subjects are at once horrifying and comic. To have written such a serious work without losing his sense of humor is in itself extraordinary, but to do so without becoming cynical is an achievement.

Over fifteen years ago, Theweleit discovered an extraordinary historical source—more than 250 *Freikorps* novels and memoirs of the 1920s. *Male Fantasies* relies largely, but not exclusively, on the writings of these men of the *Freikorps*, private armies of former imperial soldiers, anti-Communist youth, adventurers, and sundry drifters organized in the volatile atmosphere of post-World War I Germany. These "white" troops, used—and ultimately discarded—by the anxious socialist government of Friedrich Ebert to suppress the communist insurrection of 1919/20, saw the radical German working-class movement as the greatest threat to their image of the nation and German manhood. Yet, the literature of these troops, if previously investigated at all, was consulted for informational purposes or treated only as propaganda. Theweleit, however, found in this popular literature (so popular that editions ran into the hundreds of thousands) a seemingly inexhaustible vein of violent emotions, fantasies, and images, which he has mined.

Theweleit's bulky two-volume dissertation became a best-seller when it first appeared in Germany in 1977. Although surprising, and often commented on by reviewers, its success is not difficult to explain. *Male Fantasies* is one of those rare books that both sums up and, at the same time, transcends the cherished concerns of a generation. It weaves the most productive strands of the post-1968 German new left's intellectual and political preoccupations into an original, fascinating, often profound, and occasionally outrageous narrative of the fascist unconscious. But it also takes issue with much of what was said about fascism in West Germany in the decade before—and for that reason it is an original and risky undertaking.

Male Fantasies could hardly have been written in any other milieu than that of the West German student left of the late 1960s and early 1970s. The immediate postwar climate in which that generation grew up was characterized by a suffocating atmosphere of good behavior and bad faith, uneasy and pervasive shame coupled with a monumental evasion of responsibility. Until as late as 1960 Nazism was almost never publicly mentioned, and rarely discussed in private. The terms most frequently invoked to describe that era's lack of historical consciousness were "repression" and the failure of "working through." The explosion of antifascist sentiment after 1960 was both a confrontation with the silence of the previous decade and, at the same time, an expression of the first guiltless generation. Indeed, what gave the 1968 West German authoritarian revolt its "furor and pathos," the novelist Peter Schneider noted, was this "assumption of innocence" combined with an obsession with German fascism and its lingering implications for postwar German culture.[1]

For the generation of 1945 the confrontation with the Nazi past went hand in hand with the discovery of pre- and avowedly anti-Nazi German culture in which Freudian and Marxian ideas mingled in a remarkable variety of combinations. Long buried works by Ernst Bloch, Walter Benjamin, Theodor Adorno, Max Horkheimer, and Herbert Marcuse unearthed by younger intellectuals recalled the forgotten intellectual and political traditions of German antifascism. That heritage was crucial to forging a new social and political identity, and to establishing a new kind of historical memory—an anamnestic solidarity with the opponents and victims of Nazism, obscured by the almost incomprehensible amnesia of the years of reconstruction.

The West German student movement, at least in the 1960s, was probably the most intellectual of all the European (and American) new lefts. Influenced by Adorno and Horkheimer, who had returned to Germany to reestablish the Institut für Sozialforschung in the early 1950s, the German new left took seriously Adorno's warning that in Germany fascism was not merely a momentary reversion to barbarism, but a present threat. Critical Theory, with its synthesis of Marx and Freud, provided a kind of magical connection to a positive German past, and an especially powerful instrument for understanding the negative. It revealed how the ghost of fascism lingered as a psychological presence in Germany's authoritarian culture long after its political demise. A chorus of younger intellectuals warned of the dangers inherent in West Germany's strange marriage of political authoritarianism and American-style consumerism. The economic miracle, an imposed parliamentarism, a shaky ruling coalition of conservatives and Social Democrats, and an officially sanctioned anti-Communist obsession with the ''other'' Germany seemed only barely able to contain the dangerous atavistic impulses which threatened to break through at any time. In part this anxiety may have been a hallucinatory reinvocation of the past—a belated antifascism. But, it was also a response to the very real persistence and pervasiveness of an older generation still encrusted with intolerance, resentment, and that most German of all tropes ''Gehorsamkeit''—rigid obedience.

Little wonder that the concept of ''authority'' meant so much to the intellectuals of that generation. It provided the crucial link between the past and the present. On one level, authoritarianism referred to the psychological underpinnings of German fascism in the family, in character structure, in education, and in illiberal politics. A similar authoritarianism seemed to persist in the attitudes of parents raised in the Reich, especially in their fundamentally undemocratic and intolerant social attitudes, in the deeply conservative and hierarchical university, and in the highly stratified workplace. Calling themselves the ''antiauthoritarian'' student movement, German activists initiated a precocious politics of everyday life. Long before feminism they founded child-care cooperatives, introduced new pedagogical ideas (based on the Weimar Freudians) in alternative kindergartens and elementary schools, and experimented with communal living. In retrospect, many of the reforms they initiated were those associated in America with progressive education and democratic liberalism before and after World War II. In Germany, however, the subversion of the artificial normality of the postwar years, and the overthrowing of the undemocratic and punitive spare-the-rod-and-spoil-the-child culture (''kinderfeindlich'' as they said), was accomplished in large part by the new left. No other political movement so closely identified politics with psychology.

In this context we can readily see the significance of Klaus Theweleit's project of discovering the emotional core of fascism in its most virulent psychic manifestations. Theweleit's work clearly belongs to efforts to develop a "theory of fascism" which explicitly drew connections between past and present, between daily life and politics. But it also departs from that genre in its outspokenly feminist standpoint and in its critique of the exclusive focus on authority. Most important, Theweleit explicitly criticizes the Frankfurt School theorists for their lack of attention to the "attraction of fascism itself"—an attraction which is understood as the "passionate celebration of violence."[2] Indeed, it is Theweleit's insistence on the primacy of violence—originating in the fear and hatred of the feminine—that distinguishes his approach from the older social-psychological models. Moreover, where the Frankfurt School saw Freud's oedipal theory of the internalization of authority as the key to understanding fascism, Theweleit makes use of the work of Melanie Klein, Margaret Mahler, and Deleuze/Guattari, for whom preoedipal physical desires and impulses are an integral part of the psyche. It is this single-minded attention to the physical, the corporal, and the sensuous that provides the most original and provocative impulse for this work.

Theweleit belongs to an important intellectual tradition that takes fascist "irrationalism" seriously and that self-consciously rejects the kind of Marxist and liberal rationalism that reduces fascism to some "other" reality (e.g., maintaining capitalism, class interest, social structure, etc.). Fascism is not a mask but the creation of a culture by and for its adherents. As early as 1934, the German utopian philosopher Ernst Bloch wrote that the German fascists colonized a powerful "opposing landscape" of myth, which they and their followers inhabited.[3] Walter Benjamin and Georges Bataille also recognized in fascism a kind of original political dramaturgy, which was for Benjamin an illusory aesthetics of expression and for Bataille a metaphysics of sovereignty and transgression which he called "heterogeneity," a repudiation of the quotidian world.[4] Both Benjamin and Bataille saw expression as the leitmotif of fascist politics, the former in a technologically amplified aestheticism and the latter in the symbolic rituals of power. Though both allude to the body as the site of the political *ethos* of fascism and warfare—for example, when Benjamin refers to "the dreamt-of metalization of the human body" (Marinetti)— neither Benjamin (whose focus is nineteenth-century aestheticism gone berserk) nor Bataille (who is concerned with power removed from the world of work) makes the gendered world of fascist discourse the centerpiece of their analysis.[5]

Male Fantasies refuses to see fascism as "a form of government, or form of economy, or of a system in any sense"(I, 221). The crucial element of fascism is its explicit sexual language, what Theweleit calls "the conscious coding" or the "over-explicitness of the fascist language of symbol" (p. 6).

This fascist symbolization creates a particular kind of psychic economy which places sexuality in the service of destruction. Despite its sexually charged politics, fascism is an anti-eros, ''the core of all fascist propaganda is a battle against everything that constitutes enjoyment and pleasure'' (p. 8).

Male Fantasies thus goes far beyond the conventions of the genre of literature which studies the male warrior as a more or less innocent youth for whom war is a ritual of transformation into adulthood, an event which reshapes the very categories in which the self and world are considered. Even the best writing on men at war, such as Norman Mailer's *The Naked and the Dead*, Glenn Gray's *The Warriors*, and Paul Fussel's *The Great War in Modern Memory*, though they treat the mythology of war as a theme, do not fully escape this kind of narrative. Theweleit's work may be more akin to Michael Heer's evocation of the language of American pop culture that accompanied the Vietnam war in his *Dispatches* (1978), but certainly not in its unappetizing romanticization of the ''high'' of battle. Perhaps because his project is to understand men for whom war is a ''chosen'' experience, and which for them represents the most profound mirror of their identity, Theweleit is never seduced by the myths of war: that it is a spiritual experience, that it is a rite of passage that turns boys into men, that it is a confrontation with the hidden beast within us. Instead, he deconstructs these myths and their most pernicious manifestations. No other work dives so deeply into the fantasies of violence, or into warfare itself as a symbolic system of desire. He shows that in this world of war the repudiation of one's own body, of femininity, becomes a psychic compulsion which associates masculinity with hardness, destruction, and self-denial. In this sense *Male Fantasies* more properly belongs to a very small (despite the existence of a growing feminist scholarship on related themes) but serious body of literature on the social-psychology of male sovereignty. The two classic works that come to mind are the French anthropologist Michel Leiris's autobiographical *Manhood: A Journey from Childhood into the Fierce Order of Virility* (1963) and Bataille's classic *Death and Sensuality: A Study of Eroticism and the Taboo* (English, 1962). In its consistent investigation of the symbols of death and destruction Theweleit is the successor to Elias Canetti's brilliant but idiosyncratic anthropological work *Crowds and Power*, which he acknowledges as an important influence.

Male Fantasies can hardly be described as a conventional history or a conventional work of interpretation. It makes use of psychoanalytic theory, but it is not a psychohistory. As Barbara Ehrenreich emphasized in her foreword to the first volume, its boundaries are not precisely defined. The line between the *Freikorps*, Nazism, the soldiering man, and male fantasy is intentionally blurred. This blurring of historical distinctions has raised important questions about Theweleit's approach. If these desires and fantasies are not limited to the men of the *Freikorps*, if they are, as Paul Robinson and others have noted, "the common psychic property of bourgeois males—and perhaps non-bourgeois males as well," the question naturally arises: what distinguishes these *Freikorpsmen* from other men? And if, as Theweleit believes, these men were enacting the fantasies that everyone else keeps under wraps, historians will legitimately ask is there evidence "to suggest that their childhood experiences differed from those of anyone else?"[6] Theweleit leaves these questions open—precisely because he is far more interested in establishing the essential psychic constellation than in the question of degree or susceptibility. Theweleit's achievement is to have entered into the mental universe of his subjects. Beyond that he assumes a continuum between ordinary male fantasy and its violent counterpart. But there is no reason why, once the framework is established, the question of what is unique to this group of men could not be investigated by historians.

Another historical question which *Male Fantasies* raises is that of the relation of the *Freikorps*, with its pastiche of ideologies and political groupings (it included monarchists, militarists, conservatives, and radical rightist sectarians), to the eventual triumph of Nazism. The West German historian Lutz Niethammer has argued that the *Freikorps* were not "typical fascists"(he means National Socialists) since the vast majority of those who supported the Nazis after 1933 were never part of that militaristic milieu.[7] In other words, the "protofascist" core of the *Freikorps* and its ideology might be distinguished from the anti-democratic and conservative nationalist currents of the later Weimar years, on the one hand, and from mature National Socialism on the other. Although Theweleit does not claim that the emotional system that he uncovers in the *Freikorps* literature was the *only* psychological presupposition of Nazism, he leaves obscure the relationship between the success of Nazism and this earlier phase of German politics from which his texts emerge. To the extent that many of the motifs of the *Freikorps* reappear in Nazi ideology (anti-Bolshevism and misogyny) this connection is self-evident. However, judging from Theweleit's texts, the central ideological element of Nazism, anti-Semitism, seems to play a relatively minor role in the *Freikorps* literature compared to fear and hatred of women. It might then be asked: did Nazism reverse the order of priorities, investing anti-Semitism with a primacy not yet evident in the *Freikorps* or rightist literature of the 1920s, or does Theweleit's exclusive focus on the anti-feminine psyche diminish the significance of anti-Semitism?

The problem of the relation of the *Freikorps* to Nazism is no less complicated when we investigate the fate of the *Freikorps* after its disintegration in the early 1920s. There are of course many direct political, ideological, and personal ties between the *Freikorps* and National Socialism. The *Freikorps* played a crucial role in translating what George L. Mosse has called "the myth of the war experience" into a political mass movement, breaking with the nineteenth-century tradition of conservative elitism.[8] Moreover, as radical protagonists of the ideal of "revision" (of the Versailles treaty), the *Freikorps* were, and this is a crucial point, hostile to the Weimar Republic, harboring frequently articulated sentiments of restoring Germany's lost military glory. The *Freikorps* perpetuated the militarism of the war in the postwar era, participating in military action against the Polish occupation of Upper Silesia in 1921, in the Baltic states, and carried on a private war against the French occupation of the Rhineland in 1923. Three of the *Freikorps* officers Theweleit writes about—General Paul Lettow-Vorbeck (the hero of German East Africa after World War I), Heinrich Ehrhardt, and Gerhard Rossbach—participated in the abortive Kapp Putsch of 1923, the denouement of the power of the radical right in the 1920s. After their official dissolution they lived on in the dark pallet of rightist paramilitary organizations that eroded the later Weimar Republic. Entire *Freikorps* units, for example the Ehrhardt Brigade and Rossbach's unit (which introduced the Brown shirts), joined the SA *en masse* in the early 1920s and participated in Hitler's ill-fated Munich putsch in 1923.[9] Perhaps the most impressive "catch" of all, Franz Ritter von Epp, a popular military figure, who, at the head of the "*Freikorps* Epp" had "saved" Munich from the Soviet Republic in 1919, joined the NSDAP in 1928, lending it an air of respectability.[10]

The Stahlhelm, the SA, and the SS all recruited many of their most prominent leaders from the alumni of the *Freikorps*. Former *Freikorps* officers like Ernst Röhm, head of the SA (assassinated in the blood purge of July 1934) and Rudolf Höss, commandant of Auschwitz, were influential Nazis. Hans Zöberlein, one of the most popular Nazi writers, whose novels outsold even such international hits of the 1930s as Margaret Mitchell's *Gone with the Wind*, also participated in the campaign against the Munich *Räterepublik* and later joined the SA. Nevertheless, the militarism and right-wing radicalism of the early *Freikorps* did not always lead to Nazism. Many German conservatives resented the plebian character of the Nazi movement, its socialist pretenses, and its rowdyism, while local traditions, especially in Bavaria, created suspicions about the centralizing and Prussianizing character of the movement. Ironically, Hitler himself presided over the official dissolution, and integration, of the old *Freikorps* units into the Nazi state at a ceremony in November 1933.[11]

Similar ambiguities appear in the biographies of Theweleit's cast of characters. Ernst Jünger, whose literary works on the war experience are a major source and who was not involved in the *Freikorps* and did not become a Nazi party member, represented a strain of elitist German conservatism that was (if somewhat late in the game) uncomfortable with Nazism.[12] Joseph Paul Goebbels, whose novel *Michael* is another important source, was also never a *Freikorps* member, but he was certainly a Nazi of the very first rank. Martin

Niemöller, who makes a brief appearance in Volume I, was also not involved in the *Freikorps*, and later distinguished himself, as a Protestant pastor, in the resistance to the Hitler regime. The link between the *Freikorps* and Nazism is not always self-evident, especially when we take into account the very large number of followers of Hitler who had little experience of the front and the aftermath of the war. The *Freikorps* provided a recruiting ground for the Nazi elite and also gave the movement its militarist stamp in the early 1920s, yet it was only one element in the political and cultural synthesis that came to power in 1933.

Some of the key figures in *Male Fantasies*, it should be added, continued to be popular writers in the postwar period. Jünger and Ernst von Salomon (imprisoned for his part in the assassination of the liberal Jewish politician and financier Walter Rathenau in 1922) were both widely read conservative writers after 1945. Jünger's *The Marble Cliffs* (1939) was considered to be an allegory of opposition to Nazi brutality, and as recently as 1982 he was awarded the Goethe Prize by the city of Frankfurt. Von Salomon gained postwar notoriety as the author of *Der Fragebogen*, a sardonic attack on denazification and the allies, published in 1951.

What can be said is that Theweleit's discovery of this cache of early postwar rightist literature is like an archaeological find which sheds light on something in the oldest sediment of German fascism, its "martial" origins. If we dismiss our own inclinations to see German history teleologically, and remain focused on the *Freikorps*, we see a dimension of German politics perhaps obscured by the emergence of National Socialism as *the* politically successful mass movement in Germany. It might even be argued that National Socialism was not really a "fascism" at all, precisely because, and in contradistinction to all other fascism, it placed race and anti-Judaism at the very center of its political worldview. Not that fascism and anti-Semitism did not reinvigorate each other, but, as historians have frequently noted, not all fascists were anti-Semites. Thus, from another angle Theweleit may be more than justified in describing the texts he investigates as "fascist" because this literature comes closer in some ways to a wider current of intellectual European fascism of the interwar period than it does to Nazism *per se*.

The literary fascism of the *Freikorps* has numerous parallels to the literary fascism in vogue in France or even Italy in the 1920s. The elevation of militarism, male comradery, and heroic youth to a virtual cult was characteristic not only of the *Freikorps* "Männerbund" but is also evident in the writings of Drieu La Rochelle, Robert Brasillach, and Maurice Bardèche as well.[13] Fascism well describes that potent brew of anti-liberal, anti-Jewish, anti-democratic, anti-Marxist, and of course anti-feminine motifs that congealed in the radicalism of the interwar right. We can even find traces of the politically revolutionary and "non-conformist" synthesis of left and right radicalism—authoritarian and elitist, on the one hand, statist and communitarian, on the other—which Zeev Sternhell has recently claimed to be the distinctive mark of European fascism in that era.[14] Alice Kaplan, following Theweleit, has also demonstrated the degree to which misogyny was a crucial ingredient in the writings of Marinetti, Céline, and Drieu, who especially extolled virility and manliness as the central virtues of fascist politics.[15] Jünger once remarked that he had learned his nationalism from Maurice Barrès, whose influence on the generation of intellectuals who came to adulthood in the war was profound.[16]

In this sense, the *Freikorps* writers, with their admiration for the "jugglers of death" and "masters of explosive and flame" demonstrate more affinities to the intellectual nationalism of the 1920s—with its militarized ethos—than to Nazism.[17] Theweleit's *Freikorps* belong to that current of European fascism of the 1920s which venerated the war experience above all else. "Transformations undergone by the war," Jünger once remarked, "are paralleled by transformations undergone by those fighting it."[18] His comment that "fascism's most significant achievement was the resurrection and rebirth of dead life in the masses" (p. 189) captures this casuistry of combat and its mental universe, suffused with blood and power. Indeed, if we forgo the kind of thinking that makes National Socialism the apotheosis of fascism, the particular horror of the *Freikorps* is all the more chilling.

These caveats aside, Theweleit's work is not an attempt to trace the evolution of the *Freikorps* ideology into Nazism. Rather it is an effort to describe the political culture out of which Nazism eventually developed *in vitro*. His purpose is to survey the language, narrative structure, and metaphors of the *Freikorps* to reconstruct the mythical content of the fascist imagination. As a whole *Male Fantasies* is an analysis of masculine identity as a flight from the feminine, as fear of ego dissolution, and of warfare as the fulfillment of both a longing for fusion (with the military machine) and legitimate explosion in the moment of battle. The first volume is concerned with the image of women in the collective unconscious of the fascist warrior; this volume is concerned with the male body and the boundaries of the self in the experience of war and revolution. The fear of the feminine is investigated in a seemingly endless series of liquid images in which woman is associated with all that might threaten to deluge or flood the boundaries of the male ego. In this volume the armored organization of the male self in a world that constantly threatens it with disintegration provides the key to understanding the emotional underpinnings of fascist militarism. The self is mechanized through a variety of mental and physical procedures: military drill, countenance, training, operations which Foucault identified as "techniques of the self."

These operations are all in the service of what Theweleit calls the "muscle physis," a system of self-regulation arising from an implacable dread of any outside life, which threatens to fragment its own "wholeness" and integrity: "the most urgent task of the man of steel is to pursue, to dam in and to subdue any force that threatens to transform him back into the horribly disorganized jumble of flesh, hair, skin, bones, intestines, and feelings that calls itself human" (p. 160). Only in the explosion of war itself can redemption from constraint and control be risked: war is a kind of rebirth, the apocalyptic moment of battle when "the man longs for the moment when his body armor will explode"(p. 179). In killing there is a transgression against the boundaries of the other while the inner cohesion of the self remains intact. The military formation is both a kind of fusion (mass) and a denial of all fusion and pleasure. Military culture divides itself from nonmilitary culture in its equation of civilian life with femininity, the existence of "masses" or "classes" with the unpermitted pleasures of the body. The fascist warrior turns nation, race, and voïk into instruments of the militarization of the self—the "pain principle."

As a book about political symbolism and the sexual component of the idea of nationhood, masses, and power, *Male Fantasies* creates a completely unique type of psychoanalytic history. Whereas "psychohistory" has remained tied to the analytic convention of the individual biography and its constitutive etiology of oedipal circumstances as they reveal themselves in the behavior of the adult, Theweleit attempts to find in the language of his protagonists the unalloyed emotional sources of their ideological and political acts in a historical drama. He explicitly does not "use" their writing in an instrumental way, nor does he use Freudian theories to reductively delineate a scheme of developmental markers or events that generate ideology and behavior. In fact he purposely does not—and we shall return to this point—distinguish between their words and their political "beliefs" and "actions."[19] Instead, he allows his texts to express the full range of emotion without excessive commentary or overbearing interpretation (technical psychoanalytic theory is reserved for theoretical chapters which appear midway in each volume). As he admits, rather than apply Freudian categories *to* fascists, he prefers to allow his texts to speak their language. He constructs a psychic milieu, or to use the Foucauldian term, discursive field, in which the mechanisms of desire and repulsion are articulated.

Theweleit is concerned with bodies, both in their external and internal dimensions. He acknowledges his debt to Norbert Elias, and of course to Foucault, for the insight that discourse and institutional norms that transform the body into "an inscribed surface of events."[20] But Theweleit does not rest with demonstrating how the body becomes the object of abstract power relations. The body is also a mental subject. It does not remain the passive receptor of external stimuli: it is dynamic, protean, and even explosive in its need to construct systems to repel danger or absorb tensions. In fact, we might say that in Theweleit's texts the body constructs the external world in its own image. Fear of the inner body with its inchoate ''mass'' of viscera and entrails, its ''soft'' genitalia, its ''lower half,'' is translated into the threat of the ''masses'' in the social sense of classes or—especially in those chaotically mixed groups with women and children in the forefront—mass demonstrations. The mass is diametrically opposed to the need for a rigidly, hierarchically structured whole. The ''front'' is not simply the place of battle, the locale of violence, but also the site of the body's boundary against self-disintegration. The soldiering man is simultaneously armored ''enclosure'' and pure ''interior,'' the armor replacing his ''missing skin.''

Male Fantasies is interested in how the body both organizes and expresses the politics of division between gender as a totalizing framework. Fascism, in Theweleit's view, is an extreme example of the political polarization of gender (not restricted to any biological division of the sexes). Feminized men are as repellent to the fascist mentality as masculine women. But, Theweleit goes further: for the male it is the woman within that constitutes the most radical threat to his own integrity. Two basic types of bodies exemplify the corporal metaphysics at the heart of fascist perception. On the one side there is the soft, fluid, and ultimately liquid female body which is a quintessentially negative ''Other'' lurking inside the male body. It is the subversive source of pleasure or pain which must be expurgated or sealed off. On the other there is the hard, organized, phallic body devoid of all internal viscera which finds its apotheosis in the machine. This body-machine is the acknowledged ''utopia'' of the fascist warrior. ''The new man is a man whose physique has been machinized, his psyche eliminated'' (p. 162). In the first volume, the fear and revulsion of the feminine manifests itself in the incessant invocation of metaphors of an engulfing fluid, or flood, in the ''red tide,'' ''street of blood,'' ''bursting earth,'' and in dirt, effluvia, streams, lava, and emissions of all sorts. In the second volume this visceral analysis is fleshed out to include the male''physis''—the body as a mechanism for eluding the liquid, for incorporating or repelling undesired emotions, thoughts, longings. The desire of the male ego is to be freed from all that can be identified with the female body: with liquidity, with warmth, and above all with a sensuality that is responsive to other human beings. It produces a politics of ''steel hard'' (Jünger's term) men who ''struggle against the mass and femininity as a struggle to contain the soldier male's fear of the desiring production of his own unconscious'' (p. 6). The preoccupation of the warrior with the perimeters of the body is a kind of disemboweled, disembodied, dis-sensuality, what we might call ''sensuous anti-sensualism.''

The warrior utopia of a mechanized body is therefore erected against the female self within. The terrifying deluge is femininity and the interior life which cannot admit to the ''soft'' desire for maternal love. The key to the fantasy of destructive violence and rage against women is the conflict between the longing for fusion and simultaneous terror at the destructive implications for the self that such merger entails. Women represent the splitting of masculine desire into the opposites of fusion/autonomy and erotic merging/armored self. The relentless presence of this threat also explains the compulsion to violence: the "spilling of blood" in the external world is a response to the anxiety of the interior one, the warding off of a danger which demands survival. Reality for these men is something set against the experience of pleasure, "erected against our own innermost flows." For this reason they feel an extreme sense of powerlessness and defenselessness when they encounter their (also powerless) victims. Theweleit's men are killers, not out of a simple lust for blood or romantic dreams of glory, but because they want to remain whole.

The conflicts and fantasies experienced by these men lie, in Theweleit's view, outside the oedipal orbit. It is not unconscious rage at the father, whose absence is hardly noted, nor the missing paternal authority that explains this violent obsession with the female body. Infantile terrors are far more central to this dread of, and at the same time, desire for fusion. Theweleit is at pains to show that Freud's oedipal theory does little to illuminate the mentality of these fascists, an idea that is far more commonplace in England and America, where the emigre psychoanalytic communities long ago elaborated the theory of preoedipal development. Theweleit was among the first German writers on fascism to draw on this emigre work—notably of Michael Balint and Melanie Klein in England and Margaret Mahler in America—and for this reason he engages in rearguard arguments with earlier formulations about fascist psychology pioneered by Wilhelm Reich, the Frankfurt theorists, and Freud himself. He is especially critical of Adorno and Horkheimer's work on the mass psychology of fascism in the 1930s and 1940s (which closely follows Freud's theory of narcissistic identification in *Group Psychology and the Analysis of the Ego*).[21] The operative terms in that thinking, as we have already suggested, were the identification with and idealization of paternal authority, and the centrality of the "leader" in fascist movements.[22]

Of course, Theweleit's contention that fascist men were in no sense oedipal does not always contradict these earlier thinkers. Adorno, too, saw the fascist relationship to authority as a preoedipal relationship of primitive identification, "an act of devouring, of making the beloved object part of oneself."[23] But for Adorno, the lack of an oedipal father, the presence of preoedipal currents, was enough to explain the matter. Theweleit goes much further and insists on exploring the content of this preoedipal mental world. He abandons the issue of authority in favor of an analysis that begins, as he puts it, "closer to the patient," with the "clinical" material supplied by the men themselves. And there the narcissistic idealization of the leader is clearly marginal to the powerful obsession with maintaining self-cohesion through direct action on their own and others' bodies. In fact, as we have already noted, the "leader" plays a subsidiary role in this phase of the emergence of the radical right—in contrast to National Socialism—and the destructive animus against the "enemy," a far more prominent one.

To understand this destructive impulse, Theweleit relies on Margaret Mahler's theory of self-other differentiation, which she calls "separation-individuation" (conceived, we might add, as part of the ego psychology Theweleit, following European intellectual fashion, often swipes at) and which she first developed in relation to psychotic children. The fantasies of destruction which these men express are hardly unconscious. Nor are they the expression of repressed wishes for a missing ego ideal. Rather, fear and longing for fusion, the threat of fragmentation and dissolution, and the inability to tolerate animate reality are concrete expressions of a failure to differentiate. His argument that these men were not fully born (as in Mahler's concept of "psychological birth" from symbiosis), that they never entered the field of object relations between a whole ego and a whole other, is not a hollow generalization, but explains much about what impels violence and destruction. These texts document their consequent inability to distinguish self from other, the inability to feel the integrity of the self and sustain a sense of bodily boundaries without inflicting violence.

Theweleit's parallel between the defenses of psychotic children and the "maintenance mechanisms" used by his subjects to stave off self-fragmentation is not, however, entirely convincing. Perversion, a primitive, sexualized defense against psychosis, comes much closer to what Theweleit describes than does psychosis. Recent theories of perversion—e.g., Robert Stoller's work on how issues of separation from the mother are acted out—have outlined the relationship between murderous fantasies and a failure of differentiation.[24] Janine Chasseguet-Smirgel, a French psychoanalyst, has also analyzed the loss of reality and the desire for fusion in terms of perversion, explicitly drawing the connection to Nazism.[25] Chasseguet-Smirgel argues that the male pervert lacks the paternal identification which would bar the way against his wish to enter the mother, to plunder and violate her body; this missing barrier is tantamount to the reality principle itself, the lack of which means that the person's fantasy moves unimpeded through "white" space, in much the same way as Theweleit's men fantasize.

On the other hand, Theweleit's work is a helpful corrective to some of Chasseguet-Smirgel's conclusions. She insists that this fantasy of a "universe without obstacles" reflects the lack of the father, and claims that fascism is solely about fusion with the mother, the *Blut und Boden* reunion with the maternal goddess, and therefore the product of a "fatherless universe."[26] Theweleit, however, shows us that the fascist soldier's wish to destroy the mother, his desire to fuck the earth, is not so much a wish for incestuous union with the mother as it is a wish to rid himself and the earth of all those maternal qualities of warmth and sensuality that could be called mother. It is a frantic repudiation of her. As Stoller put it, perversion is that "ultimate in separation, mother murder."[27] If one calls the fascist man fatherless because his image of male strength is the opposite of the oedipal father, then surely he is also motherless. His desire for fusion is above all directed to other men exactly like himself, his soldier-brother-mirror; his fear of fusion is directed toward all that is female, and his world banishes women as much as possible.

Theweleit's description of the fascist male's fantasy life thus challenges one of the most influential shibboleths about fascism that persists in psychoanalysis today: the idea of the fatherless society. He shows that the fascist male is not merely someone in search of a father, or someone whose father has failed and who therefore wishes to overthrow all fathers. He also shows the extent to which the fascist man is a motherless child, a man who must exclude women, who is threatened by any maternal or feminine warmth and sensuality. Long ago as a child he was denied these, and he replaced them with physical pain and discipline. Thus, while Theweleit's work supports the idea that preoedipal or narcissistic pathology is operative in fascist psychology, it does not support the proposition that the all-important factor is the missing father. This is the significance of his criticism of Freud's oedipal theory, both as a normative ideal of the male ego and as an explanation of pathology, a critique which explicitly avoids any affirmation of "paternal law" as the force of individuation. Theweleit does not set up the oedipal as the normal, the preoedipal as the pathological. He never slips into the stance common to contemporary analysts, and to earlier Freudians, in which the father's role is ultimately valorized in contrast to the mother's regressive character as a temptation to fusion and regression. Theweleit's soldiering men do not act as they do because they are overwhelmed by a preoedipal desire to become one with the mother, but because they never experience union with another person. It is the repudiation of woman, not the identification with her as a primal nature, which typifies fascism.

The vast majority of texts discussed in *Male Fantasies* are the product of *Freikorps* and fascist writers, or, we might say, literary fascists. This raises two important questions. First, what does it mean for these men to write? And second, what is the status of these texts in Theweleit's own work? He answers the first question clearly and explicitly. Their writings are not distinct from experience, they are the written "form" of experience. The language of these texts betrays their purpose: not to communicate but to eradicate, to expunge every association to the fear of dissolution, a fear which obsessively takes the form of the deluge: the sea of blood, the flood, the swamp, the tidal wave. Theweleit is not interested in "ideology" as a representation of reality, but in the symbolic construction of the other as a mechanism of self-cohesion. This conspiracy of bodily imperative and political effect is not at all hidden — it lies on the surface like debris in the aftermath of battle. It would be mistaken therefore to consider these works simply as "documents" or "evidence" of their authors' state of mind or beliefs. These texts alone are the subject matter of the analysis. Theweleit remarks that "their mode of writing is no different in principle from their mode of action" (I, 218).

Elsewhere Theweleit says that Jünger does not write *about* war. The act of writing is itself synonymous with destruction. For Jünger to produce a text like *Storm of Steel* or *Battle as Inner Experience*, or for Hanns Heinz Ewald to write *Riders in the German Night* (a novel of almost 500 pages devoted to the "nurse-whore-mother" complex) has nothing to do with artistic self-expression. These texts are alien to any linguistic posture that respects the integrity of its object. The purpose of this writing is to combat the aliveness of experience, to turn it into something lifeless. These texts are acts of literary homicide: their language "cannot describe, or narrate, or represent, or argue" (I, 215). Theweleit adds: "What is striking about our male writers is that the particles of reality taken up in their language lose any life of their own. They are de-animated and turned into dying matter. They are forced to relinquish their life to a parasitic, linguistic onslaught, which seems to find 'pleasure' in the annihilation of reality. Reality is invaded and 'occupied' in that onslaught. The language of occupation: it acts imperialistically against any form of independently moving life" (I, 215).

Writing thus has as its goal the marking out of a secure terrain free of the threat of any dangerous emotion. But there is even more involved than simply destroying the experience. An alternative must simultaneously appear in its place because empty space, a hole, as Theweleit reminds us, creates dread. The language and narrative of these texts is placed in the service of a kind of wrecking ball that demolishes emotion-laden experience in order to replace it with a new and familiar landscape populated by reassuring figures of discourse. "The more intensely life (emotions) impinges on them, the more aggressively they attack it, rendering it 'harmless' in extreme cases. That is one side of the process, its destructive aspect"(I, 217). But, the other side is the creation of a new reality as crucial as the destruction. Theweleit illustrates this with a famous passage by Walter Benjamin about Jünger: "As far as the eye could see above the edges of the trenches, the land had become the terrain of German idealism itself — every shell crater a philosophical problem; every barbed wire fence a representation of autonomy; every barb a definition; every explosion an axiom" (II, p. 51).

In this metaphysics of battle, the landscape is repopulated, philosophically speaking: the act of writing becomes directly analogous to the "muscular physis" of the soldiering man. It produces a narrative physis, a protective shield that secures the boundaries of the body no less effectively than the drill. To fully become secure the threat has to be neutralized by the discourse, dissolved as it were in the storm of words. The ego, as Theweleit points out, must rise above events — the significer triumphs *over* culture. Indeed, the more successful these writers are, the more risks they take in transgressing into the no-man's-land of dangerous emotions. To destroy the life world, they must first "penetrate" it. At one point Theweleit comments that both Jünger and Von Salomon were "able to use *writing* to gain stability" because, by invoking the dread, "the threshold of collapse is raised even higher" (II, p. 228). The more intense the writing, the more effectively the phantoms produced by their own fantasies are engaged.

If for the fascist the act of writing "safeguards both writer and reader against the experiences they fear" (II, p. 6), Theweleit intends these texts to have the opposite effect in his own work. Rather than steer the reader into the safety and security of the familiar, he pushes further and further away. He tries to comprehend what cannot be grasped easily, what we naturally avoid confronting, by poking around in it, even playing with it. This undaunted quality, which is the strength of the work, also sometimes leads to its excesses, its wild quality. Anyone who gives even a cursory thumbing of the work will find that there is much more here than a psychoanalytic study: it is full of unsolicited opinions, digressions, jokes, commentaries, and political judgments. In counterpoint to its subject matter, it is "undisciplined." And this is what is so "unGerman" and at the same time perhaps so very (post-1968) German about *Male Fantasies*. The intellectual environment from which *Male Fantasies* emerged was not always known for its wit, and yet, the more playful side of the alternative scene—for example, the Greens, who refuse to wear dresses and suits, and who play cello concerts in parliament—

confronting, by poking around in it. This undaunted quality, which is the strength of the work, also sometimes leads to its excesses, its wild quality. Anyone who gives even a cursory thumbing of the work will find that there is much more here than a psychoanalytic study: it is full of unsolicited opinions, digressions, jokes, commentaries, and political judgments. In counterpoint to its subject matter, it is "undisciplined." And this is what is so "unGerman" and at the same time perhaps so very (post-1968) German about *Male Fantasies*. The intellectual environment from which *Male Fantasies* emerged was not always known for its wit, and yet, the more playful side of the alternative scene—for example, the Greens, who refuse to wear dresses and suits, and who play cello concerts in parliament—

is evident here. More conservative critics will no doubt continue to fault Theweleit for his unorthodox attitudes toward some of the conventions of scholarship. But, they will hardly be able to deny his achievement and his intellectual daring. Theweleit's gift is his fearlessness in taking his subject at its word. At one point he notes Deleuze/Guattari's apt remark that "Freud had drawn back from this world of wild production and explosive desire, wanting at all costs to restore a little order there, an order made classical owing to the Greek theater'' (I, 214). It is this refusal to draw back and impose order that distinguishes Theweleit from all his predecessors.

male fantasies

Chapter 1
The Mass and Its Counterparts

THE MASS AS EMBODIMENT OF
A SPECIFIC UNCONSCIOUS

One specific type of mass was discussed in Volume 1: a mass of diverse consistencies, from fluid to viscous, in which the soldier male "sinks and is irretrievably lost." A damp mass: all that is hybrid within, across, on, or emanating from the body; everything "filthy." If the soldier male speaks negatively, with hatred, loathing, fear, disgust, of the mass (the human mass), it is not from any direct relation to the human masses themselves that his emotions spring; they arise in relation to the "mass" that issues from his own body.*

The emergence of revolutionary masses into the public arena occurs as a consequence of the rupturing of dams. At the same time, it threatens to undermine the internal dams of these men, as if their bodily boundaries might collapse under the pressure of the masses without. Their own inner mass "dissipates" into the mass which is outside, and the external mass comes to embody their own erupted interior. The man is "inundated."

This gives us a key to the apparent contradictoriness of the fascist concept of the masses. Alongside his capacity to mobilize great masses of human beings, there exists within the fascist a simultaneous contempt for the masses; while he addresses himself to them, he feels himself at the same time to be raised above them, one of an elite standing against the lowly "man-of-the-masses."[1]

---

* "Our *direct* experience of the interior of our bodies knows nothing of organs. We perceive merely a heavy mass." (Mahler, p. 40, referring to Hartmann and Schilder, 1927.)

The contradictions cease to appear as such once we understand that the fascist has two distinct and different masses in mind, two masses that stand in mutual opposition. The mass that is celebrated is strictly formed, poured into systems of dams. Above it there towers a leader (*Führer*). To the despised mass, by contrast, is attributed all that is flowing, slimy, teeming. (The soldier feels "exposed to the incomprehensible, seething hatred of the corrupted masses.")[2]

Thus when direct reference is made in these texts to "the masses," they appear in conjunction with everything associated with the "floods" and with "filth." (The notion of the "Red Flood," for example, has been shown to refer to specific masses of human beings.) This occurs particularly when the mass in question is a revolutionary one, though the rule applies to every formless mass. The example cited below is just one of many; here, "the mass" can be, and indeed is, substituted for the "Red Flood":

> And so they went forth, the warriors of the revolution. Was it then from amongst this swarthy rabble that the burning flame was to rise, the dream of blood and barricades to be realized? Capitulating to such as these was unthinkable. Only scorn for the demands they made, demands which knew no pride, no confidence in victory, no ripples of restraint. Laughter at the threat they presented, for they marched out of a hunger, an exhaustion, an envy under whose banners none have ever triumphed. Defiance of their danger, for its countenance was formless, the face of the mass, rolling sluggishly onward, prepared to suck anything that offered no resistance into its mucous whirlpool. I had no wish to succumb to the maelstrom. I stiffened, in my mind I called them "scoundrels," a pack, a mob, a rabble, narrowed my eyes to scrutinize their mouldering, emaciated figures. Like rats, I thought, wearing the dirt of the gutter on their backs, scrabbling and grey with beady, red-rimmed eyes.[3]

The same sense of threat ("I had no desire to succumb to the maelstrom"); the same defense ("I stiffened"), the same dripping wet rabble, teeming with animals. The activities of the mass are familiar from the waves and miasma of Volume 1: we know how it roars, surges, pours out, devours, swallows, shreds, smashes, tramples, beats to a pulp—then lies calm once again.[4]

The "animal" in the mass snaps its greedy jaws and stares poisonously, paralyzingly from a thousand eyes. It has a thousand legs, a thousand heads, it can generate a thousand degrees of heat. It can metamorphose into a single creature, many-limbed: millipede, rat, snake, dragon.[5] And it is named with the same mythological names we have encountered as characterizations of the bestial terrors inhabiting what is known indiscriminately as the belly of the

"Collaboration Parfaite." Vichy Government poster.

erotic woman menstruating or "ruptured" in childbirth: the Hydra, the head of the Medusa, the Gorgon.[6]

What has however become quite clear is that the meaning of these names cannot be interpreted by reference to the mythological context from which they derive. They should instead be seen as culturally specific encodings (their origins traceable to a humanist secondary education), used to evoke feelings which the linguistic material and stylistic repertoire of the soldier male (neither of which extends beyond the limits of German essay-writing exercises) cannot even begin to describe.[*]

The easy accessibility of the symbolism in the texts of the soldier males does, however, almost succeed in persuading the reader to "interpret" them in this way. What they offer us is precisely the kind of exchange that Ulrich Sonnemann considers typical of all interpretation, in which the possibility of experience is exchanged for a meaning, an objectifying concept. "It is in the very recognition of the exchange character of interpretation that we are forced to note also the way in which this exchange itself dissipates any impulse to unleash the past."[7] It is surely in this sense that we are to understand the function of the over-explicitness of the fascist language of symbol: it safeguards both writer and reader against the experiences they fear. The *conscious* encoding[**] of the revolutionary mass with the specific configuration of "devouring femininity" successfully prevents any confrontation with an experience of the struggle against the mass and femininity as a struggle to contain the soldier male's fear of the desiring production of his own unconscious.

And yet in his role as a builder of dams, as killer, exterminator, the man draws closer to the "desire to desire," to his own unconscious, his own life. Of this alone he remains unconscious.

It is not specific contents that he represses; instead, he subjects the unconscious itself, the whole desiring production of the unconscious, to repression. Inside this man is a concentration camp, the concentration camp of his desires. The socially encoded forms of his desires and fears (the "desire" for incest, fear of the Medusa, the woman with the penis) have, however, nothing to do with repression and are in no sense unconscious; on the contrary, they are openly and obtrusively celebrated in the literature of the fascists and in the activities of the White Terror.

This recognition of the possible origin of terror perpetrated on the mass in a fear of the merging of the individual "interior" with that same mass may

---

[*]Or to put this another way, the concepts deployed by the soldier male are "more Oedipal" than the sensations he feels—a fact which confirms once again that the pathway toward the knowledge the language speaks of leads, not through the "connotations" of those concepts, their associations with other terms, nor through "translations" of latent *contents*, but through an analysis of the affects which accompany them, of their dynamic.

[**]In this case, "conscious" means accessible to consciousness, not deliberate.

L'A MARCHANDE de CHATS

337. Symbolische Darstellung der sich prostituierenden Frau

Symbolische Darstellung des Weibes als
männerfressendes Ungeheuer

serve as a useful addendum to Elias Canetti's insights in his *Crowds and Power*. The revolutionary mass may usefully be seen as an embodiment (not a symbol) of the erupted "interior" of the soldier male—an effluent that he perceives in thoroughly objectified form, as a repellent mixture of fluids streaming from the body. The unconscious emerges here no longer as a productive force, but as a product of the body, a substance which, once released, becomes ungovernable, combining itself with uncontrollable external masses and laying waste the boundaries of the body.

A number of the specific characteristics of the White Terror become visible in this relationship with the mass, as do some of the central features of fascist ideologies. It is these that we examine in the following chapter.

CONTAGIOUS LUST

The focus of repression in the soldier male is the "desire to desire"; concomitantly, the core of all fascist propaganda is a battle against everything that constitutes enjoyment and pleasure. Pleasure, with its hybridizing qualities, has the dissolving effect of a chemical enzyme on the armored body. Attitudes of asceticism, renunciation, and self-control are effective defenses. A Nazi dream:

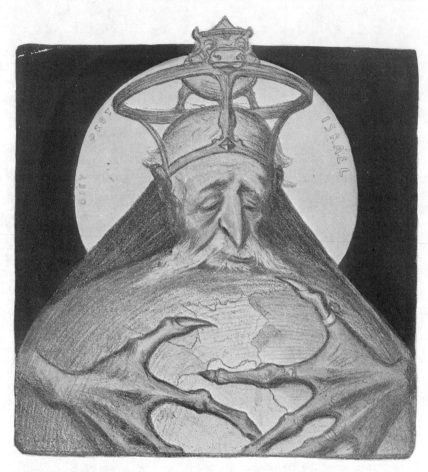

"Rothschild," by C. Leandre (France, 1898). A contagious lust undermines the "whorish masses," making them susceptible both to the Jews and to Bolshevism.

> Some intangible impulse within the masses has long wished to rid itself of the wretched belief that life is intended for pleasure—a contagious belief which is truly Jewish in nature. Today, the idyll of "heaven on earth" has lost much of its attraction.[1]

This quotation from Rosenberg is a highly explicit formulation of the Nazi program for the masses: a combating of any hope for a real "heaven-on-earth," a real life in pleasure; a naming of the desire for a better life as an illness, of human pleasures as a contagious disease whose prime carrier is the "Jewish element," with its perpetual drive toward miscegenation.

The "success" of the fascists in diverting anticapitalist sentiments among the masses toward the Jews—the rich Jew, the Jew as exploiter—has become something of a standard explanation for the persecution of the Jews.[2] Yet a

"Germany." Poster for the German Reichstag elections of 1920.

study of fascist literature and propaganda shows quite clearly that this point is secondary. What we find at the core of German anti-Semitism is instead a coupling of "Jewishness" with a "contagious" desire for a better life. Jewishness is brought into association, both with the mass of lascivious flesh and with two other masses: with mountains of money and piles of corpses.

> There are three types of parasitic Jews. You will be familiar with the first type: their home is the bank, from whence they practice their economic extortions on their host nations. The second variety is equally widely known. These are the Jews one invariably sees

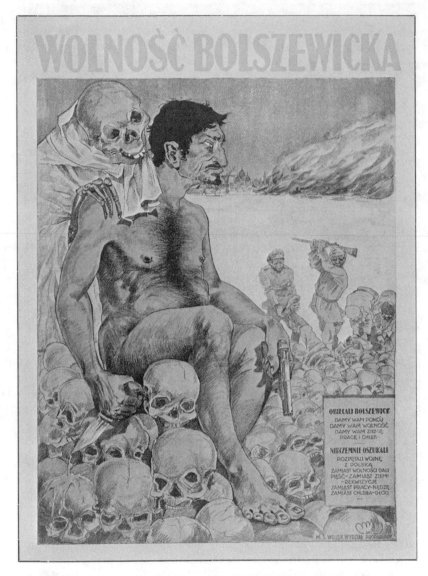

"Trotsky the Jew." Skabowski's poster from the Polish-Russian War (1920).

sitting with blonde German girls in bars and cafes, sapping the
sexual and racial strength of their host people and destroying
them.

"The Exalted Hero." Street poster from the Sailors' Rebellion, Kiel (1918). The cloth on the bayonet is red.

But there is also a third type of Jew—the kind who quite literally sap the blood of Gentiles and their children. They do so not for religious reasons, but because their own chaotic blood is in danger of decomposition; it is only in sucking the blood of other peoples that they can preserve their own life. (Robert Ley)

During coitus the male semen is fully or partially absorbed into the lining of the female uterus, where it enters the bloodstream. A single act of intercourse between a Jew and an Aryan woman is enough to poison her blood forever. . . . It now becomes clear why the Jew employs every device of the seductive art in an attempt to dishonor German girls at the earliest possible age, or why the Jewish doctor violates female patients under anaesthetic.[3]

No description of any revolutionary action is without its equivalent of comments such as, "The day ended in wine and blood, whiskey and women." (The day in question, described here by v. Berk, is the date of the seizure of the city of Essen by the workers in March 1920.)[4] Equally, it is rare for the list of professions ascribed to revolutionary activists not to include—along with "jailbird," "bum," "common criminal," "hoodlum," "shirker," "riff-raff," "traitor," "thief," and "good-for-nothing"—the title of "pimp" or "brothel-keeper." Everywhere he turns, the soldier male finds himself confronted with "sexual depravity."[5]

Never does the republican or revolutionary appear unaccompanied by his whore. His mouth is full of filthy language. (The vagabond, a girl hooked onto each arm, who bellows: "They musta forgot t'bury you in Flanders!"[6] His time will come . . .) Similar encodings surface in military reports; one account of the military's defeat of the workers talks of "those elements who had preferred to evade capture by fleeing (being) gradually rounded up in surprise raids during their nocturnal visits to family members and sundry lovers."[7]

The haunts of whores through which the revolutionaries passed in secret seem to have been intimately familiar to and closely surveyed by the *Freikorps* commandant Major Schulz. Ernst Toller, the temporary (and reluctant) commander of the Red Army of the Munich soviet republic, was widely rumored to have been apprehended in the company of one such "lover." In an attempt to avoid the fate of Landauer and others, who had been beaten to death by the White troops, Toller disguised himself in a wig. He was discovered, so the report went, hiding behind a hidden doorway in his nightshirt, the red wig still on his head.[8] Howling laughter was the form now chosen by the army of soldier males to "annihilate" a man who had hitherto eluded the death squads.

During the Nuremberg Trials, General Jodl ventured the opinion that the only element of Nazi propaganda the German people had really "fallen for" was "the identification of the Jews with Communism."[9] The success of the encoding of "contagious lust" with two qualities, Judaism and Bolshevism, clearly demonstrates both the extent to which fear of communism represents a fear of the liberation of individual desires and the extent to which, in the historical period in question, "Jewishness" must have been seen in Germany as the embodiment of dangerous desires.*

Fascism, then, waged its battle against human desires by encoding them with a particular set of attributes: with effeminacy, unhealthiness, criminality, Jewishness—all of which existed together under the umbrella of "Bolshevism." For the fascist, the most malignant force of all these seems, in fact, to have been "Jewishness." Following Rathenau's murder by Fischer, Kern, Techow, Salomon, and others, Friedrich Wilhelm Heinz offered this response to the rhetorical cry "But Rathenau loved the German people!'":

> Of course any Jew loves the German people. It draws him to itself in its very being, its spiritual nature, the physicality of its daughters and sons. He seeks to restore himself with blood that is virginal and fresh. . . . What moves us to flee from Jewry, no matter how much love we may harbour for individual Jews, is the repugnance we feel in the face of degeneracy personified.[10]

("The Eternal Jew/Leads us downward.''**)

More dangerous still is the Jewish woman, within whom all possible threats cluster together simultaneously. Hans Krafft, the hero of Zöberlein's novel *Befehl des Gewissens* (Conscience Commands), is hounded by Mirjam, the daughter of a Jewish banker; she is beauty personified, elegance, wealth, serpent, whore, and countess—not to mention opium addict. Nor is this all. She has two further traits of particular interest here. The first is her affiliation with death, with the world of the no-longer-living. When Krafft proves successful in resisting her charms, she breaks down:

> Do you know what it means to be the last in a long line rising from the darkness of millennia? To be surrounded by emptiness, night, and mortal solitude? To burn, with nothing to still your torment. To be cold as ice, with never a friendly gaze to warm you. To have wealth in millions and still to be made destitute by a heart that is only a pumping machine, worn out over thousands of years. To wish for youth and yet to have the years of a Methuselah.

---

*For any refutation of the hypothesis of projection here, it would be necessary to identify the traits in the actual behavior of "the Jews" which made it possible for viewpoints of this kind to develop. I do not feel myself to be in a position to demonstrate such traits (any more, as I indicated in Chapter 1, than I could in relation to the proletarian woman). I know of no study which describes the life situation of German Jews in Wilhelminian society, their true functions, the actual influence they exercised.

**A play on the final lines of Faust, Part 1: "The Eternal Feminine/Leads us onward." (Tr.)

"The Specter of Syphilis."

Her monotone tale of despair aroused strange thoughts. A chilling aroma of decay wafted toward Krafft, the musty odor of some timeless dungeon deep beneath the earth. So speaks the eternal curse of a people who desire heaven on earth but have hell instead. It was now that Krafft recognized the rebellion rising up within him as a dread of this darkness, the same horror of going under that grips the drowning man as every instinct within him struggles toward the light above.[11]

"A people who desire heaven on earth but have hell instead":[*] Hell is inside, in the darkness of the body; the body is a tomb, a dungeon. The mass of this ancient, pleasure-seeking people is the mass of dead desires Krafft feels moldering within himself. "Struggling toward the light"—fleeing from pleasure, from desire, from the unconscious, whose "darkness" is the realm of the dead. It is not only the mass of *human* dead that can attract and repel, as Canetti claims;[13] it is also the mass of dead *desires,* of life that has perished within the soldier male's own body.

---

[*]The same analysis played a key role in the "documentary" *Der Ewige Jude* (The Eternal Jew), a film produced at the time when the "Final Solution" was beginning to be implemented; the film was shown all over Germany. Zöberlein's works were also widely circulated. My quotations are taken from the fourteenth edition of *Befehl des Gewissens* (281,000-310,000), published by the Central Publishing House of the Nazi Party, Franz Eher, Munich (originally published in 1937). In the notes I've cited several other passages from the same chapter, "Mirjam," to show the extent to which the various threats of "Jewishness" were able to be assembled within the category woman, and to demonstrate also how they change in the general movement toward the extermination of the Jews.[12]

A measure taken to prevent the deliberate infection of the German army: evacuating diseased women.

Mirjam's other interesting trait is a blood disease that makes her sterile and is highly contagious: the "Jewish pox" (*Judenpest*). One of Krafft's well-meaning friends, a pharmacist familiar with such matters, enlightens him:

> "Mirjam will capture you like the witch she is. Whatever she loves is horribly destroyed—and her love is more often than not quickly given. No man has ever been able to keep away from her after the first time—not even me. Just so you know."
>
> "Why are you telling me this? I've already explained . . ."
>
> "Because even the best of intentions are useless if you're dealing with slippery cats like this one. You need to be able to feel enormous repugnance for her. I would be sorry to see you become the next victim of her Jewish pox, her . . . syphilis!"
>
> Krafft started back in horror. "Why you . . . !" An icy horror seized him, and he cursed himself for babbling at such length with a man completely unknown to him. All for a Jewess for whom he cared so little, indeed who disgusted him. How could he do such a thing to his Berta, how could he waste as much as one single thought on such a woman?[14]

The fear of syphilis, to which Reich has ascribed such great significance,[15]appears here as a fear which is only derivative in nature. "Syphilis" is *one name only* for the dissolution to which a man falls prey if he comes into contact with the external incarnation of his devouring, dead unconscious. But it is a particularly apposite name, a rich code, containing as it does the corrosions of femininity, Jewishness, epidemic disease, criminality (the contagion is international), and emasculating death.

Witness the German Imperial Army in its battle against syphilis:

> In the early part of 1916, the incidence of disease among German soldiers in the cities of Lille and Roubaix reached such alarming proportions that the German High Command resolved to intervene. Countless women workers, deprived of their means of existence with the closure of their factories, were living on the proceeds of love. . . . As the various epidemics became increasingly widespread, individual medical treatment remained useless, particularly since the women infected never considered abandoning their trade—indeed pressure seems to have been exerted on them from some unknown source to continue to practice it in spite of all. . . . Once it had become clear on the German side that the enemy's intelligence service was responsible for the situation in the northern French industrial cities, it became necessary to implement the most stringent of measures . . . mercilessly evacuating any women who were in the least suspect, even initially at the risk of expelling numbers of innocent women in the process. This was however our only means of defense against the grave danger which had become the destiny of whole divisions now peacefully encamped in this region.

In *Spionage* (Espionage), a collection edited by Lettow-Vorbeck, Ferdinand Brack reports that at least fifteen hundred women from Lille and Roubaix were transported in this way to areas distant from the front, and indefinitely interned. Brack takes evident pleasure in describing how the French mayors of individual small towns were forced to concede entry to the freight cars marked "vegetables," in which the women were transported.

> The cargo of vegetables which the local adjutant was forced to receive—not without a slight shudder of horror—was indeed a particularly rotten one, an avenging chorus. . . . Strangely the integration of this Great Female Flood into the resident population proceeded more smoothly than expected. . . . Thus all enemy hopes of further gains by these means were dashed.

On the syphilis front at least, the German army could then claim a victory.

Even in our own homeland, in the fatherlands of the Axis powers, women of the same kind were incited by enemy agents to place their diseased bodies in the service of our foes. . . . One female carrier of venereal disease in Leipzig in 1918 has been proved beyond doubt to have spent all her time transmitting her illness to soldiers, and to have been financially supported by anonymous parties, in order to allow her to pursue her degenerative activities to greater effect. In her particular case, even sexual pleasure was no longer afforded to her visitors. Intercourse with her was practised only to the point at which infection appeared assured. This one individual is said to have had a prodigious number of infected soldiers on her conscience, several thousand men in all, by the time she was able successfully to be prevented from pursuing her trade. (Ferdinand Brack, 'Frauen als Kampfmittel,' in *Spionage*, 415ff.)

Syphilis is not simply something one *has*. It is either a condition deliberately *given*, or a function of enemy intelligence. As Hocquenghem writes:

Syphilis is more than a microbe,it is also an ideology—an ideology in the sense in which Artaud uses the term in his analysis of the plague and its symptoms as an integral complex of obsessional ideas. The idea of syphilis encapsulates a compulsive fear of contagion, of hidden collaboration between microbes and the unconscious energies of the libido.[16]

It is this latter point which will be crucial; we should note too that syphilis appears here as a mass (a swarming mass of microbes) and that it produces another mass: a seething mound of rotting flesh.

Thus the rebellious human mass gathering in the street is both an incarnation of all contagious diseases spawned by life-producing desire, and an incarnation of all the Red masses into which the man sinks and is lost: the embodiment both of pleasures that tempt and of pleasures that are dead. This may explain the soldier male's fascination with the decaying mass; for it appears to have all the features of his own externalized interior. Its attraction is irresistible:

A jumble of stakes and fragments of iron. On the ground a charred, blackish, encrusted mass. *Can this be a human being?*[*] I jabbed into it with the barrel of my gun, inexpressibly curious. There was a hiss, the outer skin ruptured, and my gun went deep inside—the lump seemed to move. My stomach heaved momentarily. The hideous stench of disease and decomposition sent me reeling backward, and I stumbled away.[17]

[*]The emphasis is mine.

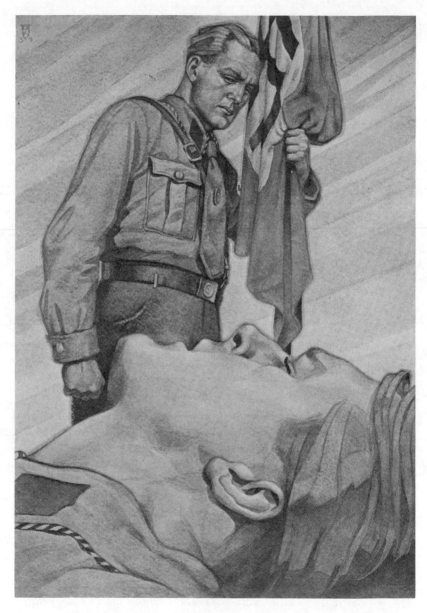

There is no other way of expressing gratitude than to swear on oath to fight on for the Germany for which you have died. From ''Germany Awake,'' cigarette-image album, Altona-Bahrenfeld (1933).

Elsewhere, as Salomon contemplates a painting of the fleshy face of Napoleon I, he feels a desire to stab into the cheek, and imagines a whitish-yellow mass pouring out.[18]

Jünger described himself as a person to whom life appeared "sometimes as a polished carbuncle, sometimes as a mysteriously shimmering opal, sometimes as the worm-eaten face of a corpse" (the sequence moves from "exterior" to "blurring of boundaries" to "interior").[19] The gaze he directs away from the trench and onto the fragments of rotting corpses seeks them out almost deliberately; his eyes remain riveted:

> Just yesterday I spent hours staring nervously, rigidly at the crumbling earthen wall opposite me. . . . There was a dead man under it, though all that could be seen was one leg. He must have been lying there like that for some time. The foot, no longer able to support the weight of his boot, had fallen off at the ankle. The anklebone and the brown, gangrenous flesh that had peeled away from it were clearly visible. Next came the crudely knitted underwear and the grey pants, which the rain had already rinsed clear of clay. One should oneself properly have been lying for no lesser length of time in some similar place.[20]

But "one" is not yet lying there, and it is this that is important. The attack: "under my hobnail boots, a chest cavity gently collapses like a bellow."[21] It is the *other* who is dead, the softness underfoot. The grinding of the boot is an affirmation of life.

On the basis of his identification of analogous features in fascist writings, Erich Fromm has attempted to describe the fascist as a "necrophiliac character," an individual who loves corpses.[22] He calls Hitler "a clinical case of necrophilia."[23] Quite apart from the fact that characterological definitions of this kind are rooted in an ideological image of human construction, the very core of Fromm's hypothesis must also be seen as mistaken. It is not corpses that this man loves; he loves his own life.[24] But he loves it—and this strikes me as Canetti's crowning insight—for its ability to survive.[25] Corpses piled upon corpses reveal him as victor, a man who has successfully externalized that which is dead within him, who remains standing when all else is crumbling.

Jünger on the *aftermath* of battle

> At such times I feel existence to be vital and intoxicating—hot, wild, insane—a fervent prayer. Expression is imperative, expression at any price, to allow myself the shuddering perception: I'm alive. I'm still alive.[26]

And just how does he "express" himself? His next sentence is one we've seen before: "I plunge my glance, quick and penetrating as a gunshot, into the eyes of passing girls."

Survival in the identity of two distinct movements: in battle the dead are "stepping stones for those who follow, whose hearts quail each time their hobnail boots sink into softness."[27] Meanwhile in the brothel, "a rising chorus of drunken laughter as metallic hands sink into soft flesh."[28]

A night march in France:

"And still the alien race dug relentlessly into this alien land."[29] "I have the war to thank for this need to penetrate life with every fiber of my being, to grasp life in all its glory. To do so requires familiarity with decay, for only he who knows the darkness of night knows also the value of the light."[30]

Light no longer brings clarity of vision—any such meaning for the metaphors of light and darkness has long since been lost. What they now describe is a movement of flight. To stand in the light—to survive—is to experience the joy of escape from the mass of the dead, the darkness within oneself. The "fibers" with which Jünger penetrates life are there to suck it dry, they pierce and destroy life. "We are the only living beings in an age of decay"[31]: so says Heinz at the end of *Sprengstoff* (Explosive). But it is the "decay" of which he speaks that is living; it is desire, dissolving all that is rigid and causing it to flow. If Heinz feels alive, it is because he has not yet disintegrated, because his armor is still intact as he marches onward, grinding his boots into gently collapsing rib cages.[32]

THE ALIEN WITHIN AS "PRIMITIVE MAN"

If the mass and whatever lives, teems, or decays within it is to appear to the soldier male as an embodiment of his own "interior," he needs to perceive his own "inner life," the state of his inner drives, as a separable entity completely divorced from him. He experiences the force that from time to time threatens to erupt and express itself from within him, as the Alien *per se*, as "primitive man" (*der Urmensch*):

> Over millennia, society has tamed our impetuous urges and
> desires; the savage, brutal, shrill tone of our instincts has been
> polished, smoothed and dampened. Growing refinement has
> enlightened and ennobled man; yet the beast still sleeps in the
> depths of his existence. There is still much of the animal in him
> . . . and when life's dial swings back to its primitive guiding line
> the mask falls; primitive man, the cave-dweller, sallies forth naked
> as ever, with all the savagery of his unfettered instincts.[1]

What appears to Jünger—however alien he may feel it to be—as the *defining quality* of his humanity is in fact the most social aspect of his being: the state of his drives as produced by the patriarchal capitalism of the nine-

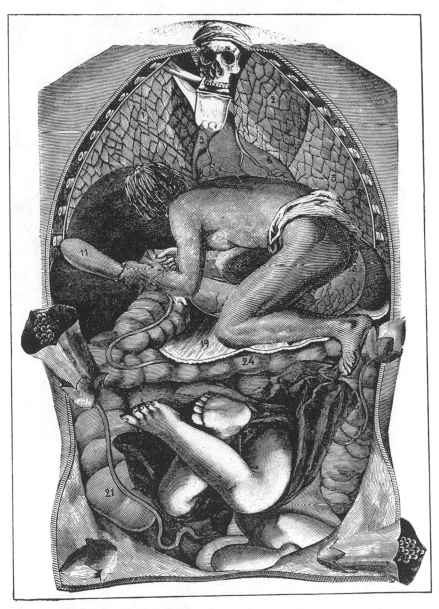

''White Week'' (Element: the Dark) by Max Ernst.

Advertisements for *Freikorps* volunteers (1919).

teenth and twentieth centuries. Jünger confronts his own society as a culture that "smooths" and "dampens"; he is aware of its existence as the armor around his own body. Yet he remains oblivious to the part played by culture in producing the "bestial" state of his drives. The soldier male is forced to turn the periphery of his body into a cage for the beast within. In so doing, he deprives it of its function as a surface for social contact. His contact surface becomes an insulated shield, and he loses the capacity to perceive the social corpus within which his insulated body moves. Though the devastation wrought on his body originates in social agencies and human "modelers," he perceives it only as an evil ("bestial") interior, which he cannot perceive as "social," and thus inevitably sees as "essentially human." This is a man who strongly senses the animal in himself; he will be hard to convert from cultural pessimism.

The passage from Jünger quoted above can also be understood as a specific means of registering the enormous distance separating Jünger's own psychic structure from any mechanism of sublimation or what Freud called "culture-work." Nothing is "transformed"; everything "internal" (or "bestial") is retained intact, and simply incarcerated to await discharge. Jünger's conclusion seems indisputable: "wars will be fought as long as this bestial legacy remains in our blood."[2] A man structured in the way he describes craves war, because only war allows him to achieve identity with his alien, "primitive," "bestial" interior, while at the same time avoiding being devoured by it. Or to put it another way, only war promises to animate the dead within him. War is rebirth, resurrection of the mass of his dead desires. And when those desires break out, they give the world their own form of life—which is death.

Dwinger, referencing a familiar quote from Büchner, voices the notion that the only way to really know a man is to kill him, to crack his skull— literally—and to scrutinize its contents. It is hard to say what makes the passage more horrifying: his polished näiveté of expression, the innocent ease with which he condemns all living matter to death, his complacent crudity, or his vacuousness:

> Hellwig pulled the book abruptly away from his face and called
> over to Pahlen in a half-whisper. "Listen to this for a moment.
> Julie asks Danton, 'Do you believe in me?' and he answers, 'How
> can I say. We know so little of each other. We have thick skins,
> the two of us; we stretch out our hands to each other but our
> trouble is in vain. All we do is wear away our coarse leather
> skins—we're very lonely creatures.' He points to her forehead and
> continues. 'But here, what's behind here? To know each other
> truly, we should have to break open each other's skulls, tease the
> thoughts out of the brain fibers!'" Half rising, Hellwig said gently,
> "Is that not quite stupendous? How often have I felt precisely
> this, in the face of the poor and needy (*die Armen*) for example?"
> "Or in my case, in confrontation with the raging mob," said
> Pahlen thoughtfully.[3]

Reading this extract from Pahlen invariably conjures up for me the image of a face—a staring face with a hollow smile around its open mouth, a face set apart from its own narcissistic sneer: omnipotent, impotent. Then there is movement: two rough hands reach out toward anything with an interior; they open it, peer inside to assure themselves that it is dead and finished, before dropping it to search further.

Hellwig refers to confrontations with "the poor" (*die Armen*): in German, the statement is ambiguous. *Die Armen* refers both to paupers and to human "arms"; arms that may belong to a human body. In the embrace of another human being, Hellwig experiences only strangeness and fear. His only means of discovering how his body functions is to take bodies apart, as a child might dismantle a mechanical toy.

The child's aim is not to fathom the functions of mechanics itself, but to find answers to the riddle of its own existence. It perceives a similarity between the tiny machines and motors it feels working in its own interior, and the motors that drive its playthings.

Analogously, the unresolved question that underlies the soldier male's impotent attempts to gain mastery over objects by tearing them apart, and thus rendering them knowable, seems to be that of the construction of his own

Advertisements for *Freikorps* volunteers (1919).

self—a question which acquires tremendous explosive force in a body never rendered capable of experiencing itself in relation to other bodies. The soldier male cannot know what impels him to tear out his own entrails, what moves him to spill his own contents in an effort to discover what species of being he may be.

But how close is the resemblance of bodies opened to view: they are all pulp and glutinous mass. Knowledge at last! Each penetration of the external alien seems to bring the soldier male into proximity with the alien within, the enemy that lurks beneath his own thick skin; it animates the mass of the dead waiting to be awakened.

One of the poems included by Curt Hotzel in his essay *Student 18*, "Botschaft des Dichters" (The Poet's Mission), seems to me more or less demonstrably to derive from this same emotional configuration. Hotzel does not give the poet's name:

> When once our race is cleansed of shame
> The chains of serfdom ripped from its arms
> Feeling only hunger for honor in its belly
> Then, on the battlefield of endless graves,
> The testament of blood will rise to life
> and blasting armies hunt from clouds
> and through the fields will roar
> the horror of horrors, the third and final storm:
> The return of the dead![4]

When dead desires rise from the grave, they are transformed into a mass earmarked for murder. Historically, there was a time when it might have been possible for a whole mass of desires to be satisfied in Germany. But they remained unrealized, reflected only in massacres of monstrous proportions, great mountains of corpses. For every desire that had been put to death, a Jew or a nigger, a nip, a communist, a woman, a child was made to die (though, as we know, there was also a form of mass murder that was random).

ASPECTS OF THE MASSES IN REALITY

What is it that actually happens in the mass to allow it to appear to the solider male as riddled with contagious lust, threatening him with dissolution? Elias Canetti has given a precise description of the processes occurring within human masses—referred to in the English version of his work as "crowds." The three I shall be citing in the following seem to me essential for our discussion.

> Ideally, all are equal there; no distinctions count, not even that of sex. The man pressed against him is the same as himself. He feels him as he feels himself. Suddenly it is as though everything were happening *in one and the same body*. This is perhaps one of the reasons why a crowd seeks to close in on itself: it wants to rid each individual as completely as possible of the fear of being touched. The more fiercely people press together, the more certain they feel that they do not fear each other. This *reversal of the fear of being touched* belongs to the nature of crowds.[1]

In contrast to this, soldiers serving in the same company are always separated by an exactly prescribed *distance*.

> In the crowd, the individual feels that he is transcending the limits of his own person.[2]

Both the above aspects of the mass lead the soldier male quite correctly to perceive an element of the sexual, of hybridity and dissolution, in mass events. A perception of the mass as body is more than a figment of the soldier male's imagination; the mass *is* one body, a body with many eyes, arms, heads, and feet. And by virtue of its very density, the mass allows human beings within it to touch and to transcend boundaries.

It would, however, be misleading to relate mass processes solely to the kind of fusion that occurs between lovers. Pleasures within the mass may be much more than mere projections of the soldier male; but they also involve a third process of pleasure—a process perhaps more significant than the others. Canetti describes it as an act of liberation:

> Every command leaves behind a painful *sting* in the person who is forced to carry it out.[3]
> It is obvious that, in a soldier, these stings must accumulate to a monstrous degree. Everything he does is done in response to a

command; he does, and must do, nothing else (. . .) All his spontaneous impulses are suppressed. He swallows order after order, and whatever he feels about it, must go on doing so. Each command he carries out—and they are innumerable—leaves a sting behind in him.[4]
The sting sinks deeper into the person who has carried out the command and remains in him unchanged. In the whole psychological structure of man, there is nothing less subject to change. The content of the command—its force, range, and definition—was fixed forever in that moment in which it was first promulgated.[5]
It may also happen, however, that a person receives one and the same command from several different sources. If this occurs often enough and order follows pitilessly close upon order, then the sting loses its clear outline and develops into a monster which endangers life. It grows until it forms the main substance of its host. He can never forget it and carries it around, seeking every opportunity to get rid of it.[6]

(Again, the features ascribed to the "interior" of the soldier male are those of a thing that is dead.) Now the crucial point:

Alone he is no longer capable of freeing himself from his burden. The emphasis is on *alone*, for liberation can be found from all stings, including the most monstrous and the most complex; it can be found within a crowd.[7]

According to Canetti's model, the soldier who pits himself against the masses experiences commands as implanted stings; but, unlike his opponents, he never achieves release. Now stings perpetually pierce him; he is at a huge disadvantage.

The soldier male has a clear perception of mass action as liberation; but it is a liberation from which he is excluded. It is this that causes him to combat the mass so vehemently through the perpetration of terror. He cannot allow himself to become mass; he must remain in formation. Only in the final stages of the civil war, when the workers are defeated and the command structure of his troop has slackened, does he himself become the mass: a dog hunting with the pack.[8] The whole military campaign is directed toward this moment, the moment of *his* liberation; it is in preparation for this moment alone that rumors are circulated about the workers, their alleged atrocities enumerated, the sinister nature of their activities emphasized, their movements observed, their forbidden pleasures scrutinized.

WOMEN TO THE FORE . . .

As we have seen above, the mass may be variously encoded—with femininity, with the bestial, with dissipating, contagious lust, and so on. But these different encodings do not necessarily occur simultaneously, nor with equal intensity. Their occurrence seems bound to specific situations; the more threatening the situation appears to any given man, the more encodings he brings into play; increase in number and intensity.

For one very common situation—confrontation on the streets of the city with unarmed, or poorly armed, mass demonstrations—it seems sufficient for the mass to be encoded with a "femininity" behind which lies concealed the castrating and/or murderous (masculine) monster. The soldier male generally has little difficulty in dealing with a mass of this kind; the threat emanating from it appears relatively low in intensity. In extreme instances, he simply presents it as comical:

> Germans will never be significantly moved by processions enacted by disparate groups of assorted men in civilian clothes, incapable of keeping in step, smoking and jabbering amongst themselves; they will never be inspired to follow groups of women and children trailing baby carriages along with them. They are likely either to perceive them as comical or as repulsive, perhaps even nauseating.[1]

The description comes from Killinger's collection of tips for aspiring SA-men; he perceives the demonstration in terms of "women and children," men out of uniform, a thoroughly confused mixture, a mass family excursion. The battle waged by Killinger and others against the mass structure of the demonstration seems to relate (in part at least) to a conflict that is familial in nature:

> Suddenly, quite without warning, the rabble was roused to storm our sentries; it advanced row upon row, with women and children in the vanguard. Our men had no choice but to pull back towards the school.[2] (Wittmann)

And suddenly, each and every militant proletarian demonstration is headed by women. "Women and children" occur with strikingly stereotypical regularity in the soldier male's descriptions; and the reason for their presence is clearly indicated. "*While the women gave cover*, machine guns were hauled out and carried to the nearest houses."[3]

But, as Wittmann suggests, "it seems likely that the women were hired

for the purpose, by cowards willing to procure their own safety by hiding behind the skirts of women. They knew no soldier would shoot at a woman.''[4]

The women are perceived to have been planted for strategic reasons; they form part of the overall tactics of the workers. As machine guns are set in place behind the women, the leaders, Wittmann stresses, "continued with negotiations.'' In an account of his negotiations with representatives of the People's Naval Brigade, whom he successfully surrounded in the Berlin Imperial Stables on 24 December 1918, Maercker stresses that it was the rebels who "thrust women and children into their fighting ranks.''[5] And von Oertzen has the following to say on the same subject: "Women and children were quite systematically moved to the front, where their bodies formed a protective wall.''[6] There are numerous similar examples.

The emphasis is clearly on the fact that women were being "moved" to the front. While the one is thrust forward, the other hides out of sight. . . . True, women did occasionally lead processions of demonstrators; indeed they staged demonstrations of their own (causing themselves to be described by one writer as "the whole great mass of the other sex'').[7] For the construction of fascist texts, it seems, however, to be crucial first that women *always* be present and second that they be depicted as present at the bidding of others — as *used* for some ulterior purpose. But why should an image of the vanguard of women be so apparently *indispensable* to the fascist text?

> The instigators never occupy the front lines of battle. They prefer to "direct the action" under the cover of women and children.*

---

*There is a remarkable resemblance between this and Maercker's own position as general.

1936: the crowd outside the prison in *Fury* (Fritz Lang).

> We have had to instruct our troops always to post a number of
> marksmen in the upper stories, so they can pick them off behind
> the front line.[8]

(This, then, is the vocation of the marksman; to shoot men who hide
under the skirts of women.) The men Maercker calls "instigators," the true
heads of the masses, are represented as a mauling beast that threatens to rise
up without warning; a penis in the swamp of the Medusae.

> The ringleaders were the same arch-cowards who had taken refuge
> under women's skirts the same morning. Under cover of darkness
> they slipped from their hideouts to whip up the masses to new
> fervor.[9]

Who is it that actually hides under women's skirts? As children, the soldier males themselves took refuge under the skirts of their mothers, frightened
of severe punishment from their fathers. On occasion, they found the protection they sought. . . . Here the "Red leaders" take refuge in the same way;
there appears to be no strong father among them who might haul them forward
into open confrontation with the enemy. (Has the father in their ranks perhaps
been defeated?)

In more than one sense, the actual father of the soldier males also "hid"
(and still hides) under the skirts of women. He and none other it was who
would slip "under cover of darkness" from his (bedroom) "hideout," to

"whip up the masses to new fervor." He used the same whip to beat his sons to prevent them at all costs from being "softened" by an excess of maternal skirts. . . . As we have seen above, the beasts within the mass of the woman's belly are seen by the soldier males to derive from men who have "occupied" those regions (in the family context, from the father). The dragon's brood guards the gates and bears the emblem of the ruler.

Ultimately, however, even the father is depicted as a man hiding (or perhaps being hidden?) under maternal skirts: hiding from the son, who, at a certain age takes up the struggle against the father—a struggle not only for the mother, but for his own independence. The mother now protects the father from the son's desire for vengeance, pleading with him to sympathize with an enfeebled old man. Invariably, the father pushes the mother to the fore when his own neck is threatened.

What we witness, then, in depictions of "women to the fore" in the mass, is an encoding of the struggle against the masses with the smoldering embers of unresolved family conflicts. The Red rabble-rouser is combated for his ability to do what has always been denied the soldier male: he can hide under skirts, can stir the mass of Woman, can push her to the fore when he needs to protect himself or to dupe his son.

The extracts cited above should thus primarily be read as encodings of conflict with the father.* But what is also combatted in the mass with "women to the fore" is the part of the mother that once allowed herself to be used by others, the part that demonstrated her refusal to take the little boy seriously by taking the father's side—if only occasionally. (The recurrent descriptions of mocking laughter resounding toward the soldiers from the front lines of demonstrations may equally derive from family memories, as may the writer's sudden recourse to the familiar "thou" when addressing the "venomous" women of the front lines: the feeling of knowing them "from somewhere or other.")[10]

What then of the claim that "no soldier will shoot at a woman"? Indeed not—at woman *as such*. But there comes a time when a woman no longer deserves to be called woman; she metamorphoses into a venomous mass, threatening the man to the point at which he is *forced* to shoot her—or he himself risks losing life. True, "the thought of having potentially to give an order to shoot Germans was thoroughly unappealing to me." Lettow-Vorbeck has scruples. And yet "the Spartacists" had already on one occasion "succeeded in gaining access to and overpowering our soldiers by sending their women and children to the head of their ranks. Thank God the reputation for ruthlessness I acquired in Africa preceded me."[11]

---

*This also makes it clear why the "ringleader theory" retains its constant attraction, even when the available evidence can be clearly and universally perceived to render it absurd. The thinking is that the masses must surely contain and conceal "heads"—for the mass would have no *possible existence* without their rabble-rousing influence.

The man who already enjoys a "reputation for ruthlessness" has no need to be perturbed by the prospect of gaining one; as a veteran of Africa, Lettow-Vorbeck in particular has more freedom of action. Many avenues are opened; when women *force* him to shoot, shooting is his only option. He may of course choose not to shoot immediately; he may initially try firing signal flares up their skirts.[12] Or this:

> The "class conscious" were forced by their leaders to drive their women and young girls along in front of them—often with babies in their arms—then periodically to fire salvos over their heads at our comrades in Company Five. Slowly but surely they drove the advance guard of women onward, each step bringing them closer to our barbed-wire barricades. . . . "Prepare the flamethrower!" With a single movement one man up front hoists the flamethrower onto another man's back, then takes a firm hold on the nozzle. These lads know what it means to look lively. The whole street scatters. Success. The crowd seethes. The trooper in charge roars the motor into action.[13]

This is only the prelude; in the end, the writer is "forced to concede" the necessity to use his guns. Forced to concede? Captain Heydebreck explains how he arrived at the same conclusion:

> We marched on. The situation was extremely serious; the squadron exceeded anything I had been led to expect by Liege officers' reports. We marched through howling mobs; the underworld had been set loose, the basest elements ruled the streets. We marched past men in German uniforms, ragged creatures attempting to court the friendship of Belgian miners; old men, the pigs that wallow at base camp, full of their own self-importance; young boys who had bolted from recruiting centers, or deserted the flag, after being called up as replacements for the front. We passed Jewish roughnecks parading in our noble uniforms, engaged in all kinds of inflammatory manipulation. Sights such as these were unfamiliar to us front-line soldiers. And the worst moment of all: marching between long lines of men in gray German fieldcoats, a rabble of Belgian men and women, volunteers from 1914, all hooked arm-in-arm, singing and swaying to the rhythm of "Victorious We'll Conquer France." The height of indignities! Savage mockery! The devil take them! It was then that we overcame our reticence at shooting Germans.[14]

Heydebreck calls his memoirs *Wir Werwolfe* (We Werewolves). The title ostentatiously flaunts the same desire that reverberates through the extract above—the *desire to be permitted to shoot.* He itemizes the elements of the

"German Girls: This Is Not a German Woman!" Caption beneath Dietrich's photographs in the clubhouses of the BDM, the Nazi organization for young women.

mob, not out of any sense of horror, but out of the joy he takes in their existence. Here at long last, his text exclaims, is an opportunity to shoot something that represents all the filthy squalor of defeat.

(What, then, is the "something" he shoots? Had he not been offered enough other opportunities to settle accounts publicly, often precisely with Germans, the Germans closest to him: members of his own family? Was he truly "reticent" at shooting Germans? Did he truly find the thought "highly unappealing"? It seems unlikely.)

For Salomon the act of shooting appears more routine—a beautiful routine. In February 1919, "unemployed demonstrators" (allegedly) attack "a small troop detachment":

> Once again, their tactics were to advance under the cover of women and children. Marching along at their head, they forced our troops to hold fire until the very last moment. In such situations, a matter of seconds can determine the outcome— though it is always bloody. If the troops don't fire at precisely the right moment, if they lose their nerve, they are crushed and trampled within seconds. In this case the troops did fire, and the demonstrators were routed.[15]

The fact that the "outcome . . . is always bloody," and that a "matter of seconds" determines that outcome is taken as given. But why? If the soldier's goal is only to disperse the demonstrators, shots fired into the air will usually suffice; equally, any human crowd is likely to clear the streets immediately after the first shot is fired into its midst, no matter from what distance. The only remaining conclusion is then that a potentially dangerous proximity to the mass is *actively sought* by soldiers; the mass is *required* to come close. Only as the soldier, rigid with tension, directly confronts the mass's "terrible countenance," does the shot he fires bring true release. Shooting from a distance constitutes no more than the activity of shooting; only shots fired at close range are true "shots in the dark." The threat of the troop "losing its nerve" must be present in the text until the very last moment; for the whole thrill of armed action derives precisely from holding fire until the danger of being disarmed by the mass becomes real.

This also explains the presence of women in the front lines. The soldiers want them, *desire* them, to be there. Their appearance allows the soldiers at last to take possession of them, to punish them for their role in allowing the enemy to hide "under their skirts." "All the way in," murmurs Dwinger's hero Donat to himself with every shot he fires. The significance of the moment *after* the shot becomes clear from a description from Dwinger.

> A scream (exploded into the sky); it was like nothing they had ever heard until this moment—would the mass now surge and engulf them in a single movement?

March 1920, Berlin. Shooting incident involving Kapp's troops.

But no! Instead, incomprehensibly, the square emptied within seconds! A few dozen, a handful of dark stains still lay scattered, trampled underfoot by the mass's own senseless flight; but the roaring, raging human wave had been magically obliterated.[16]

"Magic" indeed: one round fired into the mass, and the square is empty. The explosion produces only the *sound* of detonation (the dead bodies are attributed to the mass itself, to its "senseless flight"). For flight *is* senseless; where is there to run, when the whole nightmare dissolves into the void in a matter of seconds? I have written at several points of the soldier male's urge to turn the victim of his attacks into a "bloody mass." It is now possible to identify a further key image. What the forces of terror aim to create is an empty square, *an empty space*. A desire reaches its destination.

A three-man machine gun detachment fires into a mass of around five-thousand strong; "one minute after the order to fire," the mass is said to have "vanished without trace from the scene." The perception puts Jünger, the rifleman, into a mood priceless because it is so difficult to attain in any other fashion: "There was something magical about the image; it evoked the profound joy that holds us irresistibly in its grasp at the unmasking of some odious demon."[17]

Jünger experiences the joy of true victory. With one fell swoop, he eradicates the "odious demon," the dangerous mass in which monsters lie waiting. Nothing remains to shower the soldier with spittle, to threaten him, or rip him to pieces. The world is clean again: an empty space, untrodden territory, a virginal body. The swarthy rabble gives way to a white totality. The man is *whole* again.

A final point to note in the situations described above is that particular clarity of allusion to family conflicts (or rather to exact revenge on the mother). In all cases, the soldiers occupy a position of relative superiority vis-à-vis the familial enemy—who, in turn, is equated with a *graspable*, conquerable enemy on the street. Since the fears awakened by confrontation with this particular enemy are relatively low in intensity, it seems unlikely that the more significant fears these men also experience can be characterized in terms of the "Medusa" or the "dragon" (the devouring vagina, the mauling penis). This conclusion will be further verified in a later examination of the form taken by these men in battles.

THE UNCANNY

In certain situations, the mass fails to assemble on the street, women to the fore, in a form that the soldier male can grasp hold of. At such points, he experiences an intensification of both fear and excitement. He had no exact knowledge of the position of the mass, nor when he will encounter it, and the mass's capacity to remain invisible figures in his text alongside its capacity for metamorphosis, multiformity, transformation from one state to another:

> We went out into the night against a completely unknown opponent; we knew only that he was ruthless and unrestrained, cruel and treacherous.[*1]
> Ridding ourselves of the *Soldatesks*[**] demanded a particularly strong stomach: it took a good deal more nerve than looking a decent opponent in the eye at the front.[2]

The reds do not allow themselves to be "looked in the eye"; they approach from behind, laterally or from above. Instead, the civil war itself takes place behind the front and in the swamps, in the country's *interior*.

For Schaumlöffel, the force displayed in the workers was "uncanny"; there was a "hidden organization" in their wanton espousal of revolution.[3]

---

[*]A "completely unknown opponent," about whom it is possible to "know" anything and everything.

[**]The worker troops in the *Buch vom deutschen Freikorpskämpfer* are often referred to as "Soldateska." This particular linguistic convention can only have become current after 1933 and was clearly introduced here by the editor (Salomon).

American poster from World War II.

The different organization was not one to which they simply belonged; it was their very being. The workers are different. Schaumlöffel again:

> (T)he opponent we faced was perhaps more mysterious and more treacherous than any open enemy in open battle. The eyes of our fighting men signaled their unconditional joy in armed combat . . . a joy capable of rising to the pitch of a 1914. But their hearts were unusually troubled; they were pained by the knowledge that the enemies we now had to subdue had once belonged to our own people.[4]

The evident rage of Schaumlöffel's text is attributable to the peculiarities of urban street fighting—and it had particularly severe consequences for the workers. Street fighting has many of the qualities of guerilla warfare—though their affinities are pragmatic rather than theoretical. Men appear and disappear suddenly in the streets; there is shooting from rooftops; battle lines shift constantly. All of this corresponds precisely not only to the men's anxiety images of the multiple forms and faces of the mass/Medusa they aim to subdue, but above all to their fear of uncontrollable, unexpected stirrings in their own "interiors." By remaining invisible, the external (armed) mass becomes a particularly intense embodiment of the invisible internal mass of the soldier male.

Civil war battles against the uncanny rarely produce the "supreme delight" that rendered the battles of 1914 so splendid. The consequences were suffered by captured workers; in most cases, neither they themselves, nor even the testimonies of government supporters, were able to convince the soldiers of their innocence. "And now they attempt to pass themselves off as peaceful laborers; we should kill every last one of them." Such was the revenge exacted on any man who dared to tax the "nerve" of the soldier.[5]

By March 1920, of course, the *Freikorps* had been inactive for almost a year—a whole year without notable discharge of tension:

> We had somehow to give vent to our agitation. The best opportunities to let off steam were available in the industrial region. Here at least was a tangible opponent. In Berlin and its surroundings our enemies could sneak away into the darkness; they were free to pour scorn on us in every newspaper.[6]

After the Kapp Putsch, the Ehrhardt Brigade, for whom Rudolf Mann wrote the above report, was in fact never deployed in the Ruhr. The Social Democratic government could not afford to lose face so entirely as to send out the chief putschists against the very people responsible for keeping its party in power. Yet even in the Ruhr, the brigade would not have found the "open enemy" it was seeking. The workers were elusive; they emerged initially victorious from the first street battles. Thus Salomon could write:

Here in this convulsively bleeding region, one monstrous crater that threatened to erupt at any moment; here, surrounded by rebellion and danger, filth and blood, blown to pieces, lost, and abandoned; here divisions were irrevocably consolidated. Burned more than once to nothing, then painfully restored to full strength, the *Freikorps* fought an insane and impenetrable campaign, a struggle whose initial motives were barely discernible. Dispersed across the hundreds of towns that together formed a single gigantic city, charged with endless bitterness, hated and hating until they glowed white-hot they exchanged shots with an elusive opponent among dumps and pit-sites. Unsurprisingly, hand-grenades slipped easily from the soldier's hand; murder engendered murder. All the respect for the law hammered into these men gave way to wild, primitive instincts of the earliest hunters, the hunted animal.[7]

To Salomon, this is a struggle "whose initial motives were barely discernible"; he seems to perceive how little this massive eruption of insanity, his perception of the uncanny, his hatred, his fear, his "primitive instinct," his desire for murder has to do with his original political and military objective of "putting down the workers' rebellion."

In his texts there is no such thing as an open enemy, an open front, an open street; a boundary. The battle is internal. Three times, Salomon locates the sites of battle "within" — within the body of "a single gigantic city" (the region is "bleeding"); within the body of the earth (the crater); and within the man himself, as his body armor — the "respect for the law". . . "hammered" into him — dissipates and crumbles. Precisely because it has been "hammered" into him, and remains external, his body armor can now be cast off to allow his emotions to erupt with all their true intensity. His body armor crumbles in confrontation with "the wild, primitive instincts of the earliest hunters, the hunted animal." Initially, the fighting man himself is both hunter *and* hunted animal; he inclines toward self-mutilation; he is *always* at war with elusive enemies. But the moment the enemy comes within his grasp, the boundaries between his two personae lose their fluidity. The devils of hell have been gnawing at his liver, mashing his entrails to a pulp; but the moment the devils enter the open, his enemy is as good as dead. The blood of his victims must be made to flow free; how can they know that he rediscovers his boundaries only as a killer wading in blood? He bathes and purifies himself in blood; to call battle a "bloodbath" is then clearly appropriate (at least for the man who takes it).

It is obviously inadequate to conceptualize these processes in the triangular terms of Oedipus, the mama-papa relationship. The man described here tears the world to shreds, and is torn to shreds by it; his relation to the dis-

"Two Revolutionary Types." Drawing by Thöny (Munich, 1919).

solving world is *unmediated*. All his efforts are concentrated on his own survival.

In some cases, rebellion remains an affair fought out among men; men fight for something recognizably akin to the cause of the soldier. In such instances, a crucial boundary is re-established. Salomon views one particularly slick detachment of sailors with undisguised admiration:

> They had guns in their hands; their banded caps crowned laughing faces. Their stance was relaxed, their legs clad in wide, elegant, stylish trousers. . . . These were the young lads who had made the revolution, young ruffians with determination in their faces, strolling along with girls on their arms, singing and laughing and howling, bold and self-assured, shirts open-necked and ties flapping.[8]

One might almost have been tempted to join them.

> And as I read the posters—red posters proclaiming the establishment of the Workers and Soldiers' Council—I sensed a dangerous and enchanting energy behind their resounding force of expression, a fiery will behind their high-sounding pronouncements.[9]

Here was a front that could be perceived with some clarity; no longer the uncanny gender inversions of the invisible, whose unnaturalness caused the earth to quake and burst open.

BLACK-OUT, AND LOSS OF FLESHLY REALITY: DECOMPOSITION WITHIN THE MASS

The soldier male's most intense fear is his fear of decomposition. In what follows, I shall be drawing on two passages from Salomon to demonstrate how that fear emanates from within the soldier himself. Both passages are from *Kadetten* (Cadets); they tell of Salomon as a fifteen-year-old. In the first he confronts an image of "syphilis," in the second a human mass in a public square. Neither is a situation of wartime aggression—a fact that further reinforces my contention that the soldier's fear of dissolution is not traceable to any armed external enemy, the workers for example. His ability to perceive workers' actions as threatening is predicated on the existence of threats within his own interior.

On leave for a Sunday outing:

> Following my systematic tour of the sights of the capitol, I was magically and irresistibly drawn to a place many of my comrades had talked of in whispers, with half-derisive, half-meaningful smiles: Castan's Panopticum in the arcade. I found it more or less disagreeable even to enter a public establishment of this kind. With bowed head, slightly dizzy from the sharp transition from hot sunlight to the dust-impregnated coolness of rooms filled with all sorts of gruesome devices, I crept past immobile figures glaring suddenly wide-eyed from unsuspected corners. Standing before the wax figure of Bismarck, I felt the stabbing gaze of the thief and murderer Sternickel burning almost unendurably into my back. The odor of wax and the dust, the sour perspiration of vaguely horrified spectators, the sight of abominable execution scenes, preserved embryos, exhumed female corpses, and, most colossal of all, Dante in his inferno, with naked figures, men and women, riding down a razor blade into an ocean of blood—all of this was rather too overwhelming for a stomach whose walls were inadequately lined with pickled eggs and red cabbage. But it was the chamber of horrors that finally finished me off. The very fact of having to maintain my natural self-assurance as I walked, watched by other visitors, through a red curtain marked "Adults Only"—my curiosity competing with a severe attack of nausea— went a long way toward destroying my carefully maintained composure. I wandered from showcase to showcase; and as the final display case swam into view, presenting a vision of the tertiary stage of syphilis, one Royal Prussian Cadet, face slightly green but teeth clenched like iron to the very last, sank noiselessly to the floor.[1]

The second passage describes a situation shortly before the outbreak of war. The squares are filled with agitated crowds, swarming in on all sides:

> They clearly had no better idea than I what had drawn them here, nor what they had gone out expecting to find. The whole square was suddenly filled with a great black mass.
>
> I began to wonder why the mass should be black—the sun was shining in all its glory, the women wore summer dresses, many of the men were wearing straw hats. But the sun was now no longer shining so brightly; it must have disappeared behind the houses, for the air turned blue, then bluer, a deeper dark than the sky, like the blue that comes before a storm. And not a single cloud hung over the square; the church steeple shimmered hazy gray against the steel backdrop of the sky. There was no proper core to the mass; unsure which way to turn, I stood irresolute on the spot I had chosen. There was a certain amount of movement to begin with, and I listened, but could hear nothing.
>
> I climbed up quickly to a vantage point on a wall, and loosened my collar. My heart raced and pounded—then stood still. For a moment the mass seemed simply to disappear. It flattened out into two dimensions, then receded into the background, a gathering of ghosts mingling together—even the man at my side who stood holding my arm, a person I sensed clearly and sickeningly close to my body, even this man with the thin, unkempt moustache, staring fiercely at the square, started to swim before my eyes, to lose his fleshly reality.[2]

The same state persists until the man is able to say, ''The war is coming at last.'' The statement dissolves the tension:

> I breathed a sigh of relief. Everything was now free and simple. I knew what I had to do. Each and every one of us went swiftly on his way, silently, as if gripped by some command, yet still full of ardor.[3]

In both passages Salomon appears to withdraw from an increasingly unbearable situation: from the threat of syphilis, which he escapes by fainting, and from the threatening mass, which he hallucinates away. Everything becomes unreal: his habitual reality, his bodily boundaries, his perceptions grow hazy and unreliable; they begin dissolving. He climbs quickly to a vantage point and ''loosens his collar.'' His heart stands still. He dies within the mass; like the threat of syphilis, the mass causes him to disappear. Human beings become ghosts, and the mass turns black despite the bright sunshine and bright clothing. He cannot endure the touch of his neighbor, his unkempt moustache, swimming sickeningly before his eyes. At this point, something significant happens: presaging later developments, Salomon murders the mass. It is no longer *himself* he removes, by swooning; this time, it is *the mass* that is removed. In this second sequence, the joyous release described in an earlier passage at the sight of an empty square—or, to be more precise, an emptied square—is precisely foreshadowed. Here Salomon achieves the desired effect through hallucination; later the same effect will be achieved by the use of weapons. The word Salomon uses to describe the "disappearance" of the mass confirms that the processes are identical: he writes of the mass as "losing fleshly reality" (*sie entfleischt sich*). Later, when he and his kind face "the mass" in armed confrontation, they will indeed first strip it of its flesh before making it disappear altogether. Unlike the boy he once was, the soldier male will no longer strip himself of his own reality (*sich entwirklicken*); he will dematerialize the thing that threatens him. Killing it will cause him to erupt with exuberation: another beast laid to rest.

At this stage, however, this is not yet a possible solution for Salomon. He has instead to rescue himself from the mass in which he is helplessly entrapped by removing the source of its threat, its lack of a core, the way it swims around with no clear orientation. The moment it acquires a core, a target, it will no longer be dangerous. What organizes the mass in this instance is the announcement of imminent war; in an instant the mass begins to function as army, and Salomon can breathe a temporary sigh of relief: "Everything was now free and simple." "As if gripped *by some command*," that which is threatening becomes familiar, even beautiful.

In general, then, it seems the army has to be seen not only as an image of the mass but also as its opposite. Love of the army originates to some degree in an inability to love the mass, to love *within* the mass: reactionary formations exist as reactions to the horror that freedom potentially holds. Equally, the second passage cited above indicates the urgency with which these men experience the need for command. Command not only tames the mass in its entirety; more important, it reconstitutes the bodily mass of the soldier male, giving it direction, reassembling—or even recreating—a body in dissolution.

The first passage also shows the extent to which the man seeks out what is threatening and horrifying. Having been aroused, almost to the point where he could no longer stand up, by the eyes of murderers (stabbing him *in the back*!), by executions, embryos, the smell of sweat, razor blades streaming with blood, he simply *has* to see the syphilis. It represents something oh-so-tantalizing—but he finds it unendurable. It now begins to pursue him; later, he kills it. Only the act of killing allows him to escape the unreality of his feelings, the unfulfillment whose burning flame consumes him. The act of killing becomes a direct affirmation of his own reality: it is not I who am the ghost, but others—see how they disappear . . . (when shots are fired).

THE MASS AND CULTURE:
THE "UPSTANDING" INDIVIDUAL*

A number of the concepts central to German fascist ideology derive from a defense against what is embodied by and occurs within the mass. They include not only terms such as "culture," "race," "nation," "wholeness," but also organizations such as the army.

The broadest collective term for all that is not "mass," for its positive opposite, is "culture." Culture distinguishes what is "German" from the remaining mass of the world:

> If anything makes me doubt the infallibility of God's vaunted wisdom, it is the fact that it was left to this supremely uncultured collection of men of the masses to decide the outcome of our people's sacred struggle for living space (*Lebensraum*).[1] (Dwinger, on the Americans)**
>
> It was the Baltic tragedy of 18th March 1919 . . . that revived the genius of this one artist, and allowed him to deliver to posterity an account of the destruction of the whole European high cultural tradition, the destruction of a noble and carefree human existence by the forces of Asiatic reaction.[2] (Goltz, on the Russians)

Three oppositions are operating here: the "self" is posed against the "other," the "mass" against "culture," "high" against "low." "High culture" is seen to be threatened from "below." At one point in Captain Berthold's diary he remarks that "humanity will never be led by this socialism of the streets, which brings only the decline of all spiritual and moral values, the destruction of all higher culture."[3]

Only what is "higher" is considered capable of "leadership." "Communist doctrine" belongs down "below"; it is without question "the most uncultured crudity."

Von der Goltz:

> There is a world view, I pointed out, of cultural ennui and cultural refusal; it has found accomplished prophets in such as Tolstoy, or other Asiatics, outsiders critical of European civilization. The same view is more or less embraced by degenerate city weaklings;

---

*One of the most extraordinary texts on this theme is Uwe Nettelbeck's "Der Dolomitenkrieg" (The Dolomite War), in *Mainz wie es singt und lacht*. The book describes a battle between the Austrians and Italians over the Dolomite cliffs—whose strategic value is next to nil. The war is orchestrated at the highest level in Vienna and Rome; the men stand erect at a height that makes their weapons freeze solid.

**Göring said during the Nuremberg trials that the Americans simply lack the necessary education to understand the German standpoint. (Gilbert, *Nuremburg Diary*)

"Symbolic Representation of the Coquette," by Rodolfe (1921) in one of the volumes of *Omnipotent Woman*.

but, as I indicated in no uncertain terms, its principal support
derives from various kinds of roughnecks and criminals. Culture, I
admitted, had many weaknesses, and was currently displaying
evidence of a most regrettable decline; but the aim of these men
was to destroy culture altogether, to replace it with the most
uncivilized crudity, licentiousness and barbarism. . . . Heart,
feeling, soul, intellect, reason were to become enslaved to
coercion and bestial vulgarity.[4]

At the "height" of culture, there is nobility, morality, intellect, heart,
feeling, reason, and soul—none of which can exist "in the depths," in the
mass. (There should be no need to repeat what is seen to lurk "down below.")
Jünger expands the catalog of nonculture to include what he sees as the signs
of the mass in public life in the Weimar Republic:

Since the mass is unable to emulate the few, the few are being
called upon to emulate the mass. Politics, drama, artists, cafés,
patent-leather shoes, posters, newspapers, morality, tomorrow's
Europe, the world of the day after tomorrow: all of this is to
become thundering mass. The mass is a beast of a thousand
heads, it obstructs all movement, crushes anything it cannot
swallow or engulf; it is envious, parvenu, common. The
individual has once again been defeated, betrayed most savagely
by men born to represent him.[5]

The "individual" carves out a place for himself as the bearer of
"culture"; a handful of (male) "individuals" constitute the "few"—who
determine and sanction definitions of "culture." Mass religion works according to the same principle:

Christianity is not a religion for the many, and certainly not for
all. Cultivated and practiced by the few, it becomes one of the
most precious flowers ever to blossom from the soul of any
culture.[6] (From Goebbels's *Michael*, 1923)

The "soul," as we have seen, belongs up "above"; here, there are only
men—or women elevated to male status. Independent femininity by contrast
is the opposite of "culture." "The emancipation of women will destroy any
culture."[7]

Delmar in a similar vein: "The decline of the race begins with contraception. Pleasure and culture rise and fall in equal proportion."[8] When
"pleasure" rises (with the use of contraception), "culture" falls.

In the writings of the soldier males, the concept of culture becomes a rock
against which to break the feminine, contagious lust, dissolution—all the
threats the mass contains. It is assumed as a matter of course that the Jews are
not a "cultured people." For that "individual," a number of truths thus

become self-evident. The man of culture believes, for example, that he can never be a "barbarian": he has a sense of existing at a great height above the ground, of having no connection to the depths of femininity. So vastly superior does he consider himself to be to the depths below that even mass human slaughter cannot make him a barbarian. It remains an act of culture. Such an act would demonstrate lack of "culture" only if he were to defect to the "mass," to become, say, another democrat in the crowd, the rabble. Mass murder is in no sense considered antagonistic to the soldierly/masculine concept of culture (nor indeed does the latter surface only under fascism); on the contrary, if the world is to be formed as a landscape of culture, then it is seen as necessary to erase anything uncultured from the face of the earth—one way or another.

The Germans had a label for all Soviet military action: "Nix Kultura!" Raucous laughter, and NIX KULTURA: a refrain repeated endlessly in every report, every story, every anecdote, every joke. Thus hundreds of thousands of Russian prisoners-of-war starved to death in German camps, as official chroniclers (including Höss) looked on and noted, with slight shudders of horror, how the swine began eating one another.[9] NIX KULTURA, plain for all to see. (In that same way the death of twenty million Soviet Russians in the second Great War was no doubt considered the "highest" achievement of the German man of culture. Russians were more elusive than concentration-camp inmates.)

Certain "Asiatics" (Tolstoy, in the above example) do of course come close to the pinnacle of culture—though they have to be "towering individuals" to do so. Even Lenin is occasionally granted the dubious honor of cultural status. This device allows writers to present the failure of the German revolution as inevitable, since it lacked a leader (*Führer*) comparable to Lenin.[10] (Unfortunately, the same argument is equally familiar from the opposite camp.)

A further incidental point: when Goltz writes of "lamentable signs of decline" in culture, he is alluding to officers having more or less honorably placed their services at the disposal of the Republic. This, for him, is the beginning of the end of culture.

"Education" (*Bildung*) is also never found on the streets, but always "up above":

> A group of people stood around listening in silence to the arguments and counterarguments. It is not every man's affair to participate in street debates and the educated man is rarely equipped for the verbal torrent of Spartacist agents.[11] (Arthur Iger)

Being ill equipped to deal with "verbal torrents" is not considered a weakness. On the contrary, the man of education is "educated" precisely because he does not flow as a torrent. Thus in many of these texts, "edu-

"Monument Project," by Fidus (ca. 1900).

cation" becomes a synonym for arrogant ignorance. The position of the educated man is unassailable; he represents a social system that defines culture
exclusively in terms of relations between men. His education finds expression
in inter-male attitudes; "respect," "reverence," "courage," "discipline,"
"distance," "obedience," "integrity," and above all, "loyalty."
("Loyalty" is owed the Kaiser, the country, the *Führer*, his comrades.

"Loyalty is the backbone of honor"—and neither backbone nor honor is the business of women.)

Dwinger's Killmann inveighs against the "accursed, half-educated" mass; the mass that wants "only to live" and lacks "asceticism."[12] What is "half" belongs down below; it is only up above that the man is "whole"—with head and limb erect. At the same time, his own body is both "below" and "within"; it stubbornly refuses to be absolutely male.

It can become so—but only if held high enough by props erected in the name of the law, flagpoles reaching to the sky. The strong, sterling, solitary individual can never be anything but a man—for only men stand erect—and the German man is the most upstanding of all:

> Shall I tell you what is the scourge of our being as Germans? It is the depth of the tension between the mass and those towering individuals in whom the German essence lives and grows creative—a gulf greater than in any other people that has written its name into the stars. The individual German is sometime ethereal, a true creature of God; but precisely because the German individual towers so high above men of other countries, the German mass is all the more dreadful.[13] (W. Weigand)

Upstanding logic indeed: it is *because* the individual German stands so high that the mass is so greatly to be feared. The soldier male's fear of the mass seems in some way related to his constant fear of collapse; for him to fall from his abode in the heavens would be the end. Flaccidity is mortal danger. Possibly then, the culture-ego that strives toward the heights may be a soldierly phallus fleeing from the pleasures of co-mingling. The idea is not as fanciful as it may at first appear. In Ferenczi's "Genital theory," we find the following:

> The formation of the genitals as center of the organism should be understood in the pangenetic sense outlined by Darwin. Every part of the organism can be seen as contributing to, and being represented within, the sexual part. The genitals act more or less in the role of procurer; they attend to the business of discharging pleasure for the entire organism. . . . If we take the pangenetic hypothesis seriously, we can venture to describe the male member as a complete miniature of the ego, an embodiment of the pleasure-ego. This duplicated ego can then be regarded as the primary basis of narcissistic self-love.[14]

In his excitement at discovering his double ego—a second ego in miniature—Ferenczi "temporarily" forgets the existence of women. Women are never once mentioned throughout his discussion of psychoanalytic typology.

Sepp Rist and Leni Riefenstahl in *Storms over Montblanc*.

His work is predicated not only on an assumption of *genital** primacy in the construction of the agency of the ego within the psychic apparatus; it is based also on an assumption of phallic primacy. Within the topographical framework of psychoanalysis, there can be no such thing as a female ego (what an advantage!).[15]

Ferenczi is not alone in making this slip. Freud attempted to clarify the relationship between "ego" and "id" by comparing it to the relationship between the military "front" and the region "behind the lines."[16] In purely pragmatic terms, this comparison is unworkable (Freud claims the id, for example, to be devoid of contradictions—something that can hardly be said of the military hinterland or the home base). In emotional terms, however, the comparison does coincide with the feelings of the soldier, who sees the region "behind the lines" as a threatening state of disorder, and himself by contrast as a clear front, a boundary. The phallus on which the "ego" (the Freudian ego included) is founded is a soldier; or at least, the soldier is incipient within the phallus.[17]

In the preceding section we traced the ways in which a particular conception of culture had emerged during the course of European history, one framed in terms of a centralistic subjection of nature, of femininity, and, finally, of the individual unconscious, all of which have been banished from the male ego. Under fascism, this labor of destruction gradually extended to everything living: the fascist quality of "soldierliness" was simply an extension of existing definitions of culture.

---

*The typesetter inadvertently read this as "*genial* primacy." Everything is possible.

In "standing erect," the fascist adopts an attitude of sexual defense and mastery; his very stance was seen to produce an inevitable and unquestioned German superiority to the rest of the world, and to ground the German claim to world domination. German imperialism and missionary zeal was, then, the soldier male's "conviction" that no miniature ego in the world could ever be erected above that of the German—which was hard, unsatisfied, and impatient to discharge itself. For would not any ego standing less than fully erect have dissolved long ago within the "mass"?

For Captain Berthold this was the foundation on which the fronts of world war rested:

> The man who heaves himself out of the mass and sets larger goals for his life is universally ostracized; only a very few understand him. If you look at Germany, at the lives of nations, you see them more or less embodied within the individual. The whole enemy alliance against us is built on hatred and envy of the tirelessly forward-striving, restlessly toiling German.[18]

Ultimately, the "individual" who "heaves himself out of the mass" *becomes* the phallus. The final aspiration of the "tirelessly forward-striving, restlessly toiling German"—the man who strives to escape woman, the mass, and himself—is to embody one part of the phallus-on-high.[*]

To achieve his desired state, the soldier must fly like the fighter pilot who takes off even with his arm shot to pieces; the man who breaks all records for shooting down enemies and dispatching them to the depths, and finally, as an upstanding man, dies.[19] All his efforts must be concentrated on preventing himself from descending to the level of the invisible "woman" behind him. Raise the banner high!

But the heights are lonely. An address to the troops before the storming of the Annaberg:

> Grow beyond the norms of bravery to the unique heights of the lonely greats of the German nation! This is no mere order! These are the tidings of a new world that will begin with your victory or rise up to the stars, if we all perish, as the cherished dream of our successors! The *Freikorps* is mobilizing for a new departure![20]
> (Eggers)

For Walter Benjamin, the war landscape represented the supreme adaptation of natural forms to the towering "ego" of German idealism:

> A fact to be proclaimed with all bitterness: it was only when the landscape was totally mobilized for war that the German feeling for nature could be so unexpectedly revived. This was a landscape

---

[*]The part that will enter Valhalla.

originally settled by peaceful geniuses; but their sensuous vision was now eradicated. As far as the eye could see above the edges of the trenches, the land had become the terrain of German idealism itself—every shell-crater a philosophical problem; every barbed-wire fence a representation of autonomy; every barb a definition; every explosion an axiom. By day, the heavens were contained in the cosmic interior of the steel helmet; by night, in the morality by which it was governed. Technology had attempted to retrace the heroic features of German idealism in burning fire and trenches. Technology was wrong: for what it took to be the features of heroism were in fact the Hippocratic features of death.[21]

Even today, we are only vaguely aware of the extent to which the frozen phallic-weapon of the fascist must be seen, not as a distortion of the upstanding ego, but simply as one of its extremes. After the Second World War, the inviolate individual was simply restored to his position as bastion of so-called resistance; he was considered to have "fundamentally transcended" the events of the war. The bourgeois individual was resurrected and universally celebrated as the subject of scientific knowledge—a position he had always occupied among communist critics of fascism. Even the German student movement demanded "ego-strength" of its revolutionaries; during a period of intervening sectarianism, its books took particularly petty-minded pleasure in disseminating the fiction of themselves as the avant-garde, directing the masses from the position of the omniscient male ego.

To this day, the language of all such men is governed, and the thinking of the (male) theoretician ruled, by the signifier, as an instrument that etches order into meaning—a pointer, a prescription. To this day, it is required that the level of reflection be a high one, the level of theory higher still; the drop to lower levels of feelings and concretizations is considered precipitous.

But is there any such thing as the "height of theory," except as an element in masculine mystique?* The northern heights/deep south; deepest wil-

---

*"The imperialism of the signifier does not take us beyond the question, 'What does it mean?'; it is content to bar the question in advance, to render all the answers insufficient by relegating them to the status of a simple signified." (There *must* be answers that take us further.) "Like the young palace dogs too quick to drink the verse water, and who never tire of crying: The signifier, you have not reached the signifier, you are still at the level of the signifieds! The signifier is the only thing that gladdens their hearts." (I can still hear them crying 'Where is the basic contradiction?!') "But this master signifier remains what it was in ages past, a transcendent stock that distributes lack to all the elements of the chain, something in common for a common absence, the authority that channels all the break-flows into one and the same locus of one and the same cleavage: the detached object, the phallus-and-castration, the bar that delivers over all the depressive subjects to the great paranoiac king" (Deleuze and Guattari, *Anti-Oedipus*, 208). Bachtold's *Deutscher Soldatenbrauch* (German military customs) cites an old prophecy that war will break out when "men and women become so alike you can hardly tell them apart" (6). War accompanies the disappearance of the signifier.

"Triptych with Stake." Drawing by Vlado Kristl from *Filmkritik*, No. 233, May 1976.

derness . . . could there be such a thing as the *highest* of wildernesses? Both men and women resist such associations—a resistance that indicates the degree to which the opposition between "high" and "low" determines the ordering of our thinking. Relations of domination are stabilized through the encoding of our thought with the antitheses "masculine/feminine," "controlled/uncontrolled," "precise/vague," "external/internal," "conscious/unconscious." Anything "low" is seen as wrong, simply *because* it occupies a subordinate position. The individual of "higher culture" demands something "down below" that he can oppress as a means of actually redeeming totality and bodily wholeness.

*   *   *

His "I" struggles constantly for power; his existence is a perpetual refusal to be made subordinate, an endless celebration of the fictive phallus of the heights, a phallus possessed by none, but embodied in the organs of state power, and viewed as the yardstick of all action, of words spoken and written; monuments to the platinum yardstick, while in the individual's body an execution stake, as Vlado Kristl has called it, takes root. Yet the voice of male praise continues to soar; to be on a high even deep in the labyrinth of intoxication. As in a weather forecast, the "lows" are consistently identified with what is unpleasant.

Sometimes I'm up, sometimes I'm down—in the abstract, the abstraction is unquestionably accurate, at least as far as the male organ is concerned. But the idea that what is felt during orgasm is a "high point" has its origin in the structure of a philosophy. Did Reich and others ever question the highness of translating affective intensity into a curve with a climax? Is the mountain-climber truly pursuing "substitute satisfaction"? In the early '60s, "getting down" was introduced as a phrase for feeling good; but it never quite caught on.

Male praise, from Volker Elias Pilgrim:

> Alice Schwarzer was the first to succeed in gaining a unified vision from the standpoint of her sex; she penetrated the silent mass of women . . .

What more could a man want? Alice Schwarzer offers unification against the mass; the "standpoint" of her sex produces the vagina as an ordering eye from which the unifier gazes. Thus the very woman who writes in opposition to penetration is made to "penetrate" by the man who sings her praises. What impresses him is

> her intelligent analysis—supported by evidence from interviews with fourteen other women . . . Alice radiates beauty; her fine stance affords her the strength and clarity of vision to deliver the effective challenge men have long been waiting for.

Be this as it may, her work has in no sense been permitted to challenge the phallic writing which is the pilgrimage of V. E. Pilgrim.

Herbert Marcuse, on Angela Davis's *Marxism and Women's Liberation:*

> This piece, written in prison, is the work of a magnificent, militant, and intellectual woman. (*Konterrevolution und Revolte*, 93).

Or Ernest Borneman:

> . . . the courageous, visionary agitation of the most significant woman in the history of the trade-union movement, Clara Zetkin . . .

Clarus ZK.[*] Imperceptibly, the bearded growth of a Marx becomes visible. The visionary female homunculus is noted *en route* by men enjoying seasonal excursions to the Everests of their own thinking. Arriving, breathless with joy, at their destination, they swell with pride at their success in outstripping the new goddesses. A final example from Dieter Duhm, who is unable to resist adding a few words of guru wisdom to the introduction to *Der Mensch ist anders* (Humans Are Different): "Solidarity between the sexes is the yardstick by which we all stand or fall." His book is then dedicated to a woman.

---

[*]An abbreviation for the central committee. (Tr.)

If a male author chooses to write eulogies to the feminist movement, then he should at least recognize that the language of penetration, which he has, perhaps, used in the past to seduce long-suffering virgins, can no longer be used to take possession of virgin-white paper.

Admittedly, the problem of the language of eulogy is not confined to these individuals. It is by no means easy to find expressions of pleasure not originating in the phallus.* (Referring to a section of my manuscript that he disliked, Michael Rohrwasser wrote: "Aber wenn's gephallt" — a phallic play on "Aber wenn's gefällt," meaning "but if you like it"). "High German" (*die Hochsprache*) repudiates the multiple linguistic potentialities of colloquialism ("colloquial," or pertaining to colloquy, speaking *together*, a "conference" that may also be sexual). "High German" contents itself with the univocal.

"Prominent" (extraordinarily erect); "resplendent" (like the glans penis); and so on. "Very depressing," we say, and again it is the depths that are referenced.

In a recent interview, an aging Marcuse suggested a little anxiously that we would deprive ourselves of language were we to pay attention to the minor implications of our terms of reference. But is this really true? Do we have nothing more worthy of expression in language than the rigid shells of bodies pointing upward to the head? What is expressed in the concepts we currently use is above all a fear of the experience of difference.

Shulamith Firestone has suggested that male culture derives its power from the emotional strength of women, but gives nothing in return. The fact would be a little less objectionable were what she calls the "emotional potential" of women to remain untouched and intact as a uniquely "feminine" capacity for liberation. Unfortunately, however, men do "give" something in return: their language, a whole lethal conceptual system organized around oppositions between high and low, external and internal, subject and object. Thus women's attempts to become "themselves" are more often than not expressed in the language of male power. Women represent "standpoints"; strive for "automony"; become "one with themselves" (why not many with themselves?); these and so many other expressions derive from the abstraction of a phallus standing autonomously by its own standpoint. For some time now, I have felt uneasy about the way the notion of "uprightness" (*der aufrechte Gang*), celebrated by Bloch, Dutschke, and others on the Left, is unquestioningly applied to the "liberation of women." Tilman Moser talks of deriving his greatest strength from the supportive sensation of his analyst's phallus growing into his spine. Is then the threat that awaits us at ground level and in the confusion of existence so dreadful that we prefer our back crucified rigid?

Jünger's greatest desire was to "erect shimmering temples to the

---

*Also called *Pimmel* in German, doubtless for the simple reason that it rhymes with the word for "heaven," *Himmel*.

phallus."[22] To him the whole "culture-work" of humanity was symbolized by the construction of the tower; and he considered it *imperative* that the tower be built, the "beast" left below:

> Humanity continues to labor over the construction of a tower of immeasurable height, layer upon layer. One generation, one state of its being, follows another in blood, agony, and longing. Slowly, infinitely slowly, its square stones grow toward divinity, foisted like a saddle onto the back of the beast in wild, primitive mountain ranges. The edifice is still crude, a sweeping gesture directed toward the dim goal of a promised land.[23]

Towers foisted onto the back of the beast; to the fascist male, the whole human condition may be understood in terms of this relationship.

> The human race is a mysterious, tangled primeval forest whose treetops, cradled in the breeze of the open seas,* thrust ever more powerfully out of the sultry, gloomy haze toward the clear sun. But while the will to beauty envelops the treetops in fragrance, color, and blossoms, a confusion of strange growth proliferates in the depths. In the sun's afterglow, a string of red parrots swoops like a squadron of royal dreams into the basin of the feathery palms; then out of the depths, already dipped in darkness, there emerges a hideous profusion of creeping, crawling wildlife, the shrill cries of victims torn from their sleep, their caves, their warm nests, and consigned to death by the stealthy assaults of greedy, murderous teeth and claws.[24]

Life and (solitary) pleasure are "up above," death and terror "down below." All that is "beauty" exists among the fragrant treetops; in the depths, confusion "proliferates." What is commonly known as "beauty," as "the intellect," as "culture," exists only in the "uprights," in the vicinity of the treetops. It includes among other things all artistic productions attributable to German inhabitants of Olympus (artists who have turned their back on mis-spent coffeehouse days). The mixing of levels is strictly forbidden. In H. H. Ewers's *Reiter in deutscher Nacht* (Riders in the German Night)—the title itself sets up an opposition between high and low—the imprisoned Gerhard Scholz recalls the Mörike-Wolff songs his mother used to sing. He begins singing to himself; but it becomes clear to him after the second line: "No, impossible!—songs of this kind in a cesspool such as this?! Blasphemy!"[25]

The affairs of "culture" are conducted among men whose proper place is "in the heights"; they never mix with those "below" them. The aversion they

---

*In this case, the "open seas" are *up above*.

Postcard (Zurich, 1906).

feel for their inferiors is in part sexual, as is their attraction to other "men in high places." The concept of "culture" thus contains a further implication: individuals of the same culture are assumed to have the same sexual inclinations.

When Balla's hero, Captain Rodenholm, feels "springtime" in his blood, he "turns to Bacchus to lay Venus to rest."[26] But he fails to perceive that he

"Longing," by Hans Thoma.

will thereby fall into the hands of what he calls a "procuress." He feels the urge to celebrate but can find no one to join him. All his "unfaithful" soldiers are (allegedly) in bed with women. He can find only Holz, his orderly, asleep in his room. Since, however, Holz is unsuited to fulfill Rodenholm's needs for sexual companionship, he is sent off to seek out an equal-ranking partner for his captain:

Hahn at least was available. He was sitting on a wooden stool in his tiny room, reading Faust by the flickering light of a candle. Hahn was a man weighed down by the loneliness of those who can no longer be young and unrestrained; he joined Rodenholm gladly. And so these two aging young men sat drinking wine and talking. Hahn was a highly refined and educated man, and Rodenholm recalled a time when he too had liked to occupy himself with intellectual matters. The room soon filled with the comfortable atmosphere that develops when men of the same cultural and educational level meet together in the same connection. The wine, to which both had long been unaccustomed, heightened the congeniality of the atmosphere.[27]

Bacchus, then, appears here in the role of procurer between men.

References to Faust and to the common "educational level" of two men driven by a "springtime" renders their meeting both inoffensive, and consistent, with social conventions. At the same time, the men are referred to, somewhat awkwardly, as "meet[ing] together in the same connection": The formulation gestures obliquely toward the dominant prohibition against touching. The events taking place here must not be allowed to become openly sexual; if they do, they will no longer represent what is embodied by two men talking together over a glass of wine: "culture," "intellect," and "status."

All the above seems to me to make it easier to understand what is being said when German ignoramuses (officers, Nazi bigwigs, the landed gentry,

Comic strip by Clay Wilson in *Radical America*, a wonderful collection of American comics (Leipzig: Melzer Verlag, 1969). *Frame 1*. Head first. A tale of human weakness on the high seas and below deck. *Frame 2* . "How old are you, my friend?" / "Old enough to keep drinking this rum." *Frame 3* . "I'm just trying to strike up some light conversation. Can I feel your prick?" / "It's really enormous. Wanna see it?"

politicians, industrialists, school principals, even many professors) evoke the "intellect" with ostentatious pride and glorify "culture" — though in fact they are acutely hostile to education. It also highlights some of the reasons why the characterization of Germany as "the land of poets and thinkers" had been and remains so enormously popular among the German petite bourgeoisie, despite its aversion to the arts and thinking.[28] What the writers quoted are saying is quite simply "Down with women!" "Death to desire!" "Up with high culture!"; they demand no less than absolute control. The "people of culture" is a people of men; as the "master-race" (*Herrenvolk**), men alone are creative, intelligent, or whatever. Women are in the first instance none of these; they are not even Aryan (though they may become so if they give birth as "white women" to a quantity of master-sons).

A woman is most likely to become a "woman of culture" if she either satisfactorily fulfills her functions of representation, or if she participates in one of the few male pastimes open to women. Lettow's Danish woman, Karin Dinesen, earned the title of "woman of culture" for her success in hunting lions. It was assumed that anyone who fired enthusiastically enough at the drives embodied in an animal was necessarily taking the part of culture; indeed this was more true of women than men since their target was more obviously their own socially repressed potency. In the huntress, the riflewoman is disarmed.

Driving hunt (*battue*): a hunt against the drives.[29] Not without reason did Lettow and so many other soldier males experience hunting as so exquisitely pleasurable.

Frame 4 . "Bloody love to. Want another rum?" / "Piss on your rum. I'm proud of my prick. I'll get it out and stick it on the table." *Frame 5* . "My God. What a monster!" / "It's lovely, isn't it? Biggest on ship. When I come, I can fill up a bucket."

Herren, plural form of the common title *Herr*, means both "men" and "masters." Hence in German a "master-race" is inevitably also a "race of men." (Tr.)

Hunting gave us younger officers a welcome chance of healthy exercise. As a form of relaxation, it was infinitely preferable to strolling around the city.[30] (like whorish she-goats . . .) Once we had begun our hunting stories, we were unstoppable. I used to tell, for example, of the time I shot my first ram from the embankment of the narrow-gauge railway in Lietzow—how I slung it over my shoulder and got drenched in the ram's sweat. And the flies—almost unbearable![31]

Captain Ehrhardt's poaching abroad almost cost him his career. He was caught, but pardoned by the Kaiser (in recognition of services rendered in hunting down the Hereros in South-West Africa). His poaching, however, continued.[32]

The "congenial" meeting between Hahn and Rodenholm, two men on the same educational plane, similarly ends with an invitation to a hunt. Rodenholm is invited to spend the Easter of 1920 hunting wood grouse during the mating season.[33] (Hahn, a baron, owns a castle and adjoining forestland.) Rodenholm then returns to his quarters, where he is afflicted with what Balla calls "lockjaw of the mind." He is pursued by the image of a Latvian prisoner who has been shot and robbed the same morning. Though Rodenholm himself did not order the shooting, he was unable, or unwilling, to prevent the incident:

> There was no escaping it, it was driving him to despair. . . . The best way to find peace would be to get drunk. He tossed back half a tumbler of schnaps at a single throw. It helped, thank God, it helped. He felt his limbs slacken, and was hardly able to undress himself before he sank heavily, contentedly onto his pillow.[34]

Frame 6. "Looks brilliant, man. Let me have a taste." / CHOP! / "Hic!" *Frame 7 .* "Mmm, head tastes best."

From cultured conversation to hunting invitation to the shooting of a bol-shevist to alcoholic oblivion—this is the path traveled by the ideas and effects of one of two men who meet in the same "connection," but are unable to come close. What seems to be changing is that the soldiers' sexuality is not structured in such a way as to allow it to play itself out between persons: it appears capable only of being directed *against* persons, or of realizing itself in one of the various states of oblivion encountered above. These states are always coupled with an act of violence, or in this case with the image of a violent act (Rodenholm himself is never involved in shooting or beating; his alcoholic excesses seem to offer some kind of compensation for his exclusion from the act of shooting.)

It seems increasingly doubtful that terms such as hetero- or homosexual-ity can usefully be applied to the men we are studying. The actual sexual act is described in these writings as a trancelike act of violence; and, though it is true that any libidinal relationship is played out exclusively between men, it is also true that its context is exclusively institutional (in institutions dominated by men). It seems justified to talk of the tensions arising between men as prominently "cultural"; for they have little to do with a sexuality understood as the desire for physical love with another person (female or male).

These men seem less to possess a sexuality than to persecute sexuality itself—one way or another.

CULTURE AND THE ARMY

However far one culture may tower above others, it remains a colossus with feet of clay if its masculine nerve is extinguished. The mightier its construction, the more fearsome its fall.

But it is tempting to raise an objection:

"The good Lord may be on the side of the strongest battalions, but are the strongest battalions on the side of the highest culture?" The response is simple; the highest culture has a duty to possess the strongest battalions.[1] (Jünger)

Culture = battalions. The equation is made without hesitation. So it was that the *Freikorps* became the sole standard-bearers of "culture" after the 1918 defeat. Rudolf Mann:

It was our good fortune that the behavior of the majority of the men had remained beyond reproach. The trees were outgrown by stronger saplings and eventually eliminated by higher ranking officers. And so they became a troop of noble wanderers, who enjoyed the cultural advantage of several hundred years over their forerunners.[2]

"Insolent Sisyphus and His Followers," by W. Mattheuer (Leipzig, 1975).

Perhaps the greatest debit on the ledger of the "glorious" revolution was its merciless destruction of the cultural force that was the Prusso-German army.[3] (Goltz)

When all faith had dissipated, there remained the identity of "culture" and the weapon. Dwinger:

> I no longer believe in anything — neither in promises, nor in programs. I believe in one thing only — in the machine-gun and the bullet! Depriving us of these means delivering into (enemy) hands, forcing us at last to the wall — and not only us, but the whole of culture in our country.[4]

Actually, then, the key role played by the concept of "culture" in defining masculinity stems from its capacity to capture the whole welter of soldierly traditions in a single word. All the army's norms and code of honor, the social conventions observed in the barracks or the casino, on maneuvers, the battlefield, in theater stalls, at commanding officers' receptions, in cafes and bordellos—all are succinctly contained in this one term, culture. The high regard in which "culture" is held in Germany springs from a veneration of male dominance and militarism. There is no contradiction at all in the fact that men who hate and persecute free thought and activity, threatening its practitioners with exclusion from their professions (*Berufsverbot*), expulsion, or death, are able to do so in the name of the German culture they love and revere. The man of culture is defined as the man who knows the difference between first-lieutenant, major, and captain; a barbarian is a man who feels no love either for uniforms or death. And the "highest" form of cultural celebration is war.

> Gone are the days when battle was part of high culture. Today, even the masses are permitted to participate in games of life and death, and they bring their instincts with them. What made the British lieutenant we recently captured offer me his cigarette case? Having fought like a gentleman, he was now behaving like a baker.[5]

An alarming incident for the man of culture. The masses had now begun to encroach on the field of battle, destroying his image of a collected army of upstanding individuals, men who staunchly resisted flowing together to pulp, cake mix; and now the viscid mass had spilled over into the trenches. This is the core of the man's repeatedly voiced hatred for the bourgeoisie; for it was the bourgeoisie that had opened the trenches to the masses, and made business of war—war, the only place where a man could still be a man, the only one.

> Only one type of mass does not appear ridiculous: the army. Yet the bourgeois renders even the army ridiculous.[*6]

Jünger here chooses a favorite insult of the Marxists as the appropriate term to express his loathing: the man who is not sufficiently militaristic is "bourgeois."

Dwinger's eulogies to the *Freikorps* in *Die letzten Reiter* (The Last Horsemen) are particularly revealing. He points to the significance of the *Freikorps* for the man of culture, the elite individual, the isolated spirit, and so on:

> One last time the old days rose again with us; they rose again in three senses! In the military sense first: one last time, war here in the East forgot there had been Verdun. One last time we fought as true cavalrymen, raising a scarcely remembered weapon, a lance of old, to gleam again. Second, in a material sense: one last time

---

*Since the footwear of culture is the boot, the patent-leather shoe cannot be counted as part of culture.

"Intruder in the Land of Souls," by Fidus (1898).

we lived in wide-open spaces, spending many of our days with
men who called princely estates their own. But the space was
taken from us and the Baltic princes fell. . . . Third, in the
spiritual sense: one last time each of us could be individual, with
nothing to constrain his spirit. Yet already the masses were
announcing their presence, rolling toward us from East and
West. . . . The end of chivalrous soldiery; the end of the breadth
of the territory of the world, the end of the boundlessness of
individual spirit.[7]

Not one of the qualities apostrophized by Dwinger in his story of "one
last time" has ever pertained to these men. Not the knight's lance, nor the
prince's table, nor the broad "territory of the world" has ever been theirs—
nor, indeed, has the "boundlessness of individual spirit' (whatever that may
be). Such benefits are hardly likely to accrue to individuals living within the
confines of the Prussian drill. The only reality expressed here is that of the
youthful dreams of the youth movement's boyish romanticism; these men's
wish to flee the city, to play Red Indians; their dreams of world conquest, fantasies of nobility and King Arthur's roundtable. "One last time" = never
having been.

The source of the dream was perfectly clear to Friedrich Wilhelm Heinz.

> Here, the boyish dreams of our Karl May[*] days became reality:
> sneaking up on each other, shooting from ambush, surprise attacks
> and beatings. The silver oakleaves we wore on our collars took the
> place of feather headdresses. The only thing we couldn't find a
> practical substitute for was scalping.[8]

Apart from the colossal understatement of Heinz's concluding comment,
his description can certainly be considered accurate. What he describes is a
social process whose product is a "culture" actualized in war: a domain in
which girls figure only incidentally, bound by gangs of boys to the martyrs'
stake; total isolation from social reality—a sphere in which the city is
exchanged for the forest, and where there is little opposition to "world
conquest."[9]

In Dwinger's text above, the mass takes on a new meaning; it embodies
all the horrors of social reality. "The mass" is made synonymous with the
constraints of the everyday, with the workplace, marriage, rent, civilian life.
Even "Verdun" and the "tanks" become part of the mass; they are negative
because they are modern reality. These "men-of-the-one-last-time" want neither modern society nor modern warfare. Everything has passed them by; they
are anachronisms. What awaits them the moment they lay down their weapons
is the factory, the office, or the agricultural smallholding:

> The age of the individual is past; the age of the mass is
> approaching. . . . The choice before you is this: you may sing
> your war song here, or you may throw yourself into the stream of
> the new.[10]

The "new" is wage labor (*Lohnarbeit*), a foreign word that strikes terror into
the hearts of these last heroes. Already, the mass is swiveling its greedy finger
toward them. What to do?

> In a sense, you young men are the last of the knights. It may be
> your primordial mission to prevent the world from becoming one
> great pigsty—which to my mind, it certainly seems to be
> becoming.[11]

With the devaluation of the "upstanding individual," the world was seen
to be becoming a pigsty, where everything wallowed in the same shit. The
perception was accurate; for it was indeed a gigantic excrescence to be fos-
tered in adolescent dreams of chivalry and world conquest, then further "cultivated" in the military, if the only thing on offer to the adult male was some
pifflingly inferior post in the bourgeois administrative apparatus.

According to Alfred Sohn-Rethel, the better-placed officers did have a

---

[*]Like his American counterpart Zane Grey, Karl May has entertained several generations of
young boys with his novels of the American West. (Tr.)

Sleeve and collar insignia. Emblems of various *Freikorps*.

chance of eventually making it big—in the sparkling-wine business, as sales-men of aristocratic parentage. But the majority of our latter-day knights errant were unlikely to accumulate financial assets whose magnitude matched the magnificence of their dreams. Empty-headed as they were, they clung all the more fiercely to megalomaniacal fantasies (whose "origins" were never purely "psychic" in nature).

If they were not to play King Arthur, Siegfried of the Lowlands, or Old Shatterhand, then they could at least see themselves as poor knights errant. This army of betrayed "individuals" was ripe for enlistment against the "pigsty," first into the *Freikorps*, later the SA.[12]

Elias Canetti sees the home of the German army as the forest; by exten-sion the forest becomes a central mass symbol for Germans in general.

> The boy who is driven from the confines of his home into the forest, where he believes he can dream and be alone, experiences something which foreshadows his entry into the army. Others have arrived before him in the forest, standing loyal and true and upright as he wishes to be; one like the other, each growing *straight*, yet quite different in height and strength.

The forest (the "German" forest) seems, then, to have provided a model for the formation of the ornamented fascist mass. The forest was the shaped desire of German men, teeming woman/nature brought to order. In the forest, the *sons* were united as "members" of the rank-and-file; the army/dra-gon/snake (the penis of the *good* woman) successfully displacing the murder-ing monsters engendered (by dominant fathers) in the body of Mother Ger-many.

In escaping to the forest, the fascist male does not flee from the frying pan of women to the fire of nature; for what he finds in the forest is *culture*, male dominion made manifest in nature as the dominion of *sons*—his wishful dream.

When the fascist strolls through morning-fresh, dewy nature, he is moving through one version of the image of pure woman. When he returns to his allotment (*Schrebergarten*), by contrast he is returning to his own interior, to the Medusa he has fenced in and contained—every square inch dug up, staked out, divided into beds and paths, sections for use, sections for orna-ment. He knows every earthworm, he knows they won't bite; never a trace of desire's dissipations. Even slimy snails may live here without arousing his revulsion. Many an allotment owner patrols his sanctuary by night, gun in hand; this has less to do with the danger that he may lose half-ripe strawber-ries, than with his fear of the desecration of the tiny patch of woman/land he has fought so long and hard to purify, land he calls his own, land in which his own interior is guaranteed to remain untrodden and unthreatening.

"The Battle of Sempach" (1386). From a woodcut by Hans Rudolf Manuel Deutsch (b. 1525)

In this context, the demands of anti-pollution pressure groups appear more than usually ambivalent. What lies behind campaigns for cleaner rivers may well be a drive for purer, cleaner women; the fear of river pollution may well conceal a fear of the "dirt" of women (the dirt of sex and childbirth), or of the dirt we produce personally. Pure poetry, for once, from Biermann describing his feelings as he and his lover jump into the Elbe: "and we didn't give a damn about the crap."

UNDEFEATED IN THE FIELD?

If the individual German is to remain upstanding, he must not be laid low (*sich niederlegen*). Defeat (*Niederlage*, literally "being laid low") is out of the question. Thus German defeats consist exclusively in individual victories: Germany remains undefeated on the battlefield, until in the end the war is lost.

Throughout the war, the individual soldier never once weakened—or at least, it was impossible to tell if he had done so (or was it?). Being laid low in warfare was considered tantamount to the most monstrous of crimes; for if he allowed the dam to rupture, the man was ultimately forced to prostrate himself to Woman. Once soft, never hard again.

If a man is convinced that he who stands highest will inevitably win, simply because he is the more upstanding, he will consider defeat a form of personal exposure. He may be "laid low" by many things (including conta-

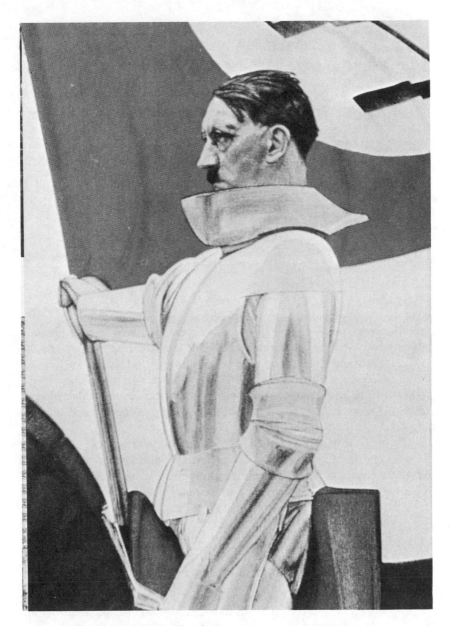

"Hitler as Flagbearer," by Hubert Lanzinger.

Italian postcard.

gious diseases): but once is enough . . . one emotion very often expressed, particularly by officers, in relation to their defeat in war was "shame." By the end of the war, the soldier was perceived as one of the sources of German military uselessness. If he was to cast off the burden of responsibility for the 1918 defeat, he had, then, to invent some kind of exonerating circumstance. Hence the story of a "stab-in-the-back" (*Dolchstoss*) perpetrated on Germany.

If a man can be proved to have been "stabbed in the back," he can also claim never to have been laid low; he can portray himself as having stood hard to face the enemy, oblivious of the scoundrels creeping up behind—to whom, of course, he was an easy target. For the soldier male, the daggers of his attackers were the first signs of revolution; he later prepared to do battle against them. "The navy is ready to recover its honor," proclaimed Captain Ehrhardt in his announcement of plans for the putsch on 13 March 1920.[1] Until now, a stain on the soldier's uniform had marked the spot where something had been momentarily allowed to seep through . . .[2]

> Undefeated in a hundred battles, unbent as all values collapsed around him, skeptical of all illusions, devoid of hope, the frontline soldier returned home. We were left only with our honor, untainted, and the unbending resolve of men whose honor and freedom were at stake. What we retained was our faith in Germany and our love for her hapless people—these were the sources from which, in the midst of collapse, the greatest frontline

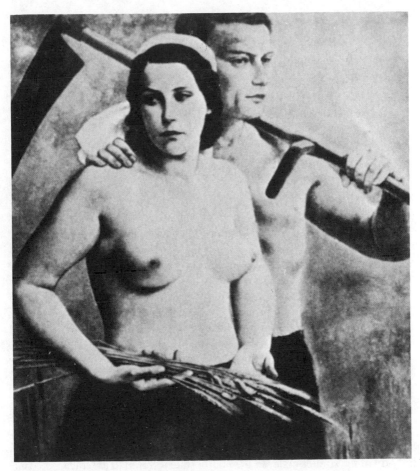

"Fruition," by Johannes Beutner (ca. 1933).

soldier of all drew the strength to begin his incomparable journey.[3]
(v. Mahnken)

Adolf Hitler, undefeated in the field. If the field were one of corn, the claim might be justified. Men determined at all costs to remain men are destined to win and to win, until the battle is lost . . .

THE MASS AND THE RACE

The qualities of "race" are in every detail the precise opposites of the terrors of "the mass." The extent to which this is the case is demonstrated by a comparative catalog of their attributes by Delmar—which needs little further comment.

Decalogue of Race
I   Race is the spirit of grace in landscape, blood, and form.
II   Race is the perfection of a possibility.
III   Race is the fate of the few who excel.
IV   Race is the exception, and the rights due to it.
V   Race is happiness and life.
VI   Race is strength, beauty, and desire.
VII   Race is battle, wisdom, and play.
VIII Race is the passionate intensity of will in a man.
IX   Race is passionate submission in a woman.
X   Race was once the hallmark of the French nation.[1]

Decalogue of the Mass
I   Mass is the death of spirit in landscape, blood, and form.
II   Mass is the eclipse of what was once real.
III   Mass is the fate of all the worst.
IV   Mass is equality and its attendant terrors.
V   Mass is suffering and death.
VI   Mass is weakness, ugliness, and fear.
VII   Mass is eternal peace, stultification, petty legalism.
VIII Mass is feminization of the will in a man.
IX   Mass is prostitution in a woman.
X   Mass is now the hallmark of the French nation.[2]

In Delmar's book, sixty-five pages separate these two "decalogues." As the comparison shows, they match line for line, and word for word.

In many of the texts already cited, the external organizational form presented as most appropriate—indeed as more or less natural—to male culture is the army. "Race" by contrast is the organizational form most appropriate to the body of the soldier male. In the bodily state referred to as "race," he finds "beauty," "desire," "play," "happiness," "wisdom," "life." Race seems to protect him from disintegration.

For Wilhelm Reich, the term "race" could clearly be seen to denote a particular sexual orientation. So unquestioningly, however, did he equate heterosexuality and genitality with sexuality in general that he tended to regard "race" as a description of "asexuality."[3] Yet the concept clearly displays "masculine" characteristics—its origin in a defense against the threats of the "mass," and its association with the masculine/soldierly concept of "culture." If "race" is compared with the various different manifestations of the "mass"—particularly the "heavy mass" of the bodily interior that threatens constantly to erupt into murder—it becomes possible to see it as the fascist's term for his own body armor: a function of his body that keeps the mass in check—and the function through which he experiences himself as living.

As Reich also recognized, the notion of the "alien race" can be read as a reference to the alien class. This is more than mere sleight of hand; for if "race" is the opposite of all that is "mass," then "race" and "proletarian" must also be opposites, since the proletarian is part of the whole larger mass of contagious pleasures.[4] It follows from this that the man who assigns himself a place in the Aryan, or any other "higher" race, is aligning himself in opposition to the lower classes, the mass, the proletarian, the woman, the animal. What he is saying is, "as a man, I am an upstanding individual, a formation, one of your kind, the upper echelons, always on the side of domination and the army."

For anyone who libidinally invests the molecular organization of the mass—not "the whole," but the "enclaves and peripheries," in the words of Deleuze and Guattari—the precise opposite may be inferred. "I am not one of you"; "I am of a race inferior for all eternity"; "I am a beast, a black."[5]

Not only does the opposition between "mass" and "race" precisely correspond to that between "mass" and "individual"; it supersedes it—which is why the mass/individual opposition has proved so unuseful in explaining any of the fascist mass phenomena.

A more useful oppositional pair is proposed by Deleuze and Guattari; they talk of "two types of mass formations, in which the collective and the individual successively enter into different relationships."[6] Their name for Canetti's type of mass formation is the "molecular," and for the other—the mass of totalities, blocks organized toward the center—the "molar": army, race, the large number as unity, macrophysics.* The molecular mass, by contrast, contains: infinite variety, multiplicity, flows beyond boundaries, microphysics.[7]

Libidinal investment in one or the other form of mass organization is not necessarily total; cathexis of both can exist in the same person, group, or party. In the soldier male, however, the two appear strictly antithetical. His unconscious is organized in ways consistent with the organization of his body; his bodily interior (the molecular ordering of the unconscious) is incarcerated by an incarcerating body armor (the molar arrangement of domination), and the two are irreconcilably opposed, one subjected to the other. The "man of superior race" needs to dominate in order to retain his body intact. He prevents himself from being "torn apart," and his bodily interior from emerging into the open, by adopting a position of absolute domination.

It now becomes evident what constitutes the horror of processes such as "racial miscegenation" for the fascist man. Miscegenation would inexorably cause him to disintegrate. His body armor would succumb to his chaoticized interior; it would be devoured by the "primitive man" within. (It is only in

---

*This may explain the soldier male's characteristic hallucination of history (described in Chapter 1) as the history of great names, great temporal unities. His "interior" is inundating him = Germany is going under, the world is going under. The "war-of-the-worlds" is a manifestation of the suffering of his body. His oblivious dream of great unities prevents him from dissipating into an infinite swarm.

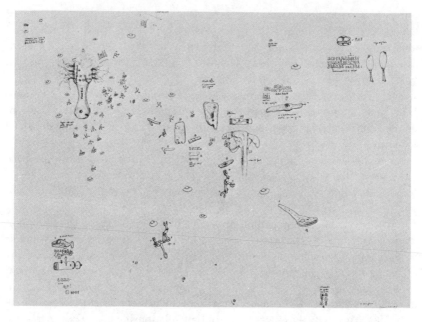

"Argument over Holding Fast to Progress," by Gianfranco Baruchello (1968).

war, in an organized act of murder, that he can expel the "primitive within" without perishing in the process. In the war context, the functions of body armor seem to be taken over by the troop formation.)[8]

The alien race appears, then, to be the most intense embodiment of the terrors represented by the mass. While it is most usual, and most often sufficient, for the mass to be encoded with threatening femininity (in which case it suffices for the mass to be made subordinate, put in its place by firing a few shots into it), the alien race is predominantly encoded with the inexorably murderous forces of the man's own interior; it must therefore be exterminated.

Three different kinds of barrier are represented in the opposition of Jewish to Aryan: barriers of class, of gender, and those between the interior and exterior of the individual body. All are torn down by *Rassenschande* (the Nazi term for miscegenation—literally, "racial disgrace"). The Nazis made miscegenation synonymous with a whole range of ideas that appeared in the marxist concept of classless society as liberating: here, they became murderous. I believe it was through their use of this concept that the fascists were able to deal the most crucial ideological blow to the marxist Utopia. For them, the notion of a classless society was overturned by bodily certainties; the body's interior *is not* external; man *is not* woman; above *is not* below; the mass cannot lead; and so on.

And above all: the one cannot be *allowed* to be the other—for this would mean death. Domination is imperative. For reasons of survival it is a necessity

Control center of the Siemens-Schuckert Concern. A racial edifice.

determined by "nature." It is "necessary" (a "natural" necessity) that the relationship between woman and man be antagonistic and that the battle-of-the-sexes be a battle for survival; it is necessary that what is "below" remain "below"; and so on and so on. For all these reasons there *cannot* be communism. Programs for "paradise on earth" surely *cannot* demand self-dissolution . . . or can they?

If imperialism is understood as what Lenin had of course to call the "highest" form of capitalism, then racism must be seen as patriarchal domination in its most intense form.[9] The internal counterpart of a nation's eternal imperialism is racism—racism as a deadly struggle against the "alien race" within, as incitement to class struggle, as an antagonistic battle-of-the-sexes, and as a struggle across the very body of the racist. The man of "race" mobilizes himself against the "mass" of pleasure; body armor versus the desiring-production of the unconscious. As long as a single drop of vulgar mass desire continues to flow, the battle is not over; somewhere, there will always be one drop seeping through. . . . Ultimately, it is toward his own death (and the death of all others with him) that the race-warrior steers; for only this, it seems, will eradicate that "alien race" in its entirety. (If there is any one circumstance that will one day cost all of us our lives, it is this one.)

THE NATION

"Parties are the mass; the *Freikorps* are fellowships of men"[1] (F. W. Heinz): A succinct expression of the unbridgeable distance that separates the

"Male Head, Disturbed by the Flight of a Non-Euclidean Fly," by Max Ernst (1947).

soldierly man from a republic (and not only that of Weimar). The republic may have a government (of men "whirled to the top"); the government, however, in no sense matches the formation required by the soldier. So, for example, Weimar is almost never referred to as a "State." Or if it is, then perhaps as follows: "When you call State, Herr Kommissar, there is not a single man among those who step up to the front—only millions of assholes." (Eggers's Lieutenant Massmann, in conversation with a plain-clothes detective who has not considered himself above serving a state concerned "only with the mass.")[2]

It is considered particularly impermissible to mention the term "nation" in connection with the republic. The nation is seen as an abandoned orphan—or one that would have been abandoned, had a handful of men not been there to hold the bastion.

What then is "nation"? It manifests itself in three forms. In the first, it is identified with the "hard core" at the "front":

> In these last battles, (the) front was mercilessly burned away to the unshakeable core (of the nation). . . . A single little finger from one of these last exhausted soldiers . . . deserved the name of the nation (more than any single man at headquarters).[3]
> (Schauwecker)

Salomon, watching frontline soldiers marching into Berlin on their way home:

> Suddenly I understood: these were not workers, farmers, students, nor artisans, office workers, tradesmen, officials: they were soldiers. Following no mission, no order, and shunning disguise, these were men responding to the call, the mysterious call of the blood, the spirit, soldiers of their own free will, men who felt the solidity of their communal bond and knew what lay below the surface of things. . . . The nation was with them.[4]

The nation was seen to have arisen more or less of its own accord in the trenches. Schauwecker:

> And suddenly, when life and death were at stake, as we waded in filth, lying under fire, sharing our filth, lice, bread, and thirst— here, now, we were finally together. We had finally found each other, we who have yearned for each other so long without the merest hint of an intimation of so doing. . . . At last our time had come! It was ours: the one-and-only, the unlearnable, the unique—the nation.[5]

Now we see: the nation has in the first instance nothing to do with questions of national borders, forms of government, or so-called nationality. The

9 November 1918: red banners through the Brandenburg Gate.

30 January 1933: SA marching through the Brandenburg Gate.

Page from a history textbook (1940).

concept refers to a quite specific form of male community, one that is "yearned for" for many a long year, that rises from the "call of the blood." Like sexual charactistics, its essential features are incapable of being "learned" or "forgotten." The nation is a community of soldiers.

> The moment Bismarck and Roon assumed the leadership of Prussia under Wilhelm I, the cause of the nation passed into the hands of the Prusso-German army. Here it remained . . . preserved and protected, until 1 August 1914. It was on that day that army and people became one, and nationalism began to emerge as the will and demand of a minority summoned to lead.[6] (Heinz)

If the army was a minority summoned to lead, then in 1914, the soldierly core of the army — and above all its nucleus, the officer caste — became nation, and leader of the people. But the "nation" suffered gravely, first in the war, then in revolution. The first officers to turn republican (if only slightly so, and in the main out of opportunism) signaled the death of the nation in its existing form. It was created anew by the *Freikorps*:

> In their struggle against the chaos of bolshevism, against the cowardice of pacifism, against the betrayal of the International, against the failure of the bourgeoisie, they gave birth to a new nation.[7]

As disarmament had signaled the death of the "old" nation, so the key to this rebirth was the arming of the *Freikorps* against the republic:

> It was Albrecht who oversaw the destruction of his company's equipment. . . . He watched case after case of cartridges plunge into the water and disappear. This then was the ultimate end. From now on, restoration was impossible. Now for the first time they were truly defenseless! The nation had resolved to bow to demands for its own castration — for what purpose would sexual organs serve in the coming age of international brotherhood, world peace, human love, universal happiness? What possible purpose?[8]

I do not believe Schauwecker intends irony here; as so often, his text is simply pointedly explicit. He deems "sexual organs" unnecessary, except in battle; thus he calls upon the nation to divest itself of them, before involving itself in brotherhood, peace, human love, happiness. Death to intermingling: the name of our love is killing. Heinz was sufficiently convinced by this argument to reformulate the sixth commandment: "Thou shalt not kill if thy conscience is not at peace before thy nation."[9] Or, to put it another way: all murder is justified so long as it is ratified by the soldierly group to which these men belong — the nation.

The second manifestation of the nation is even more narrowly defined than the first:

> "If conscience commands me to go forth, I obey for I know that the nation speaks through my conscience."[10] The nation exists in the individual man himself; it is "a soldierly rage in fervent, infallible blood, hurled forward by dark forces" (Heinz).[11] "The nation—is a spiritual value and an inner stature. The nation—is the desire of a spiritual unity desiring to surface anew." (Schauwecker)[12]

What is it that is to be "unified"?

> To fuse the separate elements of life, to reunite the polarities that threaten our ruin; to unite sober factual knowledge with unerring faith: this is the German mission. For in that unity lies the nation.[13]

The nation is created through the fusion of elements in the man himself.

> The nation first emerged from the primitive mind of a hero, struggling for inner stability on the threshold between the highest possible fulfillment and the horrible void; it penetrated to the deepest core of his being and became his vocation.[14]

In "penetrating" to the true interior of the soldier male, we discover "the deepest core of his being": the nation. If the core is absent, we plunge into the "horrible void." As Bronnen writes,

> The nationalists' task is to prepare Germany internally for total mobilization; to make ready for a battle that is to work in the deepest depths and the most enormous settings.[15]

In crucial ways, then, the battle for the nation resembles the men's own battle to become men: it takes place on the "most monstrous settings" in the body: a battle between life and death, masculinity and femininity, fulfillment and void, sense and insanity. In the battle for the nation, the man acquires the inner value that is his soul. Victory allows him to claim with absolute conviction:

> What then do we mean by nationalism? We stand by Germany because we are Germans, because Germany is our fatherland; the German soul is our soul, for we are all pieces of the soul of Germany.[16] (Goebbels)

We should not be deceived by the use of "we all" in such statements. The "we" only applies to men recognized as the possessors of a German soul, to the clearly bounded group to which the writer belongs, and in extreme cases to

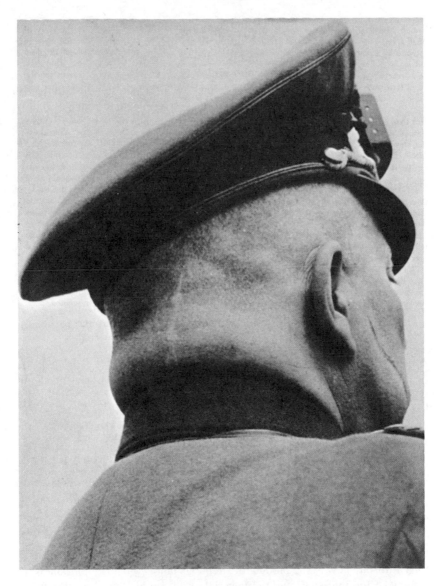

Primary sexual characteristic: German. Actor and director Erich von Stroheim developed in Hollywood a special art of playing German officers.

the writer alone. Since his soul is the soul of Germany, he speaks of Germany as if of himself. The army, high culture, race, nation, Germany—all of these appear to function as a second, tightly armored body enveloping his own body armor. They are "extensions of himself."[17]

Something of the same idea is expressed in a phrase still common in German in which individuals are described as "German to the bone" (*deutsch bis auf die Knochen*). What this formulation most clearly indicates is that the German body has to be stripped of its flesh (be encased in leather, Krupp steel, or whatever) if it is to earn the label "German." The soldierly male body is a "unified nation" at one with itself after hard-fought battles to dam its own flows: it is the ultimate form of a male sexuality at odds with itself, of a life of desires dogged by contradiction. The soldier male is a man who would doubtless be entranced to have his passport stamped "Sex: German."

Heinz sums this up for the situation in the postwar period, as nationalism began to take root once more:

> Nationalism could once be simply defined as an attitude
> expressing the extent to which corruption and cowardice,
> disloyalty and irresponsibility, dishonor, egocentrism, and
> hysteria—all the festering growths now erupting around us[18]
> —were opposed to men's character.

An attitude of the body, in the first instance.

In the third manifestation of nation, men constructed as fascists and the organizations to which they belong have already gained power—the nation has attained both internal and external "unity." Since the People (Volk) cannot be Nation, they are dominated. The Nation, meanwhile, becomes "the very core of the People."

Thus Bronnen describes Rossbach, an element within the core, as a man

> filled with a firm belief in the need to press constantly for a
> transformation that will be decisive . . . to forge a great nation
> from the lifeless block we call Germany.[19]

What is "forged" is both the people of Germany and the body of the man himself. If he is to assume the attitude that is "nation," he must repeatedly forge himself anew as the product of strenuous labor. What is important is the activity of forging itself, and the material on the anvil is among other things "the people" (*das Volk*)—not to be confused with "the mass," of which more in a moment. "Volk" is a raw material which is to be shaped into proper form by the "nation." "We do not do battle in order that the people may be happy. We do battle to force them into the shape for which they are destined" (Salomon).[20] The people conforms to its destined shape only if it is dominated by the men of "the nation." Heinz: "What is a people? A community of blood relations that endures and suffers together. But it is the nation that

shapes and rules."[21] Thus when these men portray themselves as "nation," fighting for their Germany, their homeland, their loves, their people, they are portraying themselves as fighting for their domination of all others.

Maercker talks of "the strong state . . . we need if we are to remain a people."[22] The "people," in other words, exists and arises only under the "strong state," which is the proper form of domination.

The noble values of statehood—the honor, power, and freedom of a nation—are fundamentally respected as such by the People, but only men born for freedom can live them out in reality. These warriors of Germany continued to reflect their nation's future nobility throughout an era of impotence and shame; their task, as the sons of town and country, of poverty and the old nobility, is now to reshape the history of our continent and mark it with the inexorable stamp of their domination.[23] (G. Günther)

People and continent are presented here as looking forward, in submissive anticipation, to their torture by "the nation."

The only possible response to these men's unshakeable belief in the naturalness of their need to exercise power is one of sustained incredulity. For them, their status as "nation," "soldier," "man" (noble values "respected as such by the People") is indisputable. Their self-assurance can be reduced to a single formulation: power belongs to us because we are there, because we exist. No further justification is needed. Salomon describes the state of mind this produces with the naïveté of a child who believes it has a right to its food:

We were flooded with sudden driving, gripping, explosive energy. So easy and joyous and sweet did this responsibility seem to us: power! . . . We believed power to be due us in the name of Germany; for we felt with unparalleled depth of emotion that we ourselves were Germany. If we talked of the idea, it was Germany we referred to. Whenever we said battle, deployment, life, sacrifice, duty, we meant in every case Germany. All this, we believed, was rightfully ours: the men in Berlin could in our view never rightfully claim to represent Germany.[24]

"For we *felt* . . . that we ourselves were Germany"—the comment may be taken literally. The man is flooded by a force that is easy, joyous, sweet, driving, explosive. Here something is flowing, here he feels love. He loves the power that derives from his feeling of unity, a feeling of unity with "Germany" and with himself. His blissful sense of power, of omnipotence, arises as two elements are fused together, himself and "Germany."

Nation invariably arises out of a process of fusion or, to put it another way, out of the suppression of fragmentations and separations. Nation is the fusion of the best, the toughest and most soldierly men at the front or in the *Freikorps* under the dominance of the best man of all, the *Führer*. Nation is the fusion of two antagonistic aspirations within the "heroic man" himself; it produces a "spiritual unity" in which the soldierly desire for combat remains triumphantly dominant. Nation is the binding of the man-troop to the People (Volk) and the fatherland, to the State in which the man-troop is dominant.

The bliss that accompanies the unification of "nation" is experienced by the soldier male whenever organizations of the molar order combine with other molar organizations to form larger unities, or when molecular organizations are subordinated to molar organizations within larger "unified" systems.

Clearly, then, what the fascist understands by the term "unity" is a state in which oppressor and oppressed are violently combined to form a structure of domination. For him, unity denotes a relationship not of equality, but of domination. Equality is considered synonymous with multiplicity, mass—it is thus the precise opposite of "unity," since "unity" rigidly fuses these baser elements with what is "above them," "interior" to "exterior," and so on. Unity allows the soldier male access to pleasure; it protects him from the death of splitting or decomposition.* What seems to hold the masculine-soldierly body together is his compulsion to oppress the body of another (or bodies, or the body in his own body).** His relation to the bodies he subordinates is one of violence and, in extreme cases, of murder.

The concept of nation can be seen, then, as the most explicit available foundation of male demands for domination. "Male chauvinism" — the term chosen by women's liberation movements to designate masculinity—could hardly be more appropriate. It would even be possible to leave out the word "male." Female chauvinism is a contradiction in terms.

Nation is the opposite of mass, femininity, equality, sensuous pleasure, desire, and revolution. A republican government may undertake a hundred or more initiatives that the terminology of political science would consider nationalist: none of these will ever be recognized as such (they never were, for example, in the Weimar Republic) by the soldier male. What is national is only what is undertaken by himself, or by his führer: the only national state is a state ruled by soldier manhood.

We should stress one further key quality of "the nation": its capacity for procreation. The nation is the necessary precursor of the *Reich*, of empire.[25] Produced, as we have seen, through the fusion of masculine with masculine, the "nation" proves to be fertile, productive of the future. It now becomes

---

*This man never becomes schizophrenic; he combines elements that do not belong together and becomes paranoid: the persecuted persecutor. He himself is not split, he splits others, into layers that become the material that supports him. It is in this sense that the fascist persecutor can most easily be distinguished from the "schizo." Were he to split himself (not, literally, with an ax, but along the lines laid down by desire), he would simply be engaging in an experiential process: in splitting others, he engages in murder. Deleuze and Guattari call molecular investment "paranoid-fascicizing": "The paranoic turns masses into machines; he is the artist of large molar unities, statistical formations, gregarious structures, organized mass phenomena" (*Anti-Oedipus*, 340ff.). The processes of the molecular mass appear to him by contrast as "schizo-revolutionary": they split, multiply, fuse together new multiplicities. The "schizo" remains closest to desire; in a world in which he bounces off of molar unities, dead bodies, and flat surfaces, he begins to divide himself: he continues the revolutionary process in a void and endures terrible suffering.

**Holding himself together is of paramount importance: even Faust wonders "what holds the world together in its innermost parts."

possible to understand what Jünger means when he writes, in *Kampf um das Reich* (Struggle for the *Reich*):

> It (nationalism) is more than just one idea among others. It does not seek out the measurable, but the measure. It is the surest route to the maternal being that gives birth to new forms in every century. And we have seen that there are still men who can create after the fashion of the warrior.[26]

On an initial reading, the passage is confusing: the equation it makes between the "maternal being" and "warrior procreation" seems contradictory. But no matter how it is read, the identity between the two remains. The "being" of men "who can create after the fashion of the warrior" is "maternal." It is men who procreate; they give birth to form. In the first instance, what is excluded from procreation is femininity; over and above this, there is an absence of any process of fertilization. Men create the future, the führer, power, and the *Reich*—totalities evoked in the concept of the "form" (*Gestalt*) to which they aspire.[27] Though childbirth has become masculine, it still requires a body—the body of the earth:

> Yet something is in the process of becoming, something bound to the elemental, a level of life that is deeper and closer to chaos; not yet law, but containing new laws within itself. What is being born is the essence of nationalism, a new relation to the elemental, to Mother Earth, whose soil has been blasted away in the rekindled fires of material battles and fertilized by streams of blood. Men are harkening to the secret primordial language of the people, a language they are resolved to translate into the language of the twentieth century.[28]

Procreation occurs when the hard core of men (the nation) blasts away "Mother" Earth, tearing her apart and penetrating her in warrior fashion, "fertilizing" her interior with streams of blood until "something in the process of becoming," the "new laws," issue from her. The new age, however, is dominated, as ever, by men.

War is a process that regenerates both the nation and the soldier male himself.[*] The centrality of the concept of nation to these men's structure of being is demonstrated once again by Jünger:

> It is always possible to make concessions where the material distribution of goods is concerned; but there can be no peace with any force that denies itself to the nation.[29]

Here, as elsewhere, the nation is defined in terms that are clearly sexual.

---

[*]On the subject of the war waged by men against women's fertility, see Gisela Stelly's review of the first volume of *Male Fantasies* in *Die Zeit*, 24 November 1977.

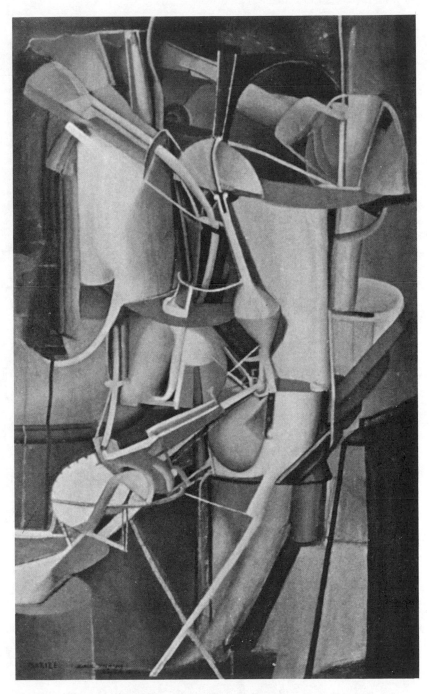

"The Bride," by Marcel Duchamp. Reproduced by permission of the Philadephia Museum of Art: Louise and Walter Arensberg Collection.

"The Lost Girl," by Felix Labisse.

"Michael (i.e., Germany) Unbound."

Men who "deny themselves" to the nation are committing the most serious crime imaginable; for to deny oneself to the nation is to refuse to be dominated by it, to refuse passive "submission."[30] There are, then, sacrifices involved in refusing to deny oneself to the nation.

> What we Germans have to recognize is that every public office we hold, every voice in our blood, every order we give or execute, every sacrifice we demand or make is given and intended by God—because it is given and intended by the nation. Only if we acknowledge this, will we be able to call the great unity of all Germans by its proper name, which is not only nation, but Reich![31] (Heinz)

The "nation" demands sacrifices—but from whom? The high-ranking Nazi who declares that sacrifices must be made never sacrifices himself, but only others, the others "below": women, the mass, the dominated classes. When Bronnen describes the men of the "nation" as "willingly offering the sacrifice of blood," he is referring to the slaughtered victims they offer to the Führer. Their own "foaming" blood is the agent, not the victim of sacrifice.[32]

This seems to me very likely to be the source of the massive attraction of propaganda demands for infinite sacrifice. The audience listening to the man above the crowd must surely sense his absolute unwillingness to make sacrifices of his own. For this very reason, they follow him gladly, in the hope that remaining with him will bring deliverance. What he means when he says "We must all make sacrifices" is always "We (the group to which I belong) must stand fast together and sacrifice others." One sacrifice is, however, demanded of men who follow the Führer and become nation. As an apparently insignificant, sacrifice to "morality," it may appear to the men themselves less as sacrifice than as virtue. What they are called upon to relinquish is their own "below," pleasurable hybridity, the productive force of the unconscious. As a result, they themselves become political victims, masochists, harried into battle by a Führer who demands that their belts be firmly tightened. It is for this particular loss that their right to murder is clearly intended to compensate. In return for something as simple as belt-tightening, they gain the right to enforce the sacrifice of all those who have refused to offer themselves as sacrificial victims.

Outside war or civil war—in "peacetime"—this right is exercised over all groups destined to remain subordinate within the state of "national unity" for which sacrifices are demanded: children, women, the dominated classes, Jews, and others.[*] The right to heap scorn on such as these, to beat and de-

---

[*]White terror in peacetime: 25,000 fatal "mishaps" among German miners between 1918 and 1931 (Steinbock-Fermor, *Deutschland von unten*); and in 1977, one fatal industrial accident every three hours in the Federal Republic (Television News Report, 23 November 1977). There are very many places with built-in razor blades.

Die Kultur

I. Jahrgang ✻ Heft 1

"Culture," Volume 1, Number 1.

ceive them, to mark them for death, is the reward accorded to men for whom sacrifice means the obligation to remain dominant. The responsibility weighs heavily on their shoulders.

THE PEOPLE (DAS VOLK)

> The people—by which I certainly do not mean the howling rabble of the asphalt cities or the mob that has torn to shreds the old banners and cockades—the great, long-suffering German *Volk*, cultivators of field and hewers of stone, stewards of the dark forests and hunters in the oceans of the world: this people demands that we remain at our posts, even in the face of government attempts to dislodge us.[1] (Bronnen)

The German *"Volk"* is erected on the foundations of subjugated nature. It is this that distinguishes it from the "mass," which whips up nature to flood and rebellion. The people is more than mass, but less than "nation":

> For the Leader (*Führer*), the mass is no more a problem than is paint for the artist. . . . The greatest aim of true politics has always been to form a people out of the mass, and a state out of the people.[2]

The suggestion that the influence of a leader (führer) turns a "mass" into a "people," quoted here from Goebbels's *Michael*, had first been advanced in an earlier text by Hans Blüher, *Volk und Führer in der Jugendbewegung* (People and Leader in the Youth Movement):

> The leader and the people differ in one important respect: the leader does not need the people to be a leader; but the people only becomes a people through its leader. In the absence of a leader, it remains a milling crowd, an arbitrary multiplicity of individuals. . . . In that form, it can never become the bearer of values . . . the crowd becomes a people only when it begins to follow; from that moment on, it has a soul; like Michelangelo's *Adam*, it extends a feeble arm toward God the Father in anticipation of divine inspiration. Thus any human crowd driven to become a people and to feel the nobility of communality requires a man as leader.[3]

The leader is a magnet organizing the mass of iron filings along lines of force: he breathes "values," a "soul," a formation into the mass; he alone penetrates and forms it.

The destiny of the "mass" is to be clubbed and bombarded into place; the "people," on the other hand, seems capable of incorporation into one or

"German Earth," by W. Peiner (1933).

another of the "unities" through which, by subordinating all "baser elements," the dominant man/race/nation secures dominance. While the "mass" teems with, among other things, devouring femininity, the "people" is encoded with the subjugated and willing white woman. She is forbidden—on pain of death—to choose the man by whom she desires to be made happy.[4]

> It is an inversion of the proper selection process to allow the people to choose what individuals of certain political persuasions term a "leader." The elected leader should properly be called a representative of interests; the people he represents is no more than a crowd. By rights, it is the leader who should elect the people to become such; he selectively penetrates the crowd, and permits part of it to become people.[5]

Selection is akin to an act of procreation: in the moment of its voluntary subjugation to the leader, the people "conceives" and gives birth:

> All the energy of the body of the people is invested in expressing itself through the army.[6] (Jünger)

At the point at which the leader makes "Volk" of the mass, he implants his seed within it and prepares it to give birth to masculine organizations.[*] Impregnation occurs in deathly paralysis: it has none of the attributes of sexual

---

[*]I wrote above that the people can never become "nation." This is not entirely true. Under conditions of imperialist war, where other peoples are exhorted to assume the role of the submissive "*Volk*" (as collaborators in the widest sense), the occupying people, insofar as it follows the leader, may be elevated to the status of "nation": "German nationalism is a conscious and unlimited demand by the German people for the political, cultural, and economic realization of its soul—defined as a unity of faith, blood, history, country, and language—within an unlimited dominion whose centre is a *Reich* encompassing all the tribes of Germany." (Heinz, *Die Nation greift an*, 9; cf. Salomon, *Die Geächteten*, 297.)

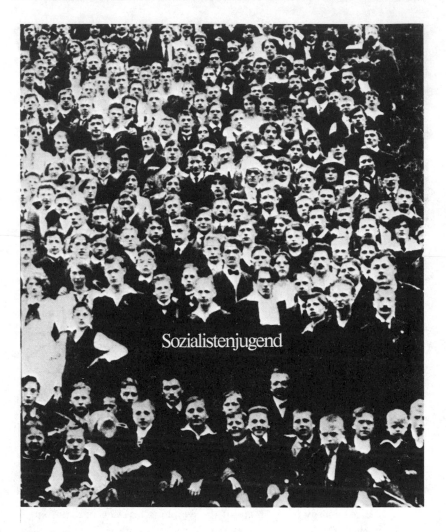

Sozialistenjugend

"People."

commingling. As it submits to an existence as *Volk*, the mass is drained of life. This union may more readily be described as incorporation: the nation, the leader, takes up the submissive mass "below" and fuses it into his own totality.

In the process, the mass below is devivified, then restored to life: it gives birth, but only to what is *made* to issue from it. Procreation is a fusing together, the birth of devivified life remolded. The phallus rises to ascendance through the fusion of leader and people, but it is the object not the agent of procreation. Like the forest that marches forth from the body of the earth, the army snake/dragon/worm (*Heerwurm*) rises out of the body of the people.

The leader attains potency by desexualizing and devivifying "the mass" (since it is the mass which contains everything that threatens to devour him). The woman of whom he is master, the white wife, keeps his prick rampant by desexualizing herself; she inserts herself into the required relation of domination by releasing to him a series of little soldiers—by dying whenever he needs an erection. *This* is what turns him on.[*]

In any democracy in which the people were to exercise true choice, this kind of man would never get it up again.

---

[*]Taking an active part in sexual intercourse is the mark and privilege of prostitutes.

"People." From the comicstrip "Love" (Frankfurt, 1974). *Frame 1.*
" Maybe it will be fun after all . . ."; *Frame 2.* "umpf!" / "Ouch! Damn—watch out,
it's still dry!"; *Frame 3.* " I'm—real gentle . . ." / "Do you have to breathe in my
face?!"; *Frame 4.* "I can't get any air air . . . not so hard!!!"

THE WHOLE

As we have seen above, the soldier male cannot stomach half measures:
the half is below and contaminates. His constant goal is to avoid the experience of fragmentation by fusing himself into a unity in which he remains on
top. Only this can make him whole. He seems to love the whole greatly,
though his love is hardly selfless—however much he may like to represent it
as such:

> In the hour of need, we must direct our gaze beyond our own
> narrow circle to the whole; we must suppress all personal interests
> and pursue common goals.

What is the significance of this recurrent German theme, rehearsed here
by Baron Major Schenk on 19 March 1920 in Marburg, as "bands of armed
men roam the country, robbing and plundering"?[1]
Like the "nation" and the men's own bodies, the "whole" consists exclusively of male soldierly formations:

Frame 6."You feel really wonderful!" / "You, too!" *Frames 7-9.* "Slurp! Smack!"

It was not personal volition that gave us the will to make our
fragmented lives whole, to rediscover the justification for
existence: it was the power of God in us, the power on which
every legitimate affirmation of this life is founded.[2] (Hotzel)

What Hotzel terms "the power of God in us" is simply another term for
the soul which is the reward bestowed upon Germans who successfully control
the fragmentation of their lives. To emerge victorious from this inner struggle,
the German must possess the will to "wholeness."

The whole had been shattered in wartime defeat; it was fused together
again in the troop, the *Freikorps:*

There were no more divisions; every man stood and died for all,
for every man had been made whole in the unity of God and
nation, spirit and deed, instinct and consciousness,
heaven-embracing faith and earth-probing life. High above the
clouds of betrayal and defeat, the signs of victory burned bright,
celebrating the inextricable union of national power and honor of
the nation with State sovereignty and dignity and with the
self-sacrifice and loyalty of the nation's adherents.[3] (Heinz)

French postcard.

"Close the circle! Join the municipal guard!" Recruiting poster (Bremen, 1919).

The whole is both the troop* and the man with whom the troop is synonymous. Relations of domination crystallize more clearly as "wholeness" is created: while "national power and honor" accrue to the fascist male, "self-sacrifice and loyalty" are demanded both of the people and of the " 'good' woman."** The whole itself is always divided into two parts, power and sacrifice, the one "above," the other "below."

Goote has one of his heroes say of Hitler that he is "struggling to make every individual see himself as part of a larger whole. The individual has to realize that he can do nothing greater than to do his duty." The "duty" of the soldier male was to rule over the larger whole;[4] for him, "doing his duty for the larger whole" was merely a more elegant way of formulating the pursuit of his own particular interests, as a member of the dominant group within the whole. The larger whole was useful to him only insofar as it contained the oppressed part without which the experience of wholeness was impossible. The harmony of the whole is never harmony among its parts; it is a harmony imposed by hierarchical orderings.

> This was the root of the will to power and it transcended all morality: it was the will to wholeness at any price.[5] (Hotzel)

---

*German troopspeak: "das Ganze (the whole)—halt!"': "What's your unit?" (Einheit: translated above as "unity.")

**As it is equally for the "white woman" of the family: the family too is "the whole"—a unit of domination.

"At any price" — the will to wholeness is the will to power. Conflicts of interest among the members of a society or contradictions fought out between diverse social organizations and groupings split the wholeness of the soldier male, his totality. When the Left argues for capitalist society to be seen in terms of class analysis, the fascist is robbed of his bodily unity, ripped in half. In his society, there can be no classes, no antagonism; for such things would demonstrate his own inability to cement his inner fractures. If there proved to be such things as classes, then he would never attain the German soul whose unity holds the promise of his satisfaction. He identifies the existence of classes with the existence of the repressed in his own body; and if the repressed has a life as class, then it gains a right to existence. If it is class, then everything he has banished to the lower regions, including woman, has a right to defend itself. None of this must be, for this man needs subordinates if he is to live. Class struggle means death, social death in the first instance: class struggle thrusts the basest elements toward the top, the soul perishes, man becomes woman, the soldier is consigned to the institution. Only domination can save him. The agent of class struggle is an agent of "suicide" within the soldier male; class struggle tears him apart from the inside. Schaumlöffel writes:

> Anyone who deserts the people and attempts to enthrone an arbitrary will born of bestial self-interest is committing the people to suicide. Today, the welfare and the existence of the people are under threat: we summon all German men to its defense.[6]

Initially, the notion that it is possible to commit others to "suicide" appears nonsensical; but the passage itself clarifies the meaning. Suicide is perpetrated on the people by its own basest elements, "deserters." In the eyes of the soldier male, the people's only legitimate function is to form the missing half of the "whole" he requires for his satisfaction. If it refuses to do so, it is accused of "bestial self-interest."

The soldier male's commitment to "the larger whole" arises, then, out of his own fear of splitting. And he is split if and when the suppressed "half" of himself, the worse "half" to whom he is married, the "lower half" of the people, the dominated on every level, demand independence.

Thus what he means by "seeing oneself as part of a larger whole" is "taking care to prevent my domination from being split asunder."

In exhorting the people to think in terms of the whole, he is warning them to remember that they are subordinate, that without him, they would have no head, no superior. Think in terms of the whole = don't forget that you are subordinate = don't forget that without us you would have no head, nothing above you. Think in terms of the whole = without us you would die = without us you would lack divinity (masculinity) and would be animals. Think in terms of the whole = without us above you, you would lose all form and become shapeless mass = without us no dams = without us you would drown in the waters at high tide.

And yet: all these are the fears of those uppermost in the whole. Only men whose own bodies consist in a "whole" comprising one part that is suppressed, and one that dominates, can "identify" with them.

More significant, the whole that is the man's body is never sufficient unto itself: it always requires larger external totalities, compressed formations of existing reality within which *he* can remain dominant. He perceives the very existence of anything living outside such totalities as threatening.

In response to that threat, the body-totality (*Ganzheitsleib*) endlessly reproduces itself in formations whose dominant parts feed off their subordinate elements. The relationship is not a symbiotic one; on the contrary, the fascist male seems to consider it necesssary to suppress any formation that threatens to activate the anxieties associated with devouring symbioses. The mass, for example, has either to be structured in a *hierarchical* formation or, at the very least, combatted by mobilizing existing hierarchical formations against it. In general terms, then, the primary function of any hierarchical formation seems to be to act as an extension of the upper level of the "self" of the soldier male.[7] In light of all this, is it not then a little incautious to call personal relationships grounded (as is marriage for example) in such formations "complementary"?* Husband and wife simultaneously or successively embody numbers of "masculine" and "feminine" positions, none of which is ever equal. What gives us the right, then, to encompass two such persons within a single whole number, the one? (To reduce them to the phallic signifier?)

"All of us are groups," as Deleuze and Foucault once agreed in a public

---

*Let us look at what is meant by "complementary" in the marital relationship between the subjugated white woman and the man who needs "totalities." Within the *whole* of this association, the white wife, on the one hand, represents the subjugated interior of the man, his "lower" regions—now rendered harmless—and, on the other, the person whose social name, "good mother," guarantees him a (hierarchical) symbiosis that will not devour him. His binding with the "good mother" has nothing to do with incest; it is oppressive and parasitically draining.

In reattaining "dual union" with the mother (a union that has become a relation of domination), the man becomes both suckling infant and master ("father") of the woman, both nourished child and despot. She nourishes him with her submission, making him full and whole; once *whole*, he immediately becomes the master, the oppressor of his own mother. He functions in this position as her father; the man becomes his own maternal grandfather. He (as child and father of the wife) and she (as his mother and daughter) bypass each other constantly: they never become a *pair*, woman and man together on an equal level. It is, as we have seen, only as a representation of his sister that she appears on an *equal* level; but from this perspective, any act of pleasurable lovemaking appears obstructed by the taboo on incest with the sister.

In terms of civil law, the two are husband and wife in bed. But what the gorilla squeezes in his arms is never the woman herself; nor is it she on whose breast the giant baby suckles (even though it is her strength that is drained). Only the child he implants in her as he lowers himself as his own grandfather onto the woman who is "mother" of his own wholeness: only the child she must bear alone.

"Sketches for the Ballet, Relache," by Francis Picabia. Copyright © S.P.A.D.E.M., Paris / V.A.G.A., New York, 1989.

interview. Historically, too, personal relationships have seldom been "complementary." Extraneous, socially defined *functions* have always maintained a ghostlike presence within them. Complementary relationships have yet to be invented as relationships between two equals touching the multiplicity of their mutual selves, rather than between bearers of socially dictated functions. In such relationships, a multiplicity of difference would mingle together; indeed the concept of a "complementary relationship" between two people as whole entities would be inadequate to describe them. The pathway to a nonfascist life is marked out a little further by every act of lovemaking in which the participants touch neither as images nor as bearers of *names* defined by the social.

If personal relationships are to be transformed, it no longer suffices simply to demand more frequent and more pleasurable orgasms, as did Reich and (more recently) David Cooper. Instead, the very notion of the orgasm as the sensation of *one* person has to be dissolved, abandoned. If human beings were to begin to achieve release through orgasms in which they experienced the other, the diverse and the different as equal, they might well become nonfascists. (Antifascism is no more than a political position that can be taken up at will; it has little significance for the defascisizing of our lives.)

And what of the divisions between genders? In the first version of this section, I wrote that sustained experiences of pleasurable commingling would begin to erase gender divisions, since they would involve one sex actually mingling with another. How, after all, can a man seriously maintain that it is *his* prick whose boundaries dissolve inside the vagina? Does it not become

Julie Christie and Oscar Werner in "Fahrenheit 451," directed by F. Truffaut. Copyright © 1989 by Universal Pictures, a Division of Universal City Studios, Inc. Reproduced by permission of MCA Publishing Rights, a division of MCA, Inc.

part of the woman's body, just as the vagina becomes part of the body of the man? And do both organs not therefore belong to both bodies? (There is of course a reverse side to this argument, for it is precisely *as a result of* difference that the sexes intermingle: and commingling never nullifies difference.)

Borneman, in his book on patriarchy, lists seven criteria by which gender can be determined, including external and internal organs, psychic, genetic, hormonal, and other factors. He stresses, however, that the distinction they establish between masculine and feminine is always approximate, and that mixtures of both are always present. A vision of the future: as genders becomes less subject to social definition, a rapprochement of the sexes and a blurring of gender distinctions is foreseeable (cf., p. 531, German original). A cry of rage from Luce Irigaray:

> Now that women's voices have begun to be heard; now women
> have become a little more forceful, a little more turbulent, the
> difference between the sexes is being called upon to disappear as
> if by magic. It is difficult to imagine a better example of cooption;
> had women not begun to raise a hue and cry, difference would
> have continued to be propagated: now they've had a chance to
> make a noise, it's to be dispensed with.

What she demands, by contrast, is the following:

> We must further reinforce a gender difference that we have yet to
> discover in all its dimensions. And if those dimensions are to be
> explored, we have also to create a space for the emergence of the
> feminine imagination.[*]

---

[*]In *Alternative* Nos. 108/109, p. 126. See also the two short works by Luce Irigaray published by Merve: *Wesen, Körper, Sprache. Der verrückte Diskurs der Frauen* and *Unbewusstes, Frauen, Psychoanalyse.*

Detail from "Fall from the Rock," by Ludwig von Carolsfeld (1833).

The prospect sounds promising, not only for a future exploration of gender difference, but for the general eradication of domination, and the attainment of a true equality—an equality that has ceased to be rooted in existing phallocentric definitions of liberation, or realized through *unification*. What Irigaray is demanding is that multiplicities be explored—though never as a basis for formal legal distinctions—and that they be explored in men as well as women—in men who may no longer desire wholeness, nor the unity in which "consciousness" struggles to conquer the "drives." Men, she suggests, should begin to dismantle the "form" they have always wished to be, to make fluid its contours, to take pleasure in contradictions (death to logical consistency), opennesses, powerlessnesses (no longer to live as killers) . . .

Then perhaps we might see what could become of productive desiring-machines hitherto banished into internal exile, where they manufacture sicknesses, only occasionally exploding outward as murdering-machines, or as ticking monsters that throw man's individual components into chaos and fragment him.

Far in the distance, we might perhaps dimly perceive a humanity with many genders, none of which is named with a name that is not its own. They are nameless not because they have been laid waste, but because they could have or could be any name, but have no need to have or to be any.

EXCURSUS: THE SEXUALIZATION OF LANGUAGE

The dominant mode of address used by public voices to reach out to their audiences is a sexual one. The political terminology of capitalist male society is thoroughly sexualized; it makes recognizable references to the sexual organization of its population. When Strauss, Schmidt, Genscher, and other connoisseurs of the people's flesh conjure up their visions of diverse "causes for anxiety," they appear credible precisely because their references evoke sexual anxiety states in the listeners' own bodies. *Political* speeches are verifiable against the people's own bodily processes.

The same process lends permanent credibility to accusations of government responsibility for inflation. Since inflation devalues human labor power, it is experienced by human beings as a punishment, an undermining of human strength. And what other cause can there be for loss of strength than masturbation—since masturbation deprives the masturbator of "backbone"? Inflation is the enfeebled backbone in the body of the working people; it can always be interpreted as evidence that the government has been masturbating to excess. The "enormous interest" generated by the internal wrangles of the German Social Democratic Party (SPD) derives from the evidence they offer of masturbation. For a time, never a day passed without the press carrying stories of the "Jusos" (Young Socialists) pursuing a course of "self-in-dulgence." Accusations of masturbation are believed without question, for doesn't everybody masturbate? The believers' greatest desire is of course for a government "under" which they themselves can masturbate without fear of inflation. As is their right. (The response may be a "politics of stability" that exhorts the people to pull themselves together. Nothing must flow away; pricks stand hard.) The government has therefore to put on a convincing dis-play of action as opposed to masturbation. And action is indeed taken: se-lected members are expelled from the party. This is a good deal more effective than other methods, such as speeches pointing out higher inflation rates in other countries. What kind of comfort is it to know that we are losing a little less backbone than others, since they have less to begin with anyway: lower productivity, less stable currency, fewer football victories. They have less to lose. Instant popularity is guaranteed to those who "save" the backbone of the people in inflationary situations, no matter how.

And what of the language of German sociology? It is much maligned: but what it suffers from least is its "difficulty." People aren't stupid; they are quick to learn anything if it affects them directly. Its real fault is that it is truly antisexual. Since it never so much as skims the surface of the skin, it leaves the people it calls "stupid peasants" convinced of one thing only: that they have not the slightest idea of anything.

But the audience knows its body conceals mysteries: deep, dark places, cliffs, abysses, locks, rapids, and dams. And each politically delicate decision it makes is a balancing act across cliffs, eddies, currents, abysses. There are men who may look to a leader to guide them for they fear they will lose them-selves on, across, within their own bodies or in the far greater mysteries of other bodies—the body of the people (der Volkskörper), the body to which in some strange way (to be examined later), men who require an external "extended self" to achieve "wholeness" feel bound. For Freud, the origin of these mysteries was to be traced to the bodies of the parents[*]—whose con-cealment certainly does render more mysterious and more contradictory the secret of "the body." Yet a sense of mystery can be implanted only in indi-viduals whose own bodies have been made secret. ("You never know where that sort of thing might lead.")

Both sociological German and the everyday language of contemporary Left agitation are, by contrast, hopelessly unmysterious. Thus neither is per-ceived to be true: they are assumed to be concealing something. The only message they convey to their audience is that of having absolutely no idea of life's "essentials." This is the source of one of the many forms of mistrust encountered by the Left. The language of the Left excludes the mysteries of the body; those who feel that they are suffering are treated as ignorant; it is

---

[*]"In this case too, then, the unheimlich is what was once heimisch, familiar." (The Uncanny, S. Ed. XVII, p. 245)

"Sexual Mysticism—Sexual Ethics—
Sexual Magic," by Fidus (no date).

assumed they merely lack information. Over and over again, the Left blunders
into engagements with the language of dominant groups without realizing it
has mistaken its terrain. Such language cannot be "refuted" on the level of
"political meaning": its primary territory of effectivity is elsewhere.

Canetti, although he makes no reference to the body, writes with some
acuity on the relation between public speech and mystery:

> The doubt people feel toward all freer forms of government—a
> loathing, as if such governments were unable to function with any
> seriousness—is connected to their lack of mystery.

What Canetti sees in operation here is not an aversion to discussion or to
deliberation on problems, but a fear that "nothing new will happen, because
everything is known in advance." The argument is convincing. As long as
this continues to be the case, it seems unlikely that anything openly debated in
the parliamentary "gossip-shop" will be considered greatly significant to the
extent that the individual body still remains the subject of strictly private
debate. "The *Führer* is conferring privately" was a phrase that inspired confidence; it meant he was getting down to the essentials. In the circumstances
of his time, his large crisis staff could be seen to represent the best possible
support for German democracy.

For similar reasons, announcement of long-term news blackouts becomes
a source of pleasure for millions (in a situation in which the information content of the news is in any case negligible). Ringed with an aura of high security, politics at last becomes interesting: we are being told nothing, *ergo* we are
being governed. Oh joy!

*Not until the body has lost its mystery will a truly public political life have
any chance of survival: this alone can be its real foundation.*

A FORERUNNER ON THE ROAD TO THE REICH

Throughout the Weimar Republic, the central aim of the men of the "nation" was, in Goebbels's words, to re-make the mass as People. On 1 August 1914, there had been universal order. The mass had vanished overnight; at the very least it had become an enthusiastic crowd, an audience applauding men who marched gladly into battle. But, more than this, it had become People and army:

> New gods were raised to the throne of the day: strength, the fist, and virile courage. The long columns of armed youth thundering along the asphalt embodied all of these qualities; the crowd was suffused with jubilation and reverential awe.[1] (Jünger)

Everything was now in proper proportion; this was how life was meant to be. At the end of the war, by contrast, the people had to choke back its jubilation; in an instant, the people was transformed back into the mass it had been before.

> Even the revolution cannot be understood as a revolution of the masses rising organically under the leadership of great individuals: it was simply the vilest form of puffed-up, mindless bourgeois philistinism.[2] (Rosenberg)

The ways and means used by leaders to convert their chosen masses into peoples deserve closer scrutiny. What they point to is the significance of oratory as the mainstay of fascist propaganda. Its importance becomes clear in the following two examples of "conversions" that were almost, but ultimately not quite, successful. In both cases, the mass remained mass, and the leader—met his death. The leader in question was Rudolf Berthold, the date 16 March 1920, in Harburg.

In fascist literature, Berthold functions as the true hero of the Kapp Putsch of 13 March 1920. Kapp himself was useless for such a role. In the first instance, he was a civilian (whereas Hitler was at least already wearing an SA uniform and soldier's boots when he marched on the Feldherrnhalle on 9 November 1923—though admittedly, as Rossbach writes, he had been "dressed up" this way by Röhm[3]). Second, Kapp fled to Sweden after the failure of the putsch. And third, he neglected to arrest the central leadership of the German Social-Democratic Party on the first day of the putsch. All this was too ridiculous, hardly the stuff from which an early hero and prophet of the movement might be made.[4]

It was, then, the murdered Berthold who became the hero of a campaign that had proved premature, since the mass was not yet a People. What the Berthold portrayed by his nationalist chroniclers was able to demonstrate was the potential of the mass eventually to become a People. Even at this early stage, the mass of Harburg workers was portrayed as being no more than a hair's-breadth away from submitting to his leadership:

> The greater part of the crowd looked in wonder and admiration at the commander, who remained calmly standing beneath the entrance, transfixing the masses with his gaze. Deathly silence, a profound hush hung over the wide square: tense expectation. What would happen now? Who would demand a reckoning? Who would play the role of judge? Nothing stirred, no one moved . . .
>
> Slowly, life returned to the stately figure of the soldier beneath the entrance: he stirred, as if released from some nightmare. A deep sigh of relief passed through the crowd, as if it was awakening from its hypnotic trance. The mass was lost in wonder and admiration.
>
> With two officers following him, Berthold strode forward, head erect, into the very center of the silent multitude. *This* they had *not* expected. Timidly, the people stepped back, formed a path,* searched for some understanding of distantly stirring emotions—feelings in the most extreme conflict one with another, feelings that touched their consciences; helplessly wide-eyed, they stared after the passing officers. All of them felt the magnanimity of a man who had cheerfully sacrificed blood and health for the fatherland in countless battles, and who would at any point selflessly have given his life for his people.
>
> Berthold stopped. His gaze swept again across the crowd, his stalwart countenance announcing a will that was iron and unbending. He spoke, announcing his intention to tell the crowd, face-to-face, what he had told the envoy that same morning. The words passed his lips slowly, piercingly, beating like hammers on the ears of his listeners, visibly achieving their intended effect.
>
> "Certain conditions have been demanded," declared Berthold. "I refuse them on behalf of myself and my batallion. I shall leave as I came!"
>
> Never a sound had interrupted the compelling speech of the commander. Within the crowd there dawned the overpowering realization that the man before them was a born leader, one who would defend what was entrusted to him in any situation, who would face any danger or sacrifice for its sake. *This* was a leader who had no need of force to draw those around him under his spell; he was followed voluntarily and gladly. No friend of naked force, a man such as this would prefer to meet anyone, even his opponents, with kindness rather than harshness. Thousands of demonstrators saw the figure of this soldier with new eyes now; he

---

* The Red Sea parts to let the prophet pass.

stood perfectly erect, though he bore clear traces of severe battle
wounds. When Berthold ended his speech with a request that the
crowd disperse peacefully, they readily complied with his
demand.[5]

How then could it be that the same crowd ultimately savaged Berthold? It
happened

very suddenly, when with a raw cry a wave of the wildest young
men, the most radical workers, slammed against the receding
demonstrators from the rear, bringing them to a standstill . . .[6]

Under the influence of a "wild wave" of men who had never heard the leader
speak, the peaceful crowd becomes a raging beast again.

In this representation of Lieutenant Wittman's desire for a people submissive to the leader, the usual relationship between mass and soldier is reversed.
The mass, usually described as raging, raving, and boisterous, is "silenced."
No one moves: the mass stands "helpless"; *the people* stands back "tim-
idly": its "conscience" stirs (we were wrong, oh horror!); and it forms a
"path" through which the leader moves. The multitude becomes a front for
the leader's inspection: the mass *opens* itself to him, and allows him to penetrate. There follows an act of copulation in which the speech of the man sat-
isfies the people-as-woman: "thousands of demonstrators . . . saw the figure

of this soldier with new eyes; he stood perfectly erect.'' God reveals Himself to the beast and raises it up to His level. It is then time for him to return to business: the flesh he has subjugated is ordered to vacate his bed. It ''readily complies with his demand.'' In this representation of the leader's desire, the mass exists for no other purpose than to satisfy him—which is precisely what it is commanded to do, with the greatest matter-of-factness.

Under normal circumstances, the mass moves and initiates; here all active initiative is transferred to one man. It is he who stands; his gaze transfixes (elsewhere, the thousand eyes of the mass transfix the man); he strides forth ''into the very center of the silent multitude.'' The people stands still, radiating in the glow of his ''stalwart countenance.'' ''Kindness for harshness,'' magnanimity. Magnanimity: the phallus-on-high as the leader's inner greatness, the measure against which he assesses the degree of the people's subjugation. His gaze sweeps across the crowd. Each individual is touched by his magnanimity, feeling it in his or her own body.

And then the man scatters his seed: ''He speaks'' (oh glory, it can speak!). He is ''compelling.''[7] This god is a human being, with needs we are called upon to satisfy for him. So massively significant is the fact of his speaking that Wittman is compelled to pause for effect: ''He spoke—.'' In the course of the dash, the leader flows into a people that stands ''face-to-face'' with him (if it did not, it would lose contact with his swelling soul). Now he begins working the crowd: ''slowly''; ''beating''; ''hammers''—the spell is cast. He makes his advance, and the mass—dies. The leader copulates the mass to a corpse. The effect of his act of coitus is to deprive the mass of all movement, all flowing. It grows rigid, dries out (he absorbs it, "face to face"), and begins to trickle away. Only a wave of the wildest among them, men he has failed to keep in his sights, prevents the mass from "receding"— like water at low tide.

Thor Goote's version of Berthold's command performance as leader is rather less impressive. But even he allows Berthold to show the mass a thing or two before he walks through it to his death:

> He walked into the howling black mass rolling toward him; as his gaze met the eyes of the vanguard, they shuddered and dropped their fists, lowering their eyes, to escape the eyes of a man whom they had assumed would have to be forced to confront them. Unwilling to run the gauntlet at their command, he now advanced voluntarily, as if *he* were the victor!
>
> Timidly they moved aside, to form a path, to allow Rudolf Berthold to walk through the very center of a crowd that expected to tear him to pieces. He remembered all the times he had hurled himself with wide-open eyes into the full force of enemy machine guns. Every nerve within him felt how utterly dependent he was on the men now leading him. . . . Suddenly a blow hit him from behind, and he staggered. Even then he felt no surprise, nor even anger. The path of his destiny led through the crowd, and never had he veered even a hair's-breadth from destiny.[8]

Here, too, the gaze that causes the mass to cower, the path that forms. The time for speeches is past; his death is sealed, but the mass will leave the square as the guilty party; it is not permitted triumph. Rudolf Berthold dies as the herald of a greater leader to come. Everything is inevitable, predetermined. "Every nerve within him felt how utterly dependent he was on the men now leading him . . ."

The destiny from whose path Rudolf Berthold could not deviate "even by a hair's-breadth" is gradually becoming clear: his fate was to become the John the Baptist of the early Nazi movement. Since his task was to proclaim the imminent coming of the Greater One in whose spirit he had struggled,[9] his death in the clutches of the murderous mass, the proletarian Salome, was inevitable. But the Greater One was defeated on the day of his first coming on 9 November 1923 before the *Feldherrnhalle* in Munich. Thus the whole process had to be repeated by Horst Wessel who became John the Baptist II, second harbinger of the people's salvation. The Nazis recognized the need for some kind of heralding martyr, but since no single Nazi was ever killed by Communists, a murder victim offered up by a generous fate had to be chosen. Horst Wessel (victim of "Red murder") was well known to have been the

Berthold lying in state.

"victim" of a squabble among pimps.[10] However, the fact was somehow for-gotten—a happy accident for a man who might otherwise never have become a figure of biblical dimensions.

Dietrich Eckart, founder and first editor-in-chief of the *Völkischer Beo-bachter*, curses the failure of Hitler's 1923 putsch in Munich as no more or less than a brazen rejection by the mass of its rightful lover:

> Idiot people! Scorning all
> Whose loyal efforts are to serve you,
> Rewarding even *Hitler's* kindness
> With blasphemy, renouncing God.
> The pharisees toppled him from behind
> You only grunted.
> Now he comes, the Hebrew—
> Your master!
> Whiplash across your face
> Sparing nothing, not even the mouth.
> Born to wear the yoke of slaves,
> You think of nothing now but eating!
> Thank the lord, the plans of Hitler
> Are undermined at every turn.

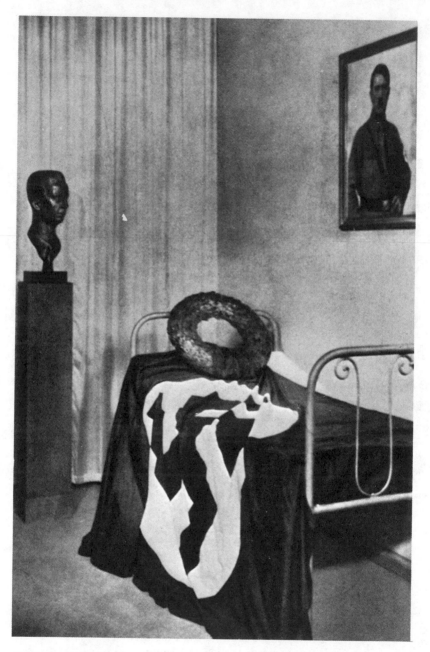

Horst Wessel's deathbed.

From *Radical America* (Frankfurt: Melzer Verlag, 1970). *Frame 1.* "Is the lumpen-proletariat a hopeless case?" *Frame 2 .* "We'll find out one day."

> So the final shame is spared him,
> Of liberating you
> The mob![11]

But still, the leader cannot leave the masses be; again and again he approaches those "below" him with offers of the grace of redemption—and this despite the words of such as Zöberlein's Schlegel . . .

> "You know, it could make you lose all desire to help the workers," said Schlegel. "They've turned into stupid flocks of sheep. I tell you, one volunteer is worth two pressed men."[12]

How happy we would be were such leaders as Zöberlein's SA-man to become sufficiently sick of their "flock" to leave it to its own devices: since, however, they can only hold themselves together by fusing others into one, they seem unlikely to neglect the arduous duty of sacrifice for very long . . .

After all, the leader asks, where would the masses be—women, children, the man's inner mass, the teeming unconscious—without him to feed them and keep them in order? They would perish, flowing out and around as miasma.

As Canetti accurately observes, the man in power does not see himself as sucking the mass dry, but as *nourishing* it.[13] The entrepreneur nourishes the workers. The man nourishes women. And the unconscious simply does not exist. Or if it does, then only as parasite. And children? These too can be dealt with; in war, if not sooner . . .

THE SPEECH

Another core element of fascist propaganda was the speech in the public hall. Modeled on the military commander's address to his troops, the speech is a crucial part of the official communication of any male society organized along military, or paramilitary, lines. Under fascism, every squadron leader, troop leader, group leader, local group leader, district leader, every candidate for state legislature or the *Reichstag* was constantly giving speeches. The written word had only secondary importance; and before the Nazis "took power," they had no direct access to radio. It was through speeches that the movement was disseminated; thus an analysis of the situation of the speech is crucial if we are to understand the expansion of popular support for Nazism.[*]

The speech delivered by Wittmann's Berthold was effective because it gave form to the mass; as the speaker touched the mass with his "magnanimity," he was said to endow it with a "soul." Soul is a term often mentioned in connection with the situation of oratory (which, incidentally, should not be seen as synonymous with the report, the narrative, or the discussion). *Soul* seems to have something to do with the *act* of speaking; the activity is more important than the message the speech conveys. How then can the act of speaking be best described, and how does the fascist experience it?

> On 29 August 1931, a prophet took the stage at the largest meeting hall in Darmstadt. Emaciated in the service of his idea, he struggled hard for the soul of his people. For over two hours he spoke to the masses, showing thousands the way to Hitler and his movement. His last words were: "Germany must and shall live, even if we must die!" Only seconds after speaking these words, he staggered behind the curtains; moments later Peter Gemeinder breathed his last in the service of the movement.[1]

Peter Gemeinder owes this record of his death-as-prophet, after over two thousand "speaking assignments," to a work by Baldur von Schirach from 1934, which gives portraits of the most prominent Nazis of the time. In the book, it emerges that the public-speaking appearances of Nazi leaders were regularly tallied and that anyone who failed to meet his quota was subject to reprimand or demotion. A man who fulfilled his quota, by contrast, only to die of exhaustion in the service of the party (assuming the story is true), was seen to be dying a hero's death, barely inferior to death at the front. In peace-

---

[*]To examine fascist oratory in terms of the rhetorical strategies of Hitler or Goebbels alone would be to distort the picture. All fascist phenomena are phenomena of groups, strata, organizations. It does make sense, on the other hand, to direct attention to the "Führer" from the perspective of fascism in general; almost every phenomenon examined in this book can be found in either *Mein Kampf* or Hitler's speeches. Hitler is not some unique monster, but rather the most significant condensation of the drives motivating the average soldier male after 1918. We may assume that inveterate personalizers personalize not because they are stupid, but because they *resist* this insight; in partitioning Hitler from fascism in general, they are partitioning fascism from its place within themselves.

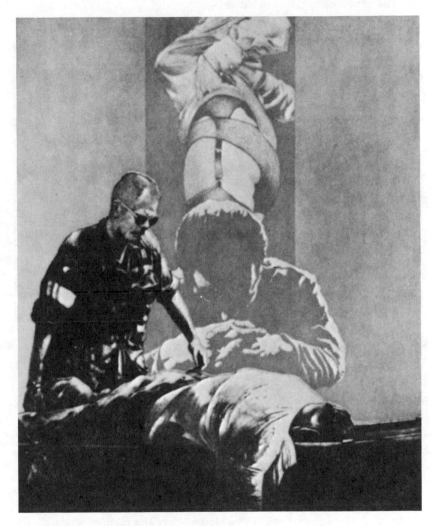

"Sex and Crime V," by Klaus Böttger (1970).

time, then, the decisive front in the struggle "for the soul of the people" was the front of oratory. It was here that the new heroes could prove themselves— as prophets.

Conversion by one such prophet later became almost obligatory for Nazis. Hardly a single novel or biography by any of the soldier fascists fails to detail some experience of conversion through oratory.

Illuminating in this context is a book by Theodore Abel containing German Nazis' accounts of their "conversions."[2] Two circumstances appear crucial: one or other of them pertains in every case. There is either a troop (usually of SA men) marching by, which spellbinds the man with its virile and powerful determination; or he attends a Nazi gathering where the speaker (in earlier works any leader, in later works the *Führer* himself) does the necessary. From this point on, he is in the everlasting grip of the leader.

Ganz Deutschland
hört den Führer

mit dem Volksempfänger

The mouth of the revolt.

None of the writers considers it important to report what the leader has actually said. He is described as having left a "deep impression"; the writer is carried away by inspiration and "sees the light." These men write exclusively of the speech's effect on their emotions. The supreme experience is a feeling of oneness with the entire hall; they are uplifted, blissful, they have reached their destination. Without exception, they describe themselves as having secretly long shared the thoughts now being expressed by the speaker; the same ideas have often occurred to them, though until now they have been unable to express them. Yet his words correspond so precisely to their feelings—yes, this is how the world is, just as he describes—and all at once, these men, who came to the meeting as skeptics, find themselves clapping involuntarily, even shouting "Bravo!"

They have been won over. Life is worth living again. It is a miracle. One man writes: "I felt the urge to be a soldier again." The impulses they experience are most often described as prophetic, illuminating, unforgettable. Then there is the power of the speaker's eyes: "There is no release from Hitler once a man has looked him in the eye and heard him speak." One writer even feels Hitler's eyes as hands reaching out to him, never to release him.[3] A passage from Goebbels's novel *Michael* includes all of these features:

> I found myself sitting in a hall I had never been in before. In the midst of strangers, all poor and downtrodden. Workers, soldiers, officers, students. Such was the German people in the aftermath of war. Such uniforms as there were, were old and tattered; the insignia of the Great War lay grieving on army coats, filthy and torn. I saw everything as if in a dream.
>
> I barely noticed one man rising suddenly to begin to speak. He spoke shyly and haltingly at first, as if searching for words to express something too great to be compressed into anything less than sweeping formulations.
>
> Then all at once, his speech began to flow more freely. I was captivated. I listened intently as the man on the platform gathered momentum. A light seemed to shine somewhere above him.
>
> Honor? Work? The flag? What was I hearing? Did such things still exist among a people from whom God had withdrawn his bounty?
>
> A glow began to spread among the people. Rays of hope illuminated their tattered gray faces. One man stood up and raised a clenched fist. His neighbor began to find his gray collar constricting. There was sweat on his brow; he wiped it on his sleeve.
>
> Two seats to the left of me an old officer sat crying like a child.
>
> Shivers of hot and cold ran through me.
>
> I had no knowledge of what was happening inside me. But all at once I seemed to hear cannons thunder. I watched as if through a mist as two soldiers stood up suddenly, shouting "Hurrah!" — though no one paid any attention.
>
> As the man above us spoke, stone rolled upon stone, building the cathedral of the future. For years, something had been living inside me: it now took shape and became palpable.
>
> Revelation! Revelation!
>
> In the midst of ruin, a single man had dared to stand and raise the banner high.
>
> Suddenly those around me were no longer strangers, but brothers. One man, gray and tattered in his open soldier's coat, looked across at me and laughed.

"Comrade!" he said spontaneously.

I felt a desire to jump up and cry, "We are all comrades. We must stand together!"

I could no longer contain myself.

I walked—no, I was driven—toward the platform.

There I stood, looking long into the face of the One.

This was no speaker, but a prophet!

Sweat streamed from his forehead. His eyes, two glowing stars, lit up in his pale gray face. His fists were clenched.

Word after word, sentence after sentence thundered like the Last Judgment. I no longer knew what I was doing.

I was almost out of my mind.

I shouted "Hurrah!" No one thought anything of it.

The man above me looked at me for a brief moment. The blue stars of his eyes struck me like rays of flame. A command! In this instant I was reborn.

All the dross I carried fell away.

I now knew where my future lay; I had found the pathway to maturity.

By now, I could hear nothing; I was intoxicated.

And suddenly, I was standing on a chair above the people and shouting: "Comrades! Freedom!" What happened then, I cannot say.

I only know that I placed my hand in the pulsing hand of a man and made a lifelong vow, as my eyes sank in two great blue stars.[4]

The speech of "the man up above" is compressed into three words: Honor, Work, the Flag. Its remaining contents are assumed to be self-evident: the words of a man who can fire his listeners to this extent can only be the right ones. Even Goebbels himself, one of the leaders of National Socialism, limits his intellectual expectations in this instance.[5]

Quite rightly: for what happens here is expected to take place under the express prohibition of thinking. Michael sits "as if in a dream": "I had no knowledge of what was happening inside me"; "I was driven"; "almost out of my mind"; "intoxicated"; "What happened then, I cannot say." He hears the speech in a trancelike state.

The terms used to describe the speaker himself are not dissimilar. His speech "flows freely," as he "raises the banner high"; "his fists are clenched"; his eyes are "glowing stars" that "light up"; he shoots out "rays of flame" and, finally, a light appears "somewhere above him." He himself is barely in control of his senses. Instead, God, the supernatural, speaks through him; he is a divine manifestation in broad daylight. "Revelation! Revelation!'' Under normal circumstances, what becomes visible in the situation of the speech remains concealed, perhaps even forbidden.

Goebbels's passage recalls a number of similar descriptions of fascist mass ritual. It seems likely then that we may be encountering the public staging of processes that are ordinarily forbidden or impossible.

For Horst Warttemberg (in Ekkehard's *Sturmgeschlecht*), the absence of the forbidden represented a crucial flaw in one speech by a nationalist Reichstag representative. Warttemberg ''agreed''with the speaker, but this was not enough:

> It was like a dream. The speaker's polished formulations caused him actual physical pain. He thought back to the meeting in Munich, heard the raw, flaming voice, the beer steins flying, the pistols cracking. By comparison, this was nothing but bourgeois child's play.[6]

The speaker's ''polished formulations'' fail to penetrate the listener's body: it is this that causes him physical pain. His expectations of the speech are confounded. He had anticipated the bliss experienced, for example, by Goote's Berthold:

> It was here that the struggle for the German soul was taking place, and he surrendered with a rude elation, not caring that it might devour him.[7]

The experience sought by these men is dependent on penetration by the speaker, since their soul is ''inside'' them. The man ''surrenders,'' though he risks being devoured. What then constitutes the specific labor of the second protagonist in the speech, the ''leader'' or speaker?

The speaker is invariably portrayed as an officer, *Freikorps* leader, or SA group leader, who is overcome as he sits before his men by a sense of their need for ideological support. Perceiving their courage to be weakening, their fighting spirit wavering, he talks himself ''on fire'': viz. Zöberlein's Hans Krafft.

> And . . . as Hans continued speaking, he felt a warm glow spreading from his heart.[8]

His speech strikes a chord:

> Krafft stood surrounded by a churchlike silence so devout that it made him pause for a moment. As if awakening from a dream, he wiped a hand across his fevered brow and stammered, almost apologetically: ''Comrades, I myself find it difficult to follow the direction in which my thoughts have now led me. I myself find it hard to fathom. But the way I see it . . .''[9]

And so the stream of his speech flows on. Zöberlein presents us with a man who tends more usually to be silent and brooding; the fate of his people and country lies heavy on his shoulders. But Krafft is transformed; he becomes both orator and leader. What this involves is more than his simply acquiring the "ability" to speak or lead. Leadership is a gift temporarily bestowed on men by divine grace; the miracle of transformation occurs on both sides of the dual relationship between mass and leader:

> He sat down and stared off into the distance, numbed and glowing. Still shaken by ripples of strange excitement, he hardly noticed his comrades jumping up joyfully and pressing toward him.[10]*

Texts in which the incipient leader is thus overcome by emotion do not flinch from naming the sources of his illumination. On the contrary, they are punctiliously recorded: the fatherland, nation, German socialism, and so on. The speech performs two functions: it allows the leader to prove himself worthy of the name, and gives the listener the opportunity to display the emotion his illumination produces. The leader must therefore at some point demonstrate that he possesses the attributes he aims to implant in his audience. The audience, by contrast, is only permitted to demonstrate the effect of that implantation—never memory, nor anything resembling it.

Illumination, revelation, rebirth: again, the man is remade through successive processes of fusion.

The leader, then, becomes such only in the process of speaking. In the speech, he achieves union with the phallus-on-high; he attains the "magnanimous" state of noncastration; his soul swells to give him form. Piling stone on stone, the man himself becomes a cathedral to the future. Assembling himself into a form that is whole, he is ultimately able to commune with the god of the entire system (whose name is "the one possessed by none").

In the same way, speech fuses the individual listener into a whole. Goebbels writes: "For years, something had been living inside me: it now took shape and became palpable."[11] What is formed in this process of fusion is a people of comrades. (For Goebbels, as for other writers, the people comprises only his own group, though for propaganda purposes, he extends the definition to include "workers, soldiers, officers, students." The people are always men and never the whole collectivity of Germans.)

If, by contrast, the audience remains in conflict, if unity is not achieved, then there can be neither illumination nor revelation and rebirth. This is why parliament can never be the site of the fascist ritual of oratory. A parliament necessarily remains mass and is, as such, more abhorrent the more separate parties it houses.

---

*This model of "enlightened leader/spellbound audience" also sets the pattern for Krafft's subsequent marriage. Berta Schön, an innkeeper's daughter, presents herself to him on her wedding-day with the following words: "I thank you, Herr Krafft, for allowing me to listen to you." She subsequently leaves to dream of him elsewhere.

It is as *one* man that the audience must stand before the orator: "integrated" (*gleichgeschaltet*). The emphasis can, however, also be shifted: as a *man*. For integration involves a specific form of masculinization. In Goebbels's description, the mass loses its multiplicity and itself becomes one, a single organ at the tip of which stands the narrator; he in turn desires unity with the *Führer*, "the One." The instant he touches the "pulsing hand of a man" — the *Führer* — Germany is no longer Siegfried the impotent: the severed phallus-on-high is united with the body of the people to form a new whole in which all is made hale (*heil*): "Heil Hitler!" What seems crucial is that they unite as two bodies that are "masculine."

The climax of the *Führer*'s speech is a command — the command that Michael stand by him. Similarly, Michael's strongest formulation of his emotions in the moment of "revelation" is "we must *stand* together." What is contained in this act of mutual exhibitionism is the fascist version of impregnation. The leader conceives himself as leader — there is no father to impregnate him — he exhorts the mass to conceive itself as people, by touching the phallus-on-high that is the form of the speech. He needs the mass as a body in which he can stand erect, the body that will follow him (and will not flow away) as he exposes himself to the opponents of unity and begins his bitter struggle to make them one.

The two dynamics in operation here are absolutely central to fascist activity. Within the fascist group itself, all elements are unified in hierarchical formation; outside it, whatever resists incorporation is repulsed and murdered.

The fascist gives new form to the language of desire — "and now? What comes next? . . . So that's what that was . . . and now . . ." What his desire says is, "and this can be joined to me . . . and this *cannot* be joined to me." (Even though I am constructed so that all the world fits neatly beneath me? Away with it!) "And this one fits . . . but this one must go . . . and this one fits . . . but this one must go . . . and this one fits (beneath me) . . . but this one must go (into the concentration camp) — ." This is the discourse of the castrated patriarchal son in search of tissue to close his wound: of the son who is cloven in two, who has no boundaries, who has been violently ripped from his previous "wholeness" and now searches for his other half.

His search is conducted as a process of subjugation and through a language of exclusion, which Jean-Pierre Faye aptly describes as a language of abortion.[12]

A dominant element in the dynamic of linguistic unification is the use of *and*, often inserted as a way of forcibly joining two opposites: "brain and heart"; "passion and mathematics"; "archaism and rationality": (and-pairs from Jünger).[13] In Hitler's speeches, the *and* becomes a gesture of pure magnification, duplication ("great and gifted," for example).* Winckler reproaches him with tautology; but the criticism is both rationalistic and banal.[14]

---

*Compare the earlier quote from Heinz, p. 99.

"The *Führer* Speaks," by Paul Mathias Padua (1937). Reproduced with permission of Süddekutscher Verlag, Bilderdienst.

When Hitler talks of himself as "unshakable and unconquerable," he is precisely not repeating the same thing twice. He is creating a new totality-formation, through the unification of his audience with himself.

Mary Douglas has expressed energetic opposition to the characterization of rituals as empty or hollow; what takes place within them, she says, is always history made symbolic.[15] Her subsequent contention that rituals are therefore necessary and good is rather more difficult to accept. The history we are concerned with here is, after all, a history of oppressions, of disease, lack, and madness, all of which is precisely consolidated in fascist ritual.

The ritual staging of fascist oratory symbolically unites its congregation of men through contact with the abstract phallus-on-high. The monstrous form that is oratory emerges from the mouth of the *Führer* and closes around their open wounds.[16] The ritual of the speech protects them from castration and makes clear that men must join together with men, phallus with phallus (at the expense of whatever is socially "below" them). When the leader speaks and the audience moves into formation; when both speaker and audience have assumed the correct form and can anticipate mutual contact which cannot, must not be expressed as actual male love, since this is strictly forbidden, then the man, even as officer, is permitted to cry; indeed he is *called upon* to cry at this point. This is the orgasm of oratory—surpassed only by the orgasm of killing.

In the fascist context, persuasion is an exclusively male procreative process; what is found instead is a cerebral parthogenesis (the masculine form of the virgin birth) that has little to do with any manifestation of male love, the "upper level" of a murdering machine—a machine designed specifically to annihilate its "lower levels" in the copulatory act of state-formation.[17*]

What then of the man who does *not* cry, who refuses to consider himself blessed by the form emerging from the mouth of the *Führer*, who resists unification with the towering form that reaches up toward him? He is instantly expelled, for he is the "other" way inclined; an eavesdropper, a potential informer, an alien particle in the test-tube, who prevents the desired reaction from occurring: he embodies the threat of potential failure.

With such troublemakers in their midst, speaker and people cannot attain the state of trance necessary for unification.[**]

Like all other forms of satisfaction available to the soldier male, unification can be achieved only *in opposition to* consciousness.[18] Whenever thresholds are crossed—the ubiquitous thresholds of prohibitions across the body, thresholds of defense and control, thresholds of fear before the regions of the unknown—the transition takes place in a state of trance, intoxication, or miracle.

This applies both to killing and to participation (for this is more than mere listening) in the speeches of the leader; both represent forms of external contact through which the fascist male achieves redemption . . . and redemption includes loss of consciousness. Serge Leclaire maintains:

> In the very act of producing the spoken word, the speaker denies himself the experience of pleasure; for the experience of pleasure submerges all liberal, spoken "content" in a process of

---

*Benjamin's claim that "persuasion is fruitless" may thus be seen as a description of a relatively propitious situation. It might equally be said that "persuasion kills."

**How do we explain the strange satisfaction many comrades derive from expelling an (alleged) informer from a meeting that may include hundreds of participants? The motive certainly can't be self-protection; and truly dangerous informers are rarely discovered since they generally belong to the fascist group itself, but are rarely looked for within it. Is the men's fear of informers a fear of alien bodies, or fear that their own bodies may refuse to toe the line?

dissolution to which the individual voluntarily and unconditionally surrenders.[19]

If, as Leclaire believes, "spoken content" and the immediate experience of pleasure are mutually exclusive, then this implies either that the situation of the fascist speech-ritual cannot involve the kind of pleasurable contact I have described it as containing or that its spoken content does not—indeed cannot—be permitted to be generative of meaning.

If the latter were the case, then this would explain the writers' universal reticence on the explicit content of fascist speeches. It would also explain a central contradiction within fascist oratory—the contradiction between the rationality of its superficial organization and the "illogicality" of the arguments it pursues. Although the rhetorical stance of the fascist orator is one of substantiated argument, he makes no explicit effort to substantiate anything— he simply makes assertions. Superficially, the fascist speech is a triumph of enlightenment rationality: its antitheses are clearly defined, its rhetorical contrasts elaborate.

Questions of cause are addressed, and effects enumerated: "therefore" is one of the words most liberally used; the speaker is always ready with "answers," cross-references, connections. He is the ever-watchful teacher, his red pen poised to strike against infringements of the rules of rational, enlightened discourse.

The external form of the speech appears to function as part of the fascist body-armor. The authoritative stance adopted by the speaker offers him evidence of his own solidity; whatever he cannot tolerate within his own boundaries is torn apart, annihilated. The speech is a process of unification; no particular meaning is expressed in the laying of a handful of "foundation-stones" for some "cathedral of the future" nor in the use of a few potent words: "the flag," "work," "honor." They simply establish what it is that the speaker "stands for." They indicate too that the speaker is more than a mere lay member of the assembled company "speaking in tongues." He is an authority, a master of language. The speech itself takes the shape of the formation it aspires to produce; it marks out a solid framework for the events surrounding it.

What processes subsequently occur within that framework? Walter Benjamin, in his commentary on Jünger's anthology *Krieg und Krieger* (War and Warriors), identifies "a superficiality . . . within these cyclopean thought-constructions . . . that would guarantee them a place in any newspaper editorial. He considers the mediocrity of their substance . . . "shameful," and even more distasteful than "the glibness of their formulations."[20]

However justified Benjamin's criticism may be in respect of fascist writing, it is apparently invalid for the spoken process of persuasion. If the aim of the speech is indeed to organize the experience of desire along the lines I have described, then it cannot be reproached for lack of "substance"—not at least if the criticism refers to its quality of thought or language. For the success of the ritual is secured precisely by an absence of substance. "Unification," "contact," "conception," or "illumination" can occur only if attention is deflected from spoken content: the assembled crowd does not assemble in order to think or to be enlightened (nor is this what the fascist reader desires when he opens a book . . . indeed does any reader?).

The fascist speech ritual can more accurately be criticized for the forms of experiential organization it offers its participants. What the listeners gain is not any particular meaning; the speaker simply produces twenty or thirty versions of a statement that is in any case already familiar to and applauded by everyone present. They gain access instead to a productive process they experience as their own. Their contact with the speech-as-form constitutes them as active agents; they play a greater part in the ritual than do iron filings in the magnetic field, simply because they assume their own place in the pattern, fuse themselves into the whole. It is the participant himself who says to his neighbor, "Comrade, we must stand together."

This is why the objects "illuminated" through oratory so often emphasize the significance of events among the audience. As listeners, they experience themselves as "active"; standing in the great cathedral, the powerful temple of language formed around them by the leader, they feel an intoxication that they believe to be of their own making. The labor is *his*, the intoxication theirs.

Or, to put it another way, the fascist speaker does not reduce his listeners to the level of mere recipients. In stripping his speeches of intellectual "substance," he aims quite deliberately to speak the inexpressible, to rouse the imprisoned desire of the masses—not in order to liberate it, but to form it into a representation of the hierarchical symbiosis of "leader" and "people," a representation of his own longed-for "unity" and "wholeness."

It would be quite fruitless to contest this particular formation by tracing its origins to dominant economic or related "interests." The "historical subject" who might be "addressed" on the basis of such interests is a fiction deriving from false abstractions. Such a subject never once appears in the context we are studying (nor anywhere else for that matter).

One possible alternative means of opposition may be to create situations and political activities that allow us to perceive that the experience of collectivity in the mass's other form—as molecular mass—is more beautiful, more pleasurable, more secure than the mass in totality-formation.

Such a step would of course demand that the Left be transformed back into molecular mass . . .

EYES

Goebbels writes of his eyes sinking into "two great blue stars," the eyes of the *Führer*. This, it seems, is a further element not only of the speech ritual, but of other key fascist situations. The gaze, the meeting of eyes, is the most intense form of contact between man and mass; and it may well be qualitatively different from other forms. For any of our men, an incapacity to look the leader in the eye—or, more precisely, a leader's unwillingness to look into his eyes—is a mark of failure. The situation dates back to the time of the kaisers:

> Every man left for home convinced that the kaiser had looked into his eyes and his eyes alone.[1] (Röhm)

There was not an SA man in all of Germany whose eyes had not at some point been fixed in the gaze of the *Führer*. In the early days of the movement (for men lucky enough to find themselves in the vicinity of Munich), his gaze was the seal of acceptance into the SA.

And in the end, not a single German—not even those who had never seen him face to face—was permitted to claim never to have been looked in the eyes by the *Führer*. This at least is Walter Kempowski's apparent contention in his slim volume *Kannten Sie Hitler?* (Did You Know Hitler?), an anthology of responses to the title question by *Führer*-loving Germans. Many contributors mention the brilliant radiance of his eyes: they may never have seen him face to face, but they have felt themselves bathed in the light of his two "stars," which they know were blue (though his eyes were as brown as they come).[2]

The perception itself cannot be disputed: if people desire blueness, or want it to have been an eye that has gazed at them, then it is indeed a blue eye, an eye for the blind to see with. How, then, are eyes represented in the soldiers' writings?

> The commandant inspected the ranks on horseback, followed by his staff. He looked each man piercingly in the eye. Our hearts pounded with joy. It was an elevating picture, the whole brigade in parade formation.[3]

(The "commandant" is Wilfred Loewenfeld, the occasion the disbanding of his naval brigade; his gaze holds the promise that there will be a future. Sennelager, 31 May 1920.)

Munich, 8 November 1923:

> The jubilation of the crowd inside and outside the hall was boundless. Kahr grasped Hitler's hand with both hands, shook it long and hard and gazed emotionally into his eyes.[4]

(The following day, Kahr abandons Hitler; his action is dimly foreshadowed in this passage. The *Führer* is too inactive; he is looked in the eye rather than the reverse; his hand is shaken by the two hands of another.)

Marburg, 19 March 1920. The Student Corps is preparing to march to Thuringia, on a law-and-order mission to slaughter workers:

> The roll-call had been a splendid affair; and now the citizens of Marburg pressed forward around these young men of Germany, to catch one last glimpse of their sparkling eyes . . . some would have described themselves as touched to the marrow by this sight; true Germans (Sergeant Schaumlöffel for one) were touched to the heart.[5]

> It was the eyes, the eyes of Franz Epp that were remarkable; they had seen suffering, death, and horror, yet they still held something more—a manly triumph over suffering, death, and horror.[6] (Walter Frank, his biographer)

> Their eyes clung to Rossbach like steel slivers to a magnet. The first lieutenant stepped up to them sharply; his gaze raced through each in turn like a high-voltage current, giving us an insight that was almost physical into the spiritual tension molding *the leader and his followers* into new and remarkable forms.[7] (Bronnen, an admirer)

> Rossbach's extraordinary deep-set eyes swept over us and our silence.[8]

The experienced man holds triumph in his eyes; ''new and remarkable forms'' are created by the leader's gaze, ''racing'' through his followers; Rossbach's gaze ''sweeps'' his men, as Berthold's ''swept'' the men in Wittmann's description. This is the gaze of a leader:

> As he masters the crowd wih his eyes, binding the masses under his spell, his strong arm keeps a tight rein on their passions.[9] (He dances close.)

The gaze of the soldier:

> His gray eyes had something of the gun muzzle about them, and his cheekbones carved the angular line of the soldier into his lean face.[10] (Schauwecker describing his infantryman friend Herse.)

Jünger's trench soldiers have

> eyes petrified into a thousand horrors beneath their helmets.[11]

But ''comradeship'' infuses the lower ranks with ''a burning glow'':

> their hearts burst with feeling, fountains swelled from hidden veins, eyes staring with indifference melted into radiance.[12]

(For Jünger, the most prominent trait of the trench soldiers is their capacity for transformation: their staring eyes melt into the radiant crystal of the divine.[13])

> Weather-beaten, tattered, parched, dirt-encrusted, they stood as if rooted in the trenches. Even the light that broke from the dark depths of their eyes was lifeless.[14]

But when men have spoken their mind and come to an understanding:

> He squeezed me tightly by the hand, his face a vision of innumerable ecstatic eyes.[15] (Dwinger)

> Each man read the clear and earnest eyes of the other, and what he read was German.[16] (Rudolf Herzog's description of a gathering attended by Admiral von Reuter, "The hero of Scapa Flow.")

Reconciliation after an argument between comrades:

> Donat looked up sharply and listened, meeting his eyes directly. For one breath, they looked silently across at each other. Then Donat dropped what he was carrying, and stretched his right hand disarmingly toward him. "Come on, old boy," he bellowed, "we'll be all right."[17]

And so on. The eyes of Salomon's dead friend Kern haunt him in prison:

> I never once shrank from the apparitions of the long night hours, when the invincible eyes that watched me daily were joined by other eyes emerging from the darkness. I felt no threat in the thin, enigmatic face in which they came; the moment they appeared, I left my dreams behind me. I willed them to come so that I could be harsh in rejecting them. This, I sensed, was a battle I would wage for a lifetime, a battle that would prove most fertile if neither party emerged victorious.[18]

For Salomon, confrontation with two male eyes is a lifelong and fertile "battle"; it took around five years for Kern's eyes to stop haunting him nightly. Back now to the speech. "Michael" sees the *Führer* a second time:

> Sitting one evening in a hall with an audience of a thousand or more, I saw the man to whom I owed my awakening a second time. This time, he was speaking to a community of the converted. His being was greater, more contained; the endless streams of energy flowing from his mouth and hands were denser; a whole ocean of light flashed from his two blue stars . . . I felt a sea of energy foam through my soul . . . I was sitting among strangers and I blushed like a child as tears stole into my eyes.[19]

Now it is hardly the case that children blush when they cry. In adults, by contrast, blushing is a sign that they have summoned the courage publicly to act out forbidden desires. Another speaker: Ekkehard's "Tim Kröger, the flaming one, the modern prophet":

> A strange energy emanated from the man on the rock; his eyes shone down on the audience, and when he turned toward the sun, they flared like liquid fire.[20]

The speaker is characterized by fluidity; his abundant energy is permitted to "stream" and his eyes are "oceans." In neither case, however, is it water that flows. The eyes of the "flaming one" flare with light and "liquid fire." His eyes flash, radiate, illuminate. Like the sun to which they are somehow connected, they offer the satisfaction, not of flowing, but of irradiation. Michael "sees the light" only when he feels the impact of "rays of flame" from the "glowing stars of the speaker's eyes." When one eye sinks into another, it is not two streams that are united. The eye is the only organ capable of touching across a distance, touching without touching (viz. the gaze of a man who feels the gaze of another behind him). The meeting of eyes is meeting of two beams of light refracting and flaring in the "crystal of the divine." Far from releasing the man to flow freely, the gaze works by a process of elevation; it erects the man to verticality and greatness: "I felt a sea of energy foam through my soul."

If contact takes place at all, it is by proxy only; as two hard, warm, pulsing male hands sink together in tight embrace, lightning flashes above them from eye to eye, the lights flare into flame, gazes burn. The flaming eye is the sign of the master, descendant of the sun, the immutable "on high" — and it is capable of proliferation . . .

He "squeezed me . . . by the hand, his face a vision of innumerable ecstatic eyes."

> And you will know your fellow-born
> By the fire in their eyes . . .[21] (Stefan George)

And you will know those born against you . . . von Selchow:

> I have always judged a person first by his handshake, and my initial impression has almost always been confirmed. Shaking Erzberger by the hand was a sensation akin to grasping a dead and rotting rat. On every new occasion, I found his molelike smugness repulsive in the extreme. A pince-nez concealed his soulless eyes.[22]

"Soulless" = flameless.*

---

*The German phrase *abgeblitzt sein* (being shot down; literally "flashed away") has a particularly bitter aftertaste for these men. It implies they have been found insufficiently brilliant and thus insufficiently masculine. The other eye has failed to open. One man who was never once shot down, Hans Albers, became the darling of the Germans. He was also a man whose eyes Brecht would dearly have loved to see flashing on behalf of communism (see Brecht, *Arbeitsjournal*, entry dated 2 April 1948.)

"He wished his visitor well and took leave of him, moist eyed": an East Prussian mayor taking leave of Rossbach before his illegal border crossing into the Baltic.[23]

In the midst of fire, a drop in the ocean.*

Since the eye can be both actively "masculine" and passively "feminine," it is well suited to the game played out here between men. If its beam is hard and active, it is phallic; its gleam represents the gleaming glans of the erect penis (Abraham identified the same association among his patients, many of whom repeatedly used the masculine article "der" to refer to the eye, though its gender in German is neuter—*das* Auge).[24] But the functions of the eye may also be receptive, melting or passive; even the male eye may take on the attributes of vaginal formations (not of the castrating vagina, but the "good" one). Thus while "a great sword" may extend from one man's eye,[25] other men have eyes "staring with indifference" and "melting into radiance." What is crucial is the eye's capacity for transformation; it is simultaneously able to perform both functions. The same eye may sometimes actively radiate (and thus be "masculine") and at other times passively drink in light from elsewhere (and thus be "feminine"). In conjunction with the gaze of another, it does both—it penetrates the other eye and receives its gaze.[26]

This is perhaps why the eye of the leader must be blue. Blue is both the color closest to the light of the heavenly heights, and the color with the greatest illuminating force and capacity for transformation. Steel is dark-blue; but the light of the heavens glistens bright blue on the sea.

When the crowd looks into the eyes of the leader and is fused with him to form a whole, then the thousand eyes of the mass—lurking, crippling, gaping eyes—are gathered into a single gaze, one eye, *the* eye into which sinks the gaze of the leader, who thereby protects himself against the stake that might suddenly and swiftly be hurled from the mass, for this would cost Polyphemus his *only* eye.[27]

The eyes of the soldier male may, then, be brilliant and phallic or melting and receptive; and the look attributed to him determines the category to which he belongs. The photographs I have reproduced here from Baldur von Schirach's *Die Pioniere des Dritten Reiches* (Pioneers of the Third Reich) indicate how far the categorization of the movement's pioneers according to the phallic or receptive qualities of their gaze was a conscious maneuver.

In all the pictures, many of them visibly retouched, an excessive emphasis on the eyes is clearly evident; Schirach's representation of leading Nazis follows a model also characterized by Hans Blüher as typical of male relationships in the youth organizations, particularly the Wandervogel: shining indi-

---

*The German reads: "In all der Glut ein Tropfen auf den heissen—Stein?"—"a drop on the hot stone" being the German for a "drop in the ocean." The inference may be that the man is a man of—stone? (Tr.)

From *Germany Awake*, p. 27.

vidual heroes on the one side, while the beloved (men or women) of the hero
male form a ring of admirers around him, as a "male society of first-class
standard."[28]

The eyes of the leader's followers are actively *made* to light up and sparkle; they do not do so of their own accord, as *Freikorps* officer Franke makes
clear:

Shining eyes are a prerogative of the German soldier.[29]

Or his exclusive right—for others are not permitted to have shining eyes,
much less to light up the eyes of others. This is the privilege of the German.

Had Blüher had his way, "the eye" as hallmark of male society would
perhaps have become part of the insignia of Germany.

Edmund Heines.

(T)he *eye* of the man of spirit is deep as a chasm. Its like does not exist, nor are eyes such as *these* ever possessed by women. There is nothing more to this than an insight the Greeks considered obvious, which is that a man can be an object of Eros for another man.[30]

At the head of Blüher's state, there are hero males of "towering and resolute figure" and "effervescent vitality" whose eyes "gleam and sparkle." The direct link between the concept of *state* and conceptions of sexuality

Hermann Göring.

could hardly be more clearly demonstrated. V. Bluher's argument moves seamlessly from demands for a state in which "Eros from man to man" is dominant (since only men are creative, only they can form the state), to the development of an entire *ideology* of fascism amd so-called race "theory."

The associations he makes were, however, ultimately dismantled and denied by the groupings later dominant within Nazism. Their battle against all the various "contagious pleasures" also extended to include eroticism between men; among other things, the fascists were undoubtedly aware how

Rudolf Höss.

rapidly an unrestrained homosexuality might undermine the traditional structure of the army (as, incidentally, would unrestrained heterosexuality.)

It seems doubtful that many of Blüher's contemporaries corresponded to
his typification of the free hero-male; certainly such men were never predominant among the Nazis. What difference might it have made had they been so?
After World War II, in the preface to a new edition of *Die Rolle der Erotik in
der männlichen Gesellschaft* (The Role of Eroticism in Male Society), Blüher
accused Hitler of having betrayed and repressed what had been their common
cause, male love; indeed he had become its persecutor (Blüher makes quite

Alfred Eduard Frauenfeld.

passable use of Freud's theory of projection to examine the transformation undergone by Hitler). What Hitler lost in so doing, he argues, was the hero-male quality that might have fitted him for government. Blüher's concept of the homoerotic führer-state thus remained absolutely intact. Certainly, the führer-state had always been regarded by both groupings within Nazism as the only possible state-form. Conceivably, however, the leaders of the "hero-male" type would not have considered it imperative to their own stability to counter imminent defeat with attempts to exterminate the entire Jewish people. Something of this is indicated by Jünger in a statement he makes in the journal *Die Kommenden* (1930):

> While I acknowledge that the Jewish race itself has destructive qualities, I am tempted to ask if true destroyers would admit to a fear of the Jew. "No man can be on first name terms with the devil, and be afraid of fire" (German saying). The Jew is as unthreatening to the values of a heroic youth as he is threatening to the values of the bourgeoisie.

Jünger the destroyer seems relatively unperturbed by the destructiveness of the "Jewish race." His self-assurance suggests that the body-armor necessary to keep him "whole" was made in other men in different grades of fragility or durability; and the degree of its fragility can in fact be demonstrated to be directly related to the sexuality of the adult wearer. The armor assumes what is usually its final form in the military (the transformation of sexuality in military drill will be studied in the next chapter); what should emerge from his study is a more definitive characterization of the type(s) of sexuality found in the soldier male and of their relation to the characteristic forms of white terror.[*]

But first, a final word on the eyes of women. Jünger at one point recalls peacetime days

> suffused with a longing for brightness, warmth, love. Boyhood dreams: the noonday heathland, mother's smile, and the closed eyes of women I loved, burning on the battlements of the imagination.[31]

Women's eyes must be closed if they are to be associated with "brightness, warmth, love." If they are open, they are dark. The open eye of a woman seems to evoke the devouring abyss; between its lashes, the teeth of the *vagina dentata* glisten.

Filmic convention teaches that a woman's eyes staying open as she kisses are a sure sign of imminent betrayal; even as she lies in the arms of this one man, she is allying herself with some other object or allowing it to enter. The eyes are both entrance and exit; they have been called "windows of the soul." When eyes are closed, all possible horrors are obliterated. A glance into the eyes of a woman might reveal what it was that Siegfried found in those of Hebbel's Brunhild:

> And whoever is the man who looks you in the eye
> He will never forget, not in the most drunken stupor,
> That dark death stands beside you.

Such is the eye of Brunhild.[**]

---

[*] Numbers of workers captured by army or *Freikorps* troops were later found murdered with their eyes gouged out.

[**] The German stresses the neuter: *das Auge*. (Tr.)

What men see when they look each other in the eye is the very bottom of the soul of the other (since, as we have seen, their soul swells upward to become visible in the eye). Apparently, too, they believe absolutely in what they "see" there: brilliant, glistening clarity; the open other in which no black depths teem.

Whenever my father wanted to make sure I wasn't lying, he demanded that I look him in the eye. If I repeated what I'd said without avoiding his gaze, he believed me. In this way, he taught me to lie to him as he stared me in the eye. It worked: having refused to believe what he had heard, he believed what he *saw*.

Chapter 2:
Male Bodies and the "White Terror"

SEXUALITY AND THE DRILL

The Body Reconstructed in the Military Academy

By what means is a young boy made a soldier? How does he become what Canetti terms a "stereometric figure"?[1] How does body armor attain its final form, what are its functions, how does the "whole" man who wears it function—and above all—what is the nature of his ego, what is its site (which I believe must be identifiable)? And finally, what is the nature of the soldier's sexuality? What processes in the act of killing give him the pleasure he can apparently no longer find elsewhere?

As a rule, it was in the military academy—*the* German officer school—that the German officer acquired his finished form. One account of the changes undergone by the soldier body is given by Salomon.[2] The following precise reconstruction of his description should serve to highlight some of the differences between the language these men use in confrontation with what is alien (a language of reality destruction) and the language in which they describe their own bodily exterior—or, more specifically, the workings of their own musculature. Salomon at times waxes positively lyrical; apparently his musculature is not the site of his anxieties.

He describes the military academy as an "institution" (*Anstalt*), a place where the cadet lives behind prison bars. He has no right of exit from the prison; it is granted only in reward for strict adherence to its governing laws.

Relationships between the inmates are, without exception, hierarchical. When the cadet enters the academy, his position in the hierarchy is initially determined by his age; he has to earn any subsequent position. All the cadets have a place within a direct order of rank. Each knows exactly which cadets are "above" him and which "below." Each has the power to command and punish those below and the duty to obey those above. The occupant of the lowest position in the hierarchy must find another whom even he can dominate or he is finished.

If a cadet fails to exercise his rights over his inferiors, he is despised or demoted. Thus the situation never arises. Privilege is universally exercised. There are no gaps in the cadet's daily round of duties. Only those who have sufficiently mastered the art of demand fulfillment can squeeze a few seconds for other activities.

Everything is planned and everything is public. Withdrawal is impossible, since there is no place to retreat to. Toilet doors leave the head and feet of the seated occupant exposed. Trousers have no pockets.

When the cadet receives a letter, he has to open it and present the signature for inspection. Letters signed by women are read by the officer distributing the mail and (usually) torn up. Only letters from mothers are handed on.

None of the cadets lives in private. The dormitories have open doors. Talking from bed to bed is forbidden. The dormitory is kept under surveillance through a window in a wooden partition, behind which an officer sits and keeps watch.[3]

The beds are narrow, hard, and damp. Any boy found hiding his head under the pillows is labeled a "sissy" (*Schlappschwanz*). "Sissies" are put on "report." There are reports for every infringement; but the only way a boy can carry out the extra duties they impose is by neglecting his existing duties. If his negligence is noticed, he is put on report again. One crime punishable by report is a failure to keep equipment in order—which is unavoidable, since the regulations are too numerous to follow them all to the letter. Therefore after first report, others are bound to follow.

Boys who want to go to the toilet at night have to wake the duty officer. In this case too, punishment invariably follows. Unusual behavior of any kind is punished by forfeit; the boy is deprived of food, leave, or the opportunities for relaxation that are in any case minimal, no more than momentary easings of pressure.

In cadets who wish to remain such, all this very soon produces a "quite extraordinarily thick skin"[4] The "thick skin" should not be understood metaphorically.

On his second day in the academy, Salomon had already sensed "that here, for the first time in his life, he was not subject to arbitrary conditions, but to a single law."[5] He experiences this as good fortune. He resolves to bear every punishment meted out to him, gives himself the necessary "internal wrench," and stands stiffly erect. Everything up to now has been "arbitrary"—and school continues to be so. School is an activity performed by

From *Kling Klang Gloria. German Folk and Children's Songs* (Vienna/Leipzig, 1921).

teachers, powerless wielders of power—ridiculous. The boy enters the institution at the age of twelve. It is at the beginning of puberty and under the "pressure" of its "water" (Freud),[6] that he experiences the good fortune of subjection to a law. Freud saw puberty as a phase of transition to fully formed sexual organization, the completion of which manifests itself in the capacity for heterosexual object-choice.[7] But the military academy transforms this "unusually intense wave of the libido"[8] into something other than "object-relationships."

The cadet never receives instructions; he recognizes his mistakes only in the moment of transgression from the reactions of others who already know the score. With slight variations according to his cleverness, each newcomer thus necessarily repeats the mistakes of his predecessors, who in turn recognize and welcome the apparent opportunity to treat their successors as they themselves have previously been treated. Justice works on the principle of equal torment for all. The principle is strictly adhered to; there are no grounds on which a mistake might be considered excusable.

The punishments meted out to fellow cadets are oriented exclusively to the body. For a minor transgression on his very first day, Salomon is made to balance a tray of knickknacks on his outstretched hands (and woe betide him should any of them fall). He is then made to crouch with an open pair of compasses wedged between his heels and buttocks. If he moves even infinitesi-

mally upward or downward, the compasses will either stab him in the buttocks
or drop on the floor. But if he succeeds in staying still, the reward, as always,
will be immediate advancement. He will no longer be the lowest in the hierarchy of "sacks" (Säcke)—"sack" being the name for all newcomers who
are treated accordingly, emptied out, punched into shape, and refilled.

Younger boys courageous enough to defend themselves gain respect. But
even if they win the occasional fist-fight with older boys, punishment always
remains the prerogative of their elders.

A further first day experience reported by Salomon: he recalls a talk by an
officer on the importance of learning how to die.

Night, cold bed, cold blankets, the morning wash in cold water. The boy
who hesitates, even momentarily, is immersed and showered by others. Breakfast by hierarchy. The boy who grabs a roll before his turn gets nothing. For
the last in the pecking order, there remains the smallest portion, a crumb. To
be last is impermissible.

Physical exercise, even before breakfast:

> If I failed to pull myself up far enough for my nose to pass the
> bar, or to keep my knees straight while pulling my legs upward,
> the dormitory leader would give generous assistance by punching
> the tensed muscles of my upper arm with his clenched fist. This
> did indeed make it possible to identify the ultimate limits of my
> strength.[9]

Life in a rectangle.

Every exercise reaches the "ultimate limits," the point where pain shifts to pleasure:

> The climbing apparatus was ten meters high; it had a ladder, various perches, and smooth wooden walls. We climbed up and jumped down, hesitating for one tense moment at the top, leaping blind, tasting the full weight of the drop, slamming into the ground with a force that sent a terrible shock reverberating from the heels through the lower back, then into the rest of the body.[10]

If the cadet has any kind of choice, it is one between different punishments. He is offered the alternative of a caning on the behind, or forfeiting leave—he chooses the beating. The body swallows attack after attack until it becomes addicted. Every exertion becomes a "means of enhancing an already intoxicated consciousness, of adding strength to strength."

The boy who fails to transform rituals of bodily pain into "intoxicated consciousness"[11] (the mental intoxication of a head that crowns a powerful body) is cast out, as was the spy from the ritual speech or the unwilling participant from block parade-formations.

One passage in Salomon's book describes a certain cadet named Ulzig standing rigid with terror. He is the only nonswimmer to have failed to jump from a three-meter board. Many have already had to be pulled from the water to save them from drowning. But they continue to jump, half-blind, their limbs aching, until they can swim. Salomon learns to swim on the third day; but Ulzig leaves the institution—he is fetched away by his father, a "mountain

of a father," a major. The cadets would have liked to give him a good beating, but were stopped by the officer in charge of swimming (a leper is not for beating).

> I had gradually adapted. The service no longer appeared to me as a machine racing along mysteriously, its actions unexpected and apparently unmotivated. Instead, the few figures with whom I had any kind of relationship were now clearly and concretely emerging from the confusion. I was as determined as ever to defend myself when necessary, but my resolve was now less often broken by perplexity. Slowly, I began to lift my head higher.[12]

As Salomon himself becomes a component in the machine, he no longer perceives it as racing on its way somewhere above him. Once the machine is no longer external to him and he himself no longer its victim, it begins to protect him:

> In the end, I found myself living a life of absolute solitude. At times, I surrendered with a zeal born of desperation and unhappiness to this most painful of feelings. The only common feature in all my unrelated perceptions was (. . .) the exceptional and universal ruthlessness that underlay them. This was the only indication of any purpose behind the whole machinery of the

Academy. It was the basis on which it was constructed and imbued with life. My merciless subjection to the bitter reality of absolute isolation had originally seemed incongruous in a place where no one even momentarily escaped observation or control. But even the warmest comradeship remained far removed from simple friendship and from the brotherly stream that flows from hand to hand and heart to heart.[13]

At this point in the book, Salomon has been only partially assimilated. While he considers "exceptional ruthlessness" an acceptable goal for the workings of the machinery, he himself remains half outside it, a lonely young man in search of "the brotherly stream." He then gradually comes to realize that the stream can be found only on the outside as a stream of pain. At this point, he integrates himself entirely.

It was, I believed, my own inadequacy that erected an iron barrier between myself and my comrades. I tried repeatedly to break it down; but even the most forceful expression of my lost yearning for human warmth and clumsy intimacy would have been useless. Even outside the academy, an air of sordidness surrounded such gestures; inside, they were still more likely to offend sensibilities. My pitiful efforts to struggle free of my cocoon rebounded against rubber walls; yet I continued to search for some escape. The futility of my efforts was made bitterly clear to me; yet at the same time, doors were opened as wide, at least, as they were able.[14]

The opportunity to escape from the "cocoon" is presented on one occasion by a different kind of emission: a fart. In a rare conversation with the cadets, an officer suddenly becomes human as he remarks, in a not unfriendly tone, "What a stench! Somebody open a window!" Salomon's desire for "human warmth" grasps at this welcome evidence of a human interior, a smell that has broken the "iron barrier"; he murmurs as in a trance: "He who smelt it, dealt it"[15]—the moment the words slip from him, he realizes they have made his isolation total . . .

The officer orders Salomon to come to his room and grills him until he reveals the name of the boy who taught him the saying. Having "ratted" on a fellow-cadet, Salomon is "put in the shithouse" (in Verschiss getan)—the expression denotes the breaking off of all communication. Having spoken of something that no longer forms, or is permitted to form, part of the cadet's existence, he himself is treated as nonexistent, foul as the foulest air. "Even my own brother was now inclined to give credence to my theory that I was a foundling. 'No brother of mine' he said, 'could do anything like this'."[16]

In the end, the culprit is released from the shithouse; the effect of this particular form of punishment seems insufficiently external. The penalty takes a new form as an assault on his bodily periphery. Payment is made in the only valid currency, which is pain:

> The cadets stood around me in a semicircle. Each one held a knout in his hand, long leather thongs attached to a wooden stick that was used for beating the dirt out of clothes. Glasmacher stepped forward, took me by the arm, and led me over to the table. I climbed up, not without difficulty, and lay down on my stomach. Glasmacher took my head in his hands, pressed my eyes shut, and forced my skull hard against the surface of the table. I gritted my teeth and tensed my whole body. The first blow whistled. I jerked upward, but Glasmacher held me tight; the blows rained down on my back, shoulders, legs, a frenzied fire of hard, smacking blows. My hands were tightly gripped around the edge of the table, I beat out a rhythm with my knees, shins, and toes in an attempt to expel the excruciating pain. Now all the torment seemed to move through my body and implant itself in the table; again and again my hips and loins slammed against the wood and made it shudder with me; every blow recharged the bundle of muscles and skin, blood and bones and sinews, with slingshot force, till my whole body stretched under tension and threatened to burst in its lower regions. I gave my head over entirely to Glasmacher's hands, wrenched myself shut, and finally lay still and moaning. "Stop!" Corporal First-Class Glöcklen commanded, and the assembled company jumped back instantly. I slid slowly from the table. Glasmacher stepped up to proffer his hand, and said, "Peace! The affair is closed."[17]

More than this, he has been accepted. He has experienced the sensations that indicate other men's affection; he now numbers among their beloved.

The only site at which feelings have legitimate existence is the body as a "bundle of muscles and skin, blood and bones and sinews." This is the message hammered out by the drill; each new exercise is structured around it, as is every punishment detail. No feeling or desire remains unclarified, all are transformed into clear perception: the desire for bodily warmth into a perception of the heat of bodily pain; the desire for contact into a perception of the whiplash.

And little by little the body accepts these painful interventions along its periphery as responses to its longing for pleasure. It receives them as experiences of satisfaction. The body is estranged from the pleasure principle, drilled and reorganized into a body ruled by the "pain principle": what is nice is what hurts . . .

And, finally, the "sack" is given his equatorial baptism[*] — a form of torture that appears in German navy tales, unsurprisingly, as one of the high points in the life of a sailor:

> There was an official ceremony to mark the end of one's days as a sack. On the appointed day, to the great joy of their older comrades, the sacks were individually summoned to the company room, where a dentist from the city would be busy with his instruments. Every sack then had to sit on a small stool, while the tooth-flicker (*Zahnfips*), as the comrades called him, messed around for a while in the poor offender's wide-open mouth with a long pair of pliers; he would then take a firm grip on all his remaining baby teeth and pull them one after the other. As I stood bent over the bucket, spitting blood beneath the wicked smile of the tooth-flicker, Glasmacher consoled me by saying that it had formerly been customary to take the sacks to the dispensary and fill them with the appropriate dose of castor oil to ensure they were purged both internally and externally.[18]

As his last baby teeth swim away in a bucket of blood, so too do the residues of his anchorage in mother-ocean and a rock stretches its head from the collar of his uniform.

> I began to notice my body stiffening, my posture gaining in confidence. When I thought back to childhood games at home, I was filled with bitter shame. It had become quite impossible to move with anything other than dignity. On the rare occasions when a senseless desire for freedom surfaced, it invariably shattered against a new determination and will. My new-found capacity to follow orders to the letter was double compensation for losing the joys of roving unrestrained.[19]

Then the first visit home:

> A deep chasm divided me from the habits and customs of my so-called parental home, a chasm I felt neither the desire nor the compulsion to bridge. I found any kind of solicitous care quite intolerable, and the broad stream of my mother's empathy only made me wish to breathe the harsher air of the corps again.[20]

In becoming *capable* of following orders to the letter — he is by this point no longer forced to do so — Salomon liberates himself from the family unit. His function is now to operate within a different formation — although the "stream of his mother's empathy" is still able to reach him.

---

[*]The term refers to the custom of throwing a sailor into the ocean the first time he crosses the equator. (Tr.)

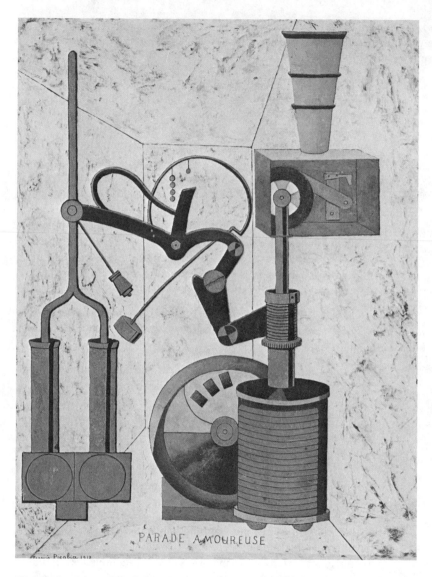

"Parade Amoureuse," by Francis Picabia (1917). Copyright © S.P.A.D.E.M. Paris/V.A.G.A., New York, 1989.

Does this stream have anything to do with the flow in the new machine of which Salomon has become a happily functioning component?

The machine's flow is continuous, a totality that maintains every component in appropriate and uninterrupted motion. It has no cut-off points, it never pauses: if the machinery of the military academy ever stops running, it is done for. To turn it off is impossible.

This machinery is the antithesis of the desiring-machine, whose principle—"the joys of roving unrestrained"—Salomon explicitly renounces. The "and now? . . . so that was that" gives way to the pleasure of existing as a component within a whole machine, a macromachine, a power machine in which the component does not invest his own pleasure, but produces that of the powerful. The man pleasurably invests his self only as a thoroughly reliable part of the machine. His line from this point on: the machine must run, the faster the better; it breaks down, it won't be my fault . . .

Remarkably enough: the component itself, in becoming a component, becomes whole—a whole that is simultaneously subordinate and dominant. It has precisely determined functions and very specific couplings to other parts; it no longer possesses its former functional multiplicity. There must have been some problem with multiplicity; its potential must have been threatening—for the component gladly accepts the wholeness it finds in the totality machine.

The machinery—and I think this is very important—transforms functions such as "thinking," "feeling," "seeing" (potential multiplicity functions with the power to develop myriad couplings) into movement, movements of the body. Salomon's new thinking follows a very specific tempo:

> Here even the most improbable actions were redolent with
> significance. The simplest salute became a symbol of submission
> to an authority that bound both parties in mutually fruitful
> association. The slow march, tempo one hundred fourteen,
> became the physical and spiritual expression of discipline to the
> brink of death.[21]

The Troop as Totality-Machine

Canetti's description of the soldier as a "stereometric figure" restricts attention to the individual soldier, to his body armor and the supporting armor surrounding it: the barrack walls, the block formations of the troop, etc. Since he neglects to consider the *function* of the soldier as machine component, he falls short of describing the construction of the machine *in toto*.[1]

> The colonel raised his hand to his helmet. The regiment
> began marking time, four thousand legs rising in unison and
> descending to stamp the ground; up and away, the first company
> pitched its legs high as if pulled by a single cord, then set them
> down on grass and soil, eighty centimeters between them, foot to
> foot—the flag approaches . . .

> A single sword hurled itself upward, flashed, and dropped
> deep to the ground; the earth turned to dust under hundreds of
> marching feet; the earth rumbled and groaned; two hundred fifty
> men were passing, touching close one after another, two hundred
> fifty rifles on their shoulders, a line sequence straight as an arrow
> above a line of helmets, shoulders, knapsacks straight as an arrow;
> two hundred fifty hands hissing back and forth; two hundred fifty
> legs tearing bodies onward in cruel, relentless rhythm.[2]

The impression of a machine being set in motion as the "finished" cadets march off to war is created quite intentionally by Salomon, as is the sense that the machine is both one of war and of sexuality ("bodies . . . in cruel, relentless rhythm"). Salomon's description of bodies as "tearing . . . onward," emphasizes the machine's violent nature.

Two aspects of its construction are stressed: the uniformity of its contours ("as if pulled by a single cord"; "a line sequence straight as an arrow") and the large number of its functionally equivalent components ("four thousand legs rising in unison"; "two hundred fifty hands hissing"; "two hundred fifty legs tearing").

The soldier's limbs are described as if severed from their bodies; they are fused together to form new totalities. The leg of the individual has a closer functional connection to the leg of his neighbor than to his own torso. In the machine, then, new body-totalities are formed: bodies no longer identical with the bodies of individual human beings.

> The brigade was a single body, destined to be bound in solidarity.[3]
> (H. Plaas, describing the Ehrhardt Naval Brigade.)

Each individual totality-component moves in precise unison with every other: "One troop, one man and one rhythm" (Plaas).[4]

The principal goal of the machine seems to be to keep itself moving. It is entirely closed to the external world. Only in combination with another machine absolutely like itself can it join together to create some larger formation.

What then produces the machine?

> The second company, the third, the fourth. Endlessly, it rolled
> onward, a broad front advancing, never wavering, wall after wall,
> the whole regiment a machine with rows ranged deep, implacable,
> precise, four thousand human beings and one regiment, whipped
> by the hymn of martial music. Who could oppose it? Who would
> set himself against this power, youth, and discipline, this eager
> thousand formed in a single will? The forest border seemed to
> tremble and retreat; the earth shook and reared, clatter of weapons
> and crunch of leather, dark eyes under brims of helmets. The

109th Regimental Grenadiers: guards' piping, white wings, a four hundred year tradition. Formed and steeled through long years, sworn to the flag, practiced in the art of death, plucked from the loins of a people and sent into war. And so the regiment marched, tempo one hundred fourteen, twelve companies, warstrong, prepared for death, ninety rounds in the cartridge case of every man, hard biscuits and ammunition in his rucksack, coat rolled and boots new. Muscles like ropes, broad-chested, tough-jointed, wall of bodies born of discipline; this was the front, the frontier, the assault, the element of storm and resistance; and behind it stood Germany, nourishing the army with men and bread and ammunition.[5]

In the first instance, what the troop-machine produces is itself—itself as a totality that places the individual soldier in a new set of relations to other bodies; itself as a combination of innumerable identically polished components.

The troop also produces an expression: of determination, strength, precision; of the strict order of straight lines and rectangles; an expression of battle, and of a specific masculinity. Or to put it another way, the surplus value produced by the troop is a code that consolidates other totality formations between men, such as the "nation."

As Salomon's text also shows with striking clarity, the troop-machine produces the front *before reaching it*: it *is* the front. As the troop sets itself in motion, the border itself is displaced. Even in peacetime, front and border are part of the troop. War is the condition of its being. It always has a border to defend, a front to advance (its own). The only thing that changes if war is declared is that the same process becomes easier and more satisfying. War offers an opportunity for discharge, for the front to be released from internal pressure. In peacetime, the front presses inward toward its own interior, compressing the individual components of the machine. It produces internal tensions of high intensity that press for discharge.

The crucial impulse behind the regeneration of the machine seems to be its desire for release—and release is achieved when the totality-machine and its components explode in battle. A strange productive principle: the machine produces its own new boundaries by transgressing the boundaries it erects around itself.

The troop machine is not independent; it has no autonomous existence. It is connected to Germany by an umbilical cord that feeds it with bread, spare parts, and munitions. Its energy-machine is "Germany."

As long as the energy circuit symbiosis with "Germany" continues to function, the machine marching to war can be presented as the supreme totality, the universal sum total. What Neruda says of the ocean ("And you lack nothing"), is realized for Jünger in the battle-machine: lack is transcended.

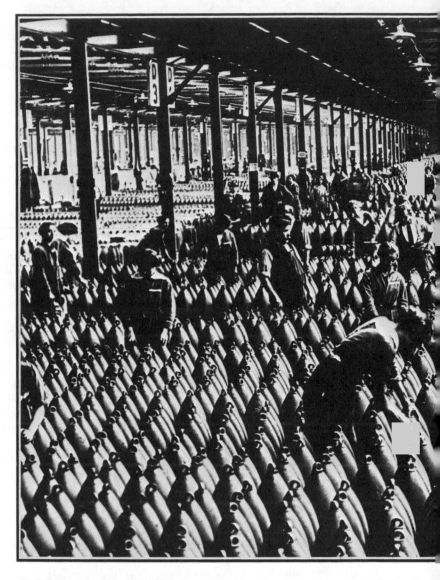

Shell-filling factory in the United States (1917).

. . . there are times when we feel light and free in our heavy armor, sensing, despite the weight, the impetus and the power which drive us forward.

We move most easily in battle-formation; for the power and will of the blood speaks most directly from the battle-machine. We are stirred as human beings are seldom stirred by (troops)

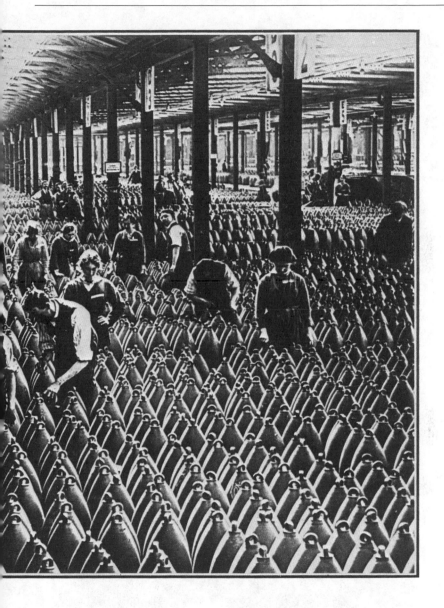

marching by . . . for they represent the will of a people to
greatness and dominance, shaped in its most effective form, as
steely hard implements. They contain all we have, all we think,
all we are; modern man marching to battle is modern man in his
most characteristic form. . . . He is a whole, not one part only.[6]

Hitler Youth motorcycle squadron.

The same utopian impulse was recognized by Foucault as part of a whole tradition of representations of the military machine.

> Historians of ideas usually attribute the dream of a perfect society to the philosophers and jurists of the eighteenth century; its fundamental reference was not to the state of nature, but to the meticulously subordinated cogs of a machine, not to the primal social contract, but to permanent coercions, not to fundamental rights, but to indefinitely progressive forms of training, not to the general will but to automatic docility. [7]

The Totality-Component: Figure of Steel

Once in battle, the formation dissolves. The macromachine separates out into its components. Each component in the soldierly totality-body has been made functional by the drill; battle gives it the opportunity to prove that its own function conform to the functioning principle of the machine itself. Each totality-component becomes a miniature of the machine.

> This was a whole new race, energy incarnate, charged with supreme energy. Supple bodies, lean and sinewy, striking features, stone eyes petrified in a thousand terrors beneath their helmets. These were conquerors, men of steel tuned to the most grisly battle. Sweeping across a splintered landscape, they heralded the final triumph of all imagined horror. Unimaginable energies were released as these brave troops broke out to regain lost outposts where pale figures gaped at them with madness in their eyes. Jugglers of death, masters of explosive and flame, glorious predators, they sprang easily through the trenches. In the moment of encounter, they encapsulated the spirit of battle as no other human beings could. Theirs was the keenest assembly of bodies, intelligence, will, and sensation. [1]

Jünger's imaginary man is portrayed as a physical type devoid of drives and of psyche; he has no need of either since all his instinctual energies have been smoothly and frictionlessly transformed into functions of his steel body. This passage seems to me to crystallize a tendency that is evident throughout Jünger's writing: a tendency toward the utopia of the body machine.

In the body-machine the interior of the man is dominated and transformed in the same way as are the components of the macromachine of the troop. For Jünger, then, the fascination of the machine apparently lies in its capacity to show how a man might "live" (move, kill, give expression) without emotion. Each and every feeling is tightly locked in steel armor.

"Discus Thrower," by Lothar Bechstein.

The "new man"* sired in the drill (the drill as organized battle of the old men against himself) owes allegiance only to the machine that bore him. He is a true child of the drill-machine, created without the help of a woman, parentless. His associations and relationships bind him instead to other specimens of the new man, with whom he allows himself to be united to form the macro-machine troop. All others belong only "under" him—never alongside, behind, or in front.

The most urgent task of the man of steel is to pursue, to dam in, and to subdue any force that threatens to transform him back into the horribly disorganized jumble of flesh, hair, skin, bones, intestines, and feelings that calls itself human—the human being of old:

> These are the figures of steel whose eagle eyes dart between whirling propellers to pierce the cloud; who dare the hellish

---

*The German is "Der neue Mensch" which could also be translated "the new human being" since Theweleit's point is however precisely that species being created is *masculine*, "men" has been used here as a general term for human beings. (Tr.)

crossing through fields of roaring craters, gripped in the chaos of tank engines; who squat for days on end behind blazing machine-guns, who crouched against banks ranged high with corpses, surrounded, half-parched, only one step ahead of certain death. These are the best of the modern battlefield, men relentlessly saturated with the spirit of battle, men whose urgent wanting discharges itself in a single concentrated and determined release of energy.

As I watch them noiselessly slicing alleyways into barbed wire, digging steps to storm outward, synchronizing luminous watches, finding the North by the stars, the recognition flashes: this is the new man. The pioneers of storm, the elect of central Europe. A whole new race, intelligent, strong, men of will. Tomorrow, the phenomenon now manifesting itself in battle will be the axis around which life whirls ever faster. A thousand sweeping deeds will arch across their great cities as they stride down asphalt streets, supple predators straining with energy. They will be architects building on the ruined foundations of the world.[2]

The new man is a man whose physique has been machinized, his psyche eliminated—or in part displaced into his body armor, his "predatory" suppleness. We are presented with a robot that can tell the time, find the North, stand his ground over a red-hot machine-gun, or cut wire without a sound. In the moment of action, he is as devoid of fear as of any other emotion. His knowledge of being able to do what he does is his only consciousness of self.

This, I believe, is the ideal man of the conservative utopia: a man with machinelike periphery, whose interior has lost its meaning (the technocrat is his contemporary manifestation).

This is not a utopia from the technologization of the means of production; it has nothing to do with the development of machine technology. That development is simply used to express a quality specific to the bodies of these men. The mechanized body as conservative utopia derives instead from men's compulsion to subjugate and repulse what is specifically human within them—the id, the productive force of the unconscious. The soldier male responds to the successful damming in and chaoticizing of his desiring-production from the the moment of his birth (if not earlier) by fantasizing himself as a figure of steel: a man of the new race.[3]

The armor of the soldier male may transform his incarcerated interior into the fuel that speeds him forward; or it may send it spinning outward. As something external to him, it can then be combatted; and it assails him constantly, as if it wished him back: it is a deluge, an invasion from Mars, the proletariat, contagious Jewish lust, sensuous woman.

The conservative utopia of the mechanized body, the body made machine in its totality, does not, then, derive from the development of the industrial means of production, but from the obstruction and transformation of human productive forces.

Preliminary Comments on the Agency of the Ego

If we now review the various functions, both of the totality armor of the "figure of steel" and of the periphery of the troop as totality, then what emerges as their most striking common feature is their function as external boundaries of the person as front: they are organs of reality-control, of control and defense against the drives. The functions of defense, both against threatening feelings and against thinking, seem to be performed by the body armor, the musculature of the individual totality component, or by the bodily form of the troop—the totality machine into which the component inserts itself.

Freud's second topographical schema of the psychic apparatus represents all these functions as fulfilled by the psychic agency of the "ego."[1] But by the

"Comradery," by Joseph Thorak. From the House of German Art (Münich).

end of the first chapter in Volume 1, it had become clear that the soldier males were incapable of possessing an "ego" in the Freudian sense. The ego is formed through processes of identification during the phase of the dissolution of the Oedipus complex, a "stage" that these men never reach. The question thus posed in Volume 1 was that of the origin of their "reality-competence"; why did these men not atrophy in "autistic" psychoses?

One possible response to that question now emerges. Since the "ego" of these men cannot form from the inside out, through libidinal cathexis of the body's periphery and identification, they must acquire an enveloping "ego" from the outside. My suspicion is that cathexis occurs as a result of coercion; it is forced upon them by the pain they experience in the onslaught of external agencies. The punishments of parents, teachers, masters, the punishment hierarchies of young boys and of the military, remind them constantly of the existence of their periphery (showing them their boundaries), until they "grow" a functioning and controlling body armor, and a body capable of seamless fusion into larger formations with armorlike peripheries. If my assumptions are correct, the armor of these men may be seen as constituting their ego.

A Freud distanced from the pleasure principle was able to write that

> the way in which we gain new knowledge of our organs during painful illnesses is perhaps a model of the way by which in general we arrive at the idea of our body.[2]

In a society that replaces the experience of pleasure in the body with its experience of pain this is irrefutably a statement of positivist truth. Drill and torture, it seems, are to be seen as the extremes of more general forms of bodily perception. (Now, in the process of being whipped, I know what my ass is capable of feeling and where exactly it's located. Now, as they kick me between the legs, I have my very first sense of my prick's enormous sensitivity . . .)

I feel pain, therefore I am. Where pain is, there "I" shall be—the psychic agency of the I as ego.

In a section entitled "The Ego and the Maintenance Mechanisms" I shall be investigating the significance of this form of the "I" for the white terror and its agents more closely. First, however, I want to examine some of the further features of the drill and the battle situation.

Blackouts

Ernst Röhm writes of his training for officer rank:

> From the very beginning, we ensigns were treated with the utmost severity. Many was the time we stumbled back to barracks thoroughly beaten down at the end of a day on duty. Once, we were all consigned to the dispensary, having fainted during exercises; we only gradually recovered.[1]

Fainting, or any related state, was no accident; it appears to have been a planned element within training. In *Sittengeschichte des Weltkrieges* (Moral History of the World War), edited by Hirschfeld, the situation is described as follows:

> The phenomena that have come to be known as "twilight states"
> (*Dämmerzustände*) can probably be interpreted as acute psychotic
> reactions to the miseries of the soldier's existence. They involve
> drowsiness, accompanied by spatial and temporal disorientation
> and loss of memory.[2]

In common soldiers, these states often culminated in angry tirades against men in uniform. This was not the case for ensigns and cadets, since they themselves hoped to become officers. What, then, happened to them during and after blackouts? Salomon as a cadet:

> And I learned to stand to "Attention!" Legs shaking, palms
> sweating slightly — and still, "Stand to attention!" Stomach walls
> straining, shoulders aching, a red wave slowly appearing before
> me, swelling and circling ponderously, then disappearing again;
> tiny dreams approaching from a distance, growing, filling out,
> grasping at my heart, my eyes, then suffocating; fleeting thoughts
> sweeping softly onward, tangling together, rolling to a ball in a
> brain that was heavy, rolling, springing away in knots together. I
> learned to "Stand to attention!"[3]

Killinger gives his all in the presence of the Kaiser, in a boat race between the crews of various navy vessels. His team wins. Then (he calls himself "Peter" in the text)

> there was a glass of champagne waiting in the cadet's mess, a
> treat from the officer in charge of naval cadets. Suddenly Peter's
> world turned black and started spinning, blood spurted from his
> nose; he remembered nothing from that moment. He awoke in the
> military hospital. The cadet officer and the staff physician were
> standing beside his cot. "Well, how do you feel now? You
> overtaxed yourself a little. But you'll get over it soon enough—
> with a constitution like yours."
> "Damn and blast," thought Peter, "I've let the side down."
> The cadet officer guessed his thoughts. "Don't worry about it. If
> the others had pushed themselves hard enough to collapse as you
> did we might have won by three lengths."[4]

Strangely enough, Peter is expressly praised for his collapse. Why? He has pushed himself beyond his own limits—but his very capacity to do so can be taken as evidence of enormous physical strength. An undrilled body would be unlikely to be able to reach "saturation point," as his does.

But this is not all. The moment at which the man enters a state of apparent blackout, or loses consciousness entirely following excessive physical exertion, seems in some way comparable to the moment of tension-and-release in orgasm.

The crucial difference between orgasm and the soldier's blackout is the absence of any intrinsic limit to the kind of physical exertion in which the soldier (or indeed the sportsman) engages. Unless exercise is voluntarily contained, or interrupted, it inevitably stretches the man beyond his limits; unlike orgasm, it does not produce bodily equilibrium, but disrupts it. Even the "ease" that Salomon experiences after "standing to attention" is the antithesis of the ease following orgasm. Standing at ease demands absolute tensing of the muscles; again, the only available form of release is loss of consciousness.

The blackout does appear momentarily to unite two normally antagonistic elements within the soldier; his body armor, as "masculine" repressor, merges with the repressed—his incarcerated "feminine" interior. Full consciousness—all the man; perceptual functions—is flooded and submerged precisely because the flow cannot be allowed to escape further. There is a clearly discernible dynamic of flow and release, yet it remains internal: a red wave approaching and disappearing; "tiny dreams" that "suffocate" in the heart; and thoughts that "spring away in knots together." The flow transforms itself and seeps away internally. The process appears intensified in the case of Killinger, whose nose spurts blood as he loses consciousness—as if his whole body had become an ejaculating phallus.

In the cases cited above, the body armor does indeed appear to become the displaced site of orgiastic potency; in the moment of blackout, at the climax of tension, the body armor surrenders to the wave that is inundating consciousness. Orgasm is not so much experienced as suffered. And, in contrast again to orgasm between lovers, the blackout threshold is raised on each new occasion. The more highly drilled the body armor, the more it must strain to reach its limits. The drill produces a heightened capacity, not for release but for tension. It digs out a new demand for the stream of the libido. The stream no longer flows as ejaculation and release of bodily tension, but pours across the sensory perception of the man and extinguishes it. The process is comparable to the man blowing a fuse in some internal short circuit; his current flows, but touches nothing external. The circuit is ingrained into the man himself, and he knows his potential; he learns to draw on it and play with it—for the point of blackout does not have to be reached in every instance.

There is also a second relationship in play here: the man's relationship to the commanding officer, or to the person for whose sake he makes physical effort—in Killinger's case, the Kaiser. The prize for the victors of the boatrace is an audience with the Kaiser ("My congratulations. You have done well.

"∞," by Roman Opalka. Detail 1:1722514-1725526 (1965).

May you continue to gain honor by your work on the *Stein*").[5] A second goal of physical exertion is, then, to see contentment in the face of the commanding officer, to be praised by a man in a superior position. And, as the man loses consciousness through overexertion, his superior does indeed appear satisfied—as if he too is reaching orgasm.

Could it be, then, that hallucinatory union with the superior (even with the Kaiser himself) occurs in the state of blackout? That the forbidden loving penetration of man into man takes place imaginarily in this blackness? (The voice and gaze of the superior have certainly always been a penetrating presence.)

Ferenczi in his genital theory draws distinctions between what he sees as three stages of unification in the sexual act. Union is achieved in "hallucinatory" form by the organism as a whole, in partial form by the penis, and in absolute form by the secretion.[6]

The "union" achieved by the soldier (with himself/his superior) is clearly limited to the hallucinatory form. In the preceding chapter, I noted the association between key situations of satisfaction (all of which were preceded by hallucinatory object-substitution) and two central perceptions: the "bloody miasma" and the "empty space." A third perception can now be added: the blackness of unconsciousness in blackout, produced when the man oversteps the limits of his strength. One of the three perceptions is dominant in every action of the White Terror; their significance will be discussed later in this chapter.

I have indicated that the bodies of the cadets were quite intentionally driven beyond their limits. But there was more; in some cases their lives were consciously endangered. Lieutenant Ehrhardt, on his year as a naval cadet:

> They saw the blazing heat as a useful means of teaching a poor naval cadet a lesson. So, for example, our crew squad was once put on punishment detail in the boat between one and two in the afternoon, at the very time when blissful sunshine turned to blistering heat.
>
> Hard labor, coupled in my case with the particular injustice of being punished when I had broken no regulations, triggered an eruption of boyish defiance: I purposely let my oar fall overboard. The NCO, who had been watching me, ordered the cutter to row back immediately and reported me to the guard officer. As punishment, I was forced to run up and down the topmast ten times—an excessive demand under any circumstances, but an act of almost horrible cruelty in the tropical heat of Brazil. Toward the end, I was already half unconscious as I groped and felt my way down along the shrouds; but I said nothing, clenched my teeth, and somehow made it to the lavatory below deck. Once

there, I dropped to the cool stone tiles, gasped for breath a few
more times, then lay unconscious.

Such tricks were often played on naval cadets. They had to be
strong as horses, or they withdrew from the service. In the end,
we were all agile as cats and tough as elephants' hides.[7]

The squirming resistance of the narrator's body is dismissed here as
"boyish." Even for the properly functionalized body, terror is "almost horrible
rible cruelty"—but only "almost." The boy withstands it. Had he fallen from
the mast—and this did happen on occasion—he would have been considered
not to have trained himself adequately for his position as machine component;
it would have been necessary to discard him. Holding out was proof of his
reliability: he could be trusted inside the machine. Von Selchow:

It was a damned hard year that lay behind us, that first year
as cadets on the HMS *Stein*. With a ruthlessness hard to match,
cadet officer Lieutenant Nordmann had driven us back and forth
between theoretical and practical duties. We were never permitted
a free moment. He had us doing every kind of filthy, heavy duty,
always longer than the sailors, always rougher than the stokers. In
those twelve months, each of us had resolved at least twelve times
to turn his back on this drudgery when we returned home.

But as cadet officer, he knew how to take young men in hand;
he knew our aim was one day to become leaders of men.[8]

One day, during an inspection of the ship, Selchow faints while hanging
from the yards. He feels dizzy and knows he has time to climb down, but he
refuses to do so and tries instead to hang on. He fails and is caught (though he
could also have smashed himself to pieces on the deck). Massive uproar, accusations
sations of drunkenness! But a number of the others are similarly overcome,
and the inspection is called off. The culprit is finally identified: contaminated
liver sausage. Still, better to fall than voluntarily vacate the yards and succumb
cumb to dizziness in the presence of the Kaiser.[9]

Selchow suffers a particularly violent blackout at the end of his training
year at sea. He returns to Kiel only weeks before the final theoretical exam
that is to make him an officer, only to be struck by some unidentified illness.
He loses consciousness and lies comatose in a military hospital for several
weeks while his doctors search in vain for the cause. As if through a mist, he
hears the doctors say that he is likely to die. But he has the "will to live" . . .
and as always, he pulls through.[10]

The drill brings the man to the very edge of dissolution. In the coma, a
new structure, a new body grows onto him. When he awakes from this process
of transformation, he has become physically and psychically another, a new
man.

From the "Pyramid Series," by Agnes Denes.

The Absorption of Sexual Desire

The most obvious consequence of the drill was its suppression of any "desire for women" (to the extent that such desire existed in the first place). The fact was an open secret; as Salomon writes, "any kind of pubescent urge was amply absorbed in the exercise of duties."[1] In response to a rumor that his food had been laced with anaphrodisiacs, Schauwecker remarks:

> But physical exertion was a far better antidote to erotic feeling than any drug could ever be. Eroticism was simply out of the question; it was a luxury of the everyday complacency of peacetime.[2] We had no time for such ridiculousness.[3]

Or if they did, it was immediately expunged. The staff sergeant in one of Vogel's stories bellows: "Toe the line, it's good for you—might stop you wanting to have a wank tonight."[4]

To most of the men, this lack of any relationship with a woman seemed in any case quite normal. That this was true for all of them make it a pleasurable position to be in.

The open obscenity of the idiom in the barracks may well have served to obscure a far more crucial transformation occurring in the soldier: the transformation of eros. By including "heterosexual" references in their repertoire of obscenities, the soldiers' language could obscure the fact that "women" and any kind of "love relationship" were no longer significant issues to the soldier. He was more likely to be interested in the following:

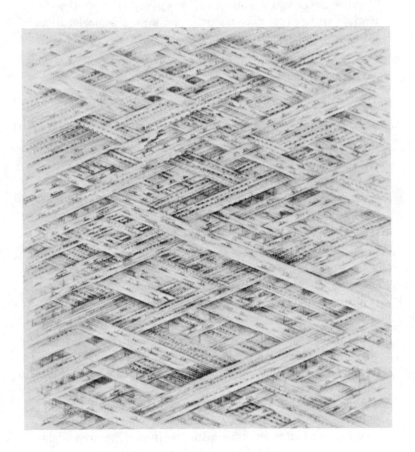

"Structure 2," by Thomas Bayrle (1976).

> A rifle in the hands of a noncommissioned officer from the
> Treptow school was a work of art. Whatever we grasped and
> twirled—rifles, beer glasses, girls—we were unbeatable. Even by
> the guards.[5] (Schauwecker)

What fascinates the soldier in drill is the activity of grasping, its synchro-
nicity, its exactitude—and not *what* is grasped.

> The very feeling of holding a rifle was rejuvenating.[6] (Salomon)

All these texts return repeatedly to the idea of the soldier as a work of art
and of his movements as "beautiful." Never an emotion, all is expression.

> Perfection: this was the crucial issue. Penetrating to the very
> limits of human ability, shaping our world to its most polished
> form. From the standpoint of the front only one kind of man could
> be seen to have achieved perfection: the professional soldier
> (*Landsknecht*).[*7]

The "polisher" referred to here is a man familiar to us as the creator of
the polished precision component within the total fascist artwork of the army:
the drill instructor.

The drill instructor sees himself unambiguously as a molder of men; a
young god at work.

> It was really the most pleasant, rewarding work, turning those
> young recruits, awkward and unpolished (they generally arrived
> from the country), into soldiers, serviceable people. . . . Mistakes
> made in their training could never have been remedied. The issue
> that the young officer in charge of recruits was called upon to
> settle was crucial both to people and fatherland: it was the
> question of whether an enthusiastic, indifferent, or even slightly
> cowed civilian would become a lifelong soldier.[8]

As General Maercker continues, the prewar army was generally successful in
crafting "lifelong soldiers"; the "cowed civilian" did indeed become a thing
of the past:

> . . . the peacetime army had schooled the German people in
> physical discipline, obedience, order, and loyalty. Their work was
> to become a source of strength for a whole army of workers in our
> industries, and of strict order and manly restraint in our German
> labor unions.[9]

---

*The term *Landsknecht* refers historically to soldiers recruited from within the German
empire.

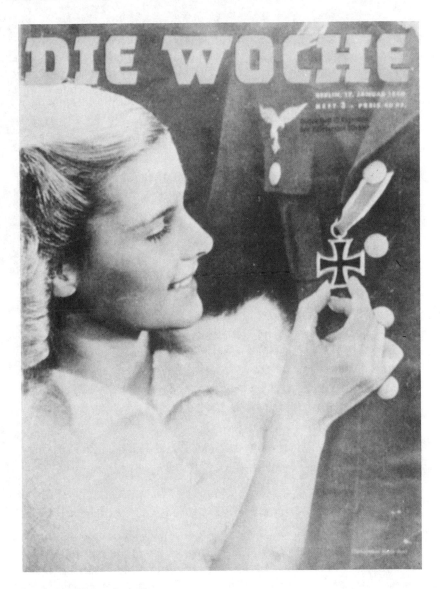

Cover of an illustrated weekly.

Such praise even pleased the occasional Wilhelminian union leader.[10] In the eyes of the soldier male, only the army was capable of creating what Röhm called "serviceable human beings": men bearing the stamp of military quality. To him, only the drill could serve as the birthplace of what he saw unquestionably as the only true human beings. The drill was a giant machine of transformation and rebirth,[11] created not only to serve the military, but society in general.

"Prussian Socialism"

> I have often wondered why this kind of education suited my taste so much better than the far easier and less disciplined life I would have had at school. My conclusion is that it was because as naval cadets we all wanted to be what our teachers and superiors had already become. As officers, they served as models for us. We assumed everything we did on their orders to be necessary. We appreciated why it had to be done.[1] (Lieutenant Ehrhardt)

Salomon, describing the teaching staff at the cadet academy:

> Instructors of officer rank were the only teachers who confounded the efforts of even the most fertile imaginations to find nicknames for them—quite simply because these men were in no way ridiculous.[2]

Ernst Röhm, on his training as infantry officer:

> . . . an ensign was required to perform every duty to perfection. However painful this might have seemed, it was of course quite proper. Our education was founded on the guiding principle that an officer had not only to have subjected his own body to the physical demands he now made of his men; he had also to have outshone his subordinates in fulfilling them. I have often looked back gratefully to the lessons I learned in my wartime schooling.[3]

Less crucial here, it seems to me, than the drilled cadet's wish to follow in the footsteps of his training officer, is the reality of the possibility that he would eventually do so (this was the essential distinction between officers and rank-and-file training). Within a matter of years, the cadet, or ensign, had real prospects of attaining whatever position would give him his desired status as torturer. This was why, unlike the common soldier, he had no need to hate the torturer as a matter of principle. (He was more likely to feel envious or jealous.)

In Röhm's description, the superior also functions as an actual physical model; he has outstripped his subordinates in subjecting his own body to the physical demands he now makes of them. Having achieved the goal of training—which is to acquire a new and better body—he now represents it to others. His new body fulfills his desire for a guarantee that he can be "in no way ridiculous." By demonstrating himself to be physically the better man, the officer can be perceived as the better lover in the martial encounters he desires between man and man.

In Freud's *Mass Psychology and Ego Analysis*, the military officer is equated with the father; but the equation is a false one.* Paternal authority derives its special terror precisely from the fact that its validity never needs to be demonstrated. A father never has to show that he can do what he demands of his son, nor is it even necessary for him to be capable of doing so—he always remains his son's better. His power is tyrannical, capricious; established by laws, axiomatic. It is unjust. The power of the training officer, by contrast, is made to appear legitimate by his capacity, and willingness, to do what he demands of others. As a son in the process of advancement, the training officer is in principle the equal of the cadet he drills—moreover the cadet is capable of one day becoming the better of his instructor.

The father commands his son: "Thou shalt become like thy father; but thou shalt never do as thy father does." In officer training this paternal double-bind is replaced by a utopian vision of justice. If the cadet overcomes the obstacles presented to him, the promise of promotion will actually be fulfilled; it is *possible* to become general. In the family in which the man has been a son, he can by contrast never become the father—not if he "eclipses" his father a million times over.

This relationship between officer and cadet is central to the "Prussian socialism" (or "socialism of the front") whose spirit pervades the writings of the soldier males. They see the military as the consummate form of socialism; for it assigns to each man his rightful place in the hierarchy.[4]

In rank-and-file training, by contrast, the notion of Prussian socialism had no material content. It was almost inconceivable that recruits would one day be superior in rank to their instructor. He would always remain superior, his seniority always perceived as bludgeoning coercion.

---

*For Freud to study army organization would have been well and good, if the type of army he described had really existed. He usually proceeded by developing theories from case studies, not the reverse. With the army, by contrast, he considered it unnecessary to start with its concrete structure, or the psychic structure of its soldiers. He contented himself with reading Le Bon's book on mass psychology, then applying its theoretical findings, together with his own from an earlier period, to the army and other hierarchical non-masses. He then drew up a whole model of the functions of an absolutely nonexistent Oedipal army—all for the stated purpose of criticizing Wilhelminian militarism (his starting point was the high suicide rate in the German army) and arguing for further improvements. He pulled a Freudian wish-fulfillment army out of a hat—an army such as Ebert himself might have wished for. The work was published in 1921, a date that clearly demonstrates how efficiently the insulating system of the father of psychoanalysis could function to exclude the actual limits of history. (Freud, *Group Psychology and the Analysis of the Ego*, Standard Edition, vol. 18.)

Even for common soldiers, the instructor never corresponded to Freud's construct of the beloved *Führer*-figure, a "father" whom the soldier identified with his "ego ideal." On the contrary, the martinet instructor was often seen as an ignoramus whose only skill lay in exploiting his borrowed power to order around grown men, men who, outside the barracks (or even on the battlefield), were in every respect his superiors.

BATTLE AND THE BODY

Speed and Explosions: Contact with the "Object"

Blackouts are a phenomenon of the drill—or, rather, of the soldier male's battle against himself, which is organized by the drill. When his libido finds itself unable to reach any external object, it pours out across his perception and extinguishes it. Any possibility of the man's libido attaining the object for whose sake his exertion is apparently undertaken—the commanding officer or Kaiser—is excluded by prohibition.

In battle, this configuration of forces is crucially transformed. Battle makes an external object (the enemy male) accessible to the soldier's overwrought body. Even when the enemy is imagined, the situation changes absolutely from that of the drill.

> We lay in the sand, chins propped on angled left arms, nestled against the ground, heads raised to spy out a distant goal. Side by side our bodies lay, row upon row anticipating the signal. Jump!— and the body tensed, left legs too were suddenly sharply angled, chests lifted easily from the sand, every fiber pressed forward. Up! March! March!—and our muscles tensed again, the earth sank and slid away behind us, our bodies were pointed arrows storming forward. Silently the ranks advanced, each man quite alone. Down! And suddenly now the earth swelled and breathed; where before a flat surface had extended beneath our stamping feet, waves and folds now grew, embracing and giving cover to our bodies as they crashed down. Our lungs labored and our eyes sought the target once more. Again the ranks worked their way forward, and yet again; but now the forest's edge was close and there were snipers in the trees. Every artery surged with fire as we prepared to storm. Then the signal, two notes only, brazenly dancing: the infantry signal to advance. All our thinking now dropped like useless ballast. Our bodies were light and wind-whipped from behind. Now the charge became a tearing pleasure, the earth smooth and sloping toward our goal, one long,

Pen and ink drawing by A. Reich of the Battle of the Marne (1914).

unobstructed pathway. Now we were upon them, breath gathering in our breasts, the broken panting of a moment earlier growing to a fearsome scream, every mouth stretched wide, our cheer exploding from blood and bones, hammering into the air in a raw, howling crescendo; now we ourselves were the storm, we were the force, unstoppable, crushing, thrust and power, breaking into the forest's edge, trampling bushes and roots to explode against the enemy. We met no resistance as we ran tumbling far beyond our target, laughing, possessed and intoxicated by this unbridled force, till we stopped, a little ashamed—for after all, our target was imaginary—and tried quickly to collect ourselves, a little shocked at the ease of our victory—and returned, abashed, to the order of the ranks.[1]

Here the soldier progresses beyond the state he achieves in blackout. The passage presages a possible union with an external object, a union that will not make his senses reel. Cadet Salomon is abashed and ashamed, as he re-enters the order of the ranks; for he has come within inches of the goal of his forbidden desires. As always, those desires are played out along the border of unconsciousness; but, in this case, a form of release is permitted: a scream.

At first glance, the goal of the assault appears to be union with the body of the earth (the earth becomes a living body: it "swells and breathes"; it has "folds" that embrace the body of the young man "crashing down"). But the earth subsequently becomes subjugated territory, across whose suddenly sloping surface he storms with "unbridled force." At this point he appears to explode. His "fearsome" scream breaks open a pathway. It screams itself

without the volition of the screamer. *It* screams:[*] "a cheer exploding from
blood and bones." He "explodes" against the enemy.

Salomon's emphasis on the *goal*, on the *speed* with which he races toward
it, and on the inner explosion that rips him apart, result in many similar evo-
cations of the pleasure of battle. In war, the soldier's pleasure appears massively intensified by the war's machinery (guns and machine-guns) to which
he is coupled, and by noise, the sound of the grenade strikes in which nature
seems to "come alive." Explosions:

> It burned its way down inside them, and remained there. . . . For
> a moment, they were all aflame. . . .[2] The alarm beat out its
> piercing message above our position, crackling electricity that
> charred anything still living; yes, yes, at last we had reached our
> objective, at last we could let go, release our own safety catches
> and prepare ourselves for discharge[3] (Schauwecker). "Eruption of
> the volcanic hearts of men possessed by war"[4] (Heinz). "It blew
> him apart, like a grenade exploding inward from his heart;[5] the
> bliss of charging the heart's roaring motor with powder."[6]

Explosion is likened to a birth, the long-awaited birth of a fleshless body, a
body that becomes the relished site of catastrophe:

> Before his very eyes, the breath of creation was descending on the
> world and remaking it in a new and different form. Inevitably, he
> too would be caught up in this destruction of all matter, for a
> moment, a second only, a tiny eternity. Already he felt it in the
> clay of his body, in the fountains of his blood vessels and nerves,
> volcanic passages. In a moment, it must surely seize him and send

---

[*]"Es schreit": it screams, or id screams. (Tr.)

him spinning cloud-high, fragmenting into atoms, himself and all around him, all no more than lumps of clay, the heart their molten center, the seeds of the future. Any second now—any second![7]

The man longs for the moment when his body armor will explode, strengthening his rigid body-ego; but a body such as his cannot atomize, as does the mass, by allowing itself to be penetrated, fragmented, and thus destroyed. His body atomizes only if he himself erupts outward. He desires to move beyond himself, bulletlike, toward an object that he penetrates. But he also desires to survive.

The marching troop as totality-armor is absent from the battle situation; but the soldier does have access to a different type of armor—one that is not destroyed by constant explosions. This second armor is the barrel of his gun or rifle, and it provides the model according to which his own eruptions function:

> . . . their bodies contracted. Curled up like great cats along the rims of shell-craters, they stretched their right arms back, joints cracking. They drew breath, pumping themselves full of compressed air(!) till it sang in their ears and hammered in their lungs. These men were living guns, with melinite muscles and tripod legs; their eyes narrowed to slits, thin blue horizons looking out toward men swarming forward between branches and tree trunks; drunk, red wine in their bellies, like tanked-up motors turned loose with no brakes to hold them.[8]

Guns have the capacity to do something of which the soldier is normally incapable: they can discharge and still remain *whole*. In Schauwecker's description above, the two are more or less indistinguishable. The metal of the gun barrels appears almost to take the place of the soldier's body armor; to function, then, as his "ego."

> What purpose would be served by all these iron weapons leveled against the universe, were they not intertwined with our nerves, were it not our blood that hissed on every axis?[9] (Jünger)

The gun barrel bundles all the energy of "hissing" blood into eruption, a shot—leveled at the *universe*, at its entire faulty structure. The men cited here are impelled by a single drive: to speed from the gun barrel (which remains intact) and to penetrate other bodies.

> It was as if I myself could feel every jolt that shook the metal parts of the gun as a bullet slicing into warm, living human bodies. A wicked pleasure; was I now perhaps one with the weapon? Was I not machine—cold metal? Into the disordered mob, straight in where a gate had been erected; for grace was accorded to the men who passed through it.[10] (Salomon)

Detail from a German poster toward the end of World War II, exhorting people to observe the blackout because of bombing raids.

Salomon is "cold metal," he is devoid of feeling, and yet he shakes as he slices into the interior of bodies. In the intoxication of power, his ego transcends its own boundaries, but remains stable; its reality-competence is secured by the machine-gun barrel. But reality-competence is not his only goal; he also anticipates overload. Dwinger's character Pahlen runs hot as his machine:

> A thousand rounds tore outward, with never an *inhibition* to hold them; Pahlen's gun glowed hot, and his fingers blistered. But he kept on shooting; he felt nothing, only death-blow raining outward from a small beast raging bloodthirsty in his hands. . . . The Bolshevists were caught unaware; their corpses were banked high before they could take cover. Then nothing stirred up ahead; all he could see was a tangled clump of dark brown. "Cease fire!" called Langsdorff loud and clear, but Pahlen did not hear him; he had to be pulled away by Wollmeier. The little baron dropped like a stone, his eyes rolling. . . .
> A question rapped out from Reimers: "Is he hit?" "Get him to cover," scowled Langsdorff, "he's only unconscious."[11] A true judge of men.

Pahlen's libido takes the opening into which it is forced by a muscle-armor ego that explodes, yet remains whole. The libido now successfully

From "The Mighty Thor," ™ Copyright © 1989 Marvel Entertainment Group, Inc. All rights reserved.

reaches its target; but even this highly effective discharge seems insufficient. A sizable portion remains inside the rifleman, once again inundating his perception: blackout. One way or another, the libido must achieve its goal, which is a discharge of tension.

"Never an inhibition" restrains Pahlen from sending his overcharged drives spinning outward. The new form of cartridge-stream lodges itself in a tangled clump of dark brown—like meets like. In the "judgment" of Langsdorff, "a true judge of men," that form is thoroughly appropriate to men such as Pahlen.

The same transformation, the same eruption outward, is sought by all soldier males in the moment of attack. Ultimately, they themselves become the shots spreading outward, bullets hurtling from the military machine toward their body-targets. At these moments, they anticipate the most intense possible sensation; but it is their own velocity they continuously evoke to legitimize their movement of eruption and penetration into the body of the enemy:

> The men started as if whipped. They crouched, ready to spring forward, like the bullets they seemed to feel themselves to be. The air turned to glass: it hissed, howled, shook, glinted, rumbled. The woods began to move, the river and the fields appeared to come alive.[12] (F. Nord)

Speed is a key category for the soldier body.[13] It needs to heat up, rev up, and race psychically, before charging physically toward the site on which it expects to experience itself in the streaming of pleasure.

"I'm no child anymore . . . and besides
. . ."

They ran on, suddenly drunkenly intoxicated by the open
space before them. They saw nothing but endless horizons, behind
whose heights lay something they were seeking . . . what was it?
. . . Onward! Ever onward!

They plunged ahead. Every second was precious. The air was
a whirlpool, the attack a maelstrom sucking them out into open
spaces. They crashed without stopping over trees and piles of
rubble; they ducked around shell-craters, screamed for the enemy,
and ran on, with tearing rage in their hearts, and tears in their
eyes. The blood shot through their bodies in massive surges.[14]

These men "screamed for the enemy" as babies scream for food, "with
tearing rage in their hearts." Now at last they can take revenge "with tears in
their eyes" for all the pain they have ever suffered. The tears they now cry are
not only tears of remembrance, tears swallowed and never cried; they are also
tears of joy. For in this moment of discharge, streams are released to flow
toward an enemy with whom penetration will be mutual, since he is intimately
familiar.

The realization dawns in a blinding flash, like an
almost-forgotten memory; this man, then, was the enemy, and we
would reach him in an instant! We were filled with the sudden
fury of savage desire, as if every pent-up, splitting tension had
found a sudden outlet and plunged like a roaring waterfall into
chasms of purple and scarlet-red.

Fast, make it fast, the killing must begin! There was now only
one deliverance, one course of fulfillment and one happiness:
flowing blood. We felt the wicked bliss of anticipation, knowing

"Whaam!"™ by Roy Lichtenstein. Copyright © S.P.A.D.E.M. Paris/V.A.G.A., New York, 1989.

we would have him in our grasp a moment later; knowing too that we would emerge the stronger, the invincible. A moment more to wait, then we would reach our target! I felt my right hand take a vicelike grip on my pistol, and my left hand grasping my short bamboo stick. I felt the blood rush seething to my face, my teeth clenching, bright tears running uncontrollably down my face.[15]

Already, a number of different elements are united in the man Jünger anticipates as his target. He is made to answer for so much that has been missed or denied; and he becomes the target of so much that can only be discharged in the battle-situation. It is impossible to equate him with any given individual; he is neither wholly the other man with whom union is sought, nor solely the tormentor who is the target of vengeance, nor indeed the equal with whom battles are fought for dominion over Mother Earth. He is an object that combines what is desired with what is hated; but above all, "this man" is *human*, a man with feelings, a man of flesh, hair, and bones; the molecular intruder who must at last be dispensed with—the old man. In penetrating him at last, the soldier male gains entry to life.

> This was our baptism by fire! The air was charged with
> overflowing virility, every breath was intoxicating, every man
> could have cried without knowing the reason. O hearts of men,
> that can feel such things![16]

Many texts make deliberate associations between "love" and "battle" —
as in the following passage from Schauwecker:

> I leave tomorrow for the front, to enjoy the embrace of burning
> grenades, the crackling kisses of gunfire under the ardent eyes of
> airplanes.[17]

Salomon invites the reader to imagine him mounting a machine-gun as he
would a woman:

> I fired — and all the day's dullness vanished. The gun wriggled and
> jerked like a fish, but I held it firmly, tenderly in my hands,
> clamping its tossing belly firmly between my knees and running
> through one strap, then the second. Steam hissed from the barrel.
> I saw nothing, but Schmitz leaped dancing, screaming, and
> howling up the bank, pushed me aside, and climbed across to take
> my place.[18]

There is nothing to be interpreted here, since everything is quite explicit.
The gun is the good whore — one man is permitted to take first turn, then the
other; they remain friends, indeed become friends in the process; and the
barrel dutifully emits its steam.

But the intensity of these moments of discharge should not mislead us
into equating them with a lover's bliss. What is crucial about them is instead
that they are the writers' streams, the streams of blood in their texts and
streams of words in their writing. More than at any other point in his writing,
the writer now rises to the literary challenge; now he desires to write great
literature. He incites his readers to be overwhelmed by the violence of his
erupting self, to let their thoughts and feelings flow with him into waterfalls of
cascading words, to be penetrated until the blood rushes to their ears. He
sends all the linguistic material at his disposal into the battle through which he
hopes to gain a place in literary history for eternity.

> And, finally, there is ecstasy — a state of mind granted not only to
> the holy man, to great writers and great lovers, but also to the
> great in spirit. . . . Ecstasy is an intoxication beyond all
> intoxications, a release that bursts all bonds. It is a madness
> without discretion or limits, comparable only to the natural
> forces. . . . A man in ecstasy becomes a violent storm, a raging
> sea, roaring thunder. He merges with the cosmos, racing toward
> death's dark gates like a bullet toward its target.[*] And should the

---

[*]"Poor death" was Christian Schaeffer's comment here.

> waves crash purple above him, he will already be long past all
> consciousness of movement or transition; he will be a wave
> gliding back into the flowing sea from whence it came.[19]

The place to which the wave returns is also the goal toward which a
single, annihilating impulse drives Jünger's great rock-words; but before he
arrives, he will have been everything, everything powerful—a violent storm,
a raging sea, roaring thunder. And he will no longer be a name, an isolated
man, but a German, a soldier, "I" absorbed into the cosmos. Such is the soldier male's oceanic feeling. Unlike Freud, he gives no intimation that he has
failed to recognize, or "repressed," the feeling. He has no urge to renounce
or sublimate his desire to dissolve in pleasure. Yet, since he has no internal or
external connection to partialities, he is incapable of drifting down the waters
of desire in search of new associations, new avenues to open: he is totality.
Only in the act of killing or dying—penetration or explosion—can he burst his
boundaries; this rule is never broken.* There must be a rush of blood, either
within him, or out of the other:

> Breath, heartbeat, engine-roar, flying grenades, and machine-gun
> clatter coalesced into one rhythm: Hot human—blood—flows—
> here—the vapors—for—all magic—dear. The rhythm caught and
> wedded itself to a text from the original verison of Goethe's
> "Walpurgisnacht," which Georg had read years before in passing.
> "Hot human blood flows here,/The vapors for all magic dear."[20]

The stream flowing here can never be associated with the names of the far
distance—ocean, Congo, or Mississippi—nor does the infinite image of
woman flow or float in its gentle embrace—for there are no still waters, but
raging, hot, spurting *interior*.

Blood** is the embodiment of the soldier male's desire for eruption and
life, and the only thing permitted to flow within him. Blood appears repeatedly throughout fascist literature as a synonym for proper feeling.[21] It may be
substituted for almost any part of the fascist's psychic apparatus; blood is the
productive force of his unconscious, the oil that pulsates through his machinized musculature, that boils when his motor runs, that foams up in the man
as machine and becomes his good interior.***

The war-machine needs blood to continue functioning. In Heinz's description, the function of "breath, heartbeat, engine-roar, flying grenades,
and machine-gun clatter" is simply to express the rhythm of "Hot human
blood." War itself is attributed to the seething of men's blood:

---

*Nor is it broken in writing, which is a kind of war (and not an easy one).

**Or ink, handwriting.

***Anyone whose feelings differ from the fascist's is thus seen to have different blood. The
"Jewish habit" of miscegenation is perceived as a ploy to poison German blood; the blood of
pacifists is seen as subversive, and so on.

It gives men form and maturity in a formless age.[22] (Heinz). The blood shot through their bodies like torrents tumbling together in a snow-thaw[23] (Schauwecker). Their blood . . . foamed and exploded and ancient rock melted back to molten fire[24] (Jünger). Battle melted the snow that had frozen our feelings; they blossomed in the surging of our blood. . . . Man's courage is the most precious of qualities. As we jangled our weapons to battle across the fields the blood surged through our veins with divine inspiration of the . . .[25]

. . . the blood whirled through our brains and pulsated through our veins, as if anticipating a long-awaited night of love — but this night would be more passionate and more furious.[26]

The enthusiasm of these virile men made their blood seethe against the walls of their veins and bubble through their hearts like fire.[27]

For Jünger, the highest category of the blood is without question the blood of men marching to battle:

Every voice ever raised in alarm, from Suttner to Kant, fades away like a child's murmur in this motoric rhythm of tension and deed. In the immutable laws of the blood, all experience sinks and is lost.[28]

One such immutable law demands that the stream of blood flow constantly toward the front,* the site of breakthrough. In world war, the stream that flows in the required direction is the army:

We were passed by endless streams (of men) — men willing to sacrifice life itself to satisfy their will to life, their will to battle and power they represented. All values were made worthless, all concepts void by this incessant nighttime flooding into battle; we sensed that we were witnessing the manifestation of something elemental and powerful, something that had always been, that would long outlive human lives and human wars.[29]

These are the final lines of *Der Kampf als inneres Erlebnis* (Battle as Inner Experience). The law perceived here behind all life is the law of the writer's own body. The "will to life" is made manifest in the eruption of his inner stream in battle — or in the battle of writing. Blood must flow . . .[30]

Our battle-cry as we meet the enemy merges into his own crying; it is a cry wrung from hearts trembling on the brink of eternity, a cry long forgotten in the sweeping tide of culture, a cry of recognition, terror, and thirst for blood.

---

*Paper.

Comic by Irons from *Radical America* (1970). *Frame 1*. "Hard Times Comics. Stories for hot-blooded real men. Not for turkeys!" *Frame 2*. "Our story begins somewhere in a no-man's-land created by tough fighters Slugger McCord and Ace Johnson. Out there on an important mission, they're crawling through the darkness, waiting . . ."

Frame 3. "Hear anything, Slugger?" "Nothing, just the frogs and crickets."

Frame 4. "You know, it reminds me of summer nights back home, so peaceful and quiet. . . . Hard to imagine there are 20,000 slit-eyes out there." *Frame 5.* "Sends chills down your spine." *Frame 6.* "Yeah, but we gotta job to do. It's almost 2 o'clock. We'll pack up in five minutes." "Let's have a smoke first. We've got enough . . ." *Frame 7.* Budda, budda . . .

Yes, the fighter thirsts for blood. This is the feeling, second only to his terror, that engulfs him in a torrent of red waves: when shivering clouds of annihilation hang heavy over fields of rage he is intoxicated, blood-thirsty. Strange as it may sound to men who have never struggled for existence, the sight of the enemy produces not only the most extreme horror, but redemption from heavy, intolerable pressure. The voluptuousness of blood hangs over war like a red storm-sail over a black man-of-war: in its limitless momentum it is comparable only to Eros itself.[31]

And not merely comparable; for the language Jünger speaks with utter clarity here is the language of these men's own transformed Eros. At moments such as these, their language no longer destroys reality; in the finest detail, it gives access to the reality of these men and their condition. It becomes impossible to call such language irrational, insane, lacking in substance; it must simply be accepted as document (as victory?), or rejected. By the Left, it has been rejected.

Frame 8. "Jeeeesus! I never imagined it'd be like this!" / "We'd better start at the beginning again."

We may at last arrive at an understanding of fascism's triumph in Germany. What the texts cited have most clearly demonstrated is a refusal by fascism to relinquish desire—desire in the form of a demand that "blood must flow," desire in its most profound distortion. In the German Communist Party (KPD) desire was never seen as the producer of a better reality; that party never so much as intimated that there might be pleasure in liberation, pleasure in new connections, pleasure in the unleashing of new streams. Instead, desire was channeled into plotting and scheming tactics and strategies—literary ones included—while fascism screamed, "Germany awaken!" What was "sleeping" had ears to hear its call as a bell-peal of immediate resurrection: "the dead" could now return from the entrails.

Fascism's most significant achievement was to organize the resurrection and rebirth of dead life in the masses—"strange as it may sound to men who have never struggled for existence." In the contemporary context, dead life can hardly be called a rarity; and its resurrection remains an imporant political process—perhaps the most important political process of all. The task of the nonfascist, however, is not to organize dead life, but to release it from its bonds, to intensify, accelerate, and transform it into a multiplicity whose best quality is that it cannot be organized as fascism, nor in any way assembled into blocks of human totality-machines, knitted into interlocking networks of order; a multiplicity that will not fit into the slot of power-hungry bodies of party formations, that refuses to function as the liver or the little finger of institutions and rulers, but instead holds the promise of a lived life that must not scream endlessly for rebirth.

Frame 9. "Our story begins when a company is heading back to base, tired and exhausted from a night patrol. Private Joe Spencer is lost in his thoughts." *Frame 10.*
"Joe was tired . . . tired of fighting, tired of killing, tired of war in the fight for survival." *Frame 12.* "KABLAM!!!" *Frame 13.* "Shit! That's not even in the script!" /
"I think we'd better start from the beginning again."

Frame 14. "Our story begins as Major 'Tuck' Bucker is returning home after a successful mission in his F-86." *Frame 15.* "He's almost reached the edge of enemy territory when suddenly . . ."

This human multiplicity will pursue its own goals and will doubtless "organize" itself in the process—always assuming it evolves in the first place.

The Site of War

The intensity of eruption in the event of war differs greatly from text to text; common to all these men's writings, however, is the central position they ascribe to the describer. He is either the source of, or is in some way connected to, every explosion; the end of the world is staged on his behalf and from within him. The arena of war is first and foremost his own body; a body poised to penetrate other bodies and mangle them in its embrace.

The man depicted as the active center of warfare[*] is an irresistible charmer hunting for sensations. His actions take place amid dying masses of humanity, between imperialist powers warring over colonial sources of raw materials or world market domination; but he remains an absolutely private individual. Though he claims repeatedly to represent the "whole," the "nation," he best fulfills that function as an isolated, self-interested individual, a man searching for the flow of desire. Within him, there must be rushing, hissing, explosion, shattering, flowing—this alone is important. Selchow feels "good and pure and happy as a child."[1] When he hears the signal announcing the Battle of Skagerak: "Trumpet and drum" (report to battle stations), the moment casts "undreamt-of bliss into (his) careworn arms." The goal of grenade-fire and machine-guns is a burning kiss for Schauwecker, the tingling Salomon feels between his thighs. Trenches are stormed again and again, simply so that Jünger may feel his blood seething; he becomes a roaring waterfall in the endless grind of trench warfare. This is his escape; not drop-

---

[*]And of literature, whose hard-hitting modern representative Jünger would be pleased to be considered.

Frame 16. "In a flash Major Bucker banks left, climbs, and . . ." / "Shit! I won't even make it through another short story. Can we start from the beginning again?"

ping out and turning on, but dropping in and bursting out ("Are you experienced?").

War is a function of the body of these men. Strangely, however, their body remains inwardly divided in the very moment in which its functioning is most intensely pleasurable. In war, the man appears not only naked, but stripped of skin; he seems to lose his body armor, so that everything enters directly into the interior of his body, or flows directly from it. He is out of control and seems permitted to be so.

But at the same time, he is all armor, speeding bullet, steel enclosure. He wears a coat of steel that seems to take the place of his missing skin. He is collected, directed toward one strict goal; in this sense he is controlled in the extreme.

As always, then, the "whole" that is the man in battle appears as two elements raging and roaring in opposition; it erupts outward, but at the same time remains compacted and contained. In fascist writing, the opposition takes the form of body versus consciousness; for unlike the body, consciousness is not dispersed in the exhilaration of assault. Jünger feels he is the stronger, he is clearly conscious of his own courage.[2] During the attack the brain takes over entirely: later on, events and landscapes surface as nothing more than dark and dreamlike recollections.[3] The man's brain "burns with an ice-cold fever, lucid and acute (Schauwecker).[4] He sees everything differently, but with absolute precision, the contours of the landscape reeling past him, no more than a hair's breadth away. He stares blankly."[5] From a distance, he

Frame 17. "Our story begins as Quan Hoy, a regular with the North Vietnamese army, is silently crawling through mud and darkness." *Frame 18.* "Further and further from his base camp. Deeper and deeper into enemy territory. His mission: sabotage!"

watches himself act, the ice-cold sting of his dying commander's voice still resounding in his ears.[6] And once again the whole magic of a landscape unparalleled in its glory is revealed in a moment of absolute lucidity, just before he falls unconscious.[7] (The ravaged landscape Heinz refers to is that of the trenches.)

A moment before his senses "reel"—before blackout, the goal of military action—the man consciously registers the perception of an object: his own consciousness. In none of the examples cited is the object of perception specifically external: even the landscape will later "surface" only dimly from memory; it reels past razor-sharp, or it is perceived not as landscape but as "magic." The "ice-cold" consciousness of these men seems icily conscious only of itself. They know the precise details of their own actions; nothing they do escapes them. As they charge, they retain a "clear consciousness of (their) own boldness"; they are conscious not only that they have feelings but that these are feelings they would never otherwise experience.

Even in battle, these men do not experience themselves: they simply register. Their breakthrough leads not to intense pleasure but to a state of intense self-observation. Their principal need in this situation is for a brain "ice-cold"—the processes occurring in their own bodies must not escape them, for they are permitted to take place only when the man is either killing or dying. Thinking ice-cold allows the man to perceive his own body in anticipation of killing or of his own death. (I kill, therefore I am. I die, therefore I was.)

The only other time individual perception may be centered on bodily processes to this extent is during orgasm; here, however, the body is not alone nor is pleasure experienced as absolute attentiveness. On the contrary, the more intense the experience of bodily pleasure, the more likely it is that psychic energy will be withdrawn from the recording process of perception. In orgasm, consciousness and bodily process are anything but opposed to each other; the brain does not observe the orgasm—unless the brain is disturbed.[8]

Frame 19. "Quan approaches noiselessly . . ." "What on earth is wrong with this comic strip? The whole thing has gotten out of control!"

In soldier males, by contrast, the perception of sensation is absolutely divorced from sensation itself. They experience their most intense feelings in isolation from themselves. They themselves are the objects of their own desire; their own brain registers their own musculature, and they achieve discharge. "Pleasure" is an intellectual quality, achieved by the head as the parasite of a body on the brink of explosion.*

This is why discharge never brings true release; its foundation has been laid by the pathway traveled by the man's libidinal energy; the drill and the pathway lead to blackout—since only blackout can mend the split between observation and experience.

Because the physical construction of his body precludes any successful discharge of psychic tension, his drives find the only available outlet; they escape in objectified form, as blood.

As blood and life flow away, the man achieves redemption.[9] (Only wait a moment more./And happines will soon be yours./Your hatchet poised./To bring you joy . . .)

Their eyes met, and a paralyzing second of silence passed.

> Then a cry went up, rising steeply, wild, blood-red, burning its fierce, unforgettable imprint into the minds of the listeners. A cry that tore the veils from dark, undreamed-of worlds of feeling, compelling all who heard it to race forward, to kill or be killed.

---

*Theweleit adds in parentheses here that the German term "Verkopfung," meaning intellectualization, appears particularly apposite in this context. It literally means "situating in the head," the head as the seat of intellect, specifically distinguished from the "rest of the body." (Tr.)

Frame 20. "Our story begins as . . . ." / "Holy shit! That's disguesting. Can we try again?"

> What meaning had hands raised in surrender here, shouts of "Mercy!" or "Comrade!"'? Only one pact mattered—the pact of blood. . . . These orgies of fury were brief, raging fever; when they burned out, the trenches were left like beds disheveled from the convulsions of the dying. Pale figures in white bandages stared at the miracle of the rising sun, unable to comprehend the reality of the world or of what they had experienced.[10]

Eyes meet, and the soldier is confronted with the seducer who has tempted him so long. The enemy surfaces as a momentary apparition of the soldier's own mirror image; Jünger once described the enemy's face as "containing all the fires of prehistory."[11] The soldier lunges "forward" and discovers his own past, the lost "reality" of the world, which he desires to penetrate again in battle. But his "breakthrough" to the real experience of pleasure is never successful: he perceives only veils, fury, fever, and convulsion. The fascist never experiences the existence of a body capable of release, his own body calm, his own self peaceful. The blackout in which he loses all memory of what he has seen, or how, is in fact a form of punishment for his attempt to obtain forbidden pleasure: but more than this, it is a function of a body incapable of the experience of pleasure in any form.

Again and again, he "awakens" from trance, mental absence, or exhilaration to discover, "in the miracle of the rising sun," that he himself is absent; he cannot feel his own self, his armor is more fragile than ever, he is about to disintegrate, "a pale figure in white bandages." Soon he will need a second dose of blood, even if this time it is his own . . .

There is a passage in Ferenczi that may enable us to define the relation between blackout and orgasm more precisely. He compares the processes of erection and ejaculation to the capacity of lower organisms for autotomy—their ability to reject and regenerate body parts that produce displeasure.[12] He speculates that this may be a forerunner of the psychic process of repression,

Frame 21. "Our story . . ." / "Oh, shit!!!!"

indeed that "erection itself may simply be an unsuccessful attempt by genitals laden with unpleasurable qualities to separate themselves from the rest of the body."[13] And he concludes:

> Compulsive scratching of the genitals may well be a response to displeasure accumulated from all areas of the body, then stored in the genitals in the form of an irritating itch — which is then eradicated through scratching. But it also seems plausible that the scratch reflex may be a vestige of the tendency to autotomy; that is, an attempt simply to tear off the itching body part with the nails. Certainly, irritation does not usually stop until the itching body part has been scratched to the point of bleeding — that is, until portions of the tissue have actually been torn away. Erection, scratching, and ejaculation may then be presumed to be autonomous processes that begin violently, and are then modified; the initial intention to tear off the entire organ is subsequently limited to scratching (*friction*), and finally to fluid emission.[14]

Let us pursue Ferenczi's argument in relation to the soldier. Since nothing flows from him, he cannot progress to the substitution stage of fluid emission. Conceivably, then, he is compelled to scratch himself away completely; this may be the only way he can stop his itching. His whole body (which is also his ego) may be both completely genitalized and incapable of discharge.[15]

To a body such as this, battle must appear not only as a unique opportunity to discover possible outlets, but also to discover what in the world is wrong with itself: to put an end to its secret. Canetti has written:

> Every secret is explosive, expanding with its own inner heat. . . .
> It does not so much matter *what* happens, as long as it happens
> with the fiery suddenness of a volcano, unexpected and
> irresistible.[16]

The same "irresistible" advance toward eruption, toward confrontation
with the enemy, and thus self-recognition (since the enemy is the soldier's mir-
ror-image), was crucial to Jünger's fantasy of the moment of battle. But a terrible recognition dawned on the pale faces he saw in the morning mist, in the
sunlight; the recognition that he had failed, as ever, to expose the secret.

This man's body remains locked from itself, a terrible secret.

The Soldierly Body, the Technological Machine, and the Fascist Aesthetic

> Our generation is the first to begin to reconcile itself to the
> machine; to perceive it as containing not utility but beauty.[1]

Jünger's use of antithesis is deceptive; for he himself desires to make use
of the machine—though his purpose is not the more usual one of production.
For him the "beauty" of the machine resides in its potential to be used to
resolve the problems of his body:

> . . . if we are to transform the flashing thunderbolts of the blood
> into conscious, logical achievements, we must imbue the machine
> with our own inner qualities; but we require distance, and
> ice-clear thinking.[2]

Jünger calls on the machine to take over from the body, to perform functions for which the body is inadequate: to function frictionlessly, quickly, pow-
erfully, brilliantly, expressively—perfectly—and to remain whole despite
internal explosions.

Jünger's program for the machine is finely detailed; he demands that it
supply him with the quantum of pleasure he considers impossible to attain by
other means:

> Yes, the machine is beautiful; its beauty is self-evident to anyone
> who loves life in all its fullness and power. Nietzsche might well
> have been writing of the machine (though it did not yet have a
> place in his Renaissance landscape) when he argued that life was
> more than Darwin's wretched struggle for existence, but a will to
> higher and deeper goals. The machine must be made more than a
> mere means of production to satisfy our pitiful basic needs; it
> should provide us with a higher and deeper satisfaction. When it
> begins to do so, many a question will be resolved; the creative

artist will suddenly perceive the machine not as a pragmatic collection of iron parts but as totality; and the strategist will be released from the spell of the war of production. These men will be as active as any technician or socialist in this process of solution.[3]

The "totality" perceived by Jünger in machines remains thoroughly meaningless unless it is understood as a category of his own physical need. He unceremoniously dismisses human desiring-production as a source of satisfaction and replaces it with the machine—which he wants for its capacity to produce the precise opposite of the desiring-machines described by Deleuze and Guattari. He too, however, describes something that can be called desiring-production, though it is a desiring-production that needs conditions he himself defines. The opposition his work sets up between desiring-machines and totality-machines reproduces that between the molecular and molar structures of mass organizations discussed in the previous chapter.

The desiring-machine of the unconscious is a molecular mass entity composed of organ-machines, well-sprung machines, energy-machines, coupled to partial objects, remnants of this and building-blocks of that; it is pure multiplicity, incapable of agglomeration, but capable of entering every possible association, producing any pleasure. The technological machine, by contrast, is a molar construction, whose individual components occupy and fulfill prescribed positions and specific functions. Since this machine can be conceived as a hierarchically organized unity, I have called it a totality-machine; a machine that is exemplary in the way it maintains the desire for a specifically constructed individual body. Within the machine "instinctual life" is controlled and transformed into a dynamic of regularized functions; it is devoid of feeling, powerful; its desiring-intensities take the form of the "velocity" of "explosion."

The human multiplicity-machine functions by manufacturing an infinity of new associations; it is always in search of accessible connections, open pathways, unforeseen spaces, powerful flows. It couples, it uncouples; each component is functionally independent; it may function here, or it may function elsewhere.

Components within the human totality-machine are hierarchized, functionalized, individual; the machine connections are standardized and unified, it flows liberated only if individual components overwhelm and explode. This machine is propelled by an engine that kicks, sparks, blacks out—motor charged . . . kick, spark, black out . . . and so on.

The multiplicity swarms outward "schizophrenically."

Totality is "paranoid" persecution, encirclement, bounding.

The machinery of war stretches every totality-machine to the limits of its capacity; day by day, war holds the promise of massive velocities, explosions without number—the promise of consummate pleasure for the totality component. The peacetime machine, by contrast, delivers no more than meager quantities of the intense pleasure of domination. Only the machinery of war allows the component to transcend its own self while remaining whole; only war produces sufficient quantities of internal explosions.

It can, of course, be demonstrated that even "peacetime" machines serve the same purpose for Jünger; he finds even "civilian" machines exhilarating:

> From time to time we sensed it, as we watched an express train thundering at lightning speed across the countryside, a race-car shooting into its lane from a banked curve, or screeching birds wheeling above our cities. Standing in great glass-roofed halls, amid pistons and gleaming flywheels, where the mercury columns of manometers rose and fell, the red dials of dynamometers quivered against the white marble of wall panels; we sensed that some surplus lived and breathed there, a luxury, an excess of energy, a will to transform all of life into energy.[4]

His life.

In Jünger's vision, the specific capabilities of the machine and the human being are inverted, and both are violated in the process. If used meaningfully, the machine, the means of production, could prove capable of improving the human condition to a point at which human beings became flesh and discarded the muscle-armor they acquired in their struggle for survival. But here, the machine is reduced to the level of a vehicle of expression for carnal desire; the human being meanwhile, producer of desire, is transformed into a muscle-machine that prohibits and persecutes the production of desire. While, on the one hand, the natural machinery of the human unconscious is abandoned, and the periphery of the human being artificially mechanized, the machine, on the other hand, abandons its natural element of production and is artificially anthropomorphized. The multiplicity of human desiring-machines is unified in the figure of the soldier male, who becomes a machine for the persecution of pleasure.

At the same time, the unity and simplicity of the object-producing machine is dissolved; the machine becomes an expressive multiplicity of semi-human aesthetic forms. Thus the human being becomes an imperfect machine, and the machine an imperfect human being, neither any longer capable of producing, only of expressing and propagating the horrors they have suffered. Perversely distorted, both now become destroyers; and real human beings, and real machines, are the victims of their mutual inversion. The expression-machine airplane drops bombs on production machines, as the mechanized bodies of soldier males annihilate bodies of flesh and blood. The libido of such men is mechanized and their flesh is dehumanized through mechanization.

From this starting point, it becomes possible to reassess and, in certain aspects, to modify one well-known passage from Benjamin's preface to his "The Work of Art in the Age of Mechanical Reproduction," in which he writes:

> All efforts to render politics aesthetic culminate in one thing: war. War and war only can set a goal for mass movements on the largest scale while respecting the traditional property system. This is the political formula for the situation. The technological formula may be stated as follows: Only war makes it possible to mobilize all of today's technical resources while maintaining the property system.[5]

What is said here of war is indisputable; there is ample evidence to support it. It is also quite correct to describe the process Benjamin terms "render[ing] politics aesthetic" as crucial to the political work of fascism. But his terminology seems to me lacking in plausibility. Benjamin's aim was to outline a formula for the "politicization of art"; the notion of an "aestheticization of politics" seems to me to have arisen more from an inversion of this original concept than from any attempt to define the activity of fascism.

Particularly dubious is the connection Benjamin makes between activity and attempts to maintain "the property system." The desire of fascists—fascist writers in particular—to "mobilize all of today's technical resources," cannot simply be traced to a wish to "maintain property relations." The fascists were out to strip "the Jewry" of property and life, to "imprint their stamp" on the face of the world; to distance themselves from castration by molding themselves as elements in monstrous blocks. Motives such as these are not equatable with the capitalist's desire to retain what he possesses. Certainly, capitalist interests can be seen to coincide to an extent with those of fascists—but they are not the same.

The fascist does not seek war as a means of maintaining property relations. What he demands is a war in which all machines are mobilized, a war in which he experiences the whole of his being and his future potential. In and across the machines with which he sets off to war, the man consolidates his existence as man; it may be in war that he becomes a man in the first place.[6] His desire speaks a language whose terms are defined not by concepts from the realm of political economy but by the bodily conditions of the soldier male. The passage from Benjamin might thus be rewritten as follows:

War and war only can set a goal for mass movements on the largest scale while respecting their molar, antirevolutionary character. This is the political formula for the situation. The technological formula may be stated as follows: War alone can mobilize all of today's technical resources while simultaneously preventing the humane deployment of the masses. For the property system, the formula might be: Only war makes it possible to set property massively in motion, to dispossess while maintaining traditional relations of ownership.

And, finally, in respect of libidinal economy: Only war makes it possible to mobilize all human psychic forces while maintaining existing types of human beings.

But even this version is relatively unsatisfactory. The problem seems to me to be the phrase "while maintaining." Even in the context of property relations the status quo is maintained only in respect of private ownership of the means of production. In all the other cases cited, what we witness is a process of transformation. What is transformed is the potential of human masses for living production; what is produced in each case is a process that is openly destructive of such production. Politics is not merely rendered "aesthetic"; more concretely and comprehensively, we can describe the process as one in which production and use are supplanted by the public display of destruction.

From our contemporary standpoint, it is possible to identify precisely what it was that was transformed (as opposed to "maintained") by the specific activity of fascism. The publicly destructive acts of molar masses take effect today in the transmuted form of a general fear of mass formation: the opposition has been resurrected and reinforced between ego and mass. In displaying the destructive potential of technology, war has transformed pleasure in technology into fear; it has further deepened the opposition between humanity and machinery. Savage and predatory expropriation has transformed pleasure in common property into repeated demands for the protection of private property. It has made ownership the touchstone of survival. And public demonstrations of false liberation, liberation through destruction, have turned pleasure in liberation into a fear of the human capacity for inhumanity. This in turn has reaffirmed the opposition between order and anarchy; the struggle for order is a battle waged against our own unconscious.

These are the negative transformations to which fascism has subjected humanity; and the attitude they most persistently foster is one of resignation: a fear of change.

Today, as ever, domination is perceived as an essential means of protection against "liberation" — for liberation is feared as a pathway to death.

In aesthetic terms, the fascist mode of reality production can best be described as a violation of material. To compress human beings into blocks is to violate them: Equally, it is a violation to mobilize technological machines — technical appliances that make our lives easier — to produce engines of destruction. Fascism never expropriates the owners of the means of production; it subjugates peoples — Jews, little people, arbitrary victims. The only thing it "liberates" is perverted desire — which it then turns loose on human beings.

The social strata most likely to produce violators of material are those whose members are denied access to the "proper" productive use of new materials. The material form against which their actions are primarily directed is the human body; a body socially excluded from the production or experience of historically available intensities and quantities of pleasure. The more absolutely the body armor is mechanized, the more its product becomes not the multiplicity of reality but an *expression* of being, the more likely it is to connect into machinery as obstruction, expression, and display, rather than machinery as means of production. The body is then fantasized as coupled not to freight aircraft—since these are not so much expressive as useful—nor to machines for aircraft construction, but to fighter aircraft as destructive display machines.

There are many moments in European history in which the technization of the body can be identified as the characteristic response of human beings denied access to sophisticated technology of the production and war technology of more powerful strata.

Such was the response of the knights, for example, to the triumphal march of the allied forces of feudalist central powers and merchant capital across the populated world. Faced with the advance of the cannon and the gun, the knights began to subject their bodies to intense physical training: suits of armor too were extended and reinforced, to produce a totality mechanization of the body. As Lippe points out, it was with the invention of the cannon that military drill came into being—at the very moment when it might have been considered historically obsolete.[7]

The cannon barrel that appears as a thick iron mantle around the body of the knight is a parody of progress. The burden of "rendering himself aesthetic" was certainly a heavy one for the knight to carry, but at least there could now be no question that he was a good soldier.

In the knight's case, then, the material of production is wrongly identified. He "mistakenly" responds to the new (cannons, guns, the greater mobility of unarmored troops) by reinforcing the old (his suit of armor), as if he hoped to make the new serve the purposes of the old. What he produces in the process is a monstrosity that expends every ounce of its energy in maintaining the appearance of invulnerability.

Arguably, it may be the case that the technicization of the body in *any* given epoch through the (differential) application of advanced productive technologies brings about the enlargement or transformation of the body armor of members of specific strata.

The alchemists' response to attempts by dominant groups to wrest wealth from the earth's body, in the form of gold and other mineral resources, was, for example, to look for their own form of "gold" as refined affect internally. They themselves owned neither ships nor mines; this, perhaps, was the principal motive for their endeavors. The rich resources they unearthed took the form of an abundance of words on inner states of existence; their particular form of body armor consisted perhaps in letters of the alphabet. Early inhabitants of the Gutenberg galaxy . . . Frieda Grafe writes of ideas, not as being

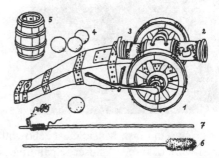

incorporated into the body, but springing from it. The state of the fascist male body is the source of a particular relationship between the artist and his material. The fascist artist models the entirety of his material on a mistaken "model" object—his own mechanized musculature. His choice of material is always false and thus persistently destructive.

He makes whole novels of a single word that never passes his lips.

He writes incessantly of himself, if possible without once saying "I."

Where knowledge fails him, we meet him as a teacher; he writes his stories as propaganda speeches.

He solves the problems of the world in twelve lines of poetry.

He does not see when he sees; he sees through . . .

Architecture, rectangular stone, are expressions of the requirement that

Designed by Albert Speer, first architect of the Reich.

his prick stand fast. Music must echo with the tramping of hobnail boots. The brushwork of fascist landscape painting works on the principle of the farmer's art: furrows neatly plowed.

Conversations take place in books, never on radio (and never live, via the direct broadcast medium of television).

The fascist's song is a response to his urge to scream. He prescribes major chords to keep his children healthy. He orders musicians to be doctors; he offers blood where milk is lacking; police where there is no freedom. And all of this with the best of intentions.

His anger is equally well intentioned. His own wounds torment him; he wants everything to be made right, all others right and whole.[8]

Ceaseless work is his principal failing. He seeks rest, but how does he seek it? Restlessly. He never lies down; he tries to progress by standing rigid, marking time.

He preserves by destroying. As a conservative, he's revolutionary.

He comes visiting with the army. Hitler learned the way of the world by

"Pearl Harbor." Japanese poster (1941).

"North Sea," by Michael Mathias Kiefer (ca. 1933).

staying at home and driving the greater proportion of Germans outward. But their reports and films infuriated him; he found them full of errors.

Satisfaction? Never. Every object resists becoming what the fascist wants to make of it.

Only when destruction is absolute is he reasonably secure that nothing remains to ruffle him. To gain knowledge of the world without shifting from his own position, he organizes it to appear absolutely uniform—which is to say, dead.

Now he can breathe a momentary sigh of relief: there's nothing in sight that might desire to penetrate him. Heil! . . . And now he turns on the radio: *Twilight of the Gods*. *Liebestod*. Eyes closed.

THE EGO OF THE SOLDIER MALE

Fragmented Armor

The picture Jünger paints of the mechanized body is more evocative than descriptive; his more extreme depictions of the "figure of steel" (*Stahlgestalt*) are never descriptions of actual soldiers. The steel figure is the soldier's utopia, a vision more general than Jünger's alone. It represents the man the soldier wished and was expected to be—though, in actuality, he barely approximated it.

This point is *crucial* for the phenomena of the White Terror. Had the soldier actually functioned as Jünger imagined, he would have devised at least some semblance of satisfaction from speed, explosion, blood-flow, and blackout in military action—even if the price of satisfaction was continual increase in the dosage. But human beings are only human; and the real body armor of these men was considerably more fragile. Precious few reached the level of "polished artwork"; most remained the fragments the drill had made them. And since armor had chinks and unevenesses, their "ego" must accordingly have remained fragmentary, prone to rapid fragmentation in situations of intense emotional pressure. To remain more or less fortified totality, the very minimum they required was the totality-armor of the troop formation:

> A man whose inner value is not absolutely above question must learn to obey to the point of idiocy, so that even in the most terrible moments, his instincts can be subdued by the strong arm of a spiritual leader (*Führer*).[1]

For Jünger to say this is interesting. For him, the value of a man was measured by his ability to "subdue . . . instincts" with his durable body armor; and he seems to doubt that the average soldier possessed such ability. His vision of a "steel figure" represented the possibility of guaranteed emotional control: in its most extreme form, it was devoid of all feelings. The figure of steel only occasionally and temporarily fragmented in blackout; but if a man's armor were itself fragmentary, it was likely to break apart much sooner, in the face of lesser external danger and less intense emotional pressures. In this context, as the affective intensity of any situation increased, external armor— the troop as totality-ego—assumed corresponding significance. Certain complaints of the troop-machine were held in place only by external pressure; and the consequences of their detachment being disbanded, of their unit (their substitute skin) being dispersed, were unimaginable. Rather, they do not have to be imagined, since we know what really became of these men. They went flying across the landscape like shrapnel from a machine blown apart at the seams, ripping to pieces whatever they encountered. This was the scenario of the civil war, where the "fronts" had collapsed and the armor of the white troops dissolved to form tiny, isolated, uncontrolled groups with no "ego" or "superego," spinning fragments whose chaoticized "id" sought escape in savage torrents.

(Released from the troop detachment and from themselves, the soldiers now beat and shot to death *whatever* they met in their vicinity, enemy and nonenemy): it was as if they were out to recapture the id, subject it anew to their own coercive totality:

> Luckily for us foreigners, it was Bavarian soldiers who initiated one very unfortunate incident, in which twenty tailor's apprentices and an innkeeper were beaten to death in the blind rage of an

anti-Spartacist mission. We might otherwise have witnessed a pogrom against us "filthy Prussians" (*die Preissen*).[2]

The site of this "unfortunate incident" is Munich; the man counting his lucky stars is Rudolf Mann of the "filthy Prussian" Ehrhardt Brigade. Munich again, in 1919:

> The embittered troops forced one of the captured civilians, one not entirely above suspicion, to stand before them with his hands up for protection—the man advanced a few steps, then the Spartacists struck him to the ground, where he lay apparently dead.[3]

The man is "apparently" dead—the text gives no further account of him. Just another civilian (they were never entirely "above suspicion") used as a decoy, a victim of Spartacist bullets. The troops were "embittered"; this was reason enough.

"We were all so happy when you came, and now look what you've done!"[4] This complaint from the wife of Meis the grocer refers to the murder of her husband and seventeen unarmed canal workers, most of them from southern Germany, in Hamm-Bossendorf, on April 1, 1920, by soldiers of the Faupel Brigade. The soldiers had moved into the area a day earlier and had found the grocer awaiting the conclusion of the Bielefeld Agreement, which granted a truce to the defeated workers. Having marched for many days with no news of anything but "red atrocities," the soldiers, under half-explicit, half-implicit orders to take no prisoners, moved in for what was clearly an illegal attack. They advanced in a loose formation that threatened to dissolve at any moment into attack.[5] The situation held a special intensity: the "object" they were to encounter was unlikely to put up any significant struggle. In the certainty of impending victory, of successful revenge for the defeats of the previous fortnight, and liberated from all other controlling armor, the men discarded a body-ego that might still have *wanted* to distinguish between friend and foe; or, rather, the ego crumbled of its own accord at the sight of a living life before which for once they did not have to flee since they had *already* dissolved and were beside themselves, poised to re-establish order in anything that moved. In the blood bath ("without skin") through which they now stumbled toward their goal, new boundaries grew around them. In his lethal penetration of other human beings, the solder male "distances" himself, "differentiates" himself in opposition to them, and thus once again escapes death by apportioning it to others. His power is so extensive that he is permitted, even expected to make "mistakes" in choosing victims . . .

Following the attack, the totality-machine of the troop is able to stand against as *one* man, obedient to the word of the leader: "In those wild and disordered times, the doors to the dark chasms of human instinctual life still opened occasionally, defying the iron bolts of strict military discipline."[6]

Rudolf Mann discreetly and hypocritically fails to mention that this occasional opening of doors was quite deliberate, that the officers themselves made sure that it occurred, that it was indeed on such occasional infringements that "normal" military discipline was founded.

If the machine does not drink in blood from time to time it creaks, grinds, and becomes defective. This is doubtless why punishments exacted by one cadet or barrack-room soldier on another were tolerated: a little blood had always to be bubbling somewhere, someone had to have their boundaries torn open, if the wheels were to shift into place and turn, now eased by a little lubrication.[7]

After the blood bath is over and thirst is quenched; when peace is restored; when the man feels content in the knowledge that every limb is in its place; he transforms himself with relative rapidity into the unfeeling but satisfied pig he once was, a man who knows that life costs money. Erhard Lucas:

> The corpses were picked clean by the murderers. The soldiers
> took several thousand marks (the canal workers had just been
> paid) as well as watches and rings. They told the villagers quite
> openly, "We can use this stuff . . . this'll be worth something."
> They even removed clothing and shoes from some of the bodies.
> The first witness was Wilhelm Dann, one of the wounded. Having
> recovered consciousness, he watched an officer "at work." The
> officer noticed that the man he had believed dead was moving
> and—however difficult this may be to believe—he asked him if he
> was carrying any money. Dann replied that his older brother, one
> of the men shot and killed, had his wages in his pocket. The
> officer had Dann point out the corpse, removed the wallet from
> the coat, "generously" withdrew a 20-mark note, gave it to
> Dann, telling him he ought to go to a hospital and get himself
> patched up, then put the wallet in his own pocket.[8]

I think the story can be believed.

The officer had become "approachable" again. Or simply "another person" than before. What seems to me absolutely clear from Lucas's description is that most of these soldiers were likely to behave ("quite openly") as if they themselves, the men now picking over the corpses for items of value, were not the men who had murdered them.

The soldiers were not always "half-drunk with exhilaration" in the moment of attack. There was sometimes an element of planning in their actions; in house searches, for example, or when they inspected the naked shoulders of workers suspected of having fought in the Red Army, looking for the marks of rifle straps and beating them to death if they found any.[9]

In the next section I intend to examine how it is possible that the soldier male's ego may switch so abruptly between a fragmented and a relatively

A. Fulneczek being led away by a member of the *Freikorps*; he was executed 23 February 1919 in Bottrop.

stable state, between bouts of bloodthirstiness and the scantest ability to take stock of reality.

The Ego and Maintenance Mechanisms

Although I have not so far used the term "maintenance mechanisms," I believe I have described a number of such mechanisms in the course of this work, in tracing the breakdown and resurrection of the "ego" of the murdering soldier male in military action.

The term "maintenance mechanisms" was coined by Margaret Mahler;[1] she introduced it to designate the aggressive behavior of psychotic children. In light of the total breakdown of all "ego functions" in aggressive acts she felt the notion of "defense mechanisms" to be particularly inadequate; she considered it inappropriate, as was all Oedipal terminology, to describe psychic processes in such children. Thus in her book *Symbiosis and Individuation*, the concept of the "superego," for example, is never once mentioned.

(I outlined my own reasons for assuming it to be similarly difficult to conceptualize the behavior of the soldier male in Oedipal terms at the end of Chapter 1 of Volume 1.)

In what follows, I shall be attempting to reconstruct Mahler's own usage of "maintenance mechanism"; this is more than simply a random enterprise. At numerous points during these investigations, it has become apparent that certain crucial phenomena of the fascist male are barely comprehensible in psychoanalytic terms; at best they can be labeled "psychotic."

Another man, unidentified, being led to execution by the *Freikorps* (Berlin, March 1919).

First, there seems to be a remarkable symmetry between terminology developed by Mahler in her work with "psychotic" children and a large number of the features of the psycho-physical construction of the soldier male: the terminology seems almost to have been developed to describe *his* behavior. I consider this nothing less than a coincidence. Mahler applies the term "psychotic" to children who live in constant danger and fear of intrusive, unpleasurable, symbiotic states from which they have never successfully been extricated.[2] Although I am not suggesting this constitutes any such thing as "predisposition" to "fascist" behavior, I do suspect that such children have little choice, under the conditions of a particular upbringing, but to become "fascist," or what clinical psychiatrists would call manifestly insane. It is perhaps justified to be distrustful of such considerations, but I think they become acceptable if we abandon the concept of "psychosis"—which is in any case deployed far too globally (often in a merely pejorative sense and rarely in a descriptive one) in traditional psychoanalysis, not to mention psychiatry.[3]

Mahler's work seems to point to the term "symbiotic" as one alternative to the notion of the psychotic type. Certainly the term would accurately reflect the principal deficiency in individuals who have never attained the security of body boundaries libidinally invested from within. But this still seems to me too clinical. I would propose a simpler description, which encompasses the various different forms of this type, without restricting them to any single def-

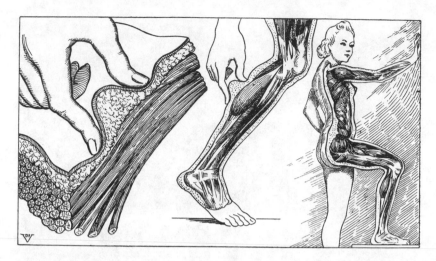

From *Plantas Medicinales*, a Spanish medical text for lay readers by Dr. Vander (Madrid, 1946).

initional tendency. My suggestion is that they be described as human beings born in a state of incompletion, or as human beings who are not-yet-fully-born.

What I would describe as "full" birth is a state Mahler calls "individuation." With individuation, the child extricates itself from the symbiosis which invariably structures its first year of life and differentiates itself from the mother and others by pleasurably cathecting its own periphery; it thereby consolidates the sense of a self different from the mother and others. The process can be successful only if the child receives loving attention from an external source;[4] the child must also learn to recognize itself in the mirror as "object," to accept that status without fear of, or longing for, re-engulfment, and to speak of all this in a language of its own.[5] This "extra-uterine birth" is seen by Mahler as taking approximately two-and-a-half years. By the end of the process, the child has certainly become "I"—but has not necessarily acquired the psychic agency known since Freud as the "ego," for the "ego" arises through identifications within Oedipus. Indeed the child does not necessarily aspire to the future possession of an ego as a means of becoming "I."

But even this stage seems never to have been reached by the men described in this study. I first attempted to specify the reasons why at the end of Chapter 2, Volume 1, when I pointed to the damming in and negativization of the men's bodily flows, to the expulsion of all pleasurable sensation from their body surface, from a skin gripped by hard and stringent hands: to the pain they have experienced in physical punishment and finally to their possible inundation as children by a mother's intermittent or sometimes constant and intense emotional stimulation. Incapable of working over (*verarbeiten*) their fear of the "devouring" mother, they seem to have escaped "inward," fleeing from the mother in the same way they have fled from pain.

By the end of their "first stage" of socialization, these men still lack any secure sense of external boundaries: in Freudian terms, they lack the psychic agency of the "ego."

The "second stage" of socialization is what, in the widest sense, I have called the "drill," and, as we have seen, the drill did impose a sense of boundaries on these men. What remains to be seen is whether the drill created anything potentially comparable to the psychic agency of the "ego." More generally, we need to establish how a psychic type capable of social functioning emerged from a type that was clinically symbiotic.

My suspicion is that only a handful of men in Wilhelmine Germany had the good fortune to be in some sense fully born—and not very many more in the rest of Europe. This seems to be borne out by the numerous parallels I have been able to trace between the behavior of the soldier males and that of the "average man." What I am suggesting, in other words, is that a psychic type whose basic structure was more or less "psychotic" may have been the norm in Germany (at the very time when Freud was writing), and that this type was far more "normal" and more common than Oedipus, for example. Oedipus seems likely to have been a highly unusual specimen: a fictional non-fascist citizen modeled on Freud himself (whose belief in himself was unshakeable).

The Oedipal route traced by Freud was the one he himself had traveled, from renunciation of the mother to "transcendence" of the father. The not-fully-born, by contrast, pays little heed to the father. The father's existence revolves around his role as the agent of socially defined power within the family, a role that diminishes as the child comes to discover his actual powerlessness. But his position bears no relation to the psychic need of the not-yet-fully-born child, for whom the father is more or less nonexistent. What this child seeks (its whole life long, if need be) is unification with maternal bodies, within which it can become "whole," born to completion. The child and the bodies themselves become progressively larger; the child's lack of boundaries allows it to fantasize itself as coupled with even the most massive of quantities. It calls upon larger bodies to nourish it and give it shelter. In this sense, rather than because of any supposed relation to the real mother, it seems legitimate to refer to those bodies as "maternal." Earlier in this volume, I described the impulse toward fusion as a key dynamic of fascist organization formation and fascist propaganda; it now seems that the source of this impulse may be the inexhaustible need of this psychic type for the missing half without which it cannot *be*: the half from which the not-yet-fully-born was once prematurely released, incomplete and violated, to "live" with open wounds. From this, the relationship with the missing half is marked by revenge, which, as we have seen, cannot fail to transform the artificial and violent symbiosis

Mary Miles Minter, Hollywood star, who was barred from films after a series of alcohol and love scandals, which ended tragically.

Sand sculpture on a beach in Monterey, California, photographed by Hedrick (23 August 1917).

that is to follow into a relationship of domination. None of this has anything to do with *regression*—a point that will be returned to as we pursue Mahler's arguments.

Even Freud accepted that the "ego" is "first and foremost a body-ego."[6]

> The ego is ultimately derived from bodily sensations, chiefly from those springing from the surface of the body. It may thus be regarded as a mental projection of the surface of the body, besides . . . representing the superficies of the mental apparatus.

Strangely enough, it is only in the English edition that this passage from *The Ego and the Id* reads as above.[7] In the German version, greater emphasis is placed on the ego ("a mental projection of the surface of the body") as psychic agency. (Might this be a concession to German anti-materialism?)

Mahler's point of departure is certainly Freud's earlier position, which does not yet represent the ego as psychic agency. When she talks of the "ego," it is to the body-ego that she refers. The body-ego arises through the "progressive displacement of libido . . . from the inside of the body (in particular from the abdominal organs) to the periphery of the body"; it emerges in response to pleasurable stimuli from an external source.[8]

> *Pari passu*, and in accordance with the pleasure-pain sequences, demarcation of representations of the body-ego within the symbiotic matrix takes place.[9]

The process of *becoming* "I" involves the child developing a sense of having a body of its own, of having ceased to be the maternal body. Mahler uses a term from Schilder to describe the idea the body develops of itself: he talks of the "body image" (Schilder's term is *Körperschema*).

> Perception of inner processes, for instance those linked with feeding, contact reception, complemented later by distance perception, form the basis of the mental representations of the body as *body image.*[*] All this constitutes *the core* of the idea of *I*
> . . .[10]

The predominant sensations experienced by the body's periphery may, however, also be unpleasurable. In this case, neither the "body-ego" nor any "idea" of the body can be formed. Mahler speaks of "delibidinization of the body image (especially its boundaries)."[11]

The interior of the body now becomes a site of ferocious emotional upheaval. Melanie Klein, discussing the same phenomena, describes feelings of unpleasure across the body's periphery, lack of affection etc., as obstacles to the formation of the internal "good object," the child's introjection of the

---

*The "body image" is not synonymous with the body as object, since it may include anything from clothing to limbs which have been amputated (Mahler, p. 40).

nourishing breast of the mother. What is introjected instead is the "bad" half of the breast—the mother's absence, or what that absence palpably conveys of her antipathy to the child. The child has no means of either integrating or discharging the affects it now experiences; thus the evil mother becomes lodged in the child's interior.[12] Mahler writes of:

> total introjection of the mother and withdrawal of libido from her and the rest of the object world.
>
> The result is a narcissistic state, in which the ego becomes fragmented and the self-boundaries blurred, fused with the mother's.
>
> The most essential failure of the fragmented ego pertains to the overall mechanisms of integration and synthesis of inside with outside stimuli.[13]

This point is crucial: for the absolute lack of any "binding" of the libido to the body's periphery, and thus to the avenues it opens to discharge, subjects the organism both internally and externally to a perpetual excess of stimulation. In a step that runs parallel to the investment of the body's periphery, there occurs "the ejection, by projection, of destructive unneutralized aggressive energy beyond the body-self boundaries."[14] In these children, by contrast, that step is never reached.

> Owing to the inability of the utterly brittle, vulnerable ego structure that the symbiotic psychotic organization entails, the problems of coping with the inundation of unneutralized instinctual drive from within, as well as with complex traumatic overstimulation from without, continually threaten the child's ego to the breaking (fragmentation) point.[15]

The child, then, is not equipped with the perceptual faculties capable of allowing it to work over (*verarbeiten*) movements external to it: the more intense the movement, the worse it is for the child. Movement penetrates directly into the child, its ego then fragments with extreme rapidity and releases destructive energies.

> With his entire body being suffused with primitive aggression, the fear of exploding and disintegrating into bits seemed his basic fear.[16]

Mahler writes this of a six-year-old patient.

This "basic fear" increases, the more alive, complex, and differentiated any external object appears. What form of defense is therefore possible?

> The fragmented ego cannot cope with changeability and complexities. It cannot integrate and it cannot synthesize. Living

objects are much more changeable, vulnerable, and unpredictable than inanimate objects.[17]

So they are rendered "inanimate":

Their psychotic defense mechanisms aim to dedifferentiate and deanimate inner and outer reality.[18]

Mahler then introduces two new concepts:

The psychotic defense of deanimation, which I also used to call devitalization, aims at rendering those "unpredictable" stimuli less threatening to the fragile ego of the prepsychotic and psychotic child.[19*]

Dedifferentiation is based upon massive denial of percepts . . .[20]

Complex stimuli, particularly those that demand a social-emotional response, are massively denied, autistically hallucinated away, so that repression may not halt before a level of perceptual dedifferentiation is reached at which that primal discrimination between living and inanimate (the *protodikrisis*[**] of von Monakow) is lost.[21]

Devivification and dedifferentiation may be effected in one of two ways. The child may either perform a destructive act that in a very real sense "takes life" as its object and manufactures undifferentiated "unity"; or it may simply perceive what is living as what is dead.

In the process, the child itself becomes "deathlike"; it no longer reacts to stimuli, appears to perceive nothing, remains entirely "wrapped up in itself"; it becomes "autistic." Autism, Mahler writes,

is an attempt at dedifferentiation and deanimation. It may be looked upon as a mechanism by which such patients try to shut out, to hallucinate away, the potential sources of sensory perception, particularly the infinitely variable ones of the *living* world, which demand emotional-social responses.[22]

It is however also directed against "inner" processes.

---

[*] Translator's note: In the German translation of Mahler, "deanimation" is rendered by "Entseelung" in which the reference to the Latin "animus" is replaced by one to "Seele," the soul. Theweleit notes: "Since the term brings intrusive and irrelevant meanings into play, obtrusive meanings which have no relevance here, I have preferred to use the single term 'Entlebendingung' to render both 'deanimation' and 'devitalization.'" In this volume and in Volume I of *Male Fantasies*, "Entlebendingung" has been translated as "devivification."

[**]The term "protodiakrisis" was coined by von Monakow in 1923 to designate primal differentiation. It refers to the primary capacity to differentiate between animate and inanimate matter. From the first day of life, new-born babies carried to full term respond with different grasping reflexes to living partial objects and to inanimate matter (Mahler, p.34).

In the wake of this kind of negative hallucinatory psychotic denial, inner percepts, saturated with aggression, gain ascendancy. Such inner excitations cannot be denied; they force themselves into the sensorium. To cope with these proprioceptive-enteroceptive stimuli the psychotic ego tries to dedifferentiate, to deanimate them.[23]

If I understand Mahler correctly, what she is suggesting is that the child attempts to simulate death—if it fails, it is saturated with aggression. The only emotions that surface are "extreme affects"; they range from "panic" to "orgastic ecstasy" and are interspersed with moments of absolute apathy. As it changes from one state to the other, the disturbed child is described by Mahler as "switching himself, as it were, from one mode of behavior into another."[24]

The goal of the child's attempts at defense is clearly to suppress both external movement and internal feeling; only in this state does its survival appear guaranteed. Mahler terms the child's efforts to achieve its goal "maintenance mechanisms": the term describes the psychotic child's substitute for "object relations" and "defense mechanisms."[25]

These children are incapable of "object relations," since, as we have seen, the libidinal, human object-world slips constantly beyond their grasp. Mahler is even loath to talk in terms of "narcissistic" relations, despite the fact that psychoanalysis commonly defines these in opposition to object relations. The "object" of narcissistic relations is the child's own "ego"—and what evidence of an ego is there here? Mahler's alternative proposal is the following:

> We must broaden and enlarge the concept of "object" as well as that of "relationship," and . . . also that of "defense." In the broadest sense, we may speak of anything as an object which in a field of interaction, physiologically or otherwise, impinges upon the organism, either *in utero* or in extrauterine life, as part of its environment.[26]

And on "defense":

> As this concept is used in analysis, it refers to mechanisms operating against the instinctual drives and their internal representations. However, from what I have previously stated in great detail, it must be clear that neither the instinctual drives themselves, nor the drives and the ego, nor the object and the subject, are differentiated. For this reason, the psychotic "maintenance mechanisms" operate against an undifferentiated "drive-object" which persists far beyond the normal dual-unity stage.[27]

Unification with the "undifferentiated drive objects" is associated with certain perceptions that the child strives continually to reproduce. These perceptions, residues of the original perception of the object of the drives, *have never been repressed*: cathexis has never been withdrawn from them. According to Freud (1915), writes Mahler, "the (different) mechanisms of repression have at least one thing in common: *a withdrawal of the cathexis of energy.*"[28] But this very process has not taken place; what has occurred is what Mahler calls "pseudo-repression." The perceptions toward which the child strives are neither conscious nor repressed; they are perfectly accessible at the right moment. Mahler describes them as retained in "syncretic memory storage," as "engram conglomerates" which are never "forgotten":[29] the child seeks repeatedly to return to the same perceptions via the mechanisms of the "primary process." The primary process (as opposed to the "secondary process," which travels the circuitous route of revision, sublimation, and so on, is identified by the child as the quickest available means of re-establishing earliest stages of infancy.[30] Referring to her patient Stanley, Mahler writes: "(H)is affective reactions were primary process reproductions of early infantile syncretic engram conglomerates, which appeared to be irreversible and irrepressible."[31]

Mahler explicitly stresses that the goal of the primary process may not only be to reproduce a central situation of pleasure from earliest infancy; the child may equally be aiming to reattain a central situation of unpleasure from which it has never fully released itself, and to which it therefore compulsively returns. The perception sought usually combines ("syncretizes") a number of different traumatic processes, which may not originally have taken place simultaneously. Syncretization occurs through what we know as the mechanisms of the primary process: condensation, displacement, substitution, simultaneity, etc.[32]

There seems to me to be a very striking correspondence between what Mahler identifies as features of "psychosis" in children and the behavioral traits of the soldier male as I have attempted to reconstruct them from his writings and actions. I can think of no single psychoanalytical term developed with reference to the psychotic child that could not equally be applied to a behavioral trait of the "fascist" male.

In both, object relations are equally impossible: both are distanced from the libidinal, human object world. Both have an "interior" that is chaoticized, saturated with aggression: both fear that their boundaries will disintegrate on contact with intense external vitality. In both the internal/external distinction is blurred, and in neither are any of the contents associated with the secret object of the drives repressed—viz., the men's hallucinatory perceptions, their object substitutions in the moment before the redemptive act of killing. The notion of unification with the "undifferentiated object of the drives" seems to me the most accurate available description of the mental absences of these men, their "being somewhere quite other," the trance-states which manifest themselves in their acts of aggression.

The bloody miasma, the empty space, the blackout toward which we have seen the soldier male persistently advancing: all of these seem to be best described as perceptual identities established by means of the primary process. We have seen quite clearly that what these perceptual states achieve is more than mere "defense": it is a moment of survival devoid of threat. The elements excluded from the notion of "defense" are precisely captured in the term "maintenance mechanism"; and, unlike "defense," a mechanism regulated by the ego, maintenance does not conflict with the "fragmentation" undergone by the ego in these cases. "Dedifferentiation" and "devivification" have appeared at work time and again in the soldier male: in his incapacity to write of what is alien, indeed to perceive it as a living object in its own right, in his capacity to "grind" it in his brain-mincer into unrecognizable mass, to perceive it as already dead, or to observe it as an object earmarked for death. The act of killing is itself the most absolute form of this dedifferentiation and devivification of living life. It is the core of the white terror, the act by which the soldier male guarantees his own survival, his self-preservation and self-regeneration. And, finally, the soldier male's insatiable need to construct totality-formations whose hierarchical structure offers potential escape from symbiosis, a need manifested in his perpetual efforts at fusion into such totalities, seems to correspond precisely to the need for dual unity identified by Mahler in the child suffering from the symbiotic-psychotic syndrome. The not-yet-fully-born needs a totality within which it can be *dominant*, since, as Mahler indicates, it needs to be able to perceive its opposite as its "functioning on his behalf."[33]

In one significant aspect, the soldier male does deviate clearly from the psychotic child. He is in no sense "autistic"; his struggles do not simply take the form of occasional eruptions, but of a constant struggle "for and on behalf of power." The soldier male's ego is differently constructed: a different reality principle has gained the upper hand within him.[34]

As Margaret Mahler has emphasized,

> We conceptualize the fear of re-engulfment as a dread of dissolution of the self (loss of boundaries) into an aggressively invested dual unity that the child cannot magically control. The subsequent psychotic defensive effort—autism—should thus be thought of as a secondary defense.[35]

If "autism" can be seen as a "secondary defense," then other forms of defense against the fear of reincorporation may conceivably be able to take its place. This, I believe, is precisely the situation in the soldier male.

In preceding sections, I have suggested that the relatively stable ego of the fascist may be, as it were, whipped and thrashed onto him: that the aggression of his various educators makes it impossible for him to become autistic: that every failure on his own part to cathect his periphery internally is accompanied by beatings administered externally.

As far as I can see, this proposition is certainly tenable in theoretical terms. The "ego" these processes seem to produce is admittedly a particularly peculiar formation: it can certainly not be conceived as a psychic agency pertaining to the person. It has, rather, to be understood as a social ego, a muscle-armor that is merely borrowed, painfully drilled into and fused onto the individual. An ego of the kind described seems likely to be incapable of escaping the danger of immediate fragmentation on contact with living life, unless it is inserted into some larger social formation that guarantees and maintains its boundaries. Any social organization, from the family to the army, might fulfill this function, as long as it functions as what I have defined above as a "totality."

If my suggestions are correct, then *whipping* has to be seen to rank alongside toilet-training—the damming in of bodily fluids—as one of the most significant educational processes. What we have seen of the German version of the not-yet-fully-born can be perceived as having been rendered fully operational through *pain*, thrashed into life. (It is a little difficult to play dead in reponse to a beating.)[36]

"Autistic" children, by contrast, seem only rarely to have a history of beatings. All the therapists and doctors I have contacted have confirmed this to be the case, and nothing to the contrary is noted in the literature. Autistic children are generally unplanned and emotionally starved; they are often rejected from birth by the mother and have had either negative or nonexistent early breast and eye contact: or they are children who have been neglected and "left out in the cold" by both parents. They have been deprived of all attention, even in the form of beatings.

One further difference to note is the conspicuous aggression of "autistic" children toward themselves. Mahler writes:

> Most autistic children have a relatively low cathexis of their body surface, which accounts for their grossly deficient pain sensitivity. Along with this cathectic deficiency of the sensorium goes a lack of hierarchic stratification, of zonal libidinization and sequence. This is evident from the relative paucity of autoerotic activities, and the ease with which they substitute one for the other. Instead of autoerotic activities, these children show such aggressive habits as head knocking, self-biting, or other self-hurting, mutilating activities, along with a mixing up of oral, anal, and phallic contents. In fact,these autoaggressive activities seem to serve the purpose of boundary cathexis of a distorted and deranged libido economy, constituting a pathological attempt to *feel alive* and

whole. Autoaggressive manipulations seem to help these children to feel their bodies; some of these activities definitely serve the purpose of sharpening the awareness of the body-self boundaries and the feeling of entity, if not of identity.[37]

Pain, then, is the only solution available to the child to resolve its predicament. If the child is willing to pay the price of self-destruction, it can use pain both to affirm the body boundaries it lacks and to accrue to itself a temporary body-ego. Autistic children often roll on the floor during therapy sessions; this is a milder form of the same affirmation of boundaries.[38] The soldier male, by contrast, has no need to bring his skin into contact with the floor to affirm his boundaries (although Hitler's response to any particularly shattering news was to lie down and roll on the carpet). The soldier carries a boundary with him, in the shape of the uniform, and the belt and crossbelt in particular. His body experiences the constant sensation of something "holding it together." His periphery, formed through external encroachments, appears to me so sharply divided from his "interior" that I am inclined to talk of his body as split into an external muscle-physique and an internal organ-physique. The muscle-physique is identical with what can be referred to as his "ego": it performs all the functions of control and defense against the drives and it is the constant determinant of his conscious thinking, his speech, his writing, his consciousness of himself as "man," his tirelessness on behalf of the "whole." All these appear to me to be functions of body-ego, a musculature originally reinforced through pain, defending itself against fragmentation.[*]

The body-ego is contained in a number of external social or organizational egos; they include various of the formations discussed above: the nation, the troop, the party. The soldier males' ego-functions are disseminated across the whole range of totality-machines within which they function, they are performed in part by the mechanical machineries to which the men "bind" themselves—by guns, for example, in military action. Another organization-ego of this kind is the family-totality, which functions in particular through the figure of the "white wife." She produces order in domestic space and functions as a barrier to ward off sexual danger; she is a subordinate and devivified buttress to the "unity" of the soldier male. He might almost be said to use her as part of his body-armor.

The "ego" described here is unremittingly dependent on external support: if it breaks down, the ego in turn disintegrates. The "maintenance mechanisms" of dedifferentiation and devivification are its only means of rescuing

---

[*]"I was fascinated by Hitler's soft, fleshy back—by the way it was so firmly packed into his uniform. Whenever I set about painting the leather strap running from his belt across his shoulder, the softness of his Hitler-flesh compressed into the jacket of his uniform would transport me into a delicious, nourishing, Wagnerian ecstasy, and my heart would begin to beat wildly." Salvador Dali, whose paintings imprison deliquesence and flow in the "body-ego" of the gilded contour, sharp relief, and glorified perspective. Dali is no more a "surrealist" than Hitler. (Dali, exhibition catalog, Kunsthalle Baden-Baden, 1971, p. 139)

Base for street lamp, designed by Albert Speer (Berlin).

itself from internal or external inundation by living life. The specific form of maintenance practiced by the soldier male will be described in a later section on "three perceptual identities."

Ego-Disintegration and Work

One problem the soldier ego finds particularly difficult to overcome is that of solitude. The moment the soldier is deprived of the support of some external organizational form, disintegration threatens. Disintegration was the threat that loomed, for example, when the army was demobilized in November 1918; it reappears in various accounts of periods of imprisonment, of sleep (dreams), of the isolation of men on the wanted list.

Lieutenant Ehrhardt, who was imprisoned as one of the leaders of the Kapp putsch, was subsequently "liberated"[1] by friends and "went underground." What most afflicted him about his life of illegality, apart from the obligation to feel indebted for every last morsel anyone gave him to eat, was

> the disorder in the natural niceties of clothes and underclothes. Socks and shirts were strewn about all over the place, shoes and suits were never moved once I had discarded them, and, above all, money was hardly easy to come by. Each day held the threat of renewed humiliation. But I kept a grip on myself. Though every evening presented me with some new source of revulsion, I fended off every urge to vomit. Any man who has successfully conquered seasickness must equally remain impervious to the nausea of life. I kept myself from slackening by issuing myself my own orders.[2]

Ehrhardt's struggle against the threat of "slackening" is a leitmotif that runs right through his postbrigade life. He feels his capacity for thought rapidly dissipating; all other mental contents are suppressed by his fear of dirt and his conviction that his persecutors are on his trail;

> I found the leisure hours I spent in coffee houses and bars quite repugnant. The older man who lives a life of this kind—even in moderation—never shakes off the sense of being swamped by dissipation.[3]

This particular "older man" has not yet turned forty: though he has "conquered seasickness," he is not yet fully born. Within a few short months of being separated from the troop, he is already being engulfed in cafés by the swamp, and all this despite the fact—which he considers it necessary to emphasize—that he abstains from alcohol.

Rathenau's murder was planned by Salomon together with Kern and Fischer. Salomon subsequently left. In the following pages, he describes how, alone in Hanover, he learned of the death of the other two. He becomes aware of his isolation and discovers a warrant for his arrest at the station. He wanders through Hanover:

> With a tingling shudder, I felt my limbs turn to glowing coal, my head detaching itself and trundling off on its own dismembered pathway. And it was my head that first came to its senses. Lying on a bench in a bed of cold ice, it awoke to find a policeman bending over it.

The policeman finds nothing untoward about Salomon, whose head he perceives as still attached to his body. Salomon continues on his way:

> I felt the pain gnawing at me in some place I could not identify; the skin it dug into was stiff and numbed as if anaesthetized, so that only my brain was able to suffer in its awareness of my irretrievable loss.[4]

In all Salomon's accounts of his relationship with Kern, the symbiosis between the two men is described as a restorative force[5] (and thus the source of a cathexis of his periphery). That whole symbiosis now breaks down, as does ultimately his "brain," the only remaining function of his body-armor. On the way to Munich by train, he falls unconscious; his temperature rises to a high fever. He describes his nerves when he arrives as "standing on end";[6] he changes his accommodation nightly.

> And so I crashed across the shimmering stones like the waters of the Isar and found myself ultimately at the place where maelstrom meets maelstrom. . . .[7]

He had experienced similar feelings in November 1918, when the world with which he was "entwined sank finally and irretrievably into the dust."[8] On this earlier occasion, he was saved by his resolution to "stand fast, whatever the cost,"[9] and by his entry into the *Freikorps*; at this later stage, his eventual arrest and five years of imprisonment draw "new boundaries" around him.

In war, the threat of disintegration is omnipresent and the formation does indeed disintegrate in periods of *waiting* between battles.

> We were on constant battle alert, always lying in ambush; straining all our senses, anticipating the next murderous encounters, as weeks and months seeped away. From the Alps to the ocean, across fields, woodland, swamps, rivers and peaks, winter and summer, day and night, there stretched a chain of men rigid with tension.[10]

Jünger consistently presents the soldier as caught between the distant threat of the uncanny and the learned securities of military activity.

It is difficult to describe any event of this more fundamental nature and this occasion is no exception. A man approaches and whispers: "Repair gang. Cable shot to pieces." No question: the brain thinks telephone, wires ripped to shreds, connection to command first duty of the troop, yes sir, yes sir. War academy, order of active service: an intimately familiar sequence. Then, suddenly all knowledge becomes ridiculous, inignificant: there begins a dialogue of shadows. Words take on second meanings; they pierce the surface and plunge into depths inaccessible to the understanding. Sensation surges around some other center; we feel our way in twilight.[11]

What Jünger describes here with some precision is what Mahler identifies as the "split of the ego into an intentional part and an experiencing part":[12]

suddenly one turns from a thinking to a feeling being, a ball tossed by phantoms; even the acutest weapon of reason becomes inadequate. Such forces are undependable and would normally be denied; but when they pounce like bats from dark dungeons, denial is fruitless.[13]

In the language of psychoanalysis, with a little less flavor:

The ego then has become the passive victim of the deneutralized, defused drives, particularly of the unmitigated destructive impulses.[14]

Jünger's text clearly does not refer to war (a fact which has hitherto been ignored by criticism). His bats flutter internally. Jünger is *not* a writer of war books.

Almost any fascist text with even minimum pretensions requires the same perception of processes as if "in a dream," the writer's sense of unrealities, the threatening knowledge that the ground on which he moves is unstable.

Escape was impossible from whatever it was that was approaching, feeling its way forward, enveloping me in stifling gloom incomprehensibly, indescribably. Then it was upon me! Overcome by paralyzing fear, a desire to run, felt some weight attach itself to me, a barrier. In swooning submission I tried to confront it directly, but it refused to make itself visible—the intangible!

It approached, inexorable. . . . I felt how it would be to anticipate murder in some dark alleyway, to suffocate slowly in a gully filled with rubble, with the last vestige of my strength, I resisted the ultimate horror: death! "All of this is a dream—only a dream!": the thought rose up as a last hope within me.[15]

And it *is* only a dream, the dream the body-armor dreams. These are moments of fragility, when the "inner dungeon" and its inhabitants surface. The same moments return in sleep. Hardly has the armor relaxed its tension than it is seized by the dream. Salomon gives the following account of a dream:

> I suddenly found myself having to escape from a confined space, pursued by some tentacled creature that continually dissipated into vague and shadowy forms. The only exit led down a steep and winding stairwell to bottomless depths. But the creature was faster than I was, I could still see its tentacles clutching at me; I extended failing legs into the darkness . . .

In his dream, he remembers "with blissful excitement" that he can fly, and he flies, always slightly above the creature from which the threat emanates—and once "over the heads of the enemies into which the figure of the demon had transformed itself," then across water:

> As I crossed the dark sea, I saw the demon in the shape of some gruesome polyp moving through the water's depths and *watching* me from a round eye that goggled mockingly from the center of its spongy stomach.* Though I was moving at some considerable height, my feet were still sodden from flailing across lashing water, and I felt the flesh on my limbs drawing in the liquid that still dragged me downward.[16]

The extreme concreteness of Salomon's description seems to me to suggest that the body-armor had become extremely well molded and functionalized; it seems unlikely to fragment in the face of minor threats such as these. Saturation by the "dragging liquid" of his interior does not immediately drown him; he does not feel the river's waves crashing above him. For the same reason, perhaps Salomon, like Jünger, seems able to use *writing* to gain stability. In both authors, the threshold of collapse is raised ever higher so that when collapse eventually comes, it is described with more than usual intensity. By contrast, in texts by such comparatively ineffectual authors as Goote, it is left to the reader to imagine collapse in the numerous spaces between hyphens. Goote "invokes" the horror from extreme distance; he dares not approach too close; this is perhaps why Goote, like the majority of fascist authors, appears particularly tedious to the critical reader.

When Rudolf Höss was imprisoned for his part in a *Vehme* murder, he developed what the prison doctor called "prison psychosis":[17]

---

*My emphasis.

I paced back and forth in my cell like a wild animal. Sleep now evaded me though I had always slept deeply and almost without dreaming the whole night through.

Höss then reports "confused anxiety dreams":

Chaotic dreams in which I was constantly being followed, or set upon, or falling into some abyss. The nights were pure agony. I heard the clock in the clocktower strike every passing hour. The closer it came to morning, the more I dreaded the day and the company it would bring—men I wished never to set eyes on again. I failed in every attempt to pull myself together; I could not fight it. I wanted to pray, but could summon only a feeble and fearful stammering, I had lost the ability to pray, and with it the pathway to God.[18]

And this was a man whose desired profession had been the priesthood. In prison, he becomes bitterly self-recriminatory; his whole past returns, approaching ever closer:

My inner agitation grew daily, indeed hourly. Something approaching frenzy threatened to take hold of me. I went into increasing physical decline.[19]

He begins to hallucinate, and returns to a state of parental symbiosis.

Can it be possible to communicate with the departed? Often, in the hours of my greatest agitation, in the moments before my mind was invaded by chaos, my parents would appear to me in flesh-and-blood, I would see them and speak to them as if they were still my guardians. I still find it impossible today to think clearly about these things; and after all these years, I have still spoken of them to no one.[20]

I had plunged to the very depths, to the verge of breakdown, but from that point on, my life here in prison continued with no particular difficulty. I settled down to a more balanced existence.[21]

Höss takes refuge in "work"; but still any reminder of the "low point" he once reached has what he describes as a "whip-like" effect on him.[22]

What happens here to Höss? I believe that what he acquires is a "substitute" ego; he makes the transition from the machinery of the troop to that of the prison and is rebuilt as a functioning component within a new totality-machine (in his later capacity as commandant of Auschwitz, his greatest concern was that the camp should run smoothly and that each individual should perform the tasks allotted to them). As his old ego, the soldier-ego, crumbles and eventually perishes, he inevitably returns to the symbiotic situation. A new

"And if the world were full of devils! . . ."

form of the ego then becomes visible in his unreserved affirmation of the daily round of prison life. This capacity to disintegrate and then re-emerge equipped with a new "ego" seems to me to be a peculiar characteristic of the not-yet-fully-born; it arises from their dependence on external egos which are first assembled around them, then dismantled, reassembled, and so on. And in the interim they experience breakdown, blackout, coma, they know nothing . . . where am I?

It should also be borne in mind that Höss, unlike Salomon for example, was not a product of the drill machinery. He left home at seventeen and immediately became a soldier. Thus his muscular body-ego is likely to have been significantly less stable, more susceptible of rapid fragmentation during imprisonment, than the body-ego of drill veterans such as Killinger. Having passed through the military academy, war, and the Ehrhardt Brigade, Killinger maintained himself as an upstanding man by putting himself through half an hour of physical training before the official start of his day. The whole process (which he called "milling") involved washing his whole body daily in "ice-cold water,"* chin-ups by clinging to the ledge of a wall only by his finger-tips. [23] He too describes "work" as crucial for his survival.

As he once wrote, having himself been through the experience of prison: "If I were in the shoes of the examining magistrate, I would give these men nothing—no books, no newspapers, no letters, nothing to write or tinker with. These men are hard as glass; they should be given no more than a piece of soap and a towel." [24] And he who admits having stolen only three apples confesses to murder for no other reason than that he desires to be put to "work" as before.

Höss hankers after work primarily as a means of discipline; what he considers important is its capacity to occupy a large part of the day to the full and to impose a certain regularity.

> My essential consideration was to impose strict, but voluntary limits on myself. (. . .) Work saved me from grueling and fruitless brooding.[25] In 1946, from his cell in Cracow, Höss wrote: "What I miss most in my current imprisonment is work. Mercifully, I have applied myself to a writing exercise that I find absolutely and completely fulfilling."[26]

The "writing exercise" Höss refers to is his autobiography, whose existence it can thus be assumed we owe to his fear of reverting to the "low point" at which, in the breakdown of his body-ego, he might potentially have had to re-live Auschwitz "from the inside." The scrupulous detail of the biographical report he wrote for the Polish court seems likely to have had little to do with any hope of milder punishment; more probably, it was a form of request

---

*Jünger's writing days begin with the same immersion in a cold bath. He once referred to this in an interview as "my formula." (Sudwestfunk 3, January 1979)

Vorlage: Hiemers, Münster

Die Zeitschrift der Arbeitsgemeinschaften entlassener Freikorpskämpfer

"The Comrade in Work." / "Hard work—the road we travel/our hope—house and home." From the *Journal of Work Collectives for Retired Freikorps Fighters.*

for mercy, a plea not at any cost to be left alone with ("I will say anything if you only allow me to write—a form of working.")

Writing—and diary writing in particular—appears to perform the same function for many soldier males: this is why we are so richly endowed with fascist biographies. In the evening when their duties are completed, they compress themselves into line upon line of methodical handwriting and compacted syntax; all the elements that threaten to rip their bodies to shreds are restrained through writing.[27] Fountain pen and paper together form a unification-machine whose totality-blocks—rows of lettering and bound pages—are devoted to the preservation of the self in body-armor.* Writing is a means of avoiding both feelings and degeneration. In descriptions of battle, by contrast, blood-ink is allowed to stream forth ecstatically. The crucial feature of the fascist understanding of work seems, then, not to be its ability, as wage labor, to guarantee his material reproduction; instead it is its capacity to keep the man living.[28]

The activity of work screens his ego against fragmentation and collapse and thus also protects it from the onset of devouring symbioses. "Arbeit macht frei" (Work makes free) was the motto that crowned the gates of Auschwitz; and it was meant more or less literally. The phrase was not coined by Höss, but he did appropriately defend it:

> The motto "Arbeit macht frei" should be understood in the sense given to it by Eicke, who resolved to release any internee from no matter what category whose consistent achievement in work raised him *above the mass*,** even in the face of opposition from the Gestapo and Reichskriminal-Polizeiamt (the Headquarters of the Criminal Police).[29]

For Höss, the intentions of such as himself had been benevolent; it was war that had thwarted them. Had he himself been a prisoner, he would have been among those for whom the Auschwitz motto was beneficial; as commandant he certainly derived support from it:

> To fulfill my duties adequately, I had to become the motor that tirelessly and restlessly regenerated impulses to work at building the camp. I had incessantly and repeatedly to drive every inmate onward, to haul SS men and prisoners forward together.[30] I was aware of nothing but my work.[31]

It was a source of pain to Höss that his SS subordinates did not hold the notion of work in sufficiently high regard.

From 1942, the concentration camp increasingly lost meaning for him, as it became no more than a site of destruction. The Hössian labor, his labor, had been one of building and extending the camp. This was how he had been able

---

*The counterpart to blood-ink gushing forth in ecstatic battle descriptions (see pp. 234-35 above).

**My emphasis.

The German dream by a French labor service (1941).

to continue to function. It had, of course, involved imposing a certain number of penalties, torture, and executions. But once these had become the principal purpose of his work, it lost its attraction. Höss had been required to move through the camp as a force of inspiration, intervention, observation, command. He had been secure in the knowledge of his own absolute control, his status as a man respected.[32] He perceived Eichmann's extermination order as a more or less flagrant sabotage of his activities (Eichmann spent his days behind a desk and lacked the unmediated satisfaction of camp labor). Extermination nullified all the efforts Höss had expended to contain the camp inmates within boundaries that can ultimately be equated with the boundaries of his own ego.[33]

The means he had used to subdue them were the same he had employed to imprison his own interior; inmates had been annihilated only if the maintenance of his boundary-order so demanded. By working on the object of his drives, Höss had been able to "stabilize" himself—to escape feeling to a point at which it was no longer necessary to exterminate the securely dammed-in forms of his interior. (What he found most threatening, by contrast, was *escape* from the concentration camp . . . taking flight. . . .)[34]

In the opening sections of Goebbels's *Michael*, "work" similarly appears as a key concept; later, however, it is revealed to be a subordinate form of battle; this, alongside war, is the most essential. "Work brings redemption,"[35] says Michael—redemption being the longed-for state toward which all his work is directed. What he means by it is redemption from humanity in its traditonal form, from the "inner swine," his "tempter" who appears in the diary at certain points in the guise of Michael's debating adversary, Iwan Wienurowsky.*

At the end of the book, Michael joins the ranks of the "workers"; he begins work in a mine. This offers him above all an opportunity to invoke the intensities of work as a form of *intoxication*, which, like the black-outs and intoxications of the drill, guarantees "redemption": "I have no wish to be a mere inheritor." The purpose of "work" is instead to allow Michael to become a new and self-born man within an apparatus that strips him of ego boundaries.[36] "I am no longer human. I am a Titan. A god!" Goebbels notes in his diary at the end of a first day of labor.[37] He is already strong enough to strangle his inner Ivan. In his invocations, the object worked on in mining figures as little as does the object worked on in his glorifications of writing: "Now the same grasp, the tone returns to me. My pen flies across the pages. Creation! Creation!"[38]

---

*It is against the bearer of this name, who gruesomely embodies Vienna and the Slav, psychoanalyis and communism together, that Goebbels marshals his forces in the battle against Bohemia. Like all "political writers" of his time (from Becher to himself), Goebbels emerges victorious from his struggle against the devouring morass of Bohemia. When Bohemia perished, the writers who had inveighed against it themselves took on the gruesome qualities they had so despised within it.

"Identity Badges for Concentration Camp Inmates—Shape and Color." Vertical columns: "Political Suspect, Professional Criminal, Emigrant, Bible Researcher, Homosexual, Anti-Social." Horizontal columns: "Basic Colors, Recidivists, Prisoners under Close Arrest, Jews, Other Distinguishing Features."

Goebbels accords to the writing process the very same function as hewing coal underground or muscle-training in the barrack square.

> My freedom was now absolute. A miracle had been enacted within me: the miracle of a new world emerging. The pathway was now open—a pathway whose foundations had been laid by my own labor. All of us are faced at some time or another with the task of performing the labor of redemption, first on ourselves, then on others.
>
> If we are to be strong enough to form the life of our era, it is our own lives that must first be mastered.[39]
>
> A new law is approaching—the law of a labor realized in battle and of the spirit that is labor. The synthesis of these three will be internally and externally liberating; labor will become battle, and spirit labor. Herein lies redemption![40]

Goebbels's use of the term synthesis is merely a rhetorical device to allow him to invoke "labor" as part of a philosophical terminology. In fact, he sees the two simply as synonymous, distinguished from each other only by the difference in their methods of functioning. Both are dams: but while "labor as battle" works through the control of the body, in "spirit as labor" the control is mental. Both forms, however, involve suppression both of the self and others. I do not believe it is at all exaggerated to claim that Höss and his contemporaries treated concentration camp internees in precisely the same way as they treated their own desires, the productive force of their unconscious: for both they had nothing to offer but incarceration, the labor of dam-building, and death.

The Nazi term "Community of Workers" *(Arbeitertum)* was used by Goebbels to describe a laboring community battling to maintain the *front* of politics. No sense was ever made of the fact that it was to this conception of *Arbeitertum* that the "A" in NSDAP referred:

> The working community *(Arbeitertum)* is not a class. While class derives from the economy, the working community is rooted in the political domain. It is a historical estate. (. . .) Its task is the internal and external liberation of the German people.[41]

Nazi references to "work" are, then, never simply nonsensical; they refer to men's actual exertions to give birth to themselves as men of stable ego; men *released* from their own history, their feelings, their origin and parents. Their escape route from their own history leads through a German history that is the product of their own labor—"we shall rise again through the efforts of the political community of workers."

The process traced here has been described psychoanalytically as a "fantasy of rebirth." In a clear attempt to defuse their significance, and with

"Storm Prayer," by Fidus. *Life Drawings* (1908).

"Women's Watch: the only official party magazine for women." / "We bear and build the Reich: Workers, Peasants, Soldiers."

some elegant side-stepping, psychoanalysis has traced fascist endeavors to escape the family by becoming "new men" to origins in the mama-papa relationship. Jung presents mama, and incest, as the actual object of these men's desires. (The symbol-seeker will have no difficulty identifying supporting evidence in Goebbels's text, where the writer in search of renewal enters the interior of the mother through the mine as vaginal passage and hammers himself out anew in the ecstasy of labor.)

In a more sophisticated account, Freud criticizes Jung's position; for him, what these men were seeking was papa, the papa inside mama. For Freud, something akin to a penis was everpresent in the (maternal) body; the man thus penetrated her in search of redemption. Freud saw the fantasy of rebirth as obscuring a latent homosexual fantasy, whose object was the father.[42] And for anyone looking for such things, they can indeed be identified in Goebbels's text: Michael is guided and directed by the pit foreman, Mathias Grötzer, who is alone among the miners in accepting and protecting him. In the interior of the earth, Michael meets an affectionate paternal friend.[43]

However, no reference is made in any of the literature to what seems to me to be the essence of the renewal desired by such as Goebbels. Since he is "no longer . . . God," he is also no longer the son of any mother; how then can he wish for incest? Or wish to love a father? Instead, he is the son of the earth and of himself, and made to dominate the earth and whatever remains in it of "humanity."

If I understand correctly, what we are dealing with here is what structural anthropology calls "direct filiation";[44] an attempted specification of origins in which any human line of descent is eradicated. In direct filiation, a single man sets himself up independently as son of God and his mother as nature.* The filiative power that thereby accrues to him supersedes all other forms of social power; the ego it engenders is massive, its limits measured only by the limits of the world. Fascism produces a construction of rebirth that is similar in structure to direct filiation, but involuted; the new-born ego is not the son of God, but the son of himself and of history. Thus, as Goebbels's novel progresses, Michael relinquishes his attempt to become Christ. In a world where fathers are nonexistent, there can be no God the Father. Under fascism, there exists only the new ego as part of a greater totality (whose boundaries are, however, synonymous with its own) and the "world": the two stand in mutual opposition. Their relationship is necessarily one of domination, since it is only from a position of dominance that this ego can endure life and avoid breakdown.

The fascist form of direct filiation appears then to create an immediate link between desire and the full body of the earth—a link theoretically capable of causing all streams to flow. Yet here, desire itself is compelled to wish to be

---

*At the beginning of Leni Riefenstahl's film *Olympia, Festival of Peoples* (completed in 1938), she has the bodies of athletes emerge equally directly from the ancient birth places of Olympia and from the body of the earth.

"The Banner Raised!"

dam, boundary, *ego*. What fascism, therefore, produces is not the microcosmic multiplicity of a desire that longs to expand and multiply across the body of the world, but a "desire" absorbed into the totality machine, and into ego-armor, a desire which wishes to *incorporate* the earth into itself. This is the basis on which the typically fascist relation between desire and politics arises: politics is made subject to *direct* libidinal investment, with no detours, no imprints of mama-papa, no encodings through conventions, institutions, or the historical situation. Under fascism, the most common form of the "I" is as a component within a larger totality-ego—the "I" as "we," pitted in opposition to the rest of the world, the whole starry galaxy . . .

> Yes, we are the masters of the world and kings upon the sea. . . .
> Masters of the air, the truest sons of Germany, men more
> battleworthy than any the earth has ever borne. . . . Our motto is
> that of the sunbird: the watchword of the Erhardt brigade.[45]

Jünger prepares for battle: "Waiting to be swept forward and formed in the grip of the world spirit itself. Here, history is lived at its very center."[46]

This, then, is "megalomania"—the desire of men to shake off what they consider to be meaningless parental origins—"history will absolve me." These men desire to execute the hidden design of history from a position of dominance within the largest of all imaginable symbiotic unities: "I/We and History. 'Freedom.' Never shall we rest until the day . . ."[47]

In their attempts to manufacture themselves as the I/We that safeguards them against threatening disintegration, the not-yet-fully-born are forced to engage in unremitting labor (the labor of subjugation). Only thus can they stave off dissolution and achieve redemption. Their ultimate need is for the whole body of the earth, as the symbiotic body that guarantees their survival. Only within the absolute totality does life arise.

To achieve that totality is the goal of all fascist "labor." "Labor, War!":[48] these are the last whispered words of Goebbels's *Michael*, as he is crushed to death by falling coal.

It seems probable that the same understanding of "work" was shared by the majority of Germans under fascism. It was, for example, not on the economic level that the fascists were successful in combating employment; their success derived from their capacity to divert unemployment into new forms, and remove it from the street. While, on the one hand, the loitering crowd was being formed into ordered columns (the "spade division" of the National Labor Service [*Spatensoldaten*]), on the other, the fascists calmly countenanced the inevitable ruin of state finances—since the latter was unlikely to agitate the masses sufficiently to disturb the vision of totality they had created. It is naïve to believe that Hjalmar Schacht's warnings were never "understood" by the fascists. They knew very well that only war could solve their problems (or demonstrate them to be insoluble). For them, "full employ-

Der Vormarſch
★ Blätter der Wikinger ★
Sondernummer zum Gedächtnis der Brigade Ehrhardt

Wir ſtießen den zerbroch'nen Schaft / Der Fahne in die Erde — — / Und ſieh! Gott gab ihm neue Kraft / Und ſprach von neuem: „Werde!" / Der Stamm ſchlug tief die Wurzeln ein, / Auf daß er ewig lebe, / Hell ſtrahlt im gold'nen Sonnenſchein / Der Flagge morſch Gewebe. / Die Herzen hoch, den Kopf empor, / Kämpft wider Schmach und Lügen, / Das Schwert zur Hand, das Banner vor! / Wir wollen, müſſen ſiegen!

Zeitſchrift für ehem. Offiziere und Mannſchaften der Marine-Brigade Ehrhardt   *Vorlage: Archiv Reiter gen Osten*

"Forward March." Newspaper for officers and troops of the Ehrhardt brigade.

"Kaiser," by Günter Brus, in *Will-o'-the-Wisp* (Frankfurt: Kohlkunstverlag, 1971)—a very beautiful book.

ment" represented a guarantee that the world was properly ordered, its boundaries secure, and their own assured. In this context, "unemployment" was much more than a purely economic problem. Indeed even many workers were more interested in warding off the threat of disintegration, by removing the swarming mass from the street than in any economic solutions to the unemployment problems. (Is this any different today?)* The fact that people freeze

*The current SPD/FDP coalition, by contrast, has successfully contained public consciousness of contemporary unemployment within the concept of *economic* catastrophe—though on a relatively insignificant scale. Since the unemployed are not permitted to be in evidence, they are more likely to be criticized for their own part in their downfall than offered help ("There's plenty of work if you go looking for it." "The Communists have brought it on themselves.") One exception is youth unemployment, which, when it occasionally overflows onto the streets, pin-

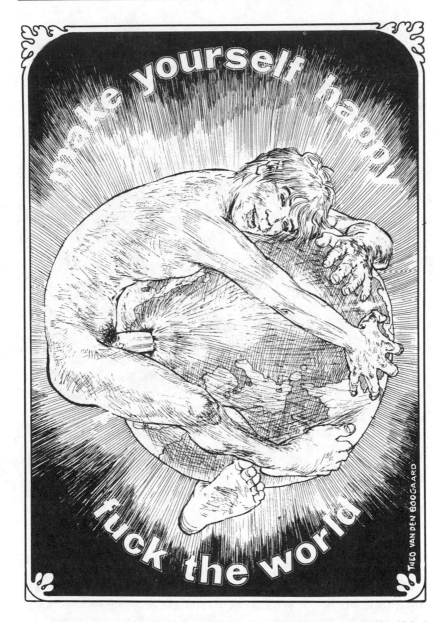

and starve without employment is still today considered marginal—if it is considered at all. A certain number of deaths are presumed to be inevitable in the unifying process whereby totalities are created and ego boundaries erected. "*We*" are here, "you" are elsewhere—who devours whom is the question, and who achieves wholeness.

points the holes in the system-armor. It is thus toward this area that the state and federal aid schemes are largely directed.

To recapitulate: "work" is a maintenance process of the ego and thus the normal mode of existence for the not-yet-fully-born. In moments of crisis, the soldier male mobilizes the maintenance mechanisms described by Mahler in her account of attempts at self-preservation on the part of the "psychotic" child. However, these are brought into play only when the normal mechanisms of ego-preservation have ceased to function, or have been temporarily suspended as a result of the boundaries of the social totality-ego being withdrawn. But in all cases, it seems to me, the principle according to which maintenance functions remains unchanged. Numbers of the activities we have witnessed in the soldier male can be conceived as structured chiefly to maintain his ego-stability; they include his imposition of commands on himself, "pulling himself together," the whole range of forms of deliberate self-control available to him; his alertness, his constant watchfulness; "keeping fit" to drill his own body; his "masculine" posture and demonstratively upright bear-

"Star-Gazer," drawing by Franz Bayros. Private printing from *Garden of Aphrodite*.

ing; his urgent longing for unification with the "we," of the house community, the neighborhood, the club, the party, the body of the people, the white race of the Aryans. They include being active for the sake of activity itself; writing for the sake of order; writing to avoid feeling; speechifying to avoid hearing, apostrophe, "piling stone upon stone." All these are the everyday, the "civilian" forms of the white terror. Lettow's frequent nighttime hunting sorties seem to fulfill the same stabilizing function; for Maercker, stabilization is achieved by the "manly discipline" he so often refers to—a discipline severe enough, according to Maercker, to drive differently structured individuals voluntarily from his *Freikorps*. Or this: " 'Our marching capacity is our best attribute. The first and the last and the most enduring!' he exclaimed aloud."

The passage is taken from the final pages of Heinz's *Sprengstoff*. The book ends: "Each man went about his work."

106. Arbeitslose vor einem Berliner Arbeitsamt

107. Arbeitsuchender in einer Berliner Straße

108. Eröffnung des Autobahnbaues durch den Führer

109. Reichsarbeitsdienst marschiert

Page from a fifth-grade history book by Walter Gehl (1940).
106. Unemployed workers outside a Berlin employment office.
107. Man looking for work on a Berlin street. "Any job accepted on offer."
108. Opening of a highway construction project by the *Führer*.
109. National labor service on the march.

"Here is my first announcement. The government is giving everyone a new home. A superb new apartment block, 200 stories, right in the center of town." From "Wonder Warthog," by Gilbert Shelton in *Radical America* (1975).

The psychic mode in which the soldier male performs any of the above activities is not fundamentally distinct from that of the overt acts of destruction and killing he perpetrates on human beings. All produce the pleasure of self-preservation; here, the pleasure is simply less intense. But the maintenance processes listed above are more obviously directed toward the men's own ego as object; in that sense they are more "narcissistic." They may perhaps destroy internal objects, but destruction is more or less incidental; it occurs — except in the intermediate case of the hunt — by oversight and exclusion only.

The term "relaxation" does not figure in the vocabulary of the incessantly self-creating and self-preserving armor-ego. The entire organism must be constantly on its toes, always under pressure; the senses always wide awake, though incapable of perception. (Deleuze and Guattari claim that monsters are not created by the sleeping of reason, but by a rationality that never sleeps and remains ever watchful.[49] But should we follow them in calling what we witness in the soldier male "rationality"?)

COLLECTED OBSERVATIONS ON THE EGO OF THE NOT-YET-FULLY-BORN

Fascism and the Family

The politics of the family under fascism created a double-bind of profoundly destructive power. Reich and others have suggested that Nazism buttressed the family,[1] but this is not unconditionally the case. Nazism also destroyed it.

The ego of the not-yet-fully-born has no psychic point of reference within the triangular configuration of the family: more concretely, the father as agency, and the mother as person, mean nothing to it. The not-yet-fully-born explodes beyond the boundaries of the family, to find itself confronted by molar unities—others, its country, the universe. It attempts either to incorporate these into itself or to be assimilated into them.

In terms of its psychic construction, it is an anti-familialist being.

Under Nazism, the father as social agency, the mother as person, and the family as a crucial site of self-location did, however, remain insistently present. They formed a part of the social armor of the not-yet-fully-born, one of the external egos into which he inserted himself—into which he was indeed forced to insert himself, since the social power of the family over its members was only partially broken. The fascist state needed, and thus reinforced, the family in its capacity as ordering force and ego boundary; but the family remained more or less an obstacle to the fascist will to world domination.

Correspondingly, fascist family policy pursued two avenues. It lent support to the formal power of the father (demanding absolute obedience of children) and to the position of the mother as the great bearer of children. But educational control was ultimately withdrawn from parents, as children within the fascist youth organizations—the Hitler Youth and German Girls League (BDM)—were made to swear *direct* obedience to the *Führer*. In the event of conflict between the *Führer* and family demands, the child was encouraged to take action against its parents as an informer in the service of the *Führer*. The youth leagues mobilized notions of the grand obligations of the future, the child's duty to participate in German world domination, to entice their members away from the enclosed privacy of the family. What these concepts contained was the promise of a psychic satisfaction of which the family offered very little.[2]

The family, then, was stripped of the only function that might have lent it human substance as a site of relationships, of communication, of protection; it became an organization for the terror of formal domination. But public denouncements of the family remained prohibited; this was the source of the fascist double-bind. While the state defended the dictum of "honoring thy father and mother" with increasing vehemence, it simultaneously deprived

Unemployment and the "annexation" of the Sudeten: two problems solved without the intervention of fathers.

parents utterly of the qualities on which a child's respect might have been founded.

It then became necessary for the respect demanded of children to be thrashed into them, as were all the other elements of their body-armor. No child with the ego of the not-yet-fully-born truly loves or respects its parents: on the contrary it hates them, since it necessarily experiences as terror the substanceless domination to which it is subjected.

Such children nurture particular hatred, not so much of the mother, but of what there is of her within themselves. Their self-hatred and auto-destructiveness finds expression in an absence of respect for their own lives, or in various kinds of physical affliction—punishments meted out to the introjected "evil" mother in revenge for her failure to protect the not-yet-fully-born from searing coldness. (The real mother as person, by contrast, is compulsively revered.) Children who grow up to perpetrate actual armed attacks on female bodies cannot then be conceived as "regressing" to the maternal body, nor to any sexual act; nor are they attempting to destroy an imaginary penis (although all these feature are often present as partial encodings in the soldier male's descriptive writing). Their aim is to annihilate what they perceive as absolute falsity and evil, in order to regenerate their ego in a better world.

The same goal is evident in attacks on pregnant women—attacks which are in no sense avoided, but rather actively sought. "Destruction for my own

Eichenrode station (1933). My parents and three older siblings.

My father, Bruno Theweleit, second from the left.

My father in the military, second from the right.

On the back of this photograph my father wrote: "New Year 1950/Bredstedt/Reconstruction!!!"

Residential dwellings owned by the railway (Bredstedt, Husum, 1948-1954).

Glückstadt, lower fifth (1957). Little boys and big women.

At the end of the war, respects are paid to grandpa.

good," is Dwinger's phrase for what his hero, Pahlen, calls destruction of "the Reds . . . down to the last child in the mother's womb."[3] More recently, the voluntary confessions of American GI's returning from Vietnam have provided similarly graphic descriptions of the killing of pregnant women; the child's embryo is subsequently ripped from the womb.[4] They have traveled the mistaken route of a woman's womb to be born.[5]

As Goebbels's Michael says,

> The wish to abolish war is tantamount to a desire to prevent mothers bringing children into the world. Both events are quite horrible—but so is the whole of life.[6]

Thus while on the one hand, the child-bearing capacity of women attracts the hatred and vengeance of the not-yet-fully-born, on the other, they *impose* child-bearing on women. Similarly today, the beauty of the pregnant body is one of the principal qualities still persistently concealed and transformed into beauty's opposite. Women accustomed to finding clothes they consider more or less wearable in boutiques or department stores are confronted with the limits to that possibility the moment they become pregnant. There is only one kind of "maternity dress"—the ugly kind.

Regression. According to Mahler,

> the psychotic child, in the light of his core deficiency, namely, his inability to use the mother to arrive at even the most primitive sense of reality, i.e., the sense of her as a need-satisfying object,

"The family is the most infamous invention of civilized countries," Lenin. Italian poster (1943).

"Expectant Mother," by Arthur Ressel. From *The Painter and German Fascism* by
Berthold Hinz et al. (Frankfurt, 1977).

cannot be thought of a having *become* alienated from reality. The fact is that he never attained a solid sense of external reality.[7]

She goes on to conclude,

that the intrapsychic situation in the psychotic child does not involve a regression to *any known phase* of redevelopment.[8]

What are the implications of this for the not-yet-fully-born, whose relatively stable ego is imposed from the outside? When his ego-armor fragments, he similarly does not "regress" to any of the familiar developmental phases (the "oral" and the "anal" stages, infancy, or the fetal situation). The psychic dynamic to which he becomes subject when maintenance mechanisms are mobilized is not one of "return" but one of *change* in psychic state. (Where, after all, is the place from which he might "return"?)

For regression to take place, it is necessary for a given level of development to have been attained. Freud conceived the psychic apparatus as a hierarchy of functions or structures. In situations of extreme conflict (including analysis), he saw the individual as "regressing" from higher psychic positions within the hierarchy—positions through which, for example, the individual had gained the capacity for sublimation or for the functions of the secondary process—to what were both qualitatively and temporarily "lower" or "earlier" stages or dynamic processes never actualized in normal behavior.[9] But these higher psychic levels are not present or are only minimally evident in the not-yet-fully born. His stabilizations derive from external sources; and when these disappear, he has no need of "regression." Instead, all the qualities otherwise concealed and dammed up in inside him are suddenly released in their original form. In the not-yet-fully-born, what we witness is not regression (which, in individuals whose psychic functions are more integrated, proceeds relatively slowly, stage by stage), but a stacatto shifting between various psychic states between which, in contrast to states of regression, there is no qualitative difference.[10]

Since the ego of the not-yet-fully-born is external to him, he develops none of the autonomous life-sustaining functions fulfilled in the fully-born by the pleasure principle, or said to be present in the Oedipal type as capacity for scrutiny, deferral, circumnavigation, and sublimation. These functions are located instead in social institutions, conventions, men in command: external totalities. Their only existence in the man himself is in the form of his bodily attitude (in the widest sense); and even in cases where the drill has worked successfully, the ego is seldom particularly stable. (Musculature is the wrong *material* for the construction of an ego.)

The only trait that could be said to be possessed by and to remain everpresent within the man himself is that of his chaoticized drives. His body-armor is imposed from outside, he has no end of trouble maintaining it intact—and the relatively stable social ego that derives from the totality to which he belongs is not in any sense his own.

The crucial point for any understanding of the white terror is that this man's aggressive potential is omnipresent, it does not need to be achieved as the result of long processes of "destructuring." In one facet of his being, he lives constantly in the state to which others "regress."

Susceptibility to Analysis. We are now better placed to understand why the soldier male was never found on the analyst's couch or in a psychiatric hospital but in politics.

First, he has no reason to consider himself sick, since he is maintained by external egos. As long as these continue to function, he too is functional, possessed of "reality competence." We have seen how the need he feels to dominate within hierarchical symbiotic structures—the most satisfying of which is the we and the body of the world—leads him inescapably to "politics."

But his insusceptibility to analysis goes much deeper than this. Unlike the "psychotic child," who is without any means of ego stabilization, this man seems to possess a capacity for speech; but what does he speak *about*? If, as I suspect, his language is a function of his body-armor, then the act of speaking is itself a defense; and if this is the case, it can no longer be assumed to produce "associations" traceable to a core of "conflicts." It is as unlikely that these men will make associative links through language as it is that their language will be a source of understanding and therefore change. Their speech is governed by a rule that defines itself as one of suppression. Speech, like all other functions of the body-ego, seems to function as the very form of "enactment" of disturbances that is expressly prohibited throughout psychoanalytic treatment. Analysis requires a capacity to regress, to return to earlier stages of development. From these starting points, and through transference onto the analyst, the process of retracing previously traveled pathways is narrated as it occurs. But the not-yet-fully-born does not regress; the state into which he relapses is one into which no distinction is made between whole persons, and in which "transference" is thus impossible. Instead, storytelling allows him to fulfill his second function, which is to achieve specific perceptual identities by way of the primary processes. His language serves here as a direct means of achieving the satisfaction we have seen him derive from his self-preservation. Though a language which fulfills this second function is relatively open to interpretation by the analyst, it is as unserviceable a tool for work with the patient as it was in its first function.

The "symbol seekers" are fundamentally misguided in assuming that fascist language is readily open to interpretation—as misguided as are the "antifascists" who characterize fascist language as "stupid" or "politically senseless." Since neither group takes account of the structure from which fascist language emanates, they inevitably underestimate its explosive political power, ignore its dynamic force; they are interested only in what it says, not in how it *functions*. And once they have framed their questions in terms of "what it says," they are able to pose fascist language in opposition to signifiers of their own preferred meanings, which they immediately claim to be "superior." "Fascism can never triumph since we are more clever"—this was the dictum on which almost all "assessments" by the 1920s Left were founded.

For psychoanalysis, one answer to the problems posed by language that functions in this way may well lie in a procedure rigorously rejected by Freud and still massively tabooed in analytic circles: the direct involvement of the patient's body in treatment.[11]

Gisela Pankow has outlined one possible avenue of treatment for "psychotic" patients who, unlike the men under scrutiny here, are not equipped with any totality ego and have no awareness whatever of their body boundaries. For her, the goal of therapy is that the patient, who often experiences a single part of the body as the whole—and perceives the whole body as dismembered—develops a recognition of her or his body boundaries. "Every new area of the body perceived is a firm piece of ground extracted from the process of psychosis."[12]

For the soldier male, by contrast, locked as he is in his totality-armor, analysis might perhaps involve guiding him toward an acknowledgment of his bodily openings and of the interior of his body, in order to protect him from immediate inundation by the fear of dissolution if his bodily periphery becomes pleasurably invested.

Consciousness. Despite the absence of "logical" or "critical" thinking in the soldier males, they are in no sense inert or stupid. It is simply that the functions of their consciousness are absorbed by their perpetual attempts to survey and control events in their immediate surroundings, or indeed in the world situation. They exist in the tortured consciousness of danger. Their body has the constant perception of an encroaching pulp in which it will founder: and in each new moment it addresses itself to its function of identifying the source from which that threat emanates.

Benn has complained of the agony of consciousness; of demands that the "watchdog" remain constantly alert. But his notion of the watchdog has little to do with the consciousness as a grasp of the process of reality. Instead, it describes a capacity to stay awake in danger, and, since danger threatens constantly, to avoid any release of tension—and thus to evade all forms of pleasure. This is indeed "agony."

Memory. Certain dates are anchored like memorial stones in the mind of the soldier male: 2 September 1871, the great Sedan victory; 1 August 1914, the immortal day of Germany's great departure for heroic battle; 9 November

1918, a day of shame, never to be forgotten! And certain places: Annaberg, and Polish defeat! The shame erased at the Feldherrnhalle! Kahr's treachery: Skagerrak—"the flag once raised." Never to be forgotten, never.

Days of remembrance are evoked in association with one of two distinct emotions: the desire for vengeance or the intense joy of events surrounding "rebirth."

The writers also represent childhood as a single great day of remembrance: youth as a golden age. There is barely a trace of true recall, either in childhood memories or in memories of schooldays. Instead, a handful of "outstanding" events is repeatedly and incessantly reproduced in unchanging form, with never the tiniest detail omitted. (It is this that makes fascist writing such a rich source of material for satire.)

Referring to a patient whom she considers typical in his incapacity to forget "certain affect-laden situations of his past," Mahler has pointed to the "uncanny *somatopsychic memory*" of many "psychotic" children.[13] Any memory of these emotive situations is, she says, always guaranteed to reproduce the same associated affects in all their original strength. She writes that:

> It would seem that because of the ego's fragmentation, the
> enteroceptive stirrings of the viscera and the hunger sensations of
> the oral cavity, the sensations experienced at defecation, the
> feeling of nausea, the urge to vomit—all these sensations and
> experiences remain unintegrated.[14]

Since these sensations are never integrated, they are able to emerge autonomously and to assert themselves with considerable energy in situations of unpleasure.

Thus 19 November 1918 becomes a massive belching vomit . . . the very thought of it turns stomachs. Other memories, by contrast, are literally heart-warming . . . the Kaiser's birthday parade, children dressed all in white . . . the man's eyes begin to shine, his body automatically stiffens. His "memory" is one that functions by tearing its elements apart, then unifying them. . . . It has faultless recourse to formulations learned by rote; to commands, prohibitions, a handful of experiential landmarks, "general knowledge," a few songs and poems. The memories of the old are similar; their eyes grow misty when certain crucial words are mentioned: ah, yes, *that* was it . . . a phrase, a name . . .

"Whispering by night in Cosenza," and now in chorus "dark waves off Busento, . . ." as long as the refrain is never forgotten, the world remains in order, every word in perfect place.

The very old, or habitual drinkers, become more or less incapable of absorbing new information. Anything they do take in is rapidly forgotten, yet they are often still able to recite school poems and other milestones of mental orientation. It is not their "brain" that seems to be speaking, but rather the residues of a fragmenting body-ego. Their memory appears as a maintenance function of a body-armor forged by traditional methods of teaching. School exercises were traditionally endlessly repeated; they were thought to have "sunk in" when the pupil finally assumed the proper contours and posture: knowledge was like a corset. (Words that "trip off the tongue" come encased in armor.)

It is absolutely misleading to define this as "good" memory. To ascertain its real inadequacy as "memory," one only need ask how much its owners have forgotten. It excels as maintenance mechanism, impenetrable insulation. The more rock-solid its memorial stones, the less capable it is of absorbing new material.

"Memory failure" in this context seems likely to be only partially a necessary consequence of aging. What seems to "fail" is the memory's capacity to be absorbed by the task of body-ego maintenance. Instead, it becomes finely tuned to a small handful of precisely selected elements which it recalls with utter clarity.

"He has it in hand . . ."

According to Michael Balint, individuals prematurely released from dual unity retain a constantly unsatisfied need for security. That need is often translated into an impulse to cling to any object that promises to dispel the feared "empty spaces" from which threatening and disruptive objects may surface at any moment. He terms this object "ocnophile" (a term containing notions of dread, hesitation, terror, "clinging"), and the psychic type the "ocnophiliac."[15] Balint writes,

> the "drowning man clutching at a straw" is a perfect paraphrase of (the ocnophiliac) attitude: it is no coincidence that this type of phrase is international.[16]

Fear of the life that inhabits "empty spaces" has been identified above as the key feature of the soldier male—as his striving to reproduce the "empty space" as perceptual identity. Both features are evident, for example, in Jünger's description of the moment when the twilight of a Brussels evening suddenly becomes dangerous. "Space slid away into cold infinity, and I saw myself as a tiny atom, spiraled restlessly to and fro by treacherous forces."[17]

The "ocnophile object" is seen by Balint as the successor to what Winnicott calls the "transitional object" (a cuddly toy or scrap of material). The infant uses the transitional object to protect itself from breakdown during the period in which it attempts to come to terms with the mother's absence. The same object then becomes a model for subsequent object relationships.[18] It functions as the direct offshoot of the maternal breast; if development proceeds unimpaired, it is discarded once the child has become capable of object relationships.

A well-known photograph of fighter pilot Rudolf Berthold, with the riding stick he carried constantly.

If it is not discarded—if the clinging impulse persists, though perhaps in a different form, into adulthood—it is assumed to indicate disturbance. The clinging impulse does not necessarily have to be expressed through the hand. It may take the form of muscular tension in the back of the neck and lower jaw (teeth clenching), or the involvement of the whole body in "posture maintenance."

Balint's long list of ocnophile objects, from pencils, paintbrushes, hammers, and violin bows to scepters, conductors' batons, crucifixes, and so on, tends to blur the distinction between manual implements and objects with no directly practical significance.[19] Their diversity becomes confusing.

What then is the actual significance of the rod in the hand of the tight-rope walker, the lion-tamer's whip, the pipe in the hand of the intellectual?

The first male hero to carry some kind of stick was Moses, whose rod became a serpent that swallowed up the serpents of the Pharaoh. Later heroes carried scepters, crucifixes, St. George's lance, Siegfried's sword; wizards had magic wands, generals a staff with which they held consultations. A man is clever if he writes in a good "style" (a message whose "point" is blunted by sublimation): teachers have the cane and the warning index finger. William II, of course, had an entire stiff arm; his pretensions as ocnophiliac were characteristically exaggerated.

The German officer was never seen without some form of stick—*Freikorps* leaders in battle did more than merely carry them:

> The battalion commander strode slowly, and with iron-faced calm, along the battlefront. The bullets that hissed around his ears,

angry vipers after his life's blood, snapped into empty air: Rodenholm seemed almost to be keeping them at bay with the riding whip he flicked up and down in his hand.[20]

The object may even be used as an offensive weapon, as it is, for example, by Freiherr von Maltzan, when under machine-gun fire in the Baltic:

I have no idea what first prompted me to threaten the Bolsheviks with my walking stick, as I shouted over to them to hold their fire immediately. But it certainly made them jump up and make good their escape, with our men giving chase.[21]

The "Bolsheviks" could have been fleeing any number of things, but Maltzan is firmly convinced it was his stick.

Iron Berthold was another *Freikorps* male whom Gangler describes as inclined to provoke republican officers by "regularly going walking with a riding whip in his hand."[22] And, more generally, German officers were as notorious for their characteristic gesture of cracking a riding whip against the heels of their boots as for tapping with their whip handle on tables or chair-arms to command respectful attention. Hitler himself carried a riding whip made of crocodile skin everywhere with him.[23]

Even guns were handled in "ocnophilic," as opposed to practical, fashion. In the aftermath of 9 November 1918, revolutionary troops were sighted carrying guns with the barrel pointing downward: "trailing in the mud, as has become customary," writes Salomon.[24] Reinhard saw "people careering round Berlin in the most vulgar of outfits, sporting red neckerchiefs and with their rifles turned downward."[25] Among the revolutionary innovations that caused the greatest irritation to the soldiers was not only the republicans' habit of tearing epaulettes from their uniforms, but also of carrying their guns "upside down." The position in which the soldiers carried their own guns—raised erect, the butt pressed against the body—was far more uncomfortable, but it was "soldierly."

Balint's interpretation of ocnophilia oscillates indecisively between oedipal analyses (he describes the ocnophile object as "in the first instance a symbol of security signifying the loving and dependable mother," or "the possession of a powerful and never flaccid penis")[26] and analyses deriving from his theory of the basic fault. By the end of his book, he has arrived at the following formulation: "One has the impression that the objects of the ocnophiliac in a certain sense constitute parts of his armor."[27]

This seems to me to be the most likely explanation, and it also accords with Mahler's view of the "psychotic" child, whom she sees not as clinging to "an adequately perceived whole person" (such as the "mother") in its acts of self-maintenance, but to a "greatly reduced, 'burned-out' often deanimated pattern-symbol, a representation of the part object."[28]

Who are you? The men under scrutiny in this study seem to exist through their insertion into the army, party, singing club, sports club, or similar association; the local or national fellowship, the voluntary fire brigade, the personnel at the workplace, the body of public officials, the teaching body, the body of regional and national state. Each man is able to give an approximate definition of the place he occupies in all these various formations. He is not the same in each organization: his place in each different hierarchy is relatively "high" or "low," but always more or less stable.

All these formations clearly act as agencies of the ego; they absolve the individual of decision-making responsibility, they act as touchstones of reality, effectuating organs, blocks defending the individual against threats internal and external. This may explain why the questions generally asked on first encounters tend to relate to their ego-bodies: where are you from, what do you do, what's your family background, your other associations? Such questions are by no means merely fatuous; as attempts to establish whether the other is of the same construction as the questioner, they are highly successful. But what if the newcomer responds, "I'm cosmopolitan, from nowhere in particular. My job? Just looking round, sometime I'll get around to . . . Family? Here and there, nothing significant. Clubs? I'm not much interested . . ."? These answers represent the lack of an ego, an uncontained interior, the horror liberated. Xenophobia is a fear of threatening confrontation with the interior; and such confrontation threatens each time an individual surfaces who is stripped of the layered armor of the supplementary external egos. In no sense can those egos be termed "extraneous."

The questioner neither initially experiences nor subsequently develops a desire to find out more about the "newcomer" than the nature of his or her social and organizational egos—for anything that lies behind them can *only* be dreadful. The only grounds on which curiosity is acknowledged ("Want to get to know me? Sure . . .") is in relation to the individual's place within organizations.

Different organizations carry different degrees of weight; they generate sensations of differing intensity according to their position within larger totality hierarchies. The network of organizational interrelationships is densely woven—"she stopped passing the time of day with me when her husband became chairman"; "the chief inspector at the tax office isn't so bad after all, you wouldn't think he was an academic"; "you get all sorts at the shooting club (*Schützenverein*), from workers right up to professors." Hybridity in the organizational context is associated with access to both "higher" and "lower" positions in the hierarchy, and it is assumed to contain the greatest possible intensity of pleasure. Individuals who exist within the totality hierarchy fail to cathect their own bodily periphery; their erogenous zones are only partially separated, graded, and defined. The effects of that failure become invisible in their attempts to substitute the hierarchies of the totality body for separate "erogenous zones." They seem to equate contact between different totality bodies, their meetings, mutual struggles, and celebrations, with the stimulation of different "erogenous zones" and with contact between the different body parts of different, hierarchically arranged bodies, all of which would otherwise be excluded from mutual contact.

This is doubtless the source of the familiar attempts by politicians to carve out a place for themselves on the "committees" of so many different associations. Their aim is not so much to demonstrate themselves to be of the same construction as other members; they occupy these positions instead as dominant erogenous zones from which they can extract pleasure. They invite caresses by invading sites that they have identified as key sources of the most beautiful sensations yielded by the totality body.

Projection. Since the ego of the not-yet-fully-born exists only in the realm of the social, it can be said less to "project" than to perceive particular forms of life as threatening to pierce its armor and shatter it. This perception is certainly *not* inaccurate. The sensual woman, for example, does *in reality* have the capacity to merge the not-yet-fully-born with himself and into herself—to "dissolve" him. The sexual freedom of the proletariat is *in reality* greater than his; dancing is something black people do better; and the son of the Jewish bourgeoisie is in reality more elegant, more charming, more worldly than the second-lieutenant. Many student parties must in reality seem like orgies to the bureaucrat who has himself been drained dry.

The scapegoats of the not-yet-fully-born thus do indeed possess qualities he finds unbearable; but they also contain a sense of the attraction of intense stimulation. He perceives those who are open to and live with stimulation as *enjoying* doing so—and as undermining and excluding him in the process. His acts of persecution are, among other things, attempts to be accepted in their midst.

In this light, it seems absolutely inadequate simply to deny the validity of such men's doubts and "projections." Given that what they perceive does indeed exist, denial simply reinforces their suspicion that something is being hidden, that there are mischievous and threatening forces lurking.

When, for example, women students are dubbed "whores," it seems to me wrong simply to assert the contrary to be the case. Denying the fact of unusually frequent sexual intercourse among students (which, in these men's terms, does indeed constitute "whoring") fractures any possible bridge between the persecutor and his object. Or to take another example: to assert for party purposes that the proletariat of the 1920s was politically and morally "pure," is in itself politically harmful. If nonmurderous relationships are ever to be established with men such as these, then the bridges they have themselves already built—the bridges of perception—have to be further buttressed by real experience.

A prerequisite for political work with potential facists would, I believe, be the acknowledgment of what they actually *perceive* in things they so avidly detest. To say "yes, it is possible to see us in this way," rather than "no, we are quite different," is the minimum requirement for rapprochement.

Aids to full birth. What is it that most clearly characterizes the majority of love relationships—first loves in particular? And would it be in any sense harmful if we were more conscious of their nature? A relationship begins when one of two, woman or man, needs the other to complete, or at least slightly to advance the process of being born. Since the demands made are often one-sided and dissimultaneous, one of the two is likely at some point to be seen to have "served their purpose." Though the individual affected feels betrayed, it is difficult to reproach the other; for these are struggles for survival. Indeed it might be more acceptable to view relationships from the outset as *supportive* in particularly characteristic ways, but not necessarily permanent. This would at least avoid the pitfalls of the duplicitous ideology that presents us all as "enlightened," "free," and "independent" individuals, permitted to go our own way when we so desire. Couples might then be in a position to develop a mutual awareness of their need for help, to fulfill that need between the two of them, and to escape the double-bind of relationships that necessarily conceal the satisfaction of what are often truly childish needs behind the mask of the truly free and independent individual. The free individual invariably keeps the other at a distance, "under control"—a recipe for psychological terror.

The "aggressive nature" of human beings. The not-yet-fully-born is unsettled not only by his own emotions, but by emotions in general—by the human potential of others. He will sacrifice anything to avoid facing the dangers he perceives in the threatening animation of human productivity. He fears the uncertain future of historical potentialities—for who knows whether they will be endurable?

Alongside the fear that is the residue of the great wars, of fascism, the concentration camps, Stalinism, torture, the bomb, the fear of human potential is one of the most significant instruments of contemporary reterritorialization. We have come to distrust the powers of humanity: "We have seen what humanity is capable of . . . now let us leave it be. Let us restrain desire, the unconscious, emotions—for they lead only to horror. We are best advised to learn to keep them under control, to master ourselves and others."

Such fears may also be the source of the immense popularity of theories of human beings as intrinsically aggressive[*]—for aggression itself is a source of relative concentration and self-collectedness.

"Hands off our interior, the desiring-production of the unconscious"; this demand is both the legacy of fascism and the form in which its effects are still

---

[*]"No," Göring sighed, "there is a curse on humanity. It is dominated by the hunger for power and the pleasure of aggression" (Göring, 9 March 1946, in his Nuremberg cell, in conversation with the American psychologist Gilbert).

"Whole generations die for what they consider legitimate causes. They believe war will somehow release them from drudgery and everyday boredom—it will save them from despair. Ha!"

felt today. Today, lack seems to be installed in men's relationships with women (and others) primarily in the form of their own distrust of themselves as the "aggressive" partner—since this makes it doubly impossible for them to trust any other.

Elaine Morgan has invited men to, "Come on in. The water's lovely";[29] but the first step must be for them to explore the waters of their own interior. Engagement with the self is one of the key demands of the women's movement.

Mountains of corpses. Television transmits endless images of the dying millions[*] (how many? two, four, five or more?): starving Pakistanis, Muslims killed by drowning, mountains of corpses in Biafra or Ethiopia, massacre in Tel Satar, strip-bombing in Vietnam, hundreds of thousands presumed killed in Cambodia . . . and we ourselves are always absent. These are images of our victories, they confirm our survival. They show us the fate of the teeming dead of the world who have screamed and still cry for revolt and upheaval. The next bank of corpses is only round the corner.

Demands that *we* be exterminated are never heard quite so loudly, perhaps precisely because of the ubiquity of visions of mountains of corpses in the Third and Fourth Worlds. Those images seem to allow us access to the psychic ecstasy of power and survival.

---

[*]Survival bacilli.

"Our home is in danger!"

Chapter 3:
The White Terror as Bounding and Maintenance of the Self

THREE PERCEPTUAL IDENTITIES ASSOCIATED WITH THE "UNDIFFERENTIATED OBJECT OF THE DRIVES"

As we have seen above, the soldier male's activity is constantly directed toward the attainment of three perceptions: the "empty space," the "bloody miasma," and the inundation of consciousness in "blackout." Through hallucination, and by the muscular activity of his body, he travels the same route as that described by Mahler in terms of the maintenance mechanisms of dedifferentiation and devivification: and his goal seems to me, as it does to Mahler, to be self-preservation.

In Freud's *Interpretation of Dreams*, the attainment of "perceptual identities"—the desired goal of the primary process—is distinguished from "thought identities," which are the means by which the secondary process attempts to achieve satisfaction.[1] Perceptual identities are presented as a "lower" means of achieving satisfactions, as routes that bypass all detours, deferrals, inhibitions, diversions, thought, word-presentations, or concepts. In the primary process, desire shoots out compulsively toward the production of an image that is either hallucinated or produced by changing the status of real objects. The image produced corresponds to an earlier situation in which the individual has experienced security and satisfaction.

Mahler's work has modified this conception of the primary process as necessarily directed toward the perception of a state of primary pleasure. From her observations of the "psychotic" child, she concludes that the activation of the primary process is equally likely to reproduce a key situation of dis-pleasure.[2] In such instances, the not-yet-fully-born child may well be attempt-ing to indicate its sense of entrapment within, and inability to transcend, a particularly destructive phase of its development. Aggressive acts of self-maintenance thus appear as intimations on the part of the child itself of a cru-cial lack within itself.

In the soldier male, both pleasurable and unpleasurable activities seem to be in evidence; the question of which is the goal of the primary process—pleasure or unpleasure—is resolved according to the degree to which his body-ego fragments in the course of activity. The degree of fragmentation varies in him according to the intensity of the threats to which he feels exposed at any given moment.

The soldier male's perception of "empty space" is produced by an act of devivification that is both concrete and hallucinatory. A shot is fired into the mass and its effects are brought into association with the hallucinatory per-ception that the space has all along been devoid of things living (save a few dead residues of what was previously alive). Devivification in this case seems predominantly to reproduce earlier situations of pleasure in which nothing swarmed around or penetrated the self, and everything was clearly bounded. The "we" and its guns are made synonymous with totality, life in the singular. The man's dominant feeling is one of glee, eruptive good-humor. His body is focused on the core action of squeezing the trigger, an act that is more magical than muscular, the flick of a switch that miraculously produces absolute emp-tiness. It switches the man into a different reality: the trigger functions as a transmission switch to a brighter life in the future.

The perceptual identity of the "empty space" eradicates the various intrusive circumstances of reality; and its production also takes a number of unarmed or "civilian forms." Reality may be discussed out of existence, or ordered away; it may be discussed with cursory phrases: "that's settled then," "problem solved." "Anyone else?" "Where?" "Aha, over there." KAPOW . . . and suddenly it's gone. Or individuals may be dismissed with a peremp-tory, "Oh him? . . . he doesn't count."

Bar-room debates are another form that leads ultimately to the "empty space"—the morning hangover that is the only residue of the previous night's feeling of having clarified the situation. It produces the real incapacity for problem-solving known at the workplace as "poor performance."

The production of the perception of the second perceptual identity, the "bloody miasma," involves devivification and dedifferentiation working simultaneously. In this process, the man seems to experience the reactivation of a central situation of unpleasure; he is stripped of boundaries, left undiffer-entiated and trapped in a symbiosis that engulfs him. He perceives flesh-and-blood exclusively as a blood-sodden mass in which he will perish; or, more extremely, he sees himself as inescapably immersed in the blood of his own

"Warning! Stay in your houses! Live ammunition on the streets! Your lives are in danger!"

childbirth. Characteristically, the bloody miasma brings the man into physical proximity with threatening elements which he both actively seeks (despite the immense danger of engulfment) and against which he differentiates himself as survivor, by smashing them to pieces (with his rifle butt, for instance) or shooting at point-blank range. He escapes by mashing others to the pulp he himself threatens to become.

The feelings he experiences are ambivalent. "Where was I?" "Was that me?" A "primal scream" wrests itself from him; he is surrounded by mists and dancing veils. But relief is imminent: ah, so this is revenge.

The perceptual identity of the "bloody miasma" is very often produced in acts of revenge following directly from the sight of the bleeding bodies of the soldier males' fallen comrades, or "news" of the effects of the "red terror" on their own people. It is as if they felt some urgent need immediately to repulse the threats of the state they here witnessed. They are explicitly willing to do violence to anyone who happens to be in immediate proximity. They need the immediate perception of *evidence* that "not I, but others" are miasma.

The key quality of the blow as an act of physical violence is its capacity to break and crack open, to smash to pieces. It produces the man as "I," not by "switching him in" to some different reality, but by an eruption of muscular activity whose goal is to crush all existing distinction and to raise the man above the undifferentiated miasma.

The civilian forms of the physical blow are many. They include verbal annihilation—also most often in revenge for "insults"; tarring with the same brush: "women are all the same" (*one* fluid and one only); thumping fists on the table (till the soup spills as evidence of others' bad manners); any number of familiar phrases: "we know your type" (the shit you really are). Most commonly, perhaps, the self is maintained by "running down" others—friends and close acquaintances if and when possible—"for no apparent reason," other than to prevent oneself merging with them in threatening proximity. Not we, but they are the diffuse crowd, indecisive, dithering, with mist and fog for brains, for all their pretensions. They are all just another disguised form of . . . miasma.

The movement toward miasma may also be disguised as criticism: the "searing critique," a rude encroachment that renders its objects unrecognizable, ripping them apart till they begin to resemble the critic's image of them as "bloody crap." It appears, too, in the impulse to "expose": the urge to tear masks from others' faces, disguise from their bodies, and to reveal, through "penetrating" intervention, that it was *right* to pursue them.[3]

The perception of the "blackout" and streaming blood, by contrast, involves processes that cannot be adequately described as devivification or dedifferentiation. Unlike the "empty space" or the "bloody miasma," the movement to "blackout" does not directly channel the man's action into acts

"Spartacus as Sentry Black Pudding (prize target)." From the "memorial volume" to
which the Ehrhardt brigade treated itself in 1920 to celebrate the first year of its existence.
This was the kind of publication made possible by the Ebert government for a troop under
its commission.

of eradication or annihilation through which he gains access to survival. It directs him instead toward a ''positive'' goal of its own.

The goal of actions leading to ''blackout'' is something resembling an object-relationship. But object-relationships themselves remain unattainable since the ''object'' the man seeks to conquer in the ecstasy of his love is part of his own body: his muscle-armor. What he seeks is the perception of his own ''interior'' and ''exterior'' merging: the fusion of organ-physique and muscle-physique. The ''enemy'' may be an object external to him; but he is identified as enemy only if his construction resembles that of the man himself (Jünger calls the enemy his ''likeness''). The nearest thing this man will enjoy to the utopian encounter of the lover and beloved is at the same time the most distant from it: a collision between the ''unbending wills of two peoples'' embodied in two men in armed confrontation. They meet to kill; and the only one to ''flow'' is the man who dies. The holes bored in his body are a signal of the murderer's own transcendence of self.[4] His self dissipates as he melts into the blood of a man of his own kind. His ecstasy takes the form of ''blackout'': perception of an end to the torment of existence as a man for whom some form of coupling is indispensable, yet who never experiences the flowing of pleasure. The mechanism at work here is less one of redemption than of ''maintenance.'' What it involves, in essence, is the quasi-ecstatic unification of a body hitherto divided into mutually antagonistic organ- and muscle-physiques—a process I propose to call ''self-coupling.'' Alongside dedifferentiation and devivification, this third central maintenance process seems to be the most intense in the soldier male. Indeed, the pleasure the man derives from ego-fragmentation seems to point to this as the moment of unification with what Mahler calls the ''undifferentiated object of the drives'' (the object being understood here, as all the above provisos and amplifications should indicate, not as an object in the Freudian sense but as the particular *state* the man wishes to attain).

Perceptions associated with self-coupling seem to hold one of two promises: restoration or utopia. Though I find it difficult to say which is predominant, the enormous energy the man expends to reach a state so absolutely distinct, both from his normal condition and from any early childhood experiences, does suggest that the utopian component is substantial. (To use the concept of ''regression'' here would, by contrast, be quite mistaken.)

The feeling the man predominantly experiences can, however, be identified; he is extinguished and inundated, he transcends boundaries, and reaches his goal.

And what of his bodily actions? He accelerates, reaches maximum speed, overloads, and penetrates (until he himself and others reach the ''bursting point'' and explode).

The ''blackout'' also takes civilian forms: work, in the acceleration of ''turnover'' to breaking point; competitiveness among relative equals in all its

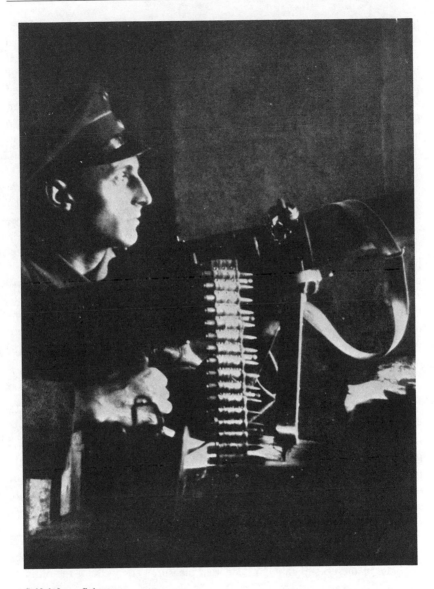

Self-defense fighter.

forms (the European male principle of mutual competition can be seen as anchored in the prohibition of love between them); momentum; verbal machine-gunning, thinking as quick as lightning, sparkling wit, "esprit," brilliant humor. Such skills are often said to be rare among women. True enough perhaps; yet the conclusion should be that what women lack men should equally abandon. The more men's polished words gather momentum, the more they distance themselves from intrusive feelings; they bask in armored brilliance. More than this, they do violence to anything similar to themselves; they identify their own faults in others with punctilious precision, and mercilessly annihilate them.

If men fail in their strenuous efforts to transcend themselves and achieve self-coupling, they revert ultimately to states of devouring symbioses: when they fail to "shake off" the man they have once been, self-disgust triumphs.

It is here that alcohol finds a place, as a possible vehicle for self-coupling through blackout. The drinker's efforts are replayed a million times daily. Yet by and large they only return him to destructive symbioses in which his attempt to escape himself expresses itself as a tormented impulse to drink every drop available—though still the acid juices of the great mother cannot be exhausted. Is it really any accident that the depths of *delerium tremens* contain the same teeming mass as the hallucinated womb of the devouring mother?

* * *

None of the maintenance processes functions in strict accordance with the pleasure principle. They subsume sexual drives under drives for self-maintenance: external objects are abandoned. The pleasure they ultimately yield is the pleasure of survival. Since the ego of the not-yet-fully-born constantly threatens to fragment, all the maintenance processes produce some form of dependency. They generate a compulsive repetition of situations of *unpleasure* as well as pleasure—a phenomenon traced by Freud, in *Beyond the Pleasure Principle*, to the "death drive."

I am loath to introduce complicated discussions of the "death drive" at this stage; it should suffice to note that the soldier male's acts of maintenance originate in attempts to gain experience of pleasure. Their goal is the ultimate form of discharge, namely self-extinction. The men's endeavors may almost invariably be unsuccessful, yet failure itself does not place them in opposition to the pleasure principle; nor does it derive from some other "principle" antagonistic to that of pleasure. A more probable cause of failure is the lack of any adequate material basis in, around, or across these particular male bodies during their quest for pleasure. Where, after all, can the capacity for pleasure be located in a body whose periphery has been de-eroticized, its interior incarcerated and objectified as flowing with filth and dangerous waters?

In our society, there is no shortage of bodies estranged from the pleasure principle. But I see no indication that the effects of the drives in a destructive society can be traced to any source opposed to that of drives toward pleasure.

*　*　*

There are by contrast very clear indications that the soldier male, in the process of differentiating himself from the "bloody miasma," or transforming the teeming mass into "empty space," organizes his own struggle for survival as a direct onslaught on femininity.

In self-coupling, men invariably produce the "bloody miasma" — a fact that is particularly revealing for their own condition. When confronted with women, by contrast, their impulse is to pierce the facade of female "innocence," to display the whole morass of blood and excrement into which they perceive the female womb to be transformed in sexual intercourse, menstruation, or childbirth. Men clearly attracted by feminine hybridity are presented, by contrast, as incurably infected. In both cases, it is a shot or a rifle butt blow that extracts the evidence.

All forms of self-maintenance are partially (though never solely) represented by the soldier males in encodings of familial relations. In this context the perception of the "bloody miasma" becomes a form of revenge extracted from the mother as whore and child-bearer, or from the erotic sister-whore who betrays the brother.

Similarly, the "empty space" presents the soldier male with a permissible vision of the purified body of the devivified "white woman" — a vision stripped of the agitated mass of erotic female flesh, and of its teeming inhabitants.

Familial encodings of all these perceptions are characterized too by the absence of the sexual father, who until now has inhabited the mother's body as monster and gatekeeper. The shot that produces empty space is among other things a means of exacting revenge upon the father as contaminator and seducer.

In the perception of blackout — in self-coupling — femininity is more indirectly combatted through exclusion. Heroic acts of killing take the place of the sexual act: and (like drinking matches or verbal duels between scintillating opponents) they take place only among men. The existence of the feminine is hallucinated away in a process whereby one man procreates himself by devouring another.

More thoughts on the familial: in various of Jünger's texts in particular, there is the occasional glimmer of the brother in the soldier's "likeness" — the man *of equal status* with whom he does battle. The question over which the "brothers" do battle is that of who is to succeed the father as master of the Mother Earth.[5] Their struggle seems likely to derive in part from real struggles over inheritance—particularly the struggles of the younger brothers. Since the latter are not their fathers' heirs, but still consider themselves their betters, they contest the injustice of the preference shown to the elder sons. The penetration of the brother in "blackout" is again a form of revenge; as Jünger writes, anticipating battle, "Justice will be done."[6] Occasionally, however, fraternal configurations take the inverse form; blackout becomes the means whereby the elder son proves his right to inheritance. Femininity, meanwhile, is never anything but absent; the subjugated Mother (Earth) is never asked to state her preferences, either in relation to her sons or in general. Her fate is decided by the combatants among themselves.

Self-coupling in blackout is the most intense of all these men's perceptions of pleasure, but it is dependent upon the availability of an opponent of more or less equal standing, with whom it is possible to engage in something more or less worthy of being called "chivalrous combat." That condition is met in frontline battle in wartime, but remains unfulfilled in civil war, since here the opponent's aspirations are immediately presumed to be presumptuous and illegitimate. (French claims to wartime victory are considered relatively legitimate by comparison.)

By and large, then, battle in civil war ends in the perception of the "empty space," or the "bloody miasma." Civil combat is fundamentally more ruthless, more terroristic, than other forms. In civil war, forces rise from the lower or inner regions, and threaten to become external; they cannot be permitted to be treated with fairness, but meet instead with suppression, damming-in, annihilation. Since, moreover, the soldier male finds battle between civilians considerably less satisfying than battle forms whose goal is "blackout" among equals, civil battles need to be repeated more frequently.

Texts describing civil war are much more likely than accounts of world war to include familial encodings, but this seems to me unsurprising. Since civil war takes place in the "interior" of the "totality," its fronts can more easily be attributed the names of the family totality; for the same reason, emotional relations between the combatants develop a particular intensity. Civil war is cloaked in an aura of obscenity, broken taboo, undefined squalor—associations that may well arise from familial encodings. Civil war appears to be a form of trespass on parental, or other strictly forbidden, territory; thus even men who desire and need it as a means of discharge retain a strange ambivalence toward it. What they do within it is not *actually* permitted. Civil war remains "perverse,"[7] despite its many advantages.

Ultimately, however, the function of battle as displaced enactment of family conflicts remains secondary to its role as a mechanism of self-maintenance. Had it been family conflicts alone that the soldier males transported into the civil war situation, fascist practice would never have produced terror of such proportions and such intensity.

*　　*　　*

"Mother Earth," by Fidus (1913).

The *Freikorps* spirit could be amply demonstrated by the butt of a rifle.[8] (Major Schulz)

The rifle-butt blow: the proudly displayed trademark of the *Freikorps* soldier. Unlike the social democratic press of the period, which tended to dismiss the terror as a Communist invention—"all this claptrap about white horror"[9]—the soldiers themselves took little trouble to hide the pleasure they experienced in killing, even documenting it in texts published at the time of the terror itself. (That it was murder they were guilty of was, however, denied in every single instance.) They denied their involvement only if the naming of particular names appeared unwise, or, to be more explicit, if doing so would lead to legal action or to unfavorable propagandistic consequences. In all other cases, the accounts of the fascist male were more likely to resemble the following:

> My brave lads from Upper Silesia returned with their rifle butts splintered, even hacked off completely—evidence of the incomparable and bitter resolve they had shown in battle.[10] (Captain Scheffel) A moment later one of his men had thrashed the Red's skull to pieces.[11] (Zöberlein)

This is more than mere retrospective exaggeration. In military action during the German revolutionary period from 1912, rifle-butt blows were second only to shooting as a method of killing workers "attempting to escape."[12]

The rifle butt was argued to be admirably suitable for hand-to-hand combat; but it was used in situations where even this rationalization became untenable. In the following account, wounded ex-fighters have been brought by Red Army soldiers to a field hospital in Dülmen:

> When *Reichswehr* troops occupied the camp the following morning and discovered that the wounded men belonged to the Red Army, they stabbed and beat them to death with rifle butts and bayonets. The corpses were unrecognizably disfigured.[13]

Or consider the following tale from a West German national service classroom, relayed to me by Karl Müller. The captain in charge once unpredictably asked why German soldiers used rifle butts in close combat, while the Japanese, for example, used short knives. Since no one could provide an answer, the captain himself supplied one. Using the rifle butt, he said, was part of the *mentality* of the German soldier. An explanation to conjure with.[14]

In the military actions of 1920, a large number of the dead were labeled "shot while attempting to escape." Prisoners with shattered skulls could not easily be presented as the victims of attempted escape—the military was not yet *quite* as powerful as it had been.

The privilege of being killed with a "decent bullet," as opposed to a rifle butt, accrues only to men. In the trial of one of Rosa Luxemburg's murderers, a witness recounts how Luxemburg was told:

> Gunpowder is too good for you. We're going to tear you open and divide you up so everyone has a piece.[15]

Identification with the bullet may well be another form of identification with genital secretion, pinpointed by Ferenczi. Like genital fluid, the bullet is never willingly released into any environment perceived as hostile. Thus unsoldierly men and women are generally said to be "not worth the expense" of a round of bullets. (The shooting of Balla's Red Marie would seem to contradict this; on the other hand, she became "white" Marie before any proper execution order was delivered.)

Once again, then, it seems that guns and weapons in general function to a large extent as part of the body-armor. The weapon is never external to the soldier body.

Black White Red

The soldier males' three perceptual identities have colors:

> "bloody mass" = red
> "empty space" = white
> melting "blackout" = black

Black is the color of forbidden love between men, of a dance of death in dark, deranged ecstasy—the ecstasy of a physical body overloaded, of mutual recognition in armed combat hand-to-hand.

White is the anti-hybrid, brilliant cold, the shroud of devivification. It is the marble body of the white countess nurse, the womb from which no teeth-gnashing monsters threaten. Whitewash: the *shot* that banishes disorder.

Red is female flesh wallowing in its blood; a reeking mass, severed from the man. Red is a mouth dripping blood—now beaten.

The soldier males love the black, white, and red of the flag with a frenzy that may be more than accidental; for it seems that the three most significant goals of their drives are represented in these same three colors.

> Any man approaching our flag with violent intent gets a bullet in the stomach (Bauchschuss). "Bauchschuss": B for Berta, A for Anna . . .

The quote is from Rudolf Mann (note that the "A" is not for Anton). He later comments:

> Depriving the German people of its flag was one of the most

Blue.   White.

unthinking and senseless of the measures taken; it was born of a
poisonous hatred of all things past.[1]

Black, white, and red appear in these men's writing as colors perpetually
to be striven after, perpetually validated. They seem to be perceived as containing all the pleasures of the past, present, and future; and they were in the
end successfully resurrected:

> With the creation of the swastika, and thus the (National Socialist)
> standard, we were able to restore the colors black, white, and
> red—perhaps the most beautiful harmony ever assembled.[2]
> (Killinger)

It has been suggested (by Brecht, and others since[3]) that the Nazi *Red* was
simply stolen from the Communists; the swastika was then added for popular
appeal. But the suggestion is misleading; for it was on this level that the fascists were *least* dependent on Communist borrowings. What, after all, had the

Red.

Republic achieved by changing the flag to black, red, and gold? Abandoning the white of the redeeming gunshot—a vehicle of "clarity" in the most literal sense—it had propagandized instead for the clarity of gold-money; for the melting-pot of the market, the hybrid world of commodities. Its aims were associated with shabby competition, petty endeavors, degradation, the men at the rear, dirty trousers—full of shit and paper money.

The "Republic" aimed to resolve social conflicts not by the gun, but through the market—a goal rightly identified by the soldier males as a dangerous source of "devaluation." *Gold* represented a demand that they coalesce into the mass into which men are transformed by the market. A diary entry from Berthold:

> Is the whole of our people depraved? The true God speaks to men from within; but our people have abandoned Him for the God of money.[4]

Common to all these writers is a rejection of both gold and money as regulatory principles. Both are equated with "bourgeois" existence. This is not to say that they had no desire for *possessions*; on the contrary, they took anything they could lay their hands on. The "national underground" of the '20s resounded with accusations of fraud and embezzlement among its members. What they *were* opposed to was the subjection of their labor power to the laws of the market.

White represented beyond question the most desirable attributes of the "peace" to come. It both offered these men bodily protection against the mass and represented their potential marital partner.

In situations where both the white of guns and that of women is absent, black and red also diminish in value. Blackout in intoxicating battle is supplanted by the lesser intoxication of alcohol; red loses the explosive intensity of the rifle-butt blow. Men are forced to content themselves with the daily round of oppressing women, and with the obligation always to know better.

In the black, red, and gold of the Weimar Republic, alcohol was brought into association with women's oppression, swaggering, with social advancement, and the market, with degradation. If "gold" had remained unadulterated, what was represented by the flag might perhaps have remained acceptable. But gold proved too weak to allow its other associations to be forgotten.

The fascists, then, held fast to the *white*, buried their weapons and went into hibernation, some in the "underground," some in prison, some abroad, some in jobs they detested. Their clamoring for whiteness was not heard again until the world economic crisis began to devalue the gold of men—their labor power. Now at last new majorities could speak for the white shot to shield bodies against dark, encroaching, dragging turbidity.

What was it in the Republic that the fascists perceived as threatening? Even the older men among them (some had already turned fifty) remained not-yet-fully-born sons striving after "break-through." Born to dominate, they seemed destined to be cast aside, branded as good-for-nothings and malingerers. Their own lack of "gold" contrasted sharply with the gold they perceived in the hands of a few rich men (the "monied Jews"). The state was as clearly dominated by gold as was the black and red of the flag—and the fascists longed for the day when both would return to their former state of sublime "harmony": to whiteness.

Just as white is devalued by gold, so also the gun is devalued by the market as domestic political medium. Fascism offered the alternative of the weapon, the white shot, the "white terror."

On the function of flags more generally, Canetti makes the following comment:

> *Flags* are wind made visible. They are like bits of color cut from clouds, nearer and more varied in color, tethered and given permanent shape. In their movement they are truly arresting.

"A plain, honest German rises from strenuous exertions, removes his nightcap, and salutes the colors black, red, and gold." German caricature (1848).

Nations use them to mark the air above them as their own, as though the wind could be partitioned.[5]

The notion that the essential attraction of the flag may consist in the apparent visibility of the invisible within it, seems highly plausible. Elsewhere, Canetti describes the wind as the incorporation of the mass of the dead in particular, and of *invisible masses* in general. In this context, the potency of the streaming flag can be seen to derive from its capacity to domesticate the spirit of the dead. (The ancestral flag: *Fahnen—Ahnen.*[*]) In the battle standard, the dead army fights alongside the living.

But the mass of human dead also contains the mass of the *inner* dead, the mass of imprisoned and deadened desires. It is these that give flags their par-

---

[*]"Fahnen" is the German term for "flags," "Ahnen" for ancestors: the suggestion is that the latter are contained in the former. (Tr.)

The Marseillaise; a stage performance by French singer Delisle (1916).

Fidus. In *Up from Below: A New Book of Freedom* (Berlin, 1911). A book of lyrics.

ticular power. The flag can be seen as containing and displaying the tamed instinctual life of the men who are its followers; its colors are those of their desires. What flutters in the flag is the flowing of desire straitjacketed in the image of a wave in motion. Flags do not move; they are expressions of move-ment—variously signified as flaming torches, the "sound of birds of prey high above," or whatever.

If the flag falls into enemy hands, it must at all costs be recaptured; if it is not, the enemy gains two masses—the mass of the internal and external dead—and control is lost over the ordering of the drives.

One element that rustles through the fabric of the flag is the tamed fem-ininity of a tame inner life. In German, skimpy dresses for women are known pejoratively as "flaglets" (Fähnchen); coupled with femininity, the flag rep-resents the whore.

Delacroix's representation of the French Revolution shows Liberty—a woman and a Jacobin—on the barricades, brandishing the tricolor; the asso-ciation with the whore is evident. Fascism, by contrast, has no flag-bran-dishing women. On the few occasions when they appear—as in Arthur Kampf's painting "The Virgin of Hemmingstedt"—the flag is explicitly encoded, not only with the sword the standard bearer invariably carries, but with some indicator of her sexual virtue.

> Warning: our standard bearer, Fräulein Rosa Hammerschmidt, has been rumored to be *in the family way*. The rumor is false: and all persons are hereby warned of the consequences of further scandalmongering. Fräulein Hammerschmidt has been mistaken for her companion Emma A., who has never once touched the flag. It can thus be considered untainted. Legal action will be taken against any person brazen enough to assert the contrary. Any such assertion is an insult to our flag and to ourselves.
>
> Directors of the Hönbach Gymnastics Association

(The quotation is taken from a Thüringen newspaper in 1907 and appears in the supplementary volume to Eduard Fuchs's *Das bürgerliche Zeitalter* [The Bourgeois Age]. The editor notes that the newspaper gives the full name of Emma A.)

The Whip

> Should all return to chaos and disorder in the Reich
> We'll whip it soft as nappies with the thrashing of its life.[1]

Whipping is an activity of a very particular kind. It differs from other acts of terror in that its primary goal does not appear to be any of the three perceptions we have identified. Ritual floggings of naked body parts certainly produce the perceptual identity of the "bloody miasma"; but the same goal could more easily be achieved by hitting the body with a rifle-butt or sticking it with a bayonet. Most particularly, flogging is not meant to kill the victim; its key characteristic seems to be something quite different.

All forms of beating are, as we have seen, intimately familiar to the soldier male. Painful encroachments by external agencies on his bodily periphery — onslaughts on his musculature — are integral to the process whereby the not-yet-fully-born acquires something approaching the psychic agency of the ego, a "stable" body-ego. It is tempting, then, to assume the beatings he himself administers to be in some way connected to the production of his own ego.

He himself certainly regards them as quite natural. In one account of the activities of the Badische Jägerbataillon, a worker is taken prisoner and beaten, then subsequently acquitted by court martial. He complains of his maltreatment to an officer and receives the following response:

> Think yourself lucky you weren't caught by the Bavarians, they beat anyone and everyone to death on the spot.[2] (The "Bavarians" referred to are the Epp Brigade.)

"Young Germany," a mural by Walter Hoeck.

The man is considered lucky to have escaped with no more than a thrashing; it is seen as a minimal punishment for someone who has fallen into the hands of the military. The soldiers expected their victims—young men in particular—to recognize beatings as valuable warnings and to display the requisite degree of gratitude:

> He assured them of his unparalleled gratitude and declared his firm intent to have no more to do with the Spartacists. His joy at the prospect of this new life was unbounded; he ran off as commanded.[3]

So much for one sixteen-year-old youth, whom Schauwecker describes here being released "after a good dressing-down" by men of the Epp Brigade. The brigade seems in fact not to have beaten "anyone and everyone" to death; their pedagogic interests in relation to "educable" young men were purely "benevolent." Witness, for example, the following remedial lesson, taught by Zöberlein's Hans Krafft to two sixteen-year-old Red Army soldiers. Following a political sermon, in which he harangues them for "pig-stupid raving," he orders,

> "Höllein! I want you to give them a sound thrashing—no sitting down for these two lads for the next three weeks. Then send them packing!"
> "So you two snotballs are too green and stupid to be shot," Höllein growled at the two lads. They grinned with visible relief.

"The Virgin of Hemmingstedt," by Arthur Kampf (1939).

Postcard from the Peking Opera (1969).

"Well, let's see if we can make up for a few of the thrashings your old man never gave you. Here we go then! Which of you wants to be the first to whistle a victory march for the proletariat?" The two lads laughed, as if they found the joke funny; after all, they were getting away with their lives.[4]

Later in the book the author comments, "the proletarians never believe in salvation unless they have it thrashed into them."[5]

Italian poster for the navy auxiliary (1936).

At moments such as these, the soldiers seem directly to replicate the beatings they themselves once received; the "dressing-down" they administer is offered to their victim as a new form of clothing, ornamented with the obligatory sermon. This precisely reproduces the process whereby they themselves once learned their own "salvation."

The proletariat is represented as a great horde of pupils and children; the soldiers, as men charged with the duty of teaching and education, or at least as elder brothers who pass on their own past lessons to their younger siblings. Canetti writes in this context of the "sting of command"—a residue of past commands that remains embedded in men incapable of liberatory mass action. Unable to rid themselves of the sting of command, they pass it on instead to those "below" them: mass action.

The fascist soldiers certainly succeeded in passing on a good proportion of the innumerable beatings they themselves received. They gave "a good thrashing" to any man they perceived as having experienced too little of the drubbing every man should have to suffer.

Beatings are administered as *gifts*: "take that!" The man with the whip exchanges the pain he has suffered for a pleasure. Every blow sends something spinning outward; he emerges a good deal lighter from the act of beating. It offers him a rare opportunity for productive externalization—the "product" of his exertions being education.

The Reds in some cases learn their lessons well. The infiltrators so much feared by the fascists reveal themselves as particularly open to instruction:

> We finally put paid to their activities by making numbers of the Red informer fraternity run the gauntlet to the camp exit. Willing volunteers could always be found to form the lines.[6]
>
> The emissaries of the various councils were given a sound thrashing; and the Red railway patrols never returned to the stretch between Lichtenfels and Saalfeld.[7]
>
> He had passed himself off—much to our relief—as a member of the third *Freikorps* battery. The beating they gave him was a lesson he would never forget.[8]
>
> I made it clear to him—with my fists—that we were now in absolute agreement.[9]
>
> There followed a session of physical instruction on the undesirability of such greetings![10]

All these writers quite unquestioningly represent beating as the clearest and most adequate means of expressing an opinion; and it is often their most direct response to external advances.

The Reds' go-between announced that he had come "to declare war." "Two men, over here," Rossbach ordered. "I want you to take the red flag from this man, pull down his trousers, and give him twenty-five of the best. I'll keep count. And the kick to finish with will be from me."[11] (Bronnen, Rossbach)

It appears that the "Red" in this passage is being punished above all for his "presumption." Beating shows him his proper place and his limits. By degrading his opponent, the soldier maintains himself; and he places the impudent who challenges him in the most humiliating of childlike positions. The question at issue seems to be which of the two is the child, and *who* can say what to *whom*."

In Zöberlein's novel, one former member of the Red Army attempts to save his own skin by casting suspicion on his brother. He believes it is possible to *pull wool over the eyes of soldiers*—poor idiot!

> "Martin?" "Over here!" "Take him to the yard, and make sure you announce loud and clear to everyone that this is the scavenger who betrayed his own brother. Then lay him across the wagon-shaft, in full view of everyone, and give him twenty-five juicy thwacks on his bare arse. Hopefully, the whole filthy lot of them will leave us in peace once you've finished with him."[12]

Looking back over these descriptions of the sensations experienced in whipping, we see three characteristic motives gradually emerging.

The first and most general is the soldier's desire to educate by beating. The principle according to which he adminsters corrective punishment is that of "doing unto others as has been done unto himself" ("a few thrashings too many have never hurt anyone"). The victim's screams are seen as necessary evidence of the effectiveness of the beating, and of his willingness to be corrected. (Double portions are administered to the inflexibly silent; everyone learns in the end.)

The second characteristic sensation is unmistakably one of relief. Whipping is the expression of a desire to escape the position of child—the desire no longer to be forced to proffer a naked arse for beating. The soldier divests himself of his burden of unpleasure by passing it on to another. In the process, he becomes a man—and his mood is correspondingly cheerful; revenge releases tension. His actions must be invested with sufficient force to allow maximum discharge; otherwise his cheerfulness is dampened.

The third distinctive sensation is one of pleasure. Pleasure reverberates through a number of the men's observations on whipping: in the description of beating as "twenty-five juicy thwacks on (a) bare arse," for example. (For the moment, I want to leave aside this third sensation; I will come back to it in the next section.)

What then of the first two sensations identified? Both appear to derive directly from the methods whereby the torturer himself was initially accorded an "ego." He seems to take beating for granted as ego-function and as a form of education; he is relieved to be able to pass on his burden of body knowledge. Unless his whole world is in immediate upheaval, he seems able to retain control of reality by determining who does and who does not deserve a good clip round the ears, and in ensuring that the requisite beatings are administered. Even his language takes on a certain lightness; insofar as he is ever witty, he becomes so in light-hearted descriptions of the heavy blows he administers.

> "Now gentlemen," said the second-lieutenant jovially, "it seems to be our turn to do the talking; you've done more than enough

for one day." He turned aside, with a curt, "Right lads, give them the usual—each man twenty-five!"[13]

The second-lieutenant's "joviality" is not incongruous; from his perspective, everything has slipped into place, the pathway to bliss is open and a note of humor obligatory.

With similar "good humor," Steinäcker describes his men as having "made themselves unpopular with the Spartacists"; their use of driving whips is described as having played a "not insignificant role."[14] In Loewenfeld's account of the Berlin railway strike at the end of June 1919, navy engineers are given "the difficult job of operating the machinery, while volunteers gave a rubber truncheon massage to pickets at the station gates."[15] Maercker reports how a man in the station hall spits at one of the pickets; "he was beaten, with delicate attention to detail, by the picket's comrades."[16] "The end of the tale (in every sense) was that none of them could sit down for a number of days."[17] (A pun from the pen of Bronnen, well, well!) Killinger describes one group of men having to "cool off in the lower quarters"[18] after a meeting with the Third Naval Brigade. Major Schulz writes of men running the gauntlet, "None of them subsequently experienced any great desire to leave the company, and head back to the barracks gate."[19] And finally, Weller refers to whipping as a gift from the Holy Ghost.[20]

Before, during, and after whipping, soldiers make demands of captured workers that similarly "replicate" demands to which they themselves were once subject. In some cases, prisoners are called upon to sing victory anthems—"Heil Dir im Siegerkranz"[21] (Hail the Victor's Garland)—or to shout "Long Live the Third Naval Brigade."[22] Prisoners on the way to execution are put through military drill—"right turn and left turn and march,"[23] or forced, like veteran soldiers, publicly to confess their shame: "I am a polack,"[24] "we are trash, trash, trash,"[25] "I am a Red Guard, I am a murderer."[26]

Numbers of workers were forced by the fascists to sing as they dug their own graves;[27] and even this can be seen as the logical extension of the pedagogic principle previously implemented against the soldiers themselves. They were all too familiar with methods that not only encouraged them to act against their own interests, but also forced them to declare publicly that they were behaving in absolute accordance with their own desires.

These were the principles that had informed the whole terroristic process of their own acquisition of "manhood." As adults, they simply "outtaught their teachers," by reduplicating their own education in slightly exaggerated form.

Whipping was often used by the fascists as a means of extracting "confessions." Prisoners who refused to give evidence were whipped because they "had to be hiding something"; but men who eventually "confessed" were considered still more deserving of whipping, since, having refused to spill the beans immediately, they could be seen not only as criminals but as liars. In many ways, the fascists' behavior mirrored the contemporary attitudes of fathers to alleged transgressions of their sons. The son who kept silence was considered a potential liar; on the other hand, it was considered unwise to allow sons who pleaded guilty to escape unpunished. Since sons inevitably occupied one of the two positions, punishment was *always* appropriate. (The beatings I myself received were administered according to the same principle.)

Since "confession" as a means of gaining exemption from punishment was something absolutely unfamiliar to the soldier males, it seems hardly surprising that they behaved as they did toward the workers. They saw them as children, playing with fire. Possibly too, they saw whipping as a way of demonstrating the precise functions of double-binds to their victims. The dog is punished for barking; but when it clenches its teeth and stops screaming, the assumption is that "it feels no pain."

The soldiers themselves had been forced to learn that some men had the power to twist anything and everything to the same conclusion. They knew only too well that human and other social agencies were always potentially able and willing not only to give palpable demonstrations of the misguidedness, or correctness, or the dangers of men's efforts to be born—and to persuade them to change accordingly—but also that the same actions were equally likely to be condemned at some later date as false or mistaken.

"Whatever we do and however we set out to do it, it's always wrong"— an "insight" that has been all too familiar to members of German strata on two fronts for the past hundred years. There can be no more than a handful among them who have never confronted the despair, resignation, and fury it produces. Indeed it seems to express the most coherently organized of all mass experiences. (It also produces one of the most effective obstacles to discussions of fascism with older generations, parents included: the argument that fascism "surely doesn't make *everything* we did wrong—we were simply doing our duty—and now we're told we were thoroughly *bad*. Wasn't at least some of what we did right and proper?")

A passage from Rudolf Mann gives some indication of the pleasure the soldiers derived from the sight of defeated "Spartacists" floundering in double-binds. The date is May 1919, in Munich. The military has set a time limit within which arms can be surrendered with no repercussions. After this, houses are to be searched for weapons. The announcement runs as follows:

> "All arms are to be surrendered immediately. Anyone caught carrying weapons will be shot!" Mann: What was any citizen of average common sense to do in this situation? He was called upon to surrender his weapons—but how? If he took his gun with him to the weapons depot, he was likely to be shot dead before even making it downstairs, since troops had already begun patroling the

houses. If he got as far as the house door, or even managed to open it, he would be shot at from all sides for being armed; if he was caught carrying a gun on the streets, he would be put up against a wall and executed. If he carried the gun under his coat, his position was yet more dangerous. and if he carried it barrel upward to indicate peaceful intent, he would be trusted by no one. In no situation was his life or his freedom secure. There were many men trapped in this unhappy dilemma.

Some were driven to the point of insanity; some no longer dared return home, since they had no way of getting rid of the guns they kept hidden there. Some came running to me for advice. I suggested they should tie their guns to a long pole and walk along the street holding them at a distance. I would of course have laughed long and loud had I seen anyone actually doing so.[28]

The last thing the reader is likely to encounter in the writings of the soldier males is any description of execution or flogging scenes in which they are presented as "passing on" to workers the terror they themselves suffered in the barracks. This absence seems to me perfectly explicable; for any such clear admission would force these men to acknowledge how they themselves have been tortured and have suffered in the process. Speaking openly of their own past would directly contradict the imperative they feel to eulogize the drill as man's ultimate birthplace.

It is not so much that the soldiers conceal their acts of terror; instead, they give accounts of it that alter its character. While they are perfectly prepared to expose their own brutality, their ecstasy at the sight of blood, and the fury of their acts of annihilation, they omit any mention of their more repugnant acts of vengeance—the moments they have waited for so long, when they finally wreak vengeance (albeit on a mistaken object). Among other things, these acts of revenge are ill-suited to the stabilizing function of diary-writing; "heroic" murder, by contrast, is the perfect object, both for the diary and for related forms.[29]

This does not mean their "lesser" deeds go unrecorded; on the contrary, they are recounted in detail—but as actions of the enemy. In terms of the key affects that agglomerate in the soldier males' evocative accounts of murder, there is no difference at all between their outraged indictments of the "Red Terror" and heroic accounts of their own "white" variety—except that the latter is defended as human necessity. All the accounts they give are celebratory.[30]

Ritual flogging and the Look

The experience of ordering "twenty-five juicy thwacks" on a man's bare buttocks, then watching the order being put into execution, clearly differs from that of administering the beating. The "relief" experienced by the spectator derives not from the physical discharge of the blow but from pleasurable aural and visual sensations. His pleasure stems partially from the production of the perceptual identity "bloody miasma"; but it contains a number of further characteristics worth noting.

The most striking difference between flogging and the physical explosion of the rifle-butt blow is the measured *duration* of the ritual beating. It has an identifiable beginning and end; the number of strokes is predetermined. Flogging seems to be organized to produce a gradual intensification of the pleasure of the spectator. Part of that pleasure derives from his perception of the effects of whipping: the metamorphosis of the victim. Initially, the victim is still capable of resistance; he screams and jerks wildly. By the end, he is left apathetic and bleeding, absolutely silenced, or softly whimpering. The attack is directed toward his skin and his flesh; his skin is made to split, his flesh to twitch convulsively. The instruments used in flogging—"horse-whips," "driving-whips," or, for soldiers occupying the Ruhr in 1920, short pieces of rubber tube[1]—leave his skeleton more or less undamaged. Sticks are used only on the buttocks, since it is only here that flesh is present in sufficient quantities.

In the following section, I will deal in greater detail with the "homosexuality" of these men; but it is important to establish at this stage whether beating of the buttocks can be seen in any way as a "homoerotic" act—since psychoanalysis and psychiatry traditionally assume it to be so.

Sadger, for example, writes in an article "Über Gesässerotik" ("On the Erotics of the Buttocks") (1931) that homoeroticism plays "perhaps the most important role of all" in beatings of the buttocks and thighs. He maintains that

> scopophilic pleasure is above all derived from the posterior, whose
> muscles flinch in an almost coital manner when violently and
> painfully beaten. The flagellant also greatly enjoys "seeing"
> (. . .) changes occurring to the skin: redness, swelling, lash marks
> or the blood which may in some cases begin to flow out. When
> the buttocks are bared in preparation for the blows which are to
> follow, the skin erotism of the individual who is to administer
> them is often (. . .) heightened, and finally the actual whipping
> can often almost produce an orgasm of muscle erotism.[2]

Some psychoanalytic case studies even represent pleasure in the *idea* of whipping as typical of "homosexual" patients.[3] The connection could be accepted as empirically substantiated were the fact of physical relations between men to be considered adequate as a defining element of "homosexuality." But our study of the soldier males' relationship to the "white wife" has taught us precisely *not* to consider physical relations a defining factor. It would be quite grotesque to argue for what is clearly a *relation of defense* against the threatening pleasures of sexuality to be seen as evidence of a "heterosexual" organization of the libido;[4] it is no more or less than *antisexual*. And it seems at least possible that certain physical relationships between men, all too glibly labeled "homosexual," are in fact manifestations of the same organization of sexuality.

Sadger's description of scopophilic pleasure in ritual beating can however be read differently. It is quite possible not to assign immediate hidden *meaning* to the exposed buttocks; they do not necessarily have to be seen as the object of the torturer's libido. Sadger's comment seems to me also to highlight the changes occurring in the flesh of the victim, his bodily movements ("twitching as in coitus"). (The description is reminiscent of the "bandera," a torture method that involves hanging prisoners and beating their limbs until they quiver like wind-blown flags from the pain.)

Ritual flogging is rarely described by the soldier males themselves in any greater detail than in the passages already cited. It seems to be one of the forms of terror considered unsuitable for displays of heroism. We do, however, have a number of accounts from individuals forced to be present as spectators. The most detailed of these are given by concentration-camp survivors.

The report I shall be quoting here comes from a homosexual ex-inmate of various concentration camps between 1939 and 1945, "Heinz Heger." Like many others, Heger was forced to witness innumerable ritual floggings. However, it was not until 1972 that he dared publish his account of them, in a book entitled *The Men of the Pink Triangle*.[5] His descriptions are not "typical"— but that is hardly the issue. The history of abomination challenges us to believe that *everything* is possible. Heger, on flogging and spectatorship:

> The victim was tied to the notorious "whipping post" in such a way as to make his buttocks arch upward above the rest of his body.[6]
>
> Prisoners condemned to punishment by flogging at the whipping post had to be watched by the assembled company of prisoners from their own block. Punishments in the roll-call square were administered with the whole prison camp in attendance.[7]
>
> The offender was required to count each stroke out loud. If the pain prevented him from calling out the number in time, or sufficiently loudly, the stroke he had missed was not counted. It was thus not uncommon for victims to receive almost double their quota.[8]

The choice of torturer was generally in the hands of the camp commandant; but, as Heger points out, "many a sadistically inclined SS platoon leader was only too glad to volunteer his services."[9] (The text makes clear that Heger's own "inclination" is homosexual.)

Heger's look, directed toward the commander as spectator:

> The SS camp commander stood close to the whipping post
> throughout the flogging and watched the penalty being exacted
> with something more than mere interest. His eyes lit up with
> every stroke; after the first few, his whole face was already red
> with lascivious excitement. His hands were plunged deep in his
> trouser pockets, and it was quite clear that he was masturbating
> throughout, apparently unembarrassed by the watching crowd.
> Having "finished himself off" and reached satisfaction, he turned
> on his heel and disappeared; perverse swine that he was, he lost
> interest at this point in the further development of the
> proceedings.
>   On more than thirty occasions, I myself have witnessed SS
> camp commanders masturbating during floggings at the whipping
> post.[10]

When a prisoner being beaten once fails to scream, the SS camp commander clearly feels himself to have been deprived of a necessary portion of his perverse enjoyment. He shouts at the prisoner, "You filthy queer, why aren't you screaming? I suppose this gives arse-fuckers like you nothing but pleasure!"[11]

He then gives the order to start the process from the beginning. As Foucault rightly says, the "celebration of torture" is not simply raging chaos; it has rules and orders.[12] More than this, the penalty meted out to the martyr is calculated—the number of whip-strokes he can survive, the level of pain he will reach, the effects of the beating among spectators who could equally well be playing the role of torture victim. But what is the significance of the SS man's masturbation? Should any importance be attached to the fact that he calls the victim who fails to scream an "arse-fucker"?

Let us look at the situation in greater detail. The prisoner at the whipping post is placed in a more or less animalistic position; head down, his limbs forced downward, hanging as if on all fours, with his buttocks at the highest, most exposed and most vulnerable point above the wood. What is displayed in his flogging is both his vulnerability and his public violation. The situation is obscene, in the sense that the victim is forced to submit to contact and invasion of every imaginable kind,* including entry into the tabooed territory of the exterritorialized anus. The buttocks are anything but sexual objects here; what attracts the torturer is the *secret* and *private* quality of the body regions he penetrates.

For me, the situation recalls a passage in which Jünger describes his sense of exposure to night-time ambushes in the trenches. He feels himself being watched:

---

*A "good hiding" administered to the back, by contrast, is not degrading; it can be the hallmark of the hero-rebel—Marlon Brando, for example, in numbers of his films.

It was like lying naked and blindfold on an executioner's block, exposed to the lusting eyes of mocking spectators.[13]

Tying the victim to the whipping post is a way of reversing the situation described by Jünger; it gives the executioner absolute control, straps the threat, and contains it. Like the eyes of Jünger's "mocking spectators," the torturer's eyes now see and lust after something outside the victim's field of vision.

Other eyes watching too: the eyes of the assembled audience of potential victims. As subordinates to the camp commandant, they have no right to witness what they see in the theater of flogging—the master of life and death masturbating.

The commandant uses his position flagrantly to violate the strictest of taboos: he affords himself sexual satisfaction in full public view. The whole camp is *forced* to watch; but any reaction is known to be punishable by death. As absolute subordinates, the prisoners represent a very specific kind of audience; they embody the concrete utopia of a *disempowered* public morality. The fascists incorporate all authority figures, including parents, into themselves. For them, the age of concealment, of renunciation, of dying is past: they need to conceal nothing. "Look at us," they seems to say, "this is what we are, men who take what we need, who should never be seen to have any kind of inhibition."

At the same time, the commandant does *not* have an audience; he situates himself as an isolated individual on a level on which he can confront the assembled mass of the dead with the threat: "Not one of you will leave here alive." What he celebrates in masturbation is an orgy of survival in defiance of the dead. With every stroke of the whip, the bundle of bound flesh at the whipping post diminishes, and the fear of the onlookers increases; but the commandant grows larger and more whole with every movement.

When the commandant voices the suspicion that his homosexual victim may be "enjoying" the beating, he is not only expressing his own pleasure in the other's degradation, he is voicing a real anxiety. Only one man is permitted to experience pleasure here; and pleasure seems only to be guaranteed if the victim *gives back* something for the pain he receives. Flogging not only allows the torturer to *rid himself* of "stings of command"—the beatings he himself has suffered—he also gains something from the victim of the torture. This is what makes the victim's sexuality important; for though he is not permitted "enjoyment" in the present, he has to have experienced it in the past to be able to pass it further. The SS man divests the man at the whipping post of the pleasure he assumes the "arse fucker" to have experienced. Flogging organizes a form of exchange of pleasures. With every stroke and every scream a substantial quantity of past pleasure is expelled from the victim and enters the spectators. The torture victim is tortured in his capacity as sexual being. (The more "experienced" he is, the better.) This may well be why old men and children are largely exempted from torture; they do not yet possess or are too old to have anything to "pass on" to others. Torture victims are called upon to surrender "information"—a term that may often be a codeword for other qualities extracted from him.

Höss writes of ritual floggings as events he attended with the greatest unwillingness. Arriving at his first concentration camp, he was ordered to watch the flogging of a "political" prisoner at close quarters. He describes how he was overcome with the urge to look away when the prisoner screamed particularly loudly.[14] His reaction was not one of disgust, nor any related emotion; he was simply unable to deal with the affects "surrendered up" by the victim of the beating. It was his own arousal that Höss found unbearable. Later he was able to resolve the problem by setting his face in what he calls a "mask of stone."[15]

Ritual flogging seems to me to be the most "sexual," the most obviously phallic of all forms of torture; one which forces the victim to participate in a form of "negative" coitus. The rhythm of the strokes offers a fair imitation of coital thrusts; the screams of the victim rise along the lines of the excitability curve, climax, then slacken. The victim is made to keep count—a demand strongly associated for me with a theory still widespread in my own day among grammar-school children, who believed that a specified number of thrusts produced the optimal orgasm. (Some men still count the number of thrusts and aim for even higher numbers.) The act of beating has *duration;* it stores up tension, defers, and heightens. And when the SS man has "finished himself off," he disappears into nothing.[*]

In the psychic economy of the not-yet-fully-born, the principal object of masturbation is to attain a state of affect in the body totality. Masturbation is an attempt temporarily to cathect the body's periphery; a number of patients who come to therapy as "homosexuals" masturbate on numerous occasions on any day.[16] Masturbation combats not only the threat of ego-disintegration, but also aggressive fantasies and searing anxiety. It offers momentary security; the head is emptied.

If the spectator's masturbation during flogging does indeed function in the way described, then it may also be seen as serving a second purpose; it absolves him of the requirement that he fantasize in order to gain pleasure. Masturbation releases him absolutely from his own threatening interior since this now takes the externalized form of the victim at the whipping post. His interior is severed from his body and strictly contained. As in all his acts of maintenance, he is now able to repress the "desire to desire," the very existence of his unconscious. And the more he can substitute external perceptions for those of the interior, the more successful repression will be.

---

[*]Might his jodhpurs also play some role here? They are certainly well suited to accommodate permanent erections and offer a certain amount of freedom to maneuver active hands.

With every blow, and every masturbatory gesture, the victim loses a part of his boundaries; for the spectator, by contrast, flogging is a means of drawing closer to an experience of his own periphery. I can find no evidence that the anus should be seen in this context as a desired sexual object. Here, as elsewhere, it seems to me that desires for specific objects are suppressed by drives for self-maintenance.

Under fascism, in contrast to the period of "enlightenment," the body of the torturer is paramount:

> In the eighteenth century, judicial torture functioned in that
> strange economy in which the ritual that produced the truth went
> side by side with the ritual that imposed the punishment. The
> body interrogated in torture constituted the point of application of
> the punishment and the locus of extortion of the truth. And just as
> presumption was inseparably an element in the investigation and a
> fragment of guilt, the regulated pain involved in judicial torture
> was a means both of punishment and of investigation.[17]

In fascist torture, punishment and interrogation have only secondary status. Its primary product is the totality of the experience of the tormentor, his absolute physical omnipotence. Torture not only involves the public display of the victim, but also of the tormentor; it is *he* and not the victim, whose actions function as "deterrent." (The victim, by contrast, is required gradually to disappear altogether; even as a model of the consequences of transgression he would still remain threatening.)

Jean Amery was tortured after his arrest in 1943 as a member of a Belgian resistance group; but he perceived his torture differently from Heger. Addressing himself to the question of whether the torturers could be considered "sadists," he suggests

> In the strict sexual pathological sense, it is my firm
> conviction that they were not; indeed I believe I never encountered
> a single true sadist throughout the two years of imprisonment by
> the Gestapo, or in the concentration camps.
>
> The men I encountered might most aptly be described as
> obtuse bureaucrats of torture. But they were also much more:
> something else was visible in the grim tension of their faces. Their
> expressions were not those of men sated by sadistic sexual
> pleasure, but of men bent on murderous self-satisfaction. They
> were committed heart and soul to the task in hand, a task whose
> name was power, domination of the flesh and the spirit, an excess
> of uninhibited self-expansion.[18]

I have no desire to contradict either Jean Amery or "Heinz Heger"; they, after all, were the ones who saw the faces of their tormentors. But when Amery writes, echoing Georges Bataille, of his inclination "'not to conceive sadism in terms of sexual pathology, but of existential psychology,'" then I find myself wondering whether this opposition is useful, particularly since the conception of torture ultimately arrived at by Amery is not dissimilar from the one I have myself developed. He defines "sadism"

> as the radical negation of the other, the simultaneous denial of both the social principle and the reality principle. In the sadist's world, torture, destruction, and death are triumphant: and such a world clearly has no hope of survival. But the sadist has no interest in global survival. On the contrary, he desires to transcend the world, to achieve total sovereignty by negating fellow human beings—which he sees as representing a particular kind of "hell."

Then comes what I consider to be the essential point:

> In torture, a fellow human being is beaten to flesh and blood; he is left close to death; or, if need be, driven beyond the frontier of death into nothingness. Unlike the martyr, the tormentor and murderer is able to gain palpable evidence of his own fleshly nature without having entirely to lose himself in the process; if need be, he can even call a halt to the torture.[19]

Like the men at the whipping post, Amery's victim is beaten to flesh and blood. But unlike Amery, I would be inclined to describe the relationship of the torturer to his victim as one in which the torturer confines his *lack* of flesh and blood. The process the two undergo is *not* the same; nor is the advantage of being able to stop a distinguishing mark of the torturer. And he only calls a halt when the victim's loss of contours has allowed his own body to gain definition. He is precisely not in danger of "losing himself"; his expression of grim tension and concentration is evidence that he has found himself as armored body-totality.

The main difference between Heger's and Amery's descriptions seems to be that while Heger's offers tormentor as spectator—a man whose physical activity is focused on himself—Amery's refers to men beating objects that are external. It seems to me to serve no purpose to play off these decriptions against each other. (Amery, by contrast, uses his recollections as a covert route into discussions of divergent philosophical and psychological traditions.)

It seems to me more important to identify adequate ways of describing and conceptualizing body processes in torture. It should be clear by now that the "desires" imputed to the torturer by Amery (world transcendence or whatever) are simply nonexistent. What torture represents is an attempt by men to maintain their own bodies; and it will continue to be used in this way as long as men are prevented from identifying other means of protecting their

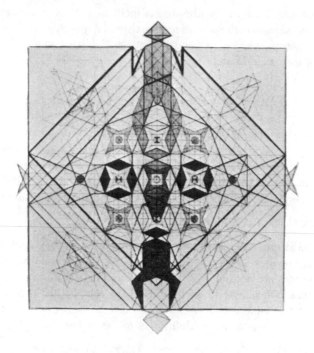

Drawing by Emma Kunz (ca. 1957).

bodies from fragmentation. (It would, in other words, be preferable to abandon the use of terms such as "sadism," since the historical baggage they carry prevents more intimate engagement with actual phenomena. Indeed the same could be said of all contemporary conceptual systems or dominant forms of abstract thinking; caught in endless spirals of historical self-reflection, none of them seems any longer to touch the manifestations of reality.)

HOMOSEXUALITY AND THE WHITE TERROR

It should be made clear from the beginning that the title of this section implies a connection that in fact does not exist. Why then, under certain conditions, does it seems possible to assert its existence?

At the beginning of the study, I avoided any discussion of the "homosexuality" of the soldier males (or indeed of men in general in a male-dominated society). My aim was in the first instance to circumvent the guilt that so often characterizes even the most "enlightened" of male responses to this particular complex of issues.[1] I was motivated, in other words, more by a wish to side-step existing prejudices than by any conviction that "homosexuality" and the white terror were connected. On the contrary, I considered it more than likely that something akin to a "latent" homosexuality, and an associated "damming up of the drives," played a constitutive part in the fascist terror.

But it has now become clear that what I consider the essential modes of operation of the white terror can be represented quite adequately without any necessary recourse to notions of either latent or overt "homosexuality." The main question now to be considered, then, is why the assertion of some connection between the two has proved so stubbornly persistent.

The following "report" from the "Münchener Post" of 6 March 1923, quoted by E. J. Gumbel in his book on the *conspiratorial* nature of the underground, should serve as a reminder of the context in which those connections are made.

> On 27 February 1923, another of Hitler's great followers, Franz Kirschtaler, was sentenced to two months' imprisonment for unnatural sexual practices. Kirschtaler has committed numerous acts of indecency; the majority of his victims are youths. A former member of the "Iron Division," Kirschtaler later served as deputy sergeant in the Ehrhardt Brigade. He saw "active service" in the Ruhr and Upper Silesia, and has a record of convictions for theft.[2]

Even this short extract begins to illustrate the way numerous different qualities are made to converge in one man.

Homosexuality and Sado-Masochism

Until relatively recently sado-masochism among homosexuals had never been empirically documented. Although a number of psychoanalytical case studies existed, none of them was open to statistical "projection"; they offered no means of quantifying the various forms of "homosexuality." It was not until 1974 that Martin Dannecker and Reimut Reiche published their *The Ordinary Homosexual*, a sociological survey of homosexuals in the Federal Republic. According to Dannecker and Reiche, eight percent of their respondents (64 men in all) "practice manifestly sado-masochistic forms of sexual activity."[3]

Though this is not a very large percentage, it is not an insignificant number in absolute terms. If the number is considered in relation to a fictional total number of homosexuals, it certainly represents a sizable pool of potential recruits for the concentration-camp garrisons—though Dannecker and Reiche do emphasize that only one of the men they interviewed corresponded to the "comic-strip image" of the SS man. A *Bundeswehr sergeant-major*,[4] he was also unusual in other respects; he gave a more or less boastful account of his "sadistic" sexual practices, and, unlike many others in the group, he did not experience his mode of satisfaction of the drives as "ego alien."

"That's really too bad," by Crumb and others in *Radical America*. "Holy men came to show us the way and all they got was a kick in the arse!!" / "Smash him in." / "Queer bastard." / "Peace brothers." / "Adolf would've sent you to the labor camp."

Examples of the split identity produced by sado-masochism were given by one respondent whose sexual practices included "beating and whipping the buttocks." He described masturbatory fantasies of "the use of flogging as a punishment in the *Bundeswehr* or in prison. I'm actually opposed to flogging; but in my fantasies, I'm the one doing the whipping."[5]

This man had a particularly ambivalent relationship to the body area he had chosen as a substitute center of pleasure—a fact demonstrated by his overriding "unmitigated failure to achieve fulfillment in sexual experiences."

"I had problems if my penis was very dirty after anal intercourse. Or if something reminded me of the real functions of the bowels after anal penetration." His choice of words clearly expresses the split he experiences; "the real function of the bowels," and "I'm actually opposed to flogging." Ultimately, he lacks any confidence that the world of self-gratification he has created can deliver "real" satisfaction.[6]

The authors conclude that some forms of homosexual practice are predominantly defensive. Homosexuality, they say, may in some cases be a form of defense against "castration anxiety" (which, as we have seen, is often an encoding of a different fear, that of self-dissolution); or it may be a response to some men's permanent compulsion to "affirm their own sexual potency."[7] Anal intercourse in general may, they suggest, be covertly sado-masochistic; indeed Dannecker and Reiche see this psychoanalytic interpretation as confirmed by several of their case studies.[8] They end their chapter on "perversion" with the comment:

> It is extremely unusual for sadistic maltreatment without the consent of the victim, or indecent assault and murder to be perpetrated by homosexuals on victims of the same sex. In clinical terms, these particularly violent acts cannot be seen as symptomatic of homosexuality. In most cases, the offender is not in any real sense homosexual; any confusion he may experience in relation to gender is of minimal psychic significance, given the far deeper disturbance he exhibits on the level of psychopathic basic structure.[9]

What emerges from this analysis is the curious picture of sado-masochism as a form of "homosexuality" that is neither openly declared as such—nor is it "homosexuality" in reality. At the same time, Dannecker and Reiche point to an unmistakable empirical convergence in a small, but identifiable group of "homosexuals" between an inclination toward homosexuality and toward acts of violence.

It seems to me unhelpful to counter with the argument that the coincidence between an inclination toward "heterosexual" acts and acts of violence is particularly rare. Such comments only serve to consolidate the prejudices of the prejudging observer: they are acts of self-maintenance, forms on which the observer depends increasingly, the more s/he resorts to the defensive ploy of rationalization. Dannecker and Reiche themselves voice the suspicion that what they call "confusion in relation to gender" plays a subordinate role in acts of violence in "homosexuals." The fact that critical psychic disturbances are encoded as homosexual should, they suggest, be understood as the product of the particular stringency of gender distinction in existing forms of social organization. This particular form of "homosexual"* practice can, in other words, not only be seen as performing functions of defense; like the attitudes of "defense" adopted by the soldier male, it seems perhaps more likely to function as what we have termed a "maintenance process."

Homosexual desire

Rather than continuing to make very imprecise distinctions between "real" and "unreal" homosexuality, I want at this point to turn to Guy Hocquenghem's book *Homosexual Desire*, which seems to offer ways of clarifying our discussion.

---

*For the moment I can see no other way of resolving the dilemma posed by a practice that gives every appearance of being what it in fact does not appear to be than to use quotation marks.

"Love," in *People's Government* (Frankfurt, 1975). As far as I'm concerned, a very popular, beautiful book. "If N = 100, then 87% have sexual contact . . . in. . . now, where are we? . . . in a ratio to friendship of . . . Never!! . . . frequency in a ratio of . . . so that makes . . . It says here, 'Not the most important thing of all, but still

important,' . . . which would mean 90% if you're talking about daily or almost daily . . . now that's interesting . . . not bad for frequency . . . boy, oh, boy! . . .'' / Cat: "This seems to me a clear case of misconceptualization of the relation between theory and praxis." / Dog: "You said it!"

Hocquenghem constructs his description of "homosexual desire"*
around two axes: on the one hand, it centers on desire in the sense defined by
Deleuze and Guattari; on the other, on the fact of exclusion of the anus from
sociality.

He sees homosexual desire as dismantling boundaries in two possible
ways. In the first instance, it represents the beginning of a return to what Hocquenghem calls the original "unformulated return of the libido."[10] (The
young Freud also assumed the libido to be in the first instance "unformulated": "It seems probable that the sexual instinct is in the first instance independent of its object."[11] Second, homosexual desire invalidates certain key
forms of repression—those consolidated by the social exterritorialization of
the anal area.

> Whereas the phallus is essentially social, the anus is
> essentially private.[12]
> The anus has no social desiring function left because all its
> functions have become excremental: that is to say, chiefly private.
> (. . .) The constitution of the private, individual, "proper" person
> is "of the anus," the constitution of the public person is "of the
> phallus." The anus does not enjoy the same ambivalence as the
> phallus, i.e., its duality as penis and Phallus. Of course, to expose
> one's penis is a shameful act, but it is also a glorious one,
> inasmuch as it displays some connection with the Great Social
> Phallus. Every man possesses a phallus which guarantees him a
> social role; every man has an anus, which is truly his own, in the
> most secret depths of his own person.[13]

As we saw at the end of Chapter 2, Volume 1, the closing of the anus and the
negativization of excrement play a crucial part in the damming-in of bodily
flows in general. The anus, the ultimate sluice, remains persistently hidden:

> The anus is so well hidden that it forms the subsoil of the
> individual, his "fundamental" core. It is his own periphery, as the

---

*The German translation of Hocquenghem more or less consistently translates *desir* as
"longing" (*Verlangen*); for reasons of clarity, Theweleit retains the term *Verlangen*. However, in
a footnote, he does state at this point: "*Desir*" in Hocquenghem is, however, expressly to be
understood in the sense in which it is used in *Anti-Oedipus*. The German translation of *Anti-Oedipus* opts for *Wunsch* as a translation of *desir*. This seems to me greatly preferable, since its
meaning is more general. *Desir* is variously rendered in German as *Verlangen*, *Wunsch*, or more
recently *Begehren*. Translation publishing seems to be beginning to work by a principle familiar
from film and television dubbing—that of maximum difference and maximum arbitrariness. Uniformity is restricted to internal house-style conventions. Suhrkamp has *Wunsch*, Hanser sometimes has *Verlangen*, sometimes *Begehren*; Merve and Alternative change according to mood or
chance circumstance; Herr Cook is to ZDF what Mr. Koch is to the ARD. ZDF recently broadcast
a Hollywood film featuring an American club band singing 'Zum Geburtstag viel Glück' to the
English tune of 'Happy Birthday to You.' "

thief's grandfather explains in Darien's *Le Voleur*, "Your thumb belongs to you, so you must not suck it; you must protect what is yours." Your anus is so totally yours that you must not use it: keep it to yourself.[14]

There are parallels here with Michel Foucault's attempt in *Discipline and Punish* to describe the individual as the product of a process of imprisonment. As Foucault points out, this form of individualization creates the paradoxical situation in which the deviant and delinquent is accorded precedence in systems of imprisonment (from hospital to prison), and thus in systems of individualization. In the minute documentation of the deviant's "abnormal" biography, s/he becomes exceptionally distinct as individual.[15]

In this context, "homosexual longing" appears not simply as one form of sexual desire among others (as the liberal reformist argument for tolerance tends to suggest). Anal penetration comes to represent the opening of social prisons, admission into a hidden dungeon that guards the keys to the recuperation of the revolutionary dimension of desire—"revolutionary" in the sense that it is a "desire to desire." Hocquenghem concludes,

What is repressed in homosexuals is not the love of woman as particular sexual object but the entire subject-object system which constitutes an oppression of desire.[16]

There is a proviso to be made here; for it seems to me fundamentally misleading to talk in this context of "homosexuals." Dannecker and Reiche's study identifies the problems of so doing with particular clarity (even if they themselves do occasionally lapse into normalization—viz., the title of their study, *The Ordinary Homosexual*).

The theoretical implications for anal penetration that Hocquenghem aims to demonstrate are likely to be relatively difficult to identify in the empirical behavior of many homosexuals. Yet this is no sense renders his comment invalid.

Homosexuality is generally dealt with in isolation, as a solely individual problem; and it is this, Hocquenghem suggests, that more or less absolutely prevents the individual homosexual from recognizing the actual motive and potential of his sexuality. To deal with homosexuality as an individual problem is the surest way to subject it to the Oedipus complex. Homosexual desire is a group desire; it groups the anus by restoring its functions as a desiring bond, and by collectively reinvesting it against a society which has reduced it to the state of a shameful little secret.[17]

If we accept Hocquenghem's definition of "true" homosexuality, then the forms associated with the white terror appear in no sense "truly" homosexual. Yet this hardly helps us in outlining clearer and potentially more useful definitions. Nor is the white terror the strict opposite of homosexuality— "here" versus "there." A number of the characteristics evoked in Blüher's descriptions of the *Wandervögel* youth movement, and even the SA, as man-loving "free men and heroes"[18] are clearly in some way connected to "homo-sexual desire." Blüher's writing—which figures Ernst Röhm as one of the most prominent representatives of this male type—displays an overt tendency to use the public display of homosexuality as a means of consolidating group formation and transgressing taboo. Blüher's men are clearly opposed to het-erosexuality as compulsory encoding; at the same time, he invariably brings eroticism between men into association with visions of a masculine society, men's state-building capacities, and so on. Blüher was the precise opposite of the advocate of the "dirty little secret"; he was not an Oedipalizer.[19]

Controversy

In a 1972 issue of the journal *Psyche* (No. 26), Reimut Reiche and Helm Stierlin exchanged views on Charles Socarides's book *The Overt Homosex-ual*—described by Reiche and acknowledged by Stierlin as the "only com-prehensive study of manifest homosexuality" in existence.[20,21]

Socarides's founding premise on the origin of homosexuality is essen-tially ratified by Reiche:

> Socarides identifies the child's failure to separate itself from the mother at the end of the initial, undifferentiated phase of mother-child unity as the key trigger of homosexuality.[22]

Potentially, then, homosexuality may originate in what Balint terms the "basic fault"; it may derive from the same source as do the problems specific to the "soldier male." The manifest homosexual may be a different phenom-enal form of the not-yet-fully-born. But how far can this comparison be taken?

Reiche rightly criticizes Socarides for his failure to perceive the theoret-ical problems his opening premise poses. The emphasis he places on a core complex at the pre-Oedipal stage

> necessarily demands a reassessment of the significance of the Oedipus complex as the core complex of all normal or pathological development. Yet at no point does Socarides acknowledge this implication.[23]

For Socarides, homosexuality is primarily to be seen as serving

> the repression of a pivotal nuclear complex: the drive to regress to a pre-Oedipal fixation in which there is a drive for and dread of merging with the mother in order to reinstate the primitive mother-child unity.[24]

As has been demonstrated above, notions of a "pivotal complex," "repression," "fixation," "regression," or "reinstatement" are inadequate as conceptualizations of the problems of the not-yet-fully-born. What remains interesting about Socarides's analysis is the way he traces "homosexuality" in general to a mechanism of *defense* against the complex of problems originating in the "basic fault." This would seem to situate homosexuality in opposition to the soldier males' attempts to resolve the same problems by *escaping* or transforming their own sexuality—which they perceive as a force that will engulf and dissolve them. Children in the process of becoming homosexual may well be seeking refuge from the same dilemma as the soldier males; for them, however, the solution lies in a particular form of *sexuality*.

This perception is not only rather startling, it is also diametrically opposed to the hypotheses advanced in previous sections on the psychic dynamics of the soldier male. (I would hardly describe the white terror as a form of "sexuality.") Let us look a little further. Homosexuals, Reiche argues in the second part of his critique, should see Socarides as the enemy in analytical sheep's clothing.

> The homophobia that pervades Socarides's work surfaces in almost unrecognizably distorted form; it is refracted variously through deliberations on issues of medical, pastoral, or humanitarian concern.[25]

Reiche's specific quarrels with Socarides are fourfold. First, he sees him as "encouraging the reader to consent to common-sense equations between health and heterosexuality, and sickness and homosexuality." Second, he makes the homosexual the "object of latent criminalization"; he presents him as a traitor to both law and marriage. Third, Reiche sees Socarides as "committed to the thoroughly nonanalytical belief in healing as mission"—a belief that becomes compulsive in particularly intense situations.

Finally—and this point is the most important—Reiche criticizes Socarides's portrayal of the homosexual as specific type (a tendency evident in his frequent and unquestioning use of the formulation "all homosexuals"). Socarides's descriptions, claims Reiche, amount to something approaching character defamation:

> [For Socarides] the super-ego of "the homosexual" is "primitive" (72); "he" is incapable of sublimation (46); "he" aggrandizes, elevates, and romanticizes his variant sexual activity (45); his ego is "poorly structured" (70), "all homosexuals" live "close to the brink of personal disaster and possible annihilation" (45). He absolutely excludes the possibility of a relatively ego-syntonic anchoring of homosexuality.[26]

Stierlin disagrees, and he points first to Socarides's analytical successes, his

> extraordinary determination, and his success in identifying the pre-Oedipal complex as the core of homosexuality. His theoretical

position is grounded in what does indeed seem to be a key feature of homosexuality.[27]

(If Socarides's method were as aggressive as Stierlin's comments, then Reiche's reservations would be quite understandable.)

As a status-conscious member of the psychoanalytical association, Stierlin's central concern in his response is to reaffirm his own position; he dismisses Reiche the critic as "outsider," and, in a footnote, denies him all credibility:

> Dr. Socarides himself once told me that, though he was often publicly attacked by homosexuals, the same men would subsequently come to him voluntarily as patients, and admit that their attacks were never genuine—or rather, that their function was defensive. The tenor of these public denouncements is in many ways echoed by the arguments advanced by Reiche.[28]

If I understand the professor's argument correctly, he is suggesting that it is possible to use an anecdote told by a "doctor"—a man firmly resolved to "penetrate further into the gray areas of therapeutic territory"[29]—as a means of dismissing the arguments of an inhabitant of the same undifferentiated regions. Not only does he discount Reiche's judgment; he also locates him in the gray no-man's-land that should, in his estimation, be the province of the "doctor." Certainly its inhabitants should not be permitted to write in *Psyche*; this is no paper for dilettante patients, but for doctors (heterosexuals).

For anyone to whom the point is not yet clear: an analysis of these forms of intellectual sparring is more than pertinent to our discussion here. Such forms no less—yet no more—"homosexual" than clashes on the football field, or the competing dogmatism of political discussion.

But let us return to the type I have described as the not-yet-fully-born. Under certain conditions, he may become the soldier male; but what does he have in common with "homosexuals"? Reiche's work suggests only that there may be certain points of similarity; but to clarify the issue further, I want at this point to look more closely at Socarides's "overt homosexual."

Socarides's Overt Homosexual

Socarides describes the men who come to him for treatment as having one thing in common: all are motivated by a *compulsion* to homosexual activity. Sexuality appears incidental or, in some cases, absolutely insignificant. What predominates in the patients' statements quoted by Socarides is something quite different.

> I can have an ejaculation the other way but it does not satisfy me. I feel it has something to do with being frightened before I go, relieved that the decision is then not made to go. I think that's

the way I go. I feel somehow I'm going to be *engulfed* and that I may lose my mind. I'm so mixed up. I've got to go. This re-establishes my sexual identity. (Patient B)[30]

I will fall apart if I don't have it. (Patient B)[31]

At these times he felt he might "crack up," fragment into a "million pieces" . . . "I feel terribly sick, as if I'm going to crack up. It's a sort of terrible fright and then a compulsion to homosexual activity. . . . Sometimes it's like I'm going to be destroyed or as if I'm going to be attacked. I'm in terrible danger. Shivers and shudders will shake my body, and I'll get into bed, pull the covers over and curl up like a fetus. It feels like if I don't then go to a homosexual activity . . . I do it for my self-preservation. At that point I'm at breaking point. If I don't I may go insane. It's not an indulgence at all. I have to do it. I might explode or I'll go crazy. It's as if all time and space are mixed up, as if things are shifted and I am in the deepest, direst trouble." (Patient B)[32]

In each case, the compulsion expresses itself as a kind of fit, accompanied by blinding headaches and loss of orientation.

When I get a sexual feeling the man must become extremely submissive and as I say this I get a dizzy feeling as though I'd like to punch these men or strangle them or strangle their genitals rather than do anything else with them. I'd like to remove their genitals by pulling them off, tearing them off, and causing them pain and enjoying their pain. I'd like to strangle them with my legs around them and I'd like to see the pain on their faces. I get a real charge out of this. I have a lot of very angry feelings within me and all this facade of being nice to people, it's all an act. And I hate my mother so. I hate her for all that she did for me, her selfishness and everything being for her. I feel like crying and I feel awful, and the hate is getting more and more about all the things that have happened to me and I guess I've wanted to kill her for a long time. (Patient A)[33]

I want to choke my partner with my legs around him or my hands around his neck just the way I wanted to choke my mother. However, I guess I substitute a man for a woman. I want to choke her by shoving my penis so far down the man's throat that he is choking and gasping for breath. I get pleasure out of that. (Patient A)[34]

And Patient A again:

Every time I engage in homosexuality I'm sure that I am enjoying a degradation with men. Also I feel that I only degrade myself in front of my mother and I really want to eat her up, eat her breasts, eat her, eat all of her. Other girls are out. Her breasts are to be eaten and they are substituted for by the penis of men.[35]

All of Socarides's patients—whom he presents as "all homosexuals"—have similar experiences to recount. For the patients he quotes, the homosexual act performs precisely the same psychodynamic function as do acts of terror for the soldier male. This may well provide a key to the question of the connection between "homosexuality" and the white terror.

If the homosexual act is indeed a compulsive act of defense against threats of devouring dissolution, then it may be possible to understand it as a *maintenance process* in the sense outlined by Margaret Mahler. Like the maintenance mechanism identified earlier, homosexual acts seem primarily to serve as means of restoring the acting subject to "totality." The homosexual, like the soldier male, displays a distinct tendency to devivify his object; the redemptive nature of the release offered by homosexual intercourse closely resembles the redemption following "blackout," in which the soldier male mingles into and intertwines with the enemy (his subjugated equal).

It seems at least possible to define "homosexual desire" in the terms outlined by Hocquenghem, or indeed in terms of the ego-syntonic homosexuality identified by Dannecker and Reiche. But if we accept these definitions, we also have to acknowledge that the one thing *not* present in Socarides's patients is homosexuality.[36] They should instead be seen as men who have reached (or been forced into) a position in which, under certain social conditions, the pleasure of object degradation in the homosexual act becomes imperative for their survival. They use the degradation of others as a means of maintaining their own services, in the face of all the threats and anxieties that typically beset the not-yet-fully-born.

The point is confirmed if we look at the meaning the patients attach to heterosexual practice. (Socarides himself perceives marriage as the ultimate cure.) In the following account of a satisfying heterosexual experience given by Patient A toward the end of his treatment, it becomes clear, for example, that it would be as misleading to talk of this as "heterosexuality" as it was to call his previous activity "homosexual":

> There's something intangible there, an overall feeling of warmth, sometimes some of the girls I find I become dependent on and I'm not frightened. It doesn't leave me guilty and dissatisfied and cold. I have something that I want. I'm left "me," I don't feel torn apart.[37]

As the soldier male needs the "white woman," so this man *needs* his "girl" as a prop for his ego, a component of his body-armor. "Not feeling torn apart" is synonymous for the patient with satisfaction. What the indomitable Socarides defines as the "cure" is a process whereby a formerly "homosexual" patient learns to use women as agents of cohesion, and thus to protect himself against disintegration. Though homosexuality itself is not a criminal offense, the "homosexual" is certainly considered delinquent; and Socarides offers his patients escape from delinquency.[38] The question of how "successful" he is is only secondary; far more significant is the fact of the transformation the patient undergoes from one form of nonsexuality to another. Thus the two forms are different only inasmuch as the second is less threatening and conforms better to the prevailing norm.

It is perhaps unjustified to reproach Socarides himself for the nature of the patients who find their way into his consulting room (or indeed for the deprecatory comments he makes on the state in which he finds them). But he *can* be criticized for using them to reconstruct a vision of "the homosexual" as a dubious type living on the brink of personal catastrophe and social delinquency. (He presents the analyst, by contrast, as the man who holds the key to deliverance from otherwise inevitable imprisonment.)

Anal intercourse as an act of maintenance

One question remains unanswered; why in existing societies based on compulsory heterosexuality does this particular form of homoerotic activity between men have the capacity to assume the psychodynamic function of self-generation; why does it seem so closely to correspond to the activities of the white terror? Under what conditions, in other words, does anal intercourse become an act of maintenance?

Two hypotheses in response:

What surfaces in various forms—including murder—in Socarides's descriptions of his patients' fantasies is a manifest impulse to devivify their passive object. Yet the violated partner is clearly not the only object of their aggression. If we accept Hocquenghem's account of anal penetration, which he sees as a means of penetrating "forbidden territory" in general—and thus as a step in the direction of the undirected, toward roaming desire—then any violent and persecuting penetration of the same area may be seen as a persecution of desire in general. Anal intercourse in its aggressive ("murderous") form may produce some form of wholeness in the persecutor; it may be in this sense that it corresponds to acts of devivification perpetrated by the white terror—acts that turn their victims to "bloody miasma." The anus is identified as the site of aggression precisely because of its potential to produce vast deterritorializations—a potential the not-yet-fully-born very clearly senses. It is for this reason that he pursues it to its ultimate physical location; its threat must be defused or it will indeed rip him to pieces.

A second reason for the anus to become a privileged site for the persecution of desires may be the opportunity it offers to circumvent devouring femininity, while continuing to persecute the threatening animation of contaminated social pleasures. It may, for example, perform this function for men whose fear of re-engulfment by erotic femininity becomes so great that they can no longer countenance the slightest contact with the dangers represented by woman—not even the forms of contact necessary to destroy them. These men seem to fear that proximity to devouring femininity will bring immediate dissolution, annihilation in symbiosis; they will lose self-control and become either violent or feeble. The escape route they seek may well be offered by anal intercourse.

Either of the above hypotheses should be seen as referring to the specific qualities of homosexual sexual organization. If either is at all plausible, then its supporting evidence is to be found exclusively in forms of social organization in which sexuality between men is prohibited. Only in such societies can the anus[39] function as the site of persecution of the "desire to desire," the place where the self plays out its struggle against dissolution. (In the same social context, taking the "passive" role in anal intercourse becomes a particularly pronounced form of degradation.)

It would thus be quite wrong to assume any absolute connection between homosexuality and the white terror—though it would not be mistaken to assume a connection between the white terror and male societies (of which more below).

And finally, it should again be stressed that homosexual acts "committed" as acts of maintenance are not necessarily attributable to what we know as homosexuality; indeed it is far more likely that acts of maintenance and devivification will be heterosexual—since these functions are far closer to what we call normal sexuality.

Homosexuality in the military academy

Following the publication of Ernst Blüher's celebration of the homoerotic sexuality of the "free man and hero," the author received numerous letters from young men weary of a clandestine love life; they now seized the opportunity to talk of it in public. One such letter, quoted below, was subsequently published by Blüher:

> The boys were not always simply good friends; some—always one elder and one younger—were lovers. The younger was known as "struck on" the other (the term derived from ideas of being "struck" or "smitten" by someone*) It was suggested at one point that the elder boy should be called "Louis" (a pimp), but the word was banned on pain of severe beating. There was genuine affection in these relationships; and we had no desire to see them vulgarized. . . . The boys would end up embracing, kissing passionately, ultimately having sexual intercourse. The

---

*The German term for the younger is *Schuss*—shot. (Tr.)

whole thing seemed quite natural; none of us thought of it as pathological or criminal; we simply took it for granted. . . . The couples never went out together in public; but you would occasionally see them standing in the corridors or exchanging a few words on the stairs. . . . The older boy had to make the first move, by asking the younger one if he wanted to be his struck-on; he was either allowed to present his case or turned down immediately if the younger boy found him unappealing. As a fourth-year pupil, at the age of fourteen-and-a-half, I myself had three requests in the space of eight days; I turned them all down. A few days later, the fourth request—which I had been expecting for some time—was finally forthcoming. My suitor was a fifth-form boy; he was slim, with fair, almost white hair, huge blue eyes and white skin. Though he had always paid me special attention, he had never harassed me particularly. . . . He said he had been fond of me for some time, but felt that I had not hitherto been sufficiently developed. But a few days earlier, he had watched me bathing: I had been standing on the diving board, and he had watched me from below. My red swimming trunks were slightly too big for me, and the wind had lifted them far enough for him to see me quite naked underneath. He noted, he then said, that I was now old enough for love. I myself had always been strongly attracted to him, and I accepted his offer without a second thought. We embraced and exchanged some kisses. From then on, we saw each other at least once a day; he would stand by the dormitory door every evening to wish me goodnight. . . . I loved him very dearly; I would have done anything he asked.[40]

Blüher takes up the story:

the military academy is saturated by the wide waters of masculine eros:[41] the eroticism of system is absolutely conscious; both the language and the tone of intercourse are completely attuned to eroticism.[42]

Blüher understands the cadets' homosexuality as a form of explicit *opposition* to their instructors:

In all their accounts of religious or academic instruction, these unadulterated young autocrats depicted themselves as nurturing the most absolute disdain for the two species of humanity to whose care they were committed: the priest and the headmaster. Their instincts told them that men such as these were their essential enemies. They were out to persecute and destroy the love lives of their charges; this was enough to condemn them. The situation

"The Judgment of Paris," by Ivo Saliger (1939).

"The Judgment of the German Paris," by
A. Guillaume (Fantasio, 1915).

among the military youth was thus quite distinct from that among
the *Wandervögel*; unlike the latter, their spirits were never broken
by hypocrisy.[43]

The question of whether Blüher's account is accurate—his tendency to
idealize is unmistakable—is less important than that of the nature of his ideal
model. He presents homosexuality among the cadets as an attempt to escape
the sexuality, or rather the paternal nonsexuality of their educators. Officers
are seen as secretly complicit in those efforts—a fact that is in no sense contradictory, since, as we have seen, the officer himself is a member of the same
fraternity, a veteran of the same system.

In the military academy, homosexuality thus acquires a very particular
quality: it offers access to power—in the first instance to the power to dismiss
the opinions and moralities of "headmasters," "hypocrites," and others. The
power that the soldier-cadet gains through homosexuality raises him above the
sexual prejudices dominant in state education, the Church, and family: he
leaves all such institutions far "below him." He is seduced by the soldier's
power to transgress the law—a power that binds him all the more tightly to the
military. While I would not wish to minimize or deny the significance of
sexual desire—particularly given the obvious capacity of pubescent adoles-
cents to shed all inhibitions once the initial thresholds have been crossed—the
crucial issue seems to me to be a different one. Homosexual love in the military academy seems to be organized in ways that make it at least possible to
reverse the process whereby the cadet gains power by freeing himself from

public morality. If, at some later date, he himself becomes an officer, if he rises to a position of "responsibility" that carries representative and socially approved functions, then his sexuality will necessarily be condemned to secrecy. For any man who becomes homosexual under the conditions outlined above, homosexuality will be increasingly subject to sanction. The more he gains in social standing, the more difficult it becomes to reconcile his "responsibilities" with his sexuality. We may assume in such cases that the *sexual* component of homosexuality becomes ever smaller with each increase in age, responsibility, and representational duties, so that in the end all that remains "perverse" is the power game played by the "homosexual."

One example that seems to support this thesis is that of the supposedly "homosexual" Eulenberg circle, of which "His Supremacy," the Kaiser himself, was a member. New material on the circle recently published by the English historian John Röhl[44] shows their homosexuality to have been little more than a secret game of the society elite. Röhl's documents include a letter from Moltke to Varnbühler in which Moltke tells of a visit to Eulenberg in Munich. Eulenberg had commissioned a well-known "medium" and mesmerist for the occasion, to tell the future to himself and his friend.

> In the midst of the session, Phili joined the circle and touched the mesmerist with one hand. He had wanted to ask a question without disturbing the medium; but she, the medium, woke instantly, with tears running down her cheeks. Something had upset her very badly. When she continued to cry, the mesmerist asked whether she had felt Phili's touch. "I felt a pain in my bowels."[45]

The connection made here between occultism and anal intercourse clearly has nothing to do with *homosexuality*: it is simply used to intensify the pleasure the powerful gain from transgression. Moltke and Eulenberg are merely enjoying the oppportunity to play hide-and-seek with the law. "If the world knew what we were doing . . . but we are doing it anyway!" It is power that yields pleasure.

What then constitutes the particular attraction of "homosexuality" to the fascist male? My suspicion is that it is its capacity to be associated with power and transgression. Homosexual practice is one of the few remaining gaps through which he can escape the compulsory encoding of feared heterosexuality; it is an escape from normality, from a whole domain of more or less permissible pleasures—all encoded with "femininity." As a homosexual, the fascist can prove, both to himself and others, that he is "nonbourgeois," and boldly defiant of normality. His "homosexuality" is strictly encoded; and for this very reason, it never becomes sexual. Like the opposite from which it flees, it is rigidly codified—as escape, transgression, boyish mischief, perverse game, or indeed ultimately as act of terror. In all these forms, it is far

So that kind of painting was allowed after all. "Leda and the Swan," by Paul Mathias Padua.

more likely to be definable in the terms of the fascist system than in terms of such things as love relationships between men. Hocquenghem defines the liberating quality of homosexuality as its capacity to decodify sexual codes; but in the fascist male, this is precisely the element that is lacking. His escape into homosexuality ultimately functions as reterritorialization: as an act prescribed by the social order, it never opens new outlets; it simply reinforces dams. It is this that makes it possible for homosexuality in general to appear connected to the white terror; any identification of the links between them is welcomed as "empirical evidence" to ground existing public defamations of homosexuality. Yet the actual connection is one between male bonding and the white terror—a connection that provides the pleasure of power. Power occupies homosexuality as it does heterosexuality; it violates both. Höss, in an account of his life in the Brandenburg prison, perceived very well what was involved in the fascist form of "homosexuality":

> Homosexuality was particularly rife. The attractive younger prisoners were much sought after as "beauties"; they were the objects of the most vicious battles and intrigues. The cleverer ones among them made their admirers pay dear for their attraction. After many years of experience and observation in these institutions, I have come to the conclusion that such widespread homosexuality can only be attributed in a handful of instances to inherited or pathological disposition. It may be caused by sexual deprivation in men whose sexual drives are particularly strong; but in the vast majority of cases, it arises out of men's more general search for activities stimulating enough, in a context in which inhibitions have almost totally been abandoned, to "add spice to their lives."[46]

The eligibility of homosexuals for release from concentration camp was assessed according to whether their "homosexuality" was real, or merely situational. It was considered imperative for "real" homosexuality—the potential for actual *homosexual* pleasure—to remain under lock and key; and interestingly enough, the *criteria* of distinction developed by the SS resemble those outlined by Socarides:

> In 1944, an order came from the *Reichsführer SS* to subject homosexuals to "aversion tests." Any homosexual not yet certified as cured was made to work alongside girls who had been secretly instructed to make subtle, but sexually stimulating advances. The men were observed from a distance. Those properly cured immediately seized the opportunity; they needed little or no encouragement. The incurables never so much as looked at the women; indeed they recoiled, shaking with disgust and nausea from particularly overt approaches. Following this

"Raincoat," by Renzo Vespignani, in *Fascism* (Berlin, 1976).

procedure, the men selcted for release were given a further opportunity to have intercourse with individuals of the same sex. In almost all cases, the opportunity was scorned, and attempted advances from real homosexuals flatly rejected. There were, however, borderline cases—men who took advanatage of both offers. The question of whether these may be characterized as bisexual remains, in my view, open.[47]

Irrespective of whether Höss's observations are accurate (they smack very much of "wish-ful" thinking), they certainly show the extent to which the concentration-camp commandant himself felt the attraction of the forbidden, and of omnipotent control. For him, human sexuality became the object of a form of behavioral science, in which he played the dual role of judge and researcher. He presents homosexuality as more or less permissible for men of "homosexual" disposition, or men who are homosexual for reasons of *transgression* (men motivated by a desire to "add spice to their lives"). But the men who are homosexual for reasons of pleasure deserve only death.

Transsexuality as regulated play

Many soldier texts employ the vehicle of a fictitious transsexuality, in which men become women, to represent the playful, apparently transgressive, but ultimately strictly regulated nature of flirtations with the homosexual.

> Munich, May 1919: We had fought together in a spirit of cheerful comradeship; and the same humor blossomed in this short spell of peace. Once, when a group of us went to the theater in the *Gärtnerplatz*, to see a delightful operetta called "The Rose of Istanbul," we all enjoyed it so much that we decided to put on our own "performance." Our chance came on May 12 when our troop was transferred. We spent the entire journey from Munich to Betzigau, our destination, playing the "Rose of Istanbul" in every possible variation. No other carriage in the whole length of the train could equal the atmosphere we created; we laughed until the tears ran down our faces. The "rose" was played by a born comedian, Anton Dilger (a "rose" of 1.80 hundredweight or more); as she trilled her aria in the sweetest falsetto, I entered the scene—staunchly supported by my warrior "choir"—to intone the refrain, "Rose of Istanbul, you alone shall be my Sche-he-re-za-de!" Even the costumes were authentic. None of us will ever forget this particular "wartime expedition." (Pitrof)[48]

> Delmar in France during the war: I woke up one morning to breathe a delicious scent drifting toward my bed in the corner; it came wafting through the dimly candlelit cellar. The tall figure of

a woman was approaching unannounced through the door—an apparition in green roccoco silk. The softly quivering ringlets of a powdered wig tumbled across her white shoulders. Her face was rouged and powdered; her lips glistened full and blood-red; her eyebrows were two delicately penciled arches. She held a fan made of strips of painted silk: a true lady.

A tantalizing smile played around her lips; she cast the occasional sidelong glance from under half-closed eyelids. She extended delicate fingers to lift her crinoline. The music box on the table—decorated with the the picture of a violinist—was playing the minuet from Mozart's great opera. And this loveliest of women began to dance the round dance, as it had been danced in France's greatest and most beautiful era. She seemed to have descended into our gloomy cellar from some glorious heaven.

As she executed the final 'pas,' the door crashed open. A private appeared and shouted, "The airman's back!"

The game was over. The room filled instead with the silence of immediate anticipation. There were sounds of men catching their breath, pulses drumming visibly. The enemy anti-aircraft gun fired the first round of delayed-action grenades; they bored their way into the lawn in front of the house. All too soon. A hollow thud, and the whole room shook around us.

The lady paled beneath her powder. She inclined her head gracefully, and left the room. Less than a quarter of an hour later the *Junker* came to sit silently in our midst. He had abandoned his mask, but the scent of the beautiful vision still hung in the room.[49]

Von Selchow decribing a school performance of Aeschylus' Agamemnon: November 21 was the happiest day of my life. The gala performance in the grammar school gymnasium at the corner of Berlinerstrasse and Cauerstrasse was not only attended by my parents, but by a minister and other high-ranking dignitaries. Even the Kaiser and his wife were intending to make an appearance. Would they come? The hall buzzed with anticipation—but they never arrived. . . . I remained quite oblivious, far away in a different world. I was playing the great daughter of the great Priamos; and as I stepped onto the stage, with a long white robe draped over the loose gown I wore underneath, sandals on my feet, a long staff in my hand, long black curls tumbling from my head to my breast, and crowned with a golden diadem to hold my white priestess's headband, I was so filled with a sense of the god himself, so absolutely the prophetess of Apollo, that I saw nothing of the events in the auditorium. I felt only one thing: that I was as

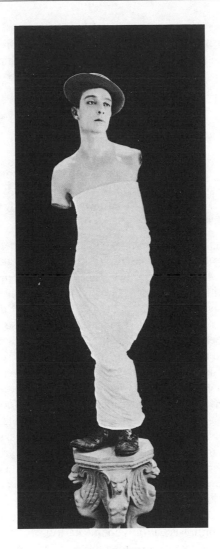

Buster von Milo.

> powerless to escape the dreadful fate decreed for me by the
> Apollo of the Light, as I was to save others from it.
> Tumultuous applause broke out as the curtain fell.[50]

Later, as sea cadet, von Selchow is unexpectedly put in charge of a difficult
maneuver. He can hardly contain his excitement. Again it was Cassandra who
came to mind:

> "Ah, ah. It is like fire, and it comes over me! Oh, Lycean Apollo,
> woe is me."
> "Go to the devil!" I called softly. The commandant stared at
> me in astonishment. (Then following the success of the
> maneuver:) As the ship sliced through the wind, Cassandra faded
> into the distance.[51]

For the soldier males, becoming a "man" involves performing functions
demanded by the military and war. The process whereby they become men is
a *social* one; while their *ego* becomes "masculine" through its insertion, as
armor, into the whole, their sex remains diffuse. Though they play at
"changing" sex, they do so only in public. All three of the above passages
describe instances of *performance*, of theater. In each case, the social context
makes a more general homosexualization of the situation impossible. The
public serves as a dam against any possible intrusion by sexuality.

Even in contexts where public control is less stringent, what the soldier
males seem to find enjoyable is the *representation* of sex-role inversion.

The fact is illustrated by a particularly illuminating comment by Göring
recorded during the Nuremberg trials. In general, Göring either summarily
dismissed any accusation of crimes committed by the Nazi leaders — himself
in particular — or simply declared them to be spurious, hypocritical, or whatever. The only exception was his response to Schach's statement that he had
once appeared at a reception in toga and sandals, with powdered face, red
painted lips, and red varnished fingernails. Clearly unsettled, Göring
declared: "It seems to me quite irrelevant." This was the only statement that
made him feel compromised (if only momentarily).[52]

Hahn describes a company of republican sailors going one step further.
They found themselves in Stuttgart for the first two months after the 1918
November Revolution; like many other groups of soldiers, they were not per-
mitted to go out alone in the evenings in search of alternative entertainment.
Hahn describes them having actual physical contact:

> A few scattered electric bulbs cast a gentle glow across the
> smoke-filled room; and the sailors' silhouettes moved in grotesque
> dance forms and figures to the rhythm of an exquisitely played
> accordion. Some danced as "ladies," the others as
> "gentlemen" — a habit they had acquired during long periods at

The "male" star of a camp theater.

sea. Dances were promised and executed with solemn *grandezza*; the refinements and formalities of the etiquette manuals were observed with absolute rigidity. The soldiers were drenched in rivers of perspiration; their eyes sparkled with the pleasure of dancing; they abandoned themselves completely to the rhythm. Naturally enough, I too felt the urge to dance. I chose a "coolie-woman," who was particularly honored. (. . .) it was

The girls from the navy. English prisoners of war during World War I.

like being on board a sailing-ship; the dancers were like ships moving with the waves. The illusion was perfect—stamping feet under strange lighting, the pipe smoke, the grotesqueness of dancers and audience, the strangely melancholic music—an extraordinary atmosphere.

The scene is described as exquisite, solemn, and melancholy; sweat flows in streams and eyes sparkle. The celebrations of men versed in etiquette may be "grotesque"; but they are anything but sexual. The sailors play heterosexual couples; for, more perhaps than any other, the preservation of this particular form is crucial.

There was no place among sailors of this kind for homosexuals—except somewhere in the darkness beyond and beside them.

The attractiveness of men as a social quality

What causes men to desire other men? It seems to me that the principal reason may well be the exclusion of women, in society as it is currently organized, from the pleasure-intensities of public activity.* In our male-dominated

---

*Men invariably dominate public life, independently of whether the existing social order can or cannot be sociologically defined as "patriarchal." Ulrike Prokop makes a similar point in relation to what she calls "antipatriarchalism"; she describes it as a mere "rhetorical strategy." (Prokop, *Weiblicher Lebenszusammenhang*, pp.36ff.). But she fails to perceive the specific problem confronted in this study, namely the survival of "patriarchal" behavior and fantasies *despite*—indeed perhaps because of—the disappearance of what might strictly be termed patriarchal relations. It is precisely this that constitutes the principal problem for fascist men. They not only wish to assume a role that is (has become) unacceptable; they actively assert their right to do so.

society, women are assumed to be far too "naïve" to compete with men's "experience." This fact alone suffices to make them less appealing. Men nurture dreams of a life of heroes, of strength and *esprit*, of rising to power and glory; they dream of the hunt, of conquering the far distance and the summit; they covet the radiant beauty of the successful "free man and hero." Many deem it impossible for such dreams to be realized in women; for women are private and enclosed beings, their lives associated, not with the world-historical deeds of great men, but with the dirt of everyday living.[53]

Only for the sake of these eight men was life worth living.

> In working with them, I forgot all the misery of the world, all the filth that the activities of the Left had generated.[54]

The whole of past and present womankind can never be a match for the dirt perceived by von Selchow. He might on occasion have dreamed of adventures — with such as the Queen of Sheba, for example — but his dreams would have ended in the bliss of abandoning her, or seeing her ripped apart by lions.

> Some of the more indifferent students display no leanings toward adult men. They should be considered worthless; there is nothing to be gained from paying attention to them.[55]

Young men such as these, according to Blüher, are destined to end on the side of the enemy. "Women-lovers" are the chaff, "men-lovers" the wheat; he separates them absolutely.

> I have no sympathy for fanny-lovers.[56] (Thor Goote)

But he has all kinds of sympathy for others:

> We spent the day basking in the sun, lying completely naked on the red-hot sand. The attack came in the afternoon; we had no time to dress. It must have been a strange sight to see naked gun-men standing in the trenches, then advancing stark-naked for counter-attack, protected only by the guns they held in their hands. Warlike as ever, these young men gleamed naked and white in the glistening sun. Even in the wood, their slim bodies shimmered through the branches. This was the swiftest and most exhilarating attack I ever experienced.[57] (Salomon)

Our generation may have difficulty in seeing our fathers as men whose allegiance to the fascists was secured by their pleasure in such visions. By the time we made their acquaintance, very little of such past investment was visible; it had long since been dispensed with. Yet in the twelve years of fascism, our fathers had experienced those images as pleasurable. Only the aftertaste was bitter — as is any experience of the dizzy heights of masculinity.

"Your health, brothers!" The girl from Kulmbach. Postcard (1910).

There are things it is only possible to talk of among men:

> Respect for one's opponent—respect that permits one to fight him, not as human being, but as pure principle. If a man cherishes an idea, he defends it with all the resources of power and spirit— resources that may include the gas attack and the flame-thrower.[58] (Ernst Jünger)

According to Elaine Morgan, any woman who attempted to participate in such things would find the whole structure designed for a different type of mind, just as she would find a gents urinal designed for a different type of body.[59]

Dannecker and Reiche have described the inclination to participate in wage labor as "the most generalized collective fate of the drives in societies under the capitalist mode of production."[60] (In view of what has been said above of the soldier body, it would seem necessary to extend this formulation.) In societies where men dominate relations of production between the sexes,[*] the most generalized collective fate of the drives—at least the drives of men—would seem to be a love channeled toward men. In women, the same erotic form is modified, to become a willingness to subordinate themselves to a man (or to men in general).

We all know men's demands that affairs be conducted "man to man," without women having to "worry their pretty little heads" about them. What I am suggesting is that the psychic disposition that produces these attitudes and formulations may not be particularly unusual. Far *more* uncommon is both the psychic disposition and the knowledge required to eradicate them.

It could even be argued that men who reject male company should be considered more homosexual than the most devoted apologists of male society; in general they are certainly likely to be more sexual.

Even the terms used to describe such men—as "latent" homosexuals— are inadequate; for what is "latent" about society's manifest demands that attraction be channeled into "the masculine"; that "femininity" be both devalued and encoded as the repository of every threat to the male "ego"? "In the depths of her being, she hides a secret trapdoor into the void. . . . But nothing will suppress the man of the *Bund;* for he has pledged the best of his being to men."[61](Blüher)

Freud and History

Freud, 1904:

> The education of boys through male persons (by slaves in antiquity) seems to encourage homosexuality. The frequency of inversion among the present-day aristocracy is made somewhat

---

[*]Relations that produce the greater part of the reality of human relationships.

more intelligible by the employment of menservants, as well as by the fact that their mothers give less personal care to their children.[62]

Freud makes this apparently insignificant and incidental comment in his *Three Essays on the Theory of Sexuality.* But the observation absolutely undermines any attempt to use Freudian psychoanalysis to explain the genesis of "inversion." Freudian explanations center on the tendentially homosexual man's identification with the mother—a theoretical construct that crumbles under the weight of even the tiniest shred of historical evidence. Such evidence is provided by Freud's comment here; it reveals the motivating impulse of psychoanalysis—and its fundamental fault—to be its desire to hold fast to its own ahistorical, indeed anti-historical character.

"Homosexuality" is not a problem for doctors; it is a political problem that touches every one of us. Any theoretical attempt to divorce homosexuality either from masculinity or from the fate of sexuality in general has to be seen as contributing to the maintenance of a *status quo* in which *specific* forms of homosexual practice are denounced and pathologized.

The struggle for power as a struggle between the homosexual and the anti-homosexual

In the absence of authentic material—or more specifically, in the absence of statements from fascist men directly involved in sexual relationships with other men—it is impossible to determine the nature of those relationships in any detail. But among the rumors circulated by the fascists, there do emerge two relatively clear characteristics.

It seems in the first instance to be a matter of fact that, before Röhm's elimination and the disempowering of the SA in 1934, many national-socialist leaders made no secret of this homosexuality—not at least to the internal public of right-wing circles. When Rossbach published his memoirs in 1950, he wrote:

> The indomitable Röhm made not the slightest secret of his homosexual inclinations. Hitler had known of them since 1926— and had still made him SA Chief of Staff.[63]

Rossbach was writing in 1950; yet he still avoided any mention of his own "homosexual" inclinations. But he does name various high-ranking SA leaders as having been "exposed" for "sexual misdemeanors"; they include Heines, Heydebreck, and Ernst. He writes of Röhm's homosexuality as "common knowledge for many months. . . . I was particularly disquieted by the cynical way in which Goebbels, of all people, elected himself to the position of moral arbiter."[64]

This brings us to our second point. Since "homosexuality" was never publicly sanctioned, it remained shrouded in obscurity; and it was this that allowed it to play a privileged role in the Right's internal power struggles. There was always the potential for "revelations" of homosexuality to be presented as evidence of depravity, or of offenses against prevailing morality. Extensive use was made of such revelations to attract hostility to the offenders, as deviants from the norm. Numbers of the ostensibly "political" wrangles that took place within national male organizations appear to have had sexual origins. Throughout the 1920s, there were reports of SA men being shot, either for having roused another man's jealousy[65] or for other unspecified reasons (the latter cases were often presented as "Red murder"). A number of these murders seem to be traceable to internal quarrels and broken friendships, further complicated by internal jostling for position. Certainly, the available evidence proves conclusively that no "reds" were involved in the majority of cases of "Red murder."[66*]

There is a significant moment in Rossbach's account, where he contests the right of Goebbels "of all people" to act as "moral Arbiter." It remains unclear what he means by "of all people"; in a way typical of the fascist writers, he assumes this to be "common knowledge" on the internal grapevine. The men take it for granted that *every one* of their number, from the highest to the lowest, has some smear on his own conscience; the extent to which the relevant information can be used against him is seen simply to depend on prevailing configurations of power. The opportunity principle alone governs the German fascists' denunciations of sexual deviance — and in their internal power struggles smear campaigns were by far the favorite weapons. Unlike Stalin, Hitler never accused men from his own ranks of betrayal — of joining the Communists, or becoming agents for the Third International. The "misdemeanors" that attracted censure were not political, but sexual; and foremost among them was "homosexuality."

Röhm was not the only man eliminated by these means. In 1938, it was the turn of General Fritsch, destined originally to succeed Blomberg as Supreme Commander of the army — a post also coveted by Hitler himself. At first, it was Göring whose help was enlisted to implicate Blomberg with a "woman of ill repute." When Göring subsequently quarreled with the SS, Hitler confronted Fritsch with "incriminating evidence" from a boy prostitute. The Supreme Commander gave his word of honor that he was not homosexual; and the accusations against him did indeed later prove to be fabricated.[67]

Even on the official level, fascist power struggles are, then, rarely encoded (as they are by contrast in the Soviet Union) with threats of infiltra-

---

*To stress the point once more: terror does not derive from homosexuality; instead, male bonding fosters a tendency toward the formation of aggressive, "homosexual" practices, which may spill over into any number of other forms of aggression. The same is, however, also true in principle of "heterosexual" practices among solder males.

Memorial Day (*Heldengedenktag*) 17 March 1935. From left to right: Field Marshal von Mackensen, the *Führer*, *Reich* War Minister Colonel General von Blomberg. Second row: Supreme Commander of the Army, Freiherr von Fritsch, General Göring, Admiral Raeder. "Soldiers and politicians . . . not even a normal madman would desire them."

tion by the wrong *political* tendency. They are conducted on the pretext of *moral* transgression.

Why is this? Political opponents, it seems, can be defeated; the threat they pose to fascist stability and domination is minimal. The Nazi ego, by contrast, is substantially threatened by any potential decoding of what constitutes normative behavior within Nazism; sexuality in the widest sense is perceived as dangerous.

Thus what Nazis in power saw as threatening in Communism was not so much its "political" force as its capacity to devour and dissolve them. Perceiving only too well that they themselves possessed the same capacities, they publicly combatted them in others, by denouncing the "immorality" of generals or party leaders—condemning men in high places.

Double double-bind

We are now in a position to establish why the fascists ultimately maintained the prohibition on homosexuality. Two reasons emerge from the above. In the first instance, the fascists feared the potential of permissible homosexuality to develop into forms of sexuality they could no longer easily organize and contain. Second, the legalization of homosexuality was seen as likely to eliminate one of the key areas of *transgression* into which the fascist had to be initiated and accepted, were he to gain access to the secrets that were the domain of a specific power elite. In other areas of social life, the Nazis were clearly denied access both to secrets and power; thus homosexuality became all the more indispensable. It replaced access to social decision-making power with the freedom to do what was *forbidden.*

But this freedom was also a shackle—in two senses. Though the fascists willingly consented to a "movement" that served their own aims, the freedom it afforded them was always potentially coercive; if they failed to do what the "movement" demanded, they risked exposure and condemnation. In the end, they faced a second double-bind, a second dilemma to parallel the double-bind that simultaneously prohibited and commanded incest between men: thou shalt love men, but thou shalt not be homosexual. A second commandment: thou shalt do what is forbidden, yet still be punished, if those in power so desire. Each carefully constructed double-bind is a time-bomb: the trapeze artist may successfully tread the "tightrope" between power relations—but he will never eradicate them. His best strategy is deferral, a repression of contradictions. For the fascist, any potential deterritorialization (in this case, the dismantling of particular bourgeois prohibitions) is channeled into a tangled system of dependencies, in which his survival depends on his acceptance of a system of unconditional obedience, or a system of endless intrigue held together by one thing only—*power.* Blüher describes the product of the system:

> What was most immediately striking about (Hitler's) bodyguards
> was their handsomeness. He surrounded himself with young men
> of extraordinary beauty—men worthy to become the pride of our
> line, with the delicate features we know as "nordic." Such was
> the male company kept by Hitler, the type to which he professed
> allegiance. At first glance, their eyes seemed empty; only on
> closer scrutiny did they seem to flicker with some distant mystery.
> Were these the men I knew from the youth movement? What had
> become of them? . . . They seemed spellbound by some
> treacherous enchantment.
>   And then it came to me . . . they were in love with the
> *Führer!*—a man who, for his part, never countenanced friendship,
> but *repressed* it instantly. These young men were banished
> unwillingly into marriage; though they were more than likely to

make their women unhappy, they would at least make mothers of them. I myself have spoken to many of these young men, and could tell endless tales of their suffering.[68]

Backbiting

The system into which the fascist enters, more or less absolutely, excludes such things as mutual respect—let alone love relationships. The fact is most clearly demonstrated at points when power structures fragment—and shatter any semblance of "love" between the system's former adherents. After the collapse of Nazism in 1945, any benevolent description of one Nazi by another seems to me to have become more or less nonexistent. Each depicts the rest (himself excepted) as a collection of reprobates whom he would gladly have restrained had he been able (which he regrettably was not). In the Nuremberg Trials, it became standard procedure for the accused voluntarily to express their distance from other Nazis, fellow defendants included; at the same time, almost all of them held fast to what they called the "idea" of Nazism. In so doing, they re-established their own sense of coherence; while others could be presented as deranged and incompetent, they themselves could be seen to have remained good Nazis. Since they needed the fascist system—it was the only one they could tolerate—they defended it as system, but condemned its individual representatives; they were insignificant and dispensable.

The point is amply demonstrated by a short extract from the notes of G. M. Gilbert, who not only interviewed all the accused during the trials, but also listened in on their private conversations.

> Goering on Ley's suicide: "Well, I'm not surprised he's dead, because he's been drinking himself to death anyway." (5) Streicher: "Oh, Goering! He couldn't even get his marriage to work. Yes, I know it was because of Goering and nobody else that I lost my post as Gauleiter in 1940 because of the story that his child was produced artificially."* (16) Goering on Ribbentrop: "Just because the wine merchants Ribbentrop associated with happened to include some English noblemen, Hitler thought he had a man with "connections." . . . But in spite of his ignorance, Ribbentrop was as arrogant as a peacock about his position." (8) Frank on Hitler: "In later years I realized what a cold-blooded, hard, insensitive psychopath he really was. That so-called fascinating look of his was nothing but the stare of an insensitive psychopath!" (13-14) . . . "And his adoration of the nude. . . . To him the nude represented merely a protest against convention

---

*Quotes marked with an asterisk do not appear in the English edition of Gilbert's diary, and thus are translations from the German volume entitled *Nürnberger Tagebuch*. (Tr.'s note.)

which he was able to understand. No, the psychopathic hatred of form and convention was the real keynote of Hitler's personality." (14) Frank on Bormann: "Bormann was his *Sekretär Wurm* (from Schiller's play *Kabale und Liebe*)—a contemptible flatterer and brutal intriguer." (14) Von Papen on Hitler: "He was a pathological liar—that is obvious." (18) Goering, on the concentration camps: "Himmler had his chosen psychopaths to carry these things out, and it was kept secret from the rest of us." (25) Streicher on Himmler: "The body structure shows the character. I'm an authority on that subject. Himmler thought he was, but he didn't know anything about it. He had Negro blood himself." (27) Goering: "People are simply egotistical and hateful—they just can't stand each other."*(65) Ribbentrop: "Himmler must have ordered those things. But I doubt if he was a real German. He had a peculiar face. We couldn't get on." (57) Von Schirach on Ribbentrop: "No one ever heard of him, and all of a sudden he turned up as an important man in the Foreign Office, practically overnight." (When Gilbert asks, "He doesn't really belong to the nobility, does he? . . . I assume there's something phony about *von* Ribbentrop," von Schirach replies, "Why no, he doesn't really belong. We've always smiled about that." He then asks Gilbert not to tell anybody about what he had said about Ribbentrop.) (82-83) Speer imputes conspiratorial motives to Goering. (94-95) Ribbentrop on mass murders: "Himmler was cruel. He must have gone mad over the past few years. I believe he talked Hitler into it."* (169) Schacht is described as "brimming over with joy" at Goering's discomfiture: "The fat one is sure taking a beating so far." (109) Smiling contemptuously, Neurath added, "The only thing he can do is smash in windows."* Expressions of malicious satisfaction by many defendants at Goering's difficulties in court, and praise for Prosecutor Jackson. (109) "Statesman! He's a bird-brained idiot!" said Schach in a tone of mocking laughter. "He's proof of Hitler's ignorance of foreign policy."* (on Ribbentrop, 190) Papen: "Ignoramus!" Neurath comments that the reason why Ribbentrop had to attend a clinic in 1943 was not known. The doctor had even "suspected an abnormal sex life."* (198) Speer expresses his irritation with Goering's "posing" as loyal patriot and hero. (148) Ribbentrop to Kaltenbrunner: "I don't know whom to trust anymore."* (201) Dönitz reserved comment, except for the remark, "He (Keitel) is an honest man." "Yes," said von Papen, "an honest man without a mind of his own." "Certainly," said Schacht sarcastically, "an honest man, but no man at all." (141)

Goering on Keitel: "The miserable weakling."[*] (237) Schacht:
"Goering told me himself even in 1933—mind you 1933—he
referred to Hitler as 'that vagabond from a Viennese cafe!'" (173)
Asked by Streicher whether he regarded the statement made by the
witness Gisevius (148) as dangerous for Goering, Frick replied
coolly: "I'm not bothered, I'm interested in looking after number
one."[*] (283) Goering: "Frick is trying to blame me for the crimes
he commited himself."[*] (284) Frick: "I could have broken

Himmler's neck myself . . . but Hitler always supported him. Besides, Hitler didn't want to do things my way. I wanted things done legally. After all, I am a lawyer.'' (177) Schacht: "Everybody was cutting him except Speer, but he didn't give a hang because they were a bunch of animals anyway, as he had always said.'' (183) Later the former admiral Raeder gives a testimony containing an annihilating attack on Goebbels. (207) Dönitz is described as an incompetent, nicknamed "Hitler Boy Dönitz'' on the basis of his final speech to the Hitler Youth. The testimony is equally negative in its portrayal of Ribbentrop, Goebbels, Himmler, and Ley. (207) Dönitz says to Gilbert: "But really they ought to add to the margin of the copy of this document that's been circulated among us, 'Jealousy, injured pride, envious rubbish.' ''* (330)

By this point, the association that has bound these men together has crumbled—and so too has any love between them. Each man unleashes and mobilizes the mechanisms of the white terror against the others. No longer bound by any "totality,'' they almost instantly lose their grip on reality; each man—even Göring—is *firmly convinced* that he may have a chance of escaping the gallows. They absolutely fail to *understand* the accusations against them. Gilbert again:

The innocence of the "white lambs'' was beginning to become a sort of joke in the Youth lunchroom. It was apparent that nobody had anything to do with anything. The foreign minister was only an office boy, the chief of staff of the high command was only an office manager, the rabid anti-Semites were all in favor of chivalrous solutions to the Jewish problem and knew nothing about the atrocities, including Gestapo Chief Kaltenbrunner; and Goering, of course, was the most chivalrous of them all.[69]

On the one hand, these men are always duplicitous; but on the other, they seem incapable of shifting even the tiniest distance from their fascist "positions.'' (Ribbentrop dismisses charges of anti-Semitism in his remarks to Minister Bonnet with the comment, "Well, I never said anything of the sort, because I always thought Bonnet was a Jew himself.''[70]

By this stage, it is quite clear that none of the men is defending what might be called an ideological position; it would be very inappropriate to condemn them for either "demagoguery'' or "sophistry.'' These men, the powerful disempowered, are capable of one thing only; they speak of what they are, in a desperate attempt to remain physically present. If backbiting—the verbal form of flagellation—were denied them, they would lose their existence. Their language cannot even be described as opportunist; it is a survival

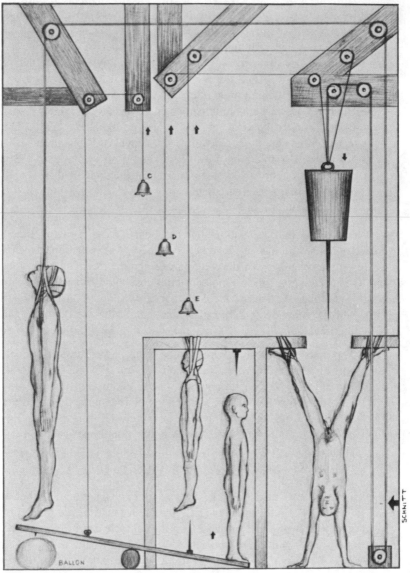

"Will-o'-the-Wisp," by Günter Brus. Finale of the Will-o'-the Wisp sonata (Frankfurt, 1971).

"Birth of Pallas Athena-Minerva," in Michael Meier, *Atalanta Fugiens, hoc est. Emblemata Nova de Secretis Naturae* (Oppenheim, 1618).

mechanism, a means of identifying the individuals these men can still position "below them." Streicher spies an opportunity:

> I warned them for 25 years, but now I see that the Jews have determination and spunk—they will still dominate the world, mark my word! And I would be glad to help lead them to victory because they are strong and tenacious. . . . And if the Jews would be willing to accept me as one of them, I would fight for them. . . . Of course they ought to give me a holiday after passing sentence.[71]

"And now tonight's news. I have to inform you folks that things are looking pretty gloomy around the world."

Conclusion

PRELIMINARY NOTE

I have to inform you that any generalizations I may make in this concluding section are not intended to erase the undeniable differences between the active military core of fascist groupings in the twenties and the large numbers of people who ultimately became their fellow-travelers in the ornamental masses of fascism. Uniformity is not the only characteristic of their writings: there are "qualitative differences," varying uses of nuance, a variety of relationships to the groupings within the national camp, different individual intentions and aims. (Jean-Pierre Faye makes these differences speak with admirable eloquence in his two-volume work, *Totalitarian Languages*—available in faulty translation from Ullstein at DM98.) There are always stray impulses in any writer that seem destined to form themselves into her or his own peculiar distinctive features; or the writer may exhibit the beginnings of an obsession with something other than simply battle and explosion. None of this has been extensively discussed in this study; but this does not mean I myself have considered it "irrelevant." It is the authors who have accorded it lesser significance; like the diverse individuals who later found their way into fascist block formations, the soldier males prefer to stress their uniformity, to ignore diversity, singularity, the specificity of their original subgroup structures, and to concentrate instead on the unities and totalities of which they were members.

Ultimately then, fascist language does appear to be unified around two main features. When the fascists write of the everyday—of their concrete physical relations to other bodies, to themselves, their work, and their sensibilities—their language is meaningless, apparently voided, "aborted." Its second feature is the precise reverse. When it becomes associated with configurations of "living intensity"—in battle, in the pursuit of world-historical missions, in contact with other classes or races, with the proletariat, blacks, lascivious or avaricious Jews, in the company of countesses, in castles, in the relationship between red beasts and white sisters—their language takes on parallel intensity and, usurping its objects, it becomes the parasite that penetrates them and dissolves their boundaries; the force that strips them of their "object-ness" and drains them of life. At these moments, fascist language resonates with desires for explosion; it becomes a function of the writer's compulsive urge to dissolve and escape his armored body, penetrate its interior. Life in the social world is ripped apart, like a planetary system exploding; and fascist language—a language of expression—is unswervingly attracted to the black holes left in reality. At this point, the something that the holes once contained begins to take effect as negative mass—the only thing alive in these men's language.

The main generalizations in these concluding pages will relate to two tendencies identifiable among many Germans under fascism. First, despite their many differences, large numbers of Germans were united in a common understanding of the German situation. In the first instance they saw themselves as Germans, German men (their family name was only secondary); as such, they considered their demand for "power" legitimate—as was their demand for forms of self-realization that pitted them against other living beings.

Their second unifying trait was their determination to rid themselves of their own tormenting feelings—the bodily stirrings that could never again be integrated once released. The Germans were united in the anti-eroticism of their marital relationships, the formal quality of their neighborly relations; in the chilly distinctions demanded by Germany's ubiquitous hierarchical systems; in their unspoken knowledge of the proximity of impenetrable prisons. They were united as the wearers of granite expressions.

What comes to light if we investigate our history is first and foremost our relatively uniform psychic investment of sites of power, our cathexis of the molar mass organizations (and our countercathexis of molecular mass formations). We ourselves might prefer to register differences; but a perception of some form of generality is inevitable.

I am not arguing for fascism's "fellow-travelers" to be seen as absolutely symmetrical with its "core." But, given what we have seen above, it seems unlikely that anyone who did not experience a need for the external block as ego—the necessary qualification for the status of macro-machine components—would voluntarily have inserted himself into any fascist mass formation.

"SA March," by Elk Eber, oil.

If we accept that fascism cannot be treated simply as a form of seduction or misrecognition, but that, as this study has attempted to demonstrate, it is a specific form of production of reality, then analyses of its "core" must be assumed to be representative—at least in part—of the condition of its "followers." Followers, in other words, do more than simply "follow"—though the extent to which they do otherwise remains to be determined. What I am offering is not proof, but a hypothesis whose plausibility seems to me substantial.

FROM THE INSIDE

> We are confronted with a puzzle: the mystery of the spirit that pours out now and then across the world, seizing whole multitudes of men together. No one knows where it originates.[1] (E. Jünger)

> The bond that joined them was stronger than any path of allegiance or institutional regulations; it beat with their hearts' own rhythm. The new commandments that urged them to pursue one line together were acknowledged by every man with the same elemental certainty. They were members of one race; and each man felt the same internal pains and flowing streams.[2]

The fascist "men of action" describe themselves as the objects of all that streamed and poured forth in their time; they experience it as rhythm, intoxication, compulsion and pain. Their comments are credible, not least because they were indeed never personally called upon to justify their actions. They experienced their time as a part of themselves, "beat[ing] with their hearts' own rhythm." "We talked on animatedly into the night, reveling in each new discovery of some similarity in our thoughts or language. We groped our way into distant spaces."[3]

These men continually found each other anew, even when temporarily separated. On a train for "Upper S." in 1921:

> With our proud features framed by shocks of blond hair, we all looked extraordinarily similar—though the reason for our similarity was imperceptible to men unaware of the identical destiny that awaited us. We recognized and greeted each other instantly. We had come from all four corners of the *Reich*; we scented battles and danger; but we knew nothing of each other, we had no marching orders, no specific destination—we knew only that we were bound for Upper Silesia. When we finally left the train, we had already formed the core of a company; the leader, chosen after a few brief minutes of conversation, was immediately and unquestioningly granted authority. One man, later destined to become company sergeant, began drawing up a roll.[4] (Salomon)

Almost all the authors discussed in this study provide similarly celebratory accounts of the sameness of the soldier males.[5] If I have avoided quoting them before, it has been in an attempt not to use them simply to bolster my method—which has consisted of distilling what might be called a "type" from written and unwritten accounts of the men's actions.

The question of whether or not that method is tenable should be assessed in relation to the method itself—and quite independently of theoretical discussion on the status of these men's fantasies as those of "groups," "classes," or "individuals."[6]

My own understanding is that these are the fantasies of very specific male groupings; not groups in the strict sense, but macro-mechanistic totality-formations. The formations reduce themselves to certain axiomatic formulations: "to smash the world to pieces, and then to perish!"[7] (Heinz's formulation for the feeling among the men of the Ehrhardt Brigade, before they march on Berlin to participate in the Kapp putsch.)

The individual, by contrast, may be described as a man "whose soul burned with relentless ardor."[8] This, at least, was the stamp that Dwinger imprinted on his Captain Berthold—a key figure in the soldier literature of the "postwar" period and the man most indelibly branded "Made in Germany." He burned with a flame that no water could extinguish.

There is a widespread assumption that the war created men of this physical and psychic construction; and, though the assumption itself is severely mistaken, its effects are clearly visible in attempts to understand and combat contemporary fascism in Germany. Yet any analysis that claims the foundations of German fascism to have been laid by war and its aftermath, or subsequently by the world economic crisis, obscures the fact that the type of man who contributed decisively to fascism's triumph existed in essence long before the beginning of the war in 1914.[9]

He was made by Wilhelmine Germany in peacetime; by the superficial peace that is the normal form of the permanent state of war waged by capitalist male society against its youth, its women, and its wage laborers—and, indeed, against its men.

Male youth—or, at least, the youth of strata fighting on two fronts—could see no future benefit in the state of "war-as-peace" that prevailed in Wilhelmine Germany. The country was solidly in the hands of abstract fathers; their schools and families were governed by paternal surrogates, who were more concrete, but unconvincing even as paternal likenesses let alone as models for emulation. There remained only the military.

But even everyday life in the Prussian military denied them true tests of strength, true victories, explosive advances. Men of strata on two fronts between the ages of around eighteen and thirty-five demanded nothing short of war; only war offered them the prospect of being recognized as adult and given adult responsibilities. In "peacetime" most men of this age were excluded from the exercise of power; yet for them, power was the only relevant function of social existence.[10] They were grown-up children, fully conversant with Karl May and dreams of world domination—or even speculations on a fourth Ice Age as a curse on contemporary morality[11]—but ignorant of, or uninterested in, the potential or desirable human uses of industry—despite the massive industrial expansion of the preceding half-century.

For these men, then, German imperialism—which both needed them and worked against their interests—took two contradictory forms. As capitalism, it appeared repugnant to them; as militarism, it was the force that promised them life.

Only rarely did they perceive these forms as motivated by the same impulse; the similarity of their underlying dynamic was obscured by divisions in state structures in Germany. Half bourgeois state, half monarchy, Germany was able to neutralize anti-bourgeois (and thus potentially anti-capitalist) sentiment among bourgeois youth by binding them to the military—the residual but glorious form of the monarchist system; and in the military, the bourgeois citizen was reduced to a figure of ridicule.[12]

According to Marx, the German bourgeoisie never fulfilled its world-historical missions; bourgeois revolution was never successful in Germany. But he is mistaken; for, despite the strength of the working-class movement, the bourgeoisie succeeded absolutely in defending its interests in Germany.[13] The

bourgeoisie was vilified by fascism—but it would be less than adequate to see their refusal to resist as "false consciousness." In one sense, fascism fulfilled their true desires—desires for war and militarism.

This is not to say that bourgeois capitalism and fascism are identical. On the economic level, there certainly is an identity between them; if the bourgeoisie considers it necessary for its survival, it can and will produce fascist organization. But from the standpoint of desire, the equation in every sense is inaccurate. The anti-bourgeois attitude of the soldier male is more than mere posturing. His hatred of the citizen as clerk or tradesman is greater even than his hatred of the worker; if he loves his master superiors, he does so not for their bourgeois character but for their association with domains of power. One writer talks of "the bourgeois rabble" as "unstable, opaque, ash-gray, and hopeless."[14]

Some writers have assumed the fascist enthusiasm for war to be a propagandistic invention of later historians and politicians; but there is clear evidence to the contrary. The following two voices speak for many:

> What had we ever known of life? We approached it with utter naïveté, troubled by a sense of inner discontent. War was the new, born of the impulse to heroism; we were fascinated by it.[15]
> (Jünger)

Jünger later talks of himself perceiving war as an "ancient drama" played out in an "era of petit-bourgeois interests." Too weak to contest "petty-bourgeois interests" in "peacetime"—or indeed to combat the terror perpetrated by the petty-bourgeoisie's paternal representatives—the fascists channeled their enthusiasms into war in a thinly disguised attempt to satisfy a desire to blow their fathers' writing desks to pieces. They had never dared plant bombs in "peacetime"—but their need for explosion remained unsated.

> We kept to our quarters, and waited with sullen resentment for the whole noxious world to burst in one great explosion. From time to time, one of our number would be moved to express our thirst for blood in a speech to the assembled company. With visionary intensity, these speeches voiced our common desire to stand the whole older generation against the wall and shoot them—for they were all so clearly corrupt and rotten to the core.[16]

So speaks Bronnen's young Rossbach of his days as a cadet. The desires he voices could be fulfilled—at best partially—by war; for him and others like him, war had bodily significance. It consolidated a male structure organized around the necessity for explosive discharge: a structure in which muscle-physique and organ-physique were locked in perpetual combat, both fearful of contact, yet longing to be coupled. In many of these men, war made that structure irreversible; yet it did not create it[17]—and it is this insight that is crucial to any discussion of fascism. In Germany, the question of fascism is often posed in terms of why the masses bacame fascist in a period of economic crisis; the conclusion from the above is that the problem cannot be understood as specific to the period in question. Only in the *most minimal sense* can fascism be seen as a problem of economic developments toward the end of the twenties. Economic crisis alone would have been as likely—if not more likely—to produce a proletarian revolution.

As Sohn-Rethel rightly remarks of the "middle and lower white-collar workers"—"for whom the party badge was a symbol of faith": "According to (their) technical and organizational function, (they) should have been able to co-operate and solidarize just as well with the workers."[18] Yet they did not do so.

The end of the war made orphans of these men; for the foreseeable future, it deprived them of the element of their lives that gave them form. They had been identical with war, and they responded to its end in this way:

> We were asked to believe that the war had now ended. We laughed—for we ourselves were the war. Its flame burned on within us and gathered all our actions under the glowing and mysterious spell of destruction.

The soldier males *needed* military opponents; it was *inevitable* that they would

"The White Week" (Element:Fire) by Max Ernst.

avidly grasp any opportunity for postwar counter-revolutionary activity. Of the years 1918-1923, Heinz is thus able to write:

> We ourselves were dynamite, explosives planted beneath the vast edifices of a materialist Ice Age that had devastated German soil for a century . . . we ourselves were "explosive"; layer upon layer of our being burned and annihilated these massed obstructions.[19]

To the fascists, the "republic" was a mere extension of the peace of Wilhelmine Germany, the "materialist Ice Age," the "era of petty-bourgeois interests." They saw it as returning to an endless preoccupation with civilian life, creditworthiness or solvency; to a whole system of bourgeois commerce and representations that war had suppressed (albeit temporarily). More crucially, however, the system of bourgeois commerce was now no longer overshadowed by the figure of a kaiser or by the monarchy, and had therefore diminished in authority.

The war had also given these men access to experiences whose memory could not easily be extinguished. What had been no more than a distant feeling in the Wilhelmine period had now crystallized in many of them into a certainty—the kind of certainty that Heinz attempts to capture, describing the men themselves as "explosive." The "massed obstructions" of the republic were experienced as an intolerable burden; and the pressure they exerted far exceeded any experienced in the prewar period. Above all, the republic threatened seriously to undermine any prospect of continued life as a soldier—and thus to eradicate what the fascists perceived as the only acceptable compensation for the general misery of their fate. Among other things then, they hated the republic as a continuation of all that was bad in the prewar period. So this was peacetime?

> Donat lifted his leg and kicked him into the snow; it went flying in all directions. "Not for me," he growled, "I make it on my own terms, or not at all!"[20]

The men's need for war had arisen on the basis of personal interest; thus they considered the conclusion of peace to be an equally personal matter. They recognized none of the negotiated accords and were particularly opposed to the Versailles Treaty.

> They think the war is over. Shit!—as long as we have lost, the war is not over.[21]

It was not only imperative that there be war—it had to be one from which these men emerged victorious.

Wars are there to be "won" or "lost." As Walter Benjamin says,

> Both these words are particularly striking for their double

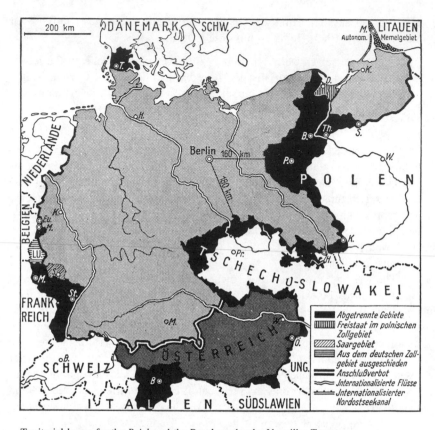

Territorial losses for the *Reich* and the People under the Versailles Treaty.
a. partitioned regions
b. Free State under Polish customs regulations
c. Saar
d. territories withdrawn from German customs control
e. annexation restriction
f. internationalized rivers
g. internationalized North Sea-Baltic canal

meaning. In their first, manifest sense, they refer, of course, to the outcome of war. In the second instance, the event referenced is the same—but its meaning is more absolute, its echoes peculiarly resonant. The words express the postwar balance between victor and vanquished; while the victor retains possession of war, the vanquished is seen to lose it. The victor appropriates war, and makes it his own; but the vanquished loses possession of war and is forced to live without it. What the loser loses is not simply war in and of itself, war in general; it is the most minute of its vicissitudes, the subtlest of its chess moves, the most peripheral of its actions. Our linguistic usage itself is a marker of the depth to which the texture of our being is penetrated by winning or losing a war; it makes our whole lives richer or poorer in representations, images, treasures. And we have lost one of the greatest wars in world history, a war intertwined with the whole material and spiritual substance of our people. The significance of that loss is immeasurable.[22]

The German psyche is not only indelibly marked by the absence or failure of Germany's revolutions; it is imprinted with the *loss of war*—the First World War in particular. The Great War touched the masculinity of several German male generations in its most sensitive area; in the conviction that German men were born to be warriors and victors. It deprived them of the victory they considered their "birthright" and subjected them, as Germans, to a narcissistic wound of the first order.

They made an absolute equation between their own needs and those of the supreme entity they encapsulated in a single little word—Germany.

Our pistols rapped out a message of protest to counter our opponents' cunning, deceit, and cowardice; we met their actions with equal measures of ferocity, honesty, and strength. Future generations will recognize that protest as the emergent form of original forces (. . .) German life in its purest form.[23] (Heinz)

Dear brother and sister-in-law! Breslau, 26 March 1920

I am writing to tell you we embark today for Westphalia. We hope to stop off and expect to make a clean sweep at Beyenburg. When the Third Naval Brigade descends, the grass itself stops growing. We fight for the essence of Germany (*das Deutschtum*).

Greetings
Your own Karl

(Text of an intercepted postcard.)[24]

These men present their assessments of self as unquestionable; they require no supporting evidence, nor can they be refuted. They are seen as necessarily endorsed by anyone "German"; detractors are perceived to be approaching the threshold beyond which they will be "unworthy" of living. The soldier males make their self-definitions appear as no more or less than factual perceptions.

The fascists were convinced of the legitimacy of their cause; and it would have been almost impossible to deflect them. They had done everything required of them; they had obeyed paternal orders, renounced freedoms and pleasures, swallowed the degradations of the drill—at least until they themselves were put in positions of command. They had gone gladly to war and given their best; they had accepted the worst and lived to tell the tale; they had honored and loved the Kaiser, "protected" their homeland . . . and so on. They had honored and cherished each and every quality presented to them as inherent in German being; they had done everything demanded of them in the name of Germany. When Germany "collapsed," the only option for these men—since they perceived themselves as the embodiment of German essence—was to represent themselves as the only Germans remaining in existence. How could they not repudiate a peace for which they had never been formed; a peace neither made for them nor in any sense *by* them; a peace that threatened to produce an exacerbated version of the slow death of the prewar period?

The most telling description we have of the fascists' compulsive urge to battle comes from Salomon. Not least because he himself never fought in the world war, he depicts the tensions to which the "soldier by nature" is subject in peacetime with particular clarity. Salomon was still in the military academy when Germany capitulated; from this time on, he channeled all his expectations of war into the military activities of the postwar situation; he took every opportunity that presented itself to him.

Salomon thus becomes a central figure among the *Freikorps* authors; for it is his case that most clearly demonstrates the extent to which the psychic structure whose imperatives and demands his writing perpetually reiterates was precisely *not* created by war. The type of men under scrutiny in this study were more than adequately produced by the form of *education* for warfare that Salomon received in the military academy. The soldier male is often presented as a type molded by the frontline experience, a man rendered incapable of peaceful civilian existence; but that image is no more than a useful myth to mystify the genesis of German fascism. The process whereby the relation between women and men becomes a perverted relation of anti-production—a process that consolidates prevailing prohibitions on the flowing of the stream of desire—is of far greater significance for the rise of fascism than any changes wrought by war on the soldier's nature.

The problem of fascism has to be seen as a problem of the "normal" organization of our lived relations—a problem for which, as yet, we have no resolution. The question of whether any given form of bourgeois-capitalist society should be defined as prefascist, not yet fascist, almost fascist, or whatever, is of only secondary significance—a definitional puzzle for political scientists.

Even Salomon himself quite clearly perceived the true nature of the target of his passion for fighting. Writing of his first substantial war mission—his participation in the Baltic campaign—he states,

> The ferocious craving we experienced as we lay ravenously anticipating battle had nothing to do with the Bolsheviks.[25]

"The New Idea," by Mölnar.

Its cause was something different:

> We lay in the sizzling darkness, searching for a gateway to the
> world. Germany lay somewhere behind us in the mist, a confused
> mass of images. We looked for firm ground to give us new
> energy; but it did not present itself willingly. We searched for the
> new, the last possible hope for Germany and ourselves; but
> somewhere in the mysterious darkness beyond, there lurked some
> unknown and formless power, the object both of our admiration
> and our hatred; it repulsed all our approaches. We had set out to
> defend a frontier; but we found no frontier here. We ourselves
> were the frontier, the men who kept all pathways open. We had
> scented an opportunity, and become pawns in a larger game
> played out on the ground beneath us.[26]

To the soldiers, the military campaign represents a pathway through the "darkness," a way of breaking through the mist and entering the world. They are *transformed* and *unified* in military action.

In Salomon's description—as so often elsewhere—the Red Army soldiers play an involuntary role; they are the "formless power" that "repulsed our approaches," the object chosen to be transformed into a perception of the "bloody mass": the monster that guards the gateway of life. Salomon openly ridicules the alleged goal of military action ("defending the frontier"); as he says, "we found no frontier here." The only frontier he finds is the boundary that delineates the self of the male soldier—a boundary he will trace, consolidate, and ultimately transgress—in battle.

> The word "advance" held a mysterious and dangerous excitement
> for those of us who set off to do battle in the Baltic. For us, the
> attack represented the ultimate, liberating intensification of energy;
> we longed for the confirmation it would bring of our sense that we
> were made for every possible destiny. In the attack, we expected
> to experience the true values of the world within us.

Salomon is *not remotely interested* in the political or strategic aspects of the "advance."

> To us, the "advance" never meant marching on military goals,
> capturing points on the map, line across the landscape. Instead, it
> meant learning the meaning of a harsh communality; experiencing
> the heights of tension to which the fighting man is projected. It
> meant relinquishing all our ties to a world that was rotten and
> sinking—a world with which the fighting man had nothing more
> in common.[27]

The texts of the soldier males perpetually revolve around the same central axes: the communality of the male society, nonfemale creation, rebirth, the rise upward to hardness and tension; the phallus climbing to a higher level. The man is released from a world that is rotten and sinking (from the morass of femaleness); he finally dissolves in battle. The biting clarity of all these images allows them to be traced to a source in these men's most intense compulsions; and indeed the writers themselves explicitly indicate that it is these compulsions, and not what are traditionally termed "political" convictions, that determine their actions.[28]

Almost every author proudly professes his ignorance of politics—the politics of parliaments, parties, newspapers, and tittle-tattle.[29]

> Comrades! We are here to defend one of the great causes of our fatherland; we see brothers of our stock, fellow Germans, in need of assistance. Our goals are lofty and sacred; they are far removed from politics or party politics, far above local, everyday wrangling and petty troubles.[30]

This is a man far enough "removed" from everything around him to be able to perceive himself as existing only for himself and for his own sake; an upstanding man indeed. Perhaps even as upstanding as the men of the Pfeffer *Freikorps*, who advertised themselves in January 1919 with the following poster:

> If the influence of politics and other pigs' filth continues to spread, we shall be finished . . . absolutely finished! It is not the people's business to be told why they should fight.[31]
>
> From the opposite side of a yawning gulf, we were constantly challenged to say what we "actually wanted"; but we could never answer. We neither understood the question, nor would the questioners have understood our answer.[32](Salomon)

This is more than empty blathering; for these men were indeed ignorant of things "political." To give one example: in novels and reports on the "Baltic campaign" they lament their "betrayal" by the Latvians. Latvian bourgeois Republican forces needed reinforcements in their campaign against the Red Army: this was the only reason they permitted German troops—the soldiers of a defeated army—to remain in the Baltic region. In the event of the Latvians winning the war, Ulmani's republican government promised settlment rights to the German soldiers. They were to be apportioned parts of the massive estates of the German Balts, whom Ulmani had promised to expropriate, indeed to eliminate. Volunteer troops from the aristocracy were also involved in the fighting; ostensibly, they were fighting not to defend their own interests but those of the Republic.

When the Red Army was finally defeated, an officer of the Baltic volunteers (who had dubbed themselves the *"Baltische Landeswehr"*—the Baltic

Fletcher, Commander of the Baltic National Army.

Manteuffel.

Commander of the German Legion.

National Army) led a putsch against the Ulmani government, with the help of Manteuffel and von Pfeffer, commander of a German *Freikorps*. The government they installed was in every sense colonial: representative only of the interests of the German Balts, it was led by a puppet president in the person of a Germanophile pastor, Needra. The putsch was neither planned by the Germans nor were the troops and commanders informed of it in advance. In the end, they accepted it as a *fait accompli*.[33]

By this point it was clear that only an unqualified German victory held any prospect of delivering the promised settlement into German hands. But victory was impossible; the German troops were few in number, and they faced armed opposition, not only from the Allies (the English), who needed a Republican government in Latvia to establish the "buffer zone" they desired. Inevitably, the Republican Latvians joined forces with the English against the "Iron Division" and the Baltic National Army; they defeated both, with predictable rapidity—whereupon the Germans howled with rage at this "breach of faith" by the Latvians.[34] The Germans demanded in all seriousness of Ulmani—now newly restored to power—that he "redeem" the Latvian promise of land for German settlement.[35]

When sections of the "Iron Division" later defected to Avaloff's White Russian troops, they did so out of anger over the attitude of the SPD/Center Party government in Berlin toward the whole affair. Unsurprisingly, the government dismissed the troops as reactionary mercenaries (though this did not subsequently prevent them from mobilizing the same troops against the German workers).

The residues of the "ID" demanded nothing less of the Berlin government than that it retain the Eastern policy of the Wilhelmine era. Refusing absolutely to acknowledge Germany's defeat, they construed the activities of the men in Berlin as a betrayal of Germany—betrayal by the "socialists."

"Any man who is not with us is a traitor. We demand victory and land—and the fulfilment of those demands should be in no sense dependent on our actual behavior." Such were the convictions of the men of the Iron Division—convictions that remained impervious to accusations of political contradiction or impossibility. The solder males were never intimidated by "inconsistencies"; witness the following telegram from the *Stahlhelm* on 4 November 1923:

> We must put an end to the current situation; this is a time for action, not negotiation. While millions starve, the greedy thousands live in luxury. A band of thugs is tearing our German Fatherland from us piece by piece. Only an immediate national dictatorship can save Germany. You are chancellor of the *Reich;* we hereby demand that you install the necessary dictator.[36]

Abb. 130. „Des Oſtens deutſcher Friede"   „Kunſt und Leben", 1918

"The German Peace of the East," "Art and Life" (1918).

The standpoint adopted by this "we" is not political; it relates purely to self-interest. The "we" that wishes to improve its own situation offers a last chance to the chancellor:

> Could our officers have been called agitators? Great heavens, what did we officers know of politics, what had we read in the six preceding years? Army reports, divisional and regimental orders, training regulations; a few Sunday novels, or letters from loved ones full of domestic complaints and worries; letters that endlessly repeated the question, "Could things not somehow be different and better?"
>
> (. . .)
>
> The above was written retrospectively by Noske and published as an open newspaper statement. The soldiering population was unified in a general nationalism; it neither belonged to, nor followed, a single party, but could itself be seen as a new form of party—one which had eradicated the divisions between right and left, and which perceived itself only as German. Its slogan was "Deutschland über alles":
>
> "Germany, crushed after world-shattering victories, Germany (in the best sense of the word) shall rule." . . . As long as a man carried a gun by his side, he would have no truck with the ugly language of party politics. Even such men as Lüttwitz were no exception—as Gröner, himself a former general under the Kaiser, has explicitly attested.[37] (Rudolf Mann)

The general in question played a leading part in preparations for the Kapp putsch; here, one of the general's own men admiringly testifies to his lack of even the slightest inkling of politics.

Mann's text also outlines a new definition of politics—one that was later to be harnessed and organized by the NSDAP. What he proposes is that the "soldiering population" be seen as a new form of party, a party joined in "blood," unified by the feelings its members share.

The Weimar Left, despite its "political acuity," never recognized the innovative quality of fascist politics; the only exception was Ernst Bloch:

> A strange and pernicious circularity is at work (in politics). The barriers erected against the "soul" by the capitalist apparatus are familiar; the soul in turn struggles for release; it strains to burst out of capitalism's dehumanizing monotony. And yet, in both the practice and the theory of vulgar Marxism, the soul is similarly segmented off—albeit in different forms. Vulgar Marxism is the form first encountered—indeed encountered often—by white-collar workers; and it produces their ultimate retrenchment to reactionary "idealism."[38]

But what concepts Bloch uses! Placing the "soul" in quotation marks, he flirts with associations of religious opposition to notions of the "unconscious." He talks of "idealism"—a term which, in its philosophical context, represents the necessary opposite of "materialism"; yet this opposition can never adequately define what Bloch (in an arbitrarily narrow definition) identifies as the problem of the "white-collar workers." And finally, it is surely necessary to dispense with the "vulgar" before "Marxism"; only then can his account begin to approximate the truth of the interwar situation.

Salomon has better ways of describing what Bloch calls "reactionary idealism."

> War and adventure, uproar and destruction: the torment of an unfamiliar urge swelling from every last corner of our hearts! Was this truly our desire—to tear a gateway through the constricting walls of the world, to march across fields glowing-hot, to stamp across rubble and scattered ashes, to hunt through tangled forest, across rolling heathland, to gnaw and jostle our way to victory in the East, in the hot, white, dark, cold country that stretched from here to Asia? I do not know if we did or did not desire such things—but we did them.[39]

Marching, stamping, scattering, hunting, jostling to victory: these are the movements into which the soldier males' desire to "flow away" transforms itself. Both in the capitalist apparatus and elsewhere, their desire is channeled into and imprisoned within double-binds, in which relations between the sexes and with the self are profoundly ruptured. These men "gnawed" their way eastward (Did Germany not need "space" for its "people"?).

For the heroes of the early bourgeois *Bildingsroman*, intervention in the world, and experience of it, were gained through *travel*; the citizen as ship navigated a path through numerous adventures before finally seeking refuge in the calmer waters of the marital streamlet. The fascists, by contrast, gain experience through *piracy*; they raid and annihilate all things alien. They do not observe—they persecute; where once a peaceful landscape gently mirrored the feelings of the wandering onlooker, the landscape now only exists in symbiosis with the body of the man racing across its surface. The fields glow red-hot, the forest is tangled, the heathland rolls; the landscape itself crouches in tense anticipation of the moment when it will devour him.

Salomon does not *look* eastward; he forces a path to victory. His text is stretched tight across numerous oppositions: he poses white against dark, hot against cold, hard against soft, standing high versus lying low. The terms are mutually exclusive; there is only yes or no, man or woman, life or death. There are no pathways to link one side to another; only *walls* and barbed-wire defenses. For Salomon, life is located in a gesture of destruction; "tearing a gateway through the constricting walls of the world." And—according to Jünger—any man whose nerve fails him "deserves shooting."[40]

The men who marched to Upper Silesia were prepared to meet death, greedy for battle; yet none of them had set out to defend the sanctity of existing treaties. Not one of the men marching in the ranks would have appealed to the forces of morality, conscience, or reason to defend his action. These young men exacted just revenge on any man who declared himself to be defending eternal justice, or some inalienable right written in the stars.[41]

Salomon speaks with the authentic and realistic voice of a suppressed and cheated desire. He quite correctly represents the soldier male's "right to revenge" as a privilege he is far more likely to realize than his right to life; these men's only resource is their compulsion for revenge (though they speak as victims reduced to this state by others on whom vengeance *can no longer be wrought*). "Revenge" is exacted instead on any being who continues to live life as such; on individuals whose "desire to desire" has never been transformed into the urge to murder. It takes two forms: either the world is incorporated into a destructive totality or it is condemned to death. The fascists formulate any legitimate grievance in terms of their "right to revenge"; indeed this seems to be the basis on which they express their right to revolution. We should beware, however, of seeing this in terms of *expression* alone; for it is surely in the transformation of legitimate revolution into legitimate revenge that the old Benjaminian formulation is finally exhausted. The transformation takes place not on the level of representation alone but on that of action. Fascist revenge is vast and expansive; it devastates the earth and annihilates human beings by the millions. Fascism may not have offered "justice" to the masses; but it did offer them the *power* to take revenge. While it may be possible to classify certain of the party congresses as expressive theater or representation, the same terms can never be applied to war or civil war, and certainly not to the concentration camp. These forms should be seen instead as orchestrating direct incursions by the fascist macromasses into the part of the earth which the fascists—quite simply by virtue of their own existence—considered their own.

The terms *revolution* and *revenge* encapsulate in political categories the two poles of desire in its left-wing and right-wing "extremes." They are similar in the sense that neither allows itself to be diluted by traveling the route normally taken by bourgeois madness—the illusory route of sublimation and guilt which would subject them to the hidden law of the double-bind. Neither voluntarily renounces its place in history.

The revolutionary is forced to *perceive* what exists and *how* (to perceive the *multiplicity* of existing phenomena); the fascist, by contrast, consumes the world—it is the material from which he constructs new macro-unities, new totalities.

All of us today are expressionists, men who wish to form the external world out of our own inner selves. The expressionist builds a new world in himself. His inner ardor is his secret and his power; but his conceptual world is repeatedly shattered on contact with reality. The soul of the impressionist is a microcosmic image of the macrocosmos. But the soul of the expressionist is a new macrocosmos, a world in and of itself.

The expressionist's perception of the world derives from his sense of his own autocratic selfhood; both he and the world are explosive.[42]

The author of this passage — it is Goebbels, in *Michael* — cannot in my view be seen as anything less than fully conscious of his own state of being.[43] The only thing he did not yet know was that he and his kind would one day have the power to impose what he calls their "conceptual world" on reality; it was reality that was to be "shattered." (At this stage, of course, the fascists themselves lacked the necessary capital.)

Jünger writes in similar vein of the war already fought by the soldier males:

We were the God of War incarnate; like other Germans who had made their periodic mark on history, we rose up with a Germanic fury that brooked no resistance. Only terror could counter the hatred of the men we confronted, yet allow us to retain our dignity. And so we stand here today as the terrible executors of an absolute justice — a justice that follows its own laws, a justice asserted against even the strongest will in a hostile world.[44]

If we concede that what men such as this demand is little more than the right to be what they are (or have become), then it seems to me more or less impossible to formulate any "moral" judgment on them. It seems we have to see their power as a right granted them by the *psychic law* to which they are subject. They may find ways of making use of the world; but they will always be acting against their own will in a world that necessarily appears "hostile." Any action, even the most insignificant, threatens to take on the quality of transgression. Every step taken by the soldier males contravenes the will of another; thus their aim is to "break" the will of the other.

These men experience their affinity with power as "natural." To them, powerlessness means the threat of permanent exclusion, both from justice and from pleasure. Their every action thus becomes an *assertion of themselves*; they are always in *opposition*. Yet their transgressions are organized within systems of absolute obedience. Their status as components within totality machines gives them the feeling of being-in-power, but the machines themselves function according to strictly hierarchical principles; each component is allotted a single position. While every component experiences a sense of power, that power is neither individual nor can it be gained in isolation. The machine partakes of, and represents, a larger social power, which it functions to maintain and celebrate. The machine—whose form recalls the supreme phallus itself—is a glittering pearl among fascism's working monuments to the power of the abstract father.

The moments in which the machine erupts are experienced by the individual component as intoxicating; and, paradoxically, these eruptions consolidate the abstract father's power. This is the only form of outburst or eruption permitted by paternal power; and indeed any totality machine component is incapable of desiring other forms, since these would undermine the hierarchical structuring principle from which it draws its energy and which defines its function.

The power of the father has little to do with the *pater familias*; it is an abstraction. The last real father projected to the apex of power was perhaps Kaiser Wilhelm II; and the position of supremacy he so pathetically abdicated remained empty; it was never filled by the fascists. Even the *Führer* preferred to remain the first SA-man of the German *Reich*, the leader of a generation of sons and brothers. And in the texts of the soldier males, real fathers are made to appear corrupt or ridiculous.[45]

This should not be seen as an argument against conceiving abstract social power as the power of the abstract *father*; for these men quite clearly *desire* a father—a man less weak than their own fathers were in reality. They wish for the father who might once have saved them from the morass into which they now feel themselves sinking. This is perhaps why their real fathers barely figure in their writings; they exist only as ambivalent and stereotypical idealizations. While real fathers are silenced by the soldier males, their texts express unmistakable desires for better ones.*

In one of Jünger's novels, for example, *Feuer und Blut* (*Fire and Blood*), published in 1929, the author represents the process of battle through the eyes of one man, second-lieutenant Jünger. At the end of the book, the man's search for a figure somehow linked to the domain of supreme power is revealed to be his dominant motivating impulse. The second-lieutenant is seriously, almost mortally, wounded; but he fights and staggers his way through the lines to headquarters. His troop has captured a strategically important road; and he delivers the news in person to the general. The general remembers Jünger as a brave and promising young man often mentioned in battle dispatches; he expresses his pleasure at finding him still alive, since he has heard he has fallen in battle. Shrapnel wounds in head and shoulder notwithstanding, the second-lieutenant has held out until reaching his goal; his efforts are now rewarded.[46] He has met the general at last and even been praised by him; at this point, he falls down unconscious.

---

*"What is the best of sea battles by comparison with the power of waves whipped by an autumn storm? How much mightier is God the Father still than humanity?" (Or than his sons?) (Capt. Ehrhardt, p.48)

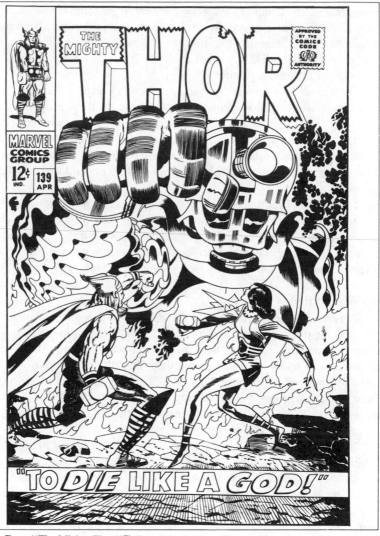

From ''The Mighty Thor.''™ Copyright © Marvel Entertainment
Group, Inc. 1989. All rights reserved.

The thrills of face-to-face combat with the "enemy" gain substance only if accorded the blessing of a supreme paternal agent. The son must be personally designated faultless, the best, by a man in immediate proximity to the father. Once accorded this status, neither his legitimacy as son nor his happiness can be contested. He is thus permitted to lose consciousness.

The soldier males are obedient sons unified in totality formation; and apparently, they long for a "father figure," both to guarantee them perpetual wholeness and to give them access to power. What they desire is access to the supreme phallus and participation in its inherent gleaming omnipotence.

The point is illustrated by Salomon in his faintly ironical description of his second-lieutenant Kay bidding farewell to his comrades in a cafe. The troop is about to be disbanded; and Kay delivers the following speech:

> "We have paused for a moment by the river of time . . . like a clique of bloodthirsty warriors who enjoy their master's favor we have sucked the honey from the bone-marrow of the people, and smeared it across their faces." He stirred his grog agitatedly.
> "When future generations ask what we achieved, we will answer that we stirred up blood. . . . They will applaud us and drink our health—but they will ask the same questions of the men we know

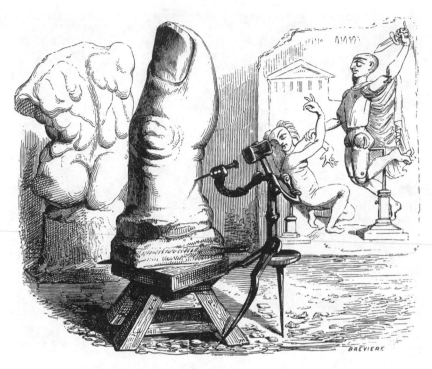

"The Finger of God—a work of enormous dimensions." From Grandville, *Un autre monde*.

as the fat, self-satisfied bourgeoisie—*Prost*! And the bourgeoisie will answer, 'We thickened the blood to soup; it tasted good, clean, and wholesome!' So future generations will send us packing: 'four, five, march!' But on the day of the Last Judgment, . . . we will collect our scattered bones and submit them for roll-call; and we will be told to advance—rightward. And what of the file-gatherers we see gathering dust before our eyes?—*Prost*, Mr. District Attorney, sir, your very good health. They will bow their heads obsequiously and beg pardon from their master; 'we cannot gather our backbones—for we never had any.' The master will recognize them as blockheads and order them leftward—as is only fitting. And I can tell you lads one thing; the division will be a clean one."[47]

As the speech progresses, "future generations" become a single "master," a man who passes sentence on a world that is perverse. Salomon makes an absolute equation between the "left" and "spinelessness." (Both Stekel and Freud have examined the sexual meaning of left and right in their dream-interpretations; they see the right as denoting correctness, the path of righteousness, and the left as synonymous with deviance, the evil and the forbidden.[48]

The son in the text desires a father who will look down on his abstract bones and pronounce him "right" — in all senses: "You have done well, my son." He needs to hear that the left-right division will be a "clean" one; and he places himself on the side of the "*we*" who have a legitimate claim to "bones" and to blood "stirred up" in warfare. He extracts a promise from the father that will be redeemed on the day of the Last Judgment — if not sooner. But the *Führer* remains the leader of sons; he embodies not paternal power but the common desire of sons for the power necessary for their survival — a power they strive to extend and consolidate.

The soldier males' reverence for the hard, upstanding, towering penis is a further sign that they cannot be seen as "homosexuals." They hold fast to the phallus as indissoluble signifier; yet, as Hocquenghem demonstrates, homosexual desire consists precisely in a subversion of phallic dominance.[49] If, as Hocquenghem suggests, anal penetration signals the return of the collectively repressed, then the preservation of phallic supremacy must surely signal a desire to return to the *past state* of the same collectivity. Under capitalism, real fathers are disempowered; thus capitalism holds out the promise of freedom. Yet for the soldier males, freedom came prematurely; they found it unbearable. Freedom transformed the flow of their desire into a torrent that engulfed them; they would have been grateful for fathers, as island rocks to cling to. When a new form of nuclear family was later established, the dead father recommended his reign of terror as a *corpse* in the body of the social. The mother meanwhile, severed from sociality, was more likely to suck life from her children than to give it. The family, one form of human association among many, was more or less guaranteed to produce human beings incapable of acting freely — at least not until they abandoned the fascism of their feelings.

How then does the *Führer* function in this system? He seems to represent a link connecting the sons to the domain of the abstract father's power. Since the *Führer* has access to the father's domain, he knows and executes his will — as indeed ostensibly do all the German fascists. They represent themselves as executors of a historic German will, whose legitimacy is open neither to doubt nor to distortion. Claiming a place for themselves at the very center of social power, they then fill that position with a shrine — the form of their desire.

The fascists meet any claim to political power — a domain they consider exclusively their own — with solemn and righteous anger. Yet they see their own right to power as realized by a system that maintains each man at an appropriate distance from power; each man is kept to his allotted place in the totality machine. Fascist egalitarianism finds expression in the subjection of all to the same jealously guarded principle of *repression*.

The key feature of conservatism seems to be its function in maintaining the balance of equality in the *status quo*. The only permissible freedoms are

Postcard (1915).

Postcard (1915).

those bestowed on fascists by their superior abstract father; in certain ambiguous situations this may mean no freedom is permissible.

This whole system is undermined at one fell swoop by any *impotent* who
possesses greater freedom than the fascist; thus when whole hordes of impo-
tents set out to conquer the domain of the abstract father's power, they are
perceived as trespassing against the holy order of the totality machine—
depriving the fascists, as it were, of their place in the heavens.

It should by this point be possible to reconstruct (though not necessarily
to relive) the shock the fascist inevitably experiences when confronted with
demands for a "dictatorship of the proletariat." He is horrifed not only by the
contents of streams flowing on the streets; he finds the nature of their *trajec-
tory* equally disturbing. He sees the proletariat as flowing into the the domain
of the abstract father's power—the terrain of his desire; into a sanctuary that
has to remain inviolable if he is to be guaranteed rebirth and totality. The only
man permitted to enter that domain is the *Führer*: he and no other.

The fascists see demand for a "dictatorship of the proletariat" as formu-
lated by the *younger* sons of the father, whom they presume to be in league
with all manner of scum and rabble. Their pretensions to "dictatorship" are
seen to indicate aspirations to the status of father. Young Germany is seen to
have joined forces with the unrepentantly striking masses; both now claim to
incorporate the supreme form of desire. A shameful display: carnival characters who seriously intend to save the whole world. And where are the soldiers?

In the totality formation, the dutiful, upright elder son is made subject to
a *Führer*; in the process, he does not simply *retain* possession of the surrogate
phallus—for the phallus which is his by right has hitherto been denied him. If
his "younger," "lower" brothers now depose him, they not only rob him of
the phallus; they immediately expose him. Like the emperor parading his new
clothes, he is forced to admit to the world that his own phallus is *nonexistent*.
When younger sons occupy the domain of paternal power, their elder brothers'
castration becomes public knowledge. More important, the elder brothers—
men once called upon to be the world's masters—are reduced to miserable
failures and banished to obscurity. For all these reasons, the elder brothers
hold fast to a "mission" they see as entrusted to them by the abstract father;
this alone can guarantee them some kind of inheritance, and can more or less
legitimate their access to power. They do not *need* a revolution of the "lower
orders"; for their freedom is power—a power that allows them moments of
eruption, on condition that they become part of the totality formation.[*]

It would be no mean feat of contortion to see nothing more than "false

---

[*]As far as the fascist novels are concerned, this seems to indicate that their hero figures
should be elder or only sons—and this is indeed what they are. Though the fact is never explicitly
emphasized, it is certainly true that sons who are, say, fourth in line never attain the status of
hero. Even heroes from proletarian backgrounds, such as Heini Völker in *Hitlerjunge Quex*
(Quex the Hitler Youth), are presented (quite inconguously) as the only sons of proletarian parents. Heini leaves the Communists to join the Nazis; he is born for better things.

"The White Week" (Prayer) by Max Ernst (text by Jacques Prévert).
"Our Father, who art in heaven—remain there! We for our part shall remain here on earth; for earthly life can be quite beautiful."

consciousness'' at work in the fascists (''they didn't know what they were missing''). For where was the revolution that would have offered them more? We have to acknowledge that the determination of men like Salomon to keep down the lower orders—and to use violence in doing so—corresponded absolutely to their own sense of self; to the demands of their own state of being.

> It was, and will always remain, our duty to fight rulers whose power is illegitimate. The order of values of illegitimate power is dictated by human needs; that of legitimate power is defined by the infinite and deep-rooted force out of which needs are first created.
>
> This force was our unique and constant point of reference; we were never ultimately directed by parties or party programs, flags or insignia, theory or dogma. If there was an identifiable direction to our thinking, it was determined by our ultimate goal: to assert the primacy of force over superficial form, of life over construction, of structured order over mere chance, of substance over falsification. Not content with deliberating the possible meaning of the future, we set about determining criteria of judgment. Such was the task entrusted to us; and the only crime we could commit was failure. We were fighting God's fight with the demons; and the field of battle was vast and open.[50]

The notion that ''human needs'' might be the basis of social existence seems, at first sight, innocuous; one might assume it to be universally acceptable. Yet the soldier male considers it both repugnant and threatening. For his own needs have been denied and repulsed, then transformed into what Salomon calls an ''infinite and deep-rooted force.'' The core of the fascist being has become a force that fuses its elements into a dominant totality. To the fascist, the needs of other human beings—or rather, human beings who retain anything identifiable as needs—are both dangerous and necessary; necessary, in the sense in which ''above'' needs ''below''—for the fascist needs to be superior. The needs of others are dangerous, in the sense that they are satisfied in direct opposition to the fascist; they threaten to undermine his *right* to domination. Every expression of human need limits the soldier male's freedom to *live his life in violence*. It curtails the right to revenge which, for him, has become synonymous with his right to life. ''Germanic rage'' is the only source of need he recognizes.

The principle of allowing ''to each according to his needs'' should be qualified in this context. The notion of need can be switched and extended *ad absurdum*—and for the soldier male, it encompasses the need to murder. There is no point in questioning the ''reality'' of that need; to the soldier male, it is the need he experiences.

To the fascist, any individual who fails to participate in "God's fight with the demons" (note the use of "with" rather than "against," which does not deny interconnectedness with the opponent) must be considered to be on the side of the demons. "God" fights on behalf of the phallus-on-high; he fights to maintain the abstract father's power, the macromass, and its individual totalities. The demons are everything in the lower and inner regions; they are the micromasses, the bacillae of social diseases, the dissipating hybridity of the female, or the unconscious of the male, transformed into negativized bodily flows, amorphous and bestial.

The demon reappears in all manner of forms, across the whole spectrum of representations of the enemy; the bellicose Communist, the lascivious Jew, or the indolent citizen. The first of these is an agent of the lower orders—and he threatens to deprive the fascist of power: the second is the agent of subversive social pleasures; and the third is an agent of death in the quicksand of inactivity. Each in his own way threatens to devour the not-yet-fully-born soldier.

The demons may equally be women—as agents of the flesh or "trapdoors into nothingness"; women as elements within the undirected streaming of pleasure that the not-yet-fully-born sees encroaching on his boundaries: the pleasure he fears will kill him. Or they may be children—the figures who embody the unregulated teeming of micromachines relentlessly seeking the configurations and spaces of desiring-intensities. Of all the devils he fears, the fascist can most readily accommodate to the indolent citizen (as long as the latter submits to domination by the male totality machine), or to the bellicose Communist (as long as he agrees to be molded to the upstanding form of man modeled on the "free man and hero"; this may not necessarily make him a Nazi, but it does remove the threat he represents to the Nazi.

A whole range of different public political terminologies serve the fascists as a source for the names they give their various fears. Their fears of anarchism and Bolshevism most often embody a fear of the castrating Hydra-Medusa; what they fear in "Communism" is the hybrid morass of whorish pleasures, in which they dissolve and sink irretrievably. The "dictatorship of the proletariat" is feared as an uprising of younger sons and lower orders.

These names are neither arbitrary nor simply "projected." In most cases, the perceived object of the men's anxiety does in reality display the characteristics they refer to; what the name allows the fascist to do is, first, to universalize those characteristics and, second, to judge them as he would, were they his own. He engages in a form of object-substitution—a form which becomes most acute in the fascist act of terror, the killer hallucinates a figure familiar to him from his *own* experience, emotion, or history. (As a substitute for his actual victim.)

As we have seen, fascist terror and aggression are organized to lead ultimately to one of three central desired perceptions: the "bloody miasma," the

Election poster (1932). "Marxism is the guardian angel of capitalism. Vote National Socialist."

"empty square," and "blackout" in self-coupling. In those perceptions, the survival of the fascist male is made dependent on the delimiting defense of his boundaries; he survives by differentiating himself as killer, in opposition to whatever he perceives as threatening.

For the "demons," by contrast, boundary-transgression is impermissible.

> Such was the task entrusted to us; and the only crime we could commit was failure.

Under fascism, men of the strata-on-two-fronts are forced "downward" by changes in the hierarchies surrounding them. The primary desire motivating such men to commit themselves *politically* to fascism is their compulsive urge to create and preserve their own selves by engaging in the dynamic process of killing. It is *quite impermissible* to ground their politics in the relations of exploitation of their labor power; they are much more than pauperized bourgeois citizens, brutalized petty-bourgeois, scum with access to power, or even bureaucrats of death. No man is forced to turn political fascist for reasons of economic devaluation or degradation. His fascism develops much earlier, from his feelings; he is a fascist from the inside.[51]

Fascism becomes the site of an existing compulsion to battle—not the reverse. As Lionel Tiger says, aggression is a function of male bonding and can as such be anticipated.[52] Jünger says the same thing, though the terms he uses are more poetic:

> "Of course our cause sanctifies battle; but how much more does battle itself sanctify the cause?"[53] And, "what could be more sacred than a man doing battle?"[54] (A woman?)

In all the situations we have seen described as "sacred," activities that are socially or officially forbidden are publicly and unashamedly practiced in ritual form, by transgressors in some way associated with power.[55] Battle, for example, is the form in which the fascists indulge in forbidden love; they leave their love-objects lying in blood.

> Love and battle are simply two forms of life; and surely both are capable of refinement?[56]

asks Jünger, laconic as ever. The different role played by the *objects* of the two seems to escape his notice.

The soldier type never forgets the terror out of which he is created; but he does accept it. It ingrains itself into his body and deprives him of all other feelings. He talks of "sensitivity"; but he is referring to a sensitivity *produced* by innumerable beatings.

> My whole being experienced the pleasure of observing (. . .) my

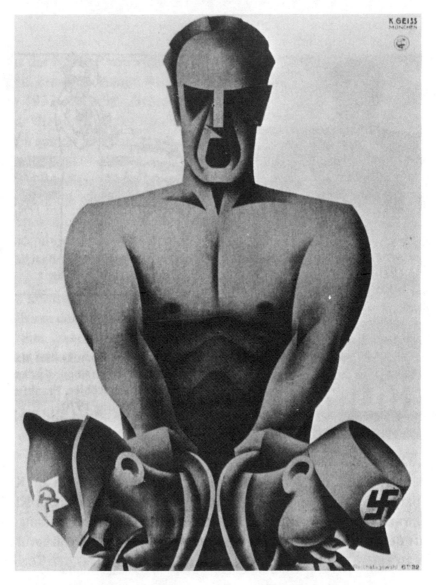

SPD poster for the parliamentary election on 6 November 1932. "These are the two responsible for the gentleman's club we have in government, for the daily worsening of the situation of the German working population. Sentence will be passed on 6 November! Vote Social Democrat!"

desires, hopes, and dreams dissipating in the daily round of pain. In the end, there remained only a bundle of flesh, its exposed nerves shrilly echoing every sound it emitted, taut as a stringed instrument, capable of vibrating with double the usual vigor in the rarefied atmosphere of my isolation.[57]

The writer takes pleasure in "observing" his body as object; like fascist battle descriptions, in which the writer's consciousness characteristically remains "ice-cold," the passage highlights the extent to which the destruction of the fascists's bodily capacity for love is pleasurably invested. The vibrations and streams of the love *he* knows have long since become inseparable from the bodily sensations of his transformation into a component of the totality machine. The fascist is a machine component composed entirely of muscle-armor; a whirring, vibrating instrument that contains its inner organs in an impenetrable inner prison. In pain, he experiences negative orgasm; he destroys himself and other objects, and produces negative revolution. Benjamin calls fascism a "parody" of revolution;[58] but the description is inadequate. Fascism is revolution's negative image; if the negative were developed, the features of the real photographic image would be those of revolution. But fascism inverts the photographic procedure; it takes the whole living social reality and forces it to approximate an image in negative. It creates by destroying, its creations are its own—and they are *deliberate*. Jünger's soldiers are distinguished by their ability "to use war as a means of creation."[59] The fascists destroy others to create themselves; they destroy things in the alien object-world and metamorphose into killing-machines and their components: a "baptism of fire." *Wreaking revenge* is their way of becoming one with themselves; and, significantly—given that what we are investigating is fascism—they experience themselves as at one with their whole era:

> I knew we could never have been wrong; we had lived our lives in accordance with the urgent will of an epoch, and had indeed been increasingly applauded for our actions. We had lived dangerously; but this was a dangerous time. Nothing we thought, did, or believed, was ever less chaotic than our time. We were haunted by our time, haunted by its destruction, haunted too by the pain we would have to suffer if destruction was to be made fruitful.[60]

We should bear in mind that these sons of their time, "haunted by its destruction," represented the most powerful of the fighting forces available to big business, the bourgeoisie and the peasantry, in their various struggles against the revolutionary proletariat. It is rare today to contest the significance of the *Freikorps* soldier males in attempts by the *Reichswehr*, or the SPD-Center Party Government, to quash armed insurrection among the workers. Without the *Freikorps*, the workers could never have been defeated—or at least, they would never have been crushed so absolutely.[61]

It is similarly unlikely that organizations such as the SA, or other sections of the "national underground," would have survived the phase of Weimar "stability" between 1924 and 1928, had it not been for the *Freikorps'* tireless quest for revenge, for murder, for *differentiation* through destruction.

I had always taken particular pleasure in destruction.[62]

A *leitmotif* can be understood not as literary technique, but as the expression of an obsession: and destruction is the *leitmotif* that runs through the whole labyrinth of emotions experienced by the not-yet-fully-born in his search for well-being. He aspires to live

> in raging wrath.[63] — The fanatical intransigence of the soldier is visible in his very features. Deep in his eyes, there glows a cold and merciless will to destruction.[64]

And in the moment of attack

> we felt only an all-consuming urge to still our blood's appetite; we planned a lightning attack on the house.[65] The whole of Tetelmünde was burning, like an enormous torch set alight by the primitive drives of men possessed. Our men felt the original human desire beating and screaming for justice inside them — the desire for destruction.[66]

How dubious is it to speculate that Freud's death-drive hypothesis may have been introduced into his psychoanalytic theory as a *defense* against the "madness" of statements and actions such as these? Certainly, the raging, destructive frenzy expressed in many such comments by Freud's contemporaries was hardly susceptible of psychoanalytic interpretation.[67] Any attempt to use existing psychoanalytic methodologies to study the agents of massive processes of contemporary destruction would have posed an enormous dilemma for psychoanalysis; for the psychoanalysts would have been required to explain why the destroyers — who, in analytical terms, would certainly have been considered "psychotic" — were so rarely associated with the psychiatric clinic, the lunatic asylum, or with what would normally be termed criminal delinquency. Instead, their context was a political one. Their particular form of libido perversion could not be contained within the analytical framework of psychoanalysis. They appeared quite excessively "reality-competent"; it would have been inaccurate to describe them as "ego-defective"; they displayed little evidence of inhibited super-ego development. Somehow, these people seemed to be allowing their lives to be directed quite overtly by the demands of the "id" — and if the id seemed bent on destruction, was it not therefore possible to perceive it as containing a "death-drive" that was only partially inhibited by culture?

But what a grave error this was. The soldier males who have been the object of this study do not in any sense "live out" their drives. The fascist terror arises out of their attempts to become "I," to attain a bounded and nonfragmentary unity. Their aim is not to give free rein to their drives, but to *escape* them. The eruption of their drives does not produce "satisfaction"; instead, it helps stabilize their totality armor. The white terror should thus be seen not so much as the function of any particular "drive" but as a function of the fragmenting and perpetually reconstituted ego, the body-ego of the soldier male.

As we saw in our analysis of some of the most widespread acts of fascist terror, the tormentor derives his triumph from his success in divesting himself of his "unconscious" — which he destroys in the person of the tormented. (It is for this reason that I consider it unjustified to see the "fascist" male as an isolated case. His development is part of a wider history, some of the details of which I attempted to trace in Volume 1, Chapter 2, where I examined the ways the European male ego develops in opposition to woman.) Men in Wilhelmine society were actively prevented from developing an ego capable of integrating their negativized unconscious into more or less peaceable social forms. The social nature of their psychic state is barely visible from the point of view of the "id"; but it becomes clearly evident once attention is focused on the ego.

But as so often happened, contemporary psychoanalysis feared its own radical potential. Had the gaze it cast on society been a little bolder, it might have recognized society's murderous nature;[68] more specifically, it would have been forced to acknowledge the significance of the mother — particularly the mothers of strata-fighting-on-two-fronts — for its analyses. Then as now, psychoanalysis largely ignored crucial maternal influences on the lives of sons of the aristocracy and the bourgeoisie, the peasantry,[69] and even to an extent the proletariat — on sons who were later only too eager to insert themselves into the deadly macromachines of fascism. Maternal labor was deemed an inappropriate object for science — and the majority of psychoanalysts were (and remain) unwilling to violate professional taboos (they have their own "society" to consider). Thus the holy cow of motherhood was never slaughtered; on the contrary, it was newly enthroned under fascism — as representation. Fascist block-formations installed a crazed order of half-born destructiveness; but that order would have been *unthinkable* without the effective support of mothers. At the very latest by 1945, there should have been some form of public acknowledgment of the mothers' part in fascism; but no such acknowledgment was forthcoming at the time; and today, even women living and working for women's liberation are reticent on the subject. (There is admittedly a danger that any overt statement could be used to reconstruct women as sources of evil; yet, given the importance ascribed by Balint, Mahler, and others to dual union, the mother-child relationship could equally well become the basis for a revolutionary perception of women as producers of nonmurderous human beings.)

Fascist writing itelf makes quite *deliberate* associations between the protagonists' acts of destruction and acts of love and self-creation. The textual evidence very strongly militates against analysis in terms of either the "deathdrive" or even "aggressive instincts." The texts can in no sense be said to conceal the origins of the soldiers' actions; the lack they experience may not always be directly admitted; but it is certainly insistently present in the sense of betrayal that permeates much of their writing.

"The omnipotence of love is perhaps never more strongly proved than in such of its aberrations as these," wrote Freud in 1904 of the "most repulsive perversions."[70] Yet this perception never informed his later investigations into the relationship between the desire for life and killing. He withdrew instead into biological speculation: a more attractive option perhaps, given the unprecedented destruction of which the civilized world had proved capable. It may even be the case, as Wilhelm Reich suggested in a 1952 interview, that Freud's death-drive hypothesis expressed his own acquiescence to death. Freud and his successor may have been more willing to face their own deaths than to take up the struggle against society's death-forces. Reich for one was certainly convinced that the appearance in Freud's face of "the first signs of cancer" coincided with the appearance of the death-drive as a feature of his theory.[71]

There are certain macabre parallels between Freud's analyses and the attempts by the fascists themselves to argue (insofar as the notion of them "arguing" is appropriate) that their destructive rage should be seen as expressing some powerful primal instinct. Ultimately, however, the two are different. For very good reasons, the fascists preferred to perceive themselves as the inheritors of millennial traditions than as the victims of their own more proximate and palpable history.

> We kept our guns in easy reach; half-drunk with sleep, we reached for them at the first sound of sudden fire, or the confused echoes of shouting somewhere above the dug-out. Clutching a weapon from the depths of sleep came easily; it was in our blood, an expression of the primitive within—the same gesture with which Ice Age man grasped his ax of stone.[72]

In a historical dimension occupied by supermen—"We are great and mighty killers"—responses must on no account appear to be *learned.*

> War was in his blood. . . . He was born for war; it was the only state in which he had ever been able to live life to the full.[73]
>
> We plunged headlong into experience . . . we were both the executors of war and its creations, men whose life led inexorably to warfare.[74]

For Goote's wounded Berthold, sick-leave turns to drudgery:

> I will only recover if my heart is in it—but I have left my
> heart at the front.[75]
> Ernst Röhm: "To the soldier, it (war) is the fount of youth,
> hope, and fulfillment in one."[76]

Heinz describes the *Freikorps* as motivated by a "burning obsession with war"; he describes "cold-blooded skill in warfare" as a feature of young German nature—a feature in which he takes the utmost pride.

> It was an element that dwelt in the magical regions where our
> brotherhood with death made life incomparably sweet and
> alluring. The French were terrified of death; and many a witness
> has told of their horror at the sight of a hell-bent Germany
> seemingly infatuated with death.[77]

And at the same time,

> We molded uncertainty into the palpable form of men capable of
> eradicating our sense of horror.[78]

The fascist has been described as a "soldier from the inside"; and he becomes such ultimately in response to his sense of the "enemy within." Contact with life—his own included—confronts him with the horrifying prospect of dissolution. "We fluttered with the anxiety of disoriented night-owls flying into the glare of early morning."[79] An appropriate image indeed for the fear experienced by these lovers of death in the face of their own desires and pleasures; they exist at loggerheads with themselves, and with the "reality" of the life that confronts them. Their response

> Everything must change . . .
> Everything must be destroyed . . .
> The world will shatter around us—but we shall march onward . . .

Such were the stated intentions of the fascists; and they saw not the slightest reason to conceal them. The best illustration of the interwar situation in Germany can perhaps be given by citing a passage from Ernst von Salomon, published in 1930 by Rowohlt (who also published Tucholsky). Newly released from prison where he had served five years for complicity in Rathenau's murder—Rathenau having been, of course, no less a figure than the Republic's foreign minister—Salomon made a triumphal entry into German literature with his novel *Die Geächteten [The Outlaws]*—what a title, on the eve of Nazi victory!):

> We smashed our way into startled crowds, raging and
> shooting and beating and hunting. We drove the Latvians across
> the fields like frightened hares; we set fire to their houses; buckled

"I dunno, is it? Maybe there's a system to it, maybe not. I don't know."

their telegraph poles, pulverized their bridges. We hurled the corpses into wells and threw hand grenades after them. Anything that came within our grasp was decimated; we burned whatever we could. We had seen red, and our hearts were emptied of human feelings. At every stage of our journey the earth groaned under the weight of our destruction. Where there had been houses, there was now only rubble and ashes, smoldering woodpiles, ulcers festering on naked terrain. Giant smoke plumes marked our passage across the landscape. We had built a funeral pyre to burn dead matter; but more than this, we burned our hopes and longings, codes of civil conduct, the laws and values of civilization, the whole burden of fusty verbiage we carried, our belief in the things and ideas of a time that had rejected us.

We withdrew, swaggering, intoxicated, and booty-laden.[80]

Such was the typical vice of the German gentleman, *anno* 1930. The only quality more excessive than his joy in destruction, his pleasure in murder, was the wide-eyed innocence of his greeting to the sonny boys from the United States in 1945: "We knew nothing." Not that the statement was in any sense inaccurate; his intoxication had indeed been great enough to eradicate memories of earlier orgies of destruction. "Please tell us, Sir, we lost the time, where are we?" "You are under the guidance of the people of God's own country." So he had made it after all to paradise.

Cardboard German tanks, for maneuvers "under Versailles."

PEACE

At the beginning of the First World War, the German officer corps comprised 22,112 officers and 29,230 reserve officers; it was very small and extremely exclusive. By Armistice Day, it had grown to over 270,000 officers.[1]

Under the Versailles Treaty, the Weimar *Reichswehr* was initially permitted to employ no more than 4,000 officers. The army High Command extracted immediate guarantees from Ebert that their autonomy would be guaranteed, as long as they could assure the republic of their "loyalty."[2] They then set about recruiting a new officer corps; and it soon became clear that they were giving preference to "real" officers, trained wherever possible in the prewar period. They were reluctant to take on officers recruited under conditions of wartime exigency, since many such men lacked even the minimum qualifications for officer status in peacetime.

Initially, then, these men were without employment: and many — boys who had joined the army from high school, for example — might return. Their only training was as soldiers; outside the military, their future prospects were dismal. Continuing their studies was one possibility — but a remote one.

> "Just imagine it, lads — having to polish up your Homer, when you've almost forgotten the Greek alphabet!" "God in heaven," sighed Herber. Seebach rocked his chair back and forth. What a prospect for a man already showing the first signs of gray![3]

So speak two old men of the *Freikorps* in Goote's *Wir tragen das Leben* (We,

The Bearers Of Life), as they face the prospect of returning to study for the *Abitur.**

Returning to the university was all the more difficult for older heroes— men who had always been soldiers but now had officer experience. They feared the university would make them look ridiculous; but some did in the end return. They soon reappeared as leaders of voluntary student militia. Von Selchow, for example, became the commander of the Marburg student corps. On his entering the university, he commented,

> I firmly believe in Germany, and in her national rebirth; scientific knowledge can only strengthen the foundations of that faith.[4]

"Studying" does not, then, appear to have been von Selchow's principal aim.

What other fates awaited the soldier males? They were offered an existence (nonexistence) as clerical workers, in banks or other offices; middle or, occasionally, higher level civil-service positions—the "slimy, clinging suffocation of bourgeois existence."

> So we are to marry calf-hearted straw-blondes from the back of beyond . . . . Gretchen-haired women with whom we spend our leisure time producing children.
>
> "A bullet through the head sounds more attractive!" sighed Lindemann.[5]
>
> "But what *do* you want?" responded Werner angrily. "To be a traveling wine salesman? To sell vacuum cleaners? Or life insurance?"
>
> Truchs gently shook his long body, then bent forward like a farm worker carrying full milk pails. "None of the above," he whispered.[6]

Truchs preferred to die a hero's death at the hands of a proletarian woman; but some of the men did become "sales representatives." In the theater of war they most detested—the market—they lent their own brand of nobility to the commonest of civilian products.

> Where once our lives were infused with the burning glow of danger, we now teetered on the brink of everyday drudgery, a paralyzing termite waiting to devour us.[7]

Höss swears an oath to his mother that he will become a priest, as his father wished; but when his mother dies,

> I . . . traveled the following day to East Prussia and joined a

---

*The German high-school-graduation certificate, which qualifies students for university entrance.

volunteer corps bound for the Baltic. The problem of my
profession was now solved; for a second time, I became a soldier.[8]

Höss's statement recalls Lettow's willingness, or rather his stated desire, to be
sent to the Baltic the day after his wedding.

Goote's Berthold rejects attempts by his father to make a forester of him;
he holds up the horror image of a future SPD superior:

> It's no good, father—it could never be, even if I said "yes" to
> you now. I know myself too well. I simply couldn't work under a
> man to whom the fatherland meant so little. It would be
> *impossible!*[9]

To work under such a man would be indecent; the officer had to remain
decent, a hero and a realist:

> The war was lost, and the old German army disbanded. What
> was I to do with myself—an old professional officer in my
> forty-sixth year?
> I was not only haunted by the disaster that had befallen our
> beloved Germany; I was worried about my own future. But
> walking along one day in Dresden, still brooding on my plight, I
> passed a small and singularly uninviting cafe, with a large poster
> on the wall. The caption read, "Applications invited for voluntary
> Eastern border patrols." My curiosity was roused; I went in and
> asked for further details.[10] (Zeschau)

For younger men with no formal qualifications, the only available options
were the farm, the artisan's workshop, or the factory. The elder sons of farmers could hope to inherit farms; but they were often too small and their owners
heavily in debt.[11] Younger sons faced the prospect of manual or artisanal
labor; or they might move to the unknown and threatening territory of the city,
in search of clerical work in the urban service industries. A conversation on
the subject of the factory in Thor Goote's *Wir tragen das Legen*:

> "We have returned to a world governed by timekeeping; our work
> moves in regular rhythm. But we are so much more used to
> sudden rhythmic bursts, than hours that creep by endlessly—until
> something again sets fire to our senses." "Yes," I said, "I
> remember being surprised by sudden, violent sensations that
> trembled and burned like gunshots shooting through my whole
> being. Civilians experienced the moments in between as peaceful
> and inoffensive; but to us, they were simply periods of mounting
> tension; and we always anticipated future release."[12]

This is what makes the soldier males so certain that they can be neither
civilians nor workers. They know they are organized to produce lethal

Göring (1923). First head of the SA.

"release"; they know others fear, or are at least indifferent to the things they desire. Their "rhythm" is different.

> Sensation is dead! The worst is upon us. We have been both overtly and covertly betrayed, condemned to the labor colony for generations to come. We have been stripped of whatever we possessed—yet we do nothing. Sensation is dead! Time rolls on— but it has lost its brilliance. We are old front-line soldiers waiting for a spark to set us alight as before. Our time has turned bourgeois![13]

Rudolf Mann summarizes the position of the (relatively few) nonofficers in the Ehrhardt Brigade as follows:

> The volunteers had the greatest of difficulty in renewing their shattered links with the factory floor or the workshop. They faced the prospect of remaining hated strangers, always out of step with their workmates' feelings.[14]

Dwinger is less precise, but waxes more lyrical:

> Even in work they remained men-at-arms in civilian clothing; . . . the grenades they have thrown will not drop into the recesses of their memories until the old order has returned forever to the German *Reich*![15]

(Texts by such as Dwinger were the preferred reading material of the Nazis. After 1933 Rudolf Mann was never reprinted; but Dwinger's books were much in demand, both as bestsellers and as classroom reading material.)

The two writers are quite right to emphasize the role of *feeling* as the soldiers' means of identifying their own difference from the workers. Weller's hero Leutner, for example, is outraged by suggestions of irregularity in his relationship to the daily round of bourgeois or proletarian labor.

> In areas of a very particular kind, the train passed close by dingy backyards and tenement gateways; and invariably, second-lieutenant Leutner would hear someone screaming "workshy loyalist." He ground his teeth in rage; for God knows there was never a German *Freikorps* in November-Germany who could be called a loyalist.[16]

Weller uses a propagandistically humorous style unique to the *Freikorps*; and his comments demonstrate, more convincingly than the best statistics, the hollowness of the *Freikorps'* claim to represent all classes in what they called the "folk community."[17] He portrays the workers as living covert lives in "areas of a very particular kind," whose "dingy backyards" the *Freikorps* enter for one purpose only: persecution.

We can, I think, conclude at this stage that what the soldier males feared in the postwar situation was a return to their prewar position of dependency. In the real restoration of patrilineage, they feared a return to the position of sons subordinated to false fathers, false superiors. In extreme cases, they feared a return to the status of children.

In the first instance, these men felt that their participation in war had proved them beyond doubt to be definable as adults. The war had permitted them to withdraw from their parents—or at the very least, to begin to do so. They were now offered various forms of training for the professions; but to them, this was simply a retrograde step into positions they had long since relinquished. In social terms, moreover, parents retained power over their children; thus any return to the past appeared particularly dangerous to the fascists, since they had no independent existence outside the home to fall back on.

Second, no position available to any twenty-two-year-old war officer was likely to offer him anything approximating to the abundance of power he had come to expect in wartime. None of the peacetime occupations on offer in the "republic" could match the opportunities characteristically provided by the German imperial army.[18] Even the lowliest military superior had been master of life and death, and thus able to exercise power arbitrarily. Yet when the war ended, its former (if relatively minor) masters were called upon to lower themselves to the degrading status of either rank-and-file soldiers or schoolboys.

Third, peacetime offered not a single opportunity for former officers, or indeed for other soldier males, to enjoy the explosive discharge without which their bodies threatened to disintegrate. Thus the end of the war condemned them not only to exclusion from their chosen profession; what they foresaw was something approaching disbarment from life.

It is inadequate to dub these men "workshy" (though the reproach is an obvious one) from a proletarian perspective. In the first instance, they can hardly be criticized for showing no great love for the labors capital allots to a white-collar workforce at the intermediate level. More important, the soldier males' hatred of available civilian forms of labor can often be traced to their fear of their own potential incapacity to adapt psychically, and thus to function properly in the civilian context: their fear of failure in a "bourgeois existence" that threatened to place intolerable limits on their perceptions of their own greatness and significance—indeed, ultimately, to make them appear ridiculous. It is likely that their stories of wartime heroics rapidly outlived their usefulness, at least as excuses for inefficiency in the office.

Given the instability of the soldiers' ego-armor, their fear of ridicule was understandable. (Many of the acts of aggression described in Volume 1, particularly those perpetrated on women, result from a man's perception of himself as object of derision.[19]) But they did have one escape route.

> Dull despair descended on many of our number; we wanted only
> to fight resolutely to an honorable end, the sooner the better—
> even in battles doomed from the outset to failure! Better dead than
> living in slavery.[20] (Captain Ehrhardt)

Gone now were the illusions of peacetime:

> When the guns first fell silent in the West, we thought life
> had regained its value. But everything that once made it light and
> beautiful has been stolen by madmen; we now see it more clearly;
> it has become less precious.
>
>> Should I die by the Danube
>> Or fall in Poland
>> What matter?
>> They will fetch away my soul
>> But I shall die as a man of the cavalry!
>
> Forward, then, to Poland! Forward, to man the frontier! There at
> least we shall hear gunfire. A man in the field can at least still be
> of value; and his heart still stirs in battle.[21]

By the time this text was written, the "value" of a "man" was actually negligible; but the soldier males were right to anticipate gunfire—since, after all, they would be the ones pulling the trigger.

A further example: Ehrhardt leaves a job as a bank clerk to protect the frontier against the incursions of upstart Poles:

No, there was nothing here to hold him. By day, the urgent cries of his German brothers echoed through the stark columns of figures he worked on; the same cries filled his head throughout his nightly labors. Bending over books dry as dust, he would sometimes start up and look around at his colleagues in the main office; had they heard the same gruesome screaming? But no; they remained crouched over papers, checks, debentures—clean-shaven faces with neatly knotted ties, amicable and contented, bored, perhaps, but little more.

The next day he found himself traveling the Görlitz line and musing on how he would never again make a good civilian. A stranger in his own country, he no longer belonged in the present. "That's it precisely; a stranger in my own country."[22]

The "gruesome screaming" of the writer's "German brothers," their presence in the muted atmosphere of the office, is an obvious fabrication; the writer needs a higher purpose to justify his flight. All the fascist texts are fastidiously deceitful; and their duplicity increases the more the men attempt to conceal their *personal interests*. ("Ilse Cornelius! To embark on a well-paid bourgeois career at such a time is . . . treachery . . . it is . . . tantamount to desertion! Great deeds must, and will be done."[23]) The actions and demands of the proletariat, by contrast, are consistently portrayed as motivated by "assertions" of "interest"; and "interests" are invariably seen as transgressions against power—its indivisibility and its totality. The fascist side is always the side of absolute command: "Conscience commands," as Zöberlein puts it. "The soldier males do what they must—as Germans."[24]

According to postwar statistics, Bavaria was left with over 9,000 officers; half later joined the *Freikorps*.[25]

Then came the announcement that the *Freikorps* were to be disbanded, starting with the naval brigades, in February-March 1920.[26] The men were shocked; participating in the putsch was the least they could do to resist threatening disbandment. The hurriedly prepared Kapp campaign was certainly triggered by the change in the *Freikorps'* fortunes. Losing the most reliable of their troops put Lüttwitz and Ehrhardt under increasing pressure; and they already knew of their troops' plans to remove Lüttwitz from office.[27]

Rudolf Mann describes reactions to the news of disbandment among Ehrhardt brigadists.

> "We would be only too happy to continue, even for the pittance Noske gives the officer corps." "We in the *Freikorps* have always been the men most committed to the soldiering profession. We're the only ones who've always refused to head homeward. And they promised . . . they promised . . ." the men stammered helplessly, standing with their arms dangling uncertainly.[28]

Soldiers of the Ehrhardt brigade distributing posters in defense of the *putsch*. Chalked onto their helmets is the sign of the future.

The men are caught unawares by the threat that the Red morass will resurface, menacing as ever. They feel themselves being severed with familiar violence from "totality" and "unity."

Their language loses its toughness; their bodies slacken. Faced with the prospect of being prohibited from attacking the enemy in *battle*, they are weakened in ways the enemy himself would envy.

And so they cling all the more fiercely to what they call the soldiering "profession." But it is more than a profession; it is a *state of being* . . . a state much sought after, and handsomely rewarded, in the postwar period. Soldiers were paid on average between 30 and 50 marks a day—enough to feed a whole family. Officers were given bonuses; Noske gave them 5 marks a day above rank-and-file wages. Naturally enough, the Ehrhardt Brigade in toto claimed an entitlement to the extra 5 marks; rather less natural was the fact that brigadists continued to be paid Noske's bonus *after* their involvement in a putsch against a government of which he himself was a member. (The *Freikorps* authors cite this with particular glee as an example of Social Democratic stupidity.[29]) And finally, the Bavarian state government paid an extra 5 marks daily to *Freikorps* under its jurisdiction.

The soldiers were clothed at government expense (the rest of the country suffered widespread clothing shortages; good shoes were a rare luxury. The quality of military boots was, of course, impeccable.) Soldiers leaving the *Freikorps* could expect a lump-sum payment comparable to the golden handshakes of any longer-serving soldier.

Food for the civilian population was rationed, and there was widespread hunger; but the *Freikorps* never suffered shortages. They were guaranteed 200g of meat and 74g of butter daily; they were also allowed beer and cigarettes, and 0.25 liters of wine a day. "A happy time."[30] (Rudolf Mann). And finally, retirement or old-age pension entitlements were calculated to take account of service in the *Freikorps*.[31]

Not surprisingly, these enviable "perks" were widely talked of; in Berlin, for example, the *Freikorps* were known as "soup troops."[32] Numbers of the unemployed, or simply men in search of easier lives, were clearly motivated to join because of the benefits enjoyed by the *Freikorps* and other temporary voluntary outfits. In the initial postwar years, before the *Freikorps* were fully established, those comforts certainly constituted part of their attraction; that attraction diminished when their political allegiances emerged more clearly.

The soldiers did, however, attempt to "purge" the *Freikorps* of such elements; and the *Freikorps* authors assure us that their efforts were successful. Maercker, the founder of the very first *Freikorps*, reports a large number of early dismissals and claims that twenty of twenty-six soldiers failed to return from leave.

"Trumped-up charge of monarchist *putsch*. End preferential treatment on class grounds—
by Left *and* Right!"

> On one occasion, I was addressing a newly formed troop and telling the men what I expected of them. After some discussion, they declared themselves unwilling to enter "a troop whose every second word is discipline."[33]

Any reader of Maercker's book is liable to sympathize; every *third* word is taken up with notions of "discipline." The overwhelming temptation is to follow his troops' example and make a closed book of the likes of Maercker.

Rudolf Mann writes of the drill driving away men unsuited to its rigors. He makes it clear that the *Freikorps* welcomed the most dubious of adventurers who surfaced from the unknown; the only requirement was that they be "soldiers."[34]

Volunteers were not only intimidated by the drill; the physical appearance of the soldier males, and their peculiar form of camaraderie, was equally alarming. It certainly sufficed to repel any man with no pressing need for the troop as a form of sociality.

What all this indicates, it seems to me, is that the soldier males' allegiance to the *Freikorps* was never won by the promise that they would be well-fed or well cared-for. It seems they would have seized the opportunity to remain or to become soldiers for half the benefits offered—most would even have taken less.[35] This was certainly true at least of the most active core of the *Freikorps*—compulsive soldiers who would have been termed delinquents in the civilian context (and would have been conspicuous as such—whereas they passed unnoticed in troop formation).

The crucial factor was a man's attitude not to "soup" but to militarism—a fact further demonstrated by the reluctance of workers—hunger, clothing shortages, and unemployment notwithstanding—to make appropriate use of opportunities to join the "people's armies." (For Maercker, their unwillingness to do so was a source of explicit amazement.[36])

Some men loved the military sufficiently to remain in it with or without the "soup" it promised; others hated it sufficiently to go without. When both the *Freikorps* and the Red Army resorted to arms, and confronted each other in March 1920, this was the *most significant difference* between them. (The privilege of naming the armed workers as "Ludendorffs of the Left" was reserved for the malicious tongue of Zickler, the Social Democratic editor of *Vorwärts*.)[37]

*　*　*

According to one explanation currently doing the rounds in theories of fascism (the "pauperization" hypothesis), susceptibility to fascism is explicable in terms of the economic degradation of large sections of the middle classes.[38]

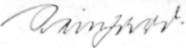

| Colonel Reinhard, Governor of the City of Berlin (1919). Pictured here in SS uniform. | N. C. O. Suppe ("Soup"), the man who gave Reinhard's "Suppe-Truppe" ("soup troop") its name. |

The economic evidence is indisputable; but the extent to which it can be cited to "explain" German fascism is a different question—on which a number of different observations may be made. First, how far was the middle-class's "loss of status" attributable to the economy? Certainly, many of the sons who had left school to go to war or interrupted professional training found it difficult in peacetime to regain socially acceptable positions. Unlike their fathers, they had lost precious years in wartime; their difficulties were attributable too to the general situation, particularly in Weimar's early years.

In principle, however, posts were still available to men of the strata-on-two-fronts qualified to intermediate or higher secondary level; there was work for them in the universities and the civil service, or as junior or senior clerical staff in businesses, banks, or department stores. All such jobs certainly involved sacrifices, and it was always necessary to earn extra money on the side, but these should not be seen as insurmountable obstacles. The soldier males were never absolutely debarred from employment.

But, more important perhaps, these were men whose parents had also never achieved "greatness." It was perhaps not so much the economic reality of postwar Germany that prevented a generation of sons from becoming civil

General Watter, Commander of Operations against the Ruhr workers in 1920.

Franz von Epp, Watter's best killer and Governor of Bavaria after 1933.

servants, pastors, shopkeepers, or officers, but rather their own *hatred* of all such occupations—with the obvious exception of that of officer.

The men most likely to be deprived of actual possessions in peacetime were the sons of large landowners from east of the Elbe. Their estates were undermechanized and lacked capital investment; this, coupled with their ignorance of agricultural principles and the increasing impossibility of exploiting farm workers to the same degree as before and during the war, threatened the farms increasingly with unprofitability—and, ultimately, with the auctioneer's hammer.

And what of men disinherited by the collapse of small businesses? They were certainly robbed of future prospects—but they already abhorred the prospect of a future as small tradesmen. The repugnance they felt for all areas of small business was more than mere fabrication; though the tradesman's life was their original destiny, their desires were now channeled in a different direction.

Alfred Sohn-Rethel writes of these young men that,

> They had no wish at all to return to their fathers' businesses, for

they regarded that kind of life as old hat, even if business were to pick up again. By contrast, a post to which they could lay claim by assisting in Hitler's "rise to power" promised them a position of dominance over the proletariat, instead of the prospect of becoming proletarian themselves, and all the sooner the more thoroughly they vanquished the "Marxists."[39]

A further substantial section of the strata-on-two-fronts to consider is the large group of relatively impecunious individuals whose problem was less that of downward mobility than of impaired upward mobility. They included farmers' sons, who had moved to the city after doing well at school; trained as skilled workers, they hoped for careers in the lower echelons of the civil service, but never actually progressed beyond exhausting and badly paid shopwork. Then there were the children of the working classes, who hoped to escape proletarian misery by rising to apparently more agreeable "middle-class" positions. In different ways, they all failed to progress *far enough* upward; they never developed the relatively stable sense of self essential for anyone attempting to overcome the extreme difficulties of moving from one social stratum to another. Their dream of a better life was shattered more or less absolutely; like many members of strata-on-two-fronts in Weimar Germany, they were left despairing and embittered. They felt themselves to be *lacking* in something they knew, or at least believed, to be due them.

The men on whom this study has focused were educated solely for war and for the tasks facing the German male after victory; in such men, the same feelings were massively exaggerated. They had marched away convinced that they could anticipate one of two futures; they would either die or they would emerge from a brief and bloody struggle to claim their rightful position as rulers of Europe, if not the world. As *Germans*, they believed in their position of supremacy.[*]

Before these men became soldiers, they lived within impenetrable circles of refusals and prohibitions. A world of terror perpetrated on their own individual bodies, a world that demanded the suppression of the slightest resistance bubbling up within them. The punishment for any refusal to acquiesce was death. They had seen fulfillment beckon—but it remained constantly distant, both geographically and temporally. Only the world outside, and the future, contained the promise of bliss; desire for anything more proximate was suppressed, then transformed into a "love" of continents and landscapes, wide-open spaces: a "love" of history, of imagined expeditions to the planets or the quaternary. They assigned the quality of greatness to all things past and to the future; they expressed "love" for the forests, for impenetrable secrets, for the warm, balmy air of the springtime days that connected them to the

---

[*]When Ewers's hero, Gerhard Scholz, is asked for details of his profession, he is initially confused. "I am no more or less than a German." (*Reiter in deutscher Nacht*, p. 246)

Triumphal procession (Munich 1937), "2000 years of German culture."

world in its entirety . . . transformations. They traveled in Napoleon's footsteps, gleamed in the warrior costume of the *Nibelungs*.

And they knew that the time would come for the long-awaited cavalry charge in the light of early morning; lance would meet lance—attack—and the enemy would crumble, walls would crumble, they would meet only vast empty spaces, devoid of danger. The world would be in their possession. "What do you want to be when you grow up?" "A Roman." "An imperialist"—the world's simplest answer.[40]

How these men would have rejoiced to conquer and possess the world, to be its masters, to march onward, winning victory upon victory, before dying for the kaiser.[41] The kaiser's "favorite" weapon was the navy—and it became the "supreme" symbol of the hopes of the fascist males.

What then of their actual postwar situation? Bullied as schoolboys, terrorized as cadets, knocked into shape in the barrack yard, then in the mud of the trenches, the soldier males ended the war as defeated soldiers, severely wounded. Deprived of promised triumphs, they were asked instead to accept the gray suit of the clerical worker; to submit to fat, lazy bosses, who never praised them for their labors—it was all they could do to give them one cigar for Christmas. This, then, was the destiny of heroes: to play the part of underdogs—men who had never made it—then to vanish into the wings, pursued by indifferent laughter from an audience of ladies. And so German imperialism faded to insignificance. It had delivered only one proper massacre—the slaughter of the Hereros in 1907. This was not only quite inadequate; it was also long past. The Boxer Rebellion in China was similarly unsatisfying—

little more than a grand hunting expedition, part of the normal round of Far Eastern duties.

A large farewell party was planned to celebrate the end of the expedition. The whole colony was to assemble in the casino. Women, thank God, were not invited—for the celebrations were

expected to be as riotous as they always are when one leaves
China.[42] (Killinger)

Not exactly the ecstasy of colonial domination. Where were the German
governors, the pleasures of colonial life; where were the guarantees that Germans too had the right to blood? The average European male protected his
dams from bursting, his equilibrium from shattering, by watching, if not
actively participating in, the spilling of a quota of blood never apportioned to
the Germans. Blood was available on demand to the rising generation of
English gentlemen; the meanest of English boot-lickers needed only to be the
right color to play the part of White God. The Germans had no access to such
unlimited opportunity.

And to crown it all, they lost the war.

Yes, we are children of our time; yes, we are weary of naked
facts. So weary.[43] (Jünger)

Shame. Treachery. A new betrayal. These men were promised domination; but how are their efforts to be rewarded? They are to be chained for life
to the office. ("So that's it.") The soldiers were told they were a *race* of masters; yet now they are offered the princely sum of 800 marks monthly to rot
away for 50 working hours in work that offends their very nature.

"Can this still be Germany?" he asked, choking with disgust.
"Are these the sons of German mothers? Or these filthy sluts their
daughters? I wouldn't touch them with a barge pole. Germans are
killing Germans — saving the enemy the trouble. And they're doing
it on the banks of what was once the Holy German Rhine."

"Listen, Volker," said Dülkingen soothingly, "think of last
year's floods. Storms pass over, the waters disperse, mud seeps
away. Our Easter is coming, Volker. You should see it as
spring-cleaning before the Day of the Resurrection."

"But Dülkingen, our resurrection doesn't follow dates in the
calendar."

"My feeling exactly. But we all know the calendar has been
adjusted in the past, by men with very specific reasons for doing
so."

"Oh ye of the sacred brotherhood," Volker said, and left the
room.[44]

But the resistance of the "sacred brotherhood" was indeed slowly consolidated in the course of the '20s. The men were perpetually poised to "grip
the spokes of the wheel of history with their own bare hands."

In those wild nights, they buried confessions and oaths, curses and
battle hymns under mountains of broken glasses. Spiked

Freikorps fighter.

boot-heels ground into dance-floors swimming in wine; then, long after cries of "women out" had driven away the waitresses; long after the men had bombarded their leader with demands for action, or gathered, quiet as mice, round a "standard bearer" who told of the hour in which they would say "yes," though all the world might be against them; then their young eyes would begin to glow with a passionate hope that mastered their drunkenness: hope for "The Day" that awaited them![45]

"The Day" came and went several times; it was never the right one. The men, meanwhile, clung to what they had learned; they *needed* the knowledge that they were masters descended from a master race whose country was, and *would remain*, Germany (no country for Jews, bolshevists, or niggers). This had always been their belief, their feeling, their desire; and it had now more than ever to remain so. . . . . They believed themselves to be the only Germans deserving of the name; yet they were denied the respect they considered due them. Things would have to change if the future *Reich* was to right the world; the *Reich* demanded nothing short of absolute destruction.

For the time being, however, the men of the "sacred brotherhood" joined the "national underground"—first the SA, then the SS (although some— 2,230 members of the Loewenfeld naval brigade, for example—did join the regular army).[46]

"As long as the war is lost, peace is impossible"; this was the implacable belief that foreshadowed fascism and paved the way for World War II in Europe. Fascism set in long before world economic crisis, before Hitler and the NSDAP, even before the November revolution. It promised its followers access to functions of domination, not only in war, but outside it:

> The whole of the new order that Hitler planned for the Europe he would never conquer was based on reserving for the "German master race" every function above the level of proletarian labor in production, extending from organization and direction, leadership and supervision right down to foreman and chief operator—while the "mixed-blooded" and "inferior races" which he had subjugated would do the manual and dirty jobs of the proletariat.[47]

Fascism made it politically and economically necessary to create a social stratum superior to the proletariat, a pseudo-elite to strip the proletariat of responsibility for the socializing functions of its own manual labor. But the policies fascism developed on the political and economic level fulfilled a second function; they answered the fascist's need for activities to satisfy his *psychic compulsion* to domination.

In 1973 Sohn-Rethel added the following footnote to his earlier comments:

The current situation with guest and immigrant workers indicates that in some parts of Germany, Switzerland, and other countries we can find striking similarities with Hitlerian ideals.[48]

(Arguably, then, migrant labor may be the organizational form in which strata-on-two-fronts gain easiest access to contemporary power.)

* * *

An anti-fascism devoid of shame is far worse than an anti-fascism devoid of power.

The brown plague will rot and die, stinking
When the Left unites in East and West, arms linking.

These lines, written by Wolf Biermann to mark the occasion of his first appearance in the "West," are a more recent document of a time-worn analysis of fascism. In various different ways, fascism is constantly denounced and ridiculed. This is more than simply an erroneous assessment of fascism's actual power; more seriously, it implies an unspoken contempt for its adherents. And it is linked to a fantasy of anti-fascist unity that suppresses perceptions of antagonism among fascism's "opponents."

No matter how the fascist leadership is portrayed: as racketeers (in Brecht's *Arturo Ui*); as stand-up comics (Chaplin, in *The Great Dictator*); as bourgeois fire-raisers (Frisch); as megalomaniacal seducers of the people, harnessing finance and monopoly capital for their own nefarious purposes (the Marburg school); as the dregs of the petty-bourgeoisie, who seized a convenient historical moment and pulled themselves up by their shirt-tails (Enzensberger)—every one of these denies the nature of fascism as a popular movement (albeit not a movement of the people in its entirety).[49]

In the early *Freikorps* period, the fascists were known only as work-shy "soup troops"; they were dubbed "bloodhounds" only when witnessed in action. An initial attitude of mocking arrogance (fascism as stuff-and-nonsense) then gave way to accusatory fury. Such was the development we traced in the German Communist Party's (KPD) attitude toward the *Freikorps*; and it was later precisely mirrored by their response to NSDAP victory: by their ill-judged "conviction" that the Nazis, incompetent as they were, would either throw in the towel after a few months in government or would be perfunctorily dismissed by a newly enlightened people. The party responded to defeat by adopting the posture of victimized innocent (of whom there were certainly many, though not necessarily among the KPD leadership); it limited its resistance to a few ineffectual insults imputing to the fascists a lack of aptitude for government.

It seems to me that the battle lines between men are repeatedly blurred by the elements of masculinity they have in common. Behind every assessment, commentary, analysis of fascism, there lies the assumption that the critic would have made a better leader than the man he ridicules. He takes it as an *insult* that his talent remains unrecognized. (And yet his ability to ridicule leaders whom he himself does not follow is simply the inverse of his reverence for those he does. The other side of the coin, so to speak.)

The *Führer* was certainly ridiculous; but only to the extent that a certain level of ridiculousness was *intended* or *accepted*. After watching Leni Riefenstahl's *Triumph of the Will*—a record of the drama of the 1934 NSDAP conference in Nuremberg—I was struck by how much more of fascism becomes visible under the impassive gaze of this one woman (the credits note that the film was "designed by Leni Riefenstahl")[50] than in many a Communist analysis.

At the beginning of the film, the screen remains blank for almost a minute; the film itself appears as if born on the ripples of the introductory symphony. The opening shot—the stone image of an Imperial Eagle—is at one and the same time the final frame of a different history: a story of confusion, now transcended.

Triumph of the Will is first and foremost a filmic celebration of protection. The eagle spreads its powerful wings and gives the audience shelter—or rather, it shelters those among the audience who acquiesce willingly. "If you agree to join us, no harm can come to you." The film situates itself from the very beginning in the realm of salvation.

The film presents fascism as a child of the heavens and of history. In the opening sequence, the camera surveys banks of high cloud from an airplane; though the spectator does not see the *Führer*, s/he knows this to be the airplane that is taking him to Nuremberg. What we see is seen for a number of minutes through the eyes of the *Führer*. We feel him gliding downward to Nuremberg, feather-light, on noiseless engines, the only sound the sober melody of a Horst Wessel arrangement. Raise the banner high.

Before the descent on Nuremberg begins, Riefenstahl etches a number of memorial inscriptions into the mind of the spectator.

> 5 September 1934.
> Twenty years after the outbreak of the Great War.
> Fifteen years after the beginning of German suffering.
> Nineteen months after the beginning of German rebirth.

On the one hand, she presents the *Führer* as an abstract being, a delegate from nonmaterial regions. Only gradually does the vehicle in which he sinks to earth materialize as a Ju 52 bomber. On the other hand, the spectator is permitted, at the beginning of the film, to see through the *Führer*'s eyes; proximity is established between *Führer* and spectator. The same intimacy persists throughout the film; it is repeatedly regenerated in numerous close-ups of the

Before take-off.

Führer's face apparently communicating with the faces of individuals in mass block formations.

The image of the *Führer*'s descent is crucially ambiguous. The spectator sees the shadow of the *Führer*-machine gliding across the assembled crowd. In the first instance, the image activates childhood fears of abduction in the predatory claws of a giant eagle. But the image turns instantly to one of protection. The shadow hovers and lands; it has come in peace, it waves to the crowd. Its intention is not to deprive them of anything, but to represent the *presence* of something hitherto lacking. It offers protection—a protection born of fear and thus experienced with double the normal intensity.[*]

What is initially most striking about Hitler as he emerges from the plane, and during his subsequent drive through the city, is his air of slight clumsiness. The penny drops: the awkwardness is either fully *intended*, or at the very least permitted. It functions as a sign of approachability. The audience sees him as a man of their own kind, a man who does not simply "descend" from the heavens. Instead, he *returns* to the people and remains there. This is no mere delegate of a "supreme power"; he is one of their kind, a man whom they themselves originally delegated heavenward.[51]

---

[*]"I saw Hitler primarily as the protector of the nineteenth-century world against the disturbing urban world that I feared was to be our common destiny." So writes Albert Speer in his *Spandau Diaries* (*Spandauer Tagebücher*, p. 219). His comments pinpoint protection and security as the key characteristics of his own monumental architecture. His buildings are monuments against the dissolution of city living.

However, this does not mean the *Führer* can be criticized. The film makes it quite clear that even the qualities it seems to ask the spectator to criticize — the *Führer*'s faintly ridiculous awkwardness — must on no account be faulted. In so doing, it lends special significance to those very qualities. Not only does it explicitly affirm the *Führer*'s absurdity; more important, it confirms the absurdity of the applauding crowd. The *Führer* is, or, rather, is required to be, flawless; but, unlike the Pope for example, his flawlessness is no gift from the heavens. It is a desire on the part of his subordinates, who derive security from the knowledge that he is above criticism.

The day ends with a pot-pourri of marching songs (*Lützows wilde verwegene Jagd* (Lützow's Bold Hunters in the Wild), *Der Gott, der Eisen wachsen liess* (The God That Made Iron Grow, etc.) and a torchlight parade outside Hitler's hotel.

Night falls and history returns, through images of a darkened Nuremberg, ancient Nuremberg, Nuremberg the idyllic and ghostly, Nuremberg the flag city — all the mythologies of German history. German being appears in all its drama and tragedy to the sleeping observer, assembling all its multitudinous elements in preparation for their regeneration in what is historically their proper location: at the party congress, here in Nuremberg.

Morning church bells: the camera fades from the bell-tower to a camp where the men who are to perform in the course of the day are still sleeping. The spectator scans endless rows of tents, ordered German Indians. Then shots of the men's morning ablutions in rapidly edited sequence: naked legs and torsos, washing in hosepipe spray, general hilarity. Cropped hair made beautiful. One man combs another's hair, another washes the back of his companion. They fetch wood, build a camp fire; a fat chef stirs enormous cauldrons. The men grab mess tins and stand in line to collect breakfast. Then they reappear as wrestlers and horseracers; five young male bodies romp across the square in chariot-formation; a sheet held by younger boys sends a comrade hurtling skyward — the Germanic Romanticism of Karl May as anti-familial game of free living. The men laugh; their ugliness makes them beautiful. These are the building blocks of all the columns the film will later show us; and we are made privy to the secret of their attraction to the NSDAP. As Riefenstahl clearly demonstrates, the Nazis attracted the most grotesque individuals, the ugliest, most dispirited of faces — men with sticking-out ears and crooked smiles, watery eyes, bulbous noses, tough and sinewy, or plump* and cheery. The very minimum the Nazis promised them was entry into the unique race of a supreme people; on occasion, they offered entry to the elite at the core of their movement.

The men they addressed were the not-yet-fully-born, men who had always been left wanting; and where was the party that would offer them more? It was certainly not the rationalist-paternalist Communist Party.

On one level, what we witness in *Triumph of the Will* is the liberation of

---

*Fatness was only a criterion for rejection if the man was too fat to fit his uniform.

"Germany: the Land of Music."

Party congress badges. From A. Speer, *Kunst im Dritten Reich* (Art in the Third Reich), Berlin (1937).

massive forces through a process of internal *amalgamation*. The men in the film submit to orders and connect into sites that promise to eliminate what they experience as lack. The word they repeatedly scream at the party congress is "whole" — heil, heil, heil, heil, heil — and this is precisely what the party makes them. They are no longer broken; and they will remain whole into infinity. Eternal life takes place in the here-and-now . . . really and truly.*

The men's reward for their efforts, and the process whereby amalgamation is consolidated, is visible in Hitler's speeches to the men of the Labor Service, the JH, the SA, or the party political leaders. In each case, his praises are precisely attuned to the wishes of his listeners. They must have exceeded his audience's boldest expectations. To his political leaders, he again evokes the notion of direct filiation; we take orders, he says, from "no earthly power." He invokes "the God who created us": "we are not ordered by the State, the State bows to our orders!" And to 52,000 men of the Labor Service, assembled in full marching order: "There will come a time when every German will have to have been part of the community you represent before he can grow into the community of our people" — a declaration that installs them as 52,000 stonemasons chiseling the bodily form of the German people. His message to youth: "And when we are no more, your task will be to hold fast to the flag we once raised from the void. And I know that you can and will do no different; for you are flesh of our flesh and blood of our blood; and the spirit that burns in your young minds is the same spirit by which we ourselves are dominated." These are speeches to spur and uplift the listeners — but at the same time, Hitler's words gently caress and woo. With every new speech, the *Führer*'s evident skill renders him more attractive and impressive; in the end,

---

*This is what gives their sense of the "beauty" of the occasion its positivity; elsewhere, the same sense is more often generated through the exclusion of everything threatening: "the steel-helmeted face is beautiful because it bears no trace of Jewishness," etc.

it becomes almost impossible not to see him, if only for passing moments, as beautiful.

It seems to me misleading to see the *Führer* as a demagogue, or his speeches as theatrical. Both terms deny not only the needs of the participating crowd but above all the undeniable fact that the *Führer* is bestowing a *gift* on his people. He offers them a religion—not a substitute, but a real one. Raising the banner high, closing ranks and standing firm: all this replaces the "foundation" of a God now abandoned. Once, when the world was populated by devils, God prevailed. Now, the struggle has passed into the hands of the youth of Germany; and the goal after which they strive is situated at the highest imaginable level. They know God is dead. The *Führer* offers a new religion. Abjuring their faith in God, they become superior to the church as currently established.

> Heralded by the streaming flag
> We march man for man to the future
> Our flag is the dawning of an era
> Our flag leads to eternity
> Our flag is more than death.[52]

(Death, where is thy sting/ Hell, where is thy victory?[53])

In his final speech to the party conference, Hitler makes overt reference to suggestions that his whole enterprise may be no more than a manipulative abuse of power. The speech is effective—and not merely on the level of "rhetoric." To me at least, it highlights his capacity to speak expertly of states and desires that were indeed massively present in the assembled blocks of his listeners—a capacity that would in fact have been wasted, had those states and desires not already been existent. His genius resided in his identification of words appropriate to heal the ravaged bodies of his listeners. Hitler was neither the mouthpiece of capital's imagination, nor was he simply its puppet. What he expressed quite explicitly was the whole configuration of existence as a "man among men,"[54] in a form appropriate to his time, namely fascism. At the very moment in history when a man's "worth" was in question, he presented himself as leader of the "most worthy."

> The Sixth Party Congress is drawing to a close. What the millions of Germans who have not joined our ranks may judge to have been no more than an ostentatious show of a growing political power has been infinitely more significant for the hundreds of thousands of those who have taken up the Party's struggle: it has been a great personal and spiritual gathering of the old stalwarts and comrades-in-arms. And, indeed, there may be those here who, despite such a compelling and splendid display of our Party's army, will have dreamed with a heavy heart back to days gone by when it was still a difficult thing to be a National

Mural from the Frankfurt Ärztehaus. In Georg Poppe, *Führerbild im Frankfurter Arztehaus* (Pictures of the *Führer* in the Frankfurt Ärztehaus).

Socialist (Heil!) For even when the Party was but seven strong it adhered to two fundamental principles: first, it was a truly ideological party (*Weltanschauungspartei*); second, it uncompromisingly sought to be Germany's sole power. (Heil!)

We had to remain the Party of the minority because we mobilized the elements most precious to the nation's struggle and sense of sacrifice. In any age these have always been displayed, not by the majority, but by the minority. (Heil!)

And because the German nation has made a proud assessment of its best racial values, and with courage and daring has demanded a leadership for the *Reich* and the people, more and more of the people have joined this leadership and placed themselves at its service. (Heil!)

The great calming influence—that regards itself as the bearer of the nation's best blood (Heil!), that has knowingly risen to lead that nation, and that is resolved to retain, nurture, and never abandon this leadership—has made the German people happy in the knowledge that things have now ceased eternally to elude them. (Heil!)

A nation is never made up exclusively of truly active fighters. Thus greater demands will be made of them than of the millions of their national comrades. It is not enough for them simply to declare, "I shall believe." They must take the oath, "I shall fight!" (Heil!) The Party of the future shall be the selected, elite political leadership of the German people. Its doctrine will not change, its organization will be as hard as steel, its tactics will be supple and adaptable, and in its entirety it will be like a holy order. (Heil!)

Yet its goal must remain this: all decent Germans shall become National Socialists, only the best will be Party comrades. (Heil, Sieg Heil, Sieg Heil!)

In the past it was our enemies who, by banning and repeatedly persecuting the Party, ensured that the movement was kept clean of the traces of flotsam that would find their way in. Today we must carry out our own inspections and eject everything that has gone bad and that thus (Heil!) . . . that thus does not belong within us. (Heil!)

It is our wish and our will for this state and this *Reich* to exist throughout the coming centuries. We can be happy in the knowledge that the entire future belongs to us. (Heil!) Even if those of the older generation become frail, we can rely on the youth, for they are committed to us and will serve us (now almost inaudible amid the cries of Heil!) with body and soul. (Heil, Sieg Hiel, Sieg Heil, Heil, Heil, Heil!) Only if we all play our part in making the Party the supreme embodiment of the thought and essence of National Socialism will it become an eternal and indestructible pillar of the German people and *Reich*. And then Germany's glorious and heralded army of old and proud bearers of arms will be joined by the Party's political leadership—for it is no less rooted in the traditions of our nation—and together these two institutions will cultivate and enhance the lives of Germans and on their shoulders shall support the German state and the German *Reich*. (Heil!)

Within the hour, tens of thousands of Party comrades will be leaving the city. While some shall still be nourished by their memories, others will be preparing for the next call to action. People will keep returning: they will never fail to be captivated, inspired with joy and enthusiasm, for the idea and the movement are the expression of the life of our people and thus the symbol of the everlasting. Long live the National Socialist movement! Long live Germany! (Cries of Heil, which turns into screaming and shouting. Hess, standing at the microphone, is for a long time unable to make himself heard. Finally, he declares:) "The Party is Hitler. Hitler is Germany, and Germany is Hitler. Sieg Heil!" (All join in, cries of Heil turn into "Die Fahne hoch.")

Benjamin has demanded of historians that they see "beauty in the most profound distortion." Riefenstahl, however, can hardly be claimed to be following Benjamin. Indeed she has no sense of the "distortion" of what she films; she has no concept of the distorted. Her wish was always to film what was "beautiful"; what she recorded at the party conference was beauty as such—not its "distortion." She perceives with a gaze that is atheoretical and unconscious. Yet in the sense that it represents what she perceives as beauty, her gaze is also radical; it makes *visible* the beauty of distortion.

(What she also makes visible is a particular distortion of "montage." Riefenstahl uses montage, a technique originally conceived to disrupt the grotesque harmonies of the "factual," as a means, precisely, of re-establishing harmony. In this respect, it seems to me, her work is close to that of Dali.)

* * *

Readers will by now be familiar with Wilhelm Reich's attempts to outline a new Communist strategy on the basis of an analysis of the psychic reality of the conditions of development of the "fascist character." Equally familiar is the reaction of the Weimar Communist Party: they expelled him. There were, of course, numerous flaws in Reich's approach, many of which he himself conceded in a 1952 interview with Dr. Eissler. He admitted, for example, that he had been mistaken in his belief in the possibility of collaborating with the Communist Party, or indeed with any party, on an enterprise such as "Sexpol."[55] Reich's original attempts to do so are commented on by Deleuze and Guattari as follows: "The leadership has a tendency rather to reply: when I hear the word 'desire,' I pull out my gun."[56] The Reich of 1952 would have shared their attitude—unlike the many contemporary "Reichians" who still idolize Lenin and declare the later Reich insane. They stem the flow through liquidation.

It was, by contrast, only on rare occasions that Reich deviated from his attempts to raise awareness among the Left of the psychic reality he labeled the "subjective factor"—a term that today remains both part of common parlance in German and dangerously erroneous, not least because of the technocratic resonances of the concept "factor."

Deleuze and Guattari pay Reich the warmest of tributes; at the same time, they develop an excellent critique of his analysis.

> Reich was the first to raise the problem of the relationship
> between desire and the social field (and went further than
> Marcuse, who treats the problem lightly). He is the true founder
> of materialist psychiatry. Situating the problem in terms of desire,
> he is the first to reject the explanations of a summary Marxism
> too quick to say the masses were fooled, mystified. But since he
> had not sufficiently formulated the concept of desiring-production,
> he did not succeed in determining the insertion of desire into the

economic infrastructure itself, the insertion of the drives into social production. Consequently, revolutionary investment seemed to him such that the desire moving within it simply coincided with an economic rationality; as to the reactionary mass investments, they seemed to him to derive from ideology, so that psychoanalysis merely had the role of explaining the subjective, the negative, and the inhibited, without participating directly as psychoanalysis in the positivity of the revolutionary movement or in the desiring-creativity. (To a certain extent, didn't this amount to a reintroduction of the error or the illusion?) The fact remains that Reich, in the name of desire, caused a song of life to pass into psychoanalysis. He denounced, in the final resignation of Freudianism, a fear of life, a resurgence of the ascetic ideal, a cultural broth of bad consciousness. Better to depart in search of the Orgone, he said to himself, in search of the vital and cosmic element of desire, than to continue being a psychoanalyst under these conditions. No one forgave him for this, whereas Freud got full pardon. Reich was the first to attempt to make the analytic machine and the revolutionary machine function together. In the end, he had only his own desiring-machines, his paranoiac, miraculous, and celibate boxes, with metallic inner walls lined with cotton and wool.[57]

The force of human desiring-production, in whatever form—whether as a force for life or for destruction—always necessarily represents a force that produces not only the organization of industrial production, but every other form of social existence (though the conditions of production are, of course, diverse and different). Even such adherents of Marx as have traditionally expected, or even continue to expect, human beings to rise in revolutionary masses as the "proletariat" on the basis of their position in the production process alone must surely concede that the massive development of industrial production in Germany has never yet proved equal to the task of releasing into social relations adequate quantities of human beings capable of freedom or productive of life: human beings capable of preventing the victory of the half-born, the victory of human beings with deathly potential, betrayed, disinherited, robbed of their capacity for life, either by the German military or by the double-bind of their existence within strata-on-two-fronts. Surely then we cannot conclude that the potential for fascism to exist among us will be eradicated only at the point at which universal industrialization "eliminates" fascist elements? Or rather: were this to be the necessary conclusion, there would be no prospect of any end to fascism.

It is more or less tantamount to a mockery of fascism's victims to assume the "true" standpoint of any class or stratum to be the basis on which political strategy should be founded. This was the very mistake initially made by the victims themselves; they paid with their lives or with emigration. The same mockery has been made by the numbers of emigrants who later took up positions as leaders of the Socialist Unity Party in the GDR. On the same issue, the "Maoist" Left in West Germany remains indistinguishable from the SED or the West German Communist Party (DKP). The real identity between the parties on the political level overrides their mutual hatred; and it originates in their common denial of human desire as a force of social production. Individuals among them may be labeled "economistic," "mechanistic and instrumentalist," "dogmatic," "pragmatic," "positivist," "Stalinist," "Leninist," "Trotskyist," "Marxist," "Communist," "liberal," "Maoist," or whatever; but they share a common and fundamental commitment to the "primacy" of "objectivity" in one form or another (be it that of a relation of production, of a historical situation, or simply the "objectivity" of what is known as "pluralism"). All organize themselves accordingly: while on the one hand excluding desire as a force of production, they perpetrate acts of terror, either on their own members or on others. Their common denominator is self-denial; they share a tendency to become or to produce macroformations, and they use exclusion as one of their principal creative means. Like guards patroling the borders of their own body-armor, they hunt down every microbe that dares appear on their unsullied theoretical territory.

The heroic male, no matter where he hails from, will always raise an anxious professorial finger to test the icy political winds he himself generates. He will anticipate a salvation that he invariably considers to have been already realized elsewhere—in the Soviet Union, in China, among the Spartans or the South Sea islanders. This land beyond the horizon does not perhaps itself function as part of the male ego or male bonding; but the "future" certainly does. (Mayakovsky, remember, cried tears of joy at the prospect of being torn from the bosom of the future—though his crying was never answered.)[58]

Anticipation blinds: this is perhaps a safer premise to work on. The figure of the Angelus Novus, driven from paradise, turns its back on the future toward which it is driven: but the angel is not a man.[59] It adopts a stance never countenanced by the owner of the penetrating gaze or the gaze from the world beyond. This man sees himself instead from the fictive perspective of a disembodied being, as the cornerstone of a monument to eternity, or the linchpin on which the monster-machine hinges. His abandoned body becomes the burden he lays on the shoulders of his colonized victims. He finds it as difficult to progress from the level of the basic fault to something as simple as conflict—contradicting parents, for instance—as others have found it to build Chinese routes to German revolution. His only solution is to abstract from his own body. For him, the body survives only in the form of occupied territory.

To the generations of young male Germans born between around 1870 and 1920, it seemed easier to blow half the world to pieces, to kill numerous millions of human beings, than to counter the demands of their various "edu-

"That's Really Too Bad." In *Radical America* by George Crumb and others. *Frame 1*.
"Daily life goes on . . . home, office, factory." *Frame 2*. "Under capitalism." "Just
another signature." *Frame 3*. " Or under communism . . ." "Is this a system . . .?" *Frame 4*. "Or in other
systems an anti-systems . . ." "Is this a system . . .?" *Frame 5*. "Dunno. Is it? Maybe
it's a system. Maybe not. . . . Dunno." *Frame 6*. "Today's news. The situation in the
world looks bad, folks." *Frame 7*. (Man) "See if there's anything good on the . . ."
(Woman) "What's the point?" *Frame 8*. "Can we hope anymore?" (Shake, shake)
"Believe me, hopelessness is the only way."

cators'' with anything identifiable as true resistance. More than this, they considered their response the *correct* one. (Any one of their numerous murder programs can be traced to an original injunction against contradicting their parents.) The group they represented was large, with no clear limits; had it not been, they would necessarily have remained ineffective.[60]

If political economy bears the traces of its origins in bourgeois science, then the same traces are still more clearly visible in its brother science, the critique of economism. Working-class parties in Germany, as in most European countries, have been dominated on the theoretical level by bourgeois individuals newly converted to "Marxism" — a fact that safely guarantees the focusing of strategy discussions on politico-economic analysis.

The emphasis on political economy seems to me an extension of a contradiction specific to the bourgeois individual: the contradiction between a capacity for strategic investigation into and exploitation of nature, on the one hand, and, on the other, ignorance of the nature of the individual. To the bourgeois ego, the world appears manipulable, controllable, knowable. It cherishes notions of the quantifiability of emotions and invests hopes in the controllability of what it terms the psychic *economy*. At the same time, it sees itself as a dark continent, uncharted territory.

Freud described the female psyche as a dark continent, both for himself and for psychoanalysis.[61] In so doing, was he not also admitting ignorance of himself as "man"? Surely the very notion that the sexes can be understood in isolation from each other is simply a typical reflection of the bourgeois male individual's isolated ego?*

The bourgeois male individual sees himself as "understanding" such things as the limits to human endurance (by which he means making them subject to surveillance, control, and comprehension), as long as he can dissect them into numbers, tables, statistics, analyses of materials, investment costs, empirical details. Seen in the most unfavorable light, Marxist political economy (like the psychic models of Freud's thinking) appears then simply as a potential complement to entrepreneurial competence in factory organization. And since Communist strategy discussions are dominated by political economy, it would appear not only that theorists of Communism find the entrepreneurial activity of organizing exploitation easier to *understand* than mass suffering, but, more than this, that they see no base in that suffering for a politics of liberation. The same deficiency is visible in psychoanalysis, which mobi-

---

*Freud's admission is, however, contradictory; it marks the limits to the "bourgeois"-masculine concept of knowledge. For was it not precisely the discoveries he made through his female patients that enabled him to develop early psychoanalysis? Did he not develop his methods of treatment in relation to the very patients he was later to describe as dark and impenetrable? Was it not precisely their "opacity" that enabled him to know? And does not the structure Freud considered a known and charted continent—the (male-oriented) ego/id/super-ego structure of the person—appear today as the most clearly ideological and most culturally determined of his "discoveries"? It seems we are dealing with an ego which, as long as it continues to live its splitting, gains its best knowledge from sites on which it never sheds light.

"That's Really Too Bad." From *Radical America* by George Crumb and others. *Frame 1.*
"Holy men came to show us the way and all they got was a kick in the arse!!" / "Smash
him in." / "Queer bastard." / "Peace brothers." / "Adolf would've sent you to the labor
camp." *Frame 2.* "In his youth, man is touchingly hopeful and optimistic." "Rah, rah,
rah . . ." *Frame 3.* " When he gets more 'mature,' he begins to recognize the gray
'reality' of life . . ." *Frame 4.* ". . . and ends up old and bitter, disappointed by
unfulfilled dreams, betrayed by fate, his days so full of pain that he is glad to die at last!"
Frame 5. "For 10,000 years many people have asked after the why and the wherefore,
and have sought salvation in a thousand ways." *Frame 6.* "It seems easier to blow the
whole planet sky high than to get on with your own wife!" *Frame 7.* "The best answer
we've ever found to all our problems is to just sit around and do nothing."

lizes inadequate notions of "health," rather than visions of human potential, as its means of combatting human suffering.

Politico-economic pressure on the Left has in the past been great enough to compel even such as Wilhelm Reich to ornament his mass psychology of fascism with figures and tables detailing quantities of human beings in particular strata and classes. The details he gives are insignificant and open to arbitrary interpretation; they remain indistinguishable from the kind of rubbish circulated in his own time by the party. Even Reich himself made no distinction; on the contrary, he drew on party literature for his own investigations. [62]

Thus, for example, he gave credence to the thoroughly unsubstantiated assumption of "class position" as a necessary determinant of human behavior. Despite his own use elsewhere of a quotation from Marx — "Man himself is the basis of his material production, as of every other production which he achieves"[63] — which he used to register a protest against the automatic conflation of the being that determines consciousness with traditional definitions of the "sphere of production," Reich himself made the self-same equation. And his is one case only, a single contradiction to demonstrate the limitations of a mere *awareness* of correct positions. The insertion of "correct" quotes in the "correct" place in any given analysis does not suffice to prevent whatever those quotes establish as false from surfacing elsewhere the moment attention wavers. The problem originates in the relation between the world and the male ego: a power relation in which pleasure is taken in violating whatever displays itself as living. Within that power relation, subject-object polarities can never be transcended; notions of a possible "synthesis," "mediation," or "sublimation" represent nothing short of a refusal to acknowledge a power relationship within which the fiction of a good totality is either simply celebrated or raised to the "higher" spheres of abstract power.

The whole is not the true, nor has it ever been so. The whole is a force that suppresses the existence of anything halved or segmented (a force for men); yet what is halved and segmented is surely what is human.

"Mediation" is an illusion that conceals its own nature from itself. It cannot, should not, will not be the whole or the "one," but only the multiple, the partial, the segmentary, the replicated, the chaotic, microanarchy, that will . . .

that will what?

that will at least not be raised to the pinnacle of theory or lowered to the level of truth at its profoundest. *Or will it?*

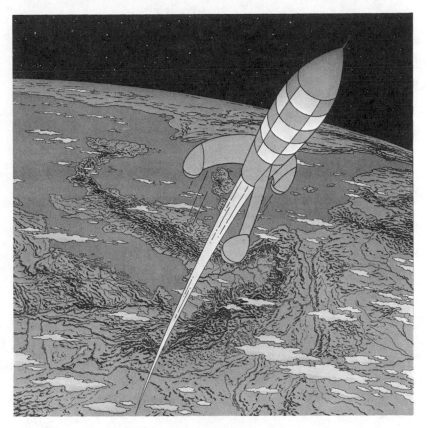

"Tintin" by Hergé. Copyright © 1989 Hergé/Casterman.

Notes

Notes

The notes cite editions of works used in the preparation of this book. Full publication information for English translations and original-language editions appears in the bibliography.

Citations to Freud's works are to *The Standard Edition of the Complete Psychological Works of Sigmund Freud* (referred to in the notes as *SE*), translated under the general editorship of James Strachey (London: Hogarth Press, 1953-74).

Abbreviations

The following abbreviations appear after the titles of works taken from the anthologies listed below:

HoDA	Hotzel, Curt. *Deutscher Aufstad*
JKR	Jünger, Ernst. *Der Kampf um das Reich*
RDS	Roden, Hans. *Deutsche Soldaten*
SB	Salomon, Ernst. *Das Buch vom deutschen Freikorpsdämpfer*

Foreword

1. Peter Schneider, "Im Todeskreis der Schuld," *Die Zeit*, Nr. 14 (March, 1987), 66.
2. See Theweleit's "Nachbemerkung" to Volume 2 of the First German Edition, 1977, p. 534. This section is not included in the American translation.
3. Ernst Bloch, *Erbschaft dieser Zeit*, 1st ed. 1935, Frankfurt am Main, 1962, p. 66. For a discussion of the political context of this work, see Anson Rabinbach, "Unclaimed Heritage: Ernst Bloch's *Heritage of Our Times* and the Theory of Fascism," *New German Critique*, No. 11 (Spring, 1977), 5-21.

4. There are a number of points of convergence between Benjamin's analysis of the metaphysics of violence in German fascism and Theweleit's own discussion. Theweleit decisively rejects Benjamin's view that war is a consequence of the expansion of the productive forces. Benjamin's perspective is neatly encapsulated in his "Theories of German Fascism," a review of a collection of writings on war edited by Jünger in 1930. A translation with an introduction by Ansgar Hillach appears in *New German Critique* 17 (Spring, 1979), 120-28. Georges Bataille, "The Psychological Structure of Fascism," appeared in *New German Critique* 16 (Winter, 1979), 64-89. It is collected, with other important writings on this theme, in Georges Bataille, *Visions of Excess: Selected Writings, 1927-1939*, ed. Allan Stoekl (Minneapolis, 1985), 137-60.

5. Walter Benjamin, "The Work of Art in the Age of Mechanical Reproduction," *Illuminations*, ed. Hannah Arendt (New York, 1969), p. 241.

6. Paul Robinson, "The Women They Feared," *The New York Times Book Review*, June 21, 1987, p. 14.

7. Lutz Niethammer, "Male Fantasies: An Argument for and with an Important New Study in History and Psychoanalysis," *History Workshop: A Journal of Socialist Historians* 7 (Spring, 1979), 176-86.

8. George L. Mosse, "Two World Wars and the Myth of the War Experience," *Journal of Contemporary History*, Vol. 21 (1986), pp. 491-513.

9. Karl Dietrich Bracher, *The German Dictatorship: The Origins, Structure and Effects of National Socialism*, trans., Jean Steinberg (New York, Washington, 1970), pp. 95, 117.

10. Geoffrey Pridham, *Hitler's Rise to Power: The Nazi Movement in Bavaria 1923-1933* (New York, Evanston, London, 1973), pp. 81, 82. Von Epp was the Nazi candidate in Upper Bavaria-Swabia for the Reichstag in 1928, opposing Gustav Stresemann, the conservative foreign minister.

11. Alan Bullock, *Hitler: A Study in Tyranny* (New York, 1962), p. 275.

12. See Jeffrey Herf, *Reactionary Modernism: Technology, Culture and Politics in Weimar and the Third Reich* (Cambridge, 1984), pp. 70-108.

13. George L. Mosse, *Nationalism and Sexuality: Respectability and Abnormal Sexuality in Modern Europe* (New York, 1985), p. 175.

14. Zeev Sternhell, *Neither Right nor Left: Fascist Ideology in France*, trans., David Maisel (Berkeley, Los Angeles, London, 1986). Also see the thoughtful review by Saul Friedländer, *The New Republic*, December 13, 1986, pp. 26-33.

15. Alice Yaeger Kaplan, *Reproductions of Banality: Fascism, Literature and French Intellectual Life* (Minneapolis, 1986). Robert Soucy's study *Fascist Intellectual: Drieu La Rochelle* (Berkeley, Los Angeles, London, 1979) also emphasizes this aspect of his ideology. See especially the chapters entitled "Women" and "The Virile Elite and Hitlerian Man."

16. Klaus-Friedrich Bastian, *Das politische bei Ernst Jünger. Nonkonformismus und Kompromiss der Innerlickeit*. Diss. Heidelberg, 1963, p. 280. Cited in Ansgar Hillach, "The Aesthetics of Politics: Walter Benjamin's 'Theories of German Fascism,'" *New German Critique* 17 (Spring, 1979), 105. On Jünger's use of language see Karl Prümm, *Die Literatur des soldatischen Nationalismus der 20er Jahre (1918-1933)*, Vol. I (Krönberg/Taunus, 1974), pp. 152-55, passim.

17. This point is intelligently argued by Robert Wohl in *The Generation of 1914* (Cambridge, MA, 1979), especially p. 60.

18. Cited in Benjamin, "Theories of German Fascism," 126.

19. In Volume I Theweleit defends Deleuze/Guattari's doctrine that desire itself is a productive force. This framework of adopting Marxist categories within the psychoanalytic model seems forced today.

20. Michel Foucault, "Nietzsche, Genealogy, History," *Language, Counter-Memory, Practice: Selected Essays and Interviews* ed. Donald F. Bourchard, trans. Donald F.

Bourchard and Sherry Simon (Ithaca, 1977), p. 148. It would be interesting to compare Foucault's later approach with that of Theweleit. The Nietzsche essay establishes a framework for the "epistemological" works, above all *The Archaeology of Knowledge*. It presages *Discipline and Punish*, which documents a genealogy of power through which discourse and technology subdue bodies: in the workplace, in the asylum, and, of course, in the prison. In this middle phase Foucault seems to have collapsed "knowledge/power" into a single concept. His later work on the *History of Sexuality*, however, restores the active moment in knowledge which is linked to desire and the body's relation to the acts that make up the ethical life. Especially *The Care of the Self* (Vol. 3), trans. Robert Hurley (New York, 1986) attempts to articulate how gendered society and its ethical constraint is itself constituted out of the changing relation of the body to the "other" and to the self, a view more consonant with Theweleit's, despite their obvious differences concerning psychoanalysis.

21. See Martin Jay, *The Dialectical Imagination: A History of the Frankfurt School and the Institute of Social Research 1923-1950* (Boston, Toronto, 1973), especially Chapters 4 and 5. More recently the Institute's discussions in this period have been further elaborated by Rolf Wiggershaus, *Die Frankfurter Schule: Geschichte, Theoretische Entwicklung, politische Bedeutung* (Munich, 1986) and Alfons Sollner, *Geschichte und Herrschaft: Studien zur materialistischen Sozialwissenschaft 1929-1942* (Frankfurt am Main, 1979).

22. Theodor W. Adorno, "Freudian Theory and the Pattern of Fascist Propaganda," *Psychoanalysis and the Social Sciences*, Geza Roheim, ed. (New York, 1951), pp. 408-33.

23. Ibid., p. 418.

24. Robert J. Stoller, *Perversion: The Erotic Form of Hatred* (New York, 1975), p. 150.

25. Janine Chasseguet-Smirgel, *Sexuality and Mind: The Role of the Father and the Mother in the Psyche* (New York and London, 1986), pp. 81-91.

26. Ibid., p. 83.

27. Stoller, *Perversion*, p.150.

Chapter 1: The Mass and Its Counterparts

The Mass as Embodiment of a Specific Unconscious

1. *Nazif̈uhrer sehen dich an* (1934), a collection of critical writings by left-wing emigres in Paris, attempts to expose the Hitlerian concept of the masses as "contradictory," citing *Mein Kampf*: 'On days like these when I pondered and mused, it was with an uneasy feeling of anguish that I saw the mass of those who no longer belonged to their people swell into a threatening army.' Thus speaks the future F̈uhrer. This hysterical fear of the mass is still with him today. (20)

2. Salomon, "Albert Leo Schlageter," in SB, 481.

3. Salomon, *Die Geaechteten (The Outlaws)*, 10-11.

4. The "mass" is described in terms of waves/femininity/bubbling/boiling/devouring/smashing in: Rossman and Schmidthuysen, "Der blutige Montage in Duisburg," in SB, 392; Gustav Goes, "Aus dem Tagebuch des letzten Kommandanten von Kowel," in SB, 131; Salomon, "Der Berliner Märzaufstand 1919," in SB, 45-46; Salomon, "Hexenkessel Deutschland," in JKR, 13, 22, 23, 27; Mahnken, "Der Kampf der Batterie Hasenclever," in RDS, 138; Wittmann, *Erinnerungen der Eisernen Schar Berthold*, 135; Dwinger, *Auf halbem Wege*, 258, 276, 367, 371, 456, 459; W. Frank, *Franz Ritter von Epp*, 95; Stoffregen, *Vaterland*, 202; Höfer, *Oberschlesien in der Aufstandszeit*, 29; Volck, *Rebellen um Ehre*, 20; Freiwald, *Der verratene Flotte*, 233;

Freiwald, *Der Weg der braunen Kämpfe*, 115ff., 313; Roden, "Hauptmann Berthold—ein Soldatenschicksal," in RDS, 140; Erbt, *Der Narr*, 91, 144; Zöberlein, *Der Befehl des Gewisens*, 165; on devouring and smashing, see an interpretation by Abraham which gives an example of how the Oedipus-incest "desire" construction is necessarily always turned upside down by manifestation of reality. He writes: "The particular method of killing the spider in the dream—crushing it—is to be explained by the sadistic theory of coitus. (Incidentally, certain of the patient's day-dreams used to culminate in a number of people being crushed to death.) The associations showed that the long broom was a phallic symbol, so that the patient's latent wish to kill his mother by copulating with her becomes unmistakable." This concerns a patient who imagines he is crushing a spider with a broom handle. The spider is identified as the mother's genitals which conceals a penis. It seems to me that the only "indisputable" compulsion is that to papa/mama/baby. K Abraham, "The Spider as Dream Symbol," in *Selected Papers* (London, 1942), 328.

5. For the mass in terms of a millipede, dragon, snake, or similar creatures, see: Fischer, "Die Räteherrschaft in München," in JKR, 155-56; Salomon, "Sturm auf Riga," in JKR, 104; Salomon, *Die Geaechteten*, 43; Nord, "Der Krieg im Baltikum," in JKR, 74; Sager, "Vom Kampf der Essener Einwohnerwehr," in SB, 385; Maltzan, "Die Spandauer stürmen Bauske," in SB, 161; Volck, *Rebellen um Ehre*, 19; Weigand, *Die rote Flut*, 92-93; von Selchow, *Hundert Tage*, 289ff., 343; Dwinger, *Auf halbem Wege*, 232, 456; Dwinger, *Die letzten Reiter*, 381; Iger, *Spartakustage*, 9; Schauwecker, *Aufbruch der Nation*, 380; Heinz, *Sprengstoff*, 34, 131; Berthold's diary in Gengler, *Rudolf Berthold*, 62; Hollenbach, *Opfergang*, 157; Bronnen, *Rossbach*, 67; Herzog, *Kameraden*, 341; Rossbach, *Mann im Sattel*, 355; Wittmann, *Erinnerungen der Eisernen Schar*, 107; Ottwald, *Ruhe und Ordnung*, 5.

On the frequent connection between women and snakes: The snake "symbolizes" neither the imaginary penis of the woman (Freud, *The Interpretation of Dreams*) nor her potency feared by the man (V. E. Pilgrim, *Der Untergang des Mannes*, unauthorized copy, Monaco, no date). Interpretations of this kind are indivisible from the encoding of the threatening with femininity. The snake seems rather to be the attribute of all that threatens to emerge from the mass or throng which can kill and yet has the power to attract. Women are merely locked into the same category. Jünger sensed the ambivalent nature of "snakes" when he tried to encapsulate the secret of spooky stories read to children (by women) on long winter evenings: "It was like getting caught up in muddy reeds and coming across a nest of speckled snakes. The disgusting coils were such a pleasure to watch, it was impossible to escape." (*Der Kampf als inneres Erlebnis*, 11.) There is more evidence here of a relationship with desire than with women. The appearance of snakes/dragons is also significant in various works of prophecy. See Bächthold, *Deutscher Soldatenbrauch und Soldatenglaube* (Strassburg, 1917), 6; Bächthold, *Aus Leben und Sprache des Schweizer Soldaten*, (Basel, 1916), 17; Grabinski, *Das Übersinnliche im Weltkriege*, (Hildesheim, 1917), 65, 81. We should also not forget the following: " 'The hissing of the snake of counterrevolution is becoming louder again,' wrote Stalin on August 13 on the slander to which Kamenev had been subjected. 'The venomous beast of reaction is coming out of its hiding place to bare its poisonous barb. It will sting, then slink back into its dark corner.'" L. Trotsky, *Stalin. Eine Biographie*, vol. 2, (Reinbek, 1971), 62.

6. Cf. von der Goltz, *Meine Sendung*, 225; von Oertzen, *Die Deutschen Freikorps*, 386; W. Frank, *Epp*, 80; Iger, *Spartakustage*, 108; Freiwald, *Die verratene Flotte*, 249.

7. U. Sonnemann, *Negative Anthropologie*, 91. F. T. Marinetti's normative formulation makes it nicely clear that such an exchange is highly deliberate and that the process has little to do with the unconscious: "Each noun should have its double; that is, the noun should be followed, with no conjunction, by the noun to which it is related by analogy.

Example: man—torpedo boat, woman—gulf, crowd—surf, piazza—funnel, door—
valve." "Technical Manifesto of Futurist Literature," in F. T. Marinetti, *Selected
Writings*, translated and edited by R. Flint and A. Coppotelli (London: Secker and
Warburg, 1972), 84-85. The game being played here is an organized one in which
forming symbols by analogy serves to block access to the unconscious rather than to
open it up.

Contagious Lust

1. Rosenberg's preface to Dietrich Eckart, *Ein Vermächtnis*, 53.
2. E.g., Rudolph Löwenstein, *Psychoanalyse des Antisemitismus*, (Frankfurt, 1967), 50;
   Klaus Horn, "Zur politischen Psychologie des Faschismus in Deutschland," in R.
   Kühnl, (ed.), *Texte zur Faschismusdiskussion*, vol. 1 (Reinbek, 1974), 164-75;
   Karl-Dietrich Bracher, *The German Dictatorship*, (Harmondsworth: Penguin, 1973),
   chapter on "The Role of Anti-Semitism," 52-65.
3. Julius Streicher in a speech of 1926, quoted by Gilbert, *Nürnberger Tagebuch*, 119. The
   Stürmer often paired contagious desire and Jewishness. See also Dietrich Eckart, "Das
   Judentum in und ausser uns," in *Ein Vermächtnis*, 193ff., and the quotations from
   issues 70-73 of the *Völkische Beobachter* of 1921, of which Eckart was the first editor,
   in Rosenberg's preface, 58. In addition, Ekkehard, *Sturmgeschlecht*, 132ff.; Zöberlein,
   Befehl des Gewissens, 296ff., 360ff., 531. The tone is as follows: "You only have to
   read carefully through the Old Testament. It's crawling with sacrificial foreskins, genitals
   that have been hacked off, people boasting of their sexual exploits, indescribably filthy
   whores, young boys being sexually abused, sodomy, incest, assassination, genocide—all
   the things we hear are happening in Russia under the Bolsheviks, mankind's modern-day
   paradise. Have you noticed something, dear reader?" (712). In a remarkable section
   from his writings from Cracow prison, Höss attempts to distinguish between "serious"
   and sexual anti-Semitism: "I used to steer clear of Streicher's anti-Semitic weekly,
   Stürmer, because its presentation was in poor taste and was designed to appeal to one's
   most basic instincts. The sexual side of things was always being emphasized, often in a
   pornographic and vulgar manner. The paper caused a great deal of damage, and did
   nothing to further the cause of serious anti-Semitism. On the contrary, it detracted from
   it in a most harmful way." In an effort to portray himself as an "unserious" anti-Semite
   after all, he goes on: "It is no wonder that after the surrender we learned it had been a
   Jew editing the paper and writing the most depraved and inflammatory articles." (Höss,
   Kommandant in Auschwitz, 112) Broszat, the editor of Höss's volume, adds a note: "We
   do not know on what Höss bases this statement, for no evidence can be found to support
   it."
4. von Berk, "Rote Armee an der Ruhr," in JKR, 211; On "contagious lust" see also
   Dwinger, *Auf halbem Wege*, 464; Höfer, *Oberschlesien in der Aufstandszeit*, 7-9;
   Stadtler, *Als Antibolschewist*, 106; Volck, *Rebellen um Ehre*, 145; Brandt, *Schlageter*,
   72; Eggers, *Vom mutigem Leben*, 34-35; Wagener, *Von der Heimat geächtet*, 157;
   Schaumlöffel, *Das Studentenkorps Marburg*, 13, 55; Lüttwitz, *Im Kampf gegen die
   Novemberrevolution*, 40; Goote, *Kamerad Berthold*, 246. On the consequences of
   "contagious lust" (weakening of moral fiber, etc.), see, for example, Eggers, *Von der
   Freiheit des Krieges*, 12; Höfer, *Oberschlesien in der Aufstandszeit*, 18.
5. For "Reds" as criminals/dirt/riff-raff, see Reinhard, "Kampf um Berlin," in SB, 32;
   Ehlers, "Die 'Bahrenfelder' Zeitfreiwilligen," in SB, 72; Zeschau, "Streiflichter aus
   den Kämpfen um Litauen," in SB, 137; Grothe/Kern, "Strassenkämpfe in München,"
   in SB, 123; Hoffmann, "Letzter Sturm," in SB, 405; Salomon, "Hexenkessel
   Deutschland," in JKR, 18, 21, 33, 36; Günther, "Hamburg," in JKR, 41; von Berk,
   "Rote Armee an der Ruhr," in JKR, 213; Mahnken, "Gegenstoss im Westen 1919," in
   RDS, 60; Loewenfeld, "Das Freikorps von Loewenfeld," in RDS, 151ff.; Pabst,

"Spartakus," in HoDA, 34; Iger, *Spartakustage*, 8, 18; Zimmermann, *Vorfrühling*, 24; Mann, *Mit Ehrhardt*, 18; Killinger, *Die SA*, 15; Killinger, *Ernstes und Heiteres aus dem Putschleben*, 22; Heinz, *Die Nation greift an*, 23, 34, 101; Schaumlöffel, *Studentenkorps Marburg*, 13; Berthold, "Tagebuch," in Gengler, *Rudolf Berthold*, 94, 102; Zöberlein, *Befehl des Gewissens*, 33, 96-97, 213ff.; Erbt, *Der Narr*, 199; Rossin, *Im roten Sumpf*, 7; Schramm, *Rote Tage*, 53; Lüttwitz, *Im Kampf gegen die Novemberrevolution*, 40; Niemöller, *Vom U-Boot*, 133; Schricker, *Rotmord*, 9; Höfer, *Oberschlesien in der Aufstandszeit*, 8, 14, 22; Engelhardt, *Ritt nach Riga*, 10; Ettighofer, *Revolver über der Stadt*, 43-44; Freiwald, *Verratene Flotte*, 90, 221, 242. Reds as pimps with whores, etc.: Kohlhaas, "Männer und Sicherheitskompanien," 96; Goes, "Aus dem Tagebuch des letzten Kommandanten von Kowel," 131ff., both in SB, Fischer, "Die Räteherrschaft in München," in JKR, 150; Rodemund, "Rote Armee an Rhein und Ruhr," in HoDA, 109; H. Schauwecker, "Freikorps Epp," in HoDA, 173; W. Frank, "Epp," in HoDA, 68, 77; Weigand, "Rote Flut," in HoDA, 161, 385; Goote, *Kamerad Berthold*, 270, 277; Schulz, "Ein Freikorps im Industriegebiet," in HoDA, 33; Maercker, "Vom Kaiderheer," in HoDA, 194, 238. With whores, etc.: Engelhardt, *Ritt nach Riga*, 28; Ettighofer, *Revolver über der Stadt*, 186; Schricker, *Rotmord*, 193; Krumbach, *Epp*, 50-51; Freiwald, *Verratene Flotte*, 245ff.; Mann, *Mit Ehrhardt*, 17.

6. Pikarski, "Zeitfreiwilligen-Regiment Pommern," in SB, 359.
7. Schulz, "Ein Freikorps im Industriegebiet," 11.
8. For example, R. Mann, *Mit Ehrhardt*, 75.
9. Gilbert, *Nürnberger Tagebuch*, 34.
10. Heinz, *Sprengstoff*, 143-44.
11. Zöberlein, *Befehl des Gewissens*, 509.
12. What is particularly terrible about the Zöberlein text is that Mirjam herself is the one who damns the Jews:

> A richly decorated table stood glowing like an island of beauty. A mountain of flowers surrounded a heavy, seven-pronged candelabra, and the flames above the wicks flickered gently, casting the only light in the otherwise dark room over the glass and silver. From the midst of this overwhelming splendor glittered the shining gold of the six points of the Star of David. And as he sat there, he could see through the bars of the seven candles above the golden star Mirjam's beaming face, and the mass of dark, curly hair that tumbled over her face. As he looked, he could not help feeling that this was no doubt the kind of place where a man could be bewitched. . . .
>
> The dim darkness all around was full of lurking secrets, and when Krafft said, "I feel just like Tannhäuser must have felt when he was in Venus's mountain," she merely nodded, her black eyes smiling invitingly, and then shook her hair cooing and laughing. He, however, had been thinking of the exile's longing for fresh air, sunlight, and such things. Somewhere he had seen a picture of a woman with a snake curled around her shiny white body, her eyes of such compelling force that one could not escape her gaze. Though the picture had chilled his spine with a ghastly feeling of horror, he had also felt a lovely sweetness flow through his veins. The picture was called "Sin." Mirjam could easily have been the model. And when she spoke, he was reminded of the tiny, darting forked tongue of a snake as it roots its victim to the spot with a hypnotic gaze, and quietly moves in for the kill. He forced himself to remember the pharmacist's words: "A sense of total disgust is the only way out." "Are you so lost in your thoughts?" she asked, her voice so full of

flattery that he looked up into her irresistibly imploring eyes and saw on her
parted lips an enchantingly disarming smile. "I feel I've seen you somewhere
before." "Me?" she said, surprised and paling slightly. "Yes, Countess, just
as I see you before me now. Only in a picture." "Oh, how interesting!" She
breathed a sigh of relief. "But don't keep calling me Countess, call me
Mirjam," she asked with endearing confidentiality. "There are only the two of
us, and I'll call you by your first name. Your health, Hans!" "Your health."
"Which picture do I look like?" "You know it, no doubt. It's by Stuck, called
'Sin.'"

He had intended to shock her, but she closed her eyes for a moment of
torrid joy. When she opened them again, a smile full of promise beamed
through the bars of the seven candles, radiating to him the glow of her burning
face. "Sin," she repeated in a bewitching tone, "what is sin?"

Her laughter and teasing brought him over to a wide opening in the room,
and she drew a curtain to one side. "This is where I play my devilish tricks!"
she laughed with a gesture beckoning him in, and rushed out of the room to
call for some coffee. He sat down with a grim and bitter laugh, looking round
her den of tricks. Above the couch on one side there was a bookshelf running
the whole length of the wall. He started—for among the various nudes, whose
purpose was unmistakable in this room, he saw a reproduction of the "Sin" he
had just been talking of. Now he knew what to expect. This damn woman was
after him and was using all her charm and force to get what she wanted. He
would have to be frank now, and be quite cold and brutal, and tell her to her
face that she was a whore even if she was a countess ten times over. And if
that failed, he would have to sling right into her face the disgust he felt at her
infested body.

He lights up an opium-flavored cigarette, then puts it out again. Looking
*round, he notices the figure of an Indian phallic god.** "Do you like the little
god?" *she asks, coming in unexpectedly*, now wearing only a gown of flowing
veils over her naked body.

After a while she stopped and said to him in a calm and pensive voice,
"I'd like to hear your opinion as an artist." "What about?" "About whether I
have a perfect figure." "Are you vain?" "No. I want to know the truth!" "I
haven't been looking." "May I?" "If you wish, Countess. Everything is pure
as far as the artist is concerned." She got up, let her gown gown slip to the
floor, stood in the light, lifted her arms and showed him her attractive body.
"That's enough!" said Krafft. "Well?" she asked, dying to hear his answer.
"You're beautiful. You've got a perfect figure for one of your kind." "For the
kind of woman I am?" "No, for your kind of race, Countess."

She looked at him in utter surprise. "My race?" she asked, slowly
articulating the words. "Which race do you mean?" "The race of your
people—Jewish!" "But I'm German, the Jewish race doesn't exist!" she
blurted out quickly, in an almost hostile tone, and then nervously swept the
figures off the board. "Stupid game!" she cried angrily, adding with
vehemence, "and there's no German race either!" "You're right," said Krafft,
"but there is a German blood!"

His tongue loosens a little and he begins a tirade against the Jews. . . .
She shuddered a little and said in a dull tone, "I'm freezing again. Why
does it always get so cold? Oh Hans, I'm such an unhappy creature. I so want
to love someone with all my heart, and I don't know what love is. Would you

---

*Italicized parts are the author's comments.

believe me if I said I hated all Jewish men?'' "I would, otherwise you would
have had a family ages ago.'' "Oh, if only I could,'' she said sadly.

Mirjam put her hands to her face and sobbed quietly. Then her ears
pricked up and she gestured to Krafft not to speak. She whispered, "Can you
hear? Can you hear it? It's my heart, it's so afraid, fluttering around looking for
me. Wandering up and down, around the room—it can't find me—I've got no
idea how I can call it back to me. Catch it for me! Bring me it! Quick—before
it runs away!''

An icy coldness surrounded him. He was trembling so much at the
intangible feeling that overcame him that he was unable to speak. Horrified,
she rushed past him into the corner and started to scream, "You! What do you
want? Go away, let me go! Leave me alone! I can't help it! No, NO! Go away!
It's your fault! Let me go! You, you, bastard!''

She had stretched her arms out stiffly in front to protect herself. Her eyes,
like shining glass, stared vacantly ahead, then gradually lost their brightness.
She slowly sank backward as if she were dying. Krafft was paralyzed by a
sense of utter terror, as if there were ghosts in the room.

Then he lifted the body which had fallen to the floor, placed her on the
couch, and covered her. But then he noticed that her eyes were showing signs
of life again, that she was trying to smile at him. "Do you feel better?'' he
asked. "You're a good man, Hans,'' she whispered in reply. She took his hand
in hers and laid it on her hot brow, closing her eyes.

*The Beast and the Dead are contained within her—Krafft is, however,
immune to them, because his name means "power" (Kraft) and because he is
immune to the attraction of pleasure. After the jaws of hell have spit even him
out in disgust at the taste, he pays a visit to his friend the pharmacist, a
mysterious fellow who had already warned him about Mirjam, the witch.* "Now
I'm beginning to understand a thing or two. Mirjam actually loves me.'' "Of
course she does, in her own way.'' "No, it's not like that—I almost felt sorry
for her. Tell me, what should I do? Should I go away?'' "There's no point in
doing that. Wait for a while. Could be the witch will try and use different
tactics this time. But you should count yourself lucky you've got out of a nasty
situation. It's always the case that the one who's infected feels healthy, while
healthy blood perhaps unconsciously becomes contaminated, and the disease
hungers after more and more healthy blood. Magic powers are evoked, forcing
the victim to spread the disease until he ends up paralyzed, overcome by raving
insanity.'' "How does that happen?'' "Take a good sip of this first. Cheers!
It'll stop you going green with nausea. I'll give you an example. Take a king
rat—the product of in-breeding, a whole load of rats with many heads and one
body, a bundle of so many entwined rat bodies. A vile creature, the stench of
its rotting corpse attracting other rats which now and agin inject fresh blood
into the family, only to be eaten up once they have inseminated the king rat. If
these other rats didn't exist, the incestuous creature would become decrepit and
die, because the law of nature wouldn't allow it to survive. You see, nature
doesn't want any rat kings.''

"That's disgusting.'' Krafft shuddered.

"Now listen carefully. Among the peoples of the world there is also a
creature that is clearly the product of in-breeding: the Jews—the king rat
among peoples. They will breed with each other, and intermarry for money and
business for so long that one day one of the many branches of the family tree
will begin to make reproduction impossible. Then nature's will shall be
ignored, and the blood of a fresh branch will have to be grafted on so that

Anti-Semitic advertising poster for a folk novel, "Sin against the Blood."

Anti-Semitic German National election flyer for the national congress election of 1919.
"Your next *Führer*!" " Do you want another?" "Then vote German National!"

growth can continue unabated. We can never perceive exactly what is going on inside, but what we see on the outside tells us what must have happened inside. That's why Jews can also have the faces of negros, Chinese, Arabs, Latins, Slavs, and Germans, even though they all look Jewish, unmistakably Jewish! The real blood of the clan—the blood of parasites—always leaves its mark. The law behind the Jews' immortality hitherto is that they don't only live off our labor, but off our blood too. They call it breeding, but it's really licentiousness it's not a process of ennoblement, but one of degeneration. If all the races refused to offer their blood to Jewish women, or if other women didn't take Jewish men, the Jew rat king would die out within foreseeable generations."

Mirjam keeps herself alive with large daily doses of arsenic. . . .

"Trees which bear poisonous fruit should be chopped down and thrown on the fire. We should feel no sympathy for them. Sympathy in this instance amounts to weakness." He was pleased to see Krafft nodding seriously in agreement, and stood up. "Look out there at our own people—there are millions of them who need your sympathy and your help. Millions of healthy beings, Krafft, who'll die otherwise. Our blood! Not that of aliens, of parasites. Even if she's Venus in person! Our gods look different. The earth will tremble when they set foot on it once again." (483-518)

If one looks at relevant popular fiction of the 1930s, it seems quite improbable that the "Final Solution" was the brainchild of a Hitler who had gone mad, or of a blood-thirsty Himmler (as even Göring tried to make out during the Nuremberg trials). The only possible explanation for the fact that between 1934 and 1941 "only" 70,000 copies of Ekkehard's *Sturmgeschlecht* were printed could be that it is not quite as disgusting as Zöberlein's book.

Judging by Dinter's best-seller of 1917 *Die Sünde wider das Blut* (*Sins against the Blood*), there is little doubt that for many people who sought escape from their state of being alive, encoding the desiring-production of the unconscious and (in the narrower sense) the "sexual" with Jewishness was very appealing. By 1922, 693,000 copies of Dinter's book had appeared, thus putting it in fifth place in Richard's table of German best-sellers between 1915 and 1940.

13. Canetti, *Crowds and Power*, 55ff.
14. Zöberlein, *Befehl des Gewissens*, 495.
15. Reich, *The Mass Psychology of Fascism*, 116ff.
16. Hocquenghem, *Homosexual Desire*, 56. He writes this in the context of a reply to a French Minister of Health who claimed that syphilis was spread more rapidly by homosexuals. *Der Spiegel* of April 21, 1975 made a similar statement in an article on a recent rise in the incidence of the disease. For Hocquenghem, these are examples of "anti-homosexual paranoia." Any enemy is also syphilitic. In Weigand, *Die rote Flut*, 464, we come across "the syphilitic scoundrel Wilson" (the one with the 14 points). In Zöberlein's *Befehl des Gewissens*, the Republican Siebentritt uncovers shady arms deals and gets beaten up for it by Zöberlein's hero Krafft and his buddies. According to Krafft, "he would never have received hospital treatment if he had not been so ill with venereal disease." (591) And so on. The usual treatment for the disease is commensurate. Ulrich Jahn, in *Hexenwesen und Zauberei in Pommern* (Wiesbaden, 1970, reprint of 1886 edition), writes: "The cure for the contagion of pleasure is to be found in sleeping with a chaste young woman. The disease is transferred from the syphilitic man to the girl." (163) And Hans Bächtold, *Aus Leben und Sprache der*

Schweizer Soldaten, (Basle, 1916): "To prevent venereal infections one should wear on one's chest a small tuft of hair from a young, innocent girl." (19) Winckler's *Studie zur gesellschaftlichen Funktion* includes a list of quotations on syphilis from *Mein Kampf* (57).

17. Salomon, "Sturm auf Riga," in Jünger, *Der Kampf um das Reich*, 107.
18. Salomon, *Die Geächteten*, 21.
19. Jünger, *Kampf als inneres Erlebnis*, 69.
20. Ibid., 64-65.
21. Ibid., 101.
22. Fromm, *The Anatomy of Human Destructiveness*, esp. 325ff.
23. This is of little help. Every "case" that may be called a "case" is in principle "clinical." It is just that the adjective "clinical" places political cases on a level for which there is no clinic (unless a world war can be described as a clinic).
24. Fromm ignores those features of "necrophiliac" behavior which show that a corpse is not necessarily the most important thing. Sadger is told by a 28-year-old medical assistant: "I also often fantasize about having intercourse with a woman who is dying, or even already dead. For I can be quite certain she won't betray me. After all, she is still and dead and can't see how lecherous I am. I can do anything I want with her. I would have done the same with women in a condition where I would have come to their aid, as it were. Suppose they'd been gagged, and I just found them lying there unconscious. (. . .) The main reason for this was that the sexual element was not the most obvious." Sadger, J., "Über den sadomasochistischen Komplex," *Jahrbuch für psychoanalytische und psychopathologische Forschungen*, 5/1, (1913), 157-232, 214.
25. Canetti, *Crowds and Power*, 266ff. Moreover, Canetti's section on "The Survivor" (265-323), which discusses survival as a form of terror, is one of the best pieces ever written on power.
26. Jünger, *Kampf als inneres Erlebnis*, 67.
27. Ibid., 21.
28. Ibid., 34.
29. Ibid., 34.
30. Ibid., 65.
31. Heinz, *Sprengstoff*, 255.
32. On the pleasure of seeing dying and death: Höss, *Kommandant in Auschwitz*, 28ff.; Salomon, *Die Geächteten*, 125-26; Stenbock-Fermor, *Freiwilliger Stenbock*, 150; Dwinger, *Auf halbem Wege*, 30, 363; Dwinger, *Die letzten Reiter*, 117, 344, 377; Bischoff, *Die letzte Front*, 71; von Killinger, *Der Kampf um Oberschlesien*, 66; Schauwecker, *Im Todesrachen*, 136ff.; Engelhardt, *Der Ritt nach Riga*, 36; Brandis, *Baltikumer*, 125-26, 266; Bochow, *Sie wurden Männer*, 77ff.; Volck, *Rebellen um Ehre*, 64; Goote, *Wir fahren den Tod*—the whole book is a celebration of survival, e.g., 74, 200ff., 353, 386; Freska, *Der Wanderer ins Nichts*, 24ff.; Krumbach, *Epp*, 80. Looking at old parks and stately homes, Delmar had a sense of the "specter of eroticism alive in its grave" (*Französische Frauen*, 43).

Dead beings are looked at in the same way in Herman Löns, *Der letzte Hansbur* (1909): ". . . and as he stood there looking at the dead animal that was lying half on the bank and half in the water, he thought to himself how singularly beautiful it must be, especially at this time of the day, when the sky above the forest would turn red, to ride slowly across the battlefield looking at those lying stiff and cold next to their dead horses. That really was the way to lead your life, and it mattered not one bit if you copped it in the process." From Günter Hartung, "Über die deutsche faschistische Literatur," in three parts, *Weimarer Beiträge*, no. 3, (1968), special edition no. 2 (1968), no. 4, (1968), quote taken from Part 1, 519. Together with Walter Linden,

Hartung cites Lön's *Der Wehrwolf* (1910) as a "standard work of national (völkisch) literature" (ibid., 519). There is no need to limit this assessment exclusively to *Wehrwolf*.

The Alien within as "Primitive Man"

1. Jünger, *Kampf als inneres Erlebnis*, 7.
2. Ibid., 8. See also the whole section entitled "*Blut*" (Blood), 5-10.
3. Dwinger, *Auf halbem Wege*, 330.
4. Stefan George, *Werke*, vol. 9, *Das Neue Reich*, (Berlin, 1928), 114. Hotzel's treatment of George's poem is no less fascistic than the poem itself. He pays attention neither to George's deliberate avoidance of capital letters, nor to his punctuation. All the commas are Hotzel's. In the original there are two full stops after the word *blutschein* (testament of blood). The poem has a second verse:

> Should this people, in its cowardly weariness,
> ever be given to recall the election of princes and noble assemblies
> to it will be revealed a sign from the gods of the most
> unspeakable horror . . . the hands will be raised
> and voices will sing in praise of dignity
> and the true emblem of the royal standard will flutter in
> the early morning wind
> and will be down to greet
> the Noble Heroes!

> (Wenn je dieses volk sich aus feigem erschlaffen
> Sein selber erinnert der kür und der sende:
> Wird sich ihm eröffnen die göttliche deutung
> Unsagbaren grauens . . . dann heben sich hände
> Und münder ertönen zum preise der würde
> Dann flattert im frühwind mit wahrhaftem zeichen
> Die königsstandarte und grüsst sich verneigend
> Die Hehren: die Helden!)

Aspects of the Masses in Reality

1. Canetti, *Crowds and Power*, 13.
2. Ibid., 21.
3. Ibid., 67.
4. Ibid., 365-66.
5. Ibid., 354.
6. Ibid., 380-81.
7. Ibid., 381.
8. Ibid., 110ff.

Women to the Fore

1. von Killinger, *Die SA*, 41.
2. Wittmann, *Erinnerungen der Eisernen Schar*, 112.
3. Ibid., 112.
4. Ibid., 106.
5. Maercker, *Vom Kaiserheer*, 30-31.
6. von Oertzen, *Die deutchen Freikorps*, 259.
7. Schramm, *Die roten Tage*, 23.

8. Maercker, *Vom Kaiserheer zur Reichswehr*, 164.
9. Wittmann, *Erinnerungen der Eisernen Schar*, 130.
10. Compare with Donat's shot into the mouth of one such woman in Chapter 1, section entitled "Attacks on Women." Women are also to the fore in Salomon, *Buch*, especially Rossmann/Schmidthuysen, *Der blutige Montag*, 392; Lützkendorf, *Aus Halles "roter Zeit,"* 369; Gengler, *Berthold*, 157; Goote, *Kamerad Berthold*, 340; Crasemann, *Freikorps Maercker*, 40; Kohlhaas, *Der Häuptling und die Republik*, 212-13; von Kessel, *Handgranaten und rote Fahnen*, 153; Volck, *Rebellen um Ehre*, 19; Schricker, *Rotmord*, 20.
11. Lettow-Vorbeck, *Mein Leben*, 183.
12. See in Chapter 1 ("Attacks on Women") Maerckers's corresponding suggestion.
13. Pikarski, "Zeitfreiwilligen-Regiment Pommern," in SB, 358-59.
14. Heydebreck, *Wir Wehrwölfe*, 31-32.
15. Salomon, "Hexenkessel Deutschland," in Jünger, *Kampf um das Reich*, 19.
16. Dwinger, *Auf halbem Wege*, 257-58.
17. Jünger, *Über den Schmerz*, 183.

The Uncanny

1. von Selchow, *Hundert Tage*, 327.
2. Hesterberg, "Felddivision und Freikorps," in Salomon, *Buch*, 223.
3. Schaumlöffel, *Das Studentenkorps Marburg*, 17.
4. Ibid., 10; Höss makes a similar comment about the battles in the Baltic (*Kommandant in Auschwitz*, 35). In SB see Maltzan, "Die Spandauer stürmen Bauske," 160; Wilden, "Durchbruch," 61. Von Selchow makes the following comparison: "The French were our enemies, but they were chivalrous enemies. The new enemies I encountered in my own country saw to it that not one remnant of my honor remained untainted." (*Hundert Tage*, 352)
5. Duisburg, recorded statements of two eyewitnesses (Ringleib and de Pree), April 13, 1920, in Severing's unpublished work *A III*.
6. Mann, *Mit Ehrhardt*, 204. Almost exactly the same words can be found in dialogue form in Dwinger, *Auf halbem Wege*, 313. Dwinger often "used" in this way texts by authors who had published before him.
7. Salomon, "Hexenkesel Deutschland," 36.
8. Salomon, *Die Geächteten*, 11.
9. Ibid., 19. On male Communism see Volck, *Rebellen um Ehre*, 55, who writes of the joy of those pursuing a fleeing Bolshevik, for he is a beautiful sight as he manages to escape through the undergrowth, driven "by the force of despair."

Blackout and Loss of Fleshly Reality: Decomposition within the Mass

1. Salomon, *Die Kadetten*, 269-70.
2. Ibid., 98.
3. Ibid., 99.

The Mass and Culture: The "Upstanding Individual"

1. Dwinger, *Auf halbem Wege*, 23.
2. von der Goltz, *Meine Sendung*, 143-44.
3. Gengler, *Rudolf Berthold*, 103.
4. von der Goltz, *Meine Sendung*, 157. See also 284-85.
5. Jünger, *Kampf als inneres Erlebnis*, 54.
6. Goebbels, *Michael*, 33.
7. Delmar, *Französische Frauen*, 22.

8. Ibid., 79-80.
9. Höss, *Kommandant in Auschwitz*, 107.
10. For example, Heinz, *Die Nation greift an*, 37-38.
11. Iger, *Spartakustage*, 25.
12. Dwinger, *Auf halbem Wege*, 464.
13. Weigand, *Die rote Flut*, 452.
14. Ferenczi, "Versuch einer Genitaltheorie," 331.
15. The French analyst Luce Irigaray put it this way in an interview:

> The sex of the women does not only have a single, but a dual form. The duality of the clitoris and the vagina (which bears a relation to male parameters) is not what is important, but rather of the two lips of the vulva, which are in constant contact, and which are a constitutive element in a woman's eroticism, and because of which she is excluded from everything that our culture affords privilege (this itself being a reflection of the male sexual imagination): the single, the unit, the individual. For the penis is also "single," there is a "sole" family name (the name of the father), the "one" in the most fundamental sense—the unity and coherence of discourse; and individualism and private property.
>
> Correspondingly, the women are looked at rather than touched. The extent to which she is accepted as a beautiful object is matched by the extent to which her sex becomes the terrible image of "blindness," of the "hole." Thus she is excluded from every level of representation. (*Alternative*, no. 108-9 [June/August, 1976], 126.)

In the original French version, Irigaray described the lips of the vulva as "constantly touching each other," whereas the German translation used *stehen in Berührung*, literally "stand in contact."

16. Freud, *The Question of Lay Analysis*, SE, vol. XX, 196.
17. Ulrich Sonnemann's description of its normal condition may apply here. He writes that Freud's "ego is a typical functionary who sees himself transferred to a career in diplomacy. Its basic disposition is characterized by suspicion and sullenness, a bourgeois and melancholy character concerned to take no risks." (*Negative Anthropologie*, 77) The war-ego, as a famous soldierly theoretician is the extension of the diplomacy-ego by other means—nothing really very different.
18. "Berthold Tagebuch," in Gengler, *Berthold*, 92.
19. As a hero, as a holder-on who holds himself up until the very end, which for him is the most valuable thing.
20. Eggers, *Berg der Rebellen*, 215.
21. Benjamin, "Theorien des deutschen Faschismus," in *Argument*, no. 30, 135.
22. Jünger, *Kampf als inneres Erlebnis*, 31.
23. Ibid., 6.
24. Ibid., 5.
25. Ewers, *Reiter in deutscher Nacht*, 287.
26. Balla, *Landsknechte wurden wir*, 126.
27. Ibid., 126-27.
28. The contrasts between higher and lower, culture and barbarism, appear in a number of different forms. For Salomon, there are "people of courage" and "people of fear." Rathenau's main crime is described as his penchant for people of fear (*Die Geächteten*, 270). Von Selchow contrasts the Hottentots (incapable of culture) with the Hereros (partially capable of a culture), because the former are nomads whereas the latter

exhibited a clear spirit of acquisitiveness. Culture derives from the planning of business (*Hundert Tage*, 203). Elsewhere the subdivision of language into a high register and colloquial speech is deemed to be a sign of culture (*Hundert Tage*, 129). Of course, the contrast between culture and machines also comes up (Delmar, *Französische Frauen*, 86). As the example of Freud showed, psychoanalysis, whose task it should have been to analyze the imperialism of such conceptions of culture as an integral part of European male madness, has proved to be far from devoid of imperialist leanings itself. Here is another example, this time from Ferenczi. He writes in connection with the "meaning of obscene words":

> From what I know of the life of inferior peoples, particularly gypsies, it would seem that the obscene words used by those who lack any cultivation place more emphasis on pleasure, but are less distinct from the rest of the language, than would appear to be the case among a cultured people.

He concludes further that obscene words are closely related to the motor activity of the body, and goes on to state that such activity is regressive. We find this train of thought again and again: renouncing the body is lauded as progress toward "culture." Whatever is related to the body is "primitive" or "regressive" ("Über obszöne Worte," in *Schriften*, vol. 1, 70ff.).

29. This can be seen in Jean Renoir's film "Die Spielregel" (The Rules of the Game) (1939). When the hunting party shoots, it seems as if they are shooting directly at feelings, shooting at the living, though the animals are not symbolic.
30. Lettow-Vorbeck, *Mein Leben*, 272.
31. Ibid., 273.
32. Freska, *Kapitän Ehrhardt*, 40ff.; on poaching see also Koll, "Die Männer von Tirschtegel," in SB, 229-30; Schramm, *Rote Tage*, 95; Eggers, *Berg der Rebellen*, 195; Maercker, *Vom Kaiserheer*, 178. On hunting, see Herzog, *Wieland der Schmied*, 49; Carl Franz, "Flieger im Baltikum," in SB, 172; Jünger, *Abenteuerliches Herz*, 123; Frank, *Epp*, 143; Lettow-Vorbeck, *Mein Leben*, 38-39, 47, 71, 77, 106, 110-11, 121-22, 196-97, 217, 223, 229, 236-37, 240, 269-76.

"In the majority of myths, swine are said to belong to the female sex and to goddesses. It can thus be assumed that hunting boar also represents this process of repression" (Kurnitzky, *Triebstruktur des Geldes*, 63).
33. The reason it is so much fun to shoot at birds in courtship becomes even clearer when we consider the peculiarities of our feathered friends: "The olfactory lobes in the brains grew smaller and their vision became relatively more important to them." Color vision, the splendor of colours. "This is also why, although birds are zoologically so far removed from us, we feel we understand their behavior and patterns of courtship, because they are based like ours on auditory and visual signals, which we can perceive, while that of mammals is conducted through odor signals, in a language to which we are largely deaf and blind" (Morgan, *The Descent of Woman*, 137-38).
34. Balla, *Landsknechte wurden wir*, 127ff.

Culture and the Army
1. Jünger, *Kampf als inneres Erlebnis*, 37.
2. Mann, *Mit Ehrhardt*, 215.
3. von der Goltz, *Meine Sendung*, 2.
4. Dwinger, *Auf halbem Wege*, 28.
5. Jünger, *Kampf als inneres Erlebnis*, 63.
6. Ibid., 56.

7. Dwinger, *Die letzten Reiter*, 436; see also Jünger, *Kampf als inneres Erlebnis*, 24-25, 41, 64, 108; Jünger, *Feuer und Blut*, 66ff.; Salomon, *Nahe Geschichte*, 19; the fifth verse of the poem *Abschied* (Farewell) by Lieutenant-Commander Kautter, on the disbanding of the Second Marine Brigade, in SB, 350; Guenther, *Deutsches Kriegertum*, 200. Wilhelm Schramm, in *Schöpferische Kritik des Krieges*, 40, writes that the ideal war would be a confrontation of the best men from each nation, untainted by technology and material interests. War should be "the highest and most noble form of the struggle between men."

8. Heinz, *Sprengstoff*, 48.

9. For a similar account, see Jünger, *Kampf als inneres Erlebnis*, 25, 41.

10. Dwinger, *Die letzten Reiter*, 359.

11. Ibid., 358.

12. The romanticism of the secret sect was an integral part of Nazi rituals from the very beginning, the most important element in the party's early days being inauguration by the flag. No SA member truly belonged until he had touched the "Flag of Blood." It was carried at the head of the march to the Feldherrnhalle on November 9, 1923, "steeped" in the blood of those who were the first to die for the "movement." The ceremony took place in secret at night. "It is a starlit night. The moon casts a silvery light on the mysterious waters of the lake whose real depth it cannot know. Yet deeper than even the deepest ocean is the love of the men who, standing amid these rocks, wish to take the *Rütlischwur* (the oath taken on the Rütli Mountain by the founders of Switzerland—Tr.). For Germany, for their Führer" (Berendt, *Soldaten der Freiheit*, 297, on the first inauguration by the flag in North Germany in 1923; the site was the tunnel of a chalk mine). From the outside it is a mass ritual, but from the inside it is a ritual of a secret sect, far removed from the city, in the heart of the earth, at the lakeside, in the mountains, in the forest.

Undefeated in the Field?

1. Plaas, "Das Kapp-Unternehmen," in JKR, 179.

2. On dishonorable stains, see also Plaas, ibid., 164, 178; von Loewenfeld, "Das Freikorps von Loewenfeld," in RDS, 149; Salomon, "Die Brigade Ehrhardt," in RDS, 120; Frey, "Die Versenkung der deutschen Kriegsflotte bei Scapa Flow," in JKR, 62; Mann, *Mit Ehrhardt*, 218; Freska, *Kapitän Ehrhardt*, 121; Niemöller, *Vom U-Boot*, 139; Förste, "Vom Freikorps zur Kriegsmarine," in RDS, 102.

3. Mahnken, "Gegenstoss im Westen, 1919," in RDS, 59.

The Mass and the Race

1. Delmar, *Französische Frauen*, 78.

2. Ibid., 143.

3. See Reich, *The Mass Psychology of Fascism*, 109ff.

4. Weigand, *Die rote Flut*, 465: "One part of our people may boast of being descendants of the master race of the Germans. The blood of the other part, to a large extent made up by the urban proletariat that is so devoid of history, is pre-Aryan."

5. Deleuze/Guattari, *Anti-Oedipus*, 340.

6. Ibid.

7. Ibid., 340ff. "Molar" is derived from the unit of measurement in physics, 1 mole, equal to 1 gram molecule. The number of molecules per gram molecule is 6×10^{23}. Hence the use of "molar" to describe the types of mass formations that can be subsumed under the notion of a large number in structured patterns. Fascism clearly employed two distinct notions of the mass: "An opponent who incites the masses and leads them onto the street (. . .) can only be countered by likewise bringing the masses

onto the street, but in a disciplined and unified form and under firm leadership" (Killinger, *Die SA*, 5).

8. "War, the father of all things, had proved to be a force capable of creating a race" (Heinz, *Die Nation greift an*, 17). In a similar vein, Jünger saw the "new race" emerge in war (Jünger, *Kampf als inneres Erlebnis*, 2, 32, 50ff.).

9. Shulamith Firestone hints at this with regard to the relationship between blacks and whites in the United States, but then, unfortunately, proceeds to frame it within the family set-up. The white man is the boss who oppresses the white woman. She consequently secretly loves the son (black man), who is despised by the black woman because of his state of slavery. She thus desires the white man, to whom she is sold by the black man (pimp complex), etc. (*The Dialectic of Sex*). The weakness of this construct is that it is equally "applicable" to the bourgeoisie/proletariat relationship, for the very reason that it reproduces the same encoding of such varied relationships with the Oedipal that is predominant in patriarchal society. The model makes it impossible to recognize that the racist is so dangerous because he is fighting against himself. Nobody wants to destroy the world because his wife is being unfaithful with the "lower race." Thus even feminists are not immune from sometimes falling into the trap of Oedipalization.

The Nation

1. Heinz, *Sprengstoff*, 162.
2. Eggers, *Berg der Rebellen*, 39.
3. Schauwecker, *Aufbruch der Nation*, 324.
4. Salomon, *Die Geächteten*, 34.
5. Schauwecker, *Aufbruch der Nation*, 209.
6. Heinz, *Die Nation greift an*, 12-13.
7. Mahnken, "Freikorps im Westen 1918/20," in HoDA, 90.
8. Schauwecker, *Aufbruch der Nation*, 369.
9. Heinz, *Sprengstoff*, 136.
10. Ibid., 177.
11. Heinz, *Die Nation greift an*, 10.
12. H. Schauwecker, "Der Aufbruch der Nation aus dem Krieg," in HoDA, 247.
13. Ibid., 246.
14. Heinz, *Die Nation greift an*, 9.
15. Bronnen, *Rossbach*, 165.
16. Goebbels, *Michael*, 113.
17. Compare Margaret Mahler, *Infantile Psychosis*, 41, who uses the term "locomotion." In her view, locomotion allows children incapable of functioning away from the symbiotic partner to use the partner (usually the mother).
18. Heinz, *Die Nation greift an*, 10.
19. Bronnen, *Rossbach*, 147.
20. Salomon, *Die Geächteten*, 203; see also ibid., 111-12.
21. Heinz, *Sprenstoff*, 143.
22. Maercker, *Vom Kaiserheer*, 355.
23. G. Günther, "Hamburg," in JKR, 51.
24. Salomon, *Die Geächteten*, 155-56.
25. See H. Schauwecker, "Aufbruch der Nation," 245ff.
26. Jünger, *Der Kampf um das Reich*, 9.
27. See, e.g., Jünger, *Der Arbeiter*, 35; Salomon, *Die Kadetten*, 66.
28. Jünger, *Der Kampf um das Reich*, Preface, 8. For war as creation see also von Schramm, *Schöpferische Kritik des Krieges*, 49, and F. G. Jünger, *Krieg und Krieger*, 56, 58, 61.

29. Jünger, *Der Kampf um das Reich*, Preface, 7; the formulation used by Salomon is almost identical in "Der verlorene Haufe," 113.

30. Of the numerous features of the "nation" (that it is male, soldierly, warlike, a creature of domination whose "upper level" and "lower level" are derived from the insecurities the soldier male has about his own body, that it will bear the future/the Reich), only one occurs to Kurt Sontheimer in his chapter on the nation (*Antidemokratisches Denken in der Weimarer Republik*, 317ff.): that it is an "upper level," connected with domination of "people." To some extent, the literature he cites (especially Ullmanns, Metzner, Moeller van der Bruck, 318ff.) allows the reader to draw the more penetrating conclusions as well. Sontheimer tends to limit himself to references to "anti-democratic thought," as he terms it, furnishing it with critical comments in the mold of scholars of the history of ideas. Concepts such as "irrationalism" are prominent. He is interested above all in the "intellectual (*geistig*) undercurrent" (46) of "new thought." Consequently most of his references are to works of cultural philosophy and political, scientific, and intellectual theory. He pays no attention to novels, biographies, and the like. It is thus even more remarkable that we agree on a number of things. Many of the intellectual configurations he illustrates can just as easily be "proved" by examining fiction, and many of the conclusions I have come to are corroborated by the sources he uses. In other words, the spread of fascist sentiments in Germany in the 1920s is confirmed everywhere. Armin Mohler's comment that just the bibliography of right-wing literature of the Weimar "Republik" would be enough to fill a dictionary may well be an understatement. I suspect it would fill a whole series of volumes (Mohler, *Die konservative Revolution in Deutschland 1818-1932. Grundriss ihrer Weltanschauungen* (Stuttgart, 1950, 212).

31. Heinz, *Sprengstoff*, 51. On the nation see also Eggers, *Von der Freiheit des Krieges*, 30 (pacifism = castration); Freiwald, *Verratene Flotte*, 248 (national self-emasculation); Volck, *Rebellen um Ehre*, 9.

32. Bronnen, *Rossbach*, 71.

The People (Das Volk)

1. Bronnen, *Rossbach*, 53.
2. Goebbels, *Michael*, 113.
3. Blüher, *Volk und Führer in der Jugendbewegung*, 3.
4. See the section on "Sisters" in Volume 1.
5. Blüher, *Volk und Führer in der Jugendbewegung*, 4. Or: "We are the ones who must act as the thorn of discontent (. . .) which in times of satiety and cowardliness (. . .) can torture the body of our people" (Eggers, *Von der Freiheit des Kriegers*, 62).
6. Jünger, *Kampf als inneres Erlebnis*, 116.

The Whole

1. Cited in von Selchow, *Hundert Tage*, 324.
2. Hotzel, "Student 1918," in HoDA, 7.
3. Heinz, *Die Nation greift an*, 17.
4. Goote, *Die Fahne hoch*, 391.
5. Hotzel, "Student 1918," 7.
6. Schaumlöffel, *Das Studentenkorps Marburg*, 55.
7. Mahler, *Infantile Psychosis*, 42. "An ego which is unable to function separately from the symbolic partner tries to re-entrench itself in the delusional fantasy of oneness with the omnipotent mother" (42). The hierarchical totality-formation, by contrast, does not replicate "oneness" with the mother. The troop is nothing like the mother's body for the

soldiers, but rather an organization helping them to *escape* the mother's body. The section entitled "The Ego and Maintenance Mechanisms" in Chapter 2 of the current work deals with this in more detail. Otto Strasser provides copious examples of totality as a program in *Der Aufbau des Sozialismus* (Leipzig, 1932). See also the series of totalities in Freska, *Der Wanderer ins Nichts*, 362: Man—Company—Regiment—Army—Fatherland; Müller, *Soldat und Vaterland*, 26; Freikorps soldiers held the Fatherland together with "an iron grip."

A Forerunner on the Road to the Reich
1. Jünger, *Kampf als inneres Erlebnis*, 30.
2. Rosenberg's preface to *Dietrich Eckart*, 11.
3. Rossbach, *Mein Weg durch die Zeit*, 215.
4. As the fabrication of the myth of Horst Wessel by Goebbels and Hans Heinz Ewers shows, these would not necessarily have been reasons preventing Kapp from becoming a hero. See Brecht, "Die Horst-Wessel-Legende," 211ff., on Ewers's novel *Horst Wessel* (Berlin, 1933). But Kapp's behavior had become too well known. The unknown Wessel, on the other hand, could be transformed into anything.
5. Wittmann, *Erinnerungen der Eisernen Schar Berthold*, 115-16.
6. Ibid., 116.
7. "To convince is to conquer without conception," says Walter Benjamin. The heading is "For Men," "One-Way Street," in *One-Way Street and Other Writings*, introduced by Susan Sontag, translated by Edmund Jephcott and Kingsley Shorter (London: New Left Books, 1979), 47.
8. Goote, *Kamerad Berthold*, 351.
9. A similar harbinger is often found in fascist literature in the shape of another tamer of the masses: the leader of the German Social-Democratic Party in 1918. The scene is the Reich Conference of the Workers' and Soldiers' Councils, Berlin, 19 December 1918. Chaos reigns. Then "Ebert rose to his feet quite calmly, walked over to the President's seat, shoved Leinert to the side and spoke in a manner so penetrating, so courageous and so clever that the red masses appeared satisfied, and within a few minutes had cleared the room." An admiring onlooker (sent by the Naval Ministry), von Selchow, *Hundert Tage*, 299.
10. Wessel was shot dead by the pimp Ali Höhler, whose "successor" he had become for the prostitute Erna J. See Scheer, *Blut und Ehre*, 150ff.; *Naziführer sehen dich an*, 177ff.
11. Cited in Rosenberg, *Dietrich Eckart*, 65.
12. Zöberlein, *Befehl des Gewissens*, 538.
13. Canetti, *Crowds and Power*, 245.

The Speech
1. Baldur von Schirach, *Pioniere des Dritten Reiches*, 75.
2. Theodore Abel, *Why Hitler Came to Power. An Answer Based on the Original Life Stories of Six Hundred of His Followers*. With the consent of the NSDAP, Abel, an American sociologist, organized a competition whose winners were to be those who had become Nazis in the nicest ways. He told the NSDAP that the point of it was to make the "movement" more popular in the United States.
3. Ibid., 116ff., 152ff.
4. Goebels, *Michael*, 101ff.
5. Killinger fails to report a single word Hitler said when he first met him in 1923: "One word led to another, and as Hitler warmed up, his eyes began to flash, and his ideas were given expression with such dialectic and persuasive power, casting a spell on

everyone. Klabautermann hung on every word that emerged from the lips of this extraordinary man" (*Der Klabautermann*, 295). See also Goote, *Die Fahne hoch*, 416.

6. Ekkehard, *Sturmgeschlecht*, 155.
7. Goote, *Kamerad Berthold*, 248; also Killinger, *Die SA*, 17.
8. Zöberlein, *Befehl des Gewissens*, 284.
9. Ibid., 285-86.
10. Ibid., 286. See also Goote, *Kamerad Berthold*, 248, where Berthold makes a speech: "Nobody was fiddling with their beer mats anymore. Nobody was looking round. Nobody called the waitress." Etc.
11. Goebbels, *Michael*, 102.
12. Jean Pierre Faye, *Theorie du recit, Introduction aux "langues totalitaires"* (Paris, 1972), 81-82.
13. Jünger, *Der Arbeiter*, 58.
14. Winckler, *Zur gesellschaftlichen Funktion faschistischer Sprache*, 36ff. For a widely read, superficial account of the process of speech, see B. Burke, *Die Rhetorik in Hitler's "Mein Kampf" und andere Essays zur Strategie der Überredung* (Frankfurt, 1967). "The sexual symbolism running through Hitler's book, which is meant to appeal to the sexual morality (sic!) of his contemporaries, can easily be summed up. The fragmentation of Germany has turned it into a Siegfried 'without a horn.' The mass of the people are 'female,' and thus want to be led by a strong man. This man assumes the form of an orator of the people, woos and, once he has won them over, dominates them." Etc. (10ff.).
15. Mary Douglas, *Natural Symbols*, 3ff.
16. Echoes of the Holy Spirit descending at Easter are surely deliberate. ("Revelation! Revelation!")
17. For similar oratory processes see: Stadtler, *Als Antibolchewist 1918/19*, 33 (making an imprint), 40 (copulation), 80 (commanding attention as a phallus); Buschbecker, *Wie unser Gesetz es befahl*, 288 (Hitler grows); Ibid., 65, the presence of a woman ("the Pole") at the back of the company being addressed prevents the speech from producing its full effect.
18. Freud makes the point that some obsessions are present in dreams as *spoken words*, containing the "undistorted text" of obsessional thought. This is a further indication that speech is a vehicle for publicly abolishing what are otherwise regarded as taboos (Freud, *The Interpretation of Dreams*, SE, vol. X, 189; Ibid., "Notes on a Case of Obsessional Neurosis," SE, vol. X, 189).
19. Serge Leclaire, *Der psychoanalytische Prozess*, 142.
20. Benjamin, "Theorien des deutschen Faschismus," in *Argument*, 30, 134.

The Eyes

1. Röhm, *Die Geschichte eines Hochverräters*, 27.
2. Walter Kempowski, *Haben Sie Hitler gesehen? Deutsche Antworten*, (Munich, 1973).
3. No author, "Die letzte Parade der III. Marine-Brigade von Loewenfeld am Skagerraktage 1920," in SB, 406-7.
4. O. Strasser, "Der Sinn des 9. Nov. 1923," in JKR, 306.
5. Schaumlöffel, *Das Studentenkorps Marburg*, 9.
6. Frank, *Epp*, 26.
7. Bronnen, *Rossbach*, 9-10.
8. Ibid., 10.
9. Wittmann, *Erinnerungen der Eisernen Schar*, 123.
10. F. Schauwecker, *Aufbruch der Nation*, 61.
11. Jünger, *Kampf als inneres Erlebnis*, 32.

12. Ibid., 26.
13. Ibid., 50ff.
14. Ibid., 23.
15. Dwinger, *Deutsches Schicksal,* vol. 1 (Jena, 1919), 536.
16. Herzog, *Mann im Sattel,* 403.
17. Dwinger, *Auf halbem Wege,* 377.
18. Salomon, *Die Geächteten,* 369.
19. Goebbels, *Michael,* 149.
20. Ekkehard, *Sturmgeschlecht,* 201.
21. Stefan George, *Gesamtwerke,* vol. 8, *Stern des Bundes* (Berlin, 1928), 85. Blüher cites the two lines in *Die Rolle der Erotik,* 324.
22. von Selchow, *Hundert Tage,* 278.
23. K. O. Bark, "Rossbachs Marsch ins Baltikum," in SB, 204.
24. K. Abraham, "Restrictions and Transformation," 169ff.
25. Lissauer, *Luther und Thomas Münzer, Drama in fünf Augenzeugen* (Berlin, 1929), 50.
26. "You weren't the only one who couldn't look me straight in the eye, you scoundrel!" says Killinger to a stoker who joins the soldier councils straightaway, in *Der Klabautermann,* 256. The most basic trait by which Germans can spot their enemies is the untrustworthy look in their eyes. Poles, Spartacists, etc. are often "pop-eyed" or they are cross-eyed. See, for example, Killinger, *Der Kampf um Oberschlesien,* 54; Hollenbach, *Opfergang,* 124-25. Or they poke German soldiers' eyes out, as in Killinger, *Die SA,* 88.
27. According to Canetti, the feeling of being watched by the thousand eyes of the mass leads "directly into the prototypal situation of paranoia. The paranoiac feels surrounded by a pack of enemies who are all after him. This is his basic experience. It is most clearly expressed in visions of *eyes;* he sees eyes everywhere and all round him; they are interested only in him and their interest is menacing in the extreme. The creatures to whom the eyes belong intend to take revenge on him. For a long time he has made them suffer and has gone unpunished; if they are animals they are relentlessly hunted and, threatened with extermination, have now suddenly risen against him" (*Crowds and Power,* 530). How wonderful, then, for the holder of power if a thousand eyes look at him as one eye would, and if instead of the stake which blinded Polyphemus, a hand stretches out toward him which he can take hold of and shake.
28. Schirach's *Die Pioniere des 3. Reichs,* was published in 1934, in other words before the power of the SA was curtailed, before Röhm was murdered, and so on. An end was put to the organization in which overt homosexual relationships were possible. The NSDAP's new core troop, the SS, was a male organization which persecuted homosexuality. The "comradeship" espoused in the SA was replaced by a most rigid hierarchical structure of internal organization (it is impossible to imagine Himmler having physical sexual relations with a *Gruppenführer*). The SS man was supposed to marry and to supervise homosexuals in concentration camps. This is not the appropriate point, however, at which to look into the question of "homosexuality" in more detail. We shall leave that until the next chapter, which describes the bodily changes that occur in military drill and combat. In *Die Rolle der Erotik in der männlichen Gesellschaft,* Blüher explains that in a "male society of the first degree," a group's consciousness of the group's own organization is of the form of a male/masculine eros, along with physical relationships. This consciousness is vitiated in male societies of the second and third degrees to the point at which such situations are repressed, and those involved persecuted. Blüher attributes the disbanding of the *Wandervogel* to the rift between the supporters and opponents of physical love between men—the opponents won (246ff.).
   In *Die Bändigung des Krieges durch den Staat,* 186ff., Gerhard Günther adopts a similar position to Blüher on maleness/warfare/formation of states. However, he omits

male love—the factor which was decisive for Blüher—and thus according to Blüher's
categories becomes a member of the "male society of the second degree."

29. Franke, *Staat im Staate*, 220; on eyes, also see Wittmann, *Erinnerungen der Eisernen
Schar*, 129; Schaumlöffel, *Das Studentenkorps Marburg*, 25; Herzog, *Wieland der
Schmied*, 25; Blüher, *Rolle der Erotik*, 185, 188-89; Blüher, *Der Wandervogel*, 32;
Höfer, *Oberschlesien in der Aufstandszeit*, 19, 26; Brandis, *Baltikumer*, 23; Bochow, *Sie
wurden Männer*, 64, 67; Kohlhaas, *Der Häuptling und die Republik*, 137; Volck,
Rebellen um Ehre, 27, 35, 53; Freiwald, *Der Weg der braunen Kämpfer*, 9; Freiwald,
Verratene Flotte, 92-93; Brandt, *Schlageter*, 101; Solf, *Deutschlands Auferstehung 1934*,
47; Mann, *Mit Ehrhardt*, 138; Balla, *Landsknechte*, 116; Salomon, *Putsch und
Verschwörung*, 15; by contrast see ibid., 15, a "mass devoid of a gaze."
Berthold's eyes in Friedrich Bodenreuth, *Das Ende der Eisernen Schar*, 34: "As if
they were forged by the anvil and hammer, they take a grip on a bloke's eyes. He can
but let them painfully sink in."
30. Blüher, *Die Rolle der Erotik in der männlichen Gesellschaft*, 188.
31. Jünger, *Der Kampf als inneres Erlebnis*, 20.

Chapter 2: Male Bodies and the "White Terror"

Sexuality and the Drill

The Body Reconstructed in the Military Academy
1. Canetti, *Crowds and Power*, 365.
2. E. von Salomon, *Die Kadetten*. The following references are taken from the first part of
the book, which describes how Salomon settles into the academy (up to 70). Further
details are given for direct quotes only.
3. For an account of how from the 18th century onward the construction of prisons came to
serve as the model for types of social supervision, see Foucault, *Discipline and Punish*,
195ff., particularly plates 3 and 4: panopticon and discipline.
4. Salomon, *Die Kadetten*, 44.
5. Ibid., 48.
6. Freud, *Analysis Terminable and Interminable*, SE, vol. XXIII 226. See also *Introductory
Lectures on Psychoanalysis*, SE, vol. XVI, 312.
7. Freud, *An Outline of Psycho-Analysis*, SE, vol. XXIII, 155; see also *Psycho-Analytic
Notes on an Autobiographical Account of a Case of Paranoia*, SE, vol. XII, 60-61.
8. As elsewhere, Freud calls such an urge: *Psycho-Analytic Notes*, SE, vol. XII, 63. On
the puberty of German boys of the time, see Erikson, "The Legend of Hitler's
Childhood," 307ff.
9. Salomon, *Die Kadetten*, 42.
10. Ibid., 68.
11. Ibid., 49.
12. Ibid., 55-56.
13. Ibid., 56.
14. Ibid., 57.
15. Ibid., 58.
16. Ibid., 61.
17. Ibid., 62-63.
18. Ibid., 63-64.
19. Ibid., 64.
20. Ibid., 69.
21. Ibid., 65.

The Troop as Totality-Machine

1. "Walls . . . in the end become part of him," Canetti emphasizes (*Crowds and Power*, 362). By contrast, his account of the command is very precise (349-50).
2. Salomon, *Die Kadetten*, 114.
3. Plaas, "Das Kapp-Unternehmen," in JKR, 178.
4. Ibid., 178. In Volck, *Rebellen um Ehre* we find the "troop with a soul of steel" (66).
5. Salomon, *Die Kadetten*, 115.
6. Jünger, *Feuer und Blut*, 84-85.
7. Foucault, *Discipline and Punish*, 169, describes how from the 18th century onward the human body was disciplined in relation to the construction of social institutions, which were meant to serve as models for the body. His description pays less attention to the body's actual physical changes. See 135-70.

The Totality-Component: Figure of Steel

1. Jünger, *Kampf als inneres Erlebnis*, 32-33; see also 55.
2. Ibid., 74. Also Buschbecker, *Wie unser Gesetz es befahl*, 132, 181; Volck, *Rebellen um Ehre*, 104, 144.
3. Manfred Nagl's *Science Fiction in Deutschland*, a survey based on extremely interesting material, shows that the attempt to create a superman in the image of the machine, by excluding women in favor of machines, is not an invention of the futurists. It is a core element of "pre-fascist" 19th century literature, which, to a large extent, has been dismissed as "trivial" by literary history (see e.g., 125ff.).

Preliminary Comments on the Agency of the Ego

1. See Volume 1, Chapter 1, Section 24, "Preliminary Findings," note 13.
2. Freud, *The Ego and the Id*, SE, vol. XIX, 25-26.

Blackouts

1. Röhm, *Die Geschichte eines Hochverräters*, 16.
2. Hirschfeld, *Sittengeschichte des Weltkrieges*, vol. 2, 180.
3. Salomon, *Die Kadetten*, 30.
4. Killinger, *Der Klabautermann*, 106.
5. Ibid., 105.
6. Ferenczi, "Versuch einer Genitaltheorie," in *Schriften*, vol. 2, 333.
7. Freska, *Kapitän Ehrhardt*, 33-34.
8. von Selchow, *Hundert Tage*, 38.
9. Ibid., 41-42.
10. Ibid., 66-67.

The Absorption of Sexual Desire

1. Salomon, *Die Kadetten*, 89 and 77-78.
2. Schauwecker, *Aufbruch der Nation*, 91-92.
3. Von Killinger, *Der Klabautermann*, 48.
4. Bruno Vogel, *Es lebe der Krieg*, cited in Hirschfeld, *Sittengeschichte des Weltkriegs*, vol. 2, 163.
5. Schauwecker, *Aufbruch der Nation*, 63. See also Goote, *Wir fahren den Tod*, 182; Eggers, *Von der Freiheit des Krieges*, 34-35. On the absorption of sexuality via drill/war, see also Freska, *Kapitän Ehrhardt*, 29-30; Jünger, *Kampf als inneres Erlebnis*, 33; Bronnen, *Rossbach*, 145; Schauwecker, *Aufbruch der Nation*, 315; Zöberlein, *Befehl des Gewissens*, 670.
6. Salomon, *Die Kadetten*, 66.

7. Jünger, *Kampf als inneres Erlebnis*, 55.
8. Röhm, *Die Geschichte eines Hochverräters*, 22.
9. Maercker, *Vom Kaiserheer*, 307. See also the section on "Ausbildung, Erziehung und inneres Leben der Truppe," 306-22.
10. See also the position on war taken by the trade union leaders Husemann and Sachse in Heinrich Tauber, *Die Sozialisierung des Ruhrbergbaus* (Frankfurt, 1973), 14ff.
11. Schramm speaks of "higher rebirth in formation" in *Schöpferische Kritik des Krieges*, 41.

"Prussian Socialism"

1. Freska, *Kapitän Ehrhardt*, 34.
2. Salomon, *Die Kadetten*, 89.
3. Röhm, *Die Geschichte eines Hochverräters*, 17-18.
4. "At that time, those of us who had been in the most complete socialist organization, the Prussian army, returned home qualified to join a movement which, founded as it was on self-discipline and obedience, endeavored to anchor the purpose of labor not in acquisition but in service, and which strove to create the kind of socialism which Spengler was shortly afterward to describe as the completion of Prussianism." Günther, "Hamburg," in JKR, 40, referring to O. Spengler, *Preussentum und Sozialismus* (Munich, 1924). See also Heinz, *Die Nation greift an*, 14; Heinz, *Sprengstoff*, 27-28; Jünger, *Feuer und Blut*, 217; Dwinger, *Auf halbem Wege*, 272-73; Gengler, *Berthold*, 103-4. It is often said that the basis of "Prussian socialism" in the *Freikorps* was the affinities that service created between officers and men. Many officers served in the ranks. See in particular Schricker, *Rotmord über München*, 190; W. von Schramm, *Schöpferische Kritik des Krieges*, complained that war was being waged "devoid of the style of natural democracy befitting its essence." (42) "Natural democracy" = the best man wins. Otto Strasser uses the term "German socialism." His intention here is to undermine the socialism of the labor movement. He wants to "make economically independent existence equally as widespread as the number of our national comrades who desire such independence." He concludes: "Anyone who recognizes the racial dangers posed by our urban conglommerations will also regard as an obligatory national duty the goal of systematically *reversing urbanization*. Reversing urbanization is a consequence of the need for autarchy and the introduction of the hereditary fief in agricultural property law. For the natural and desired outcome of both these goals is the *re-agrarianization of Germany* (Otto Strasser, *Aufbau des Sozialismus* [Leipzig, 1932] 39).

Battle and the Body

Speed and Explosions. Contact with the "Object."

1. Salomon, *Die Kadetten*, 66-67.
2. Schauwecker, *Aufbruch der Nation*, 299.
3. Ibid., 192.
4. Heinz, *Sprengstoff*, 188.
5. Schauwecker, *Aufbruch der Nation*, 243.
6. Heinz, *Sprengstoff*, 189.
7. Schauwecker, *Aubruch der Nation*, 178.
8. Ibid., 240.
9. Jünger, *Feuer und Blut*, 84.
10. Salomon, *Die Geächteten*, 100.
11. Dwinger, *Die letzten Reiter*, 109. For a similar account see Dwinger, *Auf halbem Wege*, 232; Jünger, *Kampf als inneres Erlebnis*, 9, 53, 108.

12. Nord, "Der Krieg im Baltikum," in JKR, 72.
13. There is nothing different about the notion of speed at the heart of Marinetti's Futurist Manifestos. He speaks of various human bodies when contrasting speed and slowness as a "new good" and a "new evil." For example: "Speed = synthesis of every courage in action. Aggressive and warlike." "Slowness = analysis of every stagnant prudence. Passive and pacifistic." Here, too, speed leads to an object which is to be striven for: "The intoxication of great speeds in cars is nothing but the joy of feeling oneself fused with the only *divinity*." To escape from one's own boundaries and attain the object of pleasure by way of violent, intoxicating acts is a need the armored body has, one expressed using the technological concept of speed. The "holiness of wheels and rails," to which, demands Marinetti, we should pray, bears a relation only to the untechnological side of technology. It is misused as a vehicle for describing human bodily processes. Under fascism, machines, too, achieve expression, but not their true purpose. See Marinetti's "The New Religion-Morality of Speed" in *Selected Writings*, translated by R. Flint and A. Coppotelli (London: Secker and Warburg, 1972). Fromm is quite wrong in citing this, Marinetti's "second" futurist manifesto, as evidence of Marinetti's "worship of technique" (*Anatomy of Human Destructiveness*, 345). As we have seen, futurism's conception of the machine is quite untechnical. Fromm misunderstands the machine—and deliberately so—as the polar opposite of the human, as the anti-human, in fact. The "worship of speed and the machine" are included in the "essential elements of necrophilia" (345). In so doing, he fails to take the genuinely reactionary part of Marinetti's argument to task, and shows himself to be a conservative cultural critic. More on this in the next section, *The Soldierly Body, the Technological Machine, and the Fascist Aesthetic.*
14. Schauwecker, *Aufbruch der Nation*, 299.
15. Jünger, *Feuer und Blut*, 139-40.
16. Jünger, *Kampf als inneres Erlebnis*, 12.
17. Schauwecker, *Der feurige Weg*, 185.
18. Salomon, *Die Geächteten*, 122; similarly Volck, *Rebellen um Ehre*, 84.
19. Jünger, *Kampf als inneres Erlebnis*, 53.
20. Heinz, *Sprengstoff*, 17.
21. Schauwecker says the frontline soldiers were the "nation's best": "They have instinctively what others do not even have intellectually. They have it in their blood. The tragedy of our times is that everything essential is only to be found in our blood. The important thing is that it is still there, but it is only there as a seed. It seems that the great task before us is to employ all the means at our disposal to make it grow, to make it burst forth from our blood into our spirits and thus flow into our consciousness. We must put ouselves in a position where we can think what today we can but feel!" (*Aufbruch der Nation*, 378). In Buschbecker's, *Wie unser Gesetz es befahl*, 120, all soldiers have the same blood—the "blood of steel." The right blood/instinct in men is shown in battle and their political attitudes, in women in their ability and intention to give birth to first-class Aryans. See too how the Reich Commissar for Agricultural Affairs, later to become Minister of "The State of Food and Nourishment," subdivided German women into four classes depending on the quality of the offspring they expect to produce (Walter Darre, in *Naziführer sehen dich an*, 93-94).
22. Heinz, *Sprengstoff*, 88.
23. Schauwecker, *Aufbruch der Nation*, 81.
24. Jünger, *Kampf als inneres Erlebnis*, 7.
25. Ibid., 46.
26. Ibid., 12.

27. Ibid., 53.
28. Ibid., 106.
29. Ibid., 116. See also Jünger, *Feuer und Blut*, 81, 171-72. In the same vein his brother Friedrich Georg Jünger writes "the flood of the millions, the stream of the armies . . . a gigantic wave of life," in "Krieg und Krieger," 57. On breaking down boundaries (flowing, being electrified in battle, wading through blood), see Salomon, *Die Geächteten*, 74; Killinger, *Kampf um Oberschlesien*, 42; Goote, *Kamerad Berthold*, 139; Schauwecker, *Der Feurige Weg*, 154ff.; Kohlhaas, *Der Häuptling und die Republik*, 21; Volck, *Rebellen um Ehre*, 81; Ettighofer, *Sturm 1918*, 111, 113-14; Ettighofer, *Revolver über der Stadt*, 115-16; Eggers, *Von der Freiheit des Kriegers*, 27ff.; Buschbecker, *Wie unser Gesetz es befahl*, 13; Goote, *Wir fahren den Tod*, 166ff., 193, 281.
30. By contrast with this, I have rarely come across postively charged "flows" not directly related to blood flowing in battle and troops flooding into battle—once in connection with the white woman (Erbt, *Der Narr von Kreyingen*, 68), once as a "whirlpool of foaming reality" (Salomon, *Die Geächteten*, 371), and in one instance youth is described as "a foaming torrent" (Heinz, *Sprengstoff*, 100).
31. Jünger, *Kampf als inneres Erlebnis*, 8-9; likewise Brandis, *Baltikümer*, 165-66.

The Site of War

1. Von Selchow, *Hundert Tage*, 264.
2. Jünger, *Kampf als innere Erlebnis*, 46.
3. Ibid., 12.
4. Schauwecker, *Aufbruch der Nation*, 81.
5. Ibid., 299.
6. Ibid., 243.
7. Heinz, *Sprengstoff*, 16. The brain becomes "ice cold" in Volck, *Rebellen um Ehre*, 20. See also Goote, *Wir fahren den Tod*, 168.
8. *Verkopfung* is what Bohm calls the tendency for all the processes of feeling to be intellectualized for fear of experience itself, *Lehrbuch der Rorschach-Psychodiagnostik* (Bern, 1967), 231.
9. As we can read in Bronnen, *Rossbach*, 12, he "exploded when his insides came under Germanic pressure." Or in Friedrich Jünger, "the bovista has to turn brown before it bursts, the ulcer has to be fully grown before the surgeon's shiny blade can make its relieving approach" ("Krieg und Krieger," 60).

    The mere sight of such things can bring redemption. Schauwecker, *Der feurige Weg*, 139-40: "Then I see the calix turning blood-red, growing visibly larger and blossoming through the cloth. Quick, come on! Get your coat off! And death's burning petals come blossoming between his fingers, pouring rosy-red between his shirt and his skin, damp and wet from the fertile soil of the flesh. Suddenly a face pops up, sallow, smiling. . . . It's true, he feels obliged to smile as he dies, this child, this unsuspecting, downy hero of 19 years. The kind of cadet who believes he must do this as a future officer and superior in the presence of his men and as a good soldier in the presence of me, his superior. "I've . . .," finding it hard to whisper, and looking at me, "I've . . .," and he mumbles a little more, his lips quivering. Then all of a sudden his face goes limp, ages 10 years, his mouth and eyes ringed by lines of suffering, his flesh sunken into his body, while the blood flows out, rosy and foaming, gushing out of his lungs, bubbling with oxygen, the breath of life . . . it is the source of life itself that is gushing out. Death the cannibal is pouring itself a bottle of champagne."

    I do not believe death is doing the "pouring" here. The text is part of an eight-page description of dying and corpses (136ff.), throughout which the flavor is one of enjoyment.

10. Jünger, *Kampf als inneres Erlebnis*, 29.
11. Ibid., 8.
12. Ferenczi, "Versuch einer Genitaltheorie," 342ff.
13. Ibid., 343. The fact that Ferenczi reduces sexual pleasure to a form of "separation," that the animosity shown by our age to sexuality enters into a genital theory almost as a matter of course, is not so important for our purposes, although it should at least be noted.
14. Ibid., 343-44.
15. On the possibility of the "genitalization" of parts of the body, see Ferenczi, *Schriften*, vols. 2, 11, 12, 18, 20, 73.
16. Canetti, *Crowds and Power*, 344.

The Soldierly Body, the Technological Machine, and the Fascist Aesthetic

1. Jünger, *Feuer und Blut*, 81.
2. Ibid., 75.
3. Ibid., 82.
4. Ibid., 82-83.
5. Benjamin, "The Work of Art," 299.
6. Today it is likely that the promise of intense pleasures would not be held by machines, but rather by parts of our unconscious being, shot into space at the speed of light and landing on alien planets, but still controlled by our computers; the hidden depths of our souls stored, labeled, and structured in vast data banks, countless prototypal components that can be recalled in a matter of seconds, yielding the deepest insights. I am fairly convinced that there are a number of people dotted around who are already tinkering with a fascist aesthetic of electronics.
7. Lippe, *Naturbeherrschung am Menschen*, vol. 1, 91, 101.
8. "In front of the chateau's windows, trees in blossom spread their broad branches. The general is very fond of trees and animals. The world which has slipped out of joint could be so beautiful if only people were not so enormously stupid" (Eggers, *Berg der Rebellen*, 147). This is also a survivor's fantasy—everything would be all right if he were the only one left. The blossoming on the trees would really be beautiful then because they would no longer remind one of another life.

The Ego of the Soldier Male

Fragmented Armor

1. Jünger, *In Stahlgewittern*, 237.
2. Mann, *Mit Ehrhardt durch Deutschland*, 77.
3. H. Schauwecker, "Der Kampf der Gruppe Epp," in SB, 120, also in HoDA, 182.
4. Recklinghausen civic archives, *Stadtarchiv III, Amt Marl, Verhandlungstermin vor dem Tumultschadenausschuss vom 28. März*, 1921, cited in Lucas, *Märzrevolution*, vol. 3, manuscript.
5. Details of this are given in the description of the troops marching into the Ruhr area in Lucas, *Märzrevolution*, vol. 3, manuscript.
6. Mann, *Mit Ehrhardt*, 130. Elsewhere he states quite openly: "besides, the superior next-in-line is usually responsible for excessive attacks." (207)
7. See also Paul Levi, *Luxemburg-Prozess und Soldatenmisshandlungen* (Frankfurt, 1914).
8. Recklinghausen civic archives, *Stadtarchiv III, Amt Marl, Verhandlungstermin vor dem Tumultschadenausschuss vom 28. März, 1921*, cited in Lucas, *Märzrevolution*, vol. 3, manuscript.

9. Information given to E. Lucas on 9 November 1967 by Herr Beckedahl, Registrar in Dinslaken, cited in Lucas, *Märzrevolution*, vol. 3, manuscript.

The Ego and Maintenance Mechanisms

1. Mahler, *Infantile Psychosis*, the term "maintenance mechanisms" appears for the first time on page 52.
2. Ibid., 9, 32-65.
3. See also Laplanche/Pontalis, *The Language of Psychoanalysis*, entry for "Psychosis." For Mahler's use of the word see *Infantile Psychosis*, 53, 64.
4. Ibid., 10ff.
5. Ibid., 41-42.
6. Freud, *The Ego and the Id*, SE, vol. XIX, 25, 27.
7. From Laplanche/Pontalis, *The Language*, 143.
8. Mahler, *Infantile Psychosis*, 10, referring to Phyllis Greenacre, "Problems of Infantile Neurosis: A Discussion," in *The Psychoanalytic Study of the Child*, 9, 16-71.
9. Mahler, *Infantile Psychosis*, 10.
10. Ibid., 36 (and after). See also Paul Schilder, *Das Körperschema. Ein Beitrag zur Lehre vom Bewusstsein des eigenen Körpers* (Berlin/Leipzig, 1923).
11. Mahler, *Infantile Psychosis*, 109. On the significance of epidermal sensations for human development see also Ashley Montagu, *Touching*. The fact that the mother licks her newborns is highly revealing. Montagu describes it as an action akin to stroking which completes the birth by setting the blood circulating. Animals that are not licked do not survive.
12. M. Klein, "Some Theoretical Conclusions Regarding the Emotional Life of the Infant"; "The Psycho-Analytic Play Technique."
13. Mahler, *Infantile Psychosis*, 109.
14. Ibid., 11.
15. Ibid., 233.
16. Ibid., 103.
17. Ibid., 95.
18. Ibid., 70.
19. Ibid., 229.
20. Ibid., 109.
21. Ibid., 57, 67.
22. Ibid., 69.
23. Ibid., 63.
24. Ibid., 106.
25. Ibid., 227.
26. Ibid., 52-53.
27. Ibid., 54.
28. Ibid., 92.
29. Ibid., 92.
30. See Freud, *The Interpretation of Dreams*, vol. V, 601-2. Freud wrote of *Primärvorgang*, though the German will often use *Primärprozess*, a result of the retranslation of *primary process* from other languages (English, French, Italian). (The German words *Prozess* and *Vorgang* are both usually translated as *process* in English. Tr.'s note.)
31. Mahler, 92.
32. Mahler, case history of "Stanley," 82-83.
33. Ibid., 64.
34. Fromm, *The Anatomy of Human Destructiveness*, 353, discusses the issue in a similar

manner, but when he comes to the structure of the ego he interrupts his argument to call for a comprehensive inquiry into the matter. There are no grounds for objecting to his request, but the present evidence, the statements and actions of destructive men, which Fromm fails to refer to enough, answers the question quite well.
35. Mahler, 81.
36. Without exception, beating is referred to as something taken entirely for granted. The saying "he who loves his children flogs them" must have been familiar to almost every German child over the last 150 years, and many today are bound to know it. We find it in *Kapitän Ehrhardt*, on pages 7 and 9: "My mother taught me respect for the female sex. Her hand quickly went into action and any stupidity or idleness earned me a quick box on the ears" (Freska, *Kapitän Ehrhardt*). A good idea of how much children were beaten can be gleaned from the anthology *Wir klagen an, Kinderbriefe über die Prügelstrafe*, edited by Alois Jalkotzky (Vienna, 1929).
37. Mahler, 70-71.
38. Oral communication from Dr. Margaret Berger.

Ego-Disintegration and Work
1. According to H. Hannover and E. Hannover-Druck, *Politische Justiz 1918-1933*, 136, Ehrhardt in fact had a skeleton key, and the "liberation" was merely a massive piece of propaganda. They do not cite a source, however.
2. Freska, *Kapitän Ehrhardt*, 226. For a similar account see Stadtler, *Als Anitbolschewist*, 24.
3. Freska, *Kapitän Ehrhardt*, 227.
4. Salomon, *Die Geächteten*, 330.
5. "I knew I was inseparably bound to him" (*Die Geächteten*, 322).
6. Ibid., 334.
7. Ibid., 335.
8. Ibid., 8.
9. Ibid., 9.
10. Jünger, *Kampf als inneres Erlebnis*, 23. See also Salomon, *Die Geächteten*, 380; Mann, *Mit Ehrhardt*, 204; Kohlhaas, *Der Häuptling*, 187ff.; Höfer, *Oberschlesien in der Aufstandszeit*, 153-54.
11. Jünger, *Kampf als inneres Erlebnis*, 103-4.
12. Mahler, *Infantile Psychosis*, 63.
13. Jünger, *Kampf als inneres Erlebnis*, 73. See also 72, 99, 102, 104, and likewise, Jünger, *Feuer und Blut*, 40-41; Goote, *Wir fahren den Tod*, 193ff.; Freiwald, *Verratene Flotte*, 30.
14. Mahler, *Infantile Psychosis*, 63.
15. Goote, *Wir tragen das Leben*, 128.
16. Salomon, *Die Geächteten*, 328-29.
17. Höss, *Kommandant in Auschwitz*, 48.
18. Ibid., 47.
19. Ibid., 47.
20. Ibid., 48. Von Selchow's dreams are of a similar nature, when he collapses following his training as a naval cadet (*Hundert Tage*, 66-67).
21. Höss, *Kommandant*, 49.
22. Ibid., 49.
23. Killinger, *Ernstes und Heiteres*, 111.
24. Ibid., 110. See also Weller, *Peter Mönkemann*, 314, and the volume edited by Hartmut Plaas, *Wir klagen an. Nationalisten in den Kerkern der Bourgeoisie*.
25. Höss, *Kommandant*, 65.

26. Ibid., 65.

27. "Save us from internal chaos and deliver us to the literal cosmos," demands Blüher in *Die Rolle der Erotik*, 263, also describing it as the step from "the feminine to the masculine." Berthold calls his diary his "dear diary" and "my best council, my friend in times good and bad" (Gengler, *Berthold*, 97). His entry for 21 January 1919: "I wish to continue my diary, I wish to have someone in these times to whom I can entrust my whole inner being, someone who will patiently hear me out . . ." (101-2). Fritz Kloppe: "You too, my dear and trusted diary . . ." (in JKR, 242). Goebbels, *Michael*, 146: "This diary is my best friend. I can confide in it totally. There is nobody else I can tell all these things to. And I have to be honest, I'd never get anything off my chest otherwise. It would all burn my heart out." (And so on.) It is here that the function of writing as ego maintenance is most clear. "The old must be expelled to make room for the new. The human soul is too small for things to live side-by-side." (46)

28. Perhaps prison labor in the Federal Republic of Germany is deemed as such because there is barely a need for remuneration. Prisoners work for themselves, not for money. The fact that they are allowed to do so is a sufficient blessing. On the function of prison labor when it was introduced in the eighteenth and nineteenth centuries see Foucault, *Discipline and Punish*, 231ff. It was introduced by the prison *adminstration* and its aim was to discipline individuals for the world of work (not to perform the arduous task of preventing ego disintegration).

29. Höss, *Kommandant*, 65-66.

30. Ibid., 98.

31. Ibid., 96, standard for the tenor of the whole book.

32. Ibid., 90ff. But his underlings, particularly the women prison team leaders, failed to pick that up: "They far outdid their male counterparts in their toughness, despicableness, cruelty, and depravity. Most of them were whores with a considerable number of previous convictions. Usually vile pieces . . . I don't believe men can ever turn into such creatures." (116)

33. Ibid., 131ff., 136ff.

34. Ibid., 87ff.

35. Goebbels, *Michael*, 95, 124, 149.

36. Ibid., 124.

37. Ibid., 127.

38. Ibid., 69, 137.

39. Ibid., 147.

40. Ibid., 147.

41. Ibid., 118.

42. Freud, *From the History of an Infantile Neurosis*, SE, vol. XVII, 100. Criticism of Jung is also to be found there.

43. Goebbels, *Michael*, 127.

44. See Deleuze/Guattari, *Anti-Oedipus*, 205ff.

45. Plaas, "Das Kapp-Unternehmen" in JKR, 170; also Freska, *Kapitän Ehrhardt*, 158.

46. Jünger, *Feuer und Blut*, 125.

47. See also the order for the day given by Röhm on the "Führer's" 45th birthday, in Charles Bloch, *Die SA*, 84-85; the exclusion by the leader of the Hitler Youth rituals in Hans Steinhoff's film *Hitlerjunge Quex 1933*; Dieter Thomas Heck announcing the ZDF record charts; or Salomon, *Nahe Geschichte*, 33, where the *Freikorps* member feels "needed by the forces of history itself"; or Goebbels, *Michael*, 148: "The globe belongs to whomsoever takes it." See also Crasemann, *Freikorps Maercker*, 23; Eggers, *Berg der Rebellen*, 145: "He knows a well-aimed shot can unleash a world war. That's why he wants to bear the responsibility all by himself"; Stadtler, *Als Antibolschewist*,

106; Volck, *Rebellen um Ehre*, 10; Eggers, *Von der Freiheit des Kriegers*, 48; Solf, *Deutschlands Auferstehung 1934*, 45. In addition, see the portrayal of historic battles as a direct attack on the body of the earth in Friedrich Helscher, "Die grosse Verwandlung," in *Krieg und Krieger*, 129-34.
48. Goebbels, *Michael*, 157.
49. Deleuze/Guattari, *Anti-Oedipus*.

Collected Observations on the Ego of the Not-Yet-Fully-Born

1. Reich, *The Mass Psychology of Fascism*, 92-93.
2. Hans Steinhoff's film *Hitlerjunge Quex* traces the journey taken by Heini Völker, a working-class boy, from his authoritarian family to the Hitler Youth (his mother having committed suicide, thus leaving the way free). The pro-family policies pursued in the 1930s can be understood only as components of a strategy to destroy the family by recognizing their dual character, as described by Tim Mason in *Zur Lage der Frauen in Deutschland*, 118-53. Compare further Nazi production of an elite in the "*Lebensborn* Homes" (*Lebensborn* means "spring of life"—Tr.'s note) where selected "Aryan" girls, with the aid of an SS man, were invited to give the *Führer* a child without having to officially register the birth. And, "How can you be so cruel as to leave such brilliant enemies on the other side?" (Himmler on the rounding up and "Germanization" of "gifted" Polish children.) Robert Kempner, the American prosecuting council at Nuremberg, estimated that the *Lebensborn* homes produced some 100,000 children. (From *dem Führer ein Kind schenken*, TV film by Clarissa Henry and Marc Lillel on the "*Lebensborn* Registered Association," shown on ZDF 23 March 1975.)
    In his attitude toward the family, Niemöller is quite distinct from the majority of the soldierly males. There is no trace of "direct filiation" in his case. On the contrary, in the epilogue to his book he goes to great lengths to emphasize the ties he has to his parental home, and this not in a beseeching and apologetic tone. Bidding farewell to the "time of inner rebellion," as he puts it, and with his parents not "blocking the way back home," he deliberately becomes part of a familial *tradition*—which ultimately he pursues in a professional capacity (Niemöller, *Vom U-Boot zur Kanzel*, 209). Niemöller seems to me to be a concrete example of how a familial tradition, in conjunction with the tenets of a certain religious tradition, can mark out for the individual a kind of boundary which provides a barrier between him and the destructive, absolute ego-world relationship that is typical for the fascist.
    For traditional psychoanalysis this type of "resistance" would be very much a position for the super-ego. In their study of the authoritarian personality, Adorno et al. came across a feature they described as the almost total *absence* of the super-ego in individuals prone to fascist tendencies. They meant to show that there was a lack of truly integrated prohibitions, limitations, etc., that the individual accepted. This is congruent with the findings of the present study. The difference is that I have located the causes in the absence of a body-ego capable of integration and in the reification of the unconscious into negative body flows.
    Left-wing critiques of the family tend to dismiss the possibility that a rapidly disintegrating ego willingly submitting to the claims of a terroristic state might be offered resistance in this way, even if from a very weak position.
3. Dwinger, *Auf halbem Wege*, 333.
4. The documentary *Wintersoldiers*, about a tribunal where veterans of Vietnam bring accusations against themselves, captures this. (Distributed by Arsenal Berlin.)
5. See also Hanns Johst, *Der Einsame*, 50ff.
6. Goebbels, *Michael*, 22. On 116 we read that war "is as cruel as all things living."
7. Mahler, *Infantile Psychosis*, 47.

8. Ibid., 55.

9. See Laplanche/Pontalis, *The Language of Psychoanalysis*, entry for "Regression."

10. For a critique of the Freudian concept of regression in toto, see David Cooper, *Von der Notwendigkeit der Freiheit*, (Frankfurt, 1976), 127ff., and Deleuze/Guattari, *Anti-Oedipus*, 113ff.

11. The word "body" does not appear in any of the entry headings in Laplanche/Pontalis's dictionary of psychoanalysis.

12. Gisela Pankow, *Gesprengte Fesseln der Psychose*, 17, (original French title, *L'homme et sa psychose*), provides a detailed account of her therapeutic methods. Her writings on the body image (23ff.) support and substantiate in many respects Mahler's thoughts and evidence cited in the section above on "The Ego and Maintenance Mechanisms." Without being untheoretical, Pankow's book is more concerned with describing therapeutic procedures than Mahler's, whereas the latter deals more with the conceptual understanding of child psychosis. Pankow's therapy is also suitable for adults and is the clearest, most practical evidence psychoanalysis has that many of the assumptions underlying the theories of infantile psychosis are correct. In particular, her work has clearly affirmed the prime importance of the body image for the patient's self-perception.

Currently, some nonanalytically oriented methods of treatment, such as Gestalt therapy, may well be superior forms of practice for the reason that they do not shy away from the patient's body as a matter of principle.

The likely political conclusion of this is the need to form groups and masses that allow the possibility of bodily experiences and masses different from those mediated by the unified strength of molar ordered structures and to encourage activities not based upon speech.

13. Mahler, *Infantile Psychosis*, 105.

14. Ibid., 109-10.

15. Balint, *Angstlust und Regression*, 22ff.

16. Ibid., 28.

17. Jünger, *Kampf als inneres Erlebnis*, 68.

18. Balint, *Angstlust und Regression*, 25.

19. Ibid., 24, 26.

20. Balla, *Landsknechte wurden wir*, 106.

21. Von Maltzan, "Die Spandauer stürmen Bauske," in SB, 161.

22. Gengler, *Berthold*, 126.

23. In F. S. Krauss, *Anthropophyteia IV*, an anthology of erotic verse, the riding whip sometimes appears as an attribute of the procurer, the pimp, for example, 274, to keep the mass of whores under control. Brecht's attempt to portray the Nazis as (political) pimps procuring prostitutes (the proletariat) for the punters (capitalists) is more accurate than Brecht himself realized. (*Gesamtwerke*, vol. 20, "Die Horst-Wessel-Legende," 209-19.)

24. Salomon, *Die Geächteten*, 20.

25. Reinhard, *Die Wehen der Republik*, 57. See also Rossbach, *Mein Weg durch die Zeit*, 55-56; Rotermund, "Rote Armee," in HoDA, 104.

26. Balint, *Angstlust und Regression*, 25ff., 40, 47, 66.

27. Ibid., 89.

28. Mahler, *Infantile Psychosis*, 227.

29. Morgan, *The Descent of Woman*, 281.

Chapter 3: The White Terror as Bounding and Maintenance of the Self

Three Perceptual Identities Associated with the "Undifferentiated Object of the Drives"

1. Freud, *The Interpretation of Dreams*, SE, vol. V, 601ff.
2. Mahler, *Infantile Psychosis*, 91-92.
3. Foucault, *Discipline and Punish*, on judging: "Borne along by the omnipresence of the mechanisms of discipline, basing itself on all the carceral apparatuses, it has become one of the major functions of our society. The judges of normality are present everywhere. We are in the society of the teacher-judge, the doctor-judge, the educator-judge, the 'social worker'-judge; it is on them that the universal reign of the normative is based; and each individual, wherever he may find himself, subjects to it his body, his gestures, his behavior, his aptitudes, his achievements." (304)
4. This is presumably also the situation in which part of the introjected "bad mother" can "flow away." But maybe it can't "flow away" so easily. Mahler describes the aggressive acts of children as "an attempt to re-externalize—to eject—the dangerous maternal introject." (28)
5. See, for example, Jünger, *Feuer und Blut*, 88ff.
6. Ibid., 88.
7. See, for example, Freska, *Kapitän Ehrhardt*, 191: "In civil war, which is perverse, because fellow members of the same people are at each other's throats, surrender means certain doom. The opponent will recognize the enemy only as a murderer of the people."
8. Schulz, *Ein Freikorps im Industriegebiet*, 7.
9. 4 April 1920 edition of the Duisburg *Niederrheinische Volksstimme*, an SPD paper, in an article entitled "Salvation at last!"
10. Scheffel, "Annaberg," in SB, 276.
11. Zöberlein, *Befehl des Gewissens*, 197.
12. E. J. Gumbel, *Vier Jahre politischer Mord*, e.g., 17-18, 33, 41, 60ff., 67-68, and other books by him. For the Ruhr region, Lucas, *Märzrevolution*, vol. 3, manuscript; Henning Duderstadt, *Die Tragödie von Mechterstädt*; and for the most convincing account of the fun to be had by smashing people with a rifle butt, see Schaumlöffel, *Mit dem Studentenkorps Marburg*, 23; Dwinger, *Die letzten Reiter*, 223; Schramm, *Die roten Tage*, 202; no author, in SB, 374; Fischer, "Rärteherrschaft in München" in JKR, 162; Hahn, *Der rote Hahn*, 34.
13. The *Dülmener Zeitung*, cited in the *Recklinghäuser Volks-Zeitung*, 30 March 1920; the *Lüdingshauser Zeiting*, cited in the *Lüner Zeitung*, 27 March 1920; the *Münstersche Zeitung*, 26 March 1920; statement from Krautwurst in *Volkstribüne, Organ des werktätigen Volkes von Elberfeld-Barmen*, 8 April 1920; report by Captain Guderian, 31 March 1920, in Severing's estate, *A III*, Josef Ernst, *Kapp-Tage*, 8, cited in Lucas, *Märzrevolution*, vol. 3, manuscript.
14. *"Eroberer" des "Vorwärts"-Gebäudes, Januar 1919—Der Ledebour-Prozess*, edited by Georg Ledebour (Berlin, 1919), 394, statement by the witness Steinbring.

Black White Red

1. Mann, *Mit Ehrhardt durch Deutschland*, 146.
2. Killinger, *Die SA*, 53-4.
3. Recently by Rainer Stollmann, "Faschistische Kunst als Gesamtgewerk," in Denkler/Prümm, *Die deutsche Literatur im Dritten Reich* (Stuttgart, 1976), 96-97. According to him, National Socialism simply stole its symbols from the labor movement. Bloch was more honest about it, complaining that "Marxist propaganda . . . lacks any counterweight to the myths." (*Erbschaft dieser Zeit*, 66-67)

4. Gengler, *Berthold*, 100. On money see also Goebbels, *Michael*, 122; Jünger, *Kampf als inneres Erlebnis*, 112; Mann, *Mit Ehrhardt*, 214.
5. Canetti, *Crowds and Power*, 101.
6. Ettighofer, *Revolver über den Stadt*, 64: a woman tries to save the separatists' flag (green, white, and red), but of course she fails. The flag is ripped to pieces.

The Whip

1. Benzler, a standard-bearer for the Ehrhardt Brigade in Freska, *Kapitän Ehrhardt*, 98.
2. Der Syndikalist. Organ der freien Arbeiter-Union Deutschlands, 2, no. 16, (Berlin, 1920).
3. Schauwecker, "Freikorps von Epp," in HoDA, 184.
4. Zöberlein, *Befehl des Gewissens*, 110.
5. Ibid., 425.
6. Schauwecker, "Freikorps von Epp," in HoDA, 167.
7. Ibid., 165.
8. Fischer, "Die Räteherrschaft in München," in JKR, 162.
9. Kloppe, "Kameraden," in JKR, 244.
10. Maercker, *Vom Kaiserheer*, 61.
11. Bronnen, *Rossbach*, 60.
12. Zöberlein, *Befehl des Gewissens*, 208.
13. Dwinger, *Auf halbem Wege*, 172.
14. Steinäcker, *Mit der eisernen Division im Baltenland*, 18.
15. Loewenfeld, "Das Freikorps von L.," in RDS, 153.
16. Maercker, *Vom Kaiserheer*, 144.
17. Bronnen, *Rossbach*, 68.
18. Killinger, *Ernstes und Heiteres*, 60.
19. Schulz, *Ein Freikorps*, 9.
20. Weller, *Peter Mönkemann*, 326. More whips in Ettinghofer, *Revolver*, 66; Buschbecker, *Wie unser Gesetz es befahl*, 9; Volck, *Rebellen um Ehre*, 47; Liftl-Heller, *Das Freikorps Landsberg*, 8, 27.
21. Carl Severing, *1919/20 im Wetter-und Watterwinkel*, 207.
22. *Volksfreund. Sozialdemokratisches Organ für die Kreise Recklinghausen und Borken*, 20 May 1920.
23. Testimony of an eye-witness of 13 April 1920, in Severing's estate, *A III*, cited in Lucas, *Märzrevolution*, vol. 3, manuscript.
24. Cited in Lucas, *Märzrevolution*, vol. 3, manuscript.
25. *Volksblatt. Sozialdemokratisches Organ für die Wahlkreise Bochum/Gelsenkirchen/Hattingen/Witten/Herne/, und Recklinghausen-Borken*, April 20 1920, cited in *Freiheit, Berliner Organ der Unabhängigen Sozialdemokratie Deutschlands*, 3, (Berlin), 25 April 1920.
26. *Volksblatt*, 20 April 1920.
27. *Volksfreund*, 2, no. 25, (Recklinghausen), May 25 1920, (all cited in Lucas, *Märzrevolution*, vol. 3, manuscript.
28. Mann, *Mit Ehrhardt*, 71-72; Josef Hofmiller, *Revolutionstagebuch 1918/19. Aus den Tagen der Münchener Revolution* (Leipzig, 1938), 219, reports he saw two children who had to take weapons to the collection point.
29. On white terror which openly claims to be white terror, see also Salomon, *Die Geächteten*, 76, 123; ibid., "Hexenkessel Deutschland," in JKR, 28; von Berk, "Rote Armee an Rhein und Ruhr," in JKR, 217; Nord, "Der Krieg im Baltikum," in JKR, 91; no author, "Freikorps Epp in Pelkum," in SB, 403-4; Kohlhaas, "Männer und

Sicherheitskompanien im Schwabenland 1918/19," in SB, 96-97; Schirach, *Die Pioniere des Dritten Reiches*, 110; Brandis, *Baltikumer*, 65; Schricker, *Rotmord*, 9; Karsten Curator, *Putsche, Staat und wir!* 123-24; Balla, *Landknechte*, 122-23; Fletcher, *Die Eroberung Tuckums*, in SB, 156-57; Weller, *Peter Mönkemann*, 168; Ewers, *Reiter in deutscher Nacht*, 229; Engelhardt, *Ritt nach Riga*, 42; Bischoff, *Die letzte Front*, 119-20; Mann, *Ehrhardt*, 198; Schulz, *Ein Freikorps im Industriegebiet*, 8-11; von Plehwe, *Im Kampfe gegen die Bolschewisten*, 10; Reinhard, *Die Wehen*, 69; Killinger, *Kampf um Oberschlesien*, 107, 114; Schaumlöffel, *Mit dem Marburger*, 14; von Selchow, *Hundert Tage*, 328-29, 336-37; Lüttwitz, *Im Kampf gegen die Novemberrevolution*, 57-58; Zöberlein, *Befehl des Gewissens*, 669.

30. In particular, descriptions of castration wounds and everything connected with perceptions of "the bloody miasma" can be counted as "red terror" with "white" aspects, since these are *always* perceptions of the writer. See also Nord, "Der Krieg im Baltikum," in JKR, 69-70; Salomon, *Die Geächteten*, 67; Liemann, "Sudetendeutschlands Märzgefallene," in SB, 309; Wittmann, *Erinnerungen der Eisernen Schar*, 134-35; Erbt, *Der Narr*, 234; Schricker, *Rotmord*, 131, 161; Dwinger, *Auf halbem Wege*, 423-24; Erich Czech-Jochberg, *Im Osten Feuer*, 109-10, 185ff.

Ritual Flogging and the Look

1. Reports in the *Volksfreund, Sozialdemokratisches Organ*, (Recklinghausen), 2, 4 April and 5 May 1920; *Ruhr-Echo, (USPD)*, (Essen), 2, (1920), 9 April.

2. Sadger, "Über Gesäss-Erotik," in *Internationale Zeitschrift für ärztliche Psychoanalyse*, no. 1, (1931), 354-55.

3. See the case studies in Charles Socarides, *The Overt Homosexual* (New York: Grune and Stratton, 1968); Dannecker/Reiche, *Der gewöhnliche Homosexuelle*, 261ff.; case studies in Serge Leclaire, *Das Reale entlarven*, (Freiburg and Olten, 1975); Hirschfeld, *Die Homosexualität des Mannes und des Weibes*, 291ff.

4. See Hocquenghem, *Homosexual Desire*, 103-4, on why the "object-choice" cannot be considered decisive for the type of desire.

5. Heinz Heger, *Die Männer im rosa Winkel*, the name is a pseudonym. Even today, admitting to having been a homosexual in a concentration camp is bound to cause social ruin.

6. Ibid., 67.

7. Ibid., 66.

8. Ibid., 68.

9. Ibid., 67.

10. Ibid., 68-69. In Hirschfeld, *Sittengeschichte des Weltkriegs*, vol. 2, 174-75, we find reports of officers who either collected pictures of the dead, the dying, or the tortured, or—which they preferred—took their own photographs of them. In Bruno Vogel, *Es lebe der Krieg*, 43, there is a report of a colonel who masturbated while sheltering in a dug-out in a forward position, as his troops, whom he watched through binoculars, were killed by the score in a pointless attack they had been ordered to launch. A radio-operator caught him at it (Hirschfeld, vol. 2, 176). In a milder form, "watching" a battle is described by the commander as "watching a movie" in Brandis, *Baltikumer*, 167.

11. Heger, *Männer im rosa Winkel*, 70.

12. Foucault, *Discipline and Punish*, 42. "Torture rests on a whole quantitative art of pain." (34) It is "a differentiated production of pain, an organized ritual for the marking of victims and the expression of the power that punishes; not the expression of a legal system driven to exasperation and, forgetting its principles, losing all restraint. In the 'excesses' of torture, a whole economy of power is invested" (35).

13. Jünger, *Kampf als inneres Erlebnis*, 97.
14. Höss, *Kommandant*, 56-57.
15. Ibid., 69.
16. Verbal reports from a number of therapists. See also Hirschfeld, *Die Homosexualität*, 322. In general, these are people with what is known as the "border-line" problem, as described in Rudolf Ekstein, *Grenzfallkinder. Klinische Studien über die pychoanalytische Behandlung von schwergestörten Kindern*, (Munich/Basel, 1973). See also Spitz, "Autorität and Onanie," in *Psyche*, 6/52, 2-16.
17. Foucault, *Discipline and Punish*, 42.
18. Jean Amery, *Jenseits von Schuld und Sühne*, 48-49.
19. Ibid., 48-49.

Homosexuality and the White Terror

1. See Chapter 1, "A Soldier's Love," "Excursus on 'Homosexuality,'" and "Marriage— Sisters of Comrades," and Chapter 3, "Culture and the Mass" and footnote 28 to "Eyes." See Hocquenghem, *Homosexual Desire*, section on anti-homosexual paranoia for an account of the affective judging of homosexuals as guilty. In Szasz, *The Manufacture of Madness*, the homosexual is also described as the case model of psychiatric scapegoats in both the United States and Europe.
2. Gumbel, *Verschwörer*, 188, who cites this as a matter of course in order to expose Hitler and his "hangers-on."
3. Dannecker/Reiche, *Der gewöhnliche Homosexuelle*, 272-73. Just as many had had "Sado-sex" only once "in the last few months."
4. Ibid., 275.
5. Ibid., 277.
6. Ibid., 177-78.
7. Ibid., 247.
8. Ibid., 265.
9. Ibid., 283.
10. Hocquenghem, *Homosexual Desire*, 80.
11. Freud, *Three Essays on the Theory of Sexuality*, SE, vol. 7, 148.
12. Hocquenghem, 82.
13. Ibid., 82-83.
14. Ibid., 86.
15. Foucault, *Discipline and Punish*, e.g., 233, 252.
16. Hocquenghem, 125.
17. Ibid., 97.
18. Blüher, *Die Rolle der Erotik*, passim., and *Wandervogel, Geschichte einer Jugendbewegung*, passim.
19. Stefan George is similar, for example, in *Gesamtwerke*, vol. 8, *Stern des Bundes* (Berlin, 1928), 89.
20. Reimut Reiche, "Eine Entgegnung," *Psyche*, 26, 481.
21. Helm Stierlin, "Einige Anmerkungen," *Psyche*, 26, 485.
22. Reiche, "Eine Entgegnung," *Psyche*, 26, 476 (a view, incidentally, that does not concur at all with that of Hocquenghem discussed in the last section).
23. Ibid., 476-77.
24. Ibid., 477; Socarides, *The Overt Homosexual*, 115.
25. Reiche, 478.
26. Ibid., 479-80. "Ego-syntonic" means in harmony with the ego, not rejected by the ego. Hirschfeld, *Die Homosexualität*, claims that 50% of homosexuals are what he calls "healthy" or "stable" (298).

27. Stierlin, "Einige Anmerkungen," 486.
28. Ibid., 487.
29. Ibid., 487.
30. Socarides, *The Overt Homosexual*, 148.
31. Ibid., 143.
32. Ibid., 148-9.
33. Ibid., 112.
34. Ibid., 117.
35. Ibid., 118
36. The same could be said, though perhaps with some reservations, about the patients described by Felix Boehm, "Beiträge zur Psychologie der Homosexualität," in *Internationale Zeitschrift für Psychoanalyse* (1922), 313-20. Boehm frequently found in patients who were practicing homosexuals that the "reason" they feared women and turned to men was that they were afraid of the devouring penis of women. According to Boehm, then, their "homosexuality" derived from revulsion rather than attraction. That they did not display aggression in acts of maintenance (by contrast with Socarides's patients) would suggest that their disturbance was less intense. This corresponds with the fact that their anxieties were adequately encoded with the image of a woman armed with a penis, that they thus did not feel directly exposed to the threat of being devoured. In other words, they seem to have been more effectively secondarily oedipalized. In *Die Psychoanalyse eines Falles von Homosexualität*, Nachmannsohn describes a man whose "homosexuality stems from his need to avoid women because he cannot distinguish them from the body of the maternal body/sister." (*Internationale Zeitschrift für Psychoanalyse*, 8 [1922], 45-63).
37. Socarides, 132.
38. "In homosexuality, it's a wild type, groping thing. In heterosexuality I'm left with nice feelings," he says. Ibid., 132.
39. There is not even a word like "prick" (in German *Schwanz*) for the place, only "arse" which has immediate associations with a term of abuse.
40. Blüher, *Die Rolle der Erotik*, 272-73.
41. Ibid., 273.
42. Ibid., 279.
43. Ibid., 278.
44. John Röhl, *Philip Eulenbergs politische Korrespondenz* (Boppard am Rhein, 1976).
45. Cited in *Der Spiegel*, No. 40 (1976), 215.
46. Höss, *Kommandant in Auschwitz*, 41.
47. Ibid., 81-82.
48. Pitrof, *Gegen Spartakus in München und Allgäu*, 127.
49. Demar, *Französische Frauen*, 113-14.
50. Von Selchow, *Hundert Tage*, 17-18.
51. Ibid., 55.
52. Gilbert, *Nürnberger Tagebuch*, 305-6.
53. On how fascism tried, however, to render *house work* directly significant for the maintenance of the *Reich* by suggesting there was an important link between the *Reich's* economic record and the responsible management of domestic affairs, see Mason, *Zur Lage der Frauen in Deutschland 1930 bis 1941*, 147-48. Women, too, got their fair share of the "grandeur of history," only not in the male domain.
54. Von Selchow, *Hundert Tage*, 352.
55. Blüher, *Wandervogel*, 247.
56. Goote, *Wir tragen das Leben*, 266.
57. Salomon, *Die Geächteten*, 246.

58. Jünger, *Kampf als inneres Erlebnis*, 96.
59. Morgan, *The Descent of Woman*, 229.
60. Dannecker/Reiche, *Der gewöhnliche Homosexuelle*, 327.
61. Blüher, *Die Rolle der Erotik*, 322.
62. Freud, *Three Essays on Sexuality*, SE, vol. 7, 230.
63. Rossbach, *Mein Weg durch die Zeit*, 148. See in addition, Sohn-Rethel, *Economy and Class Sructure*, 149; Charles Bloch, *Die SA*, 38, suspects Hitler was not aware of Röhm's homosexuality until 1932, which is not very credible; in Maser, *Frühgeschichte der NSDAP*, 192, Röhm is described as a "devious officer" who "indulged in homosexual vices"; "Röhm! Don't talk to me about that dirty homosexual bastard! They were all a bunch of perverse, blood-thirsty revolutionaries!" (Goering to Gilbert during the Nuremberg Trials, *Nürnberger Tagebuch*, 83.)
64. Rossbach, *Mein Weg*, 164.
65. See Waite, *Vanguard of Nazism*, 222-23.
66. On this, see Gumbel's works, but particularly Scheer, *Blut und Ehre*, and the section entitled "Die Legende der 400 Morde," 136-58 and 168ff. The principle of "the burning of the Reichstag" has a tradition right through the 1920s.
67. Gilbert, *Nuremberg Diary*, 175-80. In Gotthard Breit's dissertation, *Das Staats- und Gesellschaftsbild deutscher Generale beider Weltkriege im Spiegel ihrer Memoiren* (Freiburg, 1972), all this is referred to as the "Fritsch crisis." The word "homosexuality" is avoided entirely. There follows some academic kitsch: "The officers present were shocked and ashamed that the defamatory behavior of a Wehrmacht officer of the highest rank had made his dismissal unavoidable. In their eyes, a stain had been cast upon the honour of the entire officer corps. . . . Neither did they imagine that the head of state would send a supreme commmander of the armed forces to court on the basis of vague assertions alone" (180-84). The little angels! Four years before they had forced Hitler to get rid of Röhm because he wanted to retain power himself. But then some academic disciplines do accept trashy novels about Third Reich generals as dissertations. On Röhm and the generals see Sohn-Rethel, *Economy and Class Structure*, 140-50. Cf. Charles Bloch, *Die SA*, 71-74, 163. (At times Bloch is rather imprecise and fails to underpin large sections of factual description with evidence, 78, 94.)
68. Blüher, *Die Rolle der Erotik*, 26.
69. Gilbert, *Nuremberg Diary*, 254.
70. Gilbert, *Nürnberger Tagebuch*, 417.
71. Gilbert, *Nuremberg Diary*, 261.

Conclusion

From the Inside

1. Jünger, *Kampf als inneres Erlebnis*, 82.
2. Salomon, *Die Geächteten*, 262.
3. Ibid., 292 and 72.
4. Ibid., 240.
5. See Salomon also in *Nahe Geschichte*, 14ff. and in "Die Brigade Erhardt," in RDS, 122; von Oertzen, *Die deutschen Freikorps*, introduction and 389-90 particularly; on the officer corps, see Lettow-Vorbeck, *Mein Leben*, 35; Jünger, *Feuer und Blut*, 160; Melzer, "Die Auswirkungen des Kapp-Putsches in Leipzig," in JKR, 219; Osten, "Der Kampf um Oberschlesien," in JKR, 271; Fischer, "Die Täteherrschaft in München," in JKR, 151; Heinz, *Sprengstoff*, 87; Heinz, *Die Nation greift an*, 17; Schauwecker, *Aufbruch der Nation*, 92, 315; Killinger, *Das waren Kerle*, 19-20; Höfer, *Oberschlesien in der Aufstandszeit*, 115; Engelhardt, *Ritt nach Riga*, 10, 14; Ettighofer, *Revolver über*

der Stadt, 154; Schricker, *Rotmord*. . . , 10, 190-91; Stadtler, *Als Antibolschewist 1918/19*, 139; Buschbecker, *Wie unser Gesetz es befahl*, 21, 120, where they are not only all equal but *sons* too.

6. The first ("group") appears to be the most common and significant form. I would not maintain that the others do not arise, as Deleuze and Guattari do, following Sartre (*Anti-Oedipus*, e.g., 256-57). Individuals, at least, do exist. The most unlikely scenario is that a fantasy becomes the fantasy of an entire class. The fact that communist theoreticians have met with disaster in constructing a class consciousness should give us food for thought. At least *that* should be enough to put an end to the barbaric use of the principle that being determines consciousness.

7. Heinz, *Sprengstoff*, 161.

8. Dwinger, *Auf halbem Wege*, 209-10. "Sparks, never ceasing to spit their flames, flew from his fiery soul," writes Balla in "Rudolf Berthold," in Jünger (ed.), *Die Unvergessenen* (Berlin, 1930), 17.

9. Jünger, *Kampf als inneres Erlebnis*, 86, brings the point out in the clearest terms possible: "The spirit of the trenches is not a product of war. On the contrary, classes, races, parties, nations, all communities are countries in themselves, surrounded by walls and thick wires. Nothing but desert lies in between. Those who step outside are shot dead. Sometimes, someone will have a fit and smash their own head in." No other type of situation exists except this state of war. The armored body casts the rest of the world in its own mold.

10. See the section entitled "Germany and Versailles" in Canetti, *Crowds and Power*, 210-14. In Canetti's view, the first days of August 1914 were when "National Socialism was begotten," and the only point at which Hitler was truly part of the crowd was when he went down on his knees at the outbreak of war.

11. See in particular, Nagl, *Science Fiction in Deutschland*.

12. See Sohn-Rethel, *Economy and Class Structure*, 122, on the fatal propagandistic rivalry between the National Socialists and the German Communists against the bourgeoisie which later ensued.

13. This thought is developed in an unpublished paper by Erhard Lucas and Wolfgang Essbach, who curiously search for constructions of both bourgeois and proletarian world-historical missions in Marx.

14. Mann, *Mit Ehrhardt*, 195. Dwinger has almost exactly the same formulation in *Auf halbem Wege*, 294: the term here is the "bourgeoisie," as in Jünger's foreword to *Der Kampf um das Reich*, 7; Plaas, "Das Kapp-Unternehmen," in JKR, 172, 174; Nord, "Der Krieg im Baltikum," in JKR, 93; van Berk, "Rote Armee an der Ruhr," in JKR, 218; Melzer, *Die Auswirkungen des Kapp-Putsches in Leipzig*, 237; Mahnken, "Freikorps im Westen 1918/20," in HoDA, 94-95; Hotzel, "Der antibürgerliche Affekt," in HoDA, 345-55; Freska, *Kapitän Ehrhardt*, 93, 102, 95; Mann, *Mit Ehrhardt*, 28; von Selchow, *Hundert Tage*, 232; von Killinger, *Die SA*, 37; Salomon, *Die Geächteten*, 72-73; Dwinger, *Auf halbem Wege*, 170, 292; Delmar, *Französische Frauen*, 80; Röhm, *Geschichte eines Hochverräters*, 347; see also Röhm's remarks in Charles Bloch, *Die SA*, 12-13, 47-50, 79ff.; Goebbels, *Michael*, 119; Schauwecker, *Der feurige Weg*, 232; Eggers, *Von der Freiheit des Kriegers*, 22, 57; Eggers, *Vom mutigem Leben*, 42ff.; Ettighofer, *Revolver über der Stadt*, 23; Stadtler, *Als Antibolschewist 1918/19*, 168; Volck, *Rebellen um Ehre*, 52, 152; von Oertzen, *Die deutschen Freikorps*, 21-22; Guenther, *Kriegertum*, 197; *Die Legende von Hitlers Kindheit* portrays well the hate expressed by the phrase "nothing but a bourgeois" (192).

15. Jünger, *Feuer und Blut*, 20. For details see Schauwecker, *Aufbruch der Nation*, 9ff., 30-31, and Schauwecker's foreword to Hoeppener-Flatow, *Stosstrupp Markmann greift an;* W. von Schramm, *Schöpferische Kritik des Krieges*, 38; F. G. Jünger, *Krieg und*

Krieger, 54, 59: pre-war days seem to him in retrospect like a time of decaying old age (54).

16. Bronnen, *Rossbach*, 36.

17. The quantity and homogeneity of pre-war German literature, from which this idea emerges, means it is as relatively scrutable as it is copious and extensive—as the texts used here illustrate. I refer once again to Manfred Nagl's study of science fiction in Germany (on rebirth, macro-mechanization, exclusion of the "unconscious" complex encoded with femininity), Burte's works (*Wiltfeber, der ewige Deutsche*), or Frensen (*Jörn Uhl*), all of which Günther Hartung (of the GDR) includes in his critique of fascist literature, although he adheres to the dogmatic view that war brought out this genre's most strident features. (Hartung, "Über die deutsche faschistische Literatur," 3 parts, in *Weimarer Beiträge*, 3, 1968, special edition 2, 1968.) This is a misconception which is easily remedied by considering works such as *Das Menschenschlachthaus* by Wilhelm Lamszus, a book on the approaching war (it appeared in 1913 in Hamburg and sold 30,000 copies in its first year). For this writer, war is clearly a backdrop, a medium without which it would be impossible to articulate his condition and the fantasy of certain physical acts. The fact that war then actually broke out simplified and enhanced the process. At the same time, the Right failed to create a literature of *world war*. They did write about war, but not about *Weltkrieg*, although it is often mentioned. The most genuine book of world war is perhaps Beumelburg's *Sperrfeuer um Deutschland*, or Ettighofer's *Verdun*. For one of the many examples of comparable literature to appear after World War II, see Günter Fraschka, *Das letzte Aufgebot* (Rastatt, 1960), especially 32-59.

18. Sohn-Rethel, *Economy and Class Structure*, 136-37.

19. Heinz, *Sprengstoff*, 7; also, 9, 96, 118, 188; Heinz, *Die Nation greift an*, 74, 122; for a similar acount see Röhm, *Geschichte eines Hochverräters*, 363; Weller, *Peter Mönkelmann*, 85, 88-89; Goote, *Wir tragen das Leben*, 5; Goote, *Kamerad Berthold*, 235; Goote, *Die Fahne hoch*, 311; Salomon, "Die Gestalt des deutschen Freikorpskämpfers," in SB, 11; Solomon, *Die Geächteten*, 152; Nord, "Der Krieg im Baltikum," in JKR, 63; Gengler, *Berthold*, 131; Buschbecker, *Wie unser Gesetz es befahl*, 274-75; Freska, *Der Wanderer ins Nichts*, 13; Brandis, *Baltikumer*, 280; Bochow, *Soldaten ohne Befehl*, 251; Balla, "Rudolf Berthold," in Jünger, *Die Unvergessenen*, 15, 18; Goebbels, *Michael*, 116; Dwinger, *Auf halbem Wege*, 297; Jünger, *Kampf als inneres Erlebnis*, 45; Höss, *Kommandant in Auschwitz*, 29, 54-55, 124; Herzog, *Kameraden*, 251; Eggers, *Von der Freiheit des Kriegers*, 17ff., 29; Wrangell, *Geschichte des Baltenregiments*, 70; Werner Best, *Der Krieg und das Recht*, 152.

20. Dwinger, *Auf halbem Wege*, 10.

21. Salomon, *Die Geächteten*, 82. See also 95.

22. Benjamin, "Theorien ds deutschen Faschismus," in *Argument*, no. 30 (1964), 132.

23. Heinz, *Sprengstoff*, 10.

24. Cited in Lucas, *Märzrevolution*, vol. 3, manuscript.

25. Salomon, *Die Geächteten*, 66.

26. Ibid., 66.

27. Ibid., 69.

28. It must be emphasized once more that very little of this is "subjective." In Serge Leclaire, *La realite du desir*, 245, we read, "if one indefinitely runs up against the same set of pure singularities, one can feel confident that he has drawn near the singularity of the subject's desire" (cited in Deleuze/Guattari, *Anti-Oedipus*, 324). One almost never comes across such "singularities" in fascist literature, since they are all subject to repression. Their absence indicates that it is not simply any "ideas," "contents," that are repressed but desire, the productive power of the unconscious itself.

In our case this is expressed by the habit of all the soldierly authors to treat their subject matter in a very similar manner. The literary "capacity" of most of them is that they have written a book already in existence, one which *fits in*.

29. See Jünger's introduction to *Der Kampf um das Reich*, 6; Jünger, *Kampf als inneres Erlebnis*, 47; Plaas, "Das Kapp-Unternehmen," in JKR, 178; van Berk, "Rote Armee," in JKR, 214; Kloppe, "Kameraden," in JKR, 256; Osten, "Der Kampf," in JKR, 258; Loewenfeld, "Die Brigade L.," in RDS, 157; Heinz, "Die Freikorps retten Oberschlesien," in HoDA, 88; Heinz, *Sprengstoff*, 10, 26, 111, 163, 225; Mann, *Mit Ehrhardt*, 133, 137-38, 169, 179, 183, 194; Freska, *Kapitän Ehrhardt*, 93; Von Steinaecker, *Mit der ED ins Baltikum*, 17-18; Glombowski, *Die Organisation Heinz*, 113; Salomon, *Die Geächteten*, 15; Lettow-Vorbeck, *Mein Leben*, 182-83, 185-86, 191; Gengler, *Berthold*, 94, 107, 144; Killinger, *Ernstes und Heiteres*, 71, 78; Wittmann, *Erinnerungen der Eisernen Schar*, 102-3; Müller, *Soldat und Vaterland*, 12; Stadtler, *Als Antibolschewist 1918/19*, 114; Buschbecker, *Wie unser Gesetz*, 137-38; von Kessel, *Handgranaten und rote Fahnen*, 111; Volck, *Rebellen um Ehre*, 95; Maercker, *Vom Kaiserheer*, 65; Schulz, *Ein Freikorps im Industriegebiet*, 32, 34, 39; Rossbach, *Mein Weg durch die Zeit*, 56; Eggers, *Von der Freiheit des Kriegers*, 30; von Oertzen, *Die deutschen Freikorps*, 61-62.

30. Taken from a poster publicizing the *Westphalian "Münster" Batallion of Volunteers*, signed by Captain von Pfeffer, January 1919, in SB, 85.

31. H. Gilbert, *Landsknechte*, 144.

32. Salomon, *Die Geächteten*, 266.

33. See Waite, *Vanguard of Nazism*, Chapter 5, "The Baltic Adventure," 84ff.; Kavass/Sprudzs (eds.), *Baltic States* (Buffalo New York, 1972), 42-43; von Oertzen, *Baltenland*, 316ff.; Salomon, *Nahe Geschichte*, 47ff.; Wrangell, in *Geschichte des Baltenregiments*, encapsulates the whole story in one sentence: "After a coup on 16 April had toppled the radical Latvian government and replaced it with one more sympathetic to Germany, a fear had grown that German influence would become too great" (84); on the other hand, there are pages of the most trivial details on troop movements. In a similar vein, H. von Megede passes over the affair in one sentence without mentioning the coup in "Hakenkreuz am Stahlhelm," 21, in the anthology *Volk ans Gewehr*, published in 1934 and edited by Walter Gruber, whose title ran "Consultant at the Foreign Office of the NSDAP"; in Czech-Jochberg, *Im Osten Feuer*, we have the harmless sentence: " 'What about our eighty acres?' bellow the soldiers," (114) while three pages later he writes of Manteuffel's actions, "With only a handful of people he carried out the coup brilliantly" (117). Etc., etc.

34. E.g., Steinaecker, *Mit der ED im Baltikum*, 55; Meyer, *Das Jäger-Bataillon der ED im Kampfe*, 45.

35. SB, 478, includes a facsimile of a certificate confirming that Leo Schlageter, a lieutenant in the reserves, is entitled to "one hundred acres of settlement land" in "Kurland." It was printed as "proof" of his entitlement. The trouble is that it was issued on 1 November 1919 (long after the putsch against the Ulmanis and after the *Freikorps* were defeated in the Baltic). The certificate is signed by his own Regiment Commander and by nobody else. In other words, the Baltic campaigners had their own officers confirm their "entitlement" to settlement land (which they themselves had then thrown away), then proceeded to use the "documents" as evidence of Latvian treachery. But let's be serious about this: the document is "genuine," really.

36. Cited in Heinz Brauweiler, *Der Anteil des Stahlhelms*, in HoDA, 221.

37. Mann, *Mit Ehrhardt*, 138-39. Also, Bochow, *Soldaten ohne Befehl*, 141ff.

38. Bloch, *Erbschaft dieser Zeit*, 58-59. See 66-67 too.

Deutsche Legion
Regiment Baden.

Kurland, den 1. November 1919.

Auf Grund des am 6. Oktober 1919 zwischen der Deutschen-Legion und dem Ober-
befehlshaber der Russischen Westarmee geschlossenen Vertrages, wonach der Vertrag
zwischen der Deutschen Regierung und der provisorischen Lettländischen Regierung vom
9. und 24. Dezember 1918 (betr. Bürgerrecht und Ansiedlung deutscher Baltenkämpfer)
anerkannt wird,

wird dem:

bestätigt dass er das Anrecht auf _____ Morgen Siedlungsland in Kurland
besitzt.

Der Inhaber dieser Bescheinigung erhält hiermit nach oben genanntem Vertrage
das Russische Bürgerrecht.

Rittmeister und Kommandeur.

39. Salomon, *Die Geächteten*, 73.
40. Jünger, *Kampf als inneres Erlebnis*, 86.
41. Salomon, *Die Geächteten*, 237-38; see also Nord, "Der Krieg im Baltikum," in JKR, 91; Stoffregen, *Vaterland*, 70; Buschbecker, *Wie unser Gesetz es befahl*, 12; Volck, *Rebellen*, 58; Engelhardt, *Ritt nach Riga*, 11; Brandis, *Baltikumer*, 101-2; von Kessel, *Handgranaten und rote Fahnen*, 191; F Schauwecker, *Aufbruch der Nation*, 192, 299.
42. Goebbels, *Michael*, 77.
43. Goebbels tried in vain to have his literary manuscripts published. His application for editorship at the *Berliner Tageblatt*, "where some liberal Jews held positions of some influence," was unsuccessful. (Bloch, *Die SA*, 18.)
44. Jünger, *Feuer und Blut*, 156.
45. Erickson, "The Legend of Hitler's Childhood" develops this idea well, and his portrayal of the conflict between the German boy and his father is sensitive and precise.(298) He too concludes that Hitler's significance as *Führer* should not be looked for at the level of father. But his phrase is not quite adequate: "a glorified older brother, who took over prerogatives of the father without overidentifying with them" (304). This formulation fails to bring out the idea that the power of the *Führer* was significant because it radically *by-passed* (unjust) paternal power. Its source was derived not from the personal level but *directly* from the sphere of abstract social power. By the same token, it is right to criticize the following sort of wording because of its use of "identification": "The identification with the father which in spite of everything had been well established in early childhood" (302). Sohn-Rethel gets nearer to the heart of the matter: "Blind faith in the *Führer* is sustained when the social synthesis of private interests is transcended and it is realized that this synthesis may proceed in terms of private interests whenever this is possible. The vacuum created by this transcendence is thus filled by the enormous power of the 'leader.'" (*Ökonomie und Klassenstruktur*, 145; this passage does not

appear in the English version—Tr.'s note.) The "vacuum" of the "transcendence" of "private interests" is filled by the phallus on high.

46. Jünger, *Feuer und Blut*, 226-73. Or he can "think of a god with a smiling face through whose hands these bright fibers can slip," *Kampf als inneres Erlebnis*, 108.

47. Salomon, *Die Geächteten*, 151.

48. See Freud, *The Interpretation of Dreams*, SE, vol. 5, 357-58.

49. Hocquenghem, *Homosexual Desire*, 91.

50. Salomon, *Die Geächteten*, 472.

51. I deliberately put "he" because the fascists described here are men. The character of female fascism is an area for women to study. My suspicion is that it is fairly different from the male type. Only then would the true force of the double-binds trapping relations beween the sexes become apparent. Maria-Antonietta Macciochi's *Jungfrauen, Mütter und ein Führer, Frauen im Faschismus*, (Berlin, 1976) rises to the task in the title only.

52. L. Tiger, *Men in Groups*. Morgan, *The Descent of Woman*, 219ff.

53. Jünger, *Kampf als inneres Erlebnis*, 47.

54. Ibid., 56.

55. See the last section in Chapter 2 of the present work.

56. Jünger, *Kampf als inneres Erlebnis*, 48.

57. Salomon, *Die Geächteten*, 367.

58. See Benjamin, *Understanding Brecht*, 62.

59. Jünger's introduction to *Der Kampf um das Reich*, 9.

60. Salomon, *Die Geächteten*, 471.

61. Reflecting on his life in 1950, Rossbach proudly remarks: "Noske—in my considered opinion a truly fine fellow. He agreed three times to join us in our later involvements. Without him, the *Freikorps*, or the *Reichswehr*, the Soviet-German border would have already been running along the Elbe or the Rhein for twenty-nine years" (*Mein Weg durch die Zeit*, 59). He soon learned the best way to be "de-nazified" by the Western powers and the FRG.

62. Salomon, *Die Geächteten*, 367.

63. Ibid., 79.

64. Heinz, *Sprengstoff*, 75.

65. Salomon, *Die Geächteten*, 76.

66. Ibid., 73. See also 379, 383, and Heinz, *Die Nation*, 73; Dwinger, *Auf halbem Wege*, 239, 232.

67. This is Sohn-Rethel's assumption, quite casually asserted, in *Ökonomie und Klassenstruktur*, 189. (Omitted from English version—Tr.'s note.)

68. Freud occasionally cast that gaze. Writing on the ego in *An Outline of Psycho-Analysis*, (SE, vol. XXIII, 199) he says: "Starting from conscious perception it has subjected to its influence ever larger regions and deeper strata of the id, and, in the persistence with which it maintains its dependence on the external world, it bears the indelible stamp of its origin (as it might be 'Made in Germany')." He then proceeded, however, happily to turn his attention to the ego's ability to dam in, an ability to which he accorded such import, but failed to appreciate that the analysis of the real ego "Made in Germany" had diverted at least some of the interest shown in speculation about the "death drive."

69. Peasant mothers are included not only because so many of their sons figured in the *Freikorps* and subsequent organizations of fascist men. My view is that under capitalism, the peasantry—or at least the small peasantry—found itself in a position alllowing it in many ways to become a stratum-fighting-on-two-fronts. The term "strata-fighting-on-two-fronts," as I have used it here, by no means refers merely to differentiation within the global term "middle class," or to a position in the production

process. It signifies rather a place in the social and political hierarchy which is subject to certain pressures from both "the top" and "the bottom." These pressure brought themselves to bear no less for the small peasant than for the petty bourgeois. On the contrary, the small peasant was threatened by the unprofitability of his holding and thus stood to lose his independence, or at least his perceived independence, which made him feel far superior to the worker. Because the idea of the "free patriarch," and the adherence by the family to this idea, were part of his immediate experience, the threat that he might have to go and work in a factory was as uncomfortable for him as the threat of proletarianization was for the petty bourgeois. Simultaneously, those self-conscious sections of the proletariat, which as the class bearing the seeds of progress were "marching into the future," threatened seriously to damage the conception the peasant had of himself as an important bearer of culture. It is not surprising that in a situation typical for a stratum-fighting-on-two-fronts, such large numbers of peasant sons suddenly opted for social spheres and organizations which promised them access to POWER (which they were threatened with losing), instead of for a new position in the social production process.

On the difference between town and country, see in addition the section on the lack of timing in Bloch, *Erbschaft dieser Zeit*, 104ff.

70. Freud, *Three Essays on the Theory of Sexuality*, SE, vol. VII, 161.
71. Reich, *Reich Speaks of Freud*, 6.
72. Jünger, *Kampf als inneres Erlebnis*, 24.
73. Ibid., 55ff.
74. Ibid., 3.
75. Goote, *Kamerad Berthold*, 235.
76. Cited in anonymous, *Naziführer sehen dich an*, 45.
77. Heinz, *Die Nation greift an*, 191.
78. Jünger, *Kampf als inneres Erlebnis*, 107.
79. Erbt, *Der Narr von Kreyingen*, 170.
80. Salomon, *Die Geächteten, 144-45. For a similar account see Nord, "Der Krieg im Baltikum," in JKR, 91.*

Peace
1. Karl Demeter, *Das deutsche Heer und seine Offiziere*, 22.
2. Waite, *Vanguard*, 1-13: "The Ebert Conversations"; Wilhelm Groener, *Lebenserinnerungen, Jugend, Generalstab, Weltkrieg* (Göttingen, 1957), 473ff.; Gustav Noske, *Von Kiel bis Kapp* (Berlin, 1920), 112-13; Harold J. Gordon, *Die Reichswehr und die Weimarer Republik 1919-26* (Frankfurt, 1959), 18, 26.
3. Goote, *Wir tragen das Leben*, 51. Similarly, see Dwinger's Pahlen in *Auf halbem Wege*, 310.
4. Von Selchow, *Hundert Tage*, 304.
5. Gilbert, *Landsknechte*, 136-7.
6. Dwinger, *Auf halbem Wege*, 24-25. See also Dwinger, *Die letzten Reiter*, 386.
7. Dwinger, *Auf halbem Wege*, 293.
8. Höss, *Kommandant*, 35.
9. Goote, *Kamerad Berthold*, 244.
10. Von Zeschau, "Streiflichter aus den Kämpfen von Litauen," in SB, 135. See also Gilbert, *Landsknechte*, 237.
11. Which they often did not want. See, for example, Thor Goote, *Wir tragen das Leben*, 189.
12. Ibid., 192-93.
13. Ibid., 193.

14. Mann, *Mit Ehrhardt*, 214.
15. Dwinger, *Auf halbem Wege*, 239.
16. Weller, *Peter Mönkemann*, 50-51.
17. See, for example, Salomon, *Die Geächteten*, 246; Salomon, *Nahe Geschichte*, 18-19, 71; F. Solf, *Deutschlands Wiederauferstehung 1934*, 27; the poster in RDS, 126, put up by the putsch soldiers on 14 March 1920; Schaper, "Freikorpsgeist—Annaberg," in RDS, 165; Engelhardt, *Ritt nach Riga*, 9; Ettighofer, *Revolver über der Stadt*, 31; Buschbecker, *Wie unser Gesetz*, 5; von Kessel, *Handgranaten*, 163; Freiwald, *Der Weg der braunen Kämpfer*, 233; Guenther, *Deutsches Kriegertum*, 201.
18. Waite in particular has elucidated the extent to which the *Freikorps* met the "psychological and social needs of the junior officer," in *Vanguard of Nazism*, 48-49.
19. Jünger's fear of ridicule is most revealing. "Films" portray "an extraordinary degree of calculated cruelty." He saw in the "grotesque movie . . . merely . . . a series of painful and vicious incidents." (On pain, in *Blätter und Steine*, Hamburg, 1934, 204.) On Hasek/Schwejk: "The fact that this anarchistic buffoon has been able to delight even the informed German public is symptomatic of a condition that requires something other than literary treatment." His reaction to laughter really is to reach for a hand grenade (Jünger, "Drei Soldaten. Zur Spiegelung des Weltkriegs in der Gegenwartsdichtung," in Eckart, *Blätter für evangelische Geisteskultur*, 4, (1928), 255).
20. Freska, *Kapitän Ehrhardt*, 143-44.
21. Mann, *Mit Ehrhardt*, 11.
22. Ekkehard, *Sturmgeschlecht*, 89.
23. Weller, *Peter Mönkemann*, 242.
24. They often maintain they are not fighting for themselves. See Loewenfeld, "Das Freikorps von L.," in RDS, 156, or Salomon, "Die Brigade Ehrhardt," in RDS, 122. On the other hand, they are never contented unless they get into the position they themselves need. Their way of fighting "for themselves" is to fight "for the whole"— see the section in Chapter 3 on "The Whole." Parties are the ones fighting for interests, and the contempt shown for parties exceeds even that shown for the "political." Parties are partialities, milling masses, solvents. See, for example, the political tract of Captain Ehrhardt, *Deutschlands Zukunft*, (1921), in which constant attacks are launched on "party egoists," the powerful individuals leading the way (5, 22-23, 34). One of the demands made by the Kapp Putsch, in which Ehrhardt had a military hand, was that "specialist ministers" (as opposed to party ministers) should be appointed. Even the NSDAP regarded itself not as a "party" in the bourgeois sense but as a movement.
25. J. Nothaas, *Beiträage zur Statistik Bayerns*, cited in Waite, *Vangurd of Nazism*, 48.
26. Predominantly "on the insistence of the Allies," as Lucas emphasizes, *Märzrevolution*, vol. 1, 86ff.
27. See Lüttwitz, *Im Kampf gegen die Novemberrevolution*, 112-17; Salomon, *Nahe Geschichte*, 78; Waite, *Vanguard of Nazism*, 140ff.
28. Mann, *Mit Ehrhardt*, 206; Heydebreck, *Wehrwölfe*, 120-21.
29. For example, Mann, *Mit Ehrhardt*, 206; Freska, *Kapitän Ehrhardt*, 192; G. Krüger, *Die Brigade Ehrhardt*, 63; Gumbel, *Verschwörer*, 76; Lucas, *Märzrevolution*, vol. 2, 102.
30. Mann, *Mit Ehrhardt*, 78.
31. Details in Waite, *Vanguard of Nazism*, 40-41; Lucas, *Märzrevolution*, vol. 1, 67; Mann, *Mit Ehrhardt*, 78; Curator, *Putsche*, 102.
32. In SB, 37.
33. Maercker, *Vom Kaiserheer*, 56.
34. Mann, *Mit Ehrhardt*, 214ff.; see also Loewenfeld, "Das Freikorps von L.," in RDS, 150; Salomon, "Die Brigade Ehrhardt," in RDS, 120; Zobel, *Zwischen Krieg und Frieden*, 114.

35. Salomon regarded as "subaltern" the accusation that the *Freikorps* had joined up because of the material rewards (*Nahe Geschichte*, 21).

36. Maercker, *Vom Kaiserheer*, 39.

37. A. Zickler, *Reichswehr gegen Rote Armee, was im Ruhrgebiet geschah* (Berlin, 1920), 21.

38. See Theodor Geiger, *Die soziale Schichtung des deutschen Volkes* (Stuttgart, 1932), 1-15, 72-138; S.M. Lipset, "Fascism—Left—Right—Center," reprinted in J. Gusfield (ed.), *Protest Reform and Revolt*, (London, 1972); H. A. Winckler, *Mittelstand, Demokratie und Nationalsozialismus. Die politische Entwicklung von Handwerk und Kleinhandwerk in der Weimarer Republik* (Cologne, 1972); U. Kadritzke, *Angestellte— die geduldigen Arbeiter. Zur Soziologie und sozialen Bewegung der Angestellten* (Frankfurt, Cologne, 1973); L. Trotsky, *The Struggle Against Fascism in Germany*, introduced by E. Mandel (New York: Pathfinder, 1970).

39. See Sohn-Rethel, *Economy and Class Structure*, 132. Since at this point the English edition strays somewhat from the German original, see Sohn-Rethel, *Ökonomie und Klassenstruktur*, 191. (Tr.)

40. "My opinion is that right from the beginning Germany's adventurers, whether they have been only slightly or hardly aware of it, have always emulated Napoleon," writes Heinrich Mann, *Ein Zeitalter wird besichtigt*, 9. According to Bruno Grabinski, *Neuere Mystik. Der Weltkrieg im Aberglauben und im Lichte der Prophetie* (Hildesheim, 1916), the following "prophetic vision, clad in verse," attributed to "the poet Robert Hamerling (1830-1887)" appeared in "almost the entire press":

> Immersing my visionary eyes in eternal light
> I see faces seeped in the future rising in my soul.
> And a tall goddess stepping ever nearer
> through the darkness, shrouding you, of times distant and heavy
>   with deed.
> O you who art the twentieth since Christ's birth, rumbling with
>   weapons and commanding admiration,
> One day the worlds to come will call you the "Germanic century."
> German People, the wide world will tremble to dust before you,
> For you will soon pass stormy judgment upon your enemies.
> Your strong feet will trample upon England's untouched soil,
> And the vapors of your enemy's blood will rise as high as the
>   heavens.
> Russia, the clay giant, you shall topple and crumble,
> And the German eagle shall nest in the Baltic's rich land.
> Austria, you thought youself dead! Yet before these twenty years
>   pass,
> You will stand proud and mighty as youth before the Peoples:
> Trembling, bowing before your feats, they will call you
> Ruler of the East, the Second German Kingdom.
> A Habsburg will proudly wear the crown of the new Poland!
> And under him, in freedom new, the Ukraine will shine!
> O dear people, I can already hear the sound of cymbals,
> Violins, drums, and trumpets—the great victory parade.
> Herald the time of the heroes! You are entwined in Fate:
> Do not fear your enemies for I have given you the truth.
> (Grabinski, 226)

(Meine hellen Seheraugen tauch' ich ein in ew'gem Lichte,
Und vor meine Seele treten zukunftstrunkene Gesichte.
Durch das euch verhüllte Dunkel tatenschwangrer, ferner Zeiten
Seh ich eine hohe Göttin nah und immer näher schreiten.
Dich, o Zwanzigstes, seit Christ, waffenklirrend und bewundert,
Wird die Nachwelt einstens nennen das "Germanische Jahrhundert."
Deutsches Volk, die weite Erde wird von dir im Staub erzittern;
Denn Gericht wirst du bald halten mit den Feinden in Gewittern.
Englands unberührten Boden wird dein starker Fuss zerstampfen —
Überall wird auf zum Himmel hoch das Blut der Feinde dampfen,
Und den törnernen Giganten Russland stürzest du, zerborsten,
In der Ostsee reichen Lande wird der deutsche Adler horsten.
Österreich, du totgeglaubtes! Eh' die zwanzig Jahr vergehen,
Wirst du stolz und jugendkräftig vor den vielen Völkern stehen.
Und sie werden dich, erzitternd, beugend sich vor deinem Ruhm,
Herrscherin des Ostens nennen, zweites deutsches Kaisertum.
Mit des neuen Polens Krone wird sich stolz ein Habsburg kränzen!
Unter ihn, in junger Freiheit, wird die Ukraina glänzen!
O geliebtes Volk, ich höre stimmen schon die Zimbeln, Geigen,
Und die Pauken und Trompeten zu dem grossen Siegesreigen.
Freue dich die Heldenzeiten! Das Geschick ist dir verbündet —
Fürchte nichts von deinen Feinden, Wahrheit hab' ich dir verkündet.)

Continued in the Baltic in 1919: "Lonely, outlawed, discarded by a fatherland which no longer deserved to bear that name, the best blood of the nation, more willing than any other to be sacrificed, waged battle at this desolate outpost to save the last remnants of the dream of a German Empire." (Bronnen, *Rossbach*, 71.) See also Salomon, *Die Geächteten*, 297; Salomon, *Nahe Geschichte*, 80.

41. Schaper, for example, evokes the continuing existence of this "spirit" in "Freikorpsgeist — Annaberg," in RDS, 161ff.
42. Killinger, *Der Klabautermann*, 139.
43. Jünger, *Kampf als inneres Erlebnis*, 18.
44. Herzog, *Kameraden*, 230-31.
45. Plaas, "Das Kapp-Unternehmen," in JKR, 171. The time waiting for "the day" to come was usually spent in the military. The small number of soldiers and officers in the NSDAP before 1922 corroborates this picture (see the statistics in Maser, *Frühgeschichte der NSDAP*, 255). Around that time, the soldier males were with the active counterrevolutionary groups and paramilitary organizations (just have a look at the list for Bavaria alone in Maser, 168). Initially, there was such a general hatred of parties that those like the NSDAP were also despised. The latter became interesting only when there was no longer anything to do involving weapons.
46. Loewenfeld, "Das Freikorps von Loewenfeld," in RDS, 157.
47. Sohn-Rethel, *Economy and Class Structure*, 137.
48. Sohn-Rethel, *Ökonomie und Klassenstruktur*, footnote 4, 197. (This footnote does not appear in the English version — Tr.'s note.)
49. See — for one of the better examples — Trotsky's essays on German fascism, *The Struggle Against Fascism in Germany*, introduced by E. Mandel, (New York: Pathfinder, 1970). Apart from his being certain, by contrast with the Third International, that a fascist victory would lead to war with the Soviet Union, and apart from his more realistic assessment of the significance of the middle classes than is usually found in the writings of communist theoreticians, there is in Trotsky a strong trace of authoritarian and elitist

certainty of being better, superior. He is constantly at pains to *expose* the "deceit" of fascism. Much of this is reminiscent of the arrogance that surfaces in many of Bloch's essays on fascism (for example, *Vom Hasard zur Katastrophe*, (Frankfurt, 1972), although *Erbschaft dieser Zeit* is an exception in this respect). The "truth" of many of their insights loses force because both of them are inclined to bask in their own intellectual brilliance and occasionally to turn out a feature article written by a star-struck journalist. Clever guys.

50. Leni Riefenstahl's documentary film *Triumph des Willens*, 1934. Riefenstahl was commissioned by Hitler to film the 1934 NSDAP Party Rally in Nuremberg using eighteen cameras. The montage of the film did not correspond to the actual chronology of the rally. It was edited to produce the greatest effect and excitement, and the music played as the party members parade is often not the original sound. Riefenstahl, however, does not provide a commentary. The following quotes from the party rally are transcriptions of the original soundtrack of the speeches the film recorded.

51. The most he might be is a "delegate of his mother" — this is Helm Stierlin overextending the use of a (good) term from family therapy in his book on Hitler. Once again, world history is oedipalized. (H. Stierlin, *Adolf Hitler. Familienperspektiven*, [Frankfurt, 1975]). The basic tenet of the book is that Hitler functioned as a maternal delegate.

52. From the song of the Hitler Youth, written by Baldur von Schirach.

53. "But it was when the ritual was formally agreed upon — indeed it was almost canonized — that I first became aware the whole thing was meant to be taken literally. I had always believed all these parades, processions, and initiation cermonies to be part of a virtuoso propagandistic review. It was now clear that for Hitler it was a matter of founding a church" (Albert Speer, *Spandauer Tagebücher*, 292-93). To my mind, Bloch, who gives an account of the religious origins and traditions of Third Reich terminology (*Erbschaft dieser Zeit*, 126-60), and who called upon revolutionary propaganda to win back the religious territory which had been so carelessly left to the Nazis, emphasizes too much the idea of the "enormous fabrication" (*Falsifikat*) which the Nazis had constructed by fulfilling dreams and promising happiness. The reality of the feelings displayed by the masses of people involved is not adequately covered by the concept of "fabrication." What use is it to those who have joined the great ranks of people to escape fragmentation if he who uses the word claims to have the "right answer"? In this connection, the formulation offered by Burke seems quite inapt. He maintains that the Nazis "bastardized patterns of thought that were originally theological" (Burke, *Die Rhetorik in Hitlers "Mein Kampf"* [Frankfurt, 1967], 33).

54. As Lionel Tiger put it in *Men in Groups*. And his success in this respect was far from imaginary. See Daniel Lerner in collaboration with I. de Sola Pool and G. K. Schueller, *The Nazi Elite* (Stanford, 1951), particularly section 4, "The Rise of the Plebeian," 34ff., and 5, "Specialists on Violence," 53ff.; see also, Wolfgang Zapf, *Wandlungen der deutschen Elite. Ein Zirkulationsmodell deutscher Führungsgruppen 1919-1961* (Munich, 1965), especially 51ff.; Franz Neumann, *Behemoth, the Structure and Practice of National Socialism 1933-1944* (New York), especially 365ff. All these show that some domains of power were accessible only via promotion through party organizations. Other routes did not exist. The interesting point is that spheres which tended to hold fewer promises of the delights of male groupings, such as ministerial bureaucracies, did not usually fit in with this pattern. In such cases, the castes of academics maintained their stronghold (see Zapf, 54; Neumann, 370-71). The same was true of top-level managers in industry (see Zapf, 55; Neumann, 388). It was not until toward the end of the war that the NSDAP, taking emergency measures, began to occupy crucial positions in these spheres.

55. Reich, *Reich Speaks of Freud*, 70ff.
56. Deleuze/Guattari, *Anti-Oedipus*, 257.
57. Ibid., 118-19.
58. Mayakovsky, "To Sergei Yessenin," in *Mayakovsky*, edited and translated by H. Marshall (London: Dobson Books, 1965).
59. Walter Benjamin, "Theses on the Philosophy of History," in *Illuminations*, edited and introduced by H. Arendt, translated by H. Zohn (London: Jonathan Cape, 1970), 259-60: "A Klee painting named 'Angelus Novus' shows an angel looking as though he is about to move away from something he is fixedly contemplating. His eyes are staring, his mouth is open, his wings are spread. This is how one pictures the angel of history. His face is turned toward the past. Where we perceive a chain of events, he sees one single catastrophe which keeps piling wreckage upon wreckage and hurls it in front of his feet. The angel would like to stay, awaken the dead, and make whole what has been smashed. But a storm is blowing from paradise; it has got caught in his wings with such violence that the angel can no longer close them. This storm irresistably propels him into the future to which his back is turned, while the power of debris before him grows skyward. This storm is what we call progress."
60. At least in my opinion, it is not entirely fitting to express surprise about "the horrific acts that were, without design, to be committed by a nation which must have held the rest of the world in as much respect in 1933 as it does today" (Zmarzlik, "Die Vernichtung des Warchauer Ghettos," in *Wieviel Zukunft hat unsere Vergangenheit* (Munich, 1970), 53.
61. Freud, *The Question of Lay Analysis*, SE, vol. XX, 212.
62. Reich, *The Mass Psychology of Fascism*, 44ff.
63. Ibid., 51.

Bibliography

Bibliography

Primary sources and other works mentioned only once in context, or contributing relatively little to the progress of arguments, have generally been omitted here. The endnotes give a more complete picture of the literature I have used.

Abbreviations

The following abbreviations appear after the titles of works taken from the anthologies listed below [section 2].

HoDA	Hotzel, Curt. *Deutscher Aufstand*
JKR	Jünger, Ernst. *Der Kampf um das Reich*
RDS	Roden, Hans. *Deutsche Soldaten*
SB	Salomon, Ernst. *Das Buch vom deutschen Freikorpskämpfer*

1. Novels, Biographies, Journals

Balla, Erich. *Landsknechte wurden wir. Abenteuer aus dem Baltikum.* Berlin, 1932.

Bochow, Martin. *Soldaten ohne Befehl.* Berlin, 1933.

———. *Sie wurden Männer.* Berlin, 1935.

Brandis, Cordt von. *Baltikumer. Schicksal eines Freikorps.* Berlin, 1939.

Bronnen, Arnolt. *O.S.* Berlin, 1929. Translated under the title *O.S.* London: Secker, 1930.

———. *Rossbach.* Berlin, 1930.

Buschbecker, Karl Matthias. *Wie unser Gesetz es befehl.* Berlin, 1936.

Dwinger, Edwin Erich. *Die letzten Reiter.* Jena, 1935.

———. *Auf halbem Wege.* Jena, 1939.

Eggers, Kurt. *Der Berg der Rebellen.* Leipzig, 1937.

Ekkehard, Friedrich. *Sturmgeschlecht. Zweimal 9. November.* Munich, 1941.

Erbt, Wilhelm. *Der Narr von Kreyingen. Der Roman der deutschen Revolution.* Berlin, 1924.

Ettighoffer, Paul Coelestin. *Revolver über den Stadt. Der Kampf um Mönchengladbach 1923*. Mönchen-Gladbach, 1936.
_____. *Sturm 1918*. Gütersloh, 1941.
Ewers, Hanns Heinz. *Reiter in deutscher Nacht*. Stuttgart, 1932. Translated under the title *Riders of the Night*. New York: Day, 1939.
Freksa, Friedrich. *Der Wanderer ins Nichts*. Munich, 1920.
_____. *Kapitän Erhardt, Abenteuer und Schicksal*. Berlin, 1924.
Gengler, Ludwig F. *Rudolf Berthold, Sieger in 44 Luftschlachten. Erschlagen im Bruderkampf für Deutschlands Freiheit*. Berlin, 1934.
Gilbert, Hubert E. *Landsknechte*. Hannover, 1930.
Goebbels, Josef. *Michael. Ein deutsches Schicksal in Tagebuchblättern*. Munich, 1929.
Goote, Thor (i.e. Johannes M. Berg). *Wir fahren den Tod*. Berlin, 1930.
_____. *Wir tragen das Leben. Der Nachkriegsroman*. Berlin, 1932.
_____. *Die Fahne hoch*. Berlin, 1933.
_____. *Kamerad Berthold der "unvergleichliche Franke." Bild eines deutschen Soldaten*. Hamburg, n.d., copyright Braunschweig, 1937.
Grünberg, Karl. *Brennende Ruhr*, vol. 2. Berlin, 1952.
Hagener, Hermann. *Lava*. Berlin, 1921.
Heinz, Friedrich Wilhelm. *Sprengstoff*. Berlin, 1930.
Herzog, Rudolf. *Kameraden*. Berlin, 1944, originally published Stuttgart, 1922.
_____. *Wieland der Schmied*. Stuttgart, 1924.
_____. *Mann im Sattel*. Berlin, 1935.
Heyderbreck, Peter von. *Wir Wehrwölfe. Erinnerungen eines Freikorpsführers*. Leipzig, 1931.
Hollenbach, H H. *Opfergang*. Hamburg, 1932.
Höss, Rudolf. *Kommandant in Auschwitz*. Munich, 1963. Höss's own title for his memoirs was *Meine Psyche. Werden, Leben und Erleben*.
Jünger, Ernst. *Der Kampf als inneres Erlebnis*. Berlin, 1922.
_____. *In Stahlgewittern*. Berlin, 1922. Translated under the title *The Storm of Steel*. London: Chatto, 1929.
_____. *Feuer und Blut*. Berlin, 1929.
Killinger, Manfred von. *Der Klabautermann. Eine Lebensgeschichte*. Munich, 1936.
Kohlhaas, Wilhelm. *Der Häuptling und die Republik. Die Geschichte eines Irrtums*. Stuttgart, 1933.
Lettow-Vorbeck, Paul von. *Mein Leben*. Biberbach a. d. Riss, 1957.
Mann, Rudolf. *Mit Ehrhardt durch Deutschland*. Berlin, 1921.
Niemöller, Martin. *Vom U-Boot zur Kanzel*. Berlin, 1934. Translated under the title *From U-Boat to Pulpit*. London: Hodge, 1936.
Ottwalt, Ernst. *Ruhe und Ordnung. Roman aus dem Leben der nationalgesinnten Jugend*. Berlin, 1929.
Richter, Horst. *Freiwilliger Soltau. Mit der Eisernen Division im Baltikum*. Berlin, 1933.
Röhm, Ernst. *Die Geschichte eines Hochverräters*. Munich, 1934, fourth edition, originally published 1928.
Rossbach, Gerhard. *Mein Weg durch die Zeit. Erinnerungen und Bekenntnisse*. Weilburg/Lahn, 1950.
Salomon, Ernst. *Die Geächteten*. Berlin, 1930. Translated under the title *The Outlaws (Die Geäachteten)*. London: Cape; New York: P. Smith, 1935.
_____. *Die Kadetten*. Berlin, 1933.
Schauwecker, Franz. *Der feurige Weg*. Berlin, 1928. Translated under the title *The Fiery Way*. London: Dent, 1929.
_____. *Im Todesrachen. Die deutsche Seele im Weltkriege*. Halle, 1919.
_____. *Aufbruch der Nation*. Berlin, 1929.

Schramm, Wilhelm Ritter von. *Die Roten Tage*. Munich, 1933.
Selchow, Bogislav von. *Hundert Tage aus meinem Leben*. Leipzig, 1936.
Solf, Major Ferdinand. *Deutschlands Auferstehung: 1934*. Naumberg a. d. Saale, 1921.
Stadtler, Eduard. *Als Antibolschewist 1918/19*. Düsseldorf, 1935.
Stenbock-Fermor, Alexander. *Freiwilliger Stenbock*. Stuttgart, 1929.
Stoffregen, Götz Otto von. *Vaterland—Eine Zeitroman*. Bensheim, 1921.
Volck, Herbert. *Rebellen um Ehre. Mein Kampf und die nationale Erhebung*. Gütersloh, 1932.
Weigand, Wilhelm. *Die rote Flut*. Munich, 1935.
Weller, Tödel. *Peter Mönkemann. Ein hohes Lied des Freikorpskämpfers and der Ruhr*. Berlin, 1936.
Zöberlein, Hans. *Der Befehl des Gewissens*. Munich, 1937.

2. Battle Descriptions, Eyewitness Reports, Journal Entries, Reflections, Poems, and Songs about the Era.

Anonymous. Von. . . , "Offizier 1918," in HoDA, 9ff.
Arnold, Alfred. *Das Detachement Tüllmann*. Oldenburg, 1920.
Balla, Erich. "Rudolf Berthold." In *Die Unvergessenen*, edited by Ernst Jünger. Berlin, 1928.
Berendt, Erich F. *Soldaten der Freiheit. Ein Parolebuch des Nationalsozialismus 1918/25*. Berlin, 1935.
Berk, Hans Scwarz van. "Rote Armee and der Ruhr". JKR, 203ff.
Best, Werner. "Der Krieg und das Recht." In *Krieg und Krieger*, edited by Ernst Jünger. Berlin, 1930, 135-61.
Bischoff, Josef. *Die letzte Front*. Berlin, 1919.
Bodenreuth, Friedrich. *Das Ende der Eisernen Schar*. Leipzig, 1940.
Bose, Ulrich von. "Vormarsch gegen Essen." SB, 394ff.
Brandt, Rolf. *Albert Leo Schlageter, Leben und Sterben eines deutschen Helden*. Hamburg, 1926.
Brauweiler, Heinz. "Der Anteil des Stahlhelm." HoDA, 218ff.
Buchrucker, Franz. *Der Aufruhr bei Cottbus im März 1920*. Cottbus, 1920.
Cochenhausen, Generalleutnant von. "Deutsches Soldatentum im Weltkriege." RDS, 29ff.
Cranz, Carl. "Der Ruhreinbruch." JKR, 275.
———. "Flieger im Baltikum. Aus einem Kriegstagebuch des Kampfgeschwaders Dachsenberg." SB, 171ff.
Crasemann, Ferdinand. *Freikorps Maercker, Erlebnisse und Erfahrungen eines Freikorpsoffiziers seit der Revolution*. Hamburg, 1920.
Curator, Karsten. *Putsche, Staat und wir!*. Karlsruhe, 1931.
Czech-Jochberg, Erich. *Im Osten Feuer*. Leipzig, Zurich, 1931.
Delmar, Maximilian. *Französische Frauen. Erlebnisse und Beobachtungen, Reflexionen, Paradoxe*. Freiburg, 1925.
Eckart, Dietrich. *Ein Vermächtnis*, edited by Alfred Rosenberg, second edition, Munich, 1935, originally published 1928.
Eggers, Kurt. *Annaberg*. Berlin, 1933.
———. *Von der Freiheit des Krieges*. Berlin, 1940.
———. *Vom mutigen Leben und tapferen Sterben*. Oldenburg, 1935.
———. *Sturmsignale, Revolutionäre Sprechchöre*. Leipzig, 1934.
Ehlers, Otto August. "Die Bahrenfelder Freiwilligen." SB, 69ff.
Erhardt, Hermann. *Deutschlands Zukunft*. Munich, 1921.
Engelhardt, Freiherr Eugen von. *Der Ritt nach Riga. Aus den Kämpfen der baltischen Landeswehr gegen die rote Armee 1918-1920*. Berlin, 1938.

Ettighofer, Paul C. *Wo bis du—Kamerad?* Essen, 1938.

Ewers, Hanns-Heinz. *Deutsche Kriegslieder.* Munich, 1915.

Fiesinger, H. "Tag der Befreiung." SB, 107ff.

Fischer, Hans. "Die Räteherrschaft in München." JKR, 146ff.

Fletcher, Alfred. "Die Eroberung Tuckums." SB, 154ff.

Förste, Fregattenkapitän. "Vom Freikorps zur Kriegsmarine." RDS, 102ff.

Frank, Walter. *Franz Ritter v. Epp. Der Weg eines deutschen Soldaten.* Hamburg, 1934.

Franke, Helmut. *Staat im Staate. Aufzeichnungen eines Militaristen.* Magdeburg, 1924.

Freimüller, Wilhelm. *Die Schreckenstage in Leipzig.* Leipzig, 1920.

Freiwald, Ludwig. *Die verratene Flotte.* Munich, 1931. Translated under the title, *The Last Days of the German Fleet.* London: Constable, 1932.

_____. *Der Weg der braunen Kämpfer.* Munich, 1934.

Frey, Richard. "Die Versenkund der deutschen Kriegsflotte bei Scapa Flow." JKR, 52.

Glombowski, Friedrich. *Organisation Heinz.* Berlin, 1934. Translated under the title *Frontiers of Terror.* London: Hurst, 1935.

_____. "Der Weg ins Ruhrgebeiet." SB, 424ff.

_____. "Spezialpolizei im Einsatz." SB, 253ff.

_____. "Einsatz der Selbstschutz-Sturm-Abteiluing Heinz in Gogolin." SB, 267ff.

Goes, Gustav. "Aus dem Tagebuch des letzten Kommandanten von Kowel." SB, 129ff.

Goltz, Graf Rüdiger von der. *Meine Sendung in Finnland und im Baltikum.* Leipzig, 1920.

_____. "Baltikum." RDS, 97ff.

Grothe, G. and Kern, G. "Strassenkampf in München." SB, 121ff.

Günther, Albrecht Erich. "Die Intelligenz und der Krieg." In *Krieg und Krieger,* edited by Ernst Jünger. Berlin, 1930, 69-100.

Günther, Fritz. "Einsegnung der Wandervogelhundertschaft in Rogau." SB, 256.

Günther, Gerhard. "Hamburg." JKR, 39ff.

_____. *Deutsches Kriegertum im Wandel der Geschichte.* Hamburg, 1934.

_____. "Die Bändigung des Krieges durch den Staat." In *Krieg und Krieger,* edited by Ernst Jünger. Berlin, 1930, 163-203.

Gruppe Lifl-Heller. *Das Freikorps "Landsberg." Eine Erinnerung an den Befreiungskampf von München in den ersten Maitagen 1919.* Munich, 1919.

Hahn, Paul. *Der rote Hahn, eine Revolutionserscheinung. Erinnerungen aus der Revolution in Württemberg.* Stuttgart, 1922.

Hartmann, Georg Heinrich. "Vormarsch nach Livland." SB, 180ff.

_____. "Erinnerungen aus den Kämpfen der Baltischen Landeswehr." JKR, 116ff.

Heinz, Friedrich W. *Die Nation greift an. Geschichte und Kritik des soldatischen Nationalismus.* Berlin, 1932.

Henningsen, Fritz. "Erkundungsvorstoss nach Radziwilischky." SB, 149ff.

Hielscher, Friedrich. "Der Bauer steht auf." HoDA, 212.

_____. "Die grosse Verwandlung." In *Krieg und Krieger,* edited by Ernst Jünger. Berlin, 1930, 127-34.

Hoeppener-Flatow, Wilhelm. *Stosstrupp Markmann greift ein. Der Kampf eines Frontsoldaten.* Berlin, 1934.

Höfer, Karl. *Oberschlesien in der Aufstandszeit 1918-1921. Erinnerungen und Dokumente.* Berlin, 1938.

Hoffman, C. "Letzter Sturm." SB, 404-5.

Holtz, Friedrich Karl. *Haut ihn. Ein ernstes, lustiges, wildes und besinnliches Buch.* Berlin, 1934.

Hotzel, Curt (ed.) *Deutscher Aufstand. Die Revolution des Nachkriegs.* Stuttgart, 1934.

_____. "Student 1918." HoDA, 1ff.

_____. "Der antibürgerliche Affekt." HoDA, 345ff.

Hueg, Major a. D. *Die Ereignisse vor fünf Jahren vom 13. März bis zum 15. März 1920.* Harburg, 1925.

Hülsen, Generalleutnant von. "Freikorps im Osten." RDS, 110ff.

Iger, Arthur. *Spartakustage. Aus Berlins Bolschewistenzeit.* Berlin, 1919.

Jünger, Ernst (ed.) *Der Kampf um das Reich.* Essen, 1929.

———. *Krieg und Krieger.* Berlin, 1930.

———. *Der Arbeiter, Herrschaft und Gestalt.* Hamburg, 1932.

Jünger, Friedrich Georg. "Aufmarsch des Nationalismus." In *Aufmarsch des Nationalismus*, edited by Ernst Jünger, Berlin, 1926.

———. "Krieg und Krieger." In *Krieg und Krieger*, edited by Ernst Jünger. Berlin, 1930.

Kern, Fritz. *Das Kapp'sche Abenteuer. Eindrücke und Feststellungen.* Leipzig and Berlin, 1920.

Kessel, Hans von. *Handgranaten und rote Fahnen. Ein Taschenbericht aus dem Kampf gegen das rote Berlin 1918-1920.* Berlin, 1933.

Killinger, Manfred von. *Ernstes und Heiteres aus dem Putschleben.* Berlin, 1928.

———. *Männer und Mächte. Die SA in Wort und Bild.* Leipzig, 1933.

———. *Kampf um Oberschlesien. Bisher unveröffentlichte Aufzeichnungen des Führers der Abteilung v. Killinger, gennant "Sturmkompagnie Koppe."* Leipzig, 1934.

———. *Das waren Kerle!* Berlin, 1937.

Kloppe, Fritz. "Kameraden." JKR, 238ff.

Kohlhaas, Wilhelm. "Männer und Sicherheitskompanien 1918/19." SB, 92ff.

———. "Münchener Sturmtagebuch. Die Käampfe des Württembergischen Freiwilligen-Regiments Seutter." SB, 110ff.

Koll, Kilian. "Die Männer von Tirtschtiegel." SB, 220ff.

Krumbach, Jos. H. (ed.) *Franz Ritter von Epp. Ein Leben für Deutschland.* Munich, 1939.

Lautenbacher, Oberleutnant a. D. "Widerstand im roten München." SB, 105ff.

Lettow-Vorbeck, Paul von (ed.) *Die Weltkriegsspionage* (n.p., 1931).

Liemann, Rolf. "Felsen in roter Flut." SB, 19ff.

———. "Sudetendeutschlands Märzgefallene." SB, 307.

———. "Schwerer Kampf um Königsberg." SB, 77ff.

Loewenfeld, Wilfried von. "Das Freikorps von Loewenfeld." RDS, 149ff.

Lüttwitz, Walter. *Im Kampf gegen die Novemberrevolution.* Berlin, 1934.

———. "Einmarsch der Garde-Kavallerie-Schützendivision in Berlin." RDS, 51ff.

Lützkendorf, Dr. W. "Aus Halles 'roter Zeit', nach amtlichen Berichten zusammengestellt." SB, 369.

Maercker, Ludwig Rolf Georg. *Vom Kaiserheer zur Reichswehr.* Leipzig, 1921.

Mahnken, Heinrich. "Der erste Hammerschlag? Die Aktion des Freikorps Lichtschlag nördlich Essen 1919." SB, 81ff.

———. "Freikorps im Westen 1918/20." HoDA, 89ff.

———. "Gegenstoss im Westen 1919." RDS, 59ff.

———. "Kampf der Batterie Hasenclever. 15. März 1920." RDS, 134ff.

———. "Aufmarsch gegen die rote Armee 1920." RDS, 128ff.

Maltzan, Freiherr von. "Die Spandauer stürmen Bauske." SB, 159ff.

Megede, Hans zur. "Hakenkreuz am Stahlhelm." In *Volk ans Gewehr!* edited by Walter Gruber. Wiesbaden, 1934, 119-37.

Melzer, Gustav. "Die Auswirkungen des Kapp-Putsches in Leipzig." JKR, 219.

Meyer, Ihno. *Das Jägerbataillon der Eisernen Division im Kampf gegen den Bolschewismus.* Leipzig, 1920.

Müller, Josef. *Freikorps Haas, Soldat und Vaterland vor 15 Jahren.* Illertissen, 1934.

Nord, Franz. "Der Krieg im Baltikum." JKR, 63ff.

Oertzen, Friedrich W. von. *Kamerad, reich mir die Hände: Freikorps und Grenzschutz im Baltikum und in der Heimat.* Berlin, 1933.

————. *Baltenland. Eine Geschichte der deutschen Sendung im Baltikum.* Munich, 1933.

Oertzen, Wilhelm von. *Die deutschen Freikorps 1918-1923.* Munich, 1936.

Osten, Edmund. "Der Kampf um Oberschlesien." JKR, 257ff.

Pabst, W. "Spartakus." HoDA, 28ff.

Pikarski, Hans-Albert. "Freiwilligen-Regiment Pommern." SB, 358ff.

Pitrof, Daniel Ritter von. *Gegen Spartakus in München und im Allgäu. Erinnerungsblätter des Freikorps Schwaben.* Munich, 1937.

Plaas, Hartmut. "Das Kapp-Unternehmen. Aus dem Tagebuch eines Sturmsoldaten." SB, 344ff.

————. "Das Kapp-Unternehmen." JKR, 164ff.

————. (ed.) *Wir klagen an Nationalisten in der Kerken der Bourgeosie.* Berlin, 1928.

Plehwe, Karl von. "Von der Westfront ins Baltikum. Der Weg der 1. Garde-Reserve-Division." SB, 146ff.

————. *Im Kampf gegen die Bolschewisten. Die Kämpfer des 2. Garde-Reserveregiments zum Schutz der Grenze Ostpreussens.* Berlin, 1926.

Reetz, Walter. "Der rote Vormarsch." JKR, 190ff.

Reinhard, Wilhelm. *Die Wehen der Republik.* Berlin, 1932.

————. "Kampf um Berlin." SB, 31ff.

————. "Belagerungszustand über Moabit." RDS, 36.

————. "Sturm auf das Leipziger Volkshaus 19. März 1920." RDS, 143ff.

Roden, Hans (ed.) *Deutsche Soldaten.* Leipzig, 1935.

————. "Einmarsch in Mitteldeutschland 1921." RDS, 159.

————. "Einmarsch in Mitteldeutschland 1923." RDS, 173

————. "Einmarsch in Mitteldeutschland—Das Landesjägerkorps des Generals Maercker 1919." RDS, 65.

————. "Einmarsch in Mitteldeutschland 1920." RDS, 142.

————. "Die 'Bahrenfelder' kommen!" RDS, 108.

————. "Hauptmann Berthold—ein Soldatenschicksal." RDS, 140.

Rodermund, Eduard. "Separatismus." HoDA, 116.

————. "Rote Armee an Rhein und Ruhr." HoDA, 96ff.

Roegels, Lutz. *Aus dem rotem Sumpf. Korruptionsbilder aus der Revolution.* Berlin, 1924.

Rossmann/Schmidthuysen. "Der blutige Montag in Duisburg." SB, 392.

Roth, Bert (ed.) *Kampf. Lebensdokumente deutscher Jugend 1914-1934.* Leipzig, 1934.

Sager, Walter. "Vom Kampf der Essener Einwohnerwehr." SB, 383ff.

Salomon, Ernst von. *Nahe Geschichte.* Berlin, 1935.

————. *Putsch und Verschwörung.* Frankfurt, 1938.

————. (ed.) *Das Buch vom deutschen Freikorpskämpfer.* Berlin, 1938.

————. "Der Berliner Märzaufstand 1919." SB, 44ff.

————. "Hexenkessel in Deutschland." JKR, 13ff.

————. "Sturm auf Riga." JKR, 98.

————. "Die Versprengten." JKR, 112ff (extract from *Die Geächteten*).

————. "Die Brigade Ehrhardt." RDS, 119ff.

————. "Der verlorene Haufe." In *Krieg und Krieger*, edited by Ernst Jünger. Berlin, 1930, 101-26.

Schaper, Rittermeister a. D. "Freikorpsgeist—Annaberg." RDS, 161ff.

Schaumlöffel, Karl. *Das Studentenkorps Marburg in Thüringen. Ein Kriegstagebuch im Frieden.* Marburg, 1920.

Schauroth, von Oberst a. D. "Revolte in Libau." SB, 162ff.

Schauwecker, Franz. "Der Aufbruch der Nation aus dem Kriege." HoDA, 245.

Schauwecker, Heinz. "Freikorps Epp." HoDA, 160.

Schirach, Baldur von. *Pionere des Dritten Reiches*. Essen, 1933.

Schleisner, Sepp. "Panzerzug." SB, 327.

Schmidt-Pauli, Edgar von. *Die Männer um Hitler*. Berlin, 1932.

Schramm, Wilhelm von. "Schöpferische Kritik des Kriegers." In *Krieg und Krieger*, edited by Ernst Jünger. Berlin, 1930, 31-50.

Schricker, Rudolf. *Blut-Erz-Kohle. Der Kampf um Oberschlesien*. Berlin, 1930.

_____. *Rotmord über München*. Berlin, 1934.

Schulz, Adolf. *Ein Freikorps im Industriegebiet*. Mülheim, 1922.

Seitz, Georg. "Die Eiserne Schar Berthold in Hamburg" SB, 353.

Siegert, Max. *Aus Münchens schwerster Zeit*. Regensburg, 1928.

Spektator, (i.e., B. Wolf) *Die Schreckenstage im rheinisch-westfälischen Industriebezirk*. Hanover, 1920.

Steinaecker, Freiherr Franz Josef von. *Mit der Eisernen Division im Baltenland*. Hamburg, 1920.

Stephan, Karl. *Der Todeskampf der Ostmark 1918-1919. Die Geschichte eines grenzschutzbataillons*. Schneidemühl, 1919.

Stoffregen, Götz Otto. *Aufstand*. Berlin, 1931.

Strasser, Otto. "Der Sinn des 9. Novembers 1923." JKR, 301.

_____. "Der 9. November 1923. Erlebnisse eines Mitkämpfers." JKR, 294.

Wagener, Wilhelm Heinrich. *Von der Heimat geächtet. Im Auftrag der Deutschen Legion bearbeitet*. Stuttgart, 1920.

Watter, Freiherr von. "Die Bedeuting des Freikorps." RDS, 75.

Wiemers-Borchelhof, Dr. Franz. "Freikorps-Arbeitsdienst-Siedlung. Schicksal eines Vorkämpfers der Freikorpssiedler." SB, 40ff.

Wittmann, Hans. *Erinnerungen der Eisernen Schar Berthold*. Oberviechtach, 1926.

Wrangel, Baron Wilhelm von. *Geschichte des Baltenregiments*. Reval, 1928.

Zeschau, Major von. "Streiflichter aus den Kämpfen um Litauen." SB, 135ff.

Zimmermann, Adolf. *Vorfrühling 1920. Aus den Tagen der Kapp'schen Wirren*. Berlin, 1920.

Zobel, Johannes. *Zwischen Krieg und Frieden. Schüler als Freiwillige im Grenzschutz und Freikorps*. Berlin, 1934.

3. Other Literature and Theory

Abel, Theodore. *Why Hitler Came into Power. An Answer Based on the Original Life Stories of Six Hundred of His Followers*. New York: AMS Press, 1938.

Abraham, Karl. "Restrictions and Transformations of Scoptophilia in Psycho-Neurotics with Remarks on Analogous Phenomena in Folk Psychology." In *Selected Papers*. Translated by D. Bryan and A. Strachey. London, 1942, 169-234.

Adorno, Bettelheim, et al. *The Authoritarian Personality*. New York: Harper and Row, 1950.

Adorno, Thomas, and Horkheimer, Max. *Dialectic of Enlightenment*. New York: Herder and Herder, 1972.

Adorno, Thomas. *Minima Moralia. Reflections from a Damaged Life*. London: New Left Books, 1974.

_____. "Engagement." In *Noten zur Literatur III*. Frankfurt, 1971.

Amery, Jean. *Jenseits von Schuld und Sühne. Bewältigungsversuche eines Überwältigten*. Munich, 1970.

Anonymous. *Naziführer sehen dich an. 33 Biographien aus dem 3. Reich*. Paris, 1934.

Arendt, Henriette. *Menschen, die den Pfad verloren*. Stuttgart, 1907.

Aries, Philippe. *Geschichte der Kindheit*. Munich, 1975.

Arnold, Heinz Ludwig (ed.) *Dein Leib ist mein Gedicht. Deutsche erotische Lyrik aus fünf Jahrhunderten*. Frankfurt, 1973.

Autorenkollektiv. *Illustrierte Geschichte der deutschen Revolution*. Berlin, 1929, reprinted Frankfurt, 1970.

Balint, Michael. *The Basic Fault. Therapeutic Aspects of Regression*. London: Tavistock, 1968.

_____. *Thrills and Regressions*. London: Hogarth Press, 1959. German edition quoted here: *Angstlust und Regression*. Reinbek, 1972.

Bateson, Gregory, et al. "Towards a Theory of Schizophrenia." In *Steps to an Ecology of Mind*. San Francisco: Chandler, 1972.

Baumgarth, Christa. *Geschichte des Futurismus*. Reinbek, 1972.

Bebel, August. *Women under Socialism*. New York: Labor News, 1904.

Benjamin, Walter. "The Work of Art in the Age of Mechanical Reproduction." In *Marxism and Art*, edited by F. Williams, et al. New York, 1972, 281-300.

_____. "Theses on the Philisophy of History." In *Illuminations*, edited and introduced by H. Arendt. Translated by H. Zohn, London: Jonathan Cape,1970. 255-66.

_____. *Angelus Novus. Gesammelte Schriften*. Frankfurt, 1966. Especially "Ein Jakobiner von heute," "Der eingetunkte Zauberstab."

_____. *Understanding Brecht*. Translated by Anna Bostock. London: New Left Books, 1973.

_____. "Theorien des deutschen Faschismus." In *Das Argument*, 6, no. 30, (1964). Reprinted in *Die Gesellschaft*, edited by Rudolf Hilferding. A discussion of the anthology *Krieg und Krieger*, edited by Ernst Jünger. Berlin, 1930.

Benn, Gottfried. *Destillationen*. Wiesbaden, 1953.

_____. *Statische Gedichte*. Zurich, 1948.

Besançon, Alain. "Vers une histoire psychoanalytique." In *Histoire et experience du moi*. Flammarion, 1971.

Bierce, Ambrose. "Moxon's Master." In *The Complete Short Stories*. Garden City, New York: Doubleday, 1970.

Biermann, Wolf. *Mit Marx und Engelszungen*. Berlin, 1968.

Bloch, Charles. *Die SA und die Krise des NS-Regimes 1934*. Frankfurt, n.d.

Bloch, Ernst. *Das Prinzip Hoffnung*. Frankfurt, 1959.

_____. *Erbschaft dieser Zeit*. Frankfurt, 1962.

Blüher, Hans. *Die Rolle der Erotik in der männlichen Gesellschaft*. Stuttgart, 1962.

_____. *Wandervogel. Geschichte einer Jugendbewegung*. Prien, 1922.

_____. *Führer und Volk in der Jugendbewegung*. Jena, 1924.

Boehm, Felix. "Beiträge zur Psychologie der Homosexualität." In *Internationale Zeitschrift für Psychoanalyse*, 8 (1922).

Brecht, Bertolt. *Gesammelte Werke*, vol. 8, *Gedichte 1*. Frankfurt, 1967.

_____. *Tagebücher 1920-22. Autobiographische Aufzeichnungen 1920-1954*. Frankfurt, 1954. Translated under the title *Bertolt Brecht Diaries 1920-1922*. Translated by Herta Ramthun. London: Eyre Methuen, 1979.

_____. "Die Horst-Wessel-Legende." In *Gesammelte Werke*, vol. 20, *Schriften zur Politik und Gesellschaft*. Frankfurt, 1967.

Büchner, Georg. *Geammelte Werke*, vol. 1, *Dantons Tod*. Vienna, 1947. Translated under the title *Danton's Death*. London: Faber, 1939.

Canetti, Elias. *Crowds and Power*. Translated from the German by Carol Stewart. Harmondsworth: Penguin, 1973.

_____. *Macht und Überleben. Drei Essays*. Berlin, 1972.

Chasseguet-Smirgel (ed.) *Psychoanalyse der weiblichen Sexualität*. Frankfurt, 1974. Translated under the title *Female Sexuality*. London: Virago, 1981.

Crombie, A. C. *Von Augustinus bis Galilei. Die Emanzipation der Naturwissenschaft*. Cologne and Berlin, 1964.

Dannecker, Martin, and Reiche, Reimut. *Der gewöhnliche Homosexuelle*. Frankfurt, 1974.

Darstellungen aus den Nachkriegskämpfen deutscher Truppen und Freikorpps. Edited and published by the Forschungsanstalt für Kriegs- und Heeresgeschichte under the auspices of the Reichskriegsministerium, 7 vols. (Berlin, 1936-39).

Deleuze, Gilles, and Guattari, Felix. *Anti-Oedipus. Capitalism and Schizophrenia*. Translated from the French by Robert Hurley, Mark Seem and Helen R. Lane. Minneapolis: University of Minnesota Press, 1983.

Demeter, Karl. *Das deutsche Heer und seine Offiziere*. Berlin, 1930. Translated under the title *The German Officer-corps in Society and State*. London: Weidenfeld and Nicholson, 1965.

Douglas, Mary. *Natural Symbols*. Harmondsworth: Penguin, 1973.

Dudenstadt, Henning. *Der Schrei nach dem Recht. "Die Tragödie von Mechterstädt,"* Marburg, 1920.

Durrell, Lawrence (ed.) *The Henry Miller Reader*. New York: New Directions, 1959.

Ehrenreich, Barbara,and English, Dierdre. *Witches, Midwives and Nurses: A History of Women Healers*. Old Westbury, New York: Feminist Press, 1973.

Eisler, Hanns. *Lieder und Kantaten*. Leipzig, 1957.

Elias, Norbert. *Über den Prozess der Zivilisation*. (1936), 2 vols. Bern, 1969. Translated by Edmund Jephcott under the title *The Civilizing Process*. New York: Urizen Books, 1978.

_____. *Die höfische Gesellschaft*. Neuwied, 1969.

Enzensberger, Christian. *Grosserer Versuch über den Schmutz*. Munich, 1968. Translated under the title *Smut: An Anatomy of Dirt*. New York: Seabury, 1974.

Enzensberger, Hans M. (ed.) *Museum der modernen Poesie*. Frankfurt, 1964.

Erikson, Erik. "The Legend of Hitler's Childhood." In *Childhood and Society*, 2nd ed., revised and enlarged. New York: W.W. Norton, 1963.

Ernst, Josef. *Kapptage im Industriegebiet*. Hagen, 1921.

Ettlinger, Karl. *Die Reglemenierung der Prostitution*. Leipzig, 1903.

Fanon, Frantz. *The Wretched of Earth*. London: Macgibbon and McKnee, 1965.

Ferenczi, Sandor. *Schriften zur Psychoanalyse*, vol.1. Frankfurt, 1970.

_____. "Versuch einer Genitaltheorie." In *Schriften zur Psychoanalyse*, vol.2. Frankfurt, 1971.

Firestone, Shulamith. *The Dialectic of Sex. The Case for Feminist Revolution*. New York: Morrow, 1970.

Fischer-Eckart, Li. *Die wirtschaftliche und soziale Lage der Frauen in dem modernen Industrieort Hamborn im Rheinland*. Hagen, 1913.

Fornari, Franco. *Psychoanalyse des ersten Lebensjahres*. Frankfurt, 1970.

Foucault, Michel. *Folie et deraison: histoire de la folie a l'age classique*. Paris: Plon, 1961. Translated under the title *Madness and Civilization: A History of Insanity in the Age of Reason*. New York: Pantheon, 1965.

_____. *Surveiller et punir: naissance de la prison*. Paris: Gallimard, 1975. Translated under the title *Discipline and Punish: the Birth of the Prison*. New York: Pantheon Books, 1977.

_____. "Notes on a lecture delivered by Foucault at the College de France, 28 March, 1973." Translated as "Power and Norm," in *Power, Truth and Strategy*, Meaghan Morris and Paul Patton (eds.) Sydney: Feral Publications, 1979, 59-66.

_____. and Deleuze, Gilles. "Les intellectuels et le pouvoir." *Arc*, 49, 1972. Translated under the title "The Intellectuals and Power," in *Language, Counter-Memory, Practice: Selected Essays and Interviews*, edited by D.F. Bouchard. Ithaca, New York: Cornell University Press, 1977.

Frenzel, H. A., and Frenzel, E. *Daten deutscher Dichtung: Chronologischer Abriss der deutschen Literaturgeschichte*. Munich, 1975.

Freud, Anna. *Das Ich und die Abwehrmechanismen*. Munich, n.d. Translated under the title *The Ego and the Mechanisms of Defense*. London: Hogarth Press, 1937.

Freud, Sigmund. *The Standard Edition of the Complete Psychological Works of Sigmund Freud.* Translated from the German under general editorship of James Strachey, in collaboration with Anna Freud, assisted by Alix Strachey and Alan Tyson, 24 vols. London: Hogarth Press, 1959.

Fromm, Erich. *The Anatomy of Human Destructiveness.* New York: Holt, Rinehart and Winston, 1973.

Fuchs, Eduard. *Illustrierte Sittengeschichte vom Mittelalter bis zur Gegenwart,* 6 vols. Munich, 1909-12.

Gilbert, G. M. *Nuremberg Diary.* London: Eyre and Spottiswood, 1948. German edition *Nürnberger Tagebuch.* Frankfurt, 1962.

Goethe, J. W. von. *Faust, Parts One and Two.* Translated by Phili Wayne, 2 vols. New York: Penguin Books, 1979.

————. *Gedichte in zwei Bänden.* Frankfurt, 1964.

Grafe, Fried. "Ein anderer Eindruck vom Begriff meines Kürpers." In *Filmkritik,* 20, no. 3, 1976.

Groddek, Georg. *Das Buch vom Es.* Leipzig, 1923. Translated under the title *The Book of the It.* New York: Funk and Wagnalls, 1961.

Grützmacher, Kurt. *Liebeslyrik des deutschen Barock.* Munich, 1975.

Guillen, Nicolas. *Obra Poetica, 1920-1972.* Havana: Editorial de Arte y Literatura, 1974.

Gumbel, Emil Julius. *Vier Jahre politischer Mord.* Berlin, 1922.

————. *Verschwörer. Beiträge zur Geschichte und Soziologie der deutschen nationalistischen Geheimbünde seit 1918.* Vienna, 1924.

————. *Verräter verfallen der Feme: Opfer, Mörder, Richter.* Berlin, 1929.

————. *Vom Fememord zur Reichskanzlei.* Heidelberg, 1962.

Hannover, Heinrich, and Hannover-Drück, Elisabeth. *Politische Justiz 1918-1933.* Frankfurt, 1966.

Hauser, Arnold. *Sozialgeschichte der Kunst und Literatur.* Munich, 1969. Translated under the title *The Social History of Art.* New York: Random House, 1985.

Heger, Heinz. *Die Männer mit dem rosa Winkel.* Hamburg, 1972.

Heine, Heinrich. *Insel Heine,* vol. 1, *Gedichte.* Frankfurt, 1968.

Heintz, Günther (ed.) *Deutsche Arbeiterdichtung 1910-1933.* Stuttgart, 1974.

Hirschfeld, Magnus. *Die Homosexualität des Mannes und des Weibes: Homosexuelle Männer und Frauen als biologische Erscheinung.* Köppern i. T., 1963.

————. (ed.) *Sittengeschichte des Weltkriegs,* 2 vols. Leipzig, 1930.

Hocquenghem, Guy. *Homosexual Desire.* Translated by Danielle Dangoor, New York: Schocken, 1980.

Irigaray, Luce. "Neue Körper, neue Imagination." Interview with Martine Storti in *Alternative,* 19, nos. 108/109, June-August 1976.

————. *Wesen, Körper, Sprache: Der verrückte Diskurs der Frauen.* Berlin, 1976.

Jahn, Janheinz. *Schwarzer Orpheus: Moderne Dichtung afrikanischer Völker beider Hemisphären.* N.p., n.d.

Jean Paul (Jean Paul Friedrich Richter). "Einfältige, aber gut gemeinte Biographie einer neuen angenehmen Frau von blossem Holz, die ich längst erfunden und geheiratet." In Völker, *Künstliche Menschen,* Munich, 1971.

————. "Untertänigste Vorstellung unser, der sämtlichen Spieler und redenden Damen in Europa, entgegen und wider die Einführung der Kempelischen Spiel-und Sprachmaschinen." In Völker, *Künstliche Menschen.* Munich, 1971.

Kläber, Kurt. *Barrikaden an der Ruhr: Erzählungen.* Frankfurt, 1973.

Klein, Melanie. "The Importance of Symbol-Formation in the Development of the Ego." In *Love, Guilt, Reparation and Other Works.* London: Hogarth Press, 1975.

———. "Some Theoretical Conclusions Regarding the Emotional Life of the Infant"; "The Psycho-Analytic Play Technique: Its History and Significance." In *Envy, Gratitude and Other Works*. New York: Delta, 1975.

Klemisch, Franz Josef (ed.) *Afrikanische Lyrik aus zwei Kontinenten*. Stuttgart, 1966.

Kofler, Leo. *Zur Geschichte der bürgerlichen Gesellschaft*. Vienna, 1974.

Könnemann, Erwin. *Einwohnerwehren und Zeitfreiwilligenbände. Ihre Funktion beim Aufbau eines neuen imperialistischen Militärsystems (November 1918 bis 1920)*. East Berlin, 1971.

———. and Krusch. *Aktionseinheit contra Kapp-Putsch. Der Kapp-Putsch im März 1920 und der Kampf der deutschen Arbeiterklasse sowie anderer Werktätiger gegen die Errichtung der Militärdiktatur und für demokratische Verhältnisse*. East Berlin, 1972.

Kracauer, Siegfried. *Das Ornament der Masse*. Frankfurt, 1963.

Krauss, Friedrich Salomon (ed.) *Jahrbücher für folkloristische Erhebungen und Forschungen zur Entwicklungsgeschichte der geschlechtlichen Moral*, vol. 4, *Beiwerke zum Studium der Antropohyteia*. Leipzig, 1911.

Kurnitzky, Horst. *Triebstruktur des Geldes. Ein Beitrag zur Theorie der Weiblichkeit*. Berlin, 1974.

Lacan, Jacques. *Ecrits*. Paris: Edition du Seuil, 1966, 1970. Translated under the title *Ecrits: A Selection*. New York: Norton, 1973.

Laplanche, J., and Pontalis, J-B. *The Language of Psychoanalysis*. Translated by D. Nicholson-Smith. New York: Norton, 1973.

Lautréamont (Ducasse, Isidore Lucien). *Oeuvres completes de Lautreamont et Germain Nouveau*, edited by Pierre-Olivier Walzer. Paris: Gallimard, 1970.

Leclaire, Serge. *Der psychoanalytische Prozess*. Olten/Freiburg, 1971. Originally published as *Psychoanalyser*. Paris: Seuil, 1969.

Lipp, Herbert. *Aufschrei aus dem Asphalt*. Berlin, n.d. (ca 1920).

Lippe, Rudolf zur. *Naturbeherrschung am Menschen*, 2 vols. Frankfurt, 1974.

Lucas, Erhard. *Märzrevolution im Ruhrgebiet*, vol. 1, *Vom Generalstreik gegen den Militärputsch zum bewaffneten Arbeiteraufstand, März-April 1920*. Frankfurt, 1970.

———. *Märzrevolution im Ruhrgebiet*, vol. 2, *Der bewaffnete Arbeiteraufstand im Ruhrgebiet in seiner inneren Struktur und in seinem Verhältnis zu den Klassenkämpfen in den verschiedenen Regionen des Reiches*. Frankfurt, 1973.

———. *Märzrevolution im Ruhrgebiet*, vol. 3, Spring 1978.

———. *Zwei Formen von Radikalismus in der deutschen Arbeiterbewegung*, Frankfurt, 1976.

Mahler, Margaret. *On Human Symbiosis and the Vicissitudes of Individuation*, vol. 1, *Infantile Psychosis*. New York: International Universities Press, 1970.

Majakowski, Wladimir. *Frühe Gedichte*. Frankfurt, 1965.

———. *Politische Poesie*. Frankfurt, 1966.

Mann, Heinrich. *Ein Zeitalter wird besichtigt*. Reinbek, 1976.

Mantell, David Mark. *Familie und Aggression: Zur Einübung von Gewalt und Gewaltlosigkeit. Eine empirische Untersuchung*. Frankfurt, 1972.

Marx, Karl. *Capital*, vol. 1, *A Critique of Political Economy*. Translated by Ben Fowkes. Harmondsworth: Penguin and New Left Books, 1976.

Maser, Werner. *Die Frühgeschichte der NSDAP: Hilers Weg bis 1924*. Frankfurt, 1965.

Mason, Tim. "Zur Lage der Frau in Deutschland 1930 bis 1940: Wohlfahrt, Arbeit, Familien." In *Gesellschaft, Beiträge zur Marxschen Theorie*. Frankfurt, 1976.

Mayer, Hans. *Aussenseiter*. Frankfurt, 1975.

Melville, Herman. *Moby Dick, or the White Whale*. New York: New American Library (Signet Classic), 1961.

Michelet, Jules. *La sorciere*, edited by Lucien Refort. Paris: M. Didier, 1952. Translated under the title *Satanism and Witchcraft, a study in Medieval Superstition*. New York: Citadel Press, 1965.

Montagu, Ashley. *Touching: The Human Significance of the Skin.* New York: Columbia University Press, 1971.

Morgan, Elaine. *The Descent of Woman.* London: Souvenir, 1972.

Mörike, Eduard. *Gesammelte Werke.* Bergen, n.d. In English see *Poems*, selected and edited by Lionel Thomas. Oxford: Blackwell, 1960.

Moser, Tilmann. *Lehrjahre auf der Couch. Bruchstücke meiner Psychoanalyse.* Frankfurt, 1974.

Mostar, Gerhart (ed.) *Frederike Kempner, der schlesische Schwan.* Munich, 1965.

Nagl, Manfried. *Science-fiction in Deutschland.* Tübingen, 1972.

Neruda, Pablo. *Obras completas*, 4, edited by M. Aguirre, bibliography by A. A. Escudero H. Loyola. Buenos Aires: Editorial Losada, 1973.

Pankow, Gisela. *Gesprengte Fesseln der Psychose.* Munich, 1974.

Perse, Saint-John. *Oeuvres complete.* Paris: Gallimard, 1972.

Radical America Comix, edited by Bernd Brummbär. Frankfurt, 1970.

Reich, Wilhelm. *The Mass Psychology of Fascism.* Translated from the German by Vincent R. Carfagno. Harmondsworth: Penguin, 1983.

————. *Charakteranalyse.* Berlin, 1933. Translated by Vincent R. Carfagno under the title *Character Analysis.* New York: Farrar, Straus and Giroux, 1972.

————. *Reich Speaks of Freud*, edited by Mary Higgins and Chester M. Raphael, with translations from the German by Therese Pol. London: Souvenir Press, 1972.

————. *Die Entdeckung des Orgons/Die Funktion des Organismus.* Frankfurt, 1972. First part of the work translated by Theodore P. Wolfe under the title *The Discovery of the Orgone.* New York: Noonday Press, 1971. Second part translated by Vincent R. Carfagno under the title *The Function of the Orgasm.* New York: Farrar, Straus and Giroux, 1973.

Reiche, Reimut. "Ist der Ödipuskomplex universell?" in *Kursbuch*, 29, 1972.

————. "Eine Entgegnung: Socarides, der versteckt Anti-Homosexuelle." In *Psyche*, 26, 1972.

Reiche, Volker. *Liebe. Ein Comic.* 1974.

Richards, Donald Ray. *The German Bestseller in the Twentieth Century: A Complete Bibliography and Analysis 1915-1940.* Berne, 1968.

Roheim, Geza. "Aphrodite oder die Frau mit dem Penis." *Die Panik der Götter.* Munich, 1975.

Rohrwasser, Michael. *Saubere Mädel, starke Genossen.* Frankfurt, 1975.

Rühle, Otto. *Illustrierte Kultur-und Sitengeschichte des Proletariats.* Berlin, 1930.

Sadger, J. "Über Gesässerotik." In *Internationale Zeitschrift für ärztliche Psychoanalyse*, no. 1, 1930.

Scheer, Maximilian. *Blut und Ehre.* Paris, 1937.

Schidrowitz, Leo (ed.) *Sittengeschichte der Kulturwelt*, vol. 7, *Sittengeschichte des Proletariats.* Vienna, 1926.

Schilder, Paul. *Das Körperschema: Ein Beitrag zur Lehre vom Bewusstsein des eigenen Körpers.* Berlin, 1923. Translated under the title *The Image and Appearance of the Human Body.* International University Press, 1950.

Schmidt-Pauli, Edgar von. *Geschichte der Freikorps 1918-1924.* Stuttgart, 1936.

Schumann, Wolfgang, *Oberschlesien 1918/19, vom gemeinsamen Kampf deutscher und polnischer Arbeiter.* East Berlin, 1961.

Schwendter, Rolf. *Theorie der Subkultur.* Cologne, 1973.

Severing, Carl. *1919/20 im Wetter-und Watterwinkel: Aufzeichnungen und Erinnerungen.* Bielefeld, 1927.

Shelley, Mary. *The Annotated Frankenstein.* New York: C. N. Potter, 1977.

Sohn-Rethel, Alfred. *Ökonomie und Klassenstruktur des deutschen Faschismus.* Frankfurt, 1973. Translated by Martin Sohn-Rethel under the title *Economy and Class Structure of German Fascism.* London: CSE Books, 1978.

Sonnemann, Ulrich. *Negative Anthropologie: Vorstudien zur Sabotage des Schicksals.* Reinbek, 1969.

Sontheimer, Kurt. *Antidemokratisches Denken in der Weimarer Republik: Die politischen Ideen des deutschen Nationalismus zwischen 1918 und 1933.* Munich, 1962.

Speer, Albert. *Spandauer Tagebücher.* Frankfurt, 1975, translated under the title *Inside the Walls of Spandau: The Prison Diaries of Albert Speer.* London: Collins, 1976.

Starobinski, Jean. *Literatur und Psychoanalyse: Die Geschichte der imaginären Ströme.* Frankfurt, n.d.

Stenbock-Femor, Count Alexander von. *Meine Erlebnisse als Bergarbeiter.* Stuttgart, 1929.

———. *Deutschland von unten: Reise durch die proletarische Provinz.* Stuttgart, 1931.

Stierlin, Helm. "Einige Anmerkungen zu Reimut Reiches Kritik an Socarides' Buch 'Der offene Homosexuelle.'" *Psyche,* 26, 1972.

Szasz, Thomas. *The Manufacture of Madness.* New York: Harper and Row, 1977.

Teuber, Heinrich. *Für die Sozialisierung des Ruhrbergbaus,* a collection of articles from 1926. Reprint, Frankfurt, 1973.

Tiger, Lionel. *Men in Groups.* New York: Random House, 1969.

Träger, Klaus (ed.) *Die Französische Revolution im Spiegel der deutschen Literatur.* Frankfurt, 1975.

Verne, Jules. *Master Zacharias Amid the Ice.* Aeonian Press, n.d.

Völker, Klaus (ed.) *Künstliche Menschen: Dichtungen und Dokumente über Golems, Homunculi, Androiden und liebende Statuen.* Munich, 1971.

Waite, Robert G. L. *Vanguard of Nazism: The Free Corps Movement in Postwar Germany 1918-1923.* Cambridge, Mass, 1952.

Wenders, Wim. "Ein Genre, das es nicht gibt." *Filmkritik,* 14, no. 9, 1970.

Werner, Georg. *Ein Kumpel: Erzählung aus dem Leben eines Bergarbeiters.* Berlin, 1930.

Whitman, Walt. *Leaves of Grass.* New York: University Press, 1965.

Winckler, Lutz. *Studie zur gesellschaftlichen Funktion faschistischer Sprache.* Frankfurt, 1971.

12. Aug. 1961

Wir wissen aber, so unser irdisch
Haus dieser Hütte zerbrochen wird,
daß wir einen Bau haben, von Gott
erbauet, ein Haus, nicht mit Händen
gemacht, das ewig ist, im Himmel.

2. Korinther 5, 1

Der heilige und barmherzige Gott hat am 7. August meine
getreue Ehegefährtin, unsere geliebte Mutter und Großmutter

Else Niemöller

geb. Bremer

durch einen schnellen Tod von uns gerufen.

Mit ihr starb unsere liebe

Dora

die seit 23 Jahren ein Glied unserer Familie gewesen ist.

D. Martin Niemöller
Brigitte Johannessen, geb. Niemöller
Hermann Niemöller
Hertha von Klewitz, geb. Niemöller
Wilhelm von Klewitz
Jan Niemöller
Irene Niemöller, geb. Winter
Martin Niemöller
Käthe Wild, geb. Bremer
Hans Schulz
acht Enkelkinder

Apenrade, Wiesbaden, Königswinter, Usingen, New Haven,
den 10. August 1961

Die Trauerfeier findet am Montag, dem 14. August 1961, um
14 Uhr in der Lutherkirche in Wiesbaden (Mosbacherstraße)
statt, die Beisetzung anschließend im engsten Kreise auf dem
Südfriedhof.

A Small Postscript to Volume 1

On the opposite page, the obituary notice for "Seven Marriages." Uwe Nettelbeck gave it to me. He had got it from Rudolf Augenstein.

Else Niemöller died in a car accident. It is impossible to tell from the wording that Martin Niemöller was driving the vehicle that crashed. But apparently that was the case.

In the section "All that Flows," a few lines of poetry by Rolf Dieter Brinkmann were omitted from the illustrations to women and water:

Half of Austria came by train
kissed Eva Braun's hand, looked at her tits
sealed in by her permanent waves.

(Halb Österreich reiste mit einem Zug an,
küsste Eva Braun die Hand, sah nach den Titten,
plombiert durch Dauerwellen.)

(From: "Einige sehr populäre Songs," in *Westwärts*, 1 and 2, 132.)

Jürgen Theobaldy wrote to tell me I had misquoted him (footnote on 416 of Volume 1, "The Body as Dirt"). I'm afraid he's right. He didn't take *his* raincoat with him to Esslingen in 1968, but *the* raincoat—Bogart's, in that case. I'm probably mad at him because I didn't have a raincoat with me in Esslingen, Easter 1968. But more likely than that, it's because I think we must have been in different places when I read his so-called poem and the others. He also tells me I should not call his poems "so-called," since it is a term usually reserved for the German Democratic Republic. I won't do him the favor.

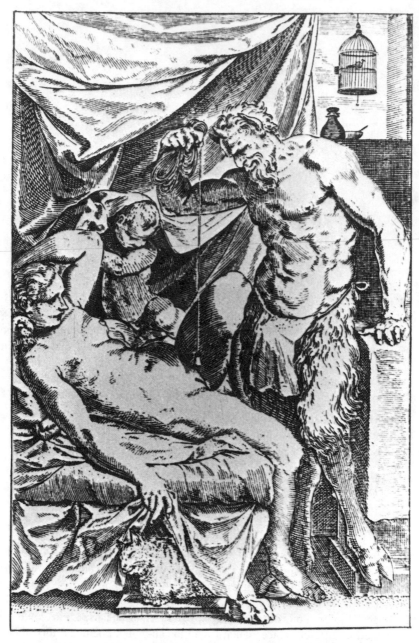

We wanted to have this engraving by Agostini Caracei, ca. 1600, in the part on women and floods. "The Dowser" (*Sendeur*, literally "one who plumbs the depths").

The Last Page

A book is "completed" not so much because the author has "finished" thinking it through and writing it, but because of a decision to do so, because of financial and other reasons.

Comparing quotes with the original, checking dates, checking whether much of what I wrote "off the top of my head" really relates to the authors I have referred to (it often doesn't), augmenting incomplete footnotes, inventing sources for quotes I can't find again, making the manuscript readable, making corrections, writing the foreword I never got round to, and so on and so on. In the process reading my own work to the point where I doubt I was all there when I wrote it.

It took six months to get the manuscript ready for publication. It was a period worse than all the previous years of writing, and it made it more difficult for Monika and I to live together than in the years before when we had been able to share the time we devoted to Daniel, to do the housework and both of our own work, Monika at the clinic and I at my desk. Towards the end, when the submission date was getting nearer and was finally agreed upon, I did not manage to do my share.

You shouldn't do this sort of thing very often; it's not worth it. Not even the odd word of approval, which is nice for me (and us) to hear, can make up for the fact that Monika had too much to bear by the end. (That I was under pressure too is neither here nor there).

I am grateful above all to Bernwald Bücheler, Michael Rohrwasser, Traute Hensch, Martin Langbein, Antje Tielebein, Horst Nitschack, Anna und Christian Schaeffer von Appen. All of them gave us the help we badly needed at the time. I would also like to thank Maria Hassenbürger, Paul Meyer, and Karin Lucas-Bosse for lending us money.

Peter Schleuning, Michael Rohrwasser, Peter Harosky, Michael Berger, Jürgen Fahle, and Hans-Peter Herrmann read the manuscript, made suggestions I often took, and discussed the texts and corrections with me. Hans-Peter Herrmann allowed me to write the thesis without bothering me with the usual academic rituals and wrote the references I needed to be given grants. Because of this, and because of the way we got on, I only rarely had the feeling that I was spending years of my life writing my own version of the certificate the police issue to confirm that the holder does not have a criminal record—although when I did, the feeling was very strong. In the end though, he could not help squeezing a pointless foreword* out of me, so that if there were any "dispute" he would not be left without a legitimate case. Well, okay, but perhaps not.

I am also grateful to the following (and others whose names have slipped my memory) who drew my attention to, or gave me, books and illustrations: Fritz Suhr, Carmen Wenk, Theresa Tschopp, Walter Mossmann, Margarete Mehmen, Paul Meyer, Gottfried Fischer, Ulf Datan, and Jürgen Ebert. I have spoken to so many people, received so many suggestions and tips, so much has changed on the Left in the last few years. The groups I used to, and still do, belong to have changed, my own life has changed—all except for the ones who go in for congresses. They call themselves freaks now and carry on as before. All this has, in various ways, gone into the revisions and reworkings of *Male Fantasies*, and I am sure that many sentences and paragraphs can be attributed to an indeterminate author, a nameless figure who has been reconstituted, then left to decay, but who no doubt really exists. At least I wish this were the case. Nor should I forget the people at Freiburg University lending library at whose counter the author was passed the many books he needed in order not to remain himself. Even though they are employees of an institution of the State of Baden-Württemberg, they are always busy, in a friendly and unbureaucratic manner, creating the conditions which make it a pleasure to use the institution they run. Right now I can't think of another institution I could say the same about, and I'm sure the instructions to put an end to it have already been issued.

---

*Not included in this edition.

Index

Index

Klaus Theweleit earned his Ph.D. in German literature at the University of Freiburg and is now a freelance writer working in West Germany.

Chris Turner is director of Material Word, a translation cooperative in Birmingham, England. He has degrees in modern languages and French from Cambridge University and the University of Sussex. Erica Carter is director of lectures and seminars at the Institute of Contemporary Arts in London. She holds degrees in French and German from the University of Birmingham. Turner and Carter co-translated, with Stephen Conway, *Male Fantasies, Volume 1* (Minnesota, 1987).

Anson Rabinbach is associate professor of history at The Cooper Union for the Advancement of Science and Art. He previously taught at Princeton University and has been a member of The Institute for Advanced Study. Rabinbach is the author of *The Crisis of Austrian Socialism: From Red Vienna to Civil War 1927-1934* (University of Chicago Press, 1983), and co-editor of *New German Critique*. His new book *The Human Motor: Energy, Fatigue and Work in Modern Europe* is forthcoming from Basic Books.

Jessica Benjamin is a psychoanalyst who practices in New York City and teaches psychoanalysis and social theory at the New School for Social Research; she is also a fellow at the New York Institute for the Humanities. She received her Ph.D. in sociology and her psychoanalytic training at New York University. Benjamin is the author of *The Bonds of Love: Psychoanalysis, Feminism and the Problem of Domination* (Pantheon Books, 1988). Her articles have appeared in *New German Critique, Feminist Studies* and the book, *The Powers of Desire* (Monthly Review Press, 1983).